POPULAR IMAGES
OF AMERICAN
PRESIDENTS

Popular Images of American Presidents

EDITED BY
William C. Spragens

GREENWOOD PRESS

NEW YORK
WESTPORT, CONNECTICUT
LONDON

Library of Congress Cataloging-in-Publication Data

Popular images of American presidents / edited by William C. Spragens.
      p.   cm.
    Bibliography: p.
    Includes index.
    ISBN 0–313–22899–X (lib. bdg. : alk. paper)
      1. Presidents—United States—Public opinion—History.   2. Public
    opinion—United States—History.   3. United States—Politics and
    government.   I. Spragens, William C., 1925–
    E176.1.P82   1988
    973′.09′92—dc19   87–24944

British Library Cataloguing in Publication Data is available.

Library of Congress Catalog Card Number: 87–24944
ISBN: 0–313–22899–X

First published in 1988

Greenwood Press, Inc.
88 Post Road West, Westport, Connecticut 06881

Printed in the United States of America

The paper used in this book complies with the
Permanent Paper Standard issued by the National
Information Standards Organization (Z39.48-1984).

10   9   8   7   6   5   4   3   2   1

CONTENTS

PREFACE

After two months of President Ronald Reagan's administration, public opinion survey data indicated that the president (despite his popular reputation as a successful president) had the lowest approval rating at that period of any modern president, and that he had the highest disapproval rating (24 percent). Similar readings were taken in 1982 at his low point, although his 1986 post-Iceland summit approval ratings were in the 70 percent plus range.

In the early months Reagan's approval rating was lower than that of Presidents Roosevelt, Truman, Eisenhower, Kennedy, Johnson, and Ford—and even President Nixon—at this early stage. How can this be explained?

The polling data probably tell us more about the state of mind of the American public in 1981 than they do about President Reagan's actual performance in the White House (after all, these data are from the early days). Why did President Reagan at that point (and at times during the 1982 recession) have relatively lower approval ratings than other presidents?

Part of the problem may have been unrealistic expectations on the American public's part. Before President Reagan took office on January 20, 1981, Wall Street had been optimistic, and the stock market began to rise markedly after the November 1980 election. Some felt that this was the result of high expectations about what Reagan could achieve as president in improving economic conditions. After the inauguration the market fell for several months; some observers felt that this was the result of dashed hopes, as it became clear that the new president would not balance the budget at an early date or keep some other campaign promises. The same phenomenon occurred after the election of previous presidents including President Carter and others.

The same psychological phenomenon that could be observed on Wall Street and in the business community could also be found among the American public, as reflected in the public opinion results. And yet the public at large at that early stage indicated some willingness to be patient with the new president. At a comparable point in 1977, four years earlier, President Carter had a similar problem, but his approval rating was higher than that of his successor after the first two months. And Carter in turn had a lower approval rating than Presidents Nixon and Ford at the early stage of their administrations.

Presidential scholar Thomas Cronin has suggested that American public opinion has been affected by development of unrealistic expectations about the presidency and about individual incumbents as a result of myth-building by the American mass media—television in particular—and also by the educational system. Professor Cronin used the concept of the "textbook presidency" to describe the way in which political socialization and training of youth tend to cause them to expect great achievements on the part of the man in the White House. When, inevitably, presidents fail to live up to the public's expectations—fed by the media and the educational system as well as some of the myths of American political folklore—a kind of disillusionment sets in. This is the problem faced by President Reagan and several of his recent predecessors.

In criticizing the "textbook presidency" and the overinflation of public expectations of American presidents, it may be wise to recognize also that a certain amount of myth-building may be described from the viewpoint of promoting the legitimacy of our elected leaders. Certainly, if the American public does not trust its presidents, it will be difficult for them to achieve their programs or even to remain in office, as the experience of Richard M. Nixon and Watergate—as well as that of Lyndon B. Johnson during the Vietnam hostilities—seems to prove.

What, then, should be the attitude of the American public toward its presidents—both those elected to office in the regular way, and those who succeed to the office from the vice presidency following the president's resignation, natural death, or assassination? This will be one of the questions examined in this book.

In this volume dealing with popular images of American presidents, a series of administrations will be analyzed, and an effort will be made to determine what the standing of each president and his administration was with the public of that historical time period. In addition, each president will be examined in terms of his image over time. Fluctuations in succeeding generations' interpretations of past presidents become noteworthy, and this historical dimension is significant in getting a better understanding of the kaleidoscopic nature of presidential images.

Those covered in the volume include all twentieth-century presidents and the most important presidents from the eighteenth and nineteenth centuries. At the conclusion of the book, an effort will be made to determine what generalizations can be drawn from this analysis and what common themes can be found in the study of each administration.

The work will employ a variety of analytical approaches, including examination of historical narrative, content analysis of editorials and news coverage, and explication of public opinion survey data. An explanation of why and how presidents have been perceived in their own time and afterward requires a sophisticated look at such public opinion data as approval ratings. These need to be interpreted by examining such questions as how the surveys are administered, the kinds of samples used, and the reliability of the data. Inferences can then be drawn about the kind of positive and negative characteristics that each president developed. Recent research has refined approaches to this analysis in terms of barometers of feelings toward political leaders. With the most recent presidents, also, data are available that reflect breakdowns of attitudes according to demographic and other characteristics. Such information is not available from contemporaries for earlier presidents, who served prior to the development of modern public opinion surveys.

For public reactions and the reactions of other leadership figures, the authors drew material from the contemporary press as well as from the writings of professional historians and political scientists. One interesting and useful facet of presidential images is the view elites or those in leadership roles held of the incumbents' performance. Evidence is taken from contemporary sources on this point, such as editorials in newspapers and magazines, but a good deal of use has been made of the writings of revisionist historians. They take a fresh look at each president in the light of changing times.

Where political scientists, in contrast to historians, have examined presidential performance, emphasis has been put on opinion dynamics and the relationship of the office to the public, to the media, and to other governmental leaders, including in some instances, where appropriate, foreign leaders in their practice of diplomacy. Historians have examined similar variables in the context of the past and have sought to explain the causes of events.

Specific conclusions about individual presidents can be found in the various case study chapters, but the reader's assessment of the contents of these chapters may be enriched by a summary of the perspectives and qualifications of the chapter authors. Specialists with expertise in a variety of academic disciplines have combined their efforts to shed light on presidential images.

In looking at George Washington, a military historian employs analysis from that specialty along with cultural history analysis, even to the point of examining how Washington appeared to the counterculture of the 1960s. A historian versed in political thought employs philosophical analysis as well as biography to provide insights into the mind of Thomas Jefferson; he also examines political history and compares prerevolutionary culture with emerging American nationalism.

An experienced historian uses exegesis of literature over a wide range of time, employing historiography as well as cultural history to explain the figure of Andrew Jackson. A political scientist uses both legal and cultural analysis to determine the contribution of Abraham Lincoln to the concept of "constitutional dictatorship" as explored by the late political scientist Clinton Rossiter; the author also examines myths surrounding Lincoln.

A skilled historian with expertise in the black studies area examines the political activities of Rutherford B. Hayes, an important transitional figure in American race relations and a key person in the development of the durable bipartisan conservative coalition of special importance in the Reagan era.

Another historian with a great skill for abstracting employs historical analysis and contemporary sources to shed light on the character of Grover Cleveland, emphasizing contextual factors.

A political scientist familiar with the character and style analysis of the James David Barber school and also factional analysis, as well as political history, develops an enhanced view of the role of William McKinley; this author also seeks to develop nuances regarding the true role of manager Mark Hanna and his relationship to McKinley, disputing some earlier writings.

A historian who is fascinated with the persona of Theodore Roosevelt examines dynastic politics along with a penetrating institutional analysis of the emerging role of the American press in relation to the White House in the early twentieth century. A journalist who developed a keen interest in the matrix of the Taft family in Cincinnati uses interviewing techniques to provide never before published insights into how William Howard Taft was viewed by those closest to him as well as by a fickle public.

A political scientist uses biographical data, close textual analysis of contemporary comments, and political theory to illuminate the significant image of Woodrow Wilson. A specialist in Ohio history digs deeply into the Harding family archives and the byzantine factional strivings of the Ohio Republican party to bring new insights into Warren Gamaliel Harding's poignant career.

A political scientist delves into the strong attachment of what would today be called Middle America to Calvin Coolidge, and examines how simplicity and identification with the man in the street enhanced Coolidge's popularity. A political scientist, with the aid of a historian, examines Herbert Hoover's amazing prepresidential career as a mining and industrial-financial genius and philanthropic prodigy and probes into the irony of how an Iowa orphan boy's shyness and seemingly retiring personality, carried over into manhood, complicated things for him in the White House at a time when flexibility, not rigidity, was required.

A skilled political scientist combines biography, media analysis, public opinion analysis, and an exploration of the linkages of political theory, pragmatism, and problem solving to give a new and more sophisticated image of Franklin D. Roosevelt. A leading historian focuses almost entirely on public opinion analysis and the linkage of polling results to events to explain the image of Harry S Truman.

A former associate and subordinate of Dwight D. Eisenhower provides important insights into the leadership traits of the general turned president and in so doing uses the tools of the historian. A political scientist analyzes interviews with members of the New Frontier staff along with reports of pioneer private polling specialists and contemporary magazine commentary as well as personal impressions to depict John F. Kennedy's image. The same political scientist, with the aid of a public relations practitioner, examines the Lyndon B. Johnson image and seeks to achieve a balance between Vietnam-era denigration of the Texas president and an appreciation of his lasting achievements in domestic policy.

A political scientist who authored a textbook on the American presidency attempts, as have others before him, to determine the strange presidential image of Richard Nixon in the light of political psychology as well as more traditional factional and ideological approaches. A political scientist examines the early materials about the transitional presidency of Gerald R. Ford to determine how the Ford image changed through his congressional and White House service.

A political scientist with special skills in the analysis of public opinion data takes a close look at polling data from several sources (with emphasis on job approval ratings) and at contemporary and recent writings in presenting interpretations of two quite different presidential images, those of Jimmy Carter and Ronald Reagan.

Finally, a young political scientist who is the author of a significant monograph on party ideologies and platforms has collaborated with the editor of this volume to examine the totality of presidential images in a more holistic, global perspective, seeking to find generalizations, trends, and distinctions in images.

As this broadbrush summary indicates, behavioral scientists with quite different skills have combined to present this introduction to constantly intriguing image-making and image analysis in the nearly two centuries of the existence of the American presidency.

The volume has been devised as a reference book intended to be useful to both scholars and lay students of the presidency. To this end, the end-of-chapter bibliographies have been constructed through a process of selection in which the relative importance of many sources has been assessed. Though space does not permit a complete listing in the instance of those presidents about whom there has been prolific writing, the volumes cited may provide further sources and were selected with that criterion in mind.

The authors hope that the reader of this reference work will use it as a starting point for a more detailed study of presidents yet to come as well as for a continuing effort to view presidential images through the lenses of events and eras yet to be experienced. All of us have greatly enjoyed making this small contribution to the constantly growing literature in the field of the American presidency.

ACKNOWLEDGMENTS

A book of this character involves a tremendous amount of work, much of it done by persons other than the editor of this volume. This acknowledgment is an effort in a small way to recognize those who contributed in any way to *Popular Images of American Presidents*.

I am first of all indebted to Marilyn Brownstein, acquisitions editor for Greenwood Press. Without her initial incentive and our working out the formula for the book, this volume might never have been written.

I shall always be indebted as well to Cynthia Harris, the Greenwood reference book editor, who was not only very professional in her work as house editor, but also provided encouragement when it was needed and prompted me to make it the best possible project.

I am grateful as well to a whole series of assistants, one of them a chapter collaborator, who helped with the nitty-gritty work that such an ambitious volume entails. These include Tammy Manahan Moss, who was instrumental in getting commitments from the authors; Melinda Taylor Swan, who not only provided some fresh insights and excellent editing ideas but also contributed to the LBJ chapter; Valerie Sacks, who provided backup details; Peggy O'Neill, an excellent manuscript typist; Pamela Columbo, a fine manuscript typist and editor; Angela Pieracini, Susan Anschutz, Julie Fauble, and Laura Raccina, manuscript typists; Heidi Brinkman, typing and proofing; and Marjan Myers, word processing specialist.

In addition to the student assistants, I am grateful to two departmental secretaries, Wilma Konecny and Marianne Kolbe, who provided assistance at several critical junctures. I am also indebted to such departmental colleagues as Professors Roger Anderson, Dennis Anderson (contributor of two chapters), D. S. Chauhan, Steven Ludd, Jerone Stephens and William Reichert, and to Dean Kendall Baker of the College of Arts and Sciences at Bowling Green State University, who provided grant assistance. The Faculty Research Committee and its secretary, Berry Cobb, former director of BGSU's Research Services Office, provided important support.

While the authors who contributed chapters deserve commendation, I am also grateful to another specialist on the presidency who was not able to contribute a chapter, Dr. Kenneth E. Davison, chair of the Department of American Civilization at Heidelberg College, who suggested several appropriate chapter authors and made other suggestions.

Researchers who contributed to the content of my own chapters deserve thanks. These included Annette and Lisa Audi, Linda Martens, Shari Graham, and Kathy Kostalnick. If I have left others unmentioned, I am grateful to them as well.

I am pleased to thank some of the staff members at the John F. Kennedy Library in Boston, including William Johnson and Deborah Greene, and at the Lyndon B. Johnson Library in Austin, among them Tina Lawson, Claudia Anderson, and others there who were also helpful on two earlier volumes.

Finally, I am grateful for my students who waited that extra moment for an answer to a question while I was sitting at the typewriter, and to my wife, Elaine, who provided constant encouragement and also did some supportive research.

POPULAR IMAGES
OF AMERICAN
PRESIDENTS

1 GEORGE WASHINGTON

David Curtis Skaggs

No American political figure has for so long dominated the national scene as George Washington. For nearly twenty-five years George Washington remained the symbol of American nationhood, commanding its armies in a war for national independence, presiding over the convention that drafted its fundamental political charter, and defining that charter's vague articles into political reality as the first chief magistrate of the Republic. In the nearly two centuries since, he has remained the First Citizen of the United States. Yet, for all his acclaim he is known to the general public more for his military achievements than his presidential ones. Still, his achievements as chief executive rate him the highest accolades from historians and political scientists. One must also remember that his popular image extends beyond when he was president and includes both a public and a scholarly reputation about which there are both differences and agreements.

WASHINGTON'S BACKGROUND

Born to a Virginia gentry family slightly below the Byrds, Carters, Lees, and Randolphs in status, Washington rose to the top rung of influence and affluence through the acquisition of the important skill of surveying, the acquaintance of the influential Fairfax family, the inheritance of the estate of an older half-brother, and marriage to a wealthy widow. Before he was thirty he had served as the envoy of the governor of Virginia to French commanders in the Ohio Valley, commanded Virginia militia in combat, accompanied General Edward Braddock on his ill-fated expedition, published two journals of his western travels, was mentioned at the court of George II, and was elected to the House of Burgesses.

"My inclinations are strongly bent to arms," he confessed, but he was refused a regular commission in the British army. This affront to his dignity undoubtedly contributed to his growing American nationalism, but the years following the French and Indian War were mostly devoted to the establishment of his estate.

His marriage in 1759 to Martha (Dandridge) Custis brought not only domestic happiness to his then-small home at Mount Vernon, but also resulted in several years of concentration not only on the expansion of the home plantation on the Potomac but also speculation on lands beyond the Appalachian chain. He pioneered in the application of the latest English scientific farming techniques to the area, invested in transportation improvement projects designed to connect the Chesapeake with the Ohio Valley, and served his constituents as their representative in the Virginia House of Burgesses. By the age of forty he was one of the most substantial and influential citizens of the Northern Neck of Virginia, but one whose reputation did not extend far beyond the boundaries of the Chesapeake region.

In these early years he also developed the essential personality characteristics that were to shape the remainder of his career. Whatever his desire for private wealth, this was not his dominant personality trait. Honor was far dearer to him than money, property, and slaves. Honor manifested itself in several ways. Washington always sought all the respect due his status. During the French and Indian War, he was deeply offended by a British army captain who claimed to outrank all provincial officers regardless of grade. Throughout his career he expected to be accorded all the entitlements and dignities of his office. Undoubtedly this contributed to his reputation for aloofness that continues to this day. This natural reserve was a definite asset for someone who commanded slaves, overseers, and troops. As he saw it, familiarity bred contempt from one's subordinates. The respect he sought could not come from familiarity. His sense of honor was the code of the gentleman; it created in him and for him respect rather than love.

Closely tied to this sense of honor was a sense of honesty. The mythical cherry tree story notwithstanding, Washington had from his earliest years a reputation for honest dealings with all. Like any sound businessman, he made hard bargains and reasonable profits. His agricultural experiments, his engrossment of western lands, and his investments in canals to open such lands to markets were all tied to his desire for personal economic well-being. At the same time, none of this can be seen as unreasonable or dishonest business practice. Throughout his life persons to whom he owed little obligation used his reputation for honesty to arbitrate disputes and to settle estates. Sometimes this required extensive expense of time and talent for which he received little or no compensation. This reputation was enhanced during his years in command of the Continental army and undoubtedly contributed to the adoption of the Constitution and to the willingness of the Founding Fathers to convey to the nation's first president the vague and undefined powers that the initial federal administration would turn into administrative reality and "traditional" policy.

Also, by the time of his appointment as commander-in-chief of the Continental army, Washington had achieved a reputation for duty. While many will argue that he failed in his filial duties to his mother, one must remember that not only did Washington assume a reasonable proportion of such family obligations, but

also that his attention to his mother, despite a busy schedule and many obligations, was greater than that of his numerous siblings. His sense of duty to his
neighbors in settling estates and disputes has already been mentioned. Early in
his career he assumed the functions of burgess and subsequently those of congressman, both of which were part of the obligations of a gentleman to his fellow
countrymen. Whatever may have been his motives in accepting public office,
he understood, as he wrote before the Constitutional Convention, that "the good
of my Country requires my reputation to be put in risque[;] regard for my own
fame will not come in competition with an object of such magnitude." Throughout his career, then, duty to family, to neighbors, to province, and to country
required his service—and he unstintingly gave of that service.

These three characteristics of honor, honesty, and duty were so well known
to his fellow delegates to the Continental Congress that, however modest his
reputation as a military leader, he was named commander of the Continental
army. During the eight years he led that force he acquired administrative talents
only slightly developed in his earlier career. So extensive and effective were his
talents in this regard that no chief executive before Dwight Eisenhower had more
administrative experience.

His administrative skills were often personal, too personal for some, for he
maintained a mastery of details, kept complete records, worked long hours,
listened patiently to the clashing opinions of subordinates before making decisions, and expected strict obedience to final decisions from his lieutenants. He
delegated authority with care, allowing distant commanders autonomy to conduct
operations as the local situation demanded. Sometimes this led to disaster as
Horatio Gates demonstrated at Camden, while at other times the independent
commander exhibited talents beyond Washington's most sanguine expectations,
such as Nathanael Greene in the southern campaign of 1781. His sense of honesty
and good administration caused him to abstain from the typical eighteenth-century
practice of nepotism.

This administrative skill was closely tied to his deep commitment to republicanism. Anyone who observed the inability of Congress to govern the nation
effectively during the war for independence wonders how it was that Washington
continued to subordinate himself to that body. No incident more exemplifies
Washington's devotion to republicanism than the so-called Newburgh conspiracy
of 1783. The inefficiency and disorganization of Congress following the victory
at Yorktown and the inability of either Congress or the states to provide for
salaries and pensions for the veterans of the Continental army led some of its
senior officers to join in threats to the very existence of the government. When
an unsigned paper circulated at the encampment at Newburgh, New York, calling
for the army to assert its "alternative" to political failures, Washington delivered
an address requesting his officers,

as you value your own sacred honor, as you respect the rights of humanity, and as you
regard the military and national character of America, to express your utmost horror and

detestation of the man who wishes, under any specious pretenses, to overturn the liberties of our country, and who wickedly attempts to open the flood gates of civil discord and deluge our rising empire in blood.

His success in thwarting this military coup d'etat left him with an integrity that undoubtedly contributed to his reputation for believing in popular government despite its failure to reward those who were most devoted to the cause of national independence.

This republicanism shaped his nationalism. When he left Virginia in 1775, he was a provincial whose basic loyalty was to the community that nourished him. Eight years of leadership of the national armed forces made him a committed nationalist. The very weakness of the Republic under the Articles of Confederation did not diminish Washington's republican ardor; rather he sought to establish a continental nation through political reform and reorganization. He desired a nation that would redistribute powers so that a central governing power would be freed from a slavish dependence upon the whims and interests of local communities. Such a concentration of power was necessary in order to preserve republicanism in North America from the divisiveness of localism. Because of this combination of republicanism and nationalism, he risked his reputation and relinquished the joys of retirement for the presidency of the Constitutional Convention in 1787. The document produced that summer in Philadelphia owes much to his patience and determination to avoid what he felt was the approach of political anarchy and national division. He staked his reputation on its ratification, and implicit in that support was his willingness to serve as the first chief executive.

As Washington rode from Mount Vernon to New York City to take the oath of office, he went through crowds of cheering citizens who lined the route to hail their national hero. They knew him as an honorable, honest citizen-soldier whose sense of duty and administrative skills were necessary if the United States was to continue as a national republic. The new president clearly understood that both his reputation and that of the new nation rested on what his administration would leave as a lasting legacy. Few men in history have had fewer guideposts to follow as they charted the future course of political, economic, and social policy.

THE PRESIDENCY

Like many of his successors, George Washington found that his presidential popularity reached a peak at the time of his inaugural. As he rowed across the Hudson River in a specially prepared barge, a mixed quartet sang a new version of "God Save the King":

. . . Joy to our native land,
Let every heart expand,

For Washington's at hand,
With glory crowned.

When the enthusiasm of his inauguration died down, the realities of governing the disparate nation arose. Washington clearly understood the nature of his problem: "I fear if the issue of public measures should not correspond with their [the public's] sanguine expectations, they will turn the extravagant [and I may say undue] praises which they are heaping upon me at this moment, into equally extravagant [though I will fondly hope] unmerited censures." His government faced difficult tasks in the fields of administrative organization, foreign relations, and economic policy. Influencing each of these areas would be both the clash of personalities and the clash of political interests. Such divisiveness would inevitably lead to a decline in the popularity of the chief executive even though he sought to remain above the political combat.

In the area of executive department organization Washington left his most lasting legacies. The essential feature consisted of presidential control of the executive offices of government. This contrasted with those who desired to use the Senate as a sort of privy council under the "advise and consent" clause and those, like Alexander Hamilton, who desired a parliamentary cabinet system with the major executive officers responsible to the Congress. The resulting independent executive system vested the chief executive with all administrative authority and responsibility for the conduct of the business of the federal government. Other factors of administration involved the creation of administrative agencies separate from the state organizations; the introduction of orderly and stable relationships between officials based on law, instructions, and precedents; the maintenance of high standards of integrity, honesty, and competence; the recognition of claims of locality upon political appointments (often called "senatorial courtesy"), and the dominance of federal authority over individuals, best expressed in the suppression of the Whiskey Rebellion. Some of Washington's administrative policies, such as the use of the veto power only in relation to constitutional questions, did not long survive his presidency. In the same vein, his use of the cabinet as a consultative body had a short life.

Other developments during his tenure can be attributed less to Washington's personal influence than to the circumstances of the time or to the role of others. The creation of the judicial branch was largely the responsibility of Roger Sherman, and the Bill of Rights was the consequence of the efforts of James Madison. The latter formulated the first national revenue system, and Alexander Hamilton created a financial system that funded the government's debts, instituted a national central bank, and established a national mint and stable currency. Washington's role in these developments was largely incidental, except that he either actively endorsed or indicated no opposition (which in itself constituted endorsement) to their implementation.

Washington played an important role in Indian affairs, often using his secretary of war as a cipher and conduit in a field where he had considerable expertise.

In military affairs, a field in which he was probably the most experienced official on the continent, Congress rejected his solutions for strategic policy and, in the Militia Act of 1793, left the nation without any effective defense posture. Moreover, his first two commanders of the U.S. Army on the northwestern frontier were defeated by the Indians. Only after Anthony Wayne took command was the Ohio country secured for white settlement. Because virtually the entire U.S. Army was employed in the Northwest Territory, Washington sought conciliation with the southeastern tribes, a policy that was often at odds with the aggressive encroachments on Indian lands by both private individuals and state governments.

In the area of foreign affairs he worked closely with Thomas Jefferson in his first administration and followed the often misguided instincts of Hamilton in the second. No single area of his administration caused greater controversy and contributed to his political decline as much as did diplomacy. The Jay Treaty was the most divisive political event of the day and did far more to encourage partisan politics than any other policy matter. Despite the political consequences of Washington's diplomacy, he is generally given appreciative accolades by modern historians for maintaining neutrality in the Anglo-French struggle that drew most of the Western world into its vortex.

Traditionally, historians have given much weight to the divisions resulting from the formation of Hamilton's financial program. However, it is clear that James Madison's opposition had few followers in a theoretical sense and that much of it revolved around local issues rather than those of public policy (such as nationalism versus localism) that Madison championed. Washington's role was that of silent endorsement, although he clearly supported the nationalistic features of Hamilton's policy.

Yet both of these last major issues—foreign affairs and financial policy— contributed to the one development Washington opposed—political parties. Although local partisan activities existed in most states, and in a few, like Pennsylvania, the rudiments of a formal party structure existed, both the president's supporters and opponents used these national issues combined with local ambitions to create the first party system. All of this ran counter to the consensual political environment desired by Washington and most of his contemporaries. For them partisan activities were divisive to national solidarity and led to corruption and personal ambition. Men like Washington sought to remain above the din of political combat, seeking the nondivisive centrist position that furthered the national best interest. Increasingly, and against his best judgment, Washington found himself drawn into such partisan contests, all of which contributed to a decrease in his popularity.

The best indication of the importance and concern Washington had for this political development appears in his Farewell Address. While we today tend to remember it as filled with advice on foreign affairs, it primarily warned against forming political parties, especially ones that supported one European nation or another. In the area of diplomacy, it is clear that Washington accepted Hamilton's emphasis on a realistic foreign policy rather than the idealism symbolized by

Jefferson. Despite his despair over the development of partisan politics, Washington increasingly came to support Federalists over Republicans, and he gradually recognized the inevitability of parties in the Republic. Too few men were as disinterested as he in their personal power or parochial influence to adopt the unfettered nationalism he felt was his. By 1799, when Governor Jonathan Trumbull of Connecticut urged Washington to run again for the presidency, he declined. He recognized the need for even the Federalists to select a partisan candidate and that it did not matter too much who it was, and, so long as he rode under the party banner, the number of votes would be approximately the same. Like Jefferson and Madison, Washington recognized the necessity of partisan activity; like them, he also deplored it. It would take the next generation of politicians to champion political parties as a positive good for the maintenance of republican government.

PRESIDENTIAL REPUTATION

As noted previously, George Washington entered the presidency with an excellent popular reputation. Even during the darkest days of the revolutionary war he remained relatively above criticism. The victory at Yorktown brought him a fame that was without any comparison in the contemporary world. His countrymen could not heap enough praise upon his virtues. Without any apologies to William Shakespare, the *Maryland Gazette* plagiarized this praise for the victor over Cornwallis when he visited Annapolis:

You would thought the very windows spoke,
So many greedy looks of young and old
Through casements darted their desiring eyes
Upon his visage; and that all the walls,
With painted imagery, had said at once,
God save thee, WASHINGTON.[1]

If the Bard of Avon were not enough to praise Washington, his countrymen soon referred to him as the American Moses or the American Cincinnatus. For them he seemed to be the embodiment of the greatest heroes of antiquity.

Obviously there were no opinion polls to ascertain the popularity of the first president. For the most part one must consult the periodicals of the day to determine his relative popular standing. In the first administration there was uniform praise of the Virginian. Even those opposition journals that became the most bitter critics of the Federalists praised the president highly. The biggest criticism during the first administration concerned his alleged aloofness. If, as David Barber argues, the most visible part of a presidential pattern is personality style, then Washington's style was one that characterized his entire career—a concerned remoteness. In an age of monarchy, he had to appear both royal and republican. There were those that felt him to be too ordinary, of which his adoption of the title "Mr. President" seems most conspicuous. On the other hand, critics on the left felt him to be "monarchical," with his liveried coachmen and other symbols of importance. Washington did not behave with familiarity toward the public, but he exhibited a character mix providing dignity and presence to an untested office.

Critics from both sides considered him to be excessively cautious. This undoubtedly was the result of long experience as a planter, businessman, and soldier, but it exasperated many who wanted quick, decisive action from him. In the midst of the diplomatic crises of the second administration, Washington recorded in his journal "that this Government ought not to go faster than it was obliged; but to walk on cautious ground." It is this prudence which he showed in the darkest days of the Revolution and which he demonstrated as he built from scratch a republican government for a diverse continent. He was doubly careful as chief executive to act in a manner which would allow his successors latitude while providing direction. Surely "walk on cautious ground" was a fitting epitaph for his administrative conduct.

Conspicuous with this prudence was his nationalism. A southern planter and slaveholder, he was not an agrarian. Perhaps this should not be surprising. However rural his Fairfax County estate, to his dock came ships from the metropolis of London, and he engaged in commercial exchanges from the Caribbean to the Thames. His was a mercantile world in which he produced a product that was part of international economic intercourse. Thus, when Alexander Hamilton proposed his economic program it was a reflection of the nationalistic views of his mentor. When he appointed men to office, Washington sought to distribute their benefits on a truly national basis. He was unmoved by political and social pressures and impervious to the claims of self-interest that ran contrary to what he felt to be the national weal.

If his domestic policy was truly nationalistic, so was his foreign policy. Washington never swerved from a maxim that it was in the best interest of the United States to avoid foreign alignments while advancing the commercial interests of the nation through trade with all belligerents. This required the United States not taking undue advantage of temporary diplomatic inconveniences confronting foreign states, since disadvantageous treaties would not bind nations together when their mutual interests did not coincide with such agreements.

Achieving these domestic and diplomatic objectives in the heat of the political revolution of the late eighteenth century created a storm of protest that adversely affected Washington's public image in his second administration.

On the domestic side, the so-called Whiskey Rebellion and the president's response to it brought about a major criticism of Washington. While Hamilton's financial system was somewhat more favorable to commercial rather than subsistence economic interests, it did not excite major opposition to the president. However, when its implementation required the imposition of an excise tax on one of the subsistence farmers' few cash crops—distilled alcohol—opposition to the administration and its enforcement of the law grew, especially in western

Pennsylvania. Washington correctly saw that the resistance to the law constituted a significant affront to the still shaky federal government. Washington decided to suppress the growing resistance through a massive imposition of federally raised state militia units who would overawe the protestors. Unfortunately, he allowed control of this effort to fall into the hands of Hamilton, the man most distrusted by the opposition. The president compounded his problems by personally accompanying the troops into central Pennsylvania in the fall of 1794. By closely associating himself with the secretary of the treasury in this expedition, Washington incurred considerable political opposition. His political support in the West was irretrievably lost.

This "Whiskey Campaign" was followed by a denunciation of the "Democratic Societies" that had sprung up throughout the country as the fomentors of the insurrection who sought to undermine legitimate government by raising "civil convulsion." The growing opposition, centered around Congressman James Madison and former Secretary of State Thomas Jefferson, saw such statements as reflecting a growing presidential drift toward the Hamiltonian faction in the cabinet and Congress and away from the consensual politics of the first administration. But since there was considerable opposition to the Whiskey Rebels, and because Washington did nothing overtly to inhibit the functioning of these Democratic Societies, this statement did not incur many personal attacks upon Washington himself.

Far more significant in lowering the president's reputation in the public mind would be the growing rage over the administration's conduct in foreign affairs. No single issue in the second administration resulted in more open opposition to the government in general and the president in particular than the role the United States played in the growing warfare between the European monarchies and republican France.

With the Neutrality Proclamation of 1793 there began attacks upon the president's character. That statement flouted both treaty obligations and popular sentiment favoring revolutionary France. Subsequent actions toward the new republic's ambassador, Edmond Genet, combined with the appearance of subservience to the British Orders in Council which restricted American commercial intercourse with the belligerents, and, finally and most importantly, the rising tide of opposition resulting from the Jay Treaty of 1765, produced extremes of vituperation against the president. He was depicted as monarchist, as a prideful aristocrat who flouted popular will, and as a new Benedict Arnold whose early patriotism was now tarnished by disloyalty to the constitutional republicanism he was pledged to uphold. Hypocritically pretending to be a republican, the president was seen in much of the opposition press as a betrayer of public trust.

While the president rode through the storm of protest over the Jay Treaty, the resulting situation was a bipolarization of politics in the country in direct opposition to the consensual style of government Washington desired. Jefferson had left the cabinet at the end of the first term, and Edmund Randolph was forced out in 1795. Increasingly, Washington's advisers were associated with

Hamilton, who was no longer an official of government but still a confidant of the president and his cabinet officers.

When Washington chose to retire from the presidency he took that opportunity to write a valedictory address to the nation which remains one of his most lasting legacies to the young Republic. Much of his motivation came from dismay over the personal attacks that characterized the previous few years. Initially taking some notes James Madison had given him four years earlier, Washington composed a draft which he sent to Hamilton for comments. The former secretary of the treasury composed what is known as Hamilton's Main Draft, which the president then redrafted in his own handwriting, making many verbal, stylistic, and organizational changes to suit his own taste.

The first of the two most important sections deals with the dangerous "spirit of party," which fostered geographic schisms, foreign intrigues, and demagoguery. Another section dealt with foreign affairs, and it became the best remembered and most influential portion of the paper. Washington was particularly pleased with Hamilton's text, which made no distinction between those Americans who favored France and those who supported Britain in the ongoing European conflict. In effect, the Farewell Address embodied a longstanding American diplomatic tradition: stay aloof from the conflicts of the Old World, follow a policy of strict neutrality and commercial intercourse with all nations, and confine the national attention to its sphere of interest, the New World.

Although initially seen by his political opponents as partisan rhetoric, the address generally received growing praise in the public press. A decade hardly passed before it became a national statement of purpose, and it was revered by all political parties. As a comprehensive and authoritative statement, the Farewell Address pleaded for an ending of domestic political factionalism (obviously ignored), for avoiding partisan conflicts over foreign policy (fitfully observed), and for maintaining an aloofness from the endless wars of European powers (the cornerstone of American foreign policy for over a century).

Despite the opposition aroused by various aspects of administrative policy in the second term, Washington left the presidency still high in public regard. His political opponents chose to attack his policies rather than him (much the same way Kennedy attacked the Eisenhower administration). Although one can truly say that he did not leave the office with the same degree of public approval with which he entered it, it can easily be argued that few presidents have enjoyed more popular approbation at the end of a second term than did George Washington. But the inauguration of John Adams on March 4, 1797, did not end Washington's popular image in the American mind; it only marked a new stage in the evolution of a national myth.

THE MYTHIC IMAGE

The myth began even before the presidential term, and by 1797 it had reached new heights. Even the mildest, most indirect criticism of the Father of His

Country evoked cries of outrage from his admirers. Thomas Jefferson learned the consequences of such conduct when a letter written to an Italian friend in the heat of controversy over the Jay Treaty was published in a slightly garbled form, the result of its being translated from English to Italian to French to English. The new vice president quietly endured the slings and arrows of the indignant press for what were perceived to be slights to the former president.

From then on, the popular image of Washington has been one of the virtually infallible hero who, in the words of an envious John Adams, sprang forth from Dr. Franklin's lightning rod a full-blown Cincinnatus ready to smite the British Empire in a stroke.

His death less than three years after retirement brought a new wave of testimony to his greatness. His name eventually graced the national capital, one state, thirty-three counties, nine colleges, and hundreds of towns, cities, and townships across an expanding continent. His visage stared out on postage stamps and on banknotes worth countless billions of dollars. His image could be found in homes and schoolrooms throughout a grateful nation. A European visitor wrote in 1815: "Every American considers it his sacred duty to have a likeness of Washington in his home, just as we have images of God's saints."

Washington iconography began during the Revolution itself and, once the fictitious prints were replaced by those based on authentic images, the portraits of Charles Willson Peale dominated the popular mind. While depictions of the president in uniform remained common during his presidential years, a number of civilian portraits emerged in the 1790s. One of the most common was *Washington's Family,* based on a painting by Edward Savage, which the artist thought would bring him the enormous sum of $10,000 in the first year of publication. Increasingly dominant was the imagery of Gilbert Stuart, which became even more popular when it served as the frontispiece to the third edition of Mason Locke Weems' *Life of Washington* (1800). Only a few days after Washington's death a New York engraver advertised for a "Portrait as natural as life" based upon a painting of the "masterly Stewart" *(sic)* for all "those who revere the Memory of the Great and Good Washington." It was an image that was to dominate the public consciousness.

While the portrait image emerged so did allegorical representations, with the latter becoming increasingly popular after the commander-in-chief's death. The most influential of these was John James Barralet's *Apotheosis of Washington* which shows "General Washington" with Stuart's face being wafted aloft by angels while at his feet a female figure representing "America" mourns over his armor along with an Indian and the virtues Faith, Hope, and Charity. Other symbols such as the defiant bald eagle and his Society of Cincinnati and Masonic decorations were included. Barralet's allegory is a tour de force in the genre of memorial portraiture.

Thus the new century had barely dawned before the essential characteristics of Washington imagery were codified. First, he was seen primarily as a military figure, and when a civilian representation appeared it was usually based upon

Stuart's dour, aging, and forbidding portraiture. Some have argued that the civilian presidential and political image dominated until the mid-nineteenth century, but aside from the Savage and Stuart portraits most depictions were martial. Second, Washington was increasingly depicted as representing the destiny of the new Republic, and various forms of embellishment were utilized to suggest this new image. Neoclassical symbols with female figures representing Liberty and ancient Roman images such as liberty caps, fasces, and laurel wreaths decorated many illustrations. Certain purely American figures such as Columbia, bald eagles, Indians, and the national flag and shield became increasingly more common. Symbolic words and phrases included "Patres Patriae," "Temperance, Prudence, Fortitude, Justice," and "The Supporter of Liberty and the Benefactor of Mankind." All this represents a third characteristic of Washington symbolism: he embodied all those honorable virtues sought by Americans, indeed, citizens of the whole world. He became an American Saint George fighting not only the dragon of British imperialism but also the monsters of demagoguery, licentiousness, irreligion, and anarchy.

The chief author of the Washington myth was a roguish Episcopal minister named Mason Locke Weems whose inclinations tended more toward entrepreneurship than evangelism. Hardly was the former president's body laid in its tomb before he sought to publish an account of Washington's life. In 1800 alone it went through four printings (editions, he called them), and by the Civil War there were at least forty-nine. "Washington, you know is gone!" he wrote a Philadelphia publisher. "Millions are gaping to read something about him." Weems sought to fill that demand. He created a folk hero mostly out of his own fertile imagination. Each of the early editions contained new and dubious anecdotes. The "Fifth edition, greatly improved" of 1806 included the first mention of his most famous "curious anecdote," the cherry tree story. Designed to illustrate the impact of his father's lessons upon the small boy, the story follows the elder Washington's admonition that "Truth, George, is the loveliest quality of youth."

In another such apocryphal story, to "startle George into a lively sense of his Maker," Augustine Washington planted cabbage seeds so that they would spell out his son's name when they matured. When the surprised youth found them the father used the phenomenon to ingraft in George's heart "that germ of piety, which filled his after life with so many of the precious fruits of morality."

Such moralistic myth-making served to reinforce the priggish image of Washington that remains with us today. He became the perfect model for emulation, epitomizimg integrity, courage, duty, leadership, service, and loyalty. The perpetuation of Weems' and the Federalists' interpretation of the Washington presidency expanded in the popular *McGuffey Readers,* which included the cherry tree incident and lauded Hamilton while excluding references to Jefferson altogether. But one must remember that Weems wrote juvenile literature, not serious biography. He sought to capture the essence of Washington's character and then to sermonize upon it.

Nothing so reinforced that imagery as Jean Antoine Houdon's statue based upon a 1785 life mask (modeled to a bust which is the standard to this day) and measurements for a full-sized representation. The emphasis in this work was the American Cincinnatus image of Washington resigning his commission. Installed in the new Virginia capitol in Richmond in 1796, Houdon's masterpiece depicted a more youthful, virile, and self-assured man than did Stuart's painting. Houdon's work was the prototype for sculptors for three-quarters of a century and remains the most copied three-dimensional image of the first president. The realism of this work, employing only a few classical allusions, appealed to the practicality of the young Republic.

When Horatio Greenough received a congressional commission for a heroic statue in the Capitol rotunda, he utilized the antique Phidian masterpiece of Zeus as his model. The result was a Greco-Roman monstrosity that outraged public sensibilities. Congress sentenced it to the Capitol Plaza, where pigeons defaced it until the Smithsonian Institution placed the work in a prominent place in one of its late twentieth-century temples on the Mall. Whatever its contribution to the evolution of American sculpture, it has never been a popular reflection of the image of the first president.

Far more significant was the utilization of equestrian statues of Washington. Following the realism of Houdon, the general-on-horseback appeared in such places as Union Square in Manhattan, the Boston Public Garden, West Point, Richmond, and the National Cathedral in the District of Columbia. The martial image of such public sculpture was part of a general refocusing of Washington the political leader to Washington the commanding general.

This had always been an important theme in Washington iconography, but Stuart's presidential image tended to dominate. The sentimentalization of much of American culture in the mid-nineteenth century, plus the impact of the Civil War, contributed to this shift of emphasis. Dominant in this era are the heroic paintings of Emanuel Leutze, epitomized by his first and most famous endeavor, *Washington Crossing the Delaware* (1851). This sentimentalization and simplification continued through and beyond the Centennial celebration in the illustrations of Howard Pyle and N. C. Wyeth.

Against all of this there was bound to be a reaction, best symbolized in the satirization of the mythic image in Grant Wood's *Parson Weems' Fable* (1939). Two things are important about this painting and its meaning. First, it attacks the mythology of Weems, not the reality of Washington. Second, it largely concerns the prepresidential aspects of Washington's career. In the popular mind George Washington was General Washington. President Washington became increasingly lost in the popular mind. The emphasis in school texts and the popular press was on the Hamilton versus Jefferson clash, which virtually ignored Washington's role during his presidency.

All this reflects the Weems tradition, which virtually dismissed the presidency. When, for instance, Enid La Monte Meadcroft wrote *The Story of George Washington* (1952) as part of Grosset & Dunlap's "Signature Books for Young Readers'' series, the book ends with his first inaugural. Only a few early biographers, such as Washington Irving, devoted much attention to the presidential years. And even Irving only gave the two terms one of five volumes.

The last great burst of traditional Washington iconography occurred during the 1930s when Congressman Sol Bloom, director of the George Washington Bicentennial Commission, organized a huge bash expending 338,000 Depression dollars and employing 125 staffers. Never one to be outdone, he even established a radio station extolling the first president's virtues via an antenna atop the Washington Monument.

For the most part the literary image of George Washington has emphasized the prepresidential years. Sometimes an author like William Gilmore Simms would note that what set Washington above Hamilton was the difference ''between smartness and wisdom.'' Much more common was the Carl Sandburg approach in *Remembrance Rock,* where the emphasis was on the future president's character at the outbreak of the Revolution.

Undoubtedly the most revolutionary literary treatment of Washington's presidential image came with Gore Vidal's *Burr* (1973), a Watergate-era historical novel that sought to elevate the voluptuary Aaron Burr to center stage while denigrating national heroes like Washington, Jefferson, and Madison for hypocrisy. Vidal's Washington is an atrocious general (aided primarily by even more inept British commanders) but a skilled and devious politician whose duplicity was easily recognizable by Americans caught in the denouement of the Nixon administration. Washington, writes Vidal, ''must be judged as an excellent politician who had no gift for warfare. History, as usual, has got it all backward.'' He was ''the supreme creator of this Union'' whose ''powerful will and serpentine cunning made of a loose confederation of sovereign states a strong federal government graven to this day in Washington's sombre Roman imperial image.''

Symbolic of the irreverence and irrelevance of some Bicentennial commentary was a *Penthouse* magazine article which named Washington to its gallery of ''Upward Failures'' because ''his lifelong muddleheadedness . . . won him the Presidency, a rich widow, slaves and the good life of a Virginia planter in retirement.'' In a snide ''interview'' this same soft-pornographic magazine found that the first president's ''fame has shrunk like the value of the dollar bill on which his face is seen.''

Part of a new cynicism brought on by the movement toward equality, the Vietnam War, and Watergate, there arose in the Bicentennial era a sarcastic critique of conventional patriotism that dominated the popular press and scholarly circles. Yet the Bicentennial image of George Washington reinforced many of the traditional impressions about him. As one might expect, the general emphasis was on his role as a military commander.

But the Bicentennial also expanded upon the ambiguity of Grant Wood's *Parson Weems' Fable* with a humorous and somewhat jaundiced view of the national birthday. Ray DeForest could depict ''George [Washington] and Mona

[Lisa] in the Baths of Caracalla'' in glazed ceramic, and Peter Saul could outrage convention with his *George Washington Crossing the Delaware,* where the general's hyperactive horse sinks the boat in the icy river. A Washington, D.C., country music station advertised itself with the first president (in the Stuart picture) wearing a cowboy hat and a bandanna. Even the august Smithsonian created an "under construction" poster using the Greenough statue topped with a hard hat.

One can, of course, overemphasize the impact of this imagery. Throughout the Bicentennial era one found a superabundance of traditional representations as Americans sought the ethos of a supposedly simpler era. In 1976 *Time* magazine created a special "September 26, 1789," issue with President Washington on its cover. "Incorruptible virtue, an unmatched sense of justice, a sound administrator's care for detail, an almost Roman stoicism when it comes to duty"—all these are variously granted to Washington. Despite two centuries of inquiry and insight, of criticism and cynicism, of caricature and humor, George Washington remains in the popular mind much as he has since his death, the very embodiment of the American ideal.

THE SCHOLARLY IMAGE

Like all chief executives, Washington has an image created by scholars. For obvious reasons that image differs somewhat from the popular one, and because of academic interest in the institution of the presidency (especially in this century), it has focused considerable attention on the years Washington served as chief magistrate.

"I walk on untrodden ground. There is scarcely any part of my conduct which may not hereafter be drawn into precedent," Washington wrote as he assumed his new position. Academics have been particularly interested in how his conduct has influenced subsequent administrations.

For nineteenth-century scholars like Chief Justice John Marshall and historian Jared Sparks and author Washington Irving supported the mythic image and turned the man into marble. Marshall's five-volume treatise was more concerned with the times than with the man. The fifth and best volume concerned the presidency and, as one would expect, Marshall wrote in the Federalist tradition, which made any criticism of Washington and his policies virtual treason.

President Jared Sparks of Harvard secured temporary control of the Washington papers then at Mount Vernon and began editing what became a twelve-volume set of Washingtonia (1834–1837). Little concerned with factual documentation, Sparks modified and deleted portions of the manuscripts that he thought should be included in the Washington canon. Sparks' Washington had no vices, even spelled correctly, and was a complete prig. According to John Bassett, Sparks "thought that a sacred halo surrounded the life of a great man, which profane hands should not break lest ordinary men should lose their proper reverence for authority, and for the noble ideals which were embraced in the higher specimens of the race." A similar "sacred halo" appeared in Washington Irving's biography. Much more readable than Marshall, Irving's study continues the Federalist bias without the chief justice's vindictive spirit.

The Federalist hagiographic tradition continued until the 1896 publication of Paul Leicester Ford's *The True George Washington*. In a series of brilliant essays, Ford sought to humanize the man by allowing Washington to speak to his readers through his own words. On subjects like religion, Ford gave both sides of the issue. Ford's book became the most popular treatment of the president since Weems. Since Ford's brother had recently edited fourteen volumes of Washington papers, no American alive had access to more of the whole corpus of the president's writings than he. Woodrow Wilson's one-volume biography is in the Weems-Sparks tradition. His future bête noire, Henry Cabot Lodge, did much better seven years earlier in a two-volume study for the "American Statesmen" series.

Key to new scholarship were better textual references. The first of the post-Sparks editions was edited by Worthington Chauncey Ford, chief of the Manuscripts Division of the Library of Congress, which possessed most of the known Washington papers. His editorial policy was to print the amended texts so as to provide the reader with what was thought to be the final authorial intent. When John C. Fitzpatrick undertook a bicentennial edition of the papers in the 1920s, he decided to read beneath the scratchouts and to return as far as possible to the original wording. Fitzpatrick's effort resulted in the publication of four volumes of *Diaries* (1925) and thirty-nine volumes of *Writings* (1931–1944).

For nearly fifty years this has been the major source of Washington papers, but in the 1960s a new edition was proposed, designed to incorporate new editorial techniques, especially in the style pioneered by Julian Boyd of *The Papers of Thomas Jefferson*. The new style will demonstrate original intent plus revisions, expand the notations extensively, and include correspondence to Washington. To date we have six volumes of *Diaries* (1976–1980) and an executive journal mostly kept during 1793. Publication of several concurrent series covering periods in Washington's life began in 1981. Under the general editorship first of Donald Jackson and now of W. W. Abbot, this series, edited at the University of Virginia, should prove the fourth and definitive edition of Washingtonia.

This century's biographies began in a muckraking tradition best represented by W. E. Woodward's *George Washington: The Image and the Man* (1926). If Weems went too far to one extreme, Woodward, who titillated the public with his iconoclastic attacks on an American idol, went just as far to the other. Although he later insisted that he admired the first president and that "there is not a debunking paragraph in the whole book," there is most certainly a derisive antihero bias throughout. In a similar vein is Rupert Hughes' uncompleted *George Washington*, but its three volumes (1926–1930) end with Yorktown, and so it makes no impact on the presidential image. Most other biographies were unexceptional and emphasized the war years while downplaying or omitting the presidential ones until the two grand biographies of the post–World War II era by Douglas Southall Freeman and James Thomas Flexner.

Fresh from his prize-winning multivolume series of the Civil War years, journalist Freeman was a scholar's scholar with a literary gift. Freeman hoped to divine the truth by uncovering the "fabric of fact" that underlay "the embroidery of fancy" surrounding his fellow Virginian. In seven volumes (1948–1957) he painstakingly and eloquently explored every facet of Washington's career. And yet, his detailed attention to documentation and his unwillingness to explore the nuances of divergent scholarly opinions on various matters means that the critical evaluation one hopes for is missing. This is particularly true of the presidential years, and the last volume had to be completed by his nonanalytical collaborators, J. A. Carroll and M. W. Ashworth.

Carroll summarized the Freeman tradition in a brief sketch of the presidential years published in 1961: "Washington's biographers . . . have put their subject first in war and second in peace. They have preferred the General's tent to the President's table." What they fail to recognize is that "Washington was a statesman fully as long as he was a soldier, and his achievements in council were fully as significant as those in the field." One of the principal reasons for this is the "fashion to regard President Washington's administration [as] not so much his as Alexander Hamilton's." All this is part of the enigma of Washington's presidency. Most will acknowledge that he was not the architect of ideas; he was essentially a man of action. Carroll lists ten particular achievements of his administration in which the president played an important and often decisive role: Washington "was neither listless nor dull, as sometimes he has been portrayed, and neither too old nor too deaf to participate fully" in policy decisions. Moreover, the neutrality policy which Carroll regards as Washington's greatest presidential achievement was in defiance of Hamilton's desires.

Unfortunately, Freeman's death prohibited the grand summation of the presidential career that we could have expected and, therefore, we do not have a full, mature evaluation of the man by one of this country's great biographers.

Perhaps a more effective biography is found in Flexner's four volumes (1965–1972). No other such study devotes more space to the presidency than does this biography. Moreover, Flexner benefited from the massive amount of historical study about the Federalist years that complemented his own study. Flexner was more interested in personality than Freeman, and he is more skilled in weaving conflicting evidence into a cohesive whole. As the first major biographer in over a hundred years to live to the project's completion, Flexner went on a few years later to condense the four volumes into one entitled *Washington: The Indispensable Man*, which aptly summarizes in its title the book's theme.

Besides these biographies there has been a veritable flood of scholarly writings related to Washington during the presidential years. Among these scholars none asks more penetrating questions of the two administrations than Joseph Charles:

How much did [Washington] understand the things being done in his name? How did those who made the greatest use of him actually regard him? Was he a responsible executive, making his own decisions after consulting his advisers, or was he something of a figurehead? Was he a sick, tired old man who went grimly through the ceremonies laid out for him, or was he an actual leader of his people, whose own deepest convictions and ultimate aims were expressed in the policies he was shaping?

Charles inclines toward the more unfavorable answers to these questions. In that he follows a pro-Jeffersonian tradition of Claude Bowers and Vernon Louis Parrington, who see a designing Hamilton behind every anti-Republican action of the president, and the pro-Hamiltonians like Forrest McDonald, who finds Jefferson and Madison small-minded agrarians with little true comprehension of the national destiny.

Unfortunately, Charles' early death never allowed this promising scholar to fully answer the questions he raised. McDonald's *The Presidency of George Washington* (1974) is the ultimate in the derision of the chief executive's effectiveness:

The harsh reality of Washington's Presidency is that the Father of his Country was not, except in a symbolic sense, particularly efficacious in establishing the permanence of his country, or even of the executive branch of his country's government. His administration was responsible for four monumental achievements: Hamilton's financial program, neutrality in a belligerent world, the opening of the Mississippi River, and the removal of the red men and redcoats in the Northwest Territory.

Washington's role in the successful outcome was negligible, according to McDonald. The first president was a national symbol but not a positive force in administrative development. But McDonald's position represents a decided minority among scholars.

Leonard D. White's administrative history entitled *The Federalists* (1948) holds an almost directly opposite opinion. He found the first president an able leader who more than Hamilton understood the broad perspective of public policy, who saw effective administration as a factor in achieving popular support, and who "understood good administration to be characterized by integrity, system, energy, reliance on facts, relative freedom from detail, and due responsibility to Congress." White concludes a list of Federalist achievements with the "recognition of the moral authority of the general government, a victory won by the character of Washington, the integrity of the public services, and the decisiveness with which the challenge to public authority in western Pennsylvania was met."

White does not see Washington as a mere figurehead, and he places much stock in the example of rectitude set by the chief executive. If Richard Nixon, Warren Harding, and Ulysses Grant are to be castigated for setting the wrong tone of leadership, then surely a George Washington deserves praise for integrity and service which continue to be held up as the example of selfless service. "The moral standards of the Federalist public service were extraordinarily high— higher by far than those prevailing in the British service or the French and approaching the austerity of the administrative system perfected by Frederick the Great in Prussia.''

In the midst of the Vietnam War and the Watergate affair, numerous scholars looked deep into the Washington precedents to see if his actions supported the creation of presidential powers claimed by Richard Nixon. For instance, Raoul Berger's *Executive Privilege: A Constitutional Myth* (1974) constituted a legal brief against such claims as made in Deputy Attorney General William P. Rogers' 1958 memorandum on this subject. Berger surveyed the two important executive privilege cases of the Washington administration—involving records pertaining to General Arthur St. Clair's 1792 defeat by the Indians and to the Jay Treaty in 1796—and found Rogers' ''precedents'' ''utterly unworthy of credence'' in justifying executive privilege.

Far more popular than Berger's legalistic briefs was Arthur Schlesinger's *Imperial Presidency* (1973), a wholesale indictment of the presumed powers of the chief executive as claimed in the mid-twentieth century. Schlesinger found Washington circumspect in his conduct and, in a matter like the controversy between Hamilton and Madison over the Neutrality Proclamation, having ''a larger vision than either of the debaters.'' This ability to find a solution to problems when his advisers were divided intrigues Norman Risjord, who finds such actions all the more indicative of Washington's control of the situation than his detractors would admit.

Garry Wills' *Cincinnatus* (1984) not only describes Washington's image, but makes a number of astute observations on how his subject foreswore Caesarism and learned to gain power by yielding it at appropriate moments. Wills also stressed Washington's importance as ''the embodiment of stability within a revolution, speaking of fixed things in a period of flux.''

One of the most forgotten Washington legacies was his refusal to stay in office until death. In a comparative study entitled *The First New Nation* (1963), Seymour Martin Lipset applauded this decision, which enabled Washington ''to set a precedent as the first head of a modern state to turn over office to a duly elected successor.'' He did not feel that his presence in the office was indispensable, and he instinctively knew that the peaceful transfer of power to a duly elected successor constituted one of the most important building blocks in erecting a stable nation-state among the diverse groups in the large space of the young Republic. For this act alone, the charismatic Father of His Country deserves credit, the more so because his closest advisers besought him to run again.

In many respects President Washington's scholarly image is like General Washington's. He was not of great creative intellectual powers and was extraordinarily cautious when making any move. When determined upon a policy he expected all to follow and abhorred public disagreement about administrative decisions. He tried to maintain diversity of opinion among his close staff. He conducted himself with circumspection and expected all who followed him to do the same. In effect he created an office which, as Marcus Cunliffe described it, was ''something between a monarch, prime minister, party chief and father figure; as a transcendental yet a representative being, a timeless Delphic oracle whose words will endure forever *and* a fallible creature who is an immediate and tempting target for abuse.''

THE MYTH AND THE PRESIDENCY

As president, George Washington was generally quite popular. It was not until his second term that public criticism emerged, and this was confined to the most vocal opposition press. He continued both the strong nationalism and devoted republicanism of his military career and combined these with an administrative skill that laid the groundwork and benchmark for the bureaucracy that developed after him.

In an age of monarchy, he was treated in the popular press much like a king. *He* could do no wrong; he had the best interest of his fellow citizens at heart. It was the evil advisers that led him astray. So the attack was directed against the evil advisers—personified in Hamilton. The secretary of the treasury became for George Washington what Robert Walpole was for George II. The opposition itself seldom attacked Washington personally. Perhaps no other president except Eisenhower enjoyed such personal bipartisan support.

Washington expected no unanimity among his advisers, but did expect acquiescence once a decision was reached. This was the characteristic of his military command style. Unfortunately, he could find few capable subordinates after Jefferson, Hamilton, and Randolph left the cabinet. The loss of the two Republicans—Jefferson and Randolph—deprived him of conflicting advice, and the remainder were mostly Hamilton's sycophants. The apogee of neo-Hamilton scholarship in the 1960s has been followed by an almost devastating critique of the most trusted Washington cabinet officer. From this has emerged the scholarly image of Washington as the effective coalition leader of the first administration and the increasingly more partisan, although never fully committed, leader of the second.

The greatest criticism of Washington's scholarly image revolves around his unwillingness to fully comprehend the political system being created around him. Washington distrusted "factions"; but no matter; so did John Adams, Alexander Hamilton, and Thomas Jefferson. The consensual politics all these men sought disintegrated in the clash of conflict politics that they all abhorred and blamed their opposition for.

One can make any number of final assessments of the man. Whether we seek a popular mythic image or a scholarly researched one, the general evaluation is the same. George Washington was one of the truly great presidents. Among scholars he has slipped to third place behind Abraham Lincoln and Franklin Delano Roosevelt. A student of the presidency like Thomas Bailey still ranks him first. Clinton Rossiter notes the peculiar circumstance in that Washington "lent his prestige to the Presidency, but today quite the reverse process takes place when a man becomes President." In Rossiter's *The American Presidency*

Washington ranks near the top of six chief executives who gave strength to the office.

Perhaps the most perceptive analysis of the first president's popular and scholarly reputation was penned by a Briton, Marcus Cunliffe, in *George Washington: Man and Monument* (1958):

He had become so merged with America that his is one of the names on the land, the presences in the air. Useless for his biographers to try to separate Washington from the myths and images surrounding him—the visage on the postage stamp and on the dollar bill, so familiar that no one sees it. . . . The man *is* the monument; the monument *is* America. *Si monumentum riquiris, circumspice.*

NOTE

1. *Richard II,* act 5, scene 2, lines 12–16.

ANNOTATED BIBLIOGRAPHY

Documents

Abbot, W. W., gen. ed. *The Papers of George Washington.* Charlottesville: University Press of Virginia, 1981–   .
  Seven volumes have been published in what should be the definitive edition of Washington's writings.
Fitzpatrick, John C., ed. *The Diaries of George Washington.* 4 vols. Boston: Houghton Mifflin, 1925.
————. *The Writings of George Washington.* 39 vols. Washington, D.C.: Government Printing Office, 1931–1944.
Ford, Worthington Chauncey, ed. *The Writings of George Washington.* 14 vols. New York: G. P. Putnam's Sons, 1889–1893.
Jackson, Donald, and Dorothy Twohig, eds. *The Diaries of George Washington.* 6 vols. Charlottesville: University Press of Virginia, 1976–1980.
Sparks, Jared, ed. *The Writings of George Washington.* 12 vols. Boston: John B. Russell, 1833–1837.

Biographies

Alden, John R. *George Washington: A Biography.* Baton Rouge: Louisiana State University Press, 1984.
  Highly complimentary of its subject, this is the best brief survey of Washington's life.
Everett, Edward. *The Life of George Washington.* New York: Sheldon and Co., 1860.
  Typically laudatory.
Flexner, James Thomas. *George Washington.* 4 vols. Boston: Little, Brown, 1965–1972.
  The latest and most perceptive of the multivolume biographies but lacking in

critical assessment of historical commentary on its subject. Much of the last two
volumes deal with the presidency.

Ford, Paul Leicester. *The True George Washington*. Philadelphia: J. B. Lippincott Co.,
1896.

Probably the best biography before Freeman.

Freeman, Douglas Southall. *George Washington*. 7 vols. New York: Charles Scribner's
Sons, 1948–1957.

John A. Carroll and Mary Wells Ashworth completed the final volume of this
detailed but non-analytical study.

Hughes, Rupert. *George Washington*. 3 vols. New York: Macmillan, 1926–1930.

A debunking account that does not reach the presidency.

Irving, Washington. *Life of George Washington*. 5 vols. New York: G. P. Putnam, 1855–
1859.

Pro-Federalist, but best of the biographies before Ford's.

Lodge, Henry Cabot. *George Washington*. 2 vols. Boston: Houghton Mifflin, 1889.

Marshall, John. *Life of Washington*. 5 vols. 1804–1807.

Ponderously written and so pro-Federalist that it outraged Jefferson.

Ramsay, David. *The Life of George Washington*. New York: Hopkins & Seymour, 1807.

The first of several editions by a popular South Carolina historian.

Reed, Anna C. *The Life of George Washington*. New York: American Sunday School
Union, 1829.

Typical of the genre and often reprinted in the nineteenth century.

Weems, Mason Locke. *The Life of Washington*. Marcus Cunliffe, ed. Cambridge, Mass.:
Harvard University Press, 1962.

Reprint of ninth edition in 1809 of a biography first published in 1800. Excellent
introduction by Cunliffe.

Wilson, Woodrow. *George Washington*. New York: Harper and Brother, 1896.

In the romantic and idolatrous Sunday School Tract tradition.

Woodward, William E. *George Washington: The Image and the Man*. New York: Charles
Scribner's Sons, 1926.

Most influential of the debunking biographies.

Special Studies

Baldwin, Leland D. *Whisky Rebels: The Story of a Frontier Uprising*. Pittsburgh: University of Pittsburgh Press, 1939.

Beard, Charles A. *Economic Origins of Jeffersonian Democracy*. New York: Knopf,
1951.

Sees Washington as part of a speculators' conspiracy against popular will.

Berger, Raoul. *Executive Privilege: A Constitutional Myth*. Cambridge, MA: Harvard
University Press, 1974.

Finds the advocates of executive privilege misusing Washington's role in the
evolution of the doctrine.

Boller, Paul F., Jr. "George Washington and Religious Liberty." *William and Mary
Quarterly*, 21 (Winter 1961): 780–91.

Reviews Washington's image in New England sermons, 1799–1800.

Boorstin, Daniel. *The Americans: The National Experience*. New York: Random House,
1965.

The legend is explored in a chapter on "The Mythologizing of George Washington."

Borden, Morton. *Parties and Politics in the Early Republic, 1789–1815*. New York: Thomas Y. Crowell, 1967.

A brief review of the scholarly literature on the subject.

————, ed. *America's Ten Greatest Presidents*. Chicago: Rand McNally, 1961.

J. A. Carroll's essay is solid but uninspired.

Bowers, Claude G. *Hamilton and Jefferson: The Struggle for Democracy*. Boston: Little, Brown, 1926.

Portrays Washington as Hamilton's lackey.

Bradley, Harold W. "The Political Thinking of George Washington." *Journal of Southern History*, 11 (1955): 469–86.

Virtually the only commentary on a much-neglected subject.

Bryan, William A. *George Washington in American Literature, 1775–1865*. New York: Columbia University Press, 1952.

Excellent literary analysis.

Chambers, William Nisbet. *Political Parties in the New Nation: The American Experience, 1776–1809*. New York: Oxford University Press, 1963.

A political scientist's successful integration of his discipline with history.

Charles, Joseph. *Origins of the American Party System*. Williamsburg, Va.: Institute of Early American History and Culture, 1956.

Neglects Washington's role.

Craven, Wesley Frank. *The Legend of the Founding Fathers*. New York: Macmillan, 1956.

Contains an excellent chapter on "A Legend Debunked and Restored."

Cunliffe, Marcus. *George Washington: Man and Monument*. Boston: Little, Brown, 1958.

Probably the best starting point on any study of Washington and the myth that surrounds him.

————. "Symbols We Made of a Man Named George Washington." *Smithsonian* (February 1982) 75–80.

A 250th anniversary update of Cunliffe's earlier study, concluding: "Washington has stood the test of time to an astonishing degree."

DeConde, Alexander. *Entangling Alliance: Politics and Diplomacy under George Washington*. Durham, N.C.: Duke University Press, 1958.

Eisen, Gustavus A. *Portraits of Washington*. 3 vols. New York: Robert Hamilton, 1932.

Along with the work by Morgan and Fielding, the best study of its subject.

Fish, Carl Russell. "George Washington, the Man." Illinois State Historical Society, *Transactions*, 39 (1932): 21–44.

Perceptive.

Fisher, Sydney George. "The Legendary and Myth-making Process in Histories of the American Revolution." *Proceedings of the American Philosophical Society*, 51 (April 1912): 53–75.

A major revisionist interpretation of the revolutionary experience.

Fishwick, Marshall W. *American Heroes: Myth and Reality*. Washington, D.C.: Public Affairs Press, 1954.

Finds that Washington, Jefferson, and Lincoln constitute a "trinity of culture heroes" who preside over the United States.

Friedman, Lawrence J. *Inventors of the Promised Land*. New York: Alfred A. Knopf,

1975.

Portrays the Washington myth as having a profound impact on the nineteenth-century American psyche.

Groseclose, Barbara S. *Emanuel Leutze, 1816–1868*. Washington, D.C.: Smithsonian Institution Press, 1975.

Discusses this nineteenth-century heroic painter and the depiction of the revolutionary experience he created.

Hofstadter, Richard. *The Idea of a Party System: The Rise of Legitimate Opposition in the United States*. Berkeley: University of California Press, 1969.

Effectively notes the place of antiparty attitudes in early America.

Jacobs, Phoebe Lloyd. "John James Barralet and the Apotheosis of George Washington." *Winterthur Portfolio,* 12 (1977): 115–37.

Kammen, Michael. *A Season of Youth: The American Revolution in Historical Imagination*. New York: Oxford University Press, 1978.

The most thorough and imaginative reappraisal of the revolutionary theme and Washington's role in it.

LaFay, Howard. "The Man Behind the Myths: Geo. Washington." *National Geographic,* 150 (July 1976): 90–111.

Typical Bicentennial appraisal which virtually ignores the presidential years.

Larned, Josephus N. *A Study of the Greatness in Men*. Boston: Houghton Mifflin, 1911.

A chapter on "Washington: Impressive in Greatness" can find no wrong in the hero in comparison with others.

Link, Eugene Perry. *Democratic-Republican Societies, 1790–1800*. New York: Columbia University Press, 1942.

Lipset, Seymour Martin. *The First New Nation: The United States in Historical and Comparative Perspective*. New York: Basic Books, 1963.

A sociologist's study that is less successful than Chambers'.

McDonald, Forrest. *The Presidency of George Washington*. Lawrence: University Press of Kansas, 1974.

Sees the president as a figurehead.

McGrane, Reginald. "George Washington: Anglo-American Hero." *Virginia Magazine of History and Biography,* 63 (1955): 3–14.

Malone, Dumas. "Was Washington the Great American?" *New York Times Magazine,* February 16, 1958.

An affirmative answer by Thomas Jefferson's biographer.

Mayo, Bernard. *Myths and Men*. Athens: University of Georgia Press, 1959.

Contains an insightful essay on Washington.

Miller, John C. *The Federalist Era*. New York: Harper and Row, 1960.

Judicious appraisal of the age.

Morgan, Edmund S. "George Washington: The Aloof American." *Virginia Quarterly Review,* 52 (Summer 1976): 410–36.

A fine appraisal of the man.

————"The Greatness of George Washington: A Sense of Power." *The New Republic* (February 21, 1981): 31–35.

One of Professor Morgan's typically insightful essays.

Morgan, John H., and Mantle Fielding. *The Life Portraits of Washington and Their Replicas*. Lancaster, Pa.: Lancaster Press, 1931.

Morison, Samuel Eliot. *By Land and By Sea*. New York: Alfred Knopf, 1953.
    Contains his excellent 1932 essay entitled "The Young Man Washington."
Murray, Robert K., and Tim H. Blessing. "The Presidential Performance Study: A
    Progress Report." *Journal of American History*, 70 (December 1983): 535–55.
    Historians rank Washington behind Lincoln and Franklin Roosevelt as one of only
    three "great" presidents.
Nettels, Curtis Putnam. "The Washington Theme in American History." Massachusetts
    Historical Society, *Proceedings*, 68 (1952): 171–98.
"The New Nation: Special Bicentennial Issue, September 26, 1789," *Time*, 197 (1976).
    Good for the current popular image of the first president.
Padover, Saul K. *The Genius of America: Men Whose Ideas Shaped Our Civilization*.
    New York: McGraw-Hill, 1960.
    Excellent treatment of Washington's role as president is included in an essay
    entitled "The American as Archetype."
———. "George Washington: Portrait of a True Conservative." *Social Research*, 22
    (1955): 199–222.
Paltsits, Victor Hugo. *Washington's Farewell Address*. New York: New York Public
    Library, 1935.
    Best introduction to the writing of this paper.
Parrington, Vernon Louis. *Main Currents in American Thought*. New York: 1927.
    Virtually ignores Washington's role.
Partin, Robert. "The Changing Images of George Washington from Weems to Freeman,"
    Social Studies, 56 (February 1965): 52–59.
Phelps, Glen A. "George Washington and the Founding of the Presidency." *Presidential
    Studies Quarterly*, 17 (Spring 1987): 345–63.
    Argues Washington relied on his wartime experiences to model his conception of
    the chief executive role.
Richardson, Edgar P. "A Penetrating Characterization of Washington by John Trumbull."
    Winterthur Portfolio, 3 (1967): 1–23.
Risjord, Norman K. *Forging the American Republic, 1760–1815*. Reading, Mass: Ad-
    dison-Wesley, 1973.
    A solid survey of the age of Washington.
Rossiter, Clinton. *The American Presidency*. New York: Harcourt, Brace & World, 1956.
    Complimentary of Washington's role in the evolution of the office.
Schlesinger, Arthur M., Jr. *The Imperial Presidency*. Boston: Atlantic Monthly Co.,
    1973.
    Generally complimentary to Washington.
Shirk, Samuel B. *The Characterization of George Washington in American Plays since
    1875*. Eastman, Pa.: J. S. Correll, 1949.
    Lacks analysis.
Sidey, Hugh. "Above All the Man Had Character." *Time*, February 21, 1983, pp. 24–
    25.
    An acute appraisal by one of the most perceptive popular commentators on the
    presidency.
Slaughter, Thomas P. *The Whiskey Rebels: Frontier Epilogue to the American Revolution*.
    New York: Oxford University Press, 1986.
    Highly sophisticated analysis of this critical event.
Stewart, Donald H. *The Opposition Press of the Federalist Period*. Albany: SUNY Press,

1969.
   Good for the Republican view of Washington's administration.
Sword, Wiley. *President Washington's Indian War: The Struggle for the Old Northwest.*
   Norman: University of Oklahoma Press, 1985.
   A solid narrative account of the Ohio campaigns of 1790–1795.
U.S. George Washington Bicentennial Commission. *History of the George Washington*
   Bicentennial Celebration, 4 vols. Washington, D.C.: Government Printing Office,
   1932.
   Congressman Sol Bloom's tribute to his hero, evoking the mythic image of Wash-
   ington.
Varg, Paul A. *Foreign Policies of the Founding Fathers.* East Lansing: Michigan State
   University Press, 1963.
   A judicious overview of American diplomacy through 1812, seeing divisions
   between the idealist and realist factions.
Vidal, Gore. *Burr.* New York: Random House, 1973.
   A novel which sees Washington as a better politician than general.
Wecter, Dixon. *The Hero in America.* New York: Charles Scribner's Sons, 1941.
   An excellent chapter on "The President and Parson Weems."
White, Leonard D. *The Federalists: A Study in Administrative History.* New York:
   Macmillan, 1948.
   Contains an excellent chapter on "George Washington as an Administrator."
Whittemore, Frances D. *George Washington in Sculpture.* New York: Harper, 1933.
Wick, Wendy C. *George Washington, an American Icon: The Eighteenth-Century*
   Graphic Portraits. Washington, DC: Smithsonian Institution, 1982.
   An excellent discussion of the early popular images of the general and president
   through 1800.
Wills, Garry. *Cincinnatus: George Washington and the Enlightenment.* Garden City,
   N.Y.: Doubleday, 1984.
   A scholar-journalist's often deft insights into Washington's self-image and popular
   image in the eighteenth and nineteenth centuries.
Wright, Esmond. *Washington and the American Revolution.* New York: Macmillan, 1957.
   Summary chapter on the presidency by an English scholar.

Television Production

"George Washington." Eight-hour miniseries featuring Barry Bostwick. CBS-TV, Feb-
   ruary 1984.
   Ignored the presidency.
"George Washington: The Forging of a Nation." Four-hour miniseries featuring Barry
   Bostwick. CBS-TV, February 1986.
   Sequel to the 1984 production, focused on the presidential years, giving Wash-
   ington a larger role than the Hamilton and Jefferson partisans would offer.

2   THOMAS JEFFERSON

Ronald L. Hatzenbuehler

Thomas Jefferson has always presented problems of interpretation. At a dinner honoring Nobel Prize winners, President John F. Kennedy caught the essence of the difficulty when he said: "I think this is the most extraordinary collection of talent, of human knowledge, that has ever been gathered together in the White House—with the possible exception of when Thomas Jefferson dined alone." The Kennedy wit aside, the president spoke an important truth about Thomas Jefferson: He is hard to understand because he did so much. Try replacing Jefferson's name in the Kennedy quote with those of other American presidents. The aphorism becomes absurd.

Perhaps because of this diversity of interests and accomplishments, most of Jefferson's biographers have confessed that they have failed to capture the essence of the man. Even Dumas Malone remarked as he recently completed the last of his six-volume life of Jefferson that he "could not hope to have done justice to a virtually inexhaustible subject." Reflecting on the numerous biographies of Jefferson since 1900 (and the same indictment applies to scholars treating single aspects of his life), Winthrop Jordan has observed, "If we regard biographers as in some measure standing in an adversary relationship with their subjects, Jefferson wins hands down." From music to gardening, from architecture to paleontology, from political theory to a tinker's inventions, we know more about Thomas Jefferson than scholars have been able to assimilate.

But if it may be said that the scholarly community has failed to deal adequately with the multitude of Jefferson's accomplishments, it must also be said that the public has fared even less well. On the eve of the 200th anniversary of his birth in April 1943, the *New York Times* reported the results of a survey indicating that of 7,000 freshmen in thirty-six colleges and universities only 16 percent could satisfactorily answer the question, "Who was Thomas Jefferson?" Worse still, two of the schools included in the survey were the College of William and Mary, Jefferson's alma mater, and the University of Virginia, the school he was instrumental in founding. One wonders if these students were part of the 16 percent who could correctly name two of Jefferson's contributions or whether they were among those who believed him to be the president of the Confederacy, founder of the *Saturday Evening Post,* originator of the Monroe Doctrine, or discoverer of electricity.

Even at the time of the Bicentennial celebration—doubly relevant for Jefferson because he died on July 4, 1826, fifty years after Independence Day—Jefferson continued to be a troublesome character for Americans. Because he thought and wrote about so many things and because his words, like the scriptures of the Bible, fit so many issues and are quoted by so many people, his writings have become a grab-bag with a prize for everyone. At this same time, however, three out of every four Americans who were asked to sign sections of the Declaration of Independence asserting that it is the right of the people to alter or abolish governments that become abusive of people's rights refused to do so because the phrases were "too radical" and part of a "subversive document."

Knowledge about the man who penned the document that more than any other defines our origins as a people simply does not touch us very deeply. Peter Stone and Sherman Edwards, the authors of the play *1776,* expressed bewilderment that so many people have asked the same question of them, "Is it true?" "What we cannot answer," they lamented, "is how such a question could possibly be asked so often by Americans. What they want to know is whether or not the story of their political origin, the telling of their national legend, is correct as presented. Don't they know? Haven't they heard it before?" Registering the same dismay concerning popular knowledge of the events of Jefferson's presidency, Gore Vidal when he finished writing *Burr* leveled this charge: For most Americans, "Thomas Jefferson was the third President of what might as well have been another country."

What are we, as scholars and Americans, to make of a man who wrote thousands of letters addressing almost every major topic of his day, who mastered the ideas of such a variety of authors, who was accomplished in so many different areas of inquiry, and who pursued several careers during his single lifetime? A starting point is his epitaph, which he chose for himself just prior to his death: "Author of the Declaration of American Independence, of the Statute of Virginia for religious freedom, & Father of the University of Virginia." But what is he trying to tell us with these words? Did he list for us what he took to be his most enduring contributions, his proudest accomplishments, his legacy to his country? If so, how are we to judge his political role as a member of the Virginia House of Burgesses, delegate to the Second Continental Congress, governor of Virginia, diplomat, secretary of state, and president of the United States—a period of time covering over one-third of his life?

In 1960 Merrill D. Peterson in his book, *The Jeffersonian Image in the American Mind,* posed the question of whether "dualities" in studies of Jefferson—contradictions, paradoxes, ironies—would persist, or whether a consensus among scholars would emerge regarding his proper place in American history. With the completion of Dumas Malone's study, it is tempting to accept that author's affirmation that the fight for freedom was the most enduring consistency in his life—freedom from English oppression, freedom of conscience, freedom for the mind. This theme, more than any other, Malone argues, gave his life meaning and ensures his place among the greatest of American leaders.

But the argument that this pursuit of freedom also governed his presidency is not persuasive. Rather, his actions as president defy formulas based on a fight for freedom in his earlier life. Ideas, which directed his behavior prior to 1800, became less and less the determinants of policy, as events moved more and more out of control. It is impossible to make his ideas and actions as president consistent in every instance. Therefore, it will be the argument of this chapter that an unresolved and persistent duality between his life as Virginian and national leader distinguishes Jefferson's presidency from those of other early presidents. Freedom must be understood not from a philosophical perspective, as has been most popular, but rather as an outgrowth of Virginia's gentry culture prior to the American Revolution. As a spokesman for that world view, Jefferson effectively chose words in the years leading to revolution that appealed to colonists from other areas than Virginia. But as president, foreign policy problems invalidated many of his provincial views, and he found he could not deal creatively with the national concerns. Only in retirement in Monticello, in reflection about the turmoil of his public life, did Jefferson succeed in restoring a sense of harmony to his life.

FREEDOM DEFINED AS RIGHTS

Jefferson was obsessed with the topic of freedom and devoted much of his correspondence and public papers to treatments of it. Yet one should not conclude, based upon Jefferson's extensive thinking about this topic, that he approached the subject from a purely philosophical perspective. Rather, the continuing vitality of his writings stems from the directness of his language and the experiential nature of his knowledge. He spoke about, but never defined the precise origins of, natural rights. He based his arguments upon, but never debated the meaning of, self-evident rights. He believed in, but never attempted to justify the existence of, a rational order in the universe. Therefore, those historians who have pushed Jefferson forward as the American epitome of Enlightenment thought err when they try to make him an ideologue. Empiricism was a method that Jefferson practiced, not a philosophy that he preached. Writing to John Adams in 1820, Jefferson spoke of the knowledge gained from "the Lockes, the Tracys, and the Stewarts." "Rejecting all organs of information, therefore, but my senses," he wrote, "I rid myself of . . . speculations hyperphysical and antiphysical [that can] so uselessly occupy and disquiet the mind." Turning Descartes completely around, Jefferson affirmed to Adams, "I feel, therefore, I exist."

VIRGINIA'S GENTRY CULTURE

There are many explanations for this material focus on life that so distinguishes Jefferson's thinking about freedom and liberty, but the origin that best illumines his practicality is found in his upbringing in the gentry culture of Virginia. To be sure, Jefferson's niche in this society is not perfect: he lived west of the tidewater area in land cleared by his father; he built his home on a hill instead of next to a river; he planted crops other than tobacco along the contours of hills and rotated them; he talked of freeing his slaves; and he was president of the American Philosophical Society. But his deviant behaviors count for less than his consistencies, and without the outlook of this group, Jefferson's writings become far less understandable. He was a man of cosmopolitan tastes but Virginia habits—French wine always tasted best at Monticello.

The gentry culture into which Jefferson came to adulthood was action-oriented. Burgesses was dominated by an articulate few, and speculative thought counted for little in the practical world of business and politics. Wealth was based on broad acres, black labor, and a weed. Law was a profession that many men like Jefferson followed, but only as a means to acquire more land, buy more slaves, and plant more tobacco.

This situation in Virginia by which 2 to 5 percent of the whites controlled the economic, social, political, and religious affairs of the colony evolved over a circuitous route involving three main factors: constant immigration throughout the seventeenth century, a high death rate of those immigrants, and the vagaries of the international market for tobacco. In the first place, without a constant stream of immigrants across the seventeenth century, there would have been no English culture in the Chesapeake Bay region. White or black, rich or poor, English or non-English, until about the 1680s, there was a net population decline in both Virginia and Maryland. Because the factor of death disrupted the normal course of an Englishman's life and because of a constant imbalance in the sexes that reversed age-old trends in European society, many cultural changes were necessary. Extended families, rather than nuclear ones, as in England or New England, were the rule. Parental and male authority were severely weakened as the premature death of one or both spouses rendered conventional ideas about family life obsolete.

But, during the late seventeenth century, those four in ten Englishmen who, on the average, lived through their period of indentured servitude could expect to make money from planting tobacco. After 1680 there was a period of stagnation in the international tobacco economy, but the Chesapeake economy was never completely ruined. And the wealth of those who had established themselves as individuals or families grew after 1720 at a steady rate, estimated at 2 to 3 percent overall real growth per year until the time of the American Revolution. Life, once so tenuous as to be disruptive personally and for society, became more predictable and more patterned.

The Virginia gentry date from this period of slow, steady growth. Those men

who gained the fertile land along the rivers had the capital to make the transition
from the labor of indentured servants to slaves, were fortunate enough to establish
a family, and were able to link their family with other successful families,
dominated Virginia society. The origins of this colonial Virginia life were hidden
in the complexities of immigration lists, death rates, and fluctuating tobacco
prices, but its unwritten history was lost in obscurity. Those people who came
to prominence as members of the gentry reckoned time from 1700, not 1607.
In the nineteenth century, descendants of these families spun a myth of the
Cavalier origins of gentry society, but the first generation was not introspective
about their natural selection. They did not care where they had been. They lived
in, and managed for, the present.

GENERATIONS, REVOLUTIONS, AND A NATURAL
ARISTOCRACY

Three of Jefferson's most troublesome sets of writings about freedom become
consistent when viewed from this perspective—his thoughts concerning the passing of generations, the need for continuing revolutions, and the existence of a
natural aristocracy among men. From Paris on the eve of the French Revolution,
Jefferson wrote to Madison, then a delegate to the Constitutional Convention,
concerning "the question whether one generation of men has a right to bind
another?" His answer: "I set out on this ground, which I suppose to be self
evident, *'that the earth belongs in usufruct to the living:'* that the dead have
neither powers nor rights over it." Debts, laws, and even constitutions should
continue for no longer than one generation, reckoned by Jefferson at nineteen
to twenty years. Nearly thirty years later, in 1816, he addressed the topic again
with a similar conclusion: "Each generation is as independent of the one preceding, as that was of all which had gone before. . . . This corporeal globe, and
everything upon it, belong to its present corporeal inhabitants, during their
generation."

Closely related to these thoughts is his advocacy of periodic revolutions. Early
in 1787, reacting again from Paris to American events (this time to Shays'
rebellion), Jefferson wrote to various correspondents that the people's censorship
of government was the only way to correct tyranny and injustice. Even if the
people were wrong in rising against some governmental act, the action would
call attention to public affairs. "I hold that a little rebellion now and then is a
good thing," he wrote to Madison, "and is necessary for the sound health of
government."

There are no more radical-sounding statements in Jefferson's writings than
these, that the earth belongs to the living generation and that "a little rebellion
now and then" is a good thing. Taken to their logical extension, Jefferson is
advocating not liberty but license. But these thoughts are grounded far less in
the soil of Jacobin France than that of prerevolutionary Virginia. The gentry
who dominated that society viewed their role as a natural development without

the class cleavages that so characterized European civilization. Without a feudal past, the dead hand that crippled every generation after the first, Virginia had evolved into the perfect society of peace and tranquility. Best of all, the wisdom of this assertion could be tested empirically. Where were the food riots, the high taxes, the encumbrances of kings and aristocrats? Virginian society, in Jefferson's view and in that of his friends, rolled placidly onward, like the James eternally unchanging, but unlike the river free to alter its course whenever the need arose.

Because of the lack of a feudal past and the fact that the gentry regarded themselves as a natural product of Virginian history, Jefferson referred to his peers as comprising a "natural aristocracy . . . the grounds of [which] are virtue and talents." "Artificial aristocrats," produced by inherited wealth, birth, or religious succession, did not exist in colonial Virginia based on Jefferson's definitions, and even if they had they were not to be feared because the people, in their votes, would correctly separate "the wheat from the chaff." This expression of trust in the people that is omnipresent in Jefferson's political writings was fostered by his political experiences among the Virginia gentry. They felt destined to control the affairs of the colony, and they exercised this control through the House of Burgesses.

NATURE OF REPRESENTATION

Representative government as practiced by the gentry in Virginia was the bulwark of society, but once again Burgesses must be understood less for what it was than for what it appeared to be. Most important, a few families dominated its activities. Wealth and status elevated a man to prominence in the society, but election to Burgesses separated those of character and distinction from the rest. Representative government was reserved for, and the responsibility of, the natural aristocrats, and those men were reelected continually. "Pseudo-aristocrats," as Jefferson tagged them, had arisen in the past, had attained positions of artificial influence and power through the King's Council, but had become "unpopular." "A Randolph, a Carter, or a Burwell must have great personal superiority over a common competitor to be elected by the people even at this day." And again, the validity of the assertion was self-evident. If circumstances had been otherwise, Burgesses would not have progressed as it had.

The harmony of the gentry's lives, then, rested in large measure in Burgesses' control of the colony's affairs. Even the royal governors deferred to Burgesses, learning that they were more likely to get what they wanted by compromise than by confrontation. This is the world in which Thomas Jefferson lived. He grew up in Albemarle but attended the College of William and Mary, studied law with the famous and influential George Wythe, was welcomed into the company of the accomodating governor Francis Fauquier, was elected to Burgesses, and married (as had his father) a woman from an appropriately well-placed tidewater family. He was, above all else, a natural aristocrat.

EARLY VIEWS OF NATURAL RIGHTS

After the French and Indian War various defenders of Virginia's orderly and harmonious life through rule by representative government arose, but none was so eloquent in written prose as Thomas Jefferson. *A Summary View of the Rights of British America* was addressed to the king, but the audience on whom the rhetoric worked best was the Virginia gentry. Written for Burgesses, the pamphlet began with a bold assertion of rights. The language Jefferson used, he told the king, was "divested of those expressions of servility which would persuade his majesty that we are asking for favors and not rights." As the Saxons chose England in which to establish freedom, so the people coming to America had exercised "a right, which nature has given to all men, of departing from the country in which chance, not choice has placed them." In America, these free-dom-loving individuals established "that system of laws under which they had hitherto lived in the mother country," retaining only their attachments to the king. Their life in America had become, however, a continual defense of these rights against arbitrary power exercised by both the Parliament and the king. The acts and decisions had, at length, begun to pile upon one another and stifle freedom. Not single acts in isolation from one another, the English government's actions were rather "a deliberate, systematical plan of reducing us to slavery."

The only defense against such usurpations of rights, Jefferson asserted, was the people's representative assemblies. Just as the Parliament had reestablished "the British constitution at the Glorious Revolution on it's *[sic]* free and ancient principles," so now Burgesses must declare that the people's rights to govern themselves are "derived from the laws of nature, and not as the gift of the chief magistrate. . . . The God who gave us life gave us liberty at the same time." No quibbling over internal or external taxes, royal charters, and Magna Carta here. Virginians through Burgesses had the right to rule themselves. It had always been this way.

VIEWS OF SLAVERY

Seen as a member of the Virginia gentry, even Jefferson's stand on slavery becomes at least understandable. As one of the chosen, the natural aristocracy, to whom was entrusted the control of Virginia's future, Jefferson was one of many after the 1760s who worried about the increasing number of slaves in Virginia. However men felt about this topic, one fact was clear to all: Burgesses would handle the problem. Jefferson raised the issue numerous times in his public proposals and his private correspondence. In the *Summary View* and the Declaration of Independence (in a passage deleted by the Congress) he blamed the king for the continuation of the slave trade. In his "Draft Constitution for Virginia" he stated that "no person hereafter (1776) coming into this country shall be held within the same in slavery under any pretext whatever." In *Notes on the State of Virginia* (1787) he proposed freeing the slaves, transporting them abroad, and replacing their labor with that of whites. But Burgesses never adopted his plans, and Jefferson never freed his own slaves, despite these writings.

Two revealing letters written late in his life clarify his attitudes. Just prior to leaving the presidency in early 1809, he wrote that his beliefs about blacks "were the result of personal observation on a limited sphere in my own State." And whenever he had proposed freedom, he wrote to Edward Coles five years later, it had been rejected by his peers. Should he in 1814, he asked rhetorically of Coles, take up the fight again? "No, I have outlived the generation with which mutual labors and perils begat mutual confidence and influence." The battle, if it were to be waged, belonged to the new generation. All he could do was treat his slaves fairly and wisely and encourage the young to take up the fight, but also within the bounds of acceptable, gentry behavior. Unless all the gentry adopted emancipation through an action of Burgesses or constitutional amendment, no good would come. If the young Coles thought otherwise, Jefferson recommended: "Reconcile yourself to your country and its unfortunate situation."

However ironical or hypocritical it may seem to us today, the best description of the Virginia gentry and Thomas Jefferson is "libertarian republicans." If free, white, Englishmen/Americans are able to act for themselves through a representative form of government, only good will result. The people can be trusted to do what is right. Natural aristocrats—men of talent and wisdom—will govern naturally and fairly, continually receiving validation from the electors, who also have a landed stake in the society. The generations pass by in orderly succession as new leaders are trained in responsibility and duty, and emerge to assume their rightful places. Change occurs naturally, and the value of this society and the need to preserve the liberty upon which it rests are self-evident to all.

APPEAL EXTENDING BEYOND VIRGINIA

Although Jefferson wrote his *Summary View* based upon his experiences in Virginia, what he said there and what he affirmed in the Declaration of Independence appealed to Americans in other localities as well. Tyranny was a word that New Englanders also understood, and indictments of a king who in 1776 overstepped his constitutional authority evoked images of Charles I's actions a century earlier. Representative government and self-determination were more than ideals for people in Massachusetts as well as in Virginia. In Pennsylvania and New York, Scots-Irish and German immigrants were also attracted to Jefferson's libertarian and egalitarian language. Anti-English and not yet fully assimilated into American life, a locally based society guaranteed the prospect of continuing ethnic identity and the promise of religious diversity.

Jefferson found common cause with these people. Their goals—seen from this perspective—were his. The promises of American life, it must have seemed to him at the time of the American Revolution, were those of Virginia, extended over a broader area. The high point of this part of his life came with the publication in 1787 of *Notes on the State of Virginia*. Written to refute European theories of American degeneracy; addressing many of the scientific and quasi-scientific theories of creation and differences among human beings; describing and analyzing Virginia's laws, customs, and natural features—Jefferson's answers to a string of questions about his native state give us a good view of gentry life as Jefferson saw it. Once again, the reader is struck by the empirical basis of Jefferson's assertions. The size of an object, for example, establishes its relationship with another. Virginia, comprising an area of 121,525 square miles, is "one third larger than the islands of Great-Britain and Ireland, which are reckoned at 88,357 square miles." Since he calculated that it was only 425 miles from Lake Erie to Alexandria via the Ohio and Potomac River systems and 825 miles to New York City, the west would be tied to Virginia rather than to New York. A middle-sized horse in Europe weighing 436 pounds, and measuring 4 feet 8.6 inches, "is deemed a small horse in America." In every case, numbers lead to conclusions about the power of the United States relative to European nations and of Virginia's stature relative to competitors. Only war, Jefferson concluded, could prevent the United States from becoming a wealthy, secure nation, and Virginia's continuing leadership of it. "Young as we are and with such a country before us to fill with people and with happiness, we should point in that direction the whole generative force of nature, wasting none of it in efforts of mutual destruction."

On the eve of being named secretary of state in Washington's first cabinet, the only problem Jefferson saw in attaining these goals for the United States and for Virginia was the American attachment to commerce. But even if wars resulted from defending American trade, the nation need not engage in an expensive war at sea or despair of asserting American rights. "Circumstances exist, which render even the stronger [European nations] weak as to us. Providence has placed their richest and most defenceless possessions at our door; has obliged their precious commerce to pass as it were in review before us." A small navy, well within the power of Virginia alone to build and outfit, would be sufficient to the task. Besides, "the value of our lands and slaves, taken conjunctly," he calculated, "doubles in about twenty years."

Even though he wrote the bulk of the *Notes* during the period of time surrounding his wife's death, Jefferson's book reeks of optimism. The period between 1787 and his election as president only confirmed the wisdom of his views. Indeed, the great problem Jefferson and Madison found with Hamilton's foreign policy was that it was based on a premise of American weakness rather than strength. European problems were the source of American opportunity. France should be used as a makeweight in the scale of international relations to break the British monopoly of American trade and credit.

RETURN OF NATURAL ARISTOCRACY

When the people removed Hamilton and his monarchical, minority faction from power, Jefferson must have sensed that national and Virginian affairs were synchronized. The people had acted. The natural aristocracy was returned to power, and artificial colonial relationships with Great Britain had once again been destroyed. Nothing stood in the way of Virginia and the United States in their mutual paths to peace and progress. Drew McCoy recently caught the essence of this feeling perfectly in the frontispiece of *The Elusive Republic*, quoting from F. Scott Fitzgerald's *The Great Gatsby:* "He had come a long way to this blue lawn, and his dream must have seemed so close that he could hardly fail to grasp it." Blueprint in hand, on March 4, 1801, Thomas Jefferson walked the short distance from his boarding house to the Capitol and outlined a Second American Revolution.

Both for contemporaries and later generations, the Inaugural Address has presented problems of interpretation. It is best understood, as all of Jefferson's writings are prior to this point, from the perspective of his life in Virginia and not as part of an emerging spirit of nationalism. His opposition to Hamilton's financial plans, his criticism of the Jay Treaty, and his defense of the right of states to interpret the constitutionality of congressional legislation expressed in the Kentucky Resolutions, were all attempts to reverse the tide of the young nation toward national integration and power. As he wrote to a friend, he viewed his presidency as presenting the opportunity for "as real a revolution in the principles of our government as that of 1776 was in its form." To accomplish this goal, there would have to be many changes.

First, he would promote "a wise and frugal government which . . . shall not take from the mouth of labor the bread it has earned" and "economy in the public expense, that labor may be lightly burdened." Unlike the Washington presidency, when Hamilton had directed the nation's course, there would be no need for heavy taxes to support a debt retirement program that benefited only creditors. Similarly, in opposition to the standing army created during Adams' presidency, "a well-disciplined militia" would obviate the need for a standing army or an expensive navy by forming "our best reliance in peace and for the first moments of war."

Second, there would be no more quasi-wars, and no more preference of Britain over France, as when the Federalist pseudo-aristocrats had held power. "Peace, commerce, and honest friendship with all nations—entangling alliances with none" would be the rule of conduct for the new, Republican administration. "A rising nation, spread over a wide and fruitful land," he asserted, need fear no foreign nations. Third, the powers of the national government would be cut drastically and control returned to the states and to the people. He would "support State governments in all their rights." Alien and Sedition Acts which had deprived Americans of basic constitutional guarantees of person, property, and liberties were not needed. State governments would be reestablished as the "surest bulwarks against anti-republican tendencies."

Finally, the president promised the "encouragement of agriculture, and commerce as its hand maid." Defending commerce against "nations who feel power and forget right" was a dangerous undertaking—a point developed in *Notes*.

When there was *already* (1801 is, one must recall, prior to the Louisiana Purchase) "room enough for our descendants to the thousandth and thousandth generation," there was no reason to risk happiness and prosperity for the interest of predominantly New England merchants. The great majority of Americans, after all, were farmers.

INCOMPLETE NATIONALISM

Because Jefferson never totally embraced nationalism while president (in contrast to the other three early presidents from Virginia), the longer he held office the less able he was to accomplish these goals. The national debt, well on the way to retirement by 1803 because of the healthy profits from the carrying trade with England and France during the lull in their wars, was greatly increased with the Louisiana Purchase, the financing of which enriched wealthy financiers. Then, when the embargo prohibited all foreign trade in 1807 in order to force a respect for American neutral rights, the powers of the national government increased dramatically. New Englanders violated the embargo by smuggling goods from Canada, and Jefferson advocated that the Secretary of the Treasury, Albert Gallatin, take all measures necessary to arrest and punish the criminals. Resistance to the national authority, he urged, must be met with force.

Speeches of Republicans in the Congress during the embargo period well capture the problems Jefferson faced in trying to defend national rights without completely abandoning state and local autonomy. Firm economic sanctions, it was hoped, would be enough to force the British to drop their hostile policies and intentions. In a letter to a friend in February 1808, Virginia congressman Burwell Bassett put the issue this way:

Having lost the continental trade that of America has become of the most importance to Britain. It is no longer a convenience. It has become necessary to the existence of the many hands hitherto employed in the commerce of the continent and America, equal to five-sixths of the whole British trade. It cannot be doubted that a judicious use of this power will bring England to her senses and convince her of the futility of attempting to appropriate . . . the common highway to her own use.

But the embargo failed to produce the desired result, and the subsequent war with England was "Mr. Madison's War" only because Jefferson did not push the issue in 1809 when, left to their own direction, Congress repealed the embargo without substituting war. In retirement, Jefferson justified the war as necessary to vindicate the nation's rights and honor and wrote letters to Republicans from all sections of the country, urging them to rally behind the national authority. The War of 1812, which was the logical extension of Jefferson's policies, greatly increased the powers of the national government at the expense of the states. During the war, public expenditures and taxes skyrocketed. Fittingly, one of the Republican taxes was on salt—even less of a luxury than the whiskey which Hamilton had taxed with dire results in 1794.

The war itself was a disaster. Militia units were unsuccessful in several attempts to invade Canada and were no match for British regulars who routed the Americans near Baltimore and invaded Washington in 1814. Jefferson himself created West Point and began the army that exists to this day, but none of those men fought with Andrew Jackson at New Orleans in January 1815. This, the only major land battle the Americans won, occurred *after* peace had been signed on the preceding Christmas Eve. In fact, the only victories of note during the war were those produced in naval battles, such as the Battle of Lake Erie, largely fought by New England sailors in ships built during the presidency of John Adams. At the end of the war, President James Madison made the move to nationalism complete. The charter for Hamilton's national bank, which had expired in 1811 and had not been renewed by the prewar Republican Congress, was now renewed at Madison's request. Also in 1816, Madison proposed and had adopted by the Congress the first protective tariff in order to shelter infant manufacturing begun during the war.

Even Jefferson's major accomplishment as president, the acquisition of the Louisiana territory, does not flow smoothly out of the Inaugural Address. In 1802 Jefferson sent Robert Livingston to Paris with the threat that French occupation of New Orleans "fixes the sentence which is to restrain her forever within her low water mark. . . . From that moment we must marry ourselves to the British fleet and nation." But European affairs more than American pressures dictated Napoleon's decision to sell not New Orleans and everything France owned *east* of the Mississippi (Florida, it was hoped) but rather New Orleans and everything *west* of the river. And in the bargain, the United States would help to finance the renewal of the wars with England, which would be only a momentary interlude in French ownership of the territory. The troops that Napolean intended for New Orleans and the territory had gone instead to Santo Dominto, where a remarkable former slave, Toussaint L'Ouverture, and tropical diseases decimated the French forces. Better, Napoleon reasoned, to allow a weak country like the United States to hold the place than to invite British aggression there. After the war with England, Napoleon would be free to deal with the Americans. Thus did a black slave and the British Duke of Wellington combine to make Jefferson's purchase one of the best land deals in American history.

There were domestic hurdles involving Louisiana as well. Many Federalists opposed so vast an acquisition of land to the west, and there was in some people's minds a question of the constitutionality of the purchase to be resolved. Nowhere in the Constitution does it allow territory to be added by treaty, without the consent of the inhabitants. Jefferson contemplated an amendment to cover all the ambiguities but opted in the end for speed and convenience. Later, John Marshall's Supreme Court—the branch of government that Jefferson constantly railed against as being the only one out of the power of the majority to control—validated the purchase in *American Insurance Company* v. *Canter* (1828).

A FAVORITE OF HISTORIANS

Ironies. Paradoxes. Contradictions. These words come to mind most readily when viewing Jefferson's presidency, especially concerning foreign policy matters. And yet, seemingly in spite of the above record, two polls of "experts," in 1947 and again in 1962, rated Jefferson among the five greatest American presidents behind Abraham Lincoln, George Washington, Franklin D. Roosevelt, and fellow Southerner Woodrow Wilson. The polls, which historian Thomas A. Bailey has likened to "something of a parlor game" similar to "pinning the tail on the donkey," are skewed in Jefferson's behalf more because of the Jefferson rebirth that reached its apogee in 1943 than his merits as president. As Bailey has noted, even "experts" can be biased.

But the trend continues. Two recent books, one by a political scientist and one by a historian, well illustrate the tendency of recent scholars to view Jefferson as an effective president. Robert M. Johnstone, Jr., in his book *Jefferson and the Presidency: Leadership in the Young Republic,* views Jefferson's presidency as a "pioneering effort in erecting a working model of presidential leadership characterized by persuasion and the cultivation of influence." Most important, Jefferson used his political party to enlarge "the horizons of acceptable political behavior." As a leader, Jefferson was a pragmatist, shrewdly calculating his decisions based on what was possible, who used his personal influence on others to promote harmony and conciliation in government. Put succinctly, the Republican party made the Congress effective, and Jefferson dominated the actions of the Republican party. Jefferson's leadership behavior with the Congress following the adoption of the embargo was an aberration, in Johnstone's view, even though the decline of presidential prestige that resulted from the embargo's ineffectiveness ushered in a shift of power from the executive to the legislative branch after Jefferson left power.

Noble E. Cunningham, Jr.'s book *The Process of Government Under Jefferson* makes similar points from a slightly different perspective. Jefferson's election brought few institutional changes into government, Cunningham argues, but rather inaugurated a fundamental change in the management of government. As the first effective party leader who became president, Jefferson exerted a stronger leadership role in the government than either of his predecessors. More than Washington or Adams did, Jefferson oversaw governmental operations by looking over a countless succession of papers submitted by the various officers and through frequent conversations with office heads. His dinners, to which he invited mainly Republican congressmen and cabinet officers, were far from informal social gatherings; they were part of Jefferson's process of government by which system, organization, and consultation prepared the way for effective legislation. Partisanship smoothed the way for every major action of the Congress. "With the national party organization depending largely on the members of Congress, with the machinery of Congress under Republican control, and with the President the head of the Republican party and his cabinet exclusively Republican, party was inseparable from the legislative process.''

Neither of these scholars, however, deals adequately with the problems of Jefferson's second term. Johnstone is more balanced than Cunningham in this regard because he criticizes Jefferson for failing to use his remarkable skills of persuasion and personal influence during the embargo period, but the effect of the criticism is to highlight Jefferson's earlier successes and to show how weakly Madison allegedly responded to the same crisis. Cunningham explains Jefferson's failure to control policy late in his administration by his decision not to tie Madison's hands as Adams had tried to tie his. But what prevented Jefferson and Madison from planning something together? If partisan feeling was so strong in the Congress, why didn't partisanship rescue the party and the nation from a drift in policy after 1809?

The best view of Jefferson's presidential leadership may be that he followed two paths as president. During the first term, a period of peace in Europe allowed the carrying trade artificially to increase the wealth of the national treasury, and prosperity made the Federalists even less popular in the nation than they had been in 1800. A strong sense of purpose in the Republican-dominated Congress made consensus and compromise between the Congress and the executive branch of government an easy task. Jefferson's style as president was well suited to this situation. He worked well with individuals who shared his goals as outlined in the Inaugural Address—goals based upon his years in Virginia and characterized by local control through strong state governments and limited powers in Washington. One-on-one at dinner parties and in informal settings, Jefferson overwhelmed his guests and rekindled their sense of unity with the party.

NO LONGER IN CONTROL

But when the events in Europe overshadowed everything else and demanded a strong, national approach to the country's problems, Jefferson could no longer control the situation. When consensus and compromise no longer produced solutions, Jefferson's past offered few viable alternatives, and he became stymied among several possibilities. He could, as Forrest McDonald has pointed out, have ''treated the British problem as a transient unpleasantness that only momentarily disrupted commerce and could have held his party, as well as the nation's honor, more or less intact.'' To do so, however, would have meant accommodation with Great Britain and ''a policy of aggressive opportunism toward Spain and its ally France.'' In short, Jefferson could have had the profits of the carrying trade, expanded territory, and a small and frugal government, but he would have had to defer to the British as Hamilton had done in the 1790s. This he could not do. Instead, as Burton Spivak and Drew McCoy have argued, Jefferson's faith in man's moral capacity for self-government in a local setting gave way to a stronger view of the powers of the national government. Jefferson thereby unwittingly transformed the embargo from a defensive strategy to buy time to work out a more effective policy for dealing with the two belligerents to a policy of economic coercion and the development of the home market and isolation from Europe. In defending the right of Americans to carry goods to Europe unhampered by either France or Great Britain, Jefferson and Madison embraced Hamilton's economic program of the 1790s and in 1812 fought, and won, the wrong war.

This "Second War for American Independence" united the country and paved the way for a period of national expansion by using Republican means to achieve Federalist ends. In the process, however, the Revolution of 1800 became an abandoned dream.

JEFFERSON'S FAILURE TO ADAPT

As president, therefore, Jefferson failed to adapt to changing circumstances. As a group-oriented, partisan leader he worked well with his followers when unity was high and foreign policy problems were few. When he was required to change his ideas or choose among plans that fell outside of the program outlined in his Inaugural Address, however, he abrogated responsibility to others. He had difficulty making decisions when the consequences of his actions meant changing directions. It is true that when he left office in 1809, the goals of his Inaugural Address had not been completely abandoned. But the wars of Europe meant that their accomplishment would require paying a heavy price—acquiescence to British foreign policy or adoption of Hamilton's financial plans. Standing up to the belligerents meant a navy and army strong enough to defend property and capture territory, or a war during which commerce, the basis of debt retirement and agrarian expansion, was destroyed, and manufacturing, paper money, and banking flourished. Either way, Jefferson lost.

As with other presidents who have come into power based upon issues born in a local or regional setting, the problems that Jefferson faced are instructive. His life as a member of the Virginia gentry made him an articulate spokesman for liberalism and republicanism, two themes that all Americans, then and now, have responded to. The farther the nation moved away from the traditional, collective, and localistic world of the Virginia gentry, however, to a modern, individualistic, and cosmopolitan orientation of the future, the less informative Jefferson's liberal republicanism became.

Back in Virginia in retirement from public office, Jefferson turned his back on the problems brought on by national expansion. His failure to accept the magnitude of the nation's changes may be seen most poignantly in his letter to Massachusetts Congressman John Holmes at the time of the Missouri Compromise. There is something very hollow in the ring of Jefferson's "fire-bell in the night." Slavery can at least be understood within the confines of the gentry culture, but its expansion over wider areas cannot. Jefferson himself had been instrumental in securing passage of the Northwest Ordinance by the Confederation Congress—legislation that prohibited the expansion of slavery into the lands of the Ohio territory—but he would not hear of the Congress acting in a similar manner in 1820. There is no logic in his assertion that a constant expansion into new areas would weaken the slave system, and when he chastised the current generation for threatening to destroy the Union over "an abstract principle," he blatantly contradicted one of the central ideas of his life—that "the earth belongs to the living."

Jefferson was fortunate to have lived until 1826. The founding of the University of Virginia and the Independence Day celebration of that year gave unity to his life, captured in his epitaph. It is the final irony of Jefferson's life that the man who sought more than anyone else to liberate man from the past in the end allowed his gentry past to ensnare him. The architectural symmetry of Monticello and the first college buildings under his mountain in Charlottesville must have been a great comfort to him. Virginians, at least, would understand what freedom meant.

JEFFERSON'S PRESIDENTIAL IMAGE

But what of his presidency? Freedom, a second time, from England? Freedom from pseudo-aristocratic tyrannies fostered by an antirepublican faction of monocrats? Freedom from an oppressive bureaucracy and an overpowering central government? Nothing consistent with his life in Virginia rings true. If Monticello and his epitaph below the hill in the family cemetery stand as the enduring symbols of Jefferson in Virginia, so the Jefferson Memorial in Washington captures the contradictions of his career as president. On the one hand, standing on the steps of the Memorial one has the sense that the spirit of Jefferson's Virginian life has been captured perfectly. Looking across the tidal basin to the other monuments to public men and public institutions, one feels isolated from official Washington. But just as his presidency promised differences and did not fulfill them, so the monument seems to stand apart from but actually is an integral part of the nation's capital.

The Memorial was controversial from the start and was completed during the administration of a man who kept a file of Jefferson's quotes, catalogued by topic, to be worked into any speech, but who firmly implemented Hamilton's plans for a strong national government. The quotation of having sworn eternal hostility toward every form of tyranny over the mind of man that encircles Jefferson's head rings of freedom, but the words taken from his writings that fill the four panels in the Memorial have been toned for modern ears. No "little rebellions" here, and even the right of people to change their governments has been excised from his Declaration of Independence.

So long as the duality between the pull of localism and the push of national integration that characterizes Jefferson's presidency remains unresolved in the United States, he will continue to be a troublesome individual. His words that all men are created equal have been a barometer by which we have measured progress toward equality before the law for all Americans, but outside of Virginia, only Alabamans celebrate his birthday along with those of Jefferson Davis, Robert E. Lee, George Washington, and *not* Abraham Lincoln.

"It has been said," as Merrill Peterson reminds us, that Americans "venerate Washington, love Lincoln, and remember Jefferson." Those Americans who visit the Jefferson Memorial to remember Thomas Jefferson should deliberately miss the difficult cut-off, however, and head south into Virginia. Today, as in Jefferson's time, both the man and his legacy make the most sense seen from that perspective.

BIBLIOGRAPHIC ESSAY

Because this chapter is intended for a general audience, I have tried to use sources which would be available to most readers through their libraries or in paperback editions. For this reason, all the quotations from Jefferson's public writings and private correspondence are taken from Merrill D. Peterson, ed., *The Portable Thomas Jefferson* (New York: Viking Press, 1975), now available as a Penguin Books paperback. The book by Peterson, who teaches at the University of Virginia, that was the most helpful in preparing this chapter is *The Jefferson Image in the American Mind* (New York: Oxford University Press, 1960). His *Thomas Jefferson and the New Nation: A Biography* (New York: Oxford University Press, 1970) remains one of the best single-volume biographies.

Winthrop Jordan's remarks are taken from his book review of Fawn Brodie, *Thomas Jefferson: An Intimate Biography,* in the *William and Mary Quarterly,* 3rd ser., 32 (July 1975). For the full results of the poll in the *New York Times,* see the April 4, 1943, edition. A letter to the editor in the *Times* for April 13, 1979, contains the references to the public refusals to sign the Declaration of Independence as well as the information about Alabama state holidays at the end of the chapter.

The quotation from the authors of *1776: A Musical Play* (New York: Penguin Books, 1976) follows the text of the play. Gore Vidal, who became intrigued with the ability of the founders to use the English language so effectively, expresses his admiration of them and his indictment of modern Americans in Stephen Koch, "Gore Vidal: Urbane Witness to History," *Saturday Review World,* December 18, 1973.

The theme of freedom for Jefferson's life runs through all of his biographies, but it is most pronounced in Dumas Malone, *Jefferson and His Time,* 6 vols. (New York: Little, Brown, 1948–1981). One of the best short articles on Jefferson that also well expresses this view is in Edmund S. Morgan, *The Meaning of Independence* (Charlottesville: University Press of Virginia, 1975).

For views of Jefferson as an embodiment of Enlightenment thought in America, see as examples Carl L. Becker, *The Declaration of Independence: A Study in the History of Political Ideas* (1922; reprint ed. New York: Vintage Books, 1970), Henry Steele Commager, *Jefferson, Nationalism and the Enlightenment* (New York: George Braziller, 1975), and Noble E. Cunningham, Jr., *In Pursuit of Reason: The Life of Thomas Jefferson* (Baton Rouge: Louisiana State University Press, 1987).

The views of the gentry culture expressed in this chapter are taken from Jack P. Greene's two essays, "Foundations of Political Power in the Virginia House of Burgesses, 1720–1776," *William and Mary Quarterly,* 3rd ser., 16 (1959), and "Society, Ideology, and Politics: An Analysis of the Political Culture of Mid-Eighteenth Century Virginia," in Richard M. Jellison, ed., *Society, Freedom, and Conscience: The Coming of the Rev-*

olution in Virginia, Massachusetts, and New York (New York: W. W. Norton and Co., 1976). Information about the high death rates in the colonial Chesapeake region, the impact of indentured servitude on Virginia and Maryland, and family life may be found in the articles in Thad W. Tate and David L. Ammerman, eds., *The Chesapeake in the Seventeenth Century: Essays on Anglo-American Society and Politics* (New York: W. W. Norton and Co., 1979). The economics of tobacco and this staple's impact on the settlement of Virginia are discussed in David W. Galenson and Russell R. Menard, "Approaches to the Analysis of Economic Growth in Colonial British America," *Historical Methods*, 13 (Winter 1980).

A good case study of one man's progress in the gentry society and his lack of interest in his historical roots is J. William T. Youngs, Jr.'s essay, "The British American: William Byrd in Two Worlds," in *American Realities*, 2 vols (New York: Little, Brown, 1981), vol. 1. The myth of Cavalier origins is found in W. J. Cash, *The Mind of the South* (New York: Alfred A. Knopf, 1941).

The view that localism in Virginia provided the foundation for federalism in the United States is expressed in Daniel Boorstin, *The Americans: The Colonial Experience* (New York: Random House, 1957). Rhys Isaac emphasizes that fundamental splits within Virginia had emerged by 1740 in *The Transformation of Virginia, 1740–1790* (Chapel Hill: University of North Carolina Press, 1982). For Burgesses' evolution to prominence in Virginia, see Jack P. Greene, *The Quest for Power: The Lower Houses of Assembly in the Southern Royal Colonies, 1689–1776* (Chapel Hill: University of North Carolina Press, 1963).

Discussions of Jefferson's attitude toward blacks differ greatly. Two good places to begin, however, are Winthrop Jordan, "Thomas Jefferson: Self and Society," in *White over Black: American Attitudes Towards the Negro, 1550–1812* (Chapel Hill: University of North Carolina Press, 1968), and John Chester Miller, *The Wolf by the Ears* (New York: The Free Press, 1977).

The literature on republican ideology is well summarized in two articles by Robert E. Shalhope, "Toward a Republican Synthesis: The Emergence of an Understanding of Republicanism in American Historiography," *William and Mary Quarterly*, 3rd ser., 29 (January 1972), and "Republicanism and Early American Historiography," *William and Mary Quarterly*, 3rd ser., 39 (April 1982). Robert Kelley labels New Englanders as "moralistic," Middle Staters as "nationalistic" and "egalitarian," and Virginians as "libertarian" republicans in *The Cultural Pattern in American Politics: The First Century* (New York: Knopf, 1979).

For the conflict between Hamilton and Jefferson regarding views of American strengths and weaknesses, see Jerald A. Combs, *The Jay Treaty: Political Battleground of the Founding Fathers* (Berkeley: University of California Press, 1970). Lawrence S. Kaplan most convincingly demonstrates Jefferson's plans for French support in *Jefferson and France: An Essay in Politics and Political Ideas* (New Haven: Yale University Press, 1967), and "Reflections on Jefferson as a Francophile," *South Atlantic Quarterly*, 79 (Winter 1980).

Drew R. McCoy's *The Exclusive Republic: Political Economy in Jeffersonian America* (Chapel Hill: University of North Carolina Press, 1980) makes Jefferson and Madison's thinking about expansion, commerce, and manufacturing relevant to today. It should be read with Burton Spivak, *Jefferson's English Crisis: Commerce, Embargo, and the Republican Revolution* (Charlottesville: University of Virginia Press, 1979).

For an extended discussion of how the Republicans developed a publicly accountable justification for war between the repeal of the embargo and the war in 1812, see Ronald L. Hatzenbuehler and Robert L. Ivie, *Congress Declares War: Rhetoric, Partisanship, and Leadership in the Early Republic* (Kent: Kent State University Press, 1983). Gallatin's role in the embargo is well described in Richard Mannix's "Gallatin, Jefferson, and the Embargo of 1808," *Diplomatic History,* 3 (Spring 1979). A graphic account of military problems in 1814 may be found in Walter Lord, *The Dawn's Early Light* (New York: W. W. Norton and Co., 1972). The classic account of how the Republicans adopted the bulk of the Federalist program of the 1790s is found in Henry Adams, *History of the United States During the Administrations of Jefferson and Madison,* 9 vols. (New York: Charles Scribner and Sons, 1889–1891), especially vol. 9. For Jefferson's creation of the army, see Richard H. Kohn, *Eagle and Sword: The Federalists and the Creation of the Military Establishment, 1787–1802* (New York: The Free Press, 1975). See also J. C. A. Stagg, *Mr. Madison's War* (Princeton: Princeton University Press, 1983).

The most recent discussion of the Louisiana Purchase is Alexander DeConde, *This Affair of Louisiana* (New York: Charles Scribner's Sons, 1976). The polls, conducted by Arthur M. Schlesinger, are reported in Thomas A. Bailey, *Presidential Greatness: The Image and the Man from George Washington to the Present* (New York: Appleton-Century, 1966).

Johnstone's book, *Jefferson and the Presidency: Leadership in the Young Republic* (Ithaca: Cornell University Press, 1978), and Cunningham's *The Process of Government Under Jefferson* (Princeton: Princeton University Press, 1978) should be read and contrasted with Forrest McDonald's *The Presidency of Thomas Jefferson* (Lawrence: University Press of Kansas, 1976) and the works of McCoy and Spivak cited earlier.

The influence of group on leaders and vice versa is addressed most directly in Fred E. Fiedler and Martin M. Chemers, *Leadership and Effective Management* (Glenview, Ill.: Scott, Foresman, 1974). The controversy over the building of the Jefferson Memorial, the reconstruction of Monticello, and the Peterson quote are all found in Peterson, *The Jefferson Image in the American Mind.* For an account of the changes in Jefferson's words in the Memorial, see Frank Whitson Fetter, "The Revision of the Declaration of Independence in 1941," *William and Mary Quarterly,* 3rd ser., 31 (January 1974). One of the most provocative collections of essays concerning the tensions of localism and nationalism in American life is found in Richard Maxwell Brown and Don E. Fehrenbacher, eds., *Tradition, Conflict, and Modernization: Perspectives on the American Revolution* (New York: Academic Press, 1977), especially the article by Kenneth Lockridge, "The American Revolution, Modernization, and Man: A Critique." See also Lockridge's book, *Settlement and Unsettlement in Early America: The Crisis of Politics Before the Revolution* (Cambridge: Cambridge University Press, 1981).

3 ANDREW JACKSON

John J. Reed

Andrew Jackson, seventh president of the United States, stands apart from his predecessors as the first person to attain that high office from outside the inner circle of presidential politics and the established procedure for advancement therein. He was the first president from a "new" West, that area beyond the Appalachian mountains, and from a state other than the original thirteen. In addition, his life and career were markedly different. Orphaned at an early age, he grew with the country, rising through the law, the military, and politics to the status of frontier gentleman concerned with commerce, vast quantities of land, and slaves. In a period of two years he served as Tennessee's representative, then senator in Congress, and soon was judge of the state superior court and major general of its militia. As Indian fighter and general he gained more than regional fame, climaxed by the decisive event of his life, the victory, on January 8, 1815, over the British at New Orleans. He had become Old Hickory and was a national hero.

After subduing Florida and serving briefly as governor of that new territory, Jackson moved easily with the changing tides of national politics and in rapid order was, again, United States senator, presidential candidate, party leader, and president-elect, the oldest person thus far elected to that office. Beginning on a chaotic Inauguration Day, the "day of the people," Jackson brought to the presidency a strong, resourceful, and ambitious personality, revealed in a commanding and dignified presence which had both a charismatic ability to charm and an ability to offend.[1] He was clearly in command of the White House and from that day to this has been a controversial figure. He early established control of his administration and pursued public policy-making in a style that can only be called forceful. His presidency, 1829–1837, is especially noted for the opposition to Henry Clay's American System and thus for his vetoes of the Maysville Road bill and the bill to recharter the Bank of the United States and for his support of a bill to lower the tariff gradually. Notable were his assertion of national authority in the face of a defiant South Carolina, his Indian removal policy, and his strong support of presidential authority in the face of censure by the Senate. With his aides he presided over the birth and growth of the modern Democratic party (soon opposed by the "Whigs of '34," standing in "patriotic" opposition to "King" Andrew Jackson). Interestingly, in 1832 Jackson became "and remains now, the only President whose reelection to a second term was marred by a decline in popular approval."[2] Jackson's foreign policy was, with the exception of his failure to acquire Texas, surprisingly successful. Amid much acclaim ("such as power never commanded, nor man in power received"), in 1837 Jackson retired to the Hermitage in Nashville, an elder statesman, and indeed a legend, until his death in 1845.[3]

The Jacksonian image was and to this day remains ambivalent. Except for extreme partisans and extreme critics it cannot be unequivocally defined. Like other historical phenomena it would vary with time, place, and observer. And it would reveal itself in many ways. Thus, for example, in the 1850s a portrait of Jackson "engraved by one T. B. Welch, Esq., after the original by T. Sully, Esq.," was issued. The next year there appeared, across from the White House, the noted equestrian statue of Jackson, "the first equestrian statue ever made in the United States . . . [and] [c]ast from cannon which Jackson captured at New Orleans . . . shows a frantically rearing horse . . . upon whose back sits a cool figure of Old Hickory tranquilly lifting his cocked hat to the cheering multitude." Jackson continued to be a political force, too, as an example to later presidents and as an attraction to voters. Robert V. Remini notes that "it is a fact that in the Presidential election of 1860 . . . a number of Americans voted for Andrew Jackson, even though he had been dead over 15 years." A similar story today circulates in the German country of eastern Pennsylvania, this one to the effect that in 1860 in that strongly Democratic area many were still voting for "Sheneral Shackson." Abraham Lincoln, himself a longtime politician, indirectly ridiculed Jackson in 1848 when the Democrats nominated General Lewis Cass for the presidency, saying that the Democrats, "like a horde of hungry ticks . . . have stuck to the tail of the Hermitage lion to the end of his life, and . . . are still sticking to it." But when it came time to prepare his First Inaugural, one of the most critical policy statements made by any president, Lincoln had before him a copy of the Constitution, Henry Clay's speech to the Senate in 1850, Daniel Webster's nationalist reply to nullifier Robert Y. Hayne in 1830—and a copy of Jackson's "Proclamation" to the people of South Carolina. It might be noted that the tone of Lincoln's address is remarkably similar to that of Jackson's "Proclamation."[4]

WILSON'S AND THE ROOSEVELTS' VIEWS OF JACKSON

Three later presidents, two of them working historians, took particular note of Jackson. Woodrow Wilson, although critical of many of Jackson's policies, concluded his section on the Jackson period in *Division and Reunion 1829–1889* with this statement: "The organic popular force in the nation came to full self-consciousness while Jackson was President. Whatever harm it may have done to put this man into the Presidency, it did the incalculable good of giving to the national spirit its first self-reliant expression of resolution and of consentaneous power.'' In Wilson's *A History of the American People* the frontispiece is that of Jackson; the opening chapter is entitled ''The Democratic Revolution,'' and it begins on a positive note. Comparing Jackson to Jefferson, Wilson writes:

General Jackson professed to be of the school of Mr. Jefferson himself; and what he professed he believed. There was no touch of the charlatan or the demagogue about him. The action of his mind was as direct, as sincere, as unsophisticated as the action of the mind of an ingenuous child, though it exhibited also the sustained intensity and the range of the mature man. . . . General Jackson was incapable of arts or deceptions of any kind. He was in fact what his partisans loved to call him, a man of the people, of the common people.

In his *Constitutional Government in the United States,* originally published in 1908, Wilson referred to Jackson's presidency and sounded the ''outsider'' theme:

When an imperious man, bred not in the deliberative assemblies or quiet councils, but in the field and upon a rough frontier, worked his own will upon affairs, with or without formal sanction of law, sustained by a clear undoubting conscience and the love of a people who had grown deeply impatient with the regime he had supplanted . . .

Wilson later notes: ''Nullification failed as even so much as an effectual protest against the power of a government of which General Jackson was the head,— never so sure he was right as when he was opposed.''

Theodore Roosevelt's correspondence contains several references in praise of Jackson. In commenting on William Dodd's *Statesmen of the Old South,* he wrote to the author: ''The two great leaders with whom I am most heartily in accord in our past are naturally Washington and Lincoln. . . . I am a great admirer of Andrew Jackson for all his faults, and it does not seem to me that you do him quite justice.'' Four years later, in a petulant mood, he wrote to his friend Henry Cabot Lodge: ''Andrew Jackson had his faults, but at least he was a fighting man, and had some idea of the proper correspondence between words and deeds. This creature [President Wilson] is not of the Jackson, but the Jefferson and Buchanan type.''

Theodore Roosevelt was one of two post–Civil War presidents to visit the Hermitage; in his ensuing annual message he asked for and received an appropriation to restore it. The other president was Franklin D. Roosevelt, who was also strongly impressed by Jackson's presidency. According to Arthur M. Schlesinger, Jr., at the Jackson Day dinner in 1936 he ''enthusiastically cast himself as the modern Andrew Jackson,'' and in the election campaign ''he saw himself increasingly as Andrew Jackson.'' He had said of Jackson: ''It is absolutely true that his opponents represented the same social outlook and the same element in the population as ours do. . . . The more I learn about Andy Jackson, the more

I love him.'' Schlesinger observes that FDR ''evidently had not learned enough to know that contemporaries never called Jackson 'Andy.' ''

John William Ward notes: ''In the depths of the Depression, in a Christmas greeting to the nation in 1934, Roosevelt reminded the people of America of the monument in the park before the White House of 'a man who will live forever as the embodiment of courage—Andrew Jackson.' '' In 1936, on election day, ''Roosevelt wore Jackson's heavy gold watch-chain . . . and he provided that the reviewing stand for the 1937 inaugural parade should be a replica of the Hermitage.'' An intriguing fact is that an earlier president, a contemporary of Jackson's, Thomas Jefferson, became, before his death on July 4, 1826, an issue in creating the Jackson image. Both pro- and anti-Jacksonians claimed the support of Jefferson. Jefferson biographer Merrill Peterson calls this part ''of a curious phenomenon in the Jackson period: the acute sensibility of political leaders to the value of Jefferson's benediction.''[5]

JACKSON AS POPULIST

A contemporary popular image of Jackson is almost impossible to determine with precision. Like all strong presidents, Jackson drew a large share of praise from his friends, his partisans, and much of the public. Conversely, he received much criticism from political opponents and those to whom Jacksonian policies were anathema. Possibly the level of popularity can be read in the election returns, but even here there are problems in using returns as a measure of popularity—or the opposite. There are many resources a study of which presumably would yield a contemporary consensus of the Jacksonian image: newspapers, correspondence, speeches in and out of Congress, diaries, and volumes of reminiscences. A sampling of these, not surprisingly, reveals a lack of agreement. Furthermore, as to the popular image, that of the people, there might be few or no records at all. And always there would be the question of how much of the printed material should, in a highly partisan age, be taken as fact or as party propaganda.

Once in office Jackson and his speechwriters naturally played upon those themes that had a broad democratic appeal. Such were his references in his first annual message to the principle of rotation in office and in the Bank veto message to the elimination of privilege and the opening of opportunity. And this course was to be echoed by his followers, as when Benton writes of the events relating to the removal of the deposits: ''There are but two parties, there never has been but two parties . . . founded in the radical question, whether PEOPLE or PROPERTY, shall govern? Democracy implies a government of the people. . . . Aristocracy implies a government of the rich.'' In the Bank veto message Jackson had a good target. The message had wide appeal, appealing to many and diverse groups. Jackson intuitively sensed the roll of the tide of public opinion. ''The spirit of the masses,'' writes Wecter, ''had captured Jackson and made him its mouthpiece. In April 1824, for the first time, Jackson [had begun] to talk about 'a moneyed aristocracy dangerous to the liberties of the country.' ''

Walt Whitman, who had younger brothers named Thomas Jefferson and Andrew Jackson Whitman, called Jackson "a noble yet simple-souled old man" and of "massive, yet most sweet and plain character." Amos Kendall, early in the presidency, wrote to Francis Blair: "He is indeed a noble, honest old man, who intends nothing but to benefit his country." And young Gideon Welles wrote that the president's " 'presence' profoundly affected him." At the time of the Bank war with Nicholas Biddle, James Fenimore Cooper noted, "hickory will prove to be stronger than gold." A senator, not named, told the German Francis Grund: "General Jackson understood the people of the United States better, perhaps, than any President before him." Henry Wise, long active in Virginia politics, met Jackson on his way to the session of Congress, 1824–1825, where the House was to choose a president. Wise recalled: "We thus knew Andrew Jackson, the greatest man, take him all in all, we have ever known among men." Even New York City merchant Philip Hone, later highly critical of Jackson, recorded in his diary in March 1830, after calling on Jackson: "We found him well and in good spirits. He received us with his usual urbanity of manner and was very agreeable." In addition, Wecter notes that the painter Ralph Earl settled "at the Hermitage and at the White House for 17 years— doing almost nothing save portraits of the General, to meet popular demand." Wecter also notes that "Jackson's mail during [his Presidency] . . . reveals not only tributes of poetry, and invitations to visit admirers or stop at hotels named for him, but also an unprecedented avalanche of presents." One letter, signed "One of the People," read:

You are now the only hope of the nation. . . . I pray you take care of yourself, & guard against poison and the dagger. Be always prepared to give yourself a vomit. The most speedy is 15 grains of white vitriol (sulphate of zinc) or 15 grains of blue vitriol (sulphate of copper). Remember that Henry 4th of France and William of Nassau founder of the Republic of Holland were assassinated.

Perhaps Jackson remembered this letter when he miraculously escaped death in January 1835 while attending a funeral in the Capitol. On that occasion neither of the assassin's pistols fired.

THE OPPOSITION DIFFERS

Needless to say, the opposition used language quite different from that suggested above. In 1831 Senator Samuel Bell of New Hampshire wrote that Jackson "is an ignorant weak superannuated man, scarcely fitted for the office he now holds, than a child of 10 years would be." Biddle, in a letter to Clay, referred to the Bank veto as "a manifesto of anarchy." And of the message in the Senate the Godlike Daniel Webster intoned: "It manifestly seeks to influence the poor against the rich. It wantonly attacks whole classes of the people, for the purpose of turning against them the prejudices and the resentments of other classes." Opponents stigmatized Jackson as a despot, unqualified for his position, and one who promoted "executive usurpation." In 1830 Senator David Barton of Missouri, defending his support of Adams in 1824, noted: "We conscientiously believed Mr. Adams the better qualified of the two principal candidates. . . . Our devotion to the civil over the military was sincere." And referring to the "people," Peleg Sprague of Maine noted: "Omnipotent as they are, they cannot have an elective monarchy and a constitutional republic at the same time." Clay called Jackson combative, and diarist Hone, having turned quite sour on Jackson, called him a "vindictive old man, whose administration of the government will be marked in the annals of the country as the period of her disgrace and humiliation." Even after Jackson's death Hone wrote: "Now, to my thinking, the country had greater cause to mourn on the day of his birth than on that of his decease. This iron-willed man has done more mischief than any man alive."

Opposition editors and cartoonists added to the anti-Jackson chorus and may have been more important in creating a negative popular image of Jackson than all of the rhetoric. There were the "Coffin Hand Bills" of the campaign of 1828, reviving graphically the charges of executions ordered by Jackson during the Creek War. There was the cartoon depicting a debilitated President Jackson from whom are scurrying rats with clearly recognizable administration faces, designed to ridicule Jackson's presidential conduct, and the classic, the one depicting "King Andrew" in royal regalia, standing on a torn copy of the Constitution, scepter in his right hand, a document labeled "veto" in his left, and a crown on his head.[6]

LEGEND AND REALITY

In a revealing and useful article entitled "Andrew Jackson: Legend and Reality," Albert Somit sought to sift fact from fiction and discern just what Jackson's character was like. Among other things, Somit indicated that there were, chronologically speaking, two Jacksons, a change being "discernible" in the early 1820s. He notes:

These [earlier] exploits and the resulting notoriety earned for Jackson a reputation which lasted his entire life and assured him the fear if not the respect of his contemporaries. His opponents, eager to discredit his fitness for the Presidency, did their best to give these stories the widest possible circulation both from the stump and in the press, an effort in which they were successful.

He adds:

Whatever truth there was in the charge that his early behavior—and the important fact is that it was only his *early* behavior—was marked by violent and undisciplined conduct, a careful study reveals that a definite change is discernible in the early 1820's.

After an extensive review of Jackson's personality traits, in a section entitled "What the People Saw in Him," Somit posed two questions. First, what in his personality made Jackson one of America's most popular presidents, and, next, "to what extent did he actually possess the attributes with which he was generally credited?" There follow seven paragraphs which in sum say: (1) "Military reputation, especially the glory of the New Orleans victory." (2) The fact that "Jackson was one of the most romantic and colorful men of his day." (3) Jackson's "awesome reputation for courage and audacity." (4) "Widespread confidence in his own probity." (5) The fact that "the masses viewed Jackson as one of their own." (6) "Jackson's steadfastness in the face of opposition." And finally:

Jackson was possessed of yet one more asset—one which all who came in contact with him instinctively sensed, yet which no one has quite successfully analyzed or described; an asset which for want of a better term can only be called personal magnetism. . . . [T]he grim warrior had something the others lacked, . . . a something which, for more than a decade, made the battle-cry of American politics the words—"Hurrah for Jackson!"

Although all of these points, years after they were written, are still being heatedly discussed, they do address the question of the public image and provide at least a partial answer to the question why, in spite of the many things about Jackson's presidency which were criticized then and can be criticized now, the presidential image for so many Americans was a positive one.[7]

JACKSON'S EUROPEAN IMAGE

In the years following the Napoleonic Wars, numerous European travelers came to the United States, some on temporary, brief visits, some on more extended ones. Some came on specific missions, some came to see what this new upstart republic was all about. Some came with minds made up, some in the reverse frame of mind. Most of them found in Andrew Jackson a person of interest, for personal or for policy reasons. It is probably likely that most of the travelers reacted favorably to Jackson and his policies, although, understandably, there was considerable criticism, depending on the person involved and on the time when Jackson was being observed. Harriet Martineau, for example, writing of a reception and dinner she had at the White House, remarked on Jackson's tendency to talk, his poor health, his austere diet, and his critical comments on the opposition majority in the Senate. She remarked on his interest in and kindness toward children and noted: "He did the honours of his house with gentleness and politeness to myself, and, as far as I saw, to every one else." She commented on Jackson's aged appearance, observing, however, "His countenance bears commonly an expression of melancholy gravity; though when aroused, the fire of passion flashes from his eyes, and his whole person looks then formidable enough." Her reaction was quite different in January 1835. She had been in the

Capitol when the attempt on Jackson's life had taken place. She had originally intended to visit Jackson the next day, but postponed the visit because Jackson seemed to be making a political affair of the assassination attempt, charging a plot and apparently ranting and raving in true paranoid fashion. When she did go, she "took the liberty of changing the subject as soon as I could." In her *Society in America,* she combines praise of Jackson with criticism of his policies, stating, for example, "He has great personal courage, much sagacity, though frequently impaired by the strength of his prejudices, violent passions, and indomitable will, and that devotion to public affairs in which no President has ever failed." Later she wrote, "The deeds of his administration remain to be justified in as far as they are sound, and undone if they are faulty." Martineau's comments, in the main, are balanced and judicious and, taken altogether, present a favorable image of Jackson. (She also reported that she had heard of the reply of a Sunday school student—in New England—who, when asked who had slain Abel, replied "General Jackson.")

Clearly the views of the many travelers who came to America during Jackson's administration cannot be readily summarized. Needless to say, as indicated previously, the image projected by Jackson was reflected both positively and negatively. The one foreign observer of this period on whose views Americans have relied more than any other was Alexis de Tocqueville, who, with his friend Gustave de Beaumont, came to the United States ostensibly to study its prisons but, using a much wider lens, produced the classic *Democracy in America.* De Tocqueville's account is interesting for a study of the presidency but disappointing in its presentation of the image of Andrew Jackson. De Tocqueville seems to have derived many of his views from Jackson's critics and to have made up his mind largely from reading *The Federalist*— before he and Beaumont met Jackson at a reception in the White House in January 1832. Hugh Brogan notes that de Tocqueville "never got, or made, anything much out of Jackson. . . . he does not seem to have been impressed" by Jackson's public papers. "Throughout *Democracy in America,*" Brogan writes, "Tocqueville underrated Jackson's significance," adding, "he went to the White House full of preconceptions." In a word, says Brogan, "Tocqueville blundered." The Jackson image for de Tocqueville seems conditioned by his fear of the military. In his *Journey to America* he writes (November 1, 1831): "How can one be in doubt about the pernicious influence of military glory in a republic? What determines the people's choice in favor of General Jackson who, as it would seem, is a very mediocre man?" In *Democracy* he writes:

It is impossible to deny the inconceivable influence that military glory exercises upon the spirit of a nation. General Jackson . . . is a man of violent temper and very moderate talents; nothing in his whole career ever proved him qualified to govern a free people; and, indeed, the majority of the enlightened classes of the Union has always opposed him.

Brogan notes that at their reception at the White House neither Beaumont nor Tocqueville was greatly impressed by Jackson, "though both young men were, in spite of themselves, a little impressed to find themselves addressing such a man as Andrew Jackson simply as 'sir.' "

Of the image of Jackson himself Beaumont gives more information than does his companion. The day after the White House reception Beaumont wrote to his mother that the French minister

presented us . . . to the President of the United States. The latter is General Jackson; he is an old man of 66 years, well preserved, and appears to have retained all the vigour of his body and spirit. He is not a man of genius. Formerly he was celebrated as a duellist and hot-head; his great merit is to have won in 1814 *[sic]* the Battle of New Orleans against the English. . . .

The President of the United States occupies a palace that in Paris would be called a fine private residence. . . . We chatted of things that were insignificant enough. He made us drink a glass of Madeira wine. . . . People in France have got an altogether false idea of the Presidency of the United States. They see in it a sort of political sovereignty and compare it constantly with our constitutional monarchies.

To de Tocqueville's credit, however, it should be noted that he made many provocative comments about the presidency under Jackson, notably: "The power of General Jackson perpetually increases, but that of the President declines; in his hands the Federal government is strong, but it will pass enfeebled into the hands of his successor."[8]

CONTINUING DEBATE AMONG HISTORIANS

The debate over Jackson and Jacksonian democracy did not end with his death in 1845. It has continued from that day to the present, thus making no easier the definition of the popular perception of Jackson and his program or just what his image was. In recent decades scholars have sought to chart the changing views of Old Hickory and his works. Charles Grier Sellers, Jr., for example, notes that the "first impartial biography," that by James Parton, revealed a "continuing disagreement" about Jackson, and that this persists to the present. Sellers points out that with Parton the "Whig" school of historians began, notable among whom was William Graham Sumner. Sellers cites several of their adverse criticisms of Jackson, including Parton's dismay at Jackson's election to the presidency. While the Whig historians were not averse to Jackson's economic policies, and while they supported his nationalism, they did not like the alleged spoils system, with which Jackson seemed to symbolize the new democracy. These historians, living in the age of Grant and in an era of extensive political corruption, understandably reflected their social backgrounds. They saw in the contemporary scene the fruits of what they believed had begun under Jackson: "These scholars," writes Sellers, " . . . displayed the class bias of an elite displaced from leadership by a vulgar and frequently corrupt democracy."

Toward the end of the nineteenth century, Sellers points out, under the leadership of frontier historian Frederick Jackson Turner, there took place a "massive shift of American historiography to a pro-democratic orientation," with historians from small-town, rural backgrounds reflecting the middle-class involvement in the reform which was to blossom in the Progressive movement. Logically, "Andrew Jackson and his Democracy were naturally among the leading beneficiaries of the new pro-democratic orientation of American historiography." The West, Turner said, produced Jacksonian democracy, and his "contemporaries quickly took up the refrain." Several historians joined in the chorus, although "the earliest major product of the democratic school . . . was John Spencer Bassett's *Life of Andrew Jackson,* published in 1911." Sellers notes that "Bassett was the first scholar since Parton to work thoroughly through the extant Jacksonian sources, . . . [and] was generally sympathetic . . . but not uncritical." There were critics, still, but as Sellers notes, "most American historians embraced the democratic orientation with only slight hesitation."

A major breakthrough came in 1904 with the publication of Carl Russell Fish's *The Civil Service and the Patronage,* in which the author defended the need for office changes in 1829 and indicated that the democratic result "was fully worth the cost." Sellers also cited "the cult of objectivity" as a factor coincidental with the growth of the democratic school, which, he says, "has continued to be the dominant influence on writings about the Jackson period ever since" although there have continued to be challengers, citing as "most embarrassing" to it the work of Thomas P. Abernethy, who "presents Jackson as a frontier nabob who took sides against the democratic movement in his own state." Sellers notes also that "the democratic historians have suffered less from these dissenting views than from their own inability to make clear just what they mean by 'democracy' " and shows in some detail how this was true in Turner's case.

Another breakthrough came in 1945, Sellers notes, with the publication of Arthur M. Schlesinger, Jr.'s *The Age of Jackson,* which shifted the emphasis from West to East, from sections to classes, and indicated that the major influence in Jacksonian democracy lay in the wage-earning classes in the East in their contests with the leaders of the business community. While writing about Jackson and Jacksonian democracy had never ceased, it may be said that Schlesinger sparked a "Jacksonian Renaissance" which continues to the present day. Sellers points out that Schlesinger almost immediately drew critics, including Bray Hammond and Richard Hofstadter, who viewed Jacksonian democracy as a phase of expanding, liberating, laissez-faire capitalism. Others, besides Hofstadter, at Columbia University, attacked Schlesinger's fundamental thesis, including especially the view that labor voted for Jackson. Sellers quite rightly in his presentation emphasizes "the profound influence of frames of reference." Probably reflecting the fact that he was writing when the so-called consensus school of historians was dominant in the late 1950s, Sellers concludes by suggesting that common ground may be taken by historians writing from different frames of reference. He indicates his support for "the paradoxical character of the Jacksonian democratic impulse,'' adding: ''Viewed in this light, the frame of reference has served a valuable purpose . . . by leading historians to the different elements of the complex Jacksonian past out of which an over-all synthesis must eventually be constructed.''

Sellers refers to one historian whose work, published in 1955, merits special attention in any discussion of the image of Andrew Jackson. This is John William Ward's *Andrew Jackson: Symbol for an Age*. What makes Ward's book unique is the methodology employed, one which helps greatly both to portray and to understand Jackson's image as seen by his contemporaries. In a word, what Ward did was to examine what contemporaries said about Jackson, especially in their funeral sermons, and including, at the beginning, a speech in the House of Representatives by Congressman George Troup of Georgia (February 16, 1815) eulogizing Jackson for his role in the victory at New Orleans. Ward's ''purpose in the book on Jackson was to distinguish the concepts that were embodied in and dramatized by the symbol 'Andrew Jackson', and to reveal them as the source of the emotional appeal of the historical person Andrew Jackson, the seventh President of the United States.'' He found embodied in Jackson, in the views of his contemporaries, certain symbols (''Nature,'' ''Providence,'' and ''Will'') which made Jackson the ''symbol for an age.'' Thus, Ward concludes, ''To describe the early nineteenth century as the age of Jackson misstates the matter. The age was not his. He was the age's.''

This brief statement does not do justice to the originality and value of Ward's book and his research. But it does suggest, in the context of this chapter, why the image of Jackson for so many contemporaries was perceived in positive terms.[9]

NEWER TRENDS IN JACKSONIAN ANALYSIS

Since Ward and Sellers wrote, other developments have occurred that relate to the apparently never ending search for the popular image of Andrew Jackson. One is the development of a more extensive and sophisticated type of quantification in historical research than had hitherto been the case. By using vast quantities of data and the computer, for more than twenty years historians have sought to sharpen their definitions of Jacksonian democracy and to determine who voted for the Old Hero. The other main development has been the advent of so-called psychohistory, an attempt to apply basic psychological knowledge and techniques in the analysis of historical figures. Writings on Jackson continue to abound, most notably at the hands of Robert V. Remini, whose recently completed three-volume study of Jackson's career merits comparison with Bassett and Parton. Remini's pro-Jackson approach has kept the debate very much alive.

The search for the Jackson images goes on, and, as Sellers says, ''as long as democracy remains pre-eminently the distinguishing feature of our society, the period and symbol of its triumph will remain controversial.'' The nature of the problem is nicely put by Parton in his Preface (and is quoted by Sellers):

If any one, at the end of a year even, had asked what I had yet discovered respecting General Jackson, I might have answered thus: "Andrew Jackson, I am given to understand, was a patriot and a traitor. He was one of the greatest of generals, and wholly ignorant of the art of war. A writer brilliant, elegant, eloquent, without being able to compose a correct sentence, or spell words of four syllables. The first of statesmen, he never devised, he never framed a measure. He was the most candid of men, and was capable of the profoundest dissimulation. A most law-defying, law-obeying citizen. A stickler for discipline, he never hesitated to disobey his superior. A democratic autocrat. An urbane savage. An atrocious saint.

Jackson was an outsider, but his election in 1828 "signaled a change in American attitudes as well as a political change, a change so important in the perceptions of later Americans that Jackson is the only American President whose name, in American historiography, is attached to an age."[10]

JACKSON'S LEADERSHIP TRAITS

Partisan and critic, both can agree that Andrew Jackson's impact on the presidential office was profound. As Edward S. Corwin wrote in an oft-quoted line, "Jackson's Presidency was, in truth, no mere revival of the office; it was a remaking of it." The reasons for this, of course, lie both in the man and in the circumstances in which he had to operate. To deny the Jacksonian influence on the office would be naive and unrealistic. This influence derived from certain personal traits, essentially summed up by the words leadership and charisma. He had the ability to command, to inspire (and to repel), and thus to lead. Much of this ability came from his military background. He had sought positions of command, had aggressively used this military power, and had gained the adulation of much of the nation. His background also demonstrated what later generations will think of as the Horatio Alger approach—the ability to rise from poverty to, in Jackson's case, the highest political position in the land. This, and more, produced in Jackson a sense of command and an ability to exercise it.

Thus, for example, he could assert the independence of the executive from the other two branches of government. In his Bank veto message, rejecting the decision of the Supreme Court in upholding the Bank's constitutionality (*McCulloch* v. *Maryland,* 1819) he noted: "The Congress, the Executive, and the Court must each for itself be guided by its own opinion of the Constitution. . . . The opinion of the judges has no more authority over Congress than the opinion of Congress has over the judges, and on that point the President is independent of both." This concept, incidentally, was not radical in 1832. It was a position held by Jefferson and is basic to the nature of the Constitution drafted in 1787. Jackson, in addition, believed in a single term for the president, and so stated in each of his annual messages to the Congress.

Furthermore, Jackson made liberal use of the presidential veto (and was the first president to use the pocket veto), vetoing more bills than all of his predecessors combined. In addition, he vetoed bills not simply for reasons of consti-tutionality but also for reasons of policy. While this produced a form of negative government, it was clearly an unprecedented use of executive power and did comport, presumably, with Jackson's philosophy of the function of the national government. In the same Bank veto message, Jackson stated that if government should "confine itself to equal protection, and, as Heaven does its rains, shower its favors alike on the high and the low, the rich and the poor, it would be an unqualified blessing." This same spirit of presidential independence animated Jackson's "Protest" to the Senate's censure for his removal of the deposits from the Bank of the United States.

The fact that Jackson was an "outsider in Washington" meant, as Theodore Lowi (differing from de Tocqueville) indicates, a strengthening of the presidential office. He broke with the prevailing pattern of succession and turned to party organization to maintain and to extend his power. *"Jackson's strategy,"* says Lowi, *"resulted in giving him and succeeding presidents a base of power independent of Congress; moreover, insofar as parties perpetuated the system of succession Jackson employed for himself, to that extent parties would perpetuate the independence"* of the presidential system of nomination by national con-vention. Thus Jackson set himself up, as Clinton Rossiter would say, as "Chief of Party," a role strong presidents since his day have played.

This commanding role was seen in Jackson's handling of the cabinet and the patronage. He reduced the former to a position of simply discussing questions or to receiving presidential decisions—not to making them. And he consulted a revolving set of advisers, "the Kitchen Cabinet," as he felt necessary. And, logically, he appointed loyal partisans to federal positions, thus further strength-ening the presidential office. He defended such action as simply democratic rotation in office:

The duties of all public officers are, or at least admit of being made, so plain and simple that men of intelligence may readily qualify themselves for their performance; and I cannot but believe that more is lost by the long continuance of men in office than is generally to be gained by their experience.

Jackson came to think of himself as a direct representative of the people. Referring to his first election, Remini indicates that Jackson "was profoundly grateful to them," adding: "Additional bonds of affection and gratitude between this crusty old soldier and the electorate formed and strengthened as a result of the presidential election. They never slackened thereafter." During the Bank war the same author notes: "Identification with the people had become fixed in his thinking."

Philip Hone (admittedly before the full tumult of the second term) was one of those chosen to receive Jackson on his visit to New York City in June 1833. In part, no doubt tongue in cheek, he wrote in his diary:

Jackson is certainly the most popular man we have ever known. . . . Here is a man who suits [the populace] exactly. . . . He is a *gourmand* of adulation, and by the assistance of the populace has persuaded himself that no man ever lived in the country to whom the country was so much indebted. Talk of him as the second Washington! It won't do now; Washington was only the first Jackson.

In his final assessment Edward Pessen views the Jacksonian impact as "a mixed blessing," pointing out that, as is obvious, presidential power can be manipulated and misused. He concludes:

My own reading of Jacksonian politics is that Jackson accomplished something very close to that, as he appealed to the people over the heads of his—and therefore their—enemies, oversimplifying complex issues and fighting the good fight against the forces of darkness though in fact the warfare was largely confined to the field of rhetoric.

There remains another point to be made in any attempt to assess the Jackson image as revealed by the events of his presidency, to wit, how shall his specific policies be judged? What does an analysis of the record reveal? With respect to the Indians, for example, Jackson might have viewed himself in the role of a father to them, but was removal necessary, sound, humane? The Bank by its very nature was related to politics, but was its destruction sound policy? Did its end not bring chaos and a multiplicity of banks and feed the inflationary fires of the early 1830s? Was support for the tariff reduction, admittedly part of a compromise over nullification, in the best interests of the nation? The end product of Jacksonian economic policies was laissez faire and the severe depression of 1837. Does not Jackson bear at least some responsibility for this result? Did he not at least have qualified power to control economic forces leading that panic? In one of the severest—and, in a way, startling—indictments of Jacksonian financial policy published in recent years, Bray Hammond, former assistant secretary of the Federal Reserve Board, wrote: "It goes without saying that Andrew Jackson himself did not understand what was happening." True?[11] What should one conclude concerning the strengthening of the presidency and the increased potential for the exercise of power at the highest level of American government?

Of these and of many other things, one may state with assurance only that while the Founding Fathers in 1787 designed the presidential office to limit power, it has become the most powerful elective office in the world and that this has happened because of the conduct of certain individuals who have occupied that office. Andrew Jackson was one of those individuals.

NOTES

1. Ralph M. Goldman, *Search for Consensus: The Story of the Democratic Party* (Philadelphia: Temple University Press, 1979), p. 30, notes that obstacles had been surmounted by the Jacksonian "outsiders," who thus "transformed the presidential se-

lection process, the national electorate, and the Presidency itself.'' A sympathetic historian calls Jackson ''the most presidential-looking figure . . . since George Washington.'' Robert V. Remini, *Andrew Jackson and the Course of American Freedom 1822–1832* (New York: Harper and Row, 1981), p. 157. And an erstwhile rival but now a strong political ally reminisced: ''The character of his mind was that of judgment, with a rapid and almost intuitive perception, followed by an instant and decisive action.'' Thomas Hart Benton, *Thirty Years' View*, 2 vols. (New York: D. Appleton and Co., 1862), 1:737.

2. James C. Curtis, *Andrew Jackson and the Search for Vindication* (Boston: Little, Brown, 1976), p. 131.

3. Benton, *Thirty Years,* 1:735. There are numerous accounts of Jackson's life and presidency, some of which will be discussed below. See the Annotated Bibliography.

4. Statue described in Dixon Wecter, *The Hero in America: A Chronicle of Hero-Worship* (New York: Charles Scribner's Sons, 1941), p. 220. Donald Smalley reports that Jackson had, literally, become a museum piece before he became president (see his introduction to Frances Trollope, *Domestic Manners of the Americans* [New York: Vintage Books, 1960], p. xxv). On 1860 votes see Remini, *Andrew Jackson,* 2:447, note 66. ''Hermitage lion'' reference in Wecter, *Hero,* p. 216. See also Edward Pessen, *Jacksonian America: Society, Personality, and Politics,* rev. ed. (Homewood, Ill.: Dorsey Press, 1978), p. 191; Wecter, *Hero,* p. 216. On Lincoln's first inaugural, see Kenneth M. Stampp, *And the War Came: The North and the Secession Crisis 1860–1861* (Baton Rouge: Louisiana State University Press), p. 198. As William Freehling writes:

In less than thirty years President Abraham Lincoln—as nationalistic, as vigorous, and as cautious as Jackson—would have his turn at enforcing the laws and maneuvering for position in Charleston harbor. Lincoln's policy would win widespread support partly because it drew on the tradition Jackson had established in the Nullification Controversy. And in the long and bitter war which followed, Jackson's nationalism would help reduce Tennessee to ashes.

Prelude to Civil War: The Nullification Controversy in South Carolina, 1816–1836 (New York: Harper and Row, 1968), pp. 294, 295.

5. ''National spirit'' cited in Woodrow Wilson, *Division and Reunion 1829–1889* (New York: Longmans, Green and Co., 1898), p. 115. ''Man of the people'' in Woodrow Wilson, *A History of the American People,* 5 vols. (New York: Harper and Brothers, 1907), 4:3, 4. On nullification failure, see Woodrow Wilson, *Constitutional Government in the United States* (New York: Columbia University Press, 1917), pp. 58, 175. TR view of Jackson in Elting E. Morison et al., eds., *The Letters of Theodore Roosevelt,* 8 vols. (Cambridge, Mass.: Harvard University Press, 1951–1954), 7:501. ''Buchanan type'' quotation, July 3, 1916, in ibid., 8:1086, 1087. Visitors to Hermitage, Wecter, *Hero,* p. 220. FDR view in Arthur M. Schlesinger, Jr., *The Age of Roosevelt: Politics of Upheaval* (Boston: Houghton Mifflin Co., 1960), pp. 503, 637. FDR on monument in John William Ward, *Andrew Jackson: Symbol for an Age* (New York: Oxford University Press, 1955), p. 257, note 28. Gold chain noted in Wecter, *Hero,* p. 461. Jefferson reference in Merrill Peterson, *The Jefferson Image in the American Mind* (New York: Oxford University Press, 1962), p. 25.

6. Benton's view of aristocracy quoted in Richard H. Brown, *The Hero and the People: The Meaning of Jacksonian Democracy* (New York: Macmillan, 1964), p. 47. On appeal of the Bank veto, see William N. Chambers, ''Andrew Jackson,'' in Morton Borden, ed., *America's Eleven Greatest Presidents* (Chicago: Rand McNally College Publishing Co., 1971), pp. 95–96, for a good, succinct statement. Talk of aristocracy,

Wecter, *Hero,* p. 206. Whitman quoted in Wecter, *Hero,* p. 213. Amos Kendall, Gideon
Welles quoted in Remini, *Andrew Jackson,* 2:167. Cooper quoted in Brown, *Hero,*
pp. 217, 218. "Greatest Man" view in Henry A. Wise, *Seven Decades of the Union*
(Philadelphia: J. B. Lippincott and Co., 1881), p. 81. "We found him well" in Allan
Nevins, ed., *The Diary of Philip Hone, 1821–1851* (New York: Dodd, Mead and Co.,
1936), p. 23. Reference to Ralph Earl in Wecter, *Hero,* p. 205. Jackson mail, letter
referring to royalty quoted in Wecter, *Hero,* pp. 212, 214. Bell in letter to William
Plumer, quoted in Remini, *Andrew Jackson,* p. 309. Biddle, Webster views quoted in
Rush Welter, *The Mind of America 1820–1860* (New York: Columbia University Press,
1975), p. 191. Sprague quoted in ibid., p. 209. Clay view, "period of her disgrace,"
in Michael Chevalier, *Society, Manners and Politics in the United States: Being a Series
of Letters on North America,* ed. John William Ward (1833. Reprint. New York: Augustus
M. Kelley, 1966), p. 176; Nevins, *Hone,* p. 492. "More mischief" in ibid., p. 732. See
replicas of Coffin Hand Bills, cartoons in Remini, *Andrew Jackson,* vol. 2, preceding
p. 257.

　　7. Jackson character analysis in Albert Somit, "Andrew Jackson: Legend and
Reality," *Tennessee Historical Quarterly,* 7 (December 1948): 291–313. Change in
Andrew Jackson, ibid., p. 301. "Grim warrior," ibid., pp. 309–313.

　　8. On "gravity of countenance," Harriet Martineau, *Retrospect of Western Travel,*
vol. 1, 1838, quoted in Robert V. Remini, ed., *The Age of Jackson* (New York: Harper
and Row, 1972), pp. 20–22. See also Allan Nevins, ed., *America Through British Eyes,*
rev. ed. (New York: Oxford University Press, 1948), pp. 151–154, citing *Society in
America,* Vol. 1, quotation, p. 154. "Violent passions" cited in Harriet Martineau,
Society in America, ed. Seymour Martin Lipset, (1837; Reprint. Garden City, N.Y.:
Doubleday, 1962), pp. 84, 85. Anecdote in Harriet Martineau, *Society in America,* 3
vols. (London: 1837), 3:166, quoted in Paul F. Boller, Jr., *Presidential Anecdotes* (New
York: Penguin Books, 1982), p. 84. A readable account of the views of foreign, mainly
English, travelers in America is John Emmett Burke, "Andrew Jackson as Seen by
Foreigners," *Tennessee Historical Quarterly,* 10 (March 1951): 25–45. There are several
excellent editions of de Tocqueville's work in English, including Phillips Bradley, ed.,
Democracy in America by Alexis de Tocqueville, 2 vols. (New York: Vintage Books,
1954), used in this section. Comment on Jackson critics in Hugh Brogan, "Tocqueville
and the American Presidency," *Journal of American Studies,* 15 (December 1981): 356–
375. See also James T. Schleifer, *The Making of Tocqueville's "Democracy in America"*
(Chapel Hill: University of North Carolina Press, 1980), pp. 155, 156. Blunder cited by
Brogan, "Tocqueville," pp. 359, 365. "Mediocre man" in Alexis de Tocqueville, *Journey to America,* ed. J. P. Mayer (New Haven: Yale University Press, 1960), pp. 157,
158. On majority view, see Bradley, *Tocqueville,* 1:299. How Jackson addressed, Brogan,
"Tocqueville," p. 358. Beaumont quoted in George Wilson Pierson, *Tocqueville and
Beaumont in America* (New York: Oxford University Press, 1938), p. 644. Comments
on presidency in Bradley, *Tocqueville,* 1:432.

　　9. One of the first recent accounts of changing views is by Charles Grier Sellers, Jr.,
"Andrew Jackson Versus the Historians," *Mississippi Valley Historical Review,* 44
(March 1958): 615–634. The present account follows Sellers closely and is essentially
based on it. Criticism cited in James Parton, *The Life of Andrew Jackson,* 3 vols. (New
York: Mason Brothers, 1860), 3:694–700. Full bibliographical citations and quotations
used by Sellers may be found in his article. Symbolism noted in John William Ward,
"Looking Backward: Andrew Jackson: Symbol for an Age," in L. P. Curtis, Jr., ed.,

The Historian's Workshop: Original Essays by Sixteen Historians (New York: Alfred A. Knopf, 1970), p. 214. "He was the age's," Ward, *Jackson,* p. 213.

10. A pioneer word using empirical data is Lee Benson, *The Concept of Jacksonian Democracy: New York as a Test Case* (Princeton: Princeton University Press, 1961). Since this volume was published many books and articles have used quantification. Two noteworthy examples of psychohistory are Curtis, *Search,* and Michael Paul Rogin, *Fathers and Children: Andrew Jackson and the Subjugation of the American Indian* (New York: Alfred A. Knopf, 1975). For Remini's many volumes on Jackson see the Annotated Bibliography, below. "Search goes on," Sellers, "Jackson," pp. 615–616. Contradictions relating to Jackson in Parton, *Jackson,* 1:vii. "Name attached to an age," James Oliver Robertson, *American Myth, American Reality* (New York: Hill and Wang, 1980), p. 80.

11. "Remaking" of presidency, Edward S. Corwin, *The President: Office and Powers 1787–1957,* 4th rev. ed. (New York: New York University Press, 1957), p. 20. On president's independence, see James D. Richardson, comp., *A Compilation of the Messages and Papers of the Presidents,* 11 vols. (Washington, D.C.: U.S. Congress, 1899–1903), 2:582. "Unqualified blessing," ibid., 2:590. "Independent power base," Theodore J. Lowi, "Party, Policy, and Constitution in America," in William Nisbet Chambers and Walter Dean Burnham, eds., *The American Party Systems: Stages of Political Development* (New York: Oxford University Press, 1967), p. 248. On chief of party role, see Clinton Rossiter, *The American Presidency,* 2nd ed. (New York: Harcourt, Brace and Co., 1960), pp. 30–32. On duties of public officers, Richardson, *Messages,* 2:449. "Identification with the people," Remini, *Andrew Jackson,* pp. 156, 339. "Washington first Jackson," Nevins, *Hone,* pp. 96, 97. On "warfare in rhetoric," see Pessen, *Jacksonian America,* p. 323. "Did not understand," Bray Hammond, *Banks and Politics in America from the Revolution to the Civil War* (Princeton: Princeton University Press, 1957), p. 359.

ANNOTATED BIBLIOGRAPHY

Books

Aronson, Sidney H. *Status and Kinship in the Higher Civil Service: Standards of Selection in the Administrations of John Adams, Thomas Jefferson and Andrew Jackson.* Cambridge, Mass.: Harvard University Press, 1964.
    Invaluable in updating Fish's work (mentioned in the text) and putting the "spoils" issue in perspective.
Bassett, John Spencer. *The Life of Andrew Jackson,* 2 vols. Garden City, N.Y.: Doubleday, Page and Co., 1911.
    Called by Sellers "the earliest major product of the democratic school of Jacksonian historiography" and "sympathetic" but "not critical." The final chapter of the second volume is recommended to seek to understand Jackson's character.
————, ed. *Correspondence of Andrew Jackson.* 7 vols. Washington, D.C.: Carnegie Institution of Washington, 1926–1935.
    Invaluable in themselves and also in underscoring the thoroughness of Bassett's research. Soon to be supplemented or superseded by a new edition of Jackson's writings currently in progress.

Benson, Lee. *The Concept of Jacksonian Democracy: New York as a Test Case*. Princeton: Princeton University Press, 1961.
  A pioneer work in the field of quantification for the Jackson period; highly critical of the concept of "Jacksonian democracy."

Chambers, William N. "Andrew Jackson." In Morton Borden, ed., *America's Eleven Greatest Presidents*. Chicago: Rand McNally College Publishing Co., 1971. Pp. 76–107.
  This chapter on Jackson is one of the best and most useful of such accounts.

Curtis, James C. *Andrew Jackson and the Search for Vindication*. Boston: Little, Brown, 1976.
  Short, well-researched, readable, and intriguing in its efforts to explain Jackson's behavior in terms of his childhood and adolescent roots.

Dangerfield, George. *The Awakening of American Nationalism, 1815–1848*. New York: Harper and Row, 1965.
  This volume, along with Van Deusen's *The Jacksonian Era* and especially Pessen's *Jacksonian America*, provides a wide range of information and references to the many-faceted developments of Jackson's emergence and activity as president and the culture of the period.

James, Marquis. *The Life of Andrew Jackson*. Vol. 1, *The Border Captain*. Vol. 2, *Portrait of a President*. Indianapolis: Bobbs Merrill Co., 1938.
  Readable, stimulating—a good survey of the life of Old Hickory.

Latner, Richard B. *The Presidency of Andrew Jackson: White House Politics, 1829–1837*. Athens, Ga.: University of Georgia Press, 1979.
  Useful for those wishing to delve into the actual functioning and the power relationships in the White House during Jackson's Presidency.

Lowi, Theodore J. "Party, Policy, and Constitution in America." In William Nisbet Chambers and Walter Dean Burnham, eds., *The American Party Systems: Stages of Political Development*. New York: Oxford University Press, 1967. Pp. 238–276.
  Explains much about the Jacksonian revolution, especially the meaning of the "outsider" theme.

Meyers, Marvin. *The Jacksonian Persuasion*. New York: Vintage Books, 1960.
  Like Ward's *Andrew Jackson* (see below), this is an effort to get at the Jackson period as one of tension between the old, the Jeffersonian, and the new emerging American, and tries to "convey the effort of Jacksonian Democracy to recall agrarian republican innocence to a society drawn fatally to the main chance" (p. 15).

Nevins, Allan, ed. *America Through British Eyes*. Rev. ed. New York: Oxford University Press, 1948.
  The Jacksonian image from a British viewpoint.

Parton, James. *Life of Andrew Jackson*. 3 vols. New York: Mason Brothers, 1860.
  Written by the "father of American biography," this is one of the most detailed and informative works on the Jackson years, published a bit more than a decade after Jackson's death. The last three chapters of the third volume deserve attention for their evaluation of Jackson.

Pessen, Edward. *Jacksonian America: Society, Personality, and Politics*. Rev. ed. Homewood, Ill.: Dorsey Press, 1978.

Prucha, Francis Paul. *American Indian Policy in the Formative Years*. Cambridge, Mass:
Harvard University Press, 1962.
Defends Jackson's Indian policy.

Remini, Robert V. *The Election of Andrew Jackson*. Philadelphia: J. B. Lippincott Co.,
1963. *Andrew Jackson*. New York: Harper and Row, 1966. *Andrew Jackson and
the Course of American Empire, 1767–1821*. New York: Harper and Row, 1977.
Andrew Jackson and the Course of American Freedom, 1822–1832. New York:
Harper and Row, 1981. *Andrew Jackson and the Course of American Democracy,
1833–1845*. New York, Harper and Row, 1984.
These are all carefully researched and written with sparkle and wit. They tend to
be pro-Jackson, although not uncritically so.

————, ed. *The Age of Jackson*. New York: Harper and Row, 1972.
A contemporary American work that sheds much light on the popular Jacksonian
image. See Nevins, ed., *America Through British Eyes,* for a foreign perspective.
The listing of an exhaustive compilation of such sources would, of course, be an
unending task.

Remini, Robert V., and Edwin A. Miles, comps. *The Era of Good Feelings and the Age
of Jackson 1816–1841*. Arlington Heights, Ill.: AHM Publishing Corp., 1979.
An extremely comprehensive bibliography of the literature of this period. Very
useful.

Schlesinger, Arthur M., Jr. *The Age of Jackson*. Boston: Little, Brown, 1945.
This book presented the new "wage-earner" thesis which sparked the renaissance
in Jacksonian studies which has continued to the present. Highly readable and
valuable in its efforts to relate Jackson and his period to the mainstream of
American political and social development.

Schlesinger, Arthur M., Jr., and Fred L. Israel, eds. *History of American Presidential
Elections*. 4 vols. New York: Chelsea House, 1971.
Has material in detail, written by specialists, on the elections in which Jackson
participated.

Sumner, William Graham. *Andrew Jackson as a Public Man*. 7th ed. Boston: Houghton
Mifflin, 1884.
This appeared a generation before Turner's volume and represents the so-called
"Whig school" of American historians. Critical of Jackson but chiefly because
of the alleged spoils systems.

Turner, Frederick Jackson. *Rise of the New West 1819–1829*. New York: Harper and
Brothers, 1906.
This volume, by America's preeminent frontier historian, provides a good statement of one of the early writers of the "democratic" approach to Jacksonian
democracy at the end of the nineteenth and the beginning of the twentieth century.

Van Deusen, Glyndon G. *The Jacksonian Era, 1828–1848*. New York: Harper and
Brothers, 1959.

Ward, John William. *Andrew Jackson: Symbol for an Age*. New York: Oxford University
Press, 1955.
Unique for its interpretation of Jackson and his period and for the research methods
employed. Readable and highly stimulating.

Wecter, Dixon. *The Hero in America: A Chronicle of Hero-Worship*. New York: Charles
Scribner's Sons, 1941.

Perhaps dated but still valuable in showing in readable, entertaining terms why, to so many, Jackson was such a popular hero in his times and later.

Articles

Burke, John Emmett. "Andrew Jackson as Seen by Foreigners," *Tennessee Historical Quarterly,* 10 (March 1951): 25–45.
This supplements material in Nevins, *America Through British Eyes,* mentioned above.

Curtis, James C. "In the Shadow of Old Hickory: The Political Travail of Martin Van Buren," *Journal of the Early Republic,* 1 (Fall 1981): 249–267.
Throws light on the problems associated with succeeding a strong president, one who for many was a national hero.

Pessen, Edward. "The Working Men's Party Revisited," *Labor History,* 4 (Fall 1963): 203–226.
Should be read in connection with Schlesinger's *The Age of Jackson.*

Prucha, Francis Paul. "Andrew Jackson's Indian Policy: A Reassessment," *Journal of American History,* 56 (December 1969): 527–539.
Written by a defender of Jackson's Indian policy. This can be read in conjunction with a so-called psychohistorical approach to the subject; Michael P. Rogin, *Fathers and Children: Andrew Jackson and the Subjugation of the American Indian* (New York: Alfred A. Knopf, 1975), and William Gilmore, "The Individual and the Group in Psychohistory: Rogin's *Fathers and Children* and the Problem of Jackson's Health," *Psychohistory Review,* 6 (Fall-Winter 1977–78): 112–126.

Sellers, Charles Grier, Jr. "Andrew Jackson Versus the Historians," *Mississippi Valley Historical Review,* 44 (March 1958): 615–634.
Recounts the changing interpretations of Jackson and Jacksonian democracy from Parton down to the near present. It should be used in connection with Alfred A. Cave, *Jacksonian Democracy and the Historians* (Gainesville: University of Florida Press, 1964), and Don F. Flatt, "Historians View Jacksonian Democracy: A Historiographical Study," Ph.D. dissertation, University of Kentucky, 1974.

Somit, Albert. "Andrew Jackson: Legend and Reality," *Tennessee Historical Quarterly,* 7 (December 1948): 291–313.
Seeks to portray and present the "real" Jackson.

4 ABRAHAM LINCOLN

L. Gerald Bursey

> Power tends to corrupt and absolute power corrupts absolutely. Great men
> are almost always bad men.[1]
>
> —Lord Acton

THE LINCOLN IMAGE

The Lincoln image—and its development—is without parallel in American history. It is unparalleled in its heights, its depths, its contrasts, its paradoxes and ironies, its reversals, and its power and influence.

That Lincoln was one of the *great* American presidents is now the standard view. Indeed, he is widely regarded as the greatest American president, not only by ordinary folk, but also by scholars. In the two most famous polls of the experts, the Arthur Schlesinger, Sr., polls of 1948 and 1962, Lincoln ranked first as the greatest president both times.[2]

That Lincoln was a *good* man is also the standard view. The popular image of Lincoln most Americans have from schooldays, the media, and popular literature is of a kindly, honest, fatherly man—a man who, though he could enjoy a joke and might at times have a twinkle in his eye, was, particularly as president, a man of sorrows and sadness. He is perceived also as a man who hated slavery and wanted freedom and justice for all. At a bare minimum, then, Lincoln is seen as a good man. Usually, however, it goes well beyond that, and Lincoln is perceived as not only good in the sense which would be applied to an ordinary man, subjected to ordinary pressures and temptations, but as a man of unusual goodness—goodness made even more remarkable by the extraordinary pressures of the office he held and the particularly unhappy time in which he held it.

Lincoln, then, is standardly seen as a man to whom Acton's dictum did not apply. If, as some contend, he held absolute power, not only did it not corrupt him absolutely, it apparently did not corrupt him at all. Quite the contrary, Lincoln is viewed as exemplifying in the highest degree the qualities of *both goodness and greatness*. That, it will be contended here, is the central feature of the dominant popular image of Lincoln, and of particular importance in its impact on the presidency.

There have, however, been other images of Lincoln. Most Americans would not recognize a Lincoln who was seen as weak, cowardly, stupid, harsh, coarse, indecisive, drunken, bloodthirsty, and tyrannical. To most people it comes as a shock to encounter descriptions of Lincoln as a "simple Susan," a "wet rag," or a "Kentucky mule," to say nothing of references to him as "the Illinois Ape," the "gorilla," the "baboon," or even "Lincoln the Beast" or "demon."[3] Yet these too have been "popular," though negative, images of Lincoln. Such views—now forgotten by all except historians—cannot be ignored in any overview of Lincoln's image, not only because they are in fact a part of the historical image, but also because they are essential to an adequate understanding of Lincoln's character, actions, and later image.

On the positive side, the first elements of the Lincoln image to emerge were the interwined themes of the *common man,* the *self-made man,* and the *honest* (i.e., good) *man.* Typical of the Lincoln paradoxes is that Lincoln, in fact a most uncommon man, came to be the supreme symbol of the common man. Though circumstances and the views of others contributed greatly to this image, Lincoln himself had a hand in its creation. In his first major political speech, he stated; "I was born and have ever remained in the most humble walks of life."[4]

No doubt his unprepossessing appearance (face, figure, and clothes) fostered a self-image which placed him with the unhandsome and inelegant. Lincoln himself spoke of "my poor, lean, lank face." Others agreed (probably more than he would have liked) with Lincoln's unflattering view of his own appearance. "He is the *homeliest . . .* and the *awkwardest* man in the Sucker State." "He is the *ungodliest* man you ever saw" (from one of Mrs. Lincoln's friends). "His phiz is truly awful."[5]

Lincoln was largely self-educated. As Lincoln himself put it (in his brief campaign "Autobiography"): "The agregate [*sic*] of all his schooling did not amount to one year"; and—referring to his legal training—"He studied with nobody."[6] Despite that background, Lincoln became a prominent Illinois attorney "with a reputation as a lawyer's lawyer—a knowledgeable jurist who argued appeal cases for other attorneys. He did his most influential legal work in the Supreme Court of Illinois, where he participated in 243 cases and won most of them."[7]

His success as a lawyer alone, to say nothing of his later political success, was enough to make Lincoln an outstanding example of a self-made man. His humble origins, ungainly appearance, and lack of formal education fitted the image of a common man. His humility and unusual honesty ("Honest Abe") suggested the image of a good man.[8]

One of the key periods in the development of the Lincoln image is that of his nomination and election to the presidency. It is a time when, in addition to major new developments in the positive image, the main themes in the negative image begin to appear, or, in one instance, reappear.

On the national scene Lincoln was not that highly regarded. He had never held top-level national office despite one congressional term, and he had been defeated in three attempts to win more prominent positions. He was virtually unknown in the South, and to thousands in the North as well. William Seward was clearly the leading contender, but he had also generated much opposition. As most historians see it, Lincoln was selected as the most available and "least objectionable of the lesser candidates."[9]

It was at this time that the image of the Railsplitter, first introduced at the Republican state convention at Decatur with the punning slogan "Abraham Lincoln, the Rail Candidate for President in 1860," was given national exposure by typical campaign techniques. There was the widespread formation in the North of the Republican Wide-Awakes, young men dressed in shiny hats and capes, carrying lamps or flaming torches attached to fence rails, who marched in a zigzag formation meant to resemble a rail fence. Clearly, behind all the hoopla was an attempt to project an image of Lincoln the hardworking pioneer farmer, the embodiment of simple frontier virtue.

In contrast, Lincoln's Democratic opponents tried to revive the "Spotty Lincoln" image. Back in 1847–1848 when Lincoln had been a one-term Whig congressman, he had joined his fellow Whigs in their denunciation of the Polk administration for involving the country in the Mexican War, which the Whigs regarded as unjust and unnecessary. Lincoln had introduced in Congress a series of resolutions which demanded that Polk indicate the "spot" where American blood was first shed. The resolutions were designed to expose the fact that "the spot where the war began" was actually Mexican territory. Back home in Illinois, Lincoln's attitude on war guilt had been ill-received, and one opposition paper, the *Illinois State Register*, had dubbed him "Spotty Lincoln." Now, in 1860, the old media-created negative image was given new life:

The Douglas Democrats were doing everything they could to smear and belittle the Republican "rail splitter." There were malicious whispers that Lincoln was a bastard, that his real father was Abraham Enloe, or Henry Clay, or even John C. Calhoun. At their rallies, Democratic orators mocked Lincoln's "traitorous" Mexican War stand and led their crowds in a chant:

> Mr. Speaker! Where's the spot?
> Is it in Spain or is it not?
> Mr. Speaker! Spot! Spot! Spot![10]

However, new negative images also arose. These images portray Lincoln as weak, incompetent, ridiculous, cowardly, contemptible, and evil.

Following the traditional practice at that time for presidential nominees, Lincoln left the campaigning to others and made no speeches himself. Seward "made what historian James Ford Rhodes has called 'the most remarkable stump-speeches ever delivered in this country.' He, rather than Lincoln, seemed to be leading the party.''[11] Under such circumstances, it is easy to see how there developed the image of a weak Lincoln who would simply be a figurehead controlled by others.

In the South, though Lincoln was at first largely unknown, hostile images were not long in developing. Lincoln was described as "a relentless, dogged free-soil border ruffian . . . a vulgar mobocrat and a Southern hater" who championed "free love, free lands and free negroes," a "horrid lookin wretch . . . sooty and scoundrelly in aspect, a cross between the nutmeg dealer, the horse swapper, and the night man." In short, as Michael Davis sums it up, Lincoln was portrayed as "the very antithesis of the Cavalier ideal"[12]—the image of the ideal southern gentleman.

After his election victory, Lincoln continued his public silence, believing that anything he said would be misrepresented and only make things worse. However, in many minds this public silence simply reinforced the image of a Lincoln lacking in leadership and inadequate for the task before him.

In February, as he started on the twelve-day trip from Springfield to Washington, public receptions had been planned for him in every major city, so he finally had to break his public silence and speak. In attempting to be publicly reassuring, he made statements such as "There is really no crisis except an *artificial one!*"[13] Like many others, Lincoln apparently overestimated the strength of Unionist sentiment in the South. Nevertheless, he was fully aware of the existence of a crisis, artificial or not, and deeply concerned about it. Thus, in the very same speech in which he said, "There is nothing going wrong," he also said, "There has fallen upon me a task such as did not rest even upon the Father of his country."[14] The overall result was not particularly reassuring and seemed to support the image of vacillation put forward by his critics.

At one brief train stop in Westfield, New York, Lincoln pleased the crowd by kissing eleven-year-old Grace Bedell who, back in October, had written Lincoln suggesting that he grow a beard.[15] Even this fatherly gesture was seized upon by some of Lincoln's critics as a further opportunity to belittle him for occupying himself with such trivia as growing whiskers and kissing little girls when so much more serious matters demanded his attention.

One can hardly avoid concluding, however, that Lincoln's decision to make such a noticeable change in his physical appearance does suggest some dissatisfaction with his existing image. It is not unreasonable to surmise that Lincoln hoped that the beard would give him greater dignity—as a letter from a number of New York Republicans had contended—and project a more fatherly image. Later, as president, Lincoln did, in fact, acquire the image of Father Abraham, and ultimately was widely perceived as a kind of second Father of His Country, surpassing even its original father, George Washington. Initially, however, the beard merely subjected him to additional criticism and ridicule.

Perhaps the most devastating blow to President-elect Lincoln's image, however, occurred in connection with the Baltimore assassination plot—an incident which also demonstrates the enormous importance of the media in image-creation. In Philadelphia, the night before he was to raise the flag at Independence Hall, Lincoln was told by Allan Pinkerton, the famous detective and head of the agency handling security for the railroad, that there was a well-organized plot to assassinate him in Baltimore. (Still later that night Seward's son, Frederick, arrived from Washington with special confidential messages from his father and General Winfield Scott containing similar warnings of the assassination plot, apparently derived from sources independent of Pinkerton's.) Though strongly urged to cancel his remaining scheduled appearances and leave immediately for Washington, Lincoln refused and insisted on keeping his Washington's Birthday speaking engagements the next day in Philadelphia and Harrisburg. Reluctantly, however, he did agree that, once his commitments were fulfilled, he would go along with the plan to slip him quietly through Baltimore ahead of schedule on a special train. Since the plan relied on secrecy and surprise, Lincoln told only his wife, Mary, who insisted that, to provide some protection, the faithful Ward Hill Lamon (armed with two pistols, two derringers, and two large knives) accompany Lincoln.[16]

Robert S. Harper described what happened:

During the first few hours after the story of the ride broke, it was treated seriously by both the Republicans and the pro-Southern press. Then the country learned what the *New York Times* said, and it rocked with laughter, bringing abuse and ridicule down on Lincoln. Joseph Howard Jr., a well-known newspaper man, was covering Lincoln for the *Times*. Upon awakening Saturday morning, February 23, in Harrisburg to find Lincoln gone, he wrote a fantastic story that was played on page one by the *Times* and given further circulation when reprinted by other newspapers. . . . The [following] sentence did the damage:

"He wore a Scotch plaid cap and a very long military cloak, so that he was entirely unrecognizable."

The *Sun* at Baltimore pounced upon the story . . . with an . . . editorial which (in part) said:

" . . . We do not believe the Presidency can ever be more degraded by any of his successors than it has by him, even before his inauguration . . . "

Because it was published in the *New York Times,* a solidly Republican paper (in Lincoln's time), the man in the street accepted Howard's story as gospel truth. In no other newspaper could it have caused so much damage to Lincoln and the cause he represented.[17]

Thus arose the image of a cowardly Lincoln sneaking into Washington in disguise. The media had a field day with the incident. There were anti-Lincoln cartoons (*Vanity Fair* showed him in kilts) and poems about Lincoln's midnight ride. The refrain of a thirteen-stanza poem, sung to the tune of "Yankee Doodle," was:

Lanky Lincoln came to town
In night and wind, and rain, sir
Wrapped in a military cloak
Upon a special train, sir.[18]

"In the midst of the greatest internal crisis it ever faced, the country burst into merriment at the thought of Lincoln in a Scotch cap."[19] Concern over the danger of possible assassination was lost in the laughter. Efforts to undo the damage were in vain.

CRISIS

Lincoln entered his presidency facing a crisis of enormous proportions. Indeed, his presidency was one long series of crises, most intertwined with other crises, and almost all part of the one great overarching crisis of secession and ultimate civil war.

The problems Lincoln faced were huge, the means available to deal with them uncertain and inadequate. Basically, Lincoln had somehow to try to keep what was left of the Union together (and ultimately bring back those who had already seceded) while at the same time ensuring that slavery was not extended (the very problem that had led to secession in the first place); to hold his own newly formed party together (despite its internal differences and loose organization) while at the same time appealing beyond party to all who might support the Union; to face a growing secessionist military capability without adequate forces of his own; to deal with a hostile chief justice, a troublesome Congress, and a critical press; and to do all this with the help of a cabinet which included some of his main rivals for the presidency, several of whom regarded themselves as better qualified than Lincoln in the first place, and with the help of government employees whose loyalties were often open to question. No wonder Lincoln later became a legendary figure; who but a legend—a folk hero or deity—could hope to accomplish such miracles?

Moreover, Lincoln enjoyed none of the advantages traditionally associated with incoming presidents. There was no honeymoon period. He did not have a favorable press, and he did not have the initial prestige with which more fortunate presidents, such as Washington and Jackson, entered the office.

Instead, it was with "incredibly low prestige" that Lincoln entered the presidency.[20] There was a widespread image of Lincoln as weak and inadequate. The very homespun qualities that had endeared him to many plain folks now increasingly became a liability. This very Lincoln had, of course, learned to talk like his neighbors. He said "howdey" to visitors. He "sot" down and "stayed a spell." He "cum" from "whar" he had been. He "keered" for his friends and "heered" the latest news.[21]

Over the years, most of the rough edges had been rubbed off. But the remaining traces of Lincoln's Indiana accent (in reference to his "inaugural," for example) sounded provincial to eastern ears and reinforced the image of inadequacy. How could such a Simple Susan possibly handle the complexities of the presidency?

Now, because of an irresponsible reporter and hostile elements in the media, there had been added the image of a cowardly Lincoln sneaking into Washington in the famous "Scotch plaid cap" and "long military cloak." Lincoln was no coward and had only with great reluctance finally been persuaded to go along with the plan to avoid his possible assassination in Baltimore. Hostility and danger had clearly existed, his protection had obviously been inadequate, the rumor had been persistent, and, moreover, if he were assassinated anywhere outside the District of Columbia the national government would have been without authority to punish the guilty party.[22]

Lincoln had only done the prudent thing. Unfortunately, the result had been to make him an object of ridicule, which, in turn, made it almost impossible for him to project the desired, and accurate, image of strength and determination. It is impossible now to determine how much of this image of weakness may have encouraged Lincoln's opponents to underestimate him, or to what extent the charge of cowardice may have made it more difficult for Lincoln to compromise or give any appearance of backing down.[23]

Except for its effect on the Lincoln image, the rumored assassination plot now seems a relatively minor incident, a possible crisis avoided, though obviously, if the assassination had actually taken place, the impact would have been enormous. It is hard to imagine what American history would have been like if there had been no President Lincoln, but instead a President Hamlin.

To add to Lincoln's woes, just two days before the inauguration, Seward precipitated a major cabinet crisis. "Long the most prominent Republican in the country,"[24] Seward had agreed to be Lincoln's secretary of state. The evidence suggests that Seward expected to be the real power in the new administration, telling the inexperienced and (in Seward's view) much less capable Lincoln what to do. (Moreover, Thurlow Weed, Seward's political manager and boss of the New York machine, apparently expected to become the national political boss and dispense the patronage.)[25] "Even as a Senator, in 1849–50, he [Seward] had dominated one administration, that of the rough soldier, Zachary Taylor."[26]

Unhappy with Lincoln's choices of Salmon P. Chase and Montgomery Blair, Seward tried to dictate the composition of the cabinet by threatening to resign. Seward apparently felt that Lincoln could not do without him. And Lincoln did not want to do without him, not only because of his great influence, but also because of his genuine ability. However, as Lincoln told his secretary; "I can't afford to let Seward take the first trick."[27] Accordingly, Lincoln hinted that perhaps he could get someone else, like Jonathan Dayton, to serve as secretary of state. Suddenly Seward discovered that he wanted the post after all, and Lincoln kept his broad-based cabinet unchanged.[28]

Seward's second challenge to Lincoln was more far-reaching and potentially much more dangerous. In the midst of the crisis over Sumter, Seward's famous memorandum, "Some Thoughts for the President's Consideration"—sent, appropriately enough, on April Fool's Day—expressed the view that after a month in office, the administration was still "without a policy." Seward, therefore, proposed one: demand explanations from Spain and France, "categorically, at once," and if the explanations were unsatisfactory, "declare war." Seward's basic idea was to *"Change the question before the Public from one upon Slavery"* to *"Patriotism or Union."* It "must be somebody's business" to direct this policy "incessantly," either "the President" or "some member of this Cabinet"—presumably Seward.[29]

Lincoln's successful handling of this matter, however accomplished, enabled him to keep Seward in the cabinet and also, apparently, to gain his respect. Two months later, Seward wrote his wife: "Executive force and vigor are rare qualities. The president is the best of us."[30]

However, Lincoln's astuteness in privately resolving cabinet problems had no effect on his public image. "Inadequacy, weakness, vacillation, even 'imbecility' (a favorite word) were attributed to the new leader."[31]

Contrary to his public image, Lincoln was in fact a talented and intelligent man with well-reasoned views on the fundamental issues and on what was really at stake. Underlying the national crisis were the two fundamental, complex, intertwined issues of slavery and the Union. Lincoln clearly believed that the more important of the two issues, and his primary responsibility as president, was to save the Union. But he also believed that the Union saved must be pointed toward freedom, not slavery.

The saving of the Union was, in turn, part of a still larger issue: upon it depended the survival of free government itself.

This issue embraces more than the fate of these United States. It presents to the whole family of man the question, whether a constitutional republic or a democracy—a government of the people, by the same people—can, or cannot, maintain its territorial integrity, against its own domestic foes. It presents the question, whether discontented individuals, too few in numbers to control administration, according to organic law, . . . can always . . . break up their Government, and thus practically put an end to free government upon the earth.[32]

It was an unfortunate fact that slavery existed within the free, democratic government that it was crucial to save. Lincoln personally believed that slavery was a great moral wrong. "If slavery is not wrong, nothing is wrong. I cannot remember when I did not so think and feel. And yet I have never understood that the presidency conferred upon me an unrestricted right to act officially upon this judgment and feeling."[33] Not only was slavery legal in many states, but, in certain respects, it was protected by the U.S. Constitution. And, both as a lawyer and as a holder of public office, Lincoln had sworn to uphold the law and the Constitution.

As realists, the Founding Fathers had, in the interests of overall unity, agreed to certain compromises on the slavery issue. But they had looked toward its ultimate extinction. And that too was Lincoln's basic position and hope. Indeed, what had particularly stimulated Lincoln's return to politics in the mid-1850's was his concern about the expansion of slavery and the threat it posed to freedom. The Kansas-Nebraska Act (and, later, the Dred Scott decision) led Lincoln to fear that the trend envisaged by the Founding Fathers was in the process of being reversed, and that an expanding slave empire might ultimately engulf free government.

Lincoln sharply distinguished between *existing* slavery (the long-range problem) and the *extension* of slavery (the intermediate problem). Lincoln frankly admitted that (as he had put it back in 1854) "if all earthly power were given me, I should not know what to do, as to the existing institution."[34] He simply could not see any realistic, quick, or simple solution to such a monumental problem without enormous, and perhaps catastrophic, upheaval. In general, Lincoln felt that the only realistic way to avoid such upheaval was by some system or policy of gradual, compensated, and, insofar as possible, voluntary emancipation. Thus, in order to avoid upheaval and calm southern fears, he tried to reassure Southerners that he intended no drastic measures but would fulfill his existing legal and constitutional obligations.

Extension of slavery, however, was a very different matter. Here Lincoln drew the line and, as president-elect, refused any compromise. "Let there be no compromise on the question of *extending* slavery. If there be, all our labor is lost, and ere long, must be done again."

"[H]old firm, as with a chain of steel." "The tug has to come and better now than later."[35] This had been the issue on which the election had been fought and won. Those who had lost had to accept the verdict of the ballot box. That was a basic principle of free government. Any movement in the direction of slavery extension had to be stopped. For Lincoln the important thing was that the nation be headed in the right direction. Once they were on the right track, men of good will could begin to work out the next steps.

The Secession Crisis

Immediately after Lincoln assumed the presidency, the secession crisis came to a focus on the issue of the forts—particularly Fort Sumter in Charleston, South Carolina, and Fort Pickens near Pensacola, Florida. On this issue, too, there was, for Lincoln, a matter of principle which ultimately could not be sacrificed: the forts and other public property of the United States belonged to it and, accordingly, should be held by it or reclaimed.

The United States clearly could not continue indefinitely to back down to secessionists' threats of force—no government could do that and survive—but, in an effort at a peaceful resolution of the problem, Lincoln would go as far as he could toward conciliation without stepping over the line of complete capitulation. Accordingly, without changing his mind on the basic principle, Lincoln significantly changed the tone of his First Inaugural, omitting any reference to *reclaiming* property, and ending with his famous appeal to "the better angels of our nature."[36]

What Lincoln certainly did not expect was to receive, on his first working day in office, communications from the commander at Fort Sumter, Major Thomas Anderson, saying that his provisions would be exhausted in a few weeks, and doubting his ability to hold onto the fort. Though it presented virtually insuperable military difficulties for Lincoln, Fort Sumter was not at bottom simply a military problem. Clearly, Major Anderson and his small band of men constituted no real military threat to the Confederacy. Their main importance to both sides was symbolic. They symbolized the right of the Union to hold the forts and other public places which they occupied.

Right was one thing; what was militarily possible was another. Lincoln was informed by General Scott and the military authorities that successfully to reinforce Fort Sumter would take 20,000 men "at a time when the whole scattered army of the United States numbered less than 16,000."[37] Lincoln thus seemed to have no military option open to him.

Moreover, for Lincoln to issue any call for troops (even if it were only to make Union resolve credible) would be interpreted in the South as provocative and evidence of intended "coercion." As the secessionists saw it, secession itself was not coercive, building up the armed forces of the Confederacy was not coercive, seizing forts and other United States property was not coercive, and even firing upon United States ships was apparently not coercive.[38] From the secessionist point of view, the United States had long ago committed the first act of aggression by authorizing Major Anderson's move from the less defensible Fort Moultrie to Fort Sumter.[39] Merely to stay in the fort and starve was, in Confederate eyes, aggression. For his part, Lincoln was determined to adhere to the statement in his First Inaugural: "The government will not assail *you*. You can have no conflict, without being yourselves the aggressors."[40]

Throughout, Fort Sumter was a problem in image as much as in reality. Not only must the United States not take aggressive action, but it must also not be perceived as taking aggressive action. However, the men could not be left to starve, and Fort Sumter had become such an important symbol that the United States could not be perceived as abjectly capitulating either. Lincoln's final decision was to attempt to send provisions only (and no armaments) to the beleaguered men in Fort Sumter, and to notify the South Carolina governor in advance of that decision. Thus the onus for hostilities, if there were any, would rest squarely upon South Carolina and the Confederacy.

They [the secessionists] knew—they were expressly notified—that the giving of bread to the few brave and hungry men of the garrison, was all which would on that occasion be attempted, unless themselves, by resisting so much, should provoke more. They knew that this Government desired to keep the garrison in the Fort, not assail them, but merely to maintain visible possession, and thus to preserve the Union from actual, and immediate dissolution—"trusting, as herein-before stated, to time, discussion, and the ballot-box, for final adjustment."[41]

Even before Lincoln had assumed office, the Confederacy had committed itself to the use of force if its objectives could not be obtained peacefully. On February 15, 1861, the Confederate Congress had in secret resolutions enacted its policy that "immediate steps should be taken to obtain possession of Forts Sumter and Pickens . . . either by negotiations or force."[42] Jefferson Davis had started with the dual policy of attempting to negotiate and simultaneously building up the military to be prepared to use force, if necessary. As a result, by the beginning of April, he "was far readier for military action than Lincoln was . . . [and] had more armed men at his call . . . four or five thousand at Pensacola, five or six thousand at Charleston."[43] As soon as he learned on April 8 that negotiations for United States surrender of the forts had failed, Davis reacted. The Confederates attacked Fort Sumter before the attempt to provision it was even made. "And the war came."[44]

Background of "Constitutional Dictatorship"

Lincoln's actions after the fall of Fort Sumter, particularly those taken in the first "eighty days," have been the source of considerable debate and controversy. They have, for example, been described as "constitutional dictatorship" by Clinton Rossiter, and, more recently, viewed by some as contributing to the emergence of what Arthur Schlesinger, Jr., has termed "the imperial presidency." In a chapter section entitled, "The Lincoln Dictatorship," Rossiter wrote: "The simple fact that one man was the government of the United States in the most critical in all its 165 years, and that he acted on no precedent and under no restraint, makes this the paragon of all democratic, constitutional dictatorship."[45] Whether this is indeed just a "simple fact" or whether instead it involves some overstatement by Rossiter is a question which can legitimately be raised.

First, however, it is important to avoid the misunderstanding that can arise from the use of such terms as "dictatorship," and, particularly, the more recent term "constitutional dictatorship." To most contemporary ears, "constitutional dictatorship" sounds like a contradiction in terms. Nowadays, the word "dictator" immediately conjures up images of unconstitutional dictators like Benito Mussolini, Adolf Hitler, Joseph Stalin, and their ilk. It is of the utmost importance not to confuse such unconstitutional dictatorship with either the original concept of dictatorship in ancient Rome, or the more recent concept of "constitutional dictatorship" (derived in part from the original Roman model) as used by some political scientists and historians, such as Carl J. Friedrich, Frederick M. Watkins, and Rossiter. What has happened is that in the course of history there has been a drastic change, indeed, basically a reversal, in the meaning of the term "dictator." Not too surprisingly, this reversal in meaning and image has tended to obscure some aspects of historical reality and has led to some confusion.

The original dictatorship was an institution of *republican* (not imperial) Rome. The ancient Roman Republic had an even more complex constitutional system of checks and balances than the United States, and a correspondingly greater possibility of deadlock. Nevertheless, the constitution of the Roman Republic was adequate for dealing with emergencies. In the event of a major crisis, constitutional practice provided for the appointment of a dictator. What the Romans standardly did was to turn to some highly respected private citizen and *temporarily* give him extraordinary—almost absolute—power to deal with the crisis.

Two points should be emphasized: (1) The early Roman dictatorship was a *constitutional* office, and the early Roman dictators were *constitutional* dictators. (They were, however, referred to simply as "dictators," because no unconstitutional dictators had yet arisen.) (2) The *purpose* of the dictatorship was to *save* the constitutional system from the threat of destruction, and, once the crisis was over, return to normal constitutional procedures.

To be selected as dictator was, therefore, about the highest compliment a citizen could be paid by his fellow citizens. It meant that he was *trusted*—indeed, trusted to the point where his fellow citizens were willing to put their lives in his hands. It also meant that they had confidence in his *ability* to provide the leadership necessary to deal with the crisis and save the system. In short, his fellow citizens regarded him as trustworthy ("good") and of unusual ability ("great").

The legendary Cincinnatus is the classic symbol of the ideal Roman constitutional dictator (or crisis leader). According to tradition, Cincinnatus was called from his plow to become dictator and save Rome, which he did in a mere sixteen days, and, having accomplished the purpose for which the dictatorship was instituted, he immediately relinquished his power and returned to the plow.

Dictatorship in the Roman Republic worked well for several centuries. As Watkins points out; "So long as Rome was a truly constitutional state, dictatorship remained an indispensable resource. . . . The abandonment of dictatorship . . . is thus in itself a significant symptom of diminishing constitutional vitality."[46]

It is crucial to distinguish between *name* and *reality* if we are to understand the matter. Where dictatorship first acquired its bad image was when, almost two hundred years after the last instance of the original dictatorship (which, as we have seen, was in accordance with the constitution), the *name*—but not the *reality*—was revived by Sulla and Caesar, who tried to capitalize on the good image of the original institution at the very time they were undermining the last vestiges of the Republic it was designed to preserve. The name was the same; the reality was not. Both *purpose* and *result* were reversed.

The reality of the original Roman republican institution of the dictatorship was the constitutional provision for a crisis leader with emergency powers who could legitimately take extraordinary measures (which in normal times would not be constitutional). Similar emergency powers are found in modern constitutional and democratic systems under a wide variety of names, including "state of siege," "state of emergency," "martial law," "war government," and so on.

In scholarly writings in the 1930s and 1940s, Friedrich and Watkins used the term "constitutional dictatorship" as a general label to include these various types of crisis government, and, following their lead, Clinton Rossiter chose the term as the title for his book, broadly regarded as the main work in the field. The term, however, never attained widespread popular usage, and even among scholars its use has been limited. Moreover, in recent decades the term "dictator" has been so constantly linked in both scholarly and popular usage to unconstitutional or totalitarian dictatorship that to attempt to use it now in any other sense is to invite misunderstanding.

What we have, then, is an enormously important historical reality—legitimate, powerful, crisis government in constitutional systems—but no appropriate term to describe it. The term "crisis government" is too broad, since crises are not limited to constitutional systems, and terms like "constitutional (democratic) crisis government" or "crisis government in constitutional (and/or democratic) systems" are awkward. "Crisis presidency" might perhaps serve for the United States, but not for other constitutional systems where the chief executive is a prime minister, a chancellor, or a premier.

Perhaps, however, we can borrow from the experience, not of imperial, but of republican Rome, and speak of a "Cincinnatan presidency" in the United States, and, more generally, of "Cincinnatan government," to include other constitutional systems.

Often, it seems, we lack not only a term, but an adequate understanding of the issues involved. In essence, what is involved in a "Cincinnatan presidency" or "Cincinnatan government" is the ultimate right of self-defense in a constitutional system. It is the temporary use of extraordinary power in a legitimate effort to deal with a crisis. As we shall see, Lincoln's ultimate conception of his own presidency was of this nature, though, of course, he did not use the term.

It is thus against the broad historical background of Cincinnatan government that Lincoln's actions can best be understood. Conversely, since it is the single most important example of a Cincinnatan presidency, analysis of the Lincoln presidency may shed some light on the more general problems involved.

Perhaps the most fundamental question about the U.S. Constitution was raised by those who regarded it as inadequate to deal with the crisis. Some (particularly those sympathetic with the South) held the view that there were no emergency powers in the Constitution, and that all the negatives in the Constitution must be strictly adhered to even though that meant that nothing could be done. Others felt that great measures were necessary but could only be undertaken by ignoring the Constitution, which was irrelevant. Many Europeans felt that this simply demonstrated that the American system was defective.[47]

If in great crisis, the only choices available to "free governments" ("democracies" or "constitutional republics") were either to do nothing or to act (illegally and unconstitutionally) *outside* the constitutional system, then such systems were manifestly unable to deal with crises. In sharp contrast to such views, Lincoln strongly asserted the adequacy of the Constitution—and was supported in this view by some eminent lawyers like Timothy Farrar and Horace Binney.[48] Indeed, Lincoln saw his fundamental responsibility as upholding the Constitution, preserving the Union, and once again heading it in the direction the Founding Fathers had intended (looking to the ultimate extinction of slavery). Clearly, in his view the Founding Fathers had not meant to set up a system that was inherently inadequate or incapable of dealing with crisis, nor had they in fact done so. Rather, the Framers had clearly foreseen and provided for the possibility of emergencies arising which might require such traditional martial law measures as the suspension of habeas corpus. And, in designating the president as commander-in-chief, the Framers had clearly specified who was to be crisis leader, issue orders to the military, and exercise what Lincoln himself, in reporting to Congress on July 4, labeled "the war-power."[49]

After the attack on Fort Sumter, Lincoln's first actions (April 15, 1861) were to call out the militia (75,000 for three months) and to summon a special session of Congress to convene on July 4. Lincoln then proceeded to proclaim a blockade (April 19, subsequently extended), add ships to the navy (April 20), authorize the spending for military purposes of $2 million of unappropriated Treasury funds by three private citizens (April 20), suspend the privilege of habeas corpus (April 27, later extended), enlarge the army and the navy (May 3), close the post office to "treasonable correspondence," order the arrest of "persons . . . about to engage in disloyal and treasonable practices," and so on.[50]

This was clearly no ordinary series of presidential actions. But it was clearly no ordinary situation either. Action was necessary, and strong arguments can be made that these were reasonable actions under the circumstances. In ordinary times, many of them (including the suspension of the privilege of the writ of habeas corpus) would have been unconstitutional. But the constitution itself provided that such suspension could become constitutional under certain circumstances. In Lincoln's opinion those circumstances existed. And, in Lincoln's opinion (and that of many others), it was reasonable to assume that other necessary actions could legitimately be taken to meet such a dire emergency. Indeed, it would be utterly unreasonable to assume that the Founding Fathers had meant to provide that no matter how dire the emergency, only one emergency action (suspension of habeas corpus) could be taken.

The first major constitutional challenge to Lincoln's actions came from the decision in *Ex parte Merryman*[51] by Chief Justice Roger B. Taney (of Dred Scott fame). Taney denied that Lincoln had the authority to suspend the privilege of the writ of habeas corpus, asserting that only Congress could do that. On narrow and strictly technical grounds, such as textual location, a case can be made for Taney's interpretation (though the "legislative" history of the clause raises doubts about the textual argument), but a good case can also be made for Lincoln's position, and these were particularly strong grounds for upholding Lincoln's view in the prevailing circumstances. The decision clearly had major *political* implications.

Taney's actions on this case, including his striking out the original petition's reference to him as "presiding Judge of the United States Circuit Court" in Baltimore (thus emphasizing his role as chief justice of the U.S. Supreme Court), his unusual special trip to Baltimore (apparently for the special purpose of hearing this case in a one-man court and making his personal view of the matter the *final* decision on it), and his emotional oral remarks made after reading his prepared statement, all suggest that something more than calm, impartial judicial decision was involved.[52] Whether or not Taney had actually "expressed the hope that in the war in Virginia the Virginians would wade to their waists in Northern blood," as reported in the *New York Times,* there is no doubt that Taney's sympathies were with the South.[53]

"The opinion had the impact of a military victory for the South and was hailed with delight by the enemies of the Administration."[54] In Harold Hyman's view, "Taney intended the decision to be the last word,"[55] the final judgment.

If Taney's intention was to halt the Lincoln administration's program and impose instead from the bench his own view of what national policy (including military policy) should be, it is hard to see why he is not open to the charge of attempting to establish an "imperial judiciary" or "imperial chief justiceship." Additional evidence supporting such a charge could be found in the fact that "during 1862–63, Taney prepared opinions-without-cases declaring unconstitutional the nation's conscription, emancipation, and legal-tender policies."[56]

Taney's order in the *Merryman* case was disregarded, and similar arrests continued to be made. Since it is so common today for Americans to accept without question the doctrine of "judicial review" (or "judicial supremacy," as it is also called), according to which courts make the final decision on what is constitutional, and thus on what is legal, it should be noted that Lincoln doubted or denied judicial claims to such power. (In no other country in the world do the courts have as much political power as they claim for themselves under the American doctrine of "judicial review.") Lincoln had long been one of the most vigorous critics of the proslavery Dred Scott decision on which the Supreme Court had tried to impose its view of the hot political issue of slavery in the territories. To Lincoln, this smacked of judicial "despotism."[57]

To consider the judges as the ultimate arbiters of all constitutional questions [is] a very dangerous doctrine indeed and one which would place us under the despotism of an oligarchy. . . . The Constitution has erected no such single tribunal, knowing that to whatever hands confided, with the corruptions of time and party, its members would become despots. It has more wisely made all the departments co-equal and co-sovereign within themselves.

Lincoln also quoted with approval Andrew Jackson's famous Bank Veto Message of July 10, 1832 (of which, ironically, Taney was the real author), which stated:

It [the opinion of the Supreme Court] ought not to control the co-ordinate authorities of this Government. The Congress, the executive, and the court, must each for itself be guided by its own opinion of the Constitution. Each public officer, who takes an oath to support the Constitution, swears that he will support it as he understands it, and not as it is understood by others.

As Lincoln put it (obviously with Dred Scott in mind) in his First Inaugural:

If the policy of the government, upon vital questions, affecting the whole people, is to be irrevocably fixed by decisions of the Supreme Court, the instant they are made, in ordinary litigation between parties, in personal actions, the people will have ceased to be their own rulers, having, to that extent, practically resigned their government, into the hands of that eminent tribunal.[58]

In Lincoln's view, the Framers did not intend to establish government by the judiciary.

Lincoln indirectly responded to criticism of his policy on habeas corpus in his report to Congress on July 4, when he posed his famous question:

Are all the laws, *but one,* to go unexecuted, and the government itself go to pieces, lest that one be violated? Even in such a case, would not the official oath be broken, if the government should be overthrown, when it was believed that disregarding the single law, would tend to preserve it? But . . . it was not believed that any law was violated. . . . The Constitution itself, is silent as to which, or who, is to exercise the power; and as the provision was plainly made for a dangerous emergency, it cannot be believed the framers of the instrument intended, that in every case, the danger should run its course, until Congress could be called together; the very assembling of which might be prevented, as was intended in this case, by the rebellion. [59]

Although Lincoln continued to exercise habeas corpus authority, Congress seemed much less concerned about the matter than Taney had been, allegedly on their behalf. It could hardly escape notice that Congress took no definitive action on the matter until 1863, and even then only "created arrangements to supplement (not replace) those which Lincoln had worked out."[60] Some interpret this as tacit approval of Lincoln's position.

Lincoln's policy, though unorthodox, is generally regarded as having been much less severe than more orthodox approaches would have been.

The actual treatment of prisoners (arrest, detention, and release) was milder than the rapid completion of all the steps of a severe summary process, including the execution of the sentence. It was even milder than regular civil justice as usually applied in time of war.[61]

Little injustice resulted. The moderation which Lincoln exhibited in the use of this power and his clemency towards Northern advocates of rebellion are a matter of historical record.

Freedom of speech and press flourished almost unchecked, and no leader of a country at war ever received such shocking and vituperative treatment from prominent citizens and journalists alike as did Abraham Lincoln.[62]

Lincoln also explained and provided a justification for most of his other actions. He regarded the calling out of the militia and the blockade as "strictly legal." The large additions to the army and navy, and the call for three-year volunteers, were justified by Lincoln as follows:

These measures, whether strictly legal or not, were ventured upon, under what appeared to be a popular demand, and a public necessity; trusting, then, as now, that Congress would readily ratify them. It is believed that nothing has been done beyond the constitutional competency of Congress.[63]

Lincoln's view here is apparently that, in an emergency, when Congress is not in session, the president can take the necessary action and have Congress ratify it later. President Jefferson had made a similar argument in 1807 when he, too, took action which was contrary to a specific constitutional prohibition (against spending unappropriated funds). After the *Chesapeake* was attacked, Jefferson, like Lincoln later, spent the money for necessary military supplies.[64]

Even after Congress came back into session, however, Lincoln continued to exercise extraordinarily broad emergency powers. He instituted the first draft program in American history, authorized Francis Lieber to draw up the famous "Lieber Code" (General Orders No. 100) for the conduct of the armed forces (despite the power given to Congress in Article I, section 8, clause 14), set up military governments and established provisional units in conquered southern territories, and drew up nonpunitive plans for reconstruction.

Most dramatic of all, of course, was Lincoln's Emancipation Proclamation, issued "by virtue of the power in me vested as Commander-in-Chief . . . as a . . . necessary war measure." [65] Lincoln believed that Congress did not have the constitutional authority to free the slaves.[66] However, he regarded his own proclamation as an act "warranted by the Constitution, upon military necessity."[67] His order applied only to slaves in rebel areas. Lincoln's conception of the breadth of his power is often illustrated by quoting his statement: "As commander-in-chief . . . in time of war, I suppose I have a right to take any measure which may best subdue the enemy."[68]

Not so often noted is Lincoln's view of the limitations of his power. He believed that the military necessity must be genuine. And he did not believe that he could use his powers to advance his own personal moral views.

Nor was it my view that I might take an oath to get power, and break the oath in using the power. I understand, too, that in ordinary civil administration this oath even forbade me to practically indulge my primary abstract judgment on the moral question of slavery. . . . And I aver that, to this day, I have done no official act in mere deference to my abstract judgment and feeling on slavery. I did understand however, that my oath to preserve the Constitution to the best of my ability, imposed upon me the duty of preserving, by every indispensable means, that government—that nation—of which the Constitution was the organic law. Was it possible to lose the nation and yet preserve the Constitution? By general law, life *and* limb must be life; but a life is never wisely given to save a limb. I felt that measures, otherwise unconstitutional, might become lawful, by becoming indispensable to the preservation of the Constitution, through the preservation of the nation.[69]

In short, Lincoln's view was that his oath obliged him to do whatever was necessary to preserve the Constitution and the nation, and that in an emergency his powers as commander-in-chief enabled him to take the necessary action. That action might include disregarding specific laws or constitutional provisions. In any system of order or rules, there is a hierarchy of importance. Some rules are of lesser importance, and subordinate to others. When the whole system is threatened, it is the system itself that must be saved—not some relatively less important rule which may have to be sacrificed.

Lincoln's view in this respect is within the basic common law tradition. As Watkins states:

Martial law is nothing more than a special application of the general common law principle that, whenever the reign of law is interrupted by a display of illegal force, it is the duty of all citizens, including government officials, to take all necessary steps for the restoration of legitimate authority. "Reasonable necessity" is the only recognized test for determining the legitimacy of actions taken on this basis.[70]

It was Lincoln's further contention that if a state of war already existed it was up to him to recognize it and take the appropriate action, and that he did not have to wait for a formal declaration of war by Congress in order to exercise his constitutional powers.

The decision of the Supreme Court in the *Prize Cases,* the most important court decision during the Lincoln administration, basically upheld Lincoln's view in this respect. Speaking for the majority, Justice Robert C. Grier took the view that the existence of a war was a matter of fact rather than of formal legal declaration. "The President was bound to meet it in the shape it presented itself, without waiting for Congress to baptize it with a name."[71]

As to how far the president could go without specific congressional authorization, Grier stated:

Whether the President is fulfilling his duties as Commander-in-Chief, in suppressing an insurrection, has met with such armed hostile resistance, and a civil war of such alarming proportions as will compel him to accord to them the character of belligerents, is a question to be decided by him, and this court must be governed by the decisions and acts of the Political Department of the government to which this power was intrusted. He must determine what degree of force the crisis demands. The proclamation of blockade is, itself, official and conclusive evidence to the court that a state of war existed which demanded and authorized a recourse to such a measure.[72]

As to the status of individuals in the rebellious states and their property, Grier said:

All persons residing within this territory whose property may be used to increase the revenues of the hostile power are, in this context, liable to be treated as enemies, though not as foreigners. They have cast off their allegiance and made war on their government, and are none the less enemies because they are traitors.[73]

Thus the majority of the Court upheld Lincoln's actions against the most important legal challenge to them. This, of course, should not be interpreted as a blanket endorsement of all of Lincoln's actions or of Lincoln's view of his presidential powers. It was, however, an endorsement of some of his most important actions when it counted most.

Negative and Positive Images

That Lincoln, faced with crisis and civil war, took a broad view of his powers as commander-in-chief is clear. No doubt his views and actions in this role have been instrumental in establishing the dominant *scholarly* image of Lincoln as a strong president, as well as the charges by a few scholars that he was excessively strong or "despotic." The dominant *popular* image is of a Lincoln who was strong, but properly so—who was firm but kindly. In his own time this emphasis tended to be reversed: he was seen as kindly, but not quite strong enough. Typical of this view is the statement by the *New York Times* on November 7, 1862:

The very qualities which have made Abraham Lincoln so well liked in private life— . . . his kindheartedness, his concern for fair play, . . . —in a manner unfit him for the stern requirements of deadly war. Quick, sharp, summary dealings don't suit him at all. He is all the while haunted with the fear of doing some injustice. . . . The very first necessity of war is extreme rigor, and yet every impulse of our constitutional Commander-in-Chief has been to get rid of it.[74]

Of course, the view from the South—predictably the most hostile—was very different. There Lincoln became the personal symbol of the enemy. Thus the North was "Lincolndom," Republicans were "Lincolnites," Union soldiers were "Lincolnpoop," and so on. Lincoln continued to be vilified and portrayed as a coarse buffoon, as the worst tyrant and dictator of all time, an "American Nebuchadnezzar," and, sometimes simultaneously, as a wretched weakling and coward.[75] Similar views were also expressed by Northerners who sympathized with the South, and by some other northern critics.

But, while these negative images of Lincoln continued throughout his presidency, one should not ignore the fact that the major new images of Lincoln which emerged in this period were positive. The most exalted image of all was also held in the South—among blacks. This was the image of "Massa Linkum," the emancipator. Its most dramatic expression was in the reception Lincoln received from blacks when he entered Richmond at the end of the war. This black image of Lincoln was, of course, negatively perceived and ridiculed by southern whites, as can be seen in Hewitt's musical satire, *King Linkum the First*, "one of the few plays actually staged in the war-time South."[76]

The other new positive image, "Father Abraham," has roots that go far back in Lincoln's career. Something about Lincoln, even in his early years, seemed to associate him with age, and to inspire nicknames like "Old Abe." As we have seen, this was even part of Lincoln's own self-image when he was only in his thirties (although he never liked the nickname "Abe"). Moreover, by growing a beard as he entered the presidency, Lincoln seemed to be trying to create a new, more fatherly, presidential image of himself. Given all this, and the general tendency for the leaders of countries to become father-figures, it is hardly surprising that the image of Father Abraham flowered in Lincoln's presidency. To the music of Stephen Foster, thousands sang "We are coming, Father Abraham." In the summer of 1864 a newspaper sprang up at Reading, Pennsylvania, called *Father Abraham;* its faith and creed were simply Abraham Lincoln.[77]

In the political arena, Lincoln's image at any given time tended to reflect whether things were going well or badly, particularly on the battlefield. Thus, at two of the lowest points—late 1862 and the summer of 1864—an image of ineffectiveness and weakness became sufficiently pervasive in certain influential circles that there were serious attempts to push Lincoln aside and put someone else in charge. Again, however, the complaint was not of a dictatorial Lincoln, but of one who was not dictatorial enough.

Actually, Lincoln's task was so enormous, so complex, and, in some of its aspects, so delicate, that it required strengths of many different kinds. Lincoln's strength consisted as much in his refusal to be pushed into harsh and vindictive uses of power as in the vigorous use of it when necessary. It consisted also in refusing to move until the time was ripe (in general, Lincoln had an excellent sense of timing). And, of course, it consisted in that understated eloquence of language that was peculiarly his. The most important image that Lincoln successfully delineated and projected was that of the nation itself, and of the ideals for which it stood.

That Lincoln was in fact the paragon depicted by legend, who had no weaknesses and possessed all of the needed strengths in incomparable measure, is obviously exaggeration. Yet even a self-styled "revisionist" like J. G. Randall, who did not hesitate to point out what he regarded as Lincoln's mistakes, blunders, and failures, ended up concluding that it was "doubtful whether any other leader of the North could have matched" Lincoln in a long list of specific strengths.[78]

One Lincoln strength which can hardly be denied, though it is often insufficiently appreciated, is his remarkable performance as a politician. This is one facet of the real Lincoln which has not adequately been incorporated into his popular image. Without his consummate political skills, Lincoln could never have accomplished the very things for which he is now so highly praised. Yet, then and now, it has been difficult for many people (including even some scholars) to accept that it is possible to combine politics and principle. No matter how important the purpose to be achieved by the use of political skill, it is particularly hazardous in times of national crisis to be *perceived* as politicking. Just how hazardous may be gauged from the following editorial (which can also serve to illustrate how far major media criticism of Lincoln could go):

The Lincoln meeting at the Cooper Institute last Friday evening was one of the most disgraceful exhibitions of human depravity ever witnessed in this wicked world. It was a gathering of ghouls, vultures, hyenas and other feeders upon carrion, for the purpose of surfeiting themselves upon the slaughter of the recent battles. We remember nothing like it in the history of politics. The great ghoul at Washington, who authorized the meeting, and the little ghouls and vultures who conducted it, have succeeded in completely disgusting the people of this country, and have damaged themselves irretrievably.

In the midst of the terrible conflicts of the past three weeks, while thousands of lives were being sacrificed for the national cause, and while every patriotic man was watching with intense and anxious interest the painful progress of events, these ghouls thought only of Lincoln's renomination, the control of the Baltimore Convention and their own chances for petty offices. At the sound of the cannon which was to decide the fate of the country these ghouls hurried down from the mountains, these vultures flocked from the plains, these hyenas sneaked out of their holes, to feast upon the bodies of the slain and gorge themselves with the best blood of the land. They met in horrible conclave in the Cooper Institute, and proceeded to dig up the graves of our soldiers, to tear open the wounds of the wounded, to riot and carnage and make themselves fat with gore.

There was Clay Smith, the Kentucky ghoul, and Oglesby, the military ghoul, and Arnold, the Congressional ghoul, and Spencer, the legal ghoul. These were the orators of the meeting and they all devoted themselves to praising Lincoln, the great Presidential ghoul, and advocating his renomination and re-election. Their arguments were corpses. Their rhetoric was blood. Their similes were drawn from death and wounds. Their logic was, that because Lincoln had killed so many men he ought to be allowed another term to kill as many more. They cared nothing for the country, for the nation, for the Union; but they rejoiced in carnage, because they hoped it would advance their fortunes, and they gloated over the red river of blood, because they hoped that it would float them into power again. We repeat that so disgraceful and disgusting an exhibition is nowhere chronicled in the history of politics before. It is without a parallel or comparison, and we lack words to stigmatize it as it deserves.[79]

Incredibly, this paper, James Gordon Bennett's *New York Herald,* ended up *supporting* Lincoln for reelection.

The 1864 election provides a good example of Lincoln as simultaneously a shrewd politician and a man of principle. By astute use of the patronage, Lincoln had built a much stronger party organization, which was a major factor in insuring his renomination.[80] Lincoln's concern with image is evident in his arranging to run on a "Union" ticket (for the 1864 campaign, the "National Union party" label replaced that of the Republican party), and apparently also (though there is dispute about it) in arranging to have as his running mate, Andrew Johnson, a Southern Democrat of 1860, to appeal to the "War Democrats."[81]

However, even in an election year, Lincoln stuck to his own nonpunitive plan for reconstruction, and pocket vetoed the much more punitive Wade-Davis bill of the powerful congressional Radicals. This so angered them that the result was an unheard-of phenomenon in American politics—leading Republicans (in the "Wade-Davis Manifesto") actually attacking their own candidate *after* his renomination and in the middle of a presidential campaign. This, added to the already existing factors of general war-weariness and the lack of a major military victory, led to an even more extraordinary situation—a growing movement among prominent Republican leaders to dump Lincoln in the middle of the campaign. As one New York Unionist put it, "There are *no* Lincoln men." Lincoln himself expected to lose, as is indicated by his famous sealed memorandum on what would have to be done in the transition period.[82] However, as usual, Lincoln persevered. William Tecumseh Sherman's occupation of Atlanta finally provided the military victory that Lincoln needed, and, in the end, he won handily.

After his reelection, Lincoln again showed the value of political skill. His Emancipation Proclamation "actually led to freedom for some 200,000 slaves," but "the rest of the more than 3,500,000 slaves would have remained in bondage" without the passage of the Thirteenth Amendment, abolishing slavery. "Lincoln was largely responsible for this. The Amendment had been held up in the House of Representatives until, in January 1865, he used his resources of patronage and persuasion upon reluctant Democrats, so as to obtain the needed two-thirds majority for its passage."[83]

As Richard Current so astutely sums it up:

There is a certain irony in Lincoln's reputation as the Great Emancipator, since he was so slow to take effective steps for freeing the slaves. There is even greater irony in the fact that he deserves his reputation. He deserves it because of his very slowness, his unwillingness to move until the time was ripe, until Northern opinion and the fortunes of war had advanced to a point where he could act without jeopardizing everything, including emancipation itself.[84]

Even William Lloyd Garrison gave Lincoln the credit for the passage of the Thirteenth Amendment. "The great job is ended," said Lincoln himself.[85] It is well that he celebrated the victory at that time, since he did not live to see its final ratification.

AFTERIMAGE

Of all American presidents, Lincoln must surely be the only one who has in all seriousness been compared to Jesus Christ. This part of his image received its main impetus immediately after his assassination. Oddly enough, one of the first to make such a comparison was none other than James A. Garfield, destined himself to be the second assassinated president. "It may be almost impious to say it, but it does seem that Lincoln's death parallels that of the Son of God."[86]

There were indeed some unusual parallels. Lincoln was assassinated on Good Friday, the anniversary of Christ's crucifixion. The previous Sunday was the day of Lee's surrender to Grant, and thus the day of triumph for the North. It was also Palm Sunday, the day celebrating Jesus' triumphant entry into Jerusalem. An additional parallel is often drawn here to Lincoln's triumphant entry into Richmond in April 1865 (as described by Dixon Wecter),

through a mile and a half of sobbing, and exulting blacks, shouting for the "year of jubilo," kneeling about him and praying. . . . Widely quoted were the words of an old "praise man" in South Carolina. . . . : "Mass Linkum, he eberywhar. He know eberything. *He walk de earth lak de Lawd!"* No greater reverence than this . . . has ever been laid at an American hero's feet.[87]

Thus the image of "Massa Linkum" paralleled that of the Master of Galilee, and Lincoln was seen as a kind of second Messiah, a heaven-sent deliverer of blacks, leading them to freedom.

The parallels could be multiplied, and were. Lincoln, like Christ, started from humble beginnings. As the dean of the Yale Divinity School later summarized it: "Lincoln's birthplace was a log cabin, and Jesus was born in the manger of a stable. Lincoln's father was a carpenter by trade and Jesus is referred to in the Gospels as 'the son of the carpenter.' "[88] Both Jesus and Lincoln were fond of using stories (parables in Jesus' case, usually humorous anecdotes in Lincoln's) to make their points. Jesus was reviled and mocked by his enemies; Lincoln was similarly treated. Both discussed impending death. There were even rumors, and ultimately a persistent myth, that Lincoln's tomb, like Christ's, was empty.[89]

More important than all the surface similarities, however intriguing, were, of course, the perceived similarities in character and role. Lincoln was now seen as Christlike: compassionate, long-suffering, and forgiving even his enemies. Lincoln's life, like Jesus', can be seen as a sacrifice in atonement for the sins of others—in this case the sin of slavery. Lincoln too (in his Second Inaugural), though wishing that the cup might pass, accepted the divine will and judgment as just.

Once Lincoln's character and role were perceived as Christlike, there remained only the final step—so common in the development of legendary folk heroes—of making Lincoln himself a god. Apparently, this first took place among American blacks. As one newly freed slave put it, in the picturesque idiom of the Sea

Islands; "Lincoln died for we, Christ died for we, and me believe him the same mans."[90] Decades later, another admirer, Denton J. Snider, described Lincoln as born "not of Tom Lincoln, but of God the Father."[91] Whether the deification was taken literally, as apparently it was among some simpler folk, or whether it was merely figurative, its development after Lincoln's death was of truly legendary proportions.

Lincoln has thus become the greatest of American folk heroes. However, his role has not been limited to the United States, but extended worldwide. Particularly fascinating is the view of Leo Tolstoy: "Of all the great national heroes and statesmen of history, Lincoln is the only real giant." Others, like Alexander, Frederick the Great, Caesar, Napoleon, and so on, were outstanding figures in history. But "in greatness of character, in depth of feeling and in a certain moral power," they stand far behind Lincoln. "If one would know the greatness of Lincoln one should listen to the stories which are told about him in other parts of the world." To illustrate that Lincoln "is known by the most primitive nations of Asia," Tolstoy told of his experience in the Caucasus where, after dinner, the chief of the wild-riding Circassians said:

But you have not told us a syllable about the greatest general and greatest ruler of the world. We want to know something about him. He was a hero. He spoke with a voice of thunder; he laughed like the sunrise and his deeds were strong as the rock and as sweet as the fragrance of roses. The angels appeared to his mother and predicted that the son whom she would conceive would become the greatest the stars had ever seen. He was so great that he even forgave the crimes of his greatest enemies and shook brotherly hands with those who had plotted against his life. His name was Lincoln.[92]

In Tolstoy's view,

the highest heroism is that which is based on humanity, truth, justice and piety. . . . The greatness of Aristotle or Kant is significant compared with the greatness of Buddha, Moses and Christ. The greatness of Napoleon, Caesar or Washington is only moonlight by the sun of Lincoln. His example is universal and will last thousands of years. Washington was a typical American, Napoleon was a typical Frenchman, but Lincoln was a humanitarian as broad as the world. He was bigger than his country—bigger than all the Presidents together.[93]

He was what Beethoven was in music, Dante in poetry, Raphael in painting, and Christ in the philosophy of life. He aspired to be divine—and he was.

EXPLANATIONS, DEVELOPMENTS, IMPLICATIONS, CONCLUSIONS

Obviously, the more extreme claims of Lincoln legend and mythology do not have to be accepted in order to recognize that even among the presidents, the Lincoln image is extraordinary. Of all the presidents, only Lincoln has been seen as a kind of American Christ. Clearly, no other presidential image has reached such heights. Nor has any other presidential image reached the depths of Lincoln's in the Civil War South—where he was depicted as destroyer, devil, and veritable anti-Christ.

The reasons for the hostile image of Lincoln in the Civil War South are obvious and require no explanation. What does need to be explained is the remarkable change in the Lincoln image apart from the South.[94]

Unlike Washington, Jefferson, and Jackson, Lincoln had no real claim to public greatness before he became president. Quite the contrary. To much of the country, the question was not whether Lincoln was great, but whether he could somehow struggle up to being adequate. How, then, did Lincoln come to be regarded as the greatest of the presidents?

The most obvious explanation is based on the magnitude of the crisis he faced and his success in handling it. The American Civil War was the greatest and most destructive war between the Napoleonic Wars and World War I. Many regard it as the greatest crisis in American history. As president, Lincoln led the victorious side, restored the Union (thereby ensuring the continued existence of the United States), and, in the course of the conflict, took actions which led to the abolition of slavery in the United States. As Lincoln saw it, the future of free government, of democracy itself, hung in the balance. Certainly the role of the United States (''the last best hope of earth'')[95] as a model for democracy was at issue.

Greatness is classically considered to consist in great deeds or great words. Lincoln had both. The major deeds have already been mentioned. The words hardly need to be. Lincoln's timeless phrases and great speeches are familiar to us all. Lincoln had no peer among the presidents in his use of language. The magnitude of this accomplishment is all the more remarkable when one remembers his extremely limited formal schooling—a total of about one year by his own account.

The crisis was great, the deeds were great, the words were great. Nothing more was needed. But something more was perceived to be there—great character.

No man suffered greater abuse as president. And no president was ever more ridiculed. It would be difficult to say which of the two was harder to bear.

If the public blows were almost unbearable, the private ones were equally so. First, Elmer Ellsworth, a former law student in Lincoln's office who had become almost like a member of the family, was killed in May 1861. Then, in October, Edward Baker, a very close friend of Lincoln's for many years (and after whom Lincoln's second son ''Eddie'' had been named) was killed. Worst of all, in February 1862 Lincoln's son Willie, only eleven, took sick and died.[96] Willie appears to have been the brightest and most promising of Lincoln's four children, and, some think, was the family favorite.

Lincoln's wife, Mary, never did fully recover from the shock, and Lincoln, rightly, feared for her sanity. When she discontinued White House social functions, Washington society, which previously "had criticized her wartime social activities," now "callously denounced her for neglecting her social duties."[97] And when, later in 1862, and then in 1863, Mary Lincoln lost two of her brothers (both on the Confederate side), "she suppressed her grief for fear of being thought disloyal."[98] Thus, both Lincoln and his wife were subjected to enormous strains in their personal as well as in their public lives.

Merely to survive under such pressure requires great strength of character. But Lincoln did much more. He functioned well on many fronts, and with consummate skill in some, and all that despite his lifelong tendency to suffer from the "hypo," or periods of melancholy or depression. However impressive his fortitude, it was his attitude that had the greatest impact. He was never petty. Through it all, he held to the larger, more humane view. No matter what the provocation, he did not become vindictive. It was typical of Lincoln that his original plan for reconstruction was mild and encouraging, not harsh and vengeful. His goal was genuine reunion and a healing of the wounds. Lincoln himself was the best example of one "with malice toward none; with charity for all."[99]

Important as greatness is, it is the image of goodness which really sets Lincoln apart. Character is at the very core of his image. It is one key to the Lincoln legend.

The other key is symbolic appropriateness. Lincoln was simply the most suitable symbol of American democracy. With his log cabin birth, early poverty, and pioneer upbringing, Lincoln qualified as a common man in a way that neither the austere Washington nor the bookish Jefferson ever could.

Among previous presidents, only Andrew Jackson could provide any serious competition to Lincoln as a symbol of democracy. Jackson also had a frontier image, and he did have qualities that Lincoln lacked: he was a genuine military hero and immensely popular. Ultimately more significant, however, were the qualities Lincoln had which Jackson lacked. Thus Lincoln's image as "humble Abraham Lincoln" tied him more closely to humble folk; no one had ever accused Jackson of undue humility. And particularly important in the long run was Lincoln's image of goodness, especially his magnanimity (Jackson was hardly noted for forgiving his enemies).

In the end, then, it is hard to avoid the conclusion that it is the spiritual qualities in Lincoln's image, and particularly his magnanimity, which, combined with his genuinely democratic features, led to his emergence as the prime democratic symbol. Perhaps it is only appropriate for the man most associated with the phrase "government of the people, by the people, for the people" to himself become the symbol of democracy.[100]

Thus it was because of his folksy reputation that Lincoln emerged as the supreme American folk hero. The Lincoln image became *both* that of the ideal common man and of the ideal uncommon leader. Lincoln was seen as the ideal American because he became a worldwide symbol of democracy. In a world which increasingly professed its commitment to democracy, and at a time of growing American influence and leadership, all of this was to be immensely powerful symbolism.

Because of the unparalleled heights to which his image has been raised, Lincoln's legitimizing role is unparalleled. It is greater than that of any other president. Indeed, for people and scholars alike, Lincoln has become the moral role model of the American presidency. As such, Lincoln is, in a sense, always with us.

Clearly, the qualities traditionally associated with Lincoln—strong leadership coupled with magnanimity, humanity, and humility—make him a presidential role model it would be hard to surpass. But his moral stature also poses a problem for those who are fearful of presidential power, and particularly of presidential emergency powers. The moral quality of his image has, at least in the popular mind, had the effect of posthumously legitimizing (if that were needed) Lincoln's own actions as president, including his conception and use of emergency powers. Indeed, it goes well beyond that: simply put, Lincoln is seen as the ideal crisis president.

Emergency powers, as used by Lincoln during the Civil War, are clearly a difficult and sensitive area of presidential powers. In the wrong hands, they pose a danger of possible abuse. However, fear of this possibility can lead to reactions which pose serious dangers of their own. One such danger is to impose so many restrictions that timely action cannot be taken to nip a crisis in the bud. The unintended result may be to encourage crises to develop and get worse. Another especially serious danger is to take so extreme an anti-emergency powers position that it has the practical effect of ruling out *legitimate* ways to deal with great crises. That, of course, would leave only illegitimate ways, or no way.

One example of what can be regarded as just such a reaction occurred shortly after Lincoln's death. In his decision in *Ex parte Milligan,* Justice David Davis seemed to take the complete opposite of Lincoln's position and assert instead that emergencies posed no special problems and required no special powers. His most famous (and most quoted) assertion is: "No doctrine involving more pernicious consequences was ever invented by the wit of man in that its [the Constitution's] provisions can be suspended during any of the great exigencies of government."[101]

Perhaps the best known recent work critical of the presidency and seeking to reduce presidential power is Arthur Schlesinger, Jr.'s, book *The Imperial Presidency*. Schlesinger contends that the presidency has too much power, that this excessive power stems primarily from presidential war powers and has been achieved at the expense of Congress, and that this power is not "within the Constitution."[102] Although much of the work is presented with appropriate scholarly qualifications and balance, Schlesinger does describe the presidency as "out of control," and flatly asserts: "By the early 1970's the American President had become on issues of war and peace the most absolute monarch (with the possible exception of Mao Tse-tung of China) among the great powers of the world."[103]

Schlesinger makes clear his view that, on matters of war and peace, the American president has fewer restraints and is more of a dictator (in the contemporary pejorative sense) than the Soviet leader.[104] It is easy to see how such statements can lead to a popular image of an "imperial president" as a dictator with virtually unlimited power.

In Schlesinger's view, the illegitimate expansion of the powers of the presidency stemmed primarily from presidential war powers. Since Lincoln played what was probably the single most important historical role in the definition and use of these powers, it is hard to see how the Schlesinger approach can avoid implying that Lincoln's presidency gave the first major impetus to what he has termed the "imperial presidency." And Schlesinger does indeed deal with Lincoln's role in expanding presidential power. In the process, he revives an old negative image and refers to Lincoln as a "despot." It is true that Schlesinger softens his charge that Lincoln was a despot by stating that "Lincoln's reputation as the greatest of democratic statesmen is well earned," and that "he obviously did not become a despot lightly."[105] Nevertheless, the charge *is* made.

(Interestingly, despite this, even the Schlesinger book itself attests to the power of Lincoln's moral authority and legitimizing role. For Schlesinger turns to Lincoln for support of the Schlesinger position, and quotes the statements of young Congressman Lincoln in his criticism of President Polk's actions in the Mexican War. In effect, what Schlesinger does here is revive yet another old negative Lincoln image, namely, "Spotty Lincoln," and transform it into a new, positive Lincoln image—Lincoln the Antiwar Leader.)[106]

Despite the historical sweep of Schlesinger's treatment (he speaks of the imperial presidency as "born in the 1940's and 1950's")[107] the book itself came out in 1973 in the era of Vietnam and Watergate (and, one suspects, primarily in a reaction against them). It is therefore not surprising that the term "imperial presidency" is widely used to refer primarily to the presidency of that period, and particularly to its most objectionable features. Even presidential scholars may sometimes use the term "Watergate presidency" as a synonym for "imperial presidency."[108] Since burglary—third-rate or not—was involved, this obviously leads to an image of a "criminal presidency."

To put Lincoln in such a class, to lump him in—even terminologically—either as an antecedent of those involved in petty crime, or with dictators like Hitler and Stalin, or despots and imperial leaders like Alexander, Caesar, and Napoleon, is clearly to suggest a misleading image both of Lincoln and of his presidency. Lincoln's similarity is to Cincinnatus, not to Caesar, and the affinity of his presidency is with republican, not imperial, Rome. It is for this reason that Lincoln's presidency has been described here as a Cincinnatan presidency, not an imperial one.

As we have seen, the concept of a Cincinnatan presidency is based on the view, common to republican and democratic political systems throughout history, that in a crisis, governments constitutionally acquire (and may legitimately exercise) additional power sufficient to deal successfully with the crisis.

Lincoln belongs in the same general category as the leaders of other Cincinnatan governments—leaders like Woodrow Wilson or Franklin Roosevelt, Lloyd George or Winston Churchill. Whatever faults or mistakes may be ascribed to these leaders, they do not belong with the likes of Hitler and Stalin. The concept of Cincinnatan leaders does not mean that such leaders cannot act improperly or are beyond criticism, or that there cannot be what in retrospect may be viewed as overreactions or excesses. It does mean that there is a presumption of legitimacy in favor of the reasonable actions of constitutional leaders in response to a major crisis, particularly one which threatens the system itself. And the standard of judgment needs to be what seemed reasonable and necessary in the heat of the crisis when the decision had to be made, not what may later be deemed reasonable with the wisdom of hindsight in a crisisless situation.[109]

The fact that power can be abused does not necessarily lead to the conclusion that the power should not exist in the first place. Schlesinger's stated ideal is "a strong Presidency *within the Constitution*," yet, paradoxically, his argument seems to put what are usually regarded as the best of the strong presidencies *outside* the Constitution, and to lead to the conclusion that in the greatest crises of all it may be *necessary* to act outside the Constitution.[110]

The conception of the imperial presidency was precipitated by concern about possible abuse of power—admittedly an important concern. But it is surely an unhappy result when it seems to lead to the conclusion that those who handle the greatest crises successfully, or even superbly, must end up labeled as "despots" or charged with having the abuse of power as their legacy. This seems to fasten responsibility for the abuse of power on the wrong people; and to make the power itself wrong, rather than its misuse.[111]

Clearly, in a crisis, the ideal situation is to have the leadership of a strong president, who consults widely, acts wisely, and is backed by a supportive but watchful and potentially critical Congress, and by a wide popular consensus. However, crises often divide, rather than unite, both Congress and the people, and they often do not permit the luxury of time to build a consensus. There is a great danger in starting from too strong a presumption against extraordinary crisis measures. It is the danger that in times of crisis we may unduly inhibit the moral, responsible president from doing what is necessary to achieve a successful result.[112]

Madison, himself the primary architect of the system of checks and balances, stated the basic point well: "It is in vain to oppose constitutional barriers to the impulse of self-preservation. It is worse than in vain; because it plants in the Constitution itself necessary usurpations of power."[113]

In great crises, great power may be indispensable. But it does not necessarily follow that the greater the power the greater the abuse. For good men, great power imposes great responsibilities. Great men *can* be good men.

NOTES

1. Letter to Mandell Creighton in John Emerich Edward Dalberg-Acton, First Baron Acton, *Essays on Freedom and Power*, ed. Gertrude Himmelfarb (Boston: Beacon, 1948), p. 364.

2. The Schlesinger polls were first published in two popular magazines: *Life*, 25 (November 1, 1948): 65–66, and *New York Times Magazine*, July 29, 1962. See also Arthur M. Schlesinger, *Paths to the Present* (New York: Macmillan, 1948), pp. 93–111. For a convenient summary and commentary see Thomas A. Bailey, *Presidential Greatness: The Image and the Man from George Washington to the Present* (New York: Appleton-Century, 1966), pp. 23–34, 337–339, 346.

3. J. G. Randall, *Lincoln the Liberal Statesman* (New York: Dodd, Mead, 1947), pp. 65, 66; Benjamin P. Thomas, *Abraham Lincoln* (New York: Knopf, 1952), pp. 262, 263; Robert S. Harper, *Lincoln and the Press* (New York: McGraw-Hill, 1951), p. 92.

4. *The Collected Works of Abraham Lincoln*, 8 vols. plus index, ed. Roy P. Basler, (New Brunswick, N.J.: Rutgers University Press, 1953–1955), 1:8, 9 (hereafter cited as *Collected Works*).

5. J. G. Randall, *Lincoln the President*, 4 vols. (New York: Dodd, Mead, 1945), 1:25–27; Richard Hofstadter, *The American Political Tradition and the Men Who Made It* (New York: Knopf, 1970), p. 94.

6. *Collected Works*, 4:62, 65.

7. Stephen B. Oates, *Our Fiery Trial* (Amherst: University of Massachusetts Press, 1979), p. 64.

8. "There was simply no deception in him; he was not only honest as most men are honest, but integrity became so much a part of his nature that acquaintances and observers who wrote about him invariably mention it. . . . people believed him."—Thomas, *Abraham Lincoln*, pp. 134, 135. "With his morbid compulsion for honesty he was too modest to pose coarsely and blatantly as a Henry Clay or James G. Blaine might pose. (When an 1860 campaign document announced that he was a reader of Plutarch, he sat down at once to validate the claim of reading the *Lives*.)" —Hofstadter, *American Political Tradition*, p. 93.

9. Eugene H. Roseboom, *A History of Presidential Elections*, 2nd ed. (New York: Macmillan, 1964), p. 179.

10. Stephen B. Oates, *With Malice Toward None* (New York: Harper, 1977), p. 186. See also pp. 77–84, and Thomas, *Abraham Lincoln*, pp. 112, 113, 118–121.

11. Roseboom, *History of Presidential Elections*, pp. 181, 182.

12. Michael Davis, *The Image of Lincoln in the South* (Knoxville: University of Tennessee Press, 1971), pp. 14, 15.

13. *Collected Works*, 4:211.

14. Ibid. 4:204.

15. Ibid., 4:129, 130, 219.

16. Thomas, *Abraham Lincoln*, pp. 242–244; Oates, *With Malice Toward None*, pp. 205, 210–212.

17. Robert S. Harper, *Lincoln and the Press* (New York: McGraw-Hill, 1957), pp. 89, 90.

18. Ibid. p. 91.

19. Ibid. pp. 89, 90.

20. Randall, *Lincoln the Liberal Statesman*, p. 66.

21. Oates, *With Malice Toward None*, p. 12.

22. Randall, *Lincoln the President*, 1:290.

23. *Collected Works*, 4:341.

24. Randall, *Lincoln the President*, 1:227.

25. Ibid., 1:248.

26. Richard N. Current, *Lincoln and the First Shot* (Philadelphia: Lippincott, 1963), p. 22.

27. Ibid., p. 37; John G. Nicolay and John Hay, *Abraham Lincoln: A History,* 10 vols. (New York: Century, 1890), 3:369–371.

28. Oates, *With Malice Toward None,* p. 215.

29. *Collected Works,* 4:316–318.

30. Thomas, *Abraham Lincoln,* p. 254. Lincoln is generally perceived to have been firm but considerate. His written response to Seward contains the often-quoted phrase: "I remark that if this must be done, *I* must do it" (emphasis in original). It is not known, however, whether this written response was actually sent, or whether the matter was handled orally. *Collected Works,* 4:317.

31. Randall, *Lincoln the Liberal Statesman,* p. 67.

32. *Collected Works,* 4:426.

33. Ibid., 7:281.

34. Ibid., 2:255.

35. Ibid., 4:149–151 (from letters to Trumbull, Kellogg, and Washburne).

36. Ibid., 4:271. In the first draft, Lincoln had put the very strong statement: "All the power at my disposal will be used to reclaim the public property and places which have fallen" (4:254), and ended with the challenging question: "Shall it be peace, or a sword?" (4:261). In the final version, he basically followed Browning's suggestion to omit any reference to reclaiming the forts, and Seward's suggestion to end on a less challenging note.

37. Randall, *Lincoln the President,* 1:320.

38. On January 9, 1861, South Carolina fired upon the United States ship *The Star of the West.* President Buchanan chose to do nothing about the incident.

39. This had occurred on December 26, 1860, in the Buchanan administration. As Randall points out:

Of the three men who had most to do with the removal from Moultrie, President Buchanan was a conciliatory and non-aggressive sympathizer with the South, Floyd was a Southern secretary of war at Washington, and Anderson, a Kentuckian, was above all anxious to avoid provocation and violence. South Carolina quickly seized Pinckney and Moultrie, and commissioners from that state demanded that the Federal authorities move back from Sumter to Moultrie, though on the latter fort the palmetto flag was then flying.

Randall, *Lincoln the President,* 1:316. On the Confederate view of aggression, see Current, *Lincoln and the First Shot,* pp. 129, 138, 207.

40. *Collected Works,* 4:271.

41. Ibid., 4:425.

42. Current, *Lincoln and the First Shot,* p. 139.

43. Ibid., p. 144.

44. *Collected Works,* 8:332 (Second Inaugural).

45. Clinton L. Rossiter, *Constitutional Dictatorship* (Princeton: Princeton University Press, 1948), p. 224. The Schlesinger treatment of Lincoln can be found in Arthur M. Schlesinger, Jr., *The Imperial Presidency* (Boston: Houghton Mifflin, 1973), pp. 58–67 and passim.

46. Frederick M. Watkins, "The Problem of Constitutional Dictatorship," in C. J. Friedrich and Edward S. Mason, eds., *Public Policy* (Cambridge, Mass.: Harvard University Press, 1940), p. 336.

47. Harold M. Hyman, *A More Perfect Union* (New York: Knopf, 1973), pp. 99–123.

48. Ibid., pp. 103, 127, 129–131, and, in general, pp. 124–140.

49. *Collected Works*, 440.

50. James D. Richardson, ed., *Messages and Papers of the Presidents* (Washington, D.C.: Bureau of National Literature and Art, 1789–1897), 6:13–19, 77–79, 102–104; Rossiter, *Constitutional Dictatorship*, pp. 224–228.

51. *Ex parte Merryman*, 17 Fed. Cas. 114 (No. 9478) (C.C.D. Md. 1861).

52. Taney's oral remarks included the threat to imprison the district commander, General, Cadwalader, if he could get him before his court. General Cadwalader was himself an attorney, and his brother was a federal district judge in Philadelphia.

53. Carl B. Swisher, *The Taney Period 1836–64: History of the Supreme Court of the United States* (New York: Macmillan, 1974), 5:848.

54. Ibid., 5:850.

55. Hyman, *A More Perfect Union*, p. 89.

56. Ibid., p. 256.

57. *Collected Works*, 2:517.

58. Ibid., 2:268.

59. Ibid., 4:430, 431.

60. Hyman, *A More Perfect Union*, p. 93. However, see also James G. Randall, *Constitutional Problems Under Lincoln*, rev. ed. (Urbana: University of Illinois Press, 1951), pp. 128–131.

61. J. G. Randall, "The Rule of Law Under Lincoln," in *Lincoln the Liberal Statesman*, p. 131.

62. Rossiter, *Constitutional Dictatorship*, pp. 236, 237.

63. *Collected Works*, 4:429.

64. Richardson, *Messages and Papers of the Presidents*, 5:2416.

65. *Collected Works*, 6:29.

66. Randall, *Constitutional Problems Under Lincoln*, p. 377.

67. *Collected Works*, 6:30.

68. Ibid., 5:421.

69. Ibid., 7:281 (letter to Albert G. Hodges).

70. Watkins, "Constitutional Dictatorship," p. 349.

71. *Prize Cases*, 2 Black 635, at 699 (1863).

72. Ibid., p. 670. Justice Samuel Nelson delivered the dissenting opinion in which he was joined by Chief Justice Taney, Justice John Catron, and ultimately by a somewhat embarrassed Justice Nathan Clifford, who seemed to be contradicting his own opinion delivered in the circuit court. In the view of the dissenters, the conflict was not war until it was declared by Congress, and the blockade was not lawful until the July 13, 1861, Act of Congress closing the ports.

73. Ibid., p. 674.

74. Quoted in J. G. Randall and David Donald, *The Divided Union* (Boston: Little, Brown, 1961), p. 461.

75. Davis, *The Image of Lincoln in the South*, pp. 72, 80.

76. Ibid., p. 70.

77. Dixon Wecter, *The Hero in America* (New York: Scribner's, 1972), p. 252.

78. *Dictionary of American History*, s.v. "Lincoln, Abraham" (11:258).

79. *New York Herald*, May 20, 1864, quoted in Herbert Mitgang, *Lincoln as They Saw Him* (New York: Rinehart, 1956), pp. 391, 392.

80. For an example of a fancy political maneuver in Indiana, see J. G. Randall and Richard N. Current, *Lincoln the President: Last Full Measure* (vol. 4 of J. G. Randall, *Lincoln the President*, completed by Richard N. Current (New York: Dodd, Mead, 1955), pp. 122, 123.

81. Ibid., 4:130–134, 241.

82. *Collected Works*, 7:514. See also Randall and Current, *Lincoln the President*, 4:188–197, 207–222; Randall, *Lincoln the Liberal Statesman*, p. 80.

83. Richard N. Current, ''Abraham Lincoln,'' in Morton Borden, ed., *America's Ten Greatest Presidents* (Chicago: Rand McNally, 1961), pp. 149, 150.

84. Ibid., p. 150.

85. Randall and Current, *Lincoln the President*, 4:314.

86. Lloyd Lewis, *Myths After Lincoln* (New York: Harcourt, Brace, 1929), pp. 112, 113.

87. Wecter, *The Hero in America*, pp. 251, 252.

88. Charles Reynolds Brown, *Lincoln: The Greatest Man of the Nineteenth Century* (New York: Macmillan, 1922), pp. 76, 77.

89. Lewis, *Myths After Lincoln*, pp. 299, 300. There was also a plot to steal Lincoln's body (pp. 307–323).

90. Benjamin Quarles, *Lincoln and the Negro* (New York: Oxford, 1962), p. 245.

91. Denton J. Snider, *Lincoln at Richmond* (1914), p. 17, quoted in Wecter, *The Hero in America*, p. 225.

92. From an interview with Tolstoy by Count S. Stakelberg, *New York World*, February 7, 1909, as quoted in Albert A. Woldman, *Lincoln and the Russians* (Cleveland: World, 1952), pp. 272–276. See also Carl Sandburg, *Abraham Lincoln: The War Years*, 4 vols. (New York: Harcourt, Brace, 1939), 4:375–378.

93. Woldman, *Lincoln and the Russians*, pp. 272–276.

94. Even in the South there has been a major change in the Lincoln image. Davis, for example, concludes that the South ''has accepted Lincoln as an authentic American hero, and in some cases, as a Southern Hero.'' Davis, *The Image of Lincoln in the South*, p. 4. It is assumed here that the reasons for such changes in Lincoln's image in the South are basically the same as for changes elsewhere, and thus require no additional explanation.

95. *Collected Works*, 5:537.

96. Oates, *With Malice Toward None*, pp. 64, 93, 263, 264, 289–293; Thomas, *Abraham Lincoln*, pp. 302–304, 278–280.

97. Thomas, *Abraham Lincoln*, p. 480.

98. Ibid.

99. *Collected Works*, 8:333.

100. Lincoln apparently took the phrase from Theodore Parker. See Hofstadter, *The American Political Tradition*, p. 361.

101. 4 Wallace 2 (1866), 120. The implications (and interpretations) of the *Milligan* case are unusually complex and varied. ''The needless breadth of language in *Milligan* should be reckoned as the starting point in the sequence of actions whereby Congress took away the Court's jurisdiction in *Ex parte McCardle*, deliberately to forestall a decision on the constitutionality of the Reconstruction Acts''—Charles Fairman, *Reconstruction and Reunion 1864–88 (History of the Supreme Court of the United States)*, vol. 6 (New York: Macmillan, 1971), Part One, p. 237. Although the Court deferred to Congress in

Ex parte McCardle (1869) and *Texas* v. *White* (1869), this was also the period when "the modern conception of judicial review began to make its appearance"—Alfred H. Kelly and Winfred A. Harbison, *The American Constitution* (New York: Norton, 1948), p. 481. Thus, in this period, all three branches of government—the Court, Congress, and the president—made claims to enlarged power.

102. Schlesinger, *The Imperial Presidency*, pp. viii–x.

103. Ibid., p. ix.

104. Ibid., p. 279.

105. Ibid., p. 59. Lincoln's role is specifically treated at pp. 58–67, though there are references to him throughout the book. In support of his view, Schlesinger quotes (in addition to Benjamin R. Curtis) Wendell Phillips' description of Lincoln as an "unlimited despot." Phillips, hardly noted for temperate statements, also referred to Lincoln as "that slavehound from Illinois," which was regarded as somewhat unfair even by so vigorous a critic of Lincoln's position as Hofstadter. See Hofstadter, *The American Political Tradition*, p. 109.

106. "A Whig in the White House," in David Donald, *Lincoln Reconsidered*, 2nd ed. (New York: Alfred A. Knopf, 1965), p. 191.

107. Schlesinger, *The Imperial Presidency*, p. 212.

108. E.g., Thomas E. Cronin in his article "An Imperiled Presidency?" in Vincent Davis, *The Post-imperial Presidency* (New Brunswick, NJ: Transaction, 1980), pp. 137–151, speaks of the "reaction to the imperial or Watergate presidency" (p. 149).

109. Schlesinger, *The Imperial Presidency*, p. x.

110. Ibid., p. 59.

111. Ibid., p. 174.

112. Ibid., p. 176.

113. *The Federalist*, No. 41.

ANNOTATED BIBLIOGRAPHY

Books

Angle, Paul M. *A Shelf of Lincoln Books: A Critical Selective Bibliography of Lincolniana.* New Brunswick, N.J.: Rutgers University Press, 1946.
  The best short annotated bibliography.
Angle, Paul M., and Earl Schenck Miers, eds. *The Living Lincoln*. New Brunswick, N.J.: Rutgers University Press, 1955.
  A good selection of Lincoln's writings.
Ballard, Colin R. *The Military Genius of Abraham Lincoln*. London: Oxford University Press, 1926.
  A British general makes the case that Lincoln was, in fact, a military genius. (Another fine study is T. Harry Williams, *Lincoln and His Generals* [New York: Alfred A. Knopf, 1952].)
Baringer, William E. *Lincoln's Rise to Power*. Boston: Little, Brown, 1937.
  A significant study.
Basler, Roy P. *The Lincoln Legend: A Study in Changing Conceptions*. 1935. Reprint. New York: Octagon, 1969.

The most extensive treatment of the subject. Pays particular attention to literary interpretations.

Beveridge, Albert J. *Abraham Lincoln, 1809–1858*. 2 vols. Boston: Houghton Mifflin, 1928.

A major but unfinished work, with considerable impact on Lincoln historiography. An example of scholarly "revisionism," which finds little greatness in the pre-presidential Lincoln.

Boritt, G. S. *Lincoln and the Economics of the American Dream*. Memphis: Memphis University Press, 1978.

The best treatment of Lincoln's economic views. Also contains a useful historiographical essay with special attention to the paucity of treatment of Lincoln's views on economics.

Carman, Harry J. and Reinhard J. Luthin. *Lincoln and the Patronage*. New York: Columbia University Press, 1943.

The best book on the subject.

Current, Richard N. *The Lincoln Nobody Knows*. New York: McGraw-Hill, 1958.

A useful collection of essays.

———. *Lincoln and the First Shot*. Philadelphia: Lippincott, 1963.

An excellent treatment of the subject—careful and balanced. Though good on comparing the leading alternative views and pointing out weaknesses in them, it does not, of course, point out any weaknesses in Current's own view.

Davis, Michael. *The Image of Lincoln in the South*. Knoxville: University of Tennessee Press, 1971.

An excellent treatment; covers the subject to 1909.

DeWitt, David Miller. *The Assassination of Abraham Lincoln and Its Expiation*. New York: Macmillan, 1909.

Still the classic treatment.

Donald, David. *Lincoln Reconsidered,* 2nd ed. New York: Alfred A. Knopf, 1965.

Contains a number of very useful essays, including "The Folklore Lincoln."

Fehrenbacher, Don E. *Prelude to Greatness: Lincoln in the 1850's*. Stanford, Calif. Stanford University Press, 1962.

Challenges the revisionist view of Beveridge that the prepresidential Lincoln showed no signs of greatness. Maintains instead that Lincoln showed greatness as early as 1854.

———. *The Changing Image of Lincoln in American Historiography*. Oxford: Oxford University Press, 1968.

Perceptive and useful.

Frank, John P. *Lincoln as a Lawyer*. Urbana: University of Illinois Press, 1961.

An illuminating attempt to understand how Lincoln's mind worked by analyzing his approach to the practice of law.

Graebner, Norman A., ed. *The Enduring Lincoln*. Urbana: University of Illinois Press, 1959.

A small book of good essays.

Harper, Robert S. *Lincoln and the Press*. New York: McGraw-Hill, 1951.

The best and most complete treatment of the subject.

Hesseltine, William B. *Lincoln and the War Governors*. New York: Alfred A. Knopf, 1948.

A useful study.

Hofstadter, Richard. "Abraham Lincoln and the Self-made Myth," Chapter 5 of *The American Political Tradition*. New York: Alfred A. Knopf, 1948.

An influential but somewhat cynical interpretation.

Hyman, Harold M. *A More Perfect Union: The Impact of the Civil War and Reconstruction on the Constitution*. New York: Alfred A. Knopf, 1973.

A careful and balanced treatment. The best book on the subject.

Jaffa, Harry V. *Crisis of the House Divided*. Garden City, N.Y.: Doubleday, 1959.

A challenging interpretation of Lincoln and political thought through an analysis of the Lincoln-Douglas debates.

Lincoln, Abraham. *The Collected Works of Abraham Lincoln*. Roy P. Basler, ed.; Marion Dolores Pratt and Lloyd A. Dunlap, assistant eds. 8 vols. plus index. New Brunswick, N.J.: Rutgers University Press, 1953–1955. *Supplement, 1832–1865*. Roy P. Basler, ed. Westport, Conn.: Greenwood Press, 1974.

The definitive edition of Lincoln's works.

Luthin, Reinhard H. *The First Lincoln Campaign*. Cambridge, Mass.: Harvard University Press, 1944.

An excellent study of Lincoln in the 1860 election.

Mitgang, Herbert, ed. *Lincoln as They Saw Him*. New York: Rinehart, 1956.

A collection of press comments about Lincoln by his contemporaries.

Monaghan, Jay. *Lincoln Bibliography, 1839–1939*. 2 vols. Springfield, Ill.: Illinois State Historical Library, 1943–45.

The standard bibliography.

———. *Diplomat in Carpet Slippers: Abraham Lincoln Deals with Foreign Affairs*. Indianapolis: Bobbs-Merrill, 1945.

A lively account, slightly overdramatized.

Nicolay, John G., and John Hay. *Abraham Lincoln: A History*. 10 vols. New York: Century, 1890.

A combined history by Lincoln's secretaries.

Oates, Stephen B. *With Malice Toward None: The Life of Abraham Lincoln*. New York: Harper and Row, 1977.

Along with Thomas, a candidate for the best one-volume biography.

Potter, David M. *The South and the Sectional Conflict*. Baton Rouge: Louisiana State University Press, 1968.

Chapter 5: "The Lincoln Theme and American National Historiography" (pp. 151–176) is of special interest.

Pressly, Thomas J. *Americans Interpret Their Civil War*. Princeton, N.J.: Princeton University Press, 1954.

Especially helpful in providing perspective on the various trends of "schools" of interpretation of Lincoln, as well as the Civil War.

Randall, James G. *Lincoln the President*. 4 vols. New York: Dodd, Mead, 1945–1955.

Vol. 4 completed by Richard Current. Randall's magnum opus. The most complete study of Lincoln's presidency. Despite Randall's revisionism, Lincoln emerges as a great figure.

———. *Lincoln the Liberal Statesman*. New York: Dodd, Mead, 1947.

A useful collection of essays.

———. *Constitutional Problems Under Lincoln*. Rev. ed. Urbana: University of Illinois Press, 1951.

A classic treatment. Should be read in conjunction with Hyman, *A More Perfect Union*.

Sandburg, Carl. *Abraham Lincoln: The Prairie Years*. 2 vols. New York: Harcourt, Brace, 1926.

The most famous of all modern Lincoln biographies—widely read, but controversial. It has evoked both superlatives for its style and severe criticisms from scholars, not only because of such scholarly deficiencies as the absence of footnotes, but particularly because Sandburg did not limit himself to the historical evidence, but relied on his imagination to "describe" the thoughts running through Lincoln's head. Sandburg attempts to present not only Lincoln, but his time (i.e., history) through what can perhaps be described as a sort of panoramic collage which critics charge includes unnecessary and unrelated material. Some critics regard it as too much in the hero-worshipping tradition. Nevertheless, Paul Angle states: "If the word 'incomparable' be given its literal meaning, only this book among the thousands which deal with the life of Lincoln deserves it" *(Shelf, p. 49).

———. *Abraham Lincoln: The War Years*. 4 vols. New York: Harcourt, Brace, 1939.

Avoids the controversial reliance on imagination of *The Prairie Years*. In the eleven years he devoted to it, Sandburg is said to have "read more Lincoln material than any other man living or dead." (Benjamin Thomas, *Portrait*, p. 294).

———. *Abraham Lincoln: The Prairie Years and the War Years*. One-volume ed. New York: Harcourt, Brace, 1954.

A useful one-volume condensation.

Thomas, Benjamin P. *Portrait for Posterity*. New Brunswick, N.J.: Rutgers University Press, 1947.

An especially useful treatment of most of the major Lincoln biographers. Should be read before reading the classic biographies.

———. *Abraham Lincoln*. New York: Alfred A. Knopf, 1951.

Regarded by many Lincoln scholars as the best one-volume biography.

Documentary Recordings and Tapes

Abe Lincoln in Illinois. Black and White. 1939. Raymond Massey, Gene Lockhart, Ruth Gordon. 110 min. Beta. VHS. Produced by Nostalgia Merchant, Hollywood, Calif.

Videotape release of the movie classic.

Harris, Julie, Hal Holbrook, Kevin McCarthy, and Edward Woodward. *The White House Saga*. Directed by Harold Stone. Produced by Caedmon from the book by Nanette Kutner. Narrators: Hal Holbrook and Kevin McCarthy. Caedmon Stereo TC 1194S. New York: Caedmon Records, n. d.

Contains a segment featuring Lincoln's private secretary (William Stoddard) and the jacket features a cutaway drawing of the White House showing the site of the signing of the Emancipation Proclamation, the room in which Lincoln reached the decision to continue the war after the defeat at Chancellorsville and the East Room where Lincoln's body lay in state.

5   RUTHERFORD B. HAYES

Leslie H. Fishel, Jr.

If there were a verifiable measure of the degrees of caustic condemnation of presidents, the name-calling directed at Rutherford B. Hayes would undoubtedly appear high on the list. From his June 1876 nomination, the breadth of the critics' views and vocabulary demonstrates, at the very least, an imaginative array of words and phrases. The acerb Henry Adams—newly settled in Washington—first referred to Hayes as "a third-rate nonentity." That was before Adams knew anything about Hayes; when his wife, Clover, met the president a year later at the White House reception, she accorded him the compliment of being "amiable and respectable," but added that there was "not a ray of force of intellect in forehead, eye or mouth." Over a four-year period, it should be recorded, the Adamses' views shifted to complimentary condescension.

At Princeton, young Woodrow Wilson believed Hayes to be "that weak instrument of the corrupt Republicans." After the disputed election had been settled in Hayes' favor and his inauguration had become history, the editorial writers had their field day. He was addressed as "His Fraudulency," described as the *"de facto* President" and the "acting President," and dismissed as "The Pretender." The *Greensboro* (North Carolina) *Patriot* combined some adjectives and came up with "the bogus, fraudulent, so called President." Of course, there were exaggeratedly positive views too. Hayes, the *Bismarck Tribune* of the Dakota Territory asserted, was "winning golden opinions on every hand," and the *Greensboro* (Pennsylvania) *Tribune and Herald* admitted some "impolitic appointments" but thought Hayes' "plans and purposes . . . patriotic, high-minded and honorable."

These examples emerged just after his nomination and in the six weeks after his inauguration. The drumbeat kept up during Hayes' full term, stemming from several conditions which were peculiar to the period, his nomination, and his presidency. At a time when politics was the national pastime, political parties were significant organizations. The roots of each party in its own strongholds penetrated deeply into communities and social organizations. Party commitments were as loud and compelling as alumni pregame and postgame celebrations; the party generated torchlight parades, soirees and beer parties, entertainment and camaraderie. In such an atmosphere, the nominee of the other party was a natural target.

If, as in Hayes' case, the party's own nominee was a compromise choice between two hostile wings and if, as in Hayes' case, he was essentially an unknown, a cipher on the national scene, emotional excrescences were sure to swell. Add to that the great distaste with which the nation appeared to tolerate U.S. Grant as president and the fear that his successor would be equally casual in the face of decisions or, what for some would have been worse, more assiduous in pursuing corruption and implementing decision.

There were still more reasons for name-calling, but one obvious circumstance loomed large. The presidential election of the Centennial year was too close to call. The Democratic party had made serious inroads in northern states like New York, Ohio, and Indiana during the 1870s and, as Reconstruction governments gave way in some states of the former Confederacy, the Democrats came to power. North Carolina, Virginia, Georgia, Mississippi, Alabama, and the border states had been "redeemed," and the party match was close to being equal. With the Democrats in control of the House of Representatives, the presidency was crucial to their total redemption, political and emotional. From the Republican side, the loss of the presidency could mean a death blow to party power and the chilling perception that perhaps, after all, the Civil War had become a lost cause.

The nominee and the future president was well equipped for this hot spot. Ohio-born, he was raised by his mother and her brother, since his father had died just before his birth. He attended private preparatory schools in Ohio and New England and enrolled at Kenyon College, in Gambier, Ohio. Here, too, one biographer points out, his capacity for mediation flowered. At a time when national issues of slavery and manifest destiny accelerated the normal run of collegial tensions, Rutherford B. Hayes stood out as one who could generally reach and talk effectively with disputants on both sides of the quarrel.

After Kenyon, Hayes studied law at Harvard and returned to Ohio to practice in the little town of Lower Sandusky. He found life dull and unresponsive, even though his uncle was a leading and prosperous citizen and landowner. Hayes participated in the move to change the town's name to Fremont, in honor of the military hero. Moving to Cincinnati, where he lived during the decade of the 1850s, Hayes found a growing city, an enlarging practice, a congenial social set, a wife, and a sense of purpose. He was appointed city solicitor in 1858, reelected the next year, and then defeated when he ran again. Shortly after leaving office in 1861, he enlisted in the Union Army.

FRONT LINE OFFICER

Hayes served the regiment which he helped to form, the 23rd Ohio Volunteer Infantry (OVI), rising from the rank of major to brigadier general and brevet major-general. Wounded six times, once seriously, and having four horses shot from under him, Hayes was a front line officer. In a strange reversal from the stolid, stable image which he projected, he entered the conflict with verve, writing in a surprised tone to his uncle on April 12, 1865, "I am more glad to think my fighting days are ended than I had expected." Hayes' respect for his comrades-at-arms and the trials they suffered together emerged after the war in his dedicated attention to the reunions of the 23rd OVI, the state and national Grand Army of the Republic, and the Loyal Legion. Michael Shaara, in his gripping novel of the Battle of Gettysburg, *The Killer Angels,* captures some of Hayes's unabashed exuberance when he has Joshua Lawrence Chamberlain, Bowdoin professor and future governor of Maine, muse on top of Cemetery Hill about his presence at Fredericksburg and Gettysburg: "Not love it. Not quite. And yet I was never so alive."

While Hayes was in the army, the Republicans in the Ohio second district nominated him for Congress, and he was elected. He chose neither to campaign for the seat nor to leave the army early as a congressman-elect. Resigning his commission in June 1865, Hayes was a freshman in the Thirty-ninth Congress, which convened in December. He consistently supported the Radical Reconstruction program during the two sessions of that Congress, was reelected to the next Congress, and resigned after the first session to campaign for the gubernatorial spot in Ohio. "I don't *particularly* enjoy Congressional life," he confessed to his uncle before his decision to resign. "I have *no ambition* for Congressional reputation or influence—not a particle. I would like to be out of it creditably." He took office as governor of Ohio on January 13, 1868.

Reelected in 1869 for a second gubernatorial term, he was pressured into running for Congress in 1872 in his old district and lost the race. The next year he and Lucy Webb Hayes moved their family to Spiegel Grove, the Fremont estate developed by and transferred to Hayes by his uncle. Here the family put down its roots. Pulled away from Fremont for an unprecedented third term as governor, Hayes was nominated for the presidency during the first year of that term by the Republican National Convention, which met in Cincinnati in 1876.

The drama of the Convention nomination has been crafted by several historians and needs no retelling here. The fit and fiber of the successful candidate may be more to the point. He was, to begin with, a compromise choice: his credentials glowed with principles endorsed by old-line Republicans like James G. Blaine, yet he stood foursquare for the basic elements of the reform movement. He believed in Negro suffrage, the need for a bipartisan South, national economic health, and the importance of party discipline; he believed also in sound money, civil service, and honesty in government. Indeed, his powers of mediation, of pulling warring sides together, would be put to the test within his party and within the nation.

The challenge to these skills came even as Hayes and his supporters were basking in their success at Cincinnati. Hayes' letter of acceptance was to be his chief public statement during the campaign, and his office was bombarded with suggestions and ideas from liberals like Carl Schurz and Stalwarts who were friends of James G. Blaine. The statement Hayes produced was short and pithy, standing forthrightly for civil service reform, sound money, a liberal federal posture toward the South, and a promise to serve only one term. While there was muted carping from the Stalwart Republicans (the Old Guard) and cheering from the liberals, Hayes soon confounded both sides when he did not try to block the appointment of the Stalwart senator, Zachariah Chandler of Michigan, as chairman of the Republican National Committee. The liberals wondered, a Washington reporter wrote to Murat Halstead, "precisely how much of a party man Governor Hayes is." With more firsthand knowledge, Hayes' brother-in-law, Joseph T. Webb, informed an inquiring Virginian that "while he [Hayes] has positive opinions, I don't think him a partisan." Webb added that Hayes was "quite conservative in all things," and concluded that "his letter of Acceptance is characteristic."

His silent posture during the campaign was equally characteristic, but since this was a common stance for presidential candidates—his opponent, Samuel J. Tilden, did not make public appearances either—it was not particularly noted. The strategy allowed Hayes to disassociate himself from campaign statements and, in certain areas of the South, campaign and election tactics. He could honestly say that he was unaware of and not remotely responsible for the fraud that characterized some Republican voting activity in Louisiana, Florida, and South Carolina.

When it developed early in November that the electoral count was in dispute, party leaders and others began to look to Hayes for support of the various tactics which they proposed in order to resolve their deadlock. In the spectrum of interpretations which have been used to disentangle and explain the process which led to Hayes' eventual victory by one electoral vote, Hayes' own role has been somewhat muted. The most persuasive approach, advanced by C. Vann Woodward in 1951, suggests a bargain between Southern Democrats and Republicans which would give Hayes the needed electoral votes in dispute in three southern states and Oregon in return for the withdrawal of troops supporting state governments in two of those states (Louisiana and South Carolina); the appointment of one or more Southerners to the cabinet and the opening up of patronage positions to Southerners; and federal subsidies for the Texas and Pacific Railroad and for other internal improvements for the South. The Southerners also promised, this view holds, to swing the election of the Speaker of the House to the Republican James A. Garfield.

This interpretation was generally accepted and not seriously challenged for over two decades. During the 1970s, four historians began to raise questions. Although none of their efforts to date have dislodged the Woodward thesis, some of the bedrock has begun to chip. Two critiques questioned whether a "bargain" as such was necessary, while another primarily wondered if a bargain which was not fulfilled can really be identified as a bargain.[1] The fourth critique argued with some authority that there was no bargain, only efforts by Southern Democrats to undermine their northern counterparts, whom they regarded, in Benjamin Hill's notable phrase, as "invincible in peace and invisible in war" as well as spineless in the struggle to claim electoral votes for Tilden.[2]

In all of these accounts, the role that Hayes played in the negotiations is somewhat fuzzy, primarily because there is no specific evidence, no "smoking gun," to pin down Hayes' acquiescence in the discussions that his representatives carried on. That he was informed about these discussions directly and indirectly there is no doubt, but his response has only been inferred. Woodward paints Hayes as a Gilded Age Victorian who, when the chips were down, went along with the chicanery in order to carry out his reform program. Woodward raises and leaves unanswered, for lack of evidence, the issue of Hayes' political ethics.

GOVERNOR REMAINS ALOOF

There is another way to look at the available documentation. Hayes repeatedly rejected invitations to send representatives to Washington, that is, men who would carry his message and speak for him, commit him to specific programs. He preferred to let a few of his friends, including General James Comly of Columbus, Garfield, Representative Samuel Shellabarger, John Sherman, and some others, represent what they thought his view might be. Garfield's letters of December 9 and 12, 1876, particularly the latter, suggested responding to the overtures that he had received from moderate Southerners. "The Democratic businessmen of the country are more anxious for quiet than for Tilden," he noted, and he laid down three principles that he hoped to advance in a future speech. These included an insistence that Hayes had been legally elected, that the Republicans would be a national party, devoted to the interests of all sections, and that the liberal tone toward the South that characterized Hayes' letter of acceptance would be implemented. Buried in the letter was an additional word of advice: "I don't think anybody should be the custodian of your policy and purposes at present, or have any power to commit you in any way." Garfield added that the southern moderates should learn, "in some discreet way," that Hayes was going to deal fairly with their section.

Hayes' response to this was brief: "Your views are so nearly the same as mine that I need not say a word." He went on to add a sentiment that he repeated, in mid-December, to several of his correspondents, including John Sherman, Richard Henry Dana, William Henry Smith, and William K. Rogers. "I am *wholly uncommitted* on *persons* and *policies*," he told Garfield and the others, "except as my public letter and other *public* utterances show. There is *nothing private.*" In a Christmas Day letter to Sherman he authorized him "to speak in pretty decided terms for me whenever it seems advisable," not with a commission, "but from your knowledge of my general methods of actions." The issue was the possible alienation of President Grant and the influential New York senator, Roscoe Conkling. Hayes' authority was offered in a narrow context, not in terms of the larger sectional tensions.

From mid-December, when the early shoots of compromise first sprouted, Hayes adopted a policy of not endorsing, except in the most general way, and not denying, except where a policy was clearly contrary to his wishes, any correspondent's views. Jacob D. Cox's lengthy analysis of the Republican position on the South since the war was endorsed with words similar to those that he addressed to Garfield six weeks earlier. William E. Chandler's mid-January letter balancing off the strengths against the weaknesses of Hayes' position, quoted Lincoln to the effect that "honest statesmanship" had to control "individual meannesses for the public good" and pointedly cited Louisiana as an instance in which statesmanship should come to grips with meanness. Hayes demurred politely; he appreciated Lincoln's "wit and wisdom," he wrote Chandler, adding significantly, "I take the hint, but you must excuse me if I still stick to my own text."

And just what his "own text" was, and would be, confounded his critics and his constituents. Indeed, this was his strength and his strategy—to stay informed but removed, to keep his tactical options open, to insure that noncommitment to any specific arrangement would give him a freer hand after he, by oath of office, accepted the ultimate responsibility. On the last day of December, he responded to an earnest plea from Chandler to send an "authorized representative" to Washington, by noting, "There are several Ohio men in Wa. who know my methods of thinking and acting in public affairs. They can," he went on,

of their own motion speak confidently. Such men as Shellabarger, Comly, Noyes, Little, etc., etc., not in official position at Washington can perhaps do and say all that can properly be said. All this must, I am confident, be left to volunteers such as the men I name or allude to. Don't misunderstand me. I am ready to hear and heed the suggestion of friends.

To this Hayes scribbled a postscript: "You now see the troubles which an authorized friend could remove. If you had such a friend in Wa.," he asked, "what other and greater troubles might you not then see?" Hayes' active participation, he seemed to be saying, could tie his hands, lead to entrapment, encourage the wrong elements, and cause all other sorts of "trouble." Remaining aloof, with unauthorized hints and interpretations, but no commitments, Hayes would enter the White House with an unmarked slate.

There were a number of Hayes men who appreciated this position, whether or not they understood it. Charles Foster, Hayes' own congressman, who spoke out more than once advancing what he believed Hayes would do or say, wrote a long report toward the end of January, worrying about the possible defection of Senators Roscoe Conkling and George F. Edmunds and their friends. Yet he emphasized his support of the Hayes strategy in a one-sentence paragraph: "I heartily commend your course in refusing to take position as to policy or persons." On the very same day, Hayes confirmed to George W. Jones his determination "to keep my own counsels as to Cabinet, policy, etc." And when the "compromise" bill passed setting up a special congressional committee to investigate the electoral count and report, Hayes wrote to Carl Schurz that "I hope it will turn out well. I shall do nothing to influence the result."

Late in January, Hayes had begun to think about an inaugural address and received some suggestions from Schurz. He replied with some ideas of his own relative to improving the southern "condition." "I feel like saying," he wrote, "that the Nation will aid the people of that section 1. to the means of education, 2. to internal improvements of national character," and then, without breaking the sentence, asked Schurz if it would be appropriate to suggest a constitutional amendment limiting the presidential term to one of six years. He repeated his desire to keep himself uncommitted: "I want also to be ready to make a Cabinet—remaining to the last, free to choose as may at the time seem advisable."

But as Hayes admitted to Schurz early in February, "The South is more on my mind than anything else." He was not specific, talking about promoting "prosperity, education, emigration and immigration, improvements" as those subjects which came to mind. Wanting to "do" something, he said, he realized the need to be cautious, and in the last section of the letter made it clear that he was thinking ahead to federal policy emanating from Washington and not political policies aimed at Washington. As he told John Sherman in mid-February, "I prefer to make no new declarations." He was still uncommitted beyond his letter of acceptance of eight months earlier; "the friendly and encouraging words of that letter and all that they imply," was the way he put it.

Charles Foster and Stanley Matthews were two among many who had begun to suggest cabinet possibilities to Hayes. Foster prefaced his listing with his view that, as president, Hayes could capture a measurable cadre of southern supporters "without bargaining of any sort," adding parenthetically, "I hate bargains." Matthews, an old friend and one of the attorneys who argued several of the disputed electoral cases before the Electoral Commission of Congress, introduced his cabinet suggestions with the announcement that "the Democrats have given up the idea of defeating the election by delays. It was discussed Saturday night, urged and abandoned."

While Matthews' judgment on the Democrats' capitulation was premature, since there was a sustained effort by Southern Democrats to delay the actual electoral count, once the reports of the Electoral Commission had been received, Hayes nevertheless remained aloof. Sherman praised him for his reserve: "You have gained largely by your silence and caution since the election," adding in a letter on the following day that he thought Hayes should plan to be in Washington the week prior to the inaugural. Hayes parried the idea, asking, "Why can't friends be sent or come here?" To some the query might appear plaintive or downright naive, but it was more likely conceived as a means of keeping in touch without being committed. In the capital city, Hayes would have had to make quick decisions, fast commitments; in Columbus or through "friends," all responses could be suggestive and unspecific. Hayes maintained his control of an uncontrolled situation by what Sherman had called his silence and his caution.

During the last ten days of February, when, as Matthews wrote, Democratic efforts to delay the count loomed large, the pressures on Hayes to make commitments became intense. While Colonel Andrew Kellar of Tennessee called Hayes' silence "the chief embarrassment in the way of a victory over Tammany Hall," William Henry Smith, a chief architect in Hayes' candidacy, advised Hayes that "I think I made clear the impropriety at this time" of saying "something in addition to your Letter of Acceptance." Hayes himself expostulated over a long letter from Joseph Medill which wondered about his southern policy. "My paragraph," Hayes wrote Murat Halstead, "was short, but his eighteen pages haven't added an idea to it."

There is no documentary support for the contention that Hayes ever moved away from that position. Bargains may have been understood, perhaps as Michael Les Benedict suggests, to permit Southern Democrats to control their own party, or perhaps, as the Woodward thesis holds, to extract substantive federal support for the South, but if Hayes was not an official party to those bargains, as seems likely, were they indeed bargains? Hayes was aware of the immense variety of ideas that filled conversations and letters during the first two months of 1877, but he strictly maintained that he alone could make the final decisions. In looking at cabinet posts, for example, he received a plethora of suggestions from a spectrum of supporters and would-be supporters, including the name of David Key of Tennessee. Key ended up as postmaster general, the only Southerner in the cabinet, and his name came to Hayes in a letter from Colonel Kellar, forwarded with an endorsement by William Henry Smith. That letter was written on February 20, yet seven days later, Hayes was still considering possible candidates for that particular cabinet spot. "My idea is," he wrote Schurz on February 27, "to leave undecided, or rather uncommitted, some place until I reach W. Say War, Navy or Post Master General." It is difficult to visualize Hayes except as one who, while encouraging discussion and even mediation between the Republicans and Southern Democrats, was at the same time making plain that he would decide in due time, once he had taken the oath of office.[3]

That ceremony first took place on Saturday night, March 3, in the Red Room of the White House. Tensions were high in Washington, with rumors of military groups forming or on the march. Lucius Q.C. Lamar later called the electoral contest "the most dangerous event in our history," intimating how close the nation was to determining the election's result by force. Whether the reality was as extreme as the rumors, leaders in Washington were edgy and did not want to chance one day (Sunday) without constitutional leadership. On Monday, March 5, the public inauguration went off as scheduled.

For the first time in decades, the Executive Mansion housed a family whose close ties and unpretentious airs created a common bond with families across the land. "I can hardly realize," Lucy Hayes confessed to her oldest son after two and a half months, "that really and truly I am the same person that led an humble life in Ohio.'' She and her husband had five surviving children, the two youngest of whom came with them to Washington; Fanny was almost ten and Scott six when they left Spiegel Grove. The second son, Webb Cook Hayes, lived in the White House and served as his father's confidential secretary and general assistant. The other two boys lived away from home, one a Cornell undergraduate and the other at Harvard Law School.

The boys came home frequently, but whether they were there or not, family activities dominated the scene. Lucy had a set routine as social manager of the Executive Mansion, but her schedule included family times. The president, too, participated, whether the occasion was the brief morning scripture and prayer or an evening family sing. The family often went target shooting or riding, Scott and Fanny sometimes in tow. Fanny was the mischievous imp of the White House, exacting patience from staff and parents alike and earning love from all. On occasion she would climb on her father's lap or clump along the second floor corridors, shaking the chandeliers below. Intermingled with the family was a constant stream of guests, often relatives of Rutherford or Lucy, some of whom stayed on for weeks and joined the family circle as well as the formal entertainment.[4]

Formal entertainment was as much a part of the Hayes administration as family gatherings. Hidden beneath the twentieth-century caricature of ''lemonade Lucy'' was the fact of a vibrant, charming hostess and her reserved yet magnetic consort in a succession of receptions, dinners, soirees, teas, and other invitation-only affairs that far exceeded in number and quality the efforts of recent earlier administrations. When a guest commented to Lucy Hayes about the heavy burden of the White House social events, she replied that she liked giving parties and enjoyed herself immensely. ''I have had a particularly happy life here,'' she wrote to a niece in July 1880, adding that she would be glad to get home to Spiegel Grove. ''Four years is long enough for a woman like this one.''

For President Rutherford B. Hayes, it was a long, hard four years. Having established himself as a person to be reckoned, not trifled, with during the campaign, and having laid out the general outlines of a middle-of-the-road program that sought resolution for the major issues of the day, Hayes now faced a party that was split in three ways: the Stalwarts, who embraced the old ways of doing things, particularly vote counting and patronage, North and South; the Reformers, who looked to civil service reform and sound money as a means of wiping out corruption; and the regulars, for lack of a better name, who were enamored of the Bloody Shirt tactic, wavered on civil service reform, and were far from united on the money issue. Obviously, politicians, editors, industrialists, and others moved around within these three categories, and there were some who refused to be categorized. To this breakdown of party discipline, add an opposition party growing in strength in both houses of Congress: the Democrats controlled the House of Representatives in 1877 and added the Senate in 1879. Splinter groups like the emerging Greenbackers were a further complication for a political leader whose right to lead was reluctantly, if not skeptically, granted.

Hayes took on the southern dilemma first; indeed, it was the most intrusive issue on the nation's agenda in 1877. Whatever his friends had promised in his behalf, Hayes' public statements were few and clear, while those letters to his friends which are extant amplify only slightly his public statements: he was going to treat the South as an equal component within the Union, trusting the good will and economic hard sense of southern whites to encourage southern blacks to improve themselves through education and land ownership. The specific steps he took to remove the southern question from its agitating prominence are detailed elsewhere in admirable accounts. In 1982 Vincent De Santis raised the question of why Hayes acted as he did, and provided a useful summary of historians' views as well as a comprehensive evaluation of his own, concluding that Hayes himself made the decision. Hayes ordered the troops back to their barracks in two contested states (South Carolina and Louisiana) and allowed Democratic regimes to take over, for reasons other than the so-called bargain struck by his friends, reasons which De Santis believes are of varying plausibility.[5]

HAYES' OPTIONS LIMITED

The evidence and the rationale are reasonably clear; the choices before Hayes were limited indeed. If he did nothing, chaos would surely continue, to the detriment of the party, the nation, and the section, and eventually, as in the states which had been redeemed earlier, southern whites would take over without any check-rein. If he looked to the existing governments to resolve the crisis, he faced a record of deteriorating efficiency and decaying integrity that also seemed headed for chaos. If he took a stronger stand and tried to reassert the dominance of the military in these two and other states, he would be fighting a rearguard action in what he regarded as an unconstitutional way. Finally, he had to take into consideration a certain fatigue in the North with southern issues, an unwillingness to stand up for racial justice, and a hunger for release from the memories of war.

From Hayes' perspective, in 1877 the only sensible course was to try local self-government in the South, trusting the southern white leaders to respond faithfully to this substantive overture for a unified nation. He anticipated that they would secure "safety and prosperity for the colored people," that they would move toward a division between the two major political parties, that they would stabilize their local economies and respond positively to private and federal capital incursions. He anticipated, in short, an era of good feelings, a period of peace.

At first, the signs that he read convinced him that, as he wrote, "the better class of citizens cordially approve" in New York and New England. His trips to these states and sections, as well as to the border states, confirmed his impressions that what he called his "pacification policy" was succeeding. After returning from Richmond, Virginia, early in November, he recorded in his diary that "there are thousands of intelligent people who are not Democrats, and who would like to unite with the Conservative Republicans of the North."

Hayes was even aware of the political risks involved in establishing this policy; to several correspondents and to his diary he identified the bitter opposition which he faced, particularly within his party. Intraparty squabbles did not help his southern policy, but they were not responsible for its undoing.

Race was a major contributor to its weakness. As the atrocities and acts of physical and economic violence mounted against southern blacks, it became clear that Hayes' integrity and declarations of good intention were not enough. Black protests mounted, impelled in large part by anger and fear. Petitions, resolutions, and letters came to Hayes and others from individuals and organizations in the black community, recounting the attacks and asking for assistance. Emigration and migration were two of the safety valves that blacks examined. While Hayes apparently did not respond to several petitions and letters, he did answer the Rev. Mr. Sturks and discouraged his idea of a black community in San Domingo. "The evils which now affect you," he told the minister in January 1878, "are likely steadily and I hope, rapidly to diminish." The migration fever, particularly in Mississippi and Louisiana, would not die down, and slowly the Exodus of 1879–1880 took shape. Blacks came up the Mississippi River heading for Kansas and free soil only to find a welcome less than warm and economic conditions less than supportive. Hayes did not directly involve himself in the Exodus, although a congressional investigation aired the southern causes as well as the treatment which the western states offered the migrants. He noted in his diary that he thought its "effect is altogether favorable," and counseled that the blacks should be spread around the upper Midwest and settle down to be home-owners. But he did not try to see that his counsel was heard.[6]

The problem was larger than migration. Signs of underlying distaste for blacks were easy to see in the North long before the Exodus helped to rekindle it. When Hayes appointed Frederick Douglass as marshal of the District of Columbia at the start of his administration, he complained about the uproar this action caused. At the same time, he stripped that position of the social responsibilities which were attached to it and gave them to "a gentleman who was officially intimately connected with the President's House and family." Even those whites who considered themselves to be "friends of the race" looked at their illiteracy and different morals with contempt and condescension. "Just how the two races are to get along together by-and-by when the colored rises in the scale," mused the Washington correspondent of the *Springfield Republican,* "is not easy to see."

Some blacks blamed the racial situation in the late 1870s on the loss of political leverage, and they pointed the accusing finger at Hayes' southern policy. P.C.B. Pinchback wrote Hayes early in 1878, comparing the number and prestige of black federal appointments in New Orleans under Grant with those under Hayes, and characterized the difference as "this apparent neglect of the colored people of the state." Hayes was not yet willing to admit that his southern policy was in error. "I am confident," he wrote an old college friend a month later, "and my confidence grows stronger, that I decided wisely at the beginning."

Later in the year his confidence was shaken, but it did not falter. "The brother in the South is ugly in many ways," he told the same friend, referring to the increase in violence and repression against the blacks, adding, "But there we are making progress." A month later, a published interview following close on the heels of a conference with Stalwart leaders Zachariah Chandler and Donald Cameron headlined Hayes' admission that his southern policy was a failure and that he was changing course. Stalwart papers picked this up with a vengeance, and the Republican reform element was hard put to refute what they called the "purported" interview in a newspaper "which very frequently depended on its imagination for its facts." Historians have tended to accept this postelection November headline of a departure from Hayes' southern policy as a radical change of course at mid-term.[7]

That there was movement within his established southern policy is irrefutable, but the policy remained, and Hayes maintained his faith in it. What he proposed to do, and within narrow limits did do, was to use marshals to seek out and bring to trial violations of the law. His 1878 annual message called attention to these muted terms; in South Carolina and Louisiana and some voting districts of other states, he wrote, "the rights of the colored voters have been overriden and their participation in the election not permitted to be either general or free." Repeating his warning of a year earlier, he pledged to use "whatever authority rests with me" to see that justice was done within the law after a "full and fair investigation of the alleged crimes." In a letter to a college friend, a southerner, a month later, Hayes was more explicit:

My theory of the Southern situation is this. Let the rights of the colored people be secured and the laws enforced only by the usual peaceful methods—by the action of civil tribunals—and wait for the healing influences of time and reflection to solve and remove the remaining difficulties.

Hayes recognized that this was an evolutionary process, but he argued that the selfish politicians who kept things stirred up were "losing rapidly their hold."

RECOGNIZED "SOLID SOUTH"

It was clear that Hayes tried to tighten up enforcement within the stated limits of his southern policy. As he wrote in May 1879, the political battle cry of his opponents, "the use of troops at the polls," was pure fantasy but, like most fiction, "if not fully understood capable of mischief." There was no turning back the clock. Hayes' increased enforcement activity, somewhat impeded by Democratic moves to withhold army appropriations, was sporadic at best; it was not carried out with the conviction with which it had been pledged and fell short of results which could be called successful.

The hard fact is that the crystallization of southern opinion into a politically solid state which permitted and even encouraged the repression and subordination of blacks had begun a decade earlier, and Hayes was in no position to confront that crystallization. His party was split, and the Democrats controlled the Congress.[8] Troops did not work, and most of them had been withdrawn before he took office. Officeholders opposed to crystallization were ineffective. The other major section—the North—had set a crude example by accepting the near-dominance of the opposing political party. In short, conciliation and trust was not only a smart policy, which had not been tried before, it was the only practical policy open to Hayes. Unhappily, it did not work.

Long before Hayes acknowledged that his southern policy had collapsed, he was ready to turn to a second reform to which he had been publicly committed since his letter of acceptance of the nomination. The southern men, he believed in April 1877, were not yet ready to bolt their party, but they were well disposed toward him and, he added, "will look kindly, I think, on my plans for civil service reform." He promised to do some homework on the subject and come up with a bill for the Congress. The steps he took and the reactions that those steps generated have been carefully detailed in Ari Hoogenboom's fine monograph and need no repetition. The picture of Hayes that emerges from Hoogenboom's study resembles those evoked by historians of the preelection bargain, a mild-mannered man of integrity with the resolve and the staying power of a strong executive.

Given the political structures in the late 1870s, with the reformers pushing for civil service reform and politicians for or against it, depending on whether they were in or out of power, it was too much to expect any president to push persistently for this reform. Hayes made haste slowly. "I have heard it said," Benjamin Harrison wrote Secretary of the Navy Richard Thompson in May 1877, "Pres. Hayes was not giving us much Civil Service reform in Indiana very often." Nevertheless, as the *Detroit Tribune* summarized late in April, the president's program was public knowledge: that office was not a congressional privilege of patronage, that appointments in the South will be made without reference to party, that changes in the administration will not create massive federal job changes, and that the President's own appointments will be offered primarily to qualified persons. It was on the basis of this program that several departments in the Hayes administration, including Interior, Treasury, and the Navy, made measurable efforts to establish honest criteria for appointments, to use competitive examinations, and to eradicate fraud.

Hayes admitted that he had made some mistakes in his appointments, and his sanguine prediction of a Congress that would happily concur in a civil service bill came to pass. What Hayes did do, with some tactical advances and retreats, was to call attention with compelling consistency to the need for civil service reform and to use his presidential power to that end. Since presidential power is finite, particularly when multiple interests converge and disperse like an erratic ocean tide, what Hayes wanted to do and what he was able to do did not always coincide. He was forced by lack of support or lack of information to vary the reform course.

The most dramatic event of his administration in confronting patronage was his attack on the New York Custom House, a fortress protected by New York senator Roscoe Conkling and manned by Collector Chester Arthur and Naval Officer Alonzo Cornell. Hayes had several reasons for moving against the Custom House and removing these two officials, not the least of which were the antagonism of Conkling and the fears of William Henry Smith, a Hayes friend and adviser, who relayed to Hayes the anger of Chicago businessmen who were bilked by the New York Custom House practices. Among Hayes' reasons was the possibility of making an example of the most prominent, but not the only, corrupt federal authority. Hayes' battle with Conkling would have more rounds than one and, in accord with most of what Hayes did, rested on a principle. Hayes believed that the executive branch was charged with the power of appointments with the advice and consent of the Senate, and not the other way around. He launched his attack on the New York Custom House for all of these reasons, yet his desire to reestablish the strength of the office of the presidency is more in keeping with his character and beliefs than the more petty excursions of political revenge.

Hayes' success in the New York battle was conditional. The rules promulgated by the new, reform-minded appointments were models of their kind and were imitated in Boston and Philadelphia. Other custom houses were also moved toward reform as a result of the ouster of Arthur and Cornell, but the New York institution needed Arthur and Cornell, who went on to prestigious elective posts. Hayes' civil service reforms demonstrated that he had both the strength and the courage of his convictions. A cartoon in *Puck* summed up the results. Conkling and Hayes are looking through different ends of the same telescope, Conkling through the proper end and Hayes through the far end. "How small he looks," says Hayes. "By Jove," says Conkling, "he's a bigger man than I thought he was."

Federal employees were not then looked upon as "labor" in the same sense that industrial workers, miners, and railroad workers were laborers, yet labor's troubles in the public arena paralleled those of labor in the private sector. Where corruption brought reform efforts to the owner, corruption of a different sort brought strikes to the latter, and eventually involved the president. The absence of labor unions permitted the railroads, most of which were in federal receivership, to exploit their workers with low pay, layovers without pay or expenses, and arbitrary wage cuts. In mid-July, Baltimore & Ohio workers in Maryland could take no more and went on strike. The strike quickly spread to West Virginia, Pennsylvania, Ohio, Indiana, and Illinois, and the governors of those states turned to the White House for assistance. Hayes' response was typical; he requested information on a continuing basis, and met with his cabinet daily to determine what the federal government could do within constitutional limits. Finally, but in time to prevent widespread rioting and bloodshed, Hayes authorized federal troops to restore order, citing specific constitutional authority. By the end of July, the general strike had collapsed and the trains were moving again but, significantly, the strikers had made their point. Wages were not reduced further, and some cuts were rescinded. In many cases, wages lost because of the strike were earned back as the railroad worked overtime to catch up on delayed orders.[9]

SOCIAL VIEWS EVOLVED

Hayes' concern for the strikers was expressed as a diary entry and, as his biographer notes, was never made public; it reflected his belief in education and his suspicions of the excesses of capitalism, but his diary entry also manifests his confusion on the issue of strikes. Five times he redrafted a line affirming a man's right to determine for himself whether or not he will work, but questioning whether that right can interfere with the rights of others: "No man," he concludes in his fifth version, "has the right to decide that question for other men."

In microcosm, the strike—heralded by historians as the Great Railroad Strike—emphasized the transitional process of Hayes' thinking; to a certain extent the same holds true for other major issues that he confronted. What are the limits to individualism and to individual rights? What are the keys to societal tranquility, and what impulses will move society progressively and tranquilly? Where are the inequities in society, and how can society resolve them? Hayes' thought had not yet set; there was no time for that in his presidency. His postpresidential years would demonstrate his efforts to grapple substantively with these questions.

On a more material level, the economic health of society was a tenacious dilemma. Prosperity in the latter years of the 1870s came, but ever so slowly, and its pace puzzled the politicians. Men were divided on the issue of "sound money" that is, a currency based on a stable metal, like gold. Hayes had been elected to his third gubernatorial term on that issue; he was as strong a sound money man when he entered the White House as when he left it. There were essentially two attacks on Hayes' version of sound money. The first was an effort by Greenbacker Thomas Ewing, an Ohio congressman, to repeal the resumption clause in the Resumption Act of 1875 by which paper currency would be redeemed in metal on or after January 1, 1879. James A. Garfield argued against repeal; with a sound metal base, "there is no longer one money for the rich and another for the poor," he told the House of Representatives in the fall of 1877.

As Hayes began preparing his first annual message to the Congress, he worried about an inflation caused by the introduction of silver currency. His belief was that circulating currency had "to have intrinsic value—to be money, and not a mere promise." Early in 1878, the Bland-Allison silver bill, enlarging, within limits, the amount of silver to be coined, passed both houses of Congress. As the bill bulled its way through Congress, Hayes made up his mind to veto it.

He was concerned lest an inflated currency hike interest rates, realizing what that would do to the nation's "vast indebtedness." Before the bill had reached his desk, he knew that his veto would be overridden. His cabinet raised some doubts about the proposed veto when he discussed it with them, but in the end the Bland-Allison bill became law over Hayes' veto.

He had received a lot of pressure from the men in the East and Midwest who ordinarily would have stood firm for hard money, he told William Henry Smith. And the issue of the future, he predicted to two correspondents, was going to be "hard money against cabbage leaves," a sound currency, redeemable in metal, versus "irredeemable government paper." Hayes' forecast was correct; in less than twenty years a heated debate over free silver coinage marked the 1896 presidential canvass, with his young friend William McKinley standing stolidly for Hayes' position against the flamboyant William Jennings Bryan. If Hayes had a strategy to deal with fiscal problems at the midpoint of his administration, it was best stated in his December 2, 1878, annual message to the Congress. Prosperity and "the welfare of legitimate business and industry" can grow best if the government refrains from attempting "radical changes in the existing financial legislation." No more fiddling with silver coinage and unsupported greenbacks, he was saying; and he added that the programmed resumption of specie payment—making paper currency redeemable in coin, effective January 1, 1879—would take place on schedule.

To protect specie resumption, his tactics were conventionally political: he sent or encouraged his subordinates to beat the drum for hard money. John Sherman's strenuous efforts were challenged without reference to party alignment by labor, small businessmen, farmers, and others who needed an easier exchange medium to relieve their debt burden. Even friendly newspapers were not above taking shots at Sherman and others. The *Rochester Evening Express* pointedly suggested that Republicans not try to show "that the entire policy of the party, financial and otherwise, since 1860, is the best conceivable"—this in a thoughtful editorial commending some parts of Sherman's position and questioning some others.

Specie resumption went off as planned and without incident at the start of 1879; there was no run on the Treasury. As the year progressed and sentiment for greenbacks became more pronounced, both political parties had difficulties on where they stood on paper money. New England businessmen did not want to "have Congress meddle with the subject at all, for fear it would muddle." The upshot was inaction in the Congress and a cold shoulder to Hayes' pleas, in his annual messages of 1879 and 1880, to suspend the limited coinage of silver and return to a single, strict gold standard. In his last annual message, Hayes did not fail to point out, however, that the depression of the 1870s was over: All our industries are thriving; the rate of interest is low; new railroads are being constructed; a vast immigration is increasing our population, capital, and labor; new enterprises in great number are in progress, and our commercial relations with other countries are improving.

QUIET FOREIGN POLICY ERA

When Hayes stressed that "our commercial relations with other countries are improving," he was underlining both the major purpose and major accomplishment of American foreign policy during his tenure. It was a quiet time; Grant's secretary of state had passed on a smoothly running organization to his successor, William M. Evarts, and outside of trying to win markets for U.S. agricultural and industrial products, very little of lasting significance took place. The U.S.-Mexican border was the scene of incursions from both sides until Mexico took the initiative and eased the tension. The abortive French effort to build an isthmus canal across Panama was scheduled to begin in 1881 under the direction of Ferdinand de Lesseps, evoking from Hayes a strong statement that our national policy "is a canal under American control." This was a useful increment to the Monroe Doctrine.

The other international incident involved China. The Burlingame Treaty of 1868 permitted unrestricted immigration at a time when cheap labor was a necessity in the West. As immigration from the East began to fill that need, agitation grew to abrogate the Burlingame Treaty unilaterally. Early in 1879, Hayes vetoed a bill which, in effect, did just that, and began negotiations with the Chinese government that resulted in their agreement to limit emigration to the United States and widen trade opportunities. Though these proved to be temporary measures, they did ease nettlesome problems at the time.

Whatever causes are attributed to Chinese exclusion, one is intimately related to the genre of racism which contributed to the exploitation of the Indians and blacks. In each situation, a variety of pressures was at work: labor tensions, land ownership, and fear, for example, but in all cases the classic statements about color, inferiority, barbarism, alien cultures, and religious differences flowed freely in the press and correspondence. The Victorian reformers, among whom can be numbered Rutherford B. Hayes and his secretary of the interior, Carl Schurz, wrestled valiantly and unsuccessfully with the hostilities that racism helped to produce. Schurz's solutions were honest but, in the light of late twentieth-century developments, repressive. He worked to remove corruption from the Indian Bureau, with some success. He worked to keep the U.S. Army in a secondary role, without very much success. He persuaded the Indian tribes to move further from their homelands to reservations which were generally on low quality lands and unsuited to the economic and cultural needs of the tribes. He brought Indian chiefs to Washington to talk with him and the president to make an impression on both Indians and whites, but promises made in executive offices and the White House were not always fully implemented when executed in the field.

Hayes' own views paralleled those of Schurz. He recognized that the Indian "problem" had remained unsolved since the coming of the white man. In his diary, he elaborated on two principles. First, he wanted to deal fairly and justly with the Indians, care for their "physical wants" and provide education and religious instruction. Second, he wanted to put a stop to "the intrigues of whites" which caused Indian uprisings. "Always," he added with a touch of wonder, "the Numbers and the prowess of the Indians have been underrated." Unhappily for the Indians and the nation, neither Hayes nor Schurz nor anyone else had solutions for the tragic erosion of economic and cultural viability which was visited on America's native peoples.

As the president tussled with the nation's relationships to native Americans, southern Americans, foreign nations, and other disparate groups at home and abroad, not far from his central focus was his relationship with the major political parties. Hayes sensed what later historians confirmed: that the political process was in transition and the institutions and issues that had blanketed the nation in the mid-nineteenth century were changing. The Democrats, emboldened by their near-victory in 1876, tried to create a campaign issue for 1878 and 1880 by establishing a congressional committee, named for its chairman, Representative Clarkson N. Potter of New York, to investigate the 1876 election. The committee provided headlines during the hot summer of 1878 as it dredged up all manner of men to testify to the corruption that characterized the canvass.

Hayes remained apparently unperturbed. The *Chicago Tribune* reported that a Wilkes-Barre, Pennsylvania, reporter found him "in excellent health, bearing the fatigues of endless speeches, reviews and handshaking like a veteran." Hayes called the Potter inquiry a "farce . . . of much cry and little wool; or, more correctly, no wool at all." Privately, Hayes thought the investigation "shabby" and wondered "how men having the instincts, or culture of gentlemen" could participate or approve. There was blame enough to go around, the *New York Times* concluded, and properly so, because documented evidence of Democratic corruption embarrassed that party and undoubtedly prevented Samuel Tilden from seeking the Democratic nomination in 1880. Nevertheless, until the Potter Committee reported early in 1879, it was a clattering distraction, chorusing again the challenge to Hayes' legitimate right to office.[10]

The Democrats did not hesitate to confront Hayes with another issue almost immediately after the new Congress convened in 1879. Anxious to relieve the South of the possibility of using federal marshals in elections, House Democrats attached riders to the army appropriations bill repealing that authority and the test-oath for jurors that kept former Confederates from federal jury duty. In a six-month period, Democrats used their rider techniques seven times, only to have Hayes use his veto successfully. For Hayes, this was a legislative intrusion into executive authority. "It is my duty to guard as a trust the powers conferred on the office which has devolved on me," he told his diary in April 1879. Standing steadfast against the Congress, Hayes eventually won his point and vouchsafed for the presidency the power effectively to exercise the incumbent's "conscience and judgment."

The pressures that even nineteenth-century presidents lived with required safety valves, and prominent among the escapes used by Hayes was his enthusiasm for traveling. He literally traveled the breadth of the land, overlooking no section and generally taking the First Lady with him. One supporter wrote to Schurz in the middle of 1879 suggesting that Hayes "drift along the New Jersey coast" and, perhaps, build on the sentiment that the president should disavow his no second term pledge. Such a leisurely trip, "in a quiet, unassuming way, . . . *would do good in more ways than one,"* Schurz's correspondent asserted, adding that "Mrs. Hayes fairly captured the ladies" on her last visit. Traveling, in short, was a tonic for the president and Mrs. Hayes, and they were generally well received. Their trip to the West Coast, the first for a sitting chief executive, was a tour de force, as the couple traveled by almost every conceivable known conveyance on land and water and met with the western elite, the politicians, and the plain people. Interspersed with business, the Hayes party, like tourists, traveled to see the beauty spots of the section: Lake Tahoe, Yosemite, the Sequoias, Puget Sound, and many more. Hayes' schedule called for him to be back in time to cast his vote for James A. Garfield, the successor whom he had hoped would follow him.

His hopes about Garfield's election realized, vindicating, he believed, his own presidential term, Hayes left office in March 1881 and turned his attention to his private life as an ordinary citizen. He returned to Fremont, "this good town," he told his fellow citizens, "to bear his part in every useful work that will promote the welfare and the happiness of his family, his town, his State and his country." The next twelve years made good on his asseveration.

SPIEGEL GROVE RETREAT

The day after Hayes' death, the vitriolic *New York Sun* editorialized that he had spent his Fremont years "in the peaceful pursuit of raising chickens." While it is true that Hayes had all sorts of domestic and farm animals and fowl, the former president spent more time in Spiegel Grove with his fruit and shade trees, some of the latter of which now tower over the lovely twenty-five acres. He consumed hours in reading, although his eyes tired easily, and he thoroughly enjoyed discussing the books that he had read, whether the author was Emerson, whose essays he enjoyed, a biographer, or a contemporary novelist. His winter pastime was sleighing, and his diary was filled with notes about seasonal rides around the countryside with friends and family, brashly challenging the crisp, cold air with piles of blankets and heavy warm clothing.

Spiegel Grove rarely was without visitors. Whether they were school friends of daughter Fanny, or the local minister, old comrades from political and military wars, old friends from Cincinnati or Kenyon, or just family relatives, the stream was continuous and spirited. The Hayes were elegant hosts, warm and gracious; and their guests were urged to remain, often extending their stay to a week or two. Spiegel Grove was a busy, bubbling place, yet far enough removed from urban hubbub to be restful and peaceful.

Attractive as it was as a place to be, it was also attractive as a place to be from—and come home to. The Hayeses traveled extensively, usually to the East, but often inside of Ohio or west to Chicago and beyond. Hayes generally had meetings to attend or speeches to give. He was on the governing boards of four colleges and universities, two grant-making foundations for black education, and the National Prison Reform Association. He was loyal to the Loyal Legion, the Grand Army of the Republic, and the veterans of his own Civil War regiment. He participated in most of the Lake Mohonk conferences on the Indians in the 1880s and early 1890s, suggesting and presiding over the two Lake Mohonk conferences on the Negro in 1890 and 1891. He was a faithful Kenyon College alumnus and a typical one, remarking on the changes and lamenting the deterioration.

A recital of the organizations that involved him has little point without some understanding of the issues about which Hayes felt strongly. Hayes himself listed "three obstacles or dangers in our path" in a brief diary entry in August 1884: "1. Intemperance. 2. Illiteracy. 3. Monster accumulation of wealth in a few hands." He often ruminated about the liquor problem, at one point using his temperance stand as a reason for not stumping in 1884 for James G. Blaine, whom Hayes disliked and distrusted intensely. In seeking a culprit for the drunkenness abroad in the land, he blamed the public. It was the public, he held, who raised "fashionable and laudable" drinking to acceptable levels, and while he recognized that humanity would always be vulnerable to temptation, he felt that drunkenness—today known as alcoholism—could be made as unsavory, and as rare, as thievery. "Public opinion could dry it up, could extirpate it, as thoroughly as larceny or burglary are prevented." Yet neither he nor Lucy actively participated in any temperance movement or organization.

As David Thelen notes in his perceptive essay on Hayes as a transitional reformer, Hayes' credo was that people were differentiated as individuals, not as groups, and that the measuring rod was "character." "The school, the church and the family," Thelen writes, "encouraged his faith in unlimited social mobility, the perfectibility of man and the responsiveness of government." Illiteracy could be wiped out by universal education, and Hayes urged Whitelaw Reid, editor of the *New York Tribune,* to campaign to have "the whiskey tax to go to the States in aid of universal education." When the Blair bill for federal support of education came before the Senate, Hayes was strongly in favor of it. He believed that education would help laborers see their role in relation to capital, blacks prepare themselves for the race's rising, Indians adjust to the whites' more civilized ways, and criminals see the error of their means of livelihood. Stopping short of calling education a panacea—he served on too many university boards for that—Hayes put his trust in the educability of all human beings, and its corollary, the ability of society to educate its citizens.

The aim of public instruction, he told a Toledo audience in 1885, is to "fit, or at least tend to fit, the young for the places they are to fill in life." His special pleading was for manual training or industrial education. He liked to call it "practical education," arguing "that study of books alone may make a learned man but not an educated man." He applauded the introduction of industrial education into high schools and, through his work with the Peabody and Slater funds, supported industrial education in black institutions. "The young of all races and all conditions should be taught skilled labor—to respect labor," he advised President S. T. Mitchell of Wilberforce University, " . . . not merely as a means of self-support . . . but for the sake of the mental and moral training it furnishes."

Hayes' preoccupation with the intimate relationship between education and labor may have been myopic at a time when industrial technology and manufacturing were beginning to change the function of the laborer, but it more clearly revealed a changing relationship between capital and labor. In a word, he began to have some second thoughts about the distribution of wealth in the country and what great wealth did to individuals. Unable to focus with any clarity on that issue while in the White House, Hayes came back to it with increasing frequency during his final years. In a series that Hayes titled "Thoughts on Various Topics," he shared with his diary a number of perceptive sentences, some in the form of aphorisms. The last in the series begins, "Vast accumulations of wealth in a few hands are hostile to labor," and it goes on to rehearse the evils which flow from that condition. One of those evils he articulated after reading an article by Edward Bellamy. "Yes," Hayes concurred, "Pauperism is the shadow of excessive wealth."

Hayes' growing dissaffection with the extreme of wealth and his concern for its debilitating effect on American society were the expressions of a man who himself was well off by contemporary standards. Cash-poor and land-rich, rumor had it that he was parsimonious in the White House, yet he calculated later that in his four White House years he had saved only $1,000 out of a total salary of $200,000. Shortly after returning to Fremont, he borrowed $30,000, and when real estate sales slowed and some business ventures collapsed in the mid-1880's he felt the pinch. By 1891 he was worried by his rising debt; he had been too easy a mark for people and causes in need. *"The interest on my debt now exceeds my income,"* he underlined in his diary on September 8, 1891. But his land holdings were secure and, he thought, would increase in value more rapidly than his obligations. At his death in January 1893, he was worth close to a million dollars.

SOUTHERN POLICY AN ISSUE

Death came almost without warning. His last few months were highlighted by a series of trips; beginning in September 1892, his travels took him to Washington, D.C., New York, Lake Mohonk, Chicago, Indianapolis, Baltimore, and then, late in December, Cleveland and Columbus. His final trip, in January, was to Columbus and Cleveland; his heart signaled danger in the Cleveland railroad station, and he came right home to Spiegel Grove to die.

Although some Democratic papers used their obituary notice to rehash Hayes' election and reopen old sores, most of the articles were bland, lacking the freshness and informativeness of the commentary published as Hayes left office twelve years before. The earlier critiques spanned the spectrum from meanness to sycophancy, but those critics who took the middle ground came close to the mark. They questioned the results of his southern policy—a solidly Democratic South, a repressed and exploited black race, and a broken trust—but hovered near the sentiment expressed by the *Rochester Democrat and Chronicle:* "In the retrospect, it is not easy to see how it [Hayes' southern policy] could have been avoided." Hayes got good marks for trying to convert the federal bureaucracy to a civil service, even as he was criticized for failing in the conversions effort and for making some inept appointments. His cabinet was generally rated as excellent; indeed, some editors credited him with success only when he listened to his advisers. His financial policy, viewed from the prosperity of 1881, was declared to be a fine achievement, for the most part attributed to the secretary of the treasury, John Sherman.

Other issues, more marginal in importance, received attention also. Was the White House a dull place and Washington society somnolent during the Hayes tenure? Did Hayes accumulate a fortune while serving as president? These were among the easier queries to resolve, as Mary Clemmer did with enthusiasm, defending the very gracious and hospitable Lucy Hayes and denying with some evidence the charge of fortune accumulation. The more difficult questions dealt with Hayes' character. There was universal praise for his integrity, his sincerity, and his patriotism, but underlying, sometimes accompanying, these conclusions were hints or assertions of irresoluteness and mediocrity. The *Hartford Evening Post* accorded him the "good will and respect, if not the admiration, of most people." The *Chicago Tribune* withheld "the honor of brilliant ability" even as it lauded Hayes' "honest and pure administration." The *New York Herald* ranked him with "the respectable, commonplace Presidents, like Polk and Pierce," while the *New York Times* thought the Hayes administration's "numerous foibles and absurdities" would soon be forgotten, while "its strength and resolution in dealing with some great and vital questions of public policy will be more clearly recognized." With some latitude of expression, the "middle ground" editors affirmed Hayes' goodness and, from the perspective of history, his successful presidency, but denied him the accolade of "great" or "brilliant."

Hayes himself was sensitive to his accomplishments and his weaknesses to defend his administration, more often in his diary than in correspondence. "I believed that a radical change of policy with respect to the South," he wrote to a distinguished black minister-educator in 1883, "would bring ultimate safety and prosperity to the colored people. . . . The change did its work. Not instantly, but slowly and surely." He believed, too, that he had given civil service a forthright and sustained push in the proper direction, had begun the healing process between the sections, and had restrained the inflationary pressures exerted by the proponents of silver and paper currency. Most significantly, he believed that he restored to the office of the presidency the potency, resiliency, and dignity it deserved. He would claim, also, that he strengthened the Republican party, since he fully subscribed to his own dictum, "He serves his party best who serves his country best."

Historians judging Hayes cover a large territory; although there is one brief published evaluation of the major interpreters, it is difficult to reduce these into schools and reduce each to one-line summaries. It is enough to say that from the laudatory early works of Charles R. Williams, the pendulum swung, perhaps erratically, to the more critical views of Woodward, De Santis, Hoogenboom, and Hirshom. The return swing seems now to be in evidence, with a new generation flailing away at the Woodward thesis, a recent revisionist essay by De Santis, an earlier general favorable assessment by H. Wayne Morgan, and a hint that Hoogenboom is revising his earlier perceptions of Hayes in his forthcoming biography. From the Hayes whose ethics were an enigma, whose strength was in his vacillation, and whose impact on the office was judged to be like a pebble in a pond, the more recent scholarly works talk about a more independent, more decisive, more alert magistrate.

HAYES' TERM LACKED CRUCIBLE

In seeking a sensible judgment on Hayes as president, one can question why he has been called the "forgotten" president. Surely part of the reason that he is not well remembered, like Lincoln or Franklin Roosevelt, is the nature of the crises each man faced; Hayes had no war to fight, no depression to lick. Nor did he have the advantage of a second term, a charismatic personality, a dramatic physical appearance like Lincoln's height, Cleveland's bulk, Theodore Roosevelt's energy, or FDR's handicap. The issues of the Hayes term were issues not of confrontation but of cooperation, not of surgery but of convalescence. These called for presidential responses of a restrained, even understated tone, the kind of leadership that Hayes offered.

Critics point to the number of poor appointments in the face of his civil service reform stance, a certain public reserve beyond the stereotypical Victorian patriarch, a weakness in leadership quality manifested in a lack of aggressiveness, an inability to sustain a working relationship with dissident segments of the Republican party, and a kind of bland blindness, a Pollyanna attitude that seemed to cover every setback with an optimistic glow.

Some of these charges are grounded in fact and others in speculation. For every poor appointment, Hayes made several good appointments, beginning with his strong cabinet. For all his reserve, he and Mrs. Hayes performed gracefully as host and hostess in the White House, and Hayes himself in letters and informal conferences was relaxed, even-tempered, and good humored. He was not jovial or charismatic, nor as a leader was he dynamic. He could act quickly and firmly, but he preferred to move slowly and thoughtfully, not aggressively.

He carried one cross that has not been fabricated for presidential incumbents before or since: his claim to office was tainted. This made him an easy target for political enemies and lukewarm friends. The country was wearily and apprehensively divided when he took his oath, and the office itself had cultured a mold of miscreancy. Working with these burdens, making the mistakes allowed to human beings, suffering the insidious jealousies and pernicious rumors that inevitably beset a chief executive, and forced to work with a hostile Congress and a divided party, Hayes laid down the outline of his policies and proceeded to implement them. The results were startlingly beneficial to all except blacks and Indians. In ending an era with this qualified success, he was also instrumental in beginning a new era that stretched into the next century.

This very Victorian president was the epitome of self-control. Often provoked, he rarely flew to anger. Often challenged, he rarely laid down the gauntlet. Often frustrated, he rarely gave in to despair. Often victorious, he rarely gloated. Not that he did not feel all of these feelings, but his self-control kept him in check, even when anger, confrontation, despair, and the enjoyment of victory might have helped his cause. He was a self-confident man, yet he accepted advice, sometimes too freely, from those whom he admired, like William M. Evarts. He liked politics, but only the invigorating contest, not the pettiness and patronage that seemed to accompany political conflict. He was an enthusiastic politician.

He was also an optimist. He believed in progress. He believed, like all good Victorians, that the world was getting better and that he, Rutherford B. Hayes, had made a substantial contribution to that end. Looking back, even a non-Victorian can conclude, "Indeed he had."

NOTES

1. Keith Ian Polakoff, *The Politics of Inertia: The Election of 1876 and the End of Reconstruction* (Baton Rouge: Louisiana State University Press, 1973); Allan Peskin, "Was There a Compromise of 1877?" *Journal of American History,* 60, no. 1 (June 1973): 63–75. Woodward's response is in the same issue: "Yes, There Was a Compromise of 1877," ibid., 215–233. In a later essay, George Rable, "Southern Interests and the Election of 1876: A Reappraisal," *Civil War History,* 26, no. 4 (December 1980): 347–361, argues that the overriding tensions were in state and local politics in the South and in efforts of Southerners to establish peace (i.e., home rule) by extracting "concessions . . . from the all but certain victors" (p. 361).

2. Michael Les Benedict, "Southern Democrats in the Crisis of 1876–1877," *Journal of Southern History,* 46, no. 4 (November 1980): 489–524, should be read in conjunction with his earlier article, "Preserving the Constitution: The Conservative Basis of Radical Reconstruction," *Journal of American History,* 41, no. I (June 1974): 65–90.

3. Benedict, "Southern Democrats," pp. 518–520; C. Vann Woodward, *Reunion and Reaction: The Compromise of 1877 and the End of Reconstruction* (Boston: Little, Brown, 1951), pp. 186–189; Andrew J. Kellar to William Henry Smith, February 20, 1877, Hayes Papers, Rutherford B. Hayes Presidential Center, Fremont, Ohio, Thomas C. Donaldson, a friend and confidant of Hayes, observed privately on February 28, 1877:

The truth is the little coterie that surrounded Prest. Hayes in Ohio came to Washington thinking they had an entire mortgage on Mr. Hayes *for all* and a deed for the equities. How he has fooled some of them! and how quickly they left him when he showed his teeth and [he] did as he liked.

Watt P. Marchman, ed., "The 'Memoirs' of Thomas Donaldson," *Hayes Historical Journal*, 2, no. 3–4, (Spring-Fall 1979): 160.

4. Emily Apt Geer, "Lucy Webb Hayes and Her Family," *Ohio History*, 77 (Winter, Spring, Summer, 1968): 51–53; William H. Crook, *Through Five Administrations: Reminiscences of Col. William H. Crook*, comp. and ed. Margarita Spalding (New York: Harper and Brother, 1910), pp. 232, 250–251; Marchman, "Thomas Donaldson," pp. 214, 221. Some months earlier, in April 1879, Donaldson remarked to the president's steward, referring to the Hayes family, "I believe *that* the happiest [presidential] family ever in this house," and the steward heartily agreed. Ibid., p. 195.

5. In a lengthy diary entry for April 11, 1880, Hayes contradicts an account of his administration, beginning with his "southern policy," written for the *Philadelphia Times* by the newspaperman-cum-president-maker, General H. V. Boynton. Hayes identifies Boynton's first complaint as a southern policy which was "very different in practice from what 'his friends' understood it would be when they supported it. I know, of course," Hayes told his diary, "very little of what was expected. The truth is I have no confidants in regard to it. My judgment was that the time had come to put an end to bayonet rule." Charles R. Williams, *The Diary and Letters of Rutherford B. Hayes*, 5 vols. (Columbus: Ohio State Genealogical Society, 1922–1926), 3:594. See also Vincent P. De Santis, "Rutherford B. Hayes and the Removal of the Troops and the End of Reconstruction," in J. Morton Kousser and James M. McPherson, eds., *Region, Race and Reconstruction: Essays in Honor of C. Vann Woodward* (New York: Oxford University Press, 1982), pp. 417–450, esp. pp. 436–445.

6. Hayes to Rev. Mr. Sturks, January 14, 1878; copy in Hayes Papers from *Cincinnati Commercial*, January 16, 1978; Nell Irvin Painter, *Exoduster: Black Migration to Kansas, 1879–1880* (Lawrence: Regents Press of Kansas, 1978); May 25, 1879, T. Harry Williams, ed., *Hayes: The Diary of a President, 1875–1881* (New York: David McKay Co., 1964), p. 221. Painter faults Hayes for ignoring petitions and for his inaction, pp. 89, 94, 170–172, 229; Athearm is somewhat more sympathetic to Hayes, but finds no evidence of active support, pp. 145–147. For a critical view of Hayes' relations to blacks, as seen by the black community, see Bess Beatty, "A Revolution Gone Backward: The Black Response to the Hayes Administration," *Hayes Historical Journal*, 4, no. 1 (Spring 1983): 5–23.

7. Stanley Hirshson, *Farewell to the Bloody Shirt: Northern Republicans and the Southern Negro, 1877–1793* (Bloomington: Indiana University Press, 1962), pp. 49–51, sees Hayes' stance as an about-face, while William Gillette, *Retreat from Reconstruction*, (Baton Rouge: Louisiana State University Press, 1979), pp. 354, 362, characterizes it as the dissolution of his grand design into no policy at all.

8. Paul Kleppner, *The Third Electoral System, 1853–1892* (Chapel Hill: University of North Carolina Press, 1979), pp. 20–26, argues that a major shift in party power took place prior to 1876, from Republicans back to Democrats, which leads to the conclusion that Hayes' political problems antedated his administration and the initiation of his southern policy.

9. Kenneth E. Davison, *The Presidency of Rutherford B. Hayes* (Westport, Conn.: Greenwood Press, 1972), pp. 145–154; Harry Barnard, *Rutherford B. Hayes and His America* (Indianapolis: Bobbs-Merrill Co., 1954), pp. 445–447. Hayes made notes on his daily cabinet meetings during the crisis, July 24–28, 31, 1877, Hayes Papers. For a critical view of Hayes' handling of the strikes, see William M. Goldsmith, *The Growth*

of Presidential Power: A Documented History, vols. (New York: Chelsea House, 1974), 2:1139–1143.

10. David P. Thelen has an enlightened view of Hayes as a representative transitional reform figure in his "Rutherford B. Hayes and the Reform Tradition in the Gilded Age," *American Quarterly,* 22, no. 2, pt. 1 (Summer 1970): 150–165.

BIBLIOGRAPHIC ESSAY

Charles R. Williams has written a laudatory biography and edited the Hayes diary: *The Life of Rutherford B. Hayes,* 2 vols. (Columbus: Ohio State Genealogical and Historical Society, 1914), and *The Diary and Letters of Rutherford B. Hayes,* 5 vols. (Columbus: Ohio State Genealogical and Historical Society, 1922–1926).

Harry Barnard updated Hayes with a biographical treatment which is now updated: *Rutherford B. Hayes and His America* (Indianapolis: Bobbs-Merrill Co., 1954).

T. Harry Williams edited the presidential eras of the Hayes diary, *Hayes: The Diary of a President, 1875–1881* (New York: David McKay Co., 1964), and wrote a study of Hayes' war service, *Hayes of the Twenty-Third* (New York: Alfred A. Knopf, 1965).

Kenneth E. Davison has written the most recent study of the Hayes presidency: *The Presidency of Rutherford B. Hayes* (Westport, Conn.: Greenwood Press, 1972).

Keith Ian Polakoff, *The Politics of Inertia: The Election of 1876 and the End of Reconstruction* (Baton Rouge: Louisiana State University Press, 1973), focuses on a critical year.

Paul Kleppner's quantitative and interpretive methodology offers a different perspective on what he calls the electoral universe in *The Third Electoral System, 1853–1892* (Chapel Hill: University of North Carolina Press, 1979).

William McFeeley's *Grant: A Biography* (New York: W. W. Norton and Co., 1981) sees Hayes from the Grant perspective.

William Gillette, *Retreat from Reconstruction* (Baton Rouge: Louisiana State University Press, 1979), faults Hayes as a politician and a statesman.

C. Vann Woodward's interpretation of the "compromise" that elevated Hayes to the presidency was first published in *Reunion and Reaction: The Compromise of 1877 and the End of Reconstruction* (Boston: Little, Brown, 1951).

Ari Hoogenboom has published the definitive work on the civil service movement, *Outlaw the Spoils: A History of the Civil Service Reform Movement* (Urbana: University of Illinois Press, 1961).

Hans L. Trefousse, *Carl Schurz: A Biography* (Knoxville: University of Tennessee Press, 1982), is the most recent treatment of Schurz.

Robert T. Patterson, *Federal Debt-Management Policy, 1865–1879* (Durham: Duke University Press, 1954), is a straightforward account.

Two overviews that have stood up well over time are H. Wayne Morgan, *From Hayes to McKinley: National Party Politics, 1877–1896* (Syracuse: Syracuse University Press, 1969), and Vincent P. De Santis, *Republicans Face the Southern Question: The New Departure Years, 1877–1897* (Baltimore: Johns Hopkins Press, 1959).

6 GROVER CLEVELAND

Vincent P. De Santis

Grover Cleveland is still generally considered by American historians to be one of America's greatest presidents and the country's ablest and most important president between Lincoln and Theodore Roosevelt. Not all historians and not all of Cleveland's contemporaries would, of course, agree with this assessment of his presidency and his standing among the presidents.

Some might agree with Richard Hofstadter that Cleveland was only a "reasonable facsimile of a major president between Lincoln and Theodore Roosevelt," even though "he was the flower of American political culture in the Gilded Age."[1] Others might concur with Thomas Bailey that Cleveland, "by most meaningful tests . . . was not an outstanding President." And if he was the ablest president between Lincoln and Theodore Roosevelt, "the others might have been an indifferent lot indeed." And still others might acquiesce in the view of Rexford G. Tugwell's study of the presidency that Cleveland was a "third sort" of president and with Leonard D. White's analysis of post–Civil War administrative history that Cleveland did not "bespeak executive leadership of Congress."[2]

Cleveland was not highly regarded by two of his most prominent contemporaries, James Bryce and Henry Adams, whose observations of the Gilded Age have influenced nearly everyone who has written about this period in American history. Bryce, writing in Cleveland's day, remarked that there had not been a single presidential candidate since Lincoln's reelection in 1864, except Grant, "of whom his friends could say that he had done anything to command the gratitude of the nation." And "since the heroes of the Revolution died out . . . no President except Abraham Lincoln had displayed rare and striking qualities in the chair." Henry Adams, writing some years after Cleveland had left office, and searching "the whole list of Congress, Judiciary, and Executive during the twenty-five years from 1870 to 1895," found "little but damaged reputation. The period was poor in purpose and barren in results."[3]

Among Cleveland's other contemporaries there were, of course, varying opinions about him, as a small and random sampling shows: James Russell Lowell, one of America's leading poets and essayists at the time, called Cleveland the most typical American since Lincoln. Richard Olney, who had been Cleveland's attorney general and secretary of state, regarded Cleveland "as the very model of an American constitutional President," whose paramount consideration was "the good of the whole country" and who "resolutely sacrificed party interests in favor of those of the country at large." Though Cleveland did not court popularity and was not popular in the ordinary sense, "the people appreciated him," wrote Olney, "felt him to be one of themselves, considered his character and achievements to reflect honor upon themselves, and retained their respect and regard for him even when they differed from him."[4]

Among some of Cleveland's prominent Republican contemporaries, there were also different views about his presidency. According to George F. Hoar, a well-known Republican senator from Massachusetts, "The two Administrations of Cleveland are remembered by the businessmen and the laboring men of the country only as terrible nightmares." Orville H. Platt, an influential Republican senator from Connecticut, agreed, telling a Hartford clergyman in the 1890s that Cleveland was "so utterly wrong on most questions that I can scarcely think of a greater calamity than his re-election." But Rutherford B. Hayes, who had been president himself in the 1870s and who had some knowledge of and experience in the office, thought Cleveland did "extremely well." "I no doubt liked him better than the majority of those who elected him," Hayes confided to his diary. "He is sound on the currency, the tariff, and the reform of the civil service."[5]

Historians more so than Cleveland's contemporaries have been responsible for placing his presidency as the ablest and most important one in the post–Civil War generation. According to the widely used American history textbook by Samuel Eliot Morison, Henry Steele Commager, and William E. Leuchtenberg, "He alone of the titular leaders of either party [of the Gilded Age] had sufficient courage to defy the groups that were using the government for selfish purposes and to risk his career in defense of what he thought was right." Allan Nevins, who has made the most exhaustive study of Cleveland, albeit a favorable one, associates four achievements with his name. He restored honesty and impartiality to government; he planted deep in the American mind the idea that the evils of the protective tariff system ought to be abolished; he saved the nation from the abandonment of the gold standard at a time when abandonment might have produced economic chaos; and he taught the American people that in their handling of foreign affairs, conscience should always be the one dominant force. Morison, Commager, and Leuchtenberg see Cleveland's achievements in a slightly different way and point out that he "advanced civil service reform, challenged the predatory interests that were taking up the public lands of the nation, denounced the evils of protection and dramatized the tariff issue, and called a halt to the raid on the United States Treasury by war veterans and their lobbyists."[6]

Yet Cleveland's reputation in the presidency commonly rests, not so much upon his accomplishments or brilliance, as upon his character. "It is as a strong man, a man of character, that Cleveland will live in history," writes Nevins. "It was his personality, not his mind that made so deep an impress upon his time." And according to Richard Hofstadter, Cleveland stood out "if only for honesty and independence."[7] Thus historians have praised Cleveland for his courage, firmness, uprightness, sense of duty, and common sense. They have described him as having a steely stubbornness, or being ruggedly independent, as standing like an oak for his principles, as having the courage to scorn popularity, as rising above the needs of the party and keeping unerringly in view the needs of the country, as not being able to be bought or bullied, and as being the prototype of jut-jawed firmness. General Edward S. Bragg, in seconding the nomination of Cleveland for president in 1884, told the delegates, "They loved Cleveland for his character," and he was called "ugly-honest," that is, truculently honest. As he told one Democratic politician seeking handouts for his followers, "Well, do you want me to appoint another horse thief for you?"[8]

ARRIVED AS A REFORMER

So the portrait of Cleveland as a fearless and heroic figure hewing to the line developed. He came to the White House in 1885 with the reputation of a reformer, a man of courage and integrity, and with prodigious work habits. Actually, he was unimaginative, stubborn, brutally forthright, and candid. He was also a thoroughgoing conservative, a believer in sound money, and a defender of property rights. In his inaugural address he promised to adhere to "business principles," and his cabinet included conservatives and business-minded Democrats. His administration indicated no significant break with his Republican predecessors on fundamental issues. Yet he appealed to Americans because he seemed to be a plain man of the people and because he consistently appeared to do what he believed to be right. The public admired him for what was called his "you be damnedness," and it loved him for the enemies he had made. William Allen White described Cleveland in the following manner:

He was plain-spoken. If he thought a proposition was a steal, he said so, and he used short words. A robber . . . a thief . . . a sneak . . . a liar, and a cheat were no perfunctory titles in the bright lexicon of Cleveland's veto messages. Naturally the people were pleased. . . . What the people desired just then with a furious passion was a vigorous, uncompromising man . . . who would save the State from its statesmen. The time crying out for an obstructionist to stem corruption found young Grover Cleveland.[9]

"The office of President," Alexander Hamilton predicted in 1788, "will never fall to the lot of any man who is not in an eminent degree endowed with the requisite qualifications. . . . It will not be too strong to say, that there will be a constant probability of seeing the station filled by characters preeminent for ability and virtue."[10] While probably none of America's presidents can be described as evil or as a demagogue, most of them have not possessed the qualifications or stature portended by Hamilton. To the contrary, a number of critics of the American system of politics and government contend that it does not produce the ablest persons for the presidency. Bryce, a leading and influential observer of our system during the Gilded Age, at a time when Cleveland was president, concluded, "Great men are not chosen Presidents . . . because great men are rare in politics . . . because the method of choice does not bring them to the top . . . [and] because they are not, in quiet times, absolutely needed." And Bryce further concluded that the presidents of the Gilded Age, including Cleveland, "are not like the early presidents, the first men of the country."[11]

The most meaningful way to judge a president is on the basis of what he did as president—his achievements or his lack of achievements in the White House—and not on his popular standing, or on what he said he hoped to do, and not on what he said or did before becoming or after leaving as president. Despite the obvious usefulness of this means of assessing a president, presidents have been measured in a variety of ways and with changing values, and this has led to an assortment of conclusions about them. For example, on the basis of public popularity, for deciding America's greatest presidents, Eisenhower would rate higher than Lincoln. And if courage, devotion, and hard work were the only criteria, John Quincy Adams would be among the very top. In March 1980 a New York Times–CBS poll reported that more Republicans would elect Eisenhower president, if they could, than anyone else who has held the office, and Americans at large would elect John F. Kennedy president over anyone else who has held the office.[12]

Despite what some important contemporaries and scholars thought of Cleveland, he is considered to be one of our greatest presidents. In two polls on presidential greatness conducted by Arthur M. Schlesinger in 1948 and 1962, Cleveland was rated one of America's greatest presidents. It was the consensus of historians, political scientists, and others asked by Schlesinger that there have been eleven great presidents (ten in the 1948 poll)—five great in the order of Lincoln, Washington, FDR, Wilson, and Jefferson, and six near great in the order of Jackson, Theodore Roosevelt, Polk and Truman tied, John Adams, and Cleveland.

Cleveland was placed in the near great category on both polls, being number eight on the first and ahead of Adams and Polk and number eleven on the second. Why he dropped three notches in the interval is not clear, but Thomas Bailey suggests "that by 1962, the bloom had worn off" of Allan Nevins' admiring biography (1933) of Cleveland and that "perhaps the 19th Century rugged individualism of stubborn old Grover did not fit into the hope-freighted atmosphere of Kennedy's New Frontier."[13] Cleveland achieved his greatness in these polls, according to Schlesinger, because of his stubborn championship of tariff reform and of honesty and efficiency in the civil service.

In an extension of the Schlesinger polls, a University of Kansas sociologist polled in a random way the membership of the Organization of American Historians on an evaluation of presidents and published his findings in 1970. Overall,

Cleveland did well, being rated between twelfth and fourteenth among presidents in general prestige, strength of action, activeness, idealism, and accomplishments. Only on the matter of flexibility did Cleveland receive a low rating—twenty-seventh among the presidents.[14] But this only served to strengthen the belief about one of the great sides of his character—his unyielding determination.

Cleveland generally has remained attractive to historians. In a sampling of recent editions of some of the leading college textbooks in American history, Cleveland continues to be portrayed as (1) the ablest president between Lincoln and Theodore Roosevelt and possessing character, courage, and integrity; (2) the only outstanding president of the post–Civil War generation of chief executives; (3) a president who used his powers forthrightly and who worked fully within the Democratic tradition of the strong presidency; and (4) a president who exercised more vigorous leadership than his Republican predecessors.[15]

But other historians have reached a different conclusion about Cleveland. They maintain that he failed to give leadership to Congress and failed to provide effective leadership for the country. They contend that he had too little imagination and too narrow a conception of his powers and duties to be a successful president, that he did not understand the problems of the farmers and the workers, that he had no broad comprehension of the political and economic forces then convulsing the country. They also maintain that he was not a skillful political leader and that his presidency is associated with little significant legislation.[16]

Despite these mixed feelings about Cleveland, there has been no move to cashier him from the list of America's greatest presidents. But a poll of American historians in 1977 by the United States Historical Society did drop him another notch, to twelfth place, just below Lyndon B. Johnson, who had the number eleven position, just outside the charmed circle of our ten greatest presidents.[17] Historians probably need one great president between Lincoln and Theodore Roosevelt, and Cleveland, despite his shortcomings, continues to fill that niche and to be thought of as the flower of American political culture in the Gilded Age, as Hofstadter put it.

The main problem for any president in the Gilded Age, and thus for Cleveland too, was that it was a period in American history when politics and politicians were under heavy censure by thoughtful Americans. Seldom has any period in American history been kicked and scuffed as much as the Gilded Age. And this particularly applied to politics, which then seemed to lack the vitality and productivity of earlier decades. Most thoughtful observers believed that at no other time in American history was the moral and intellectual tone of political life so uniformly low or political contests so preoccupied with patronage.

Two contemporaries of these years, Henry Adams and James Bryce, were largely responsible for the harsh assessment of Gilded Age politics, and their emphasis on its dreariness and emptiness has had much influence on subsequent studies of the era. "No period so thoroughly ordinary has been known in American politics since Christopher Columbus first disturbed the balance of power in American society," observed Adams. "Even among the most powerful men of that generation," continued Adams, speaking of the politicians, there was "none who has a good word for it." Bryce believed that the two major parties in these years were in danger of losing their functional usefulness, because they failed to offer the electorate an opportunity to vote on issues and because they used public office to reward party workers. "Neither party has any principles, and distinctive tenets," charged Bryce. "They were like two bottles. Each bore a label denoting the kind of liquor it contained, but each was empty."[18]

Cleveland was president also during a period when the presidency was at a low ebb in power and prestige, and when national political power was largely vested in Congress. Congressional leaders had nearly overthrown Andrew Johnson, gained almost complete control of Grant, and tried to put their successors in the Gilded Age at their mercy. In these years, the Whig theory of the presidency, which held that the president must confine himself to the execution of laws enacted by an omniscient Congress, Senator John Sherman, Republican leader of Ohio and a longtime aspirant to the White House, expressed this view when he wrote: "The executive department of a republic like ours should [be] subordinate to the legislative department. The President should obey and enforce the laws, leaving to the people the duty of correcting any errors committed by their representatives in Congress." Congressional leaders acted on these principles. "The most eminent Senators," wrote George F. Hoar of Massachusetts about his colleagues in the Senate, "would have received as a personal affront a private message from the White House expressing a desire that they should adopt any course in the discharge of their legislative duties that they did not approve. If they visited the White House, it was to give, not receive advice." Henry Adams agreed, noting, "So far as the President's initiative was concerned, the President and his Cabinet might equally have departed separately or together to distant lands."[19]

PASSIVE LEADERSHIP PATTERN

Thus presidents in the Gilded Age largely held to the Whig view about the presidency. Congress would pass the laws, and they would administer them. They did not believe that they had to provide vigorous executive leadership such as we look for in our presidents today. Nor did the country expect this kind of leadership from them. The federal government in the post–Civil War generation seldom concerned itself with economic and social matters as it does now, and the predominant feeling among Americans was that it should let well enough alone.

Since Gilded Age presidents were largely passive chief executives, we do not link them with many solid and concrete achievements. In fact, another perceptive and influential observer of the Gilded Age, Moisei Ostrogorski, commented on "the shrinkage undergone by the presidential office" in these years. He noted that the president had become merely a party leader, and that mainly in name. "He was not at liberty to assert his initiative, to give the party a policy, to form comprehensive designs and far-reaching plans.'' According to John A. Garraty, who has written one of the standard books on the Gilded Age, so ineffective were the presidents in these years that many observers, forgetting the greatness of past presidents, began to think of the office as only a ceremonial one, if not a sinecure. Woodrow Wilson, contemporary observer of the American political scene and later a president himself, wrote that since ''the business of the President . . . is usually not much above routine,'' the office might ''not inconveniently'' be made entirely administrative, the occupant a kind of tenured civil servant.[20]

Though Cleveland was a Democrat, he shared the Whig-Republican view of the extent of federal power and the role of the president in domestic matters. These did not extend to the maintenance of prosperity or to the increase of well-being, and they did not include the responsibility for avoiding or ameliorating conditions that precipitated social and labor disturbances in the 1890s. Because he firmly opposed what he called paternalism, Cleveland was not too sympathetic with the problems and protests of the nation's farmers and workers when the country was afflicted during his second term with the most severe depression it had yet seen. Cleveland was, in fact, an incredibly simple man to have been president toward the end of the nineteenth century, concludes Tugwell, who says that ''he was as innocent as a child of the large thoughts in the world,'' and ''he probably had never considered, either, the role of government in an industrialized society.''[21]

The key to Cleveland's presidency was his dislike of paternalism in government. He strongly opposed the idea of the government giving aid to anyone in distress, and his political philosophy in this respect is best illustrated in his veto of the Texas seed bill early in 1887. Certain Texas countries suffering from a drought were in pressing need of grain. In response to the pleas of a number of sufferers, Congress passed a bill appropriating $10,000 to enable the commissioner of agriculture to distribute seed. The amount was trivial, but the measure sharply challenged Cleveland's belief. He had just vetoed the Dependent pensions bill, and he regarded the Texas seed bill in the same light. He returned the measure unsigned with a strong protest, because he believed that it was wrong ''to indulge a benevolent and charitable sentiment through the appropriation of public funds for that purpose.'' He went on to say that he could ''find no warrant for such an appropriation in the Constitution, and I do not believe that the power and duty of the General Government ought to be extended to the relief of individual suffering which is in no manner properly related to the public service or benefit.'' Then he added, significantly:

A prevalent tendency to disregard the limited mission of this power and duty should, I think, be steadfastly resisted, to the end that the lesson should be constantly enforced that though the people should support the Government, the Government should not support the people.

In other phrases of this memorable veto which have been quoted again and again in behalf of the same philosophy, Cleveland reminded Americans that

"Federal aid in such cases encourages the expectation of paternal care on the part of the Government and weakens the sturdiness of our national character." In his second inaugural address in 1893, Cleveland returned to this theme when he dwelt at length on the "unwholesome progeny of paternalism," and when he complacently added, "The lessons of paternalism ought to be unlearned and the better lesson taught that while people should patriotically and cheerfully support their Government, its functions do not include the support of the people."[22]

In Cleveland's opinion, Americans were entitled to economy, purity, and justice in their government and nothing more. There was to be a fair field for all and favors for none. One of Cleveland's conceptions of his role as president was that of a righteous watchdog whose business it was to look after other politicians and to prevent them from giving and taking favors. Thus he opposed tariff favors to business, pension favors to veterans, and land favors to railroads. Cleveland's two terms of obstruction mark his place in history as a largely negative president who believed that it was his duty to prevent bad things from occurring, and not to make good things happen.

But not all effective leadership is of a positive nature, contends Bailey about presidential greatness, even though the constructive leader is generally praised more than the obstructive one. Bailey commends Cleveland for his stiff-necked determination not to be stampeded by Congress into a clash with Spain over atrocities in Cuba. When a bellicose congressman reminded him that the Constitution authorized Congress to declare war, Cleveland rejoined, "Yes, but it also makes me Commander-in-Chief, and I will not mobilize the army." "Sheer negativism," adds Bailey, "or the ability to put one's foot down when it ought to be put down is often commendable in a leader."[23]

Cleveland's shining hour, argues Louis W. Koenig, occurred "in the assertion of principle . . . against the test of events." Horace Samuel Merrill thinks that "Cleveland was much more successful as a defender of the status quo than as a crusader for peace," and Tugwell is of the opinion that Cleveland "was not a leader; he was a caretaker."[24] Then, of course, there is Nevins, who relates that Cleveland, "under the heaviest attacks, and wildest abuse, with few to aid or defend him, still smote the desk with his fist and cried 'Never, never.' " To have bequeathed a nation "such an example of iron fortitude," continues Nevins, "is better than to have swayed parliaments or to have won battles or to have annexed provinces." In fact, says Nevins, Cleveland's greatest service to the country was to leave to subsequent generations an example of "courage that never yields an inch in the cause of truth and that never surrenders an iota of principle to expediency."[25] This view of Cleveland has not substantially changed. For, as Morison, Commager, and Leuchtenberg conclude about Cleveland, "If the total achievements of his administration were negative, even that was something of a virtue at a time when too many politicians were saying 'yes' to the wrong things."[26]

"THIRD KIND OF PRESIDENT"

Cleveland's conception of the presidency was a mixed or a combined one—firmly believing in the doctrine of the separation of powers, yet holding to the idea of a strong executive in which he had the duty to exercise all of his powers to protect the interests of the federal government. This is why he is sometimes called "A Third Kind of President"—one moving between the strong concept exemplified by Lincoln and the weak concept represented by Buchanan. The Cleveland presidency shuttled between these two views, although the distinctive trait in the Cleveland presidency was that its essential function lay in defensive directions. It lay in veto, in disengagement, in the negation of what others had put in motion, or in the use of only enough executive energy to maintain an existing equilibrium.[27]

Cleveland's belief in a hands-off attitude on his part toward legislation was in line with the prevalent view in the Gilded Age that the president should not attempt to shape legislation or to meddle in the affairs of Congress. He did not begin to influence the form of legislation until about halfway through his first term, and he did little to follow through on legislation. In his second term he leaned more toward the view that the president should help push laws through, and his efforts in behalf of the repeal of the Sherman Silver Purchase Act in 1893 indicated this change. But Cleveland's leadership in this instance was in behalf of negative rather than positive action. And he continued to hold the view that the president should work independently of the legislative branch if this could be done.

At times, Cleveland's different views about the presidency clashed and were tested under provocation when he acted more like a strong president than a weak one. He faced no crisis of the magnitude that confronted Jackson, Buchanan, and Lincoln, but on two occasions, the Pullman strike and the Venezuelan boundary dispute, he was not reluctant to expand the powers of the presidency. As Lincoln was called on to preserve the Union, says Tugwell, "Cleveland was asked to preserve order and to ensure the national influence in the Western Hemisphere."[28] Perhaps Cleveland's views of the presidency were also tested but found wanting in the problems created by the new industrialized society in America, especially during the depression of his second term.

In his first inaugural address Cleveland stressed such words as "responsibility," "conscience," and "duty," and these became important aspects of the tone and style of his presidency. This was clearly demonstrated by the long hours and hard work he put in, such as working until two or three in the morning, personally taking care of his own correspondence, and by answering many White House telephone calls in person. It was also shown by his meticulous attention to detail, such as his scrutiny and veto of private pension bills for Civil War veterans and by his compulsion to do just about everything himself, including minor tasks that a mere clerk could have handled. He was probably the hardest worked man in Washington in his day, and his attention to details was often considered more a fault than a virtue. Samuel Tilden observed that "he would rather do something badly for himself than have somebody else do it well."[29] Performing most of the tasks himself made it difficult for Cleveland to give the attention he should have given to some of the larger issues. And his critics complained that it would have been better for him to get a good night's sleep and then face the big problems the next day with a clear brain. His work habits, though, did not go unnoticed. "His is the intuitive instinct of the quick and alert observer," said the *New York Times,* "as well as the careful habit of conscientious investigator. He has great application, which is another name of will power."[30]

Honesty also pervaded Cleveland's style and tone. He worked to keep both major and minor matters honest, and William Allen White says, "It was all honest." For example, he insisted on personally paying for the hay supplied by the government in the barn set aside at the White House for the president's private use. And when Cleveland went on vacation he paid for his own expenses. In Cleveland's view, if business had to be done, it had to be done honestly. White observed that "as a statesman Cleveland will be remembered as one who every working hour of the working day did what he thought was exactly right, and who never attempted to guide the current of the public business, but always to see that the business was wisely and honestly done."[31]

An unswerving loyalty to duty also characterized Cleveland's presidency. Looking upon his office as a covenant with the people, he sincerely believed that he had a deep obligation to them as a whole. Thus loyalty to duty was first and foremost in his presidency, and duty in his mind was what was best for the people. "Cleveland has never governed his conduct by any other rule than his own perception of the right of the matter," wrote White.[32]

Cleveland's sense of duty made it nearly impossible for him to compromise. He might have had a quieter life in the White House, with fewer troubles and disappointments, had he been more inclined to compromise and had he been less scrupulous about the exactness or rightness of duty. He might have avoided and improved situations had he been more flexible and agreeable with those who opposed his views. "Probably his greatest weakness was his inability to meet men agreeably," observed a contemporary, "particularly those who differed in opinion with him. He was always suspicious of them, and was too easily moved to denounce them personally." What is now called "Cleveland Courage" "was in his day known in Washington in most instances as obstinacy."[33]

Cleveland's sense of duty created not only an atmosphere of courage and loyalty but also one of antagonism, bluntness, narrowness, negativism, and stubbornness. These limited or prevented Cleveland from exercising effective leadership to promote positive programs and to take positive action to ameliorate difficult situations. Such was Cleveland's loyalty to duty that an analysis of it in the *New York Times* appearing just two days before he left office in 1897 concluded: "It has completely estranged powerful Democrats who were able to deprive him of the support of great States and to turn against him their Members and Senators. It has provoked implacable enmities potent enough to obstruct or thwart his greatest designs and highest policies."[34] Commenting on Cleveland's sense of duty, another observer wrote, "But it was Cleveland's lot to alienate in turn every important interest, faction and party in the United States; and he did this always in obedience to his own matured conception of his duty."[35]

Cleveland's impact on the presidency was felt and evidenced in several ways. He was the first president to use the veto freely and to go beyond the sparing use of it by his predecessors. Washington had vetoed two bills only, and his successors down to 1830 had returned seven to Congress. Jackson made a bolder use of his power—twelve vetoes—that aroused intense opposition. Yet until the accession of Cleveland in 1885, the total number of bills vetoed was only 132, including pocket vetoes. Cleveland vetoed 301 bills in his first term, most of them private pension measures, but on occasion he vetoed an important matter, such as an act restricting Chinese immigration.

Cleveland's most notable impact on the presidency was his successful effort to restore the powers and initiative of the chief executive largely lost by Johnson in his fight with Congress during Reconstruction. There were some stirrings of presidential assertion between Johnson and Cleveland, and there had been some presidential victories, particularly on the part of Hayes and Garfield. But the Tenure of Office Act remained to harass presidents. Cleveland made a major contribution to the strengthening of the presidency not only by reasserting his prerogatives and refusing to relinquish them, but also by bringing to an end the Tenure of Office Act and its protracted aggression upon the presidency. In this contest with the Senate, Cleveland gained both a personal and a political victory, and the legislative branch was pushed out of disputed ground within the executive enclave. This reversal of Republican theory and practice was the most important gain for the presidency in the post–Civil War years.

Cleveland also strengthened the presidency by his action in the controversy with Britain over Venezuela. He did it by bringing into the presidential arena all the negotiations with another country and by keeping there the initiative in their conduct. He later told a friend that his "aim was at one sharp stroke to bring the whole matter into his own hands, compel England to yield to arbitration, and put Congress in a position where it could not interfere." In doing this, Tugwell argues, Cleveland "advanced the Presidency immensely by foreclosing the leadership in foreign affairs which might have escaped him if he had temporized."[36]

In addition to advancing the presidency, Cleveland exceeded its limits and introduced a new pattern of the employment of the military in civil disorder when he used the army to "restore law and order" in the Pullman strike of 1894, over the opposition of the governor of Illinois, John P. Altgeld. And since Cleveland was a lawyer it can be assumed that he was aware of his constitutional offense. Cleveland never consulted Altgeld on the necessity of federal intervention but instead took Attorney General Richard Olney's view that interference with the mails made it necessary for the President to see that the laws were faithfully executed. Some historians believe that Cleveland's decisions in the pullman strike and the Venezuelan boundary dispute were "unduly influenced" by Olney, "a tough-fisted and ultraconservative Cabinet member," and that in the Venezuelan matter, "Cleveland had allowed Olney to take him far on the road to war."[37]

Finally, it is significant to note the change in view that a future president had about the office after living through Cleveland's presidency. Woodrow Wilson in his critique of the American system in *Congressional Government* (1885), from observing the presidents from Johnson through Arthur, concluded that there was no hope in the presidency, that congressional supremacy would have to be recognized, and that that body would have to accept the responsibilities of leadership. But after observing Cleveland in action, Wilson altered his view. In approving the president's conduct, he said that it had been direct, fearless, and practical, and that it had "refreshed our notion of an American Chief Magistrate." Wilson noted that Cleveland in office had changed from being a president who had considered himself to be responsible only for administration to one who had risen to the challenge and had become what a president should be—a policy maker and a shaper of opinion. Wilson praised Cleveland as the only president between 1865 and 1898 who "played a leading and decisive part in the quiet drama of our national life."[38]

Cleveland, like Jackson, characterized his presidency as predominantly the people's office, and he was determined to be a president of the people. In an address he made in 1887 he emphasized this view: "If your President should not be of the people and one of your fellow citizens, he would be utterly unfit for the position, incapable of understanding the people's wants and careless of their desires." And Cleveland wanted his presidency to be of all the people. "The President and the President alone," he asserted, "represents the American citizen, no matter how humble or in how remote a corner of the globe."[39] Fully aware that the president was elected from all parts of the country while members of Congress were chosen from geographical areas, Cleveland was concerned about representing the people as a whole. This view influenced his handling of the Pullman strike when he said the strike was hindering the mails for the country as a whole, and it also influenced his thinking in regard to political machines and office seekers.

Some historians contend that while Cleveland was an outstanding person, he was not an outstanding president. He was too provincial and narrow-visioned, and he was not in tune with the times. Bailey, for instance, points out that "he left office at the end of his second term with the economy panic riddled, the Treasury in the red, his party disrupted, his Republican opponents triumphant, and himself formally repudiated by his Democratic following."[40]

There is some merit in this assessment. Cleveland acted more as an overseer than as an initiator or organizer. He preferred to have things come to him rather than proposing or pushing them through Congress. He made little effort to bring the political branches of the government into an effective unit. His reluctance to interfere with Congress was the despair of his friends. Congressman William L. Wilson of West Virginia, author of a tariff measure in the House with modest reductions in rates, was quite disappointed by the outcome of the Wilson-Gorman Tariff of 1894, and he confided in his diary that Cleveland was

woefully lacking in the tact of making ordinary men and especially representative public men feel a personal relationship and a personal loyalty to him by little social and conventional attentions. Always courteous, frequently kind, always frank and business-like, he did not seem to think of the power he had and possibly the duty he was under, to tie men to him by personal ties, rather than by political or business relations.

Wilson believed that Cleveland could have kept many members of Congress personally friendly "by a casual invitation to lunch, or a formal invitation to dinner, a stroll together or a carriage drive." In the opinion of Woodrow Wilson, Cleveland

thought it no part of his proper function to press his preference in any other way (than by recommendation in a message) upon the acceptance of Congress. . . . But he deemed his duty done when he had thus used the only initiative given him by the Constitution and expressly declined to use any other means of pressing his views on the party. He meant to be aloof, and to be President with a certain separateness as the Constitution seemed to suggest.[41]

Yet, for all his faults and limitations, Cleveland is still generally regarded by historians as one of the country's ablest presidents. This is because he showed a degree of independence and courage that is rare in public life and that was particularly rare in the Gilded Age. Fidelity to the law and to duty enhanced Cleveland's reputation as a president who stopped things rather than started them. He checked abuses, he restrained bad men from carrying out their schemes, he warded off impending calamity, and he stopped foreign aggrandizement in the Western Hemisphere. He will be remembered always as one who every hour of the working day did what he thought was right. And Cleveland performed his tasks so well that for his generation and later ones as well he became the embodiment of this kind of presidential action.

NOTES

1. Richard Hofstadter, *The American Political Tradition and the Men Who Made It* (New York: Vintage Books, 1959), pp. 180, 185.
2. Thomas A. Bailey, *Presidential Greatness: The Image and the Man from George Washington to the Present* (New York: Appleton-Century-Crofts, 1966), pp. 300, 302; Rexford G. Tugwell, *The Enlargement of the Presidency* (Garden City N.Y.: Doubleday and Co., 1960), pp. 248, 250; Leonard D. White, *The Republican Era, 1869–1901* (New York: Macmillan Co., 1958), p. 25.

3. James Bryce, *The American Commonwealth*, 2 vols. (New York: Macmillan and Co., 1895), 78, 2:224–225; Henry Adams, *The Education of Henry Adams* (New York: Random House, Modern Library Edition, 1931), p. 294.

4. Allan Nevins, *Grover Cleveland: A Study in Courage* (New York: Dodd, Mead and Co., 1933), p. 764, for Lowell view, and Richard Olney to John Fox, President, National Democratic Club, March 16, 1910, quoted in Henry James, *Richard Olney and His Public Service* (Boston and New York: Houghton Mifflin Co., 1923), pp. 315, 316.

5. George F. Hoar, *Autobiography of Seventy Years*, 2 vols. (New York: Charles Scribner's Sons, 1903), 1:249; Lewis A. Coolidge, An Old-Fashioned Senator: Orville H. Platt (New York: G. P. Putnam's Sons, 1910), p. 5; Hayes Diary, March 23, 1885, Charles R. Williams, ed., *Diary and Letters of Rutherford Birchard Hayes*, 5 vols. (Columbus: Ohio State Archaeological and Historical Society, 1922–1926), 4:198.

6. Samuel Eliot Morison, Henry Steele Commager, and William E. Leuchtenberg, *The Growth of the American Republic*, 7th ed. (New York: Oxford University Press, 1980), p. 162; Nevins, *Cleveland*, p. 766.

7. Nevins, *Cleveland*, p. 5; Hofstadter, *American Political Tradition*, p. 180.

8. Paul F. Boller, Jr., *Presidential Anecdotes* (New York: Oxford University Press, 1981), pp. 177, 179.

9. William Allen White, "Cleveland," *McClure's Magazine*, 18 (1901–1902): 324.

10. Quoted from Introduction by Morton Borden, ed., *America's Eleven Greatest Presidents*, 2nd ed. (Chicago: Rand McNally, 1971), p. v.

11. Bryce, *Commonwealth*, 1:84, 85.

12. Borden, *America's Eleven Greatest Presidents*, p. v; *New York Times*, March 18, 1980, p. 138.

13. Bailey, *Presidential Greatness*, p. 29.

14. Gary M. Maranell, "The Evaluation of Presidents: An Extension of the Schlesinger Polls," *Journal of American History*, 57 (June 1970): 104–113.

15. Richard N. Current, T. Harry Williams, and Frank Freidel, *American History: A Survey*, 4th ed., 2 vols. (New York: Alfred A. Knopf, 1975), 2:518; Oscar Handlin, *America: A History* (New York: Holt, Rinehart and Winston, 1968), p. 263; Robert Kelley, *The Shaping of the American Past*, 3rd ed., 2 vols. (Englewood Cliffs, N.J.: Prentice-Hall, 1982), 2:435; Mary Beth Norton et al., *A People and a Nation: A History of the United States*, 2 vols. (Boston: Houghton Mifflin Co., 1982), 2:559.

16. John M. Blum et al., *The National Experience: A History of the United States*, 5th ed. (New York: Harcourt Brace Jovanovich, 1981), p. 506; John A. Garraty, *The American Nation*, 4th ed. (New York: Harper and Row, 1979), p. 522; Morison, Commager, and Leuchtenberg, *Growth of the American Republic*, 2:161; Thomas A. Bailey and David M. Kennedy, *The American Pageant*, 6th ed., 2 vols. (Lexington, Mass.: D.C. Heath, 1979), 2:477–78; Carl N. Degler et al., *The Democratic Experience: An American History*. 5th ed. 2 vols. (Glenview, Ill.: Scott, Foresman and Co., 1981), 2:118.

17. *Christian Science Monitor*, February 2, 1977, p. 20.

18. Adams, *Education of Henry Adams*, p. 355; Bryce, *Commonwealth* (1910 ed.), 2:29.

19. Quoted in L.D. White, *The Republican Era*, pp. 21, 24, 41.

20. John A. Garraty, *The New Commonwealth, 1877–1890* (New York: Harper and Row, 1968), p. 227.

21. Tugwell, *Enlargement of the Presidency*, p. 247.

22. James D. Richardson, *A Compilation of the Messages and Papers of the Presidents* 20 vols. (Washington, D.C.: U.S. Congress, 1899–1917), 8:557; 9:390.

23. Bailey, *Presidential Greatness,* p. 224.

24. Louis W. Koenig, *The Chief Executive* (New York: Harcourt, Brace and World, 1964), p. 11; Horace Samuel Merrill, *Bourbon Leader: Grover Cleveland and the Democratic Party* (Boston: Little, Brown, 1957), p. 190; Tugwell, *Enlargement of the Presidency,* p. 250.

25. Nevins, *Cleveland,* p. 766.

26. Morison, Commager, and Leuchtenberg, *Growth of the American Republic,* 2:162.

27. Sidney Hyman, "What Is the President's True Role?" *New York Times Magazine,* September 7, 1958, pp. 17ff.

28. Tugwell, *Enlargement of the Presidency,* p. 248.

29. James Morgan, *Our Presidents* (New York: Macmillan Co., 1935), p. 221.

30. *New York Times,* July 17, 1884.

31. W.A. White, "Cleveland," pp. 325, 330; Joel Benton, "Retrospective Glimpses of Cleveland," *Forum,* 40 (1908): 193.

32. W.A. White, "Cleveland," p. 325.

33. Henry L. Stoddard, *As I Knew Them: Presidents and Politics from Grant to Coolidge* (New York: Harper and Brothers, 1927), p. 152.

34. *New York Times,* March 2, 1897.

35. Harry Thurston Peck, "Grover Cleveland—Some Comment and Conclusions," *Forum,* 40 (1908): 187.

36. Tugwell, *Enlargement of the Presidency,* p. 476.

37. Bailey, *Presidential Greatness,* pp. 41, 42; Tugwell, *Enlargement of the Presidency,* p. 476.

38. Tugwell, *Enlargement of the Presidency,* p. 313; Marcus Cunliffe, *American Presidents and the Presidency* (London: Eyre and Spottiswoode, 1969), p. 185.

39. Robert McElroy, *Grover Cleveland: The Man and the Statesman,* 2 vols. (New York: Harper and Brothers, 1923), 2:100.

40. Bailey, *Presidential Greatness,* p. 300.

41. Vincent P. De Santis, "Grover Cleveland," in Borden, *America's Eleven Greatest Presidents,* pp. 166–167.

ANNOTATED BIBLIOGRAPHY

Cleveland, Grover. *Presidential Problems.* New York: Century, 1904.
Cleveland's own views on some events of his presidency.

Ford, Henry J. *The Cleveland Era.* New Haven: Yale University Press, 1919.
Remains a perceptive study of Cleveland and of Gilded Age Politics.

Hillingsworth, Joseph R. *The Whirligig of Politics: The Democracy of Cleveland and Bryan.* Chicago: University of Chicago Press, 1963.
A more critical study of Cleveland than the Nevins biography.

Hirsch, Mark C. *William C. Whitney: Modern Warwick.* New York: Dodd, Mead, and Co., 1948.
An important biography of one of Cleveland's close associates during the years in Washington.

Kelley, Robert L. *The Transatlantic Persuasion: The Liberal Democratic Mind in the Age of Gladstone.* New York: Knopf, 1969.

An excellent comparative study of liberal democratic thought in the period of Gladstone and Cleveland.

McElroy, Robert M. *Grover Cleveland: The Man and the Statesman*. 2 vols. New York: Harper, 1923.

Though old, still a useful account.

Merrill, Horace S. *Bourbon Leader: Grover Cleveland and the Democratic Party*. Boston: Little, Brown, 1957.

Another more critical study.

Nevins, Allan. *Grover Cleveland: A Study in Courage*. New York: Dodd, Mead and Co., 1932.

A Pulitzer Prize biography; the most important study, although a favorable one of Cleveland.

————, ed. *Letters of Grover Cleveland, 1850–1908*. Boston: Houghton Mifflin, 1933.

Published manuscript material on Cleveland.

Parker, George F. *The Writings and Speeches of Grover Cleveland*. New York: Cassell, 1892.

Published manuscript material on Cleveland.

7 WILLIAM McKINLEY

John S. Latcham

INTRODUCTION

The twenty fifth president, at the time of his assassination in 1901, was popular and influential. William McKinley had assumed office in 1897 after a colorful campaign; he then presided over the end of a disastrous economic depression. His domestic program reversed the balance of power away from congressional domination toward the executive for the first time since Lincoln's presidency. His first term coincided with a beginning of unparalleled industrial growth and consumer prosperity.

In 1898 McKinley *personally* directed the army and navy through the rapidly victorious Spanish-American War. The Cuban people were freed from a brutal tyranny; but also, the United States came onto the world stage for the first time. Governing new foreign territories, thrusting the country into the Chinese Boxer Rebellion, McKinley became the militaristic model for a latter-day "imperial presidency." The only two-consecutive-term president from Grant to Wilson, McKinley (aided by his controversial friend and manager, Mark Hanna) formed a national electoral coalition that kept the Republicans as the majority party for three decades. Finally, at the zenith of his long political career, President McKinley was wounded by an anarchist's bullet and endured a painful death. Like the revered Lincoln's, his assassination cut short a promising second term.

Historians, however, initially did little to sustain this enviable record. Curiously, the dead McKinley received far less esteem than the living McKinley had enjoyed. Richard Bradford finds that the former president's image suffered badly from "a generation of progressive writers like Harry Thurston Peck, William Allen White, Matthew Josephson, and Charles Beard," who portrayed McKinley as a feckless leader, a pliable tool of big business, and allegedly a puppet of the wealthy unscrupulous "Boss," Mark Hanna. Contributing to McKinley's popular decline was the inevitable comparison between his calm, dignified leadership and Theodore Roosevelt's flamboyant presidency.

Lincoln's fabled climb in popularity with the general public and among historians began almost immediately after 1865. Today, Lincoln indisputably stands preeminent. By contrast, the approbation once given President McKinley's name went into a long decline. In recent decades, though, McKinley's image has gained new respectability. In 1962, in the second Schlesinger poll, the positive effects of Margaret Leech's Pulitzer Prize-winning biography, *In the Days of McKinley* (1959), were felt among scholars. Then H. Wayne Morgan in a thorough, cautiously upbeat study, *William McKinley and His America* (1963), guaranteed that McKinley's leadership could no longer be ignored or deemed inconsequential. Muckrakers' most negative images were dispelled by Leech and Morgan; particularly clarified was the erroneously perceived unwholesome mastery which Hanna supposedly had over the McKinley administration. Lewis L. Gould's perceptive new study, *The Presidency of William McKinley* (1980), argues soundly that McKinley was the first "modern" incumbent. Gould pointed to fresh data to argue that McKinley initiated numerous presidential prerogatives. These three authors' cumulative revision is reflected in perceptions of forty-nine leading historians and political scholars in the 1982 *Chicago Tribune* poll.

Table 7.1 nicely summarizes these revisions in the McKinley image among noted scholars. In 1948 he ranked only eighteenth out of twenty-nine presidents.

McKINLEY'S ACTIVE-POSITIVE CHARACTER

The most serious misconception about McKinley's personal image is that he was a "passive" leader. Undoubtedly, he was a very private individual, which seems contradictory for one who spent all of his adult life in the public limelight. He had very few intimate friends. Mark Hanna, who most likely came to know him better than any man, always preserved an air of formality in their personal relations. "My dear William," Hanna would write; McKinley's reply would begin, "My dear Hanna." McKinley's genuine character appears more inscrutable than that of his contemporaries; unlike TR, he wrote few letters and kept no diary.

Despite first impressions, McKinley had what political scientist James David Barber has termed an "active-positive" character. He had the type of personality thought safe to hold great power: aggressive enough to achieve much and generally affable. To have been the successful president that Leech, Morgan, and Gould claim he was, McKinley could only have had an active-positive character. Such leaders are viewed as hardworking, creative, and ambitious. They strive for the general welfare first, and fulfillment of their own power drives second. Character, as Barber defines it, is a product mainly of childhood. In his formative years, McKinley adopted a strategy of self-assertion to compete successfully in a large, pleasant enough family setting with two loving, strong-willed parents.[1]

Born in the frontier northeastern Ohio hamlet of Niles in 1843, McKinley was remembered as an energetic, assertive youth. Tempering this natural, competitive bent was a second strategy of compliance with authority, often misinterpreted as his dominant character trait.

Table 7.1
McKinley's Image of "Greatness" Compared: Closing the Gap of Scholarly Perceptions

	Schlesinger Polls' Rank and Categorization[a]			Chicago Tribune Poll[b]
	1948	1962	Category	1982
Respondents' N =	(55)	(75)	--------	(49)
McKinley	18	15	"Average"	10
Lincoln	1	1	"Great"	1
T. Roosevelt	7	7	"Near Great"	4
Presidents' N =	(29)	(31)		(39)

[a] Arthur M. Schlesinger, Sr., "The U.S. Presidents," *Life* (November 1, 1948), pp. 65ff.; and "Our Presidents: A Rating by 75 Historians," *New York Times Magazine* (July 29, 1962), pp.12ff. Two other less prestigious categories in Schlesinger's polls are "below average" and "failure."

[b] Steve Neal, "Our Best and Worst Presidents," *Chicago Tribune Magazine* (January 10, 1982), pp. 10ff.

All his life McKinley succeeded through an intuitive knowledge of when to shove and when to step back from confrontation. As an adolescent he had healthy self-esteem. Most evidence depicts him as affectionate—easy to love, easily reciprocating love as a child.

The young man's psychodynamics included a world view and the foundations for a political style highly compatible with the active-positive type. Aside from this good humor, McKinley early on developed a serious, though not depressing, perspective on humanity. From infancy, he had been nurtured in the Methodist faith. Christianity gave him an unflagging intolerance for human frailties and a strong moral code. He maintained a demeanor of personal integrity rarely found in public men in any era.

His ironmaster father, William, Sr., typified the self-made man of Horatio Algerism and helped shape the boy's laissez-faire world view. His father helped him learn of the "Tariff Question," an issue that involved government directly helping business prosper.

From his mother, William learned virtue. An active churchwoman, "Mother

McKinley,'' as the townsfolk called her, instilled powerful moral concerns in her seven children. She always wanted William to be a preacher. Even at his inauguration in 1897, Mother McKinley (at age eighty-seven!) told reporters that being president was not all that much compared to being a minister.

Neither parent had a formal education, but classical books and quality newspapers were on the parlor shelves along with the Bible. Schooling was highly valued and homework overseen. Both William, Sr., and Nancy Allison were devout abolitionists. As president, McKinley reflected this compassion for non-whites in Cuba, the Philippines, Puerto Rico, and China.

He learned his political style in early adulthood, displaying balanced, flexible behavior. His first practical experiences in ''politics'' were in the Union army during the Civil War. He moved from volunteer private to major by the war's end. (The title ''Major'' stayed with him all his life.) McKinley never irrationally pursued, as some negative psychological types do, a self-destructive, stubborn, one-sided political style.

Most of his adult years were spent on the stump, campaigning for himself or other Republicans. He never acquired the oratorical talent of a William Jennings Bryan; but, even speaking on the dullest of topics (like tariff schedules), the Major had an amazing capacity to captivate an audience with his logic, wit, and charm. McKinley did his political homework and was seldom embarrassed by lacking facts. He was a keen student of men. McKinley always knew who his real friends were and saw that they were honestly rewarded. He could also keep an enemy at bay without alienating him. Behind the smile and piercing gray eyes were a steel-trap will and expert political wisdom.

After four years in the army, McKinley took a brief law course in Albany. Then he settled in Canton, Ohio, and soon earned a reputation as an able attorney before running successfully for county prosecutor. In 1871 he married Ida Saxton, whose father was a banker. At first, the couple was happy; two daughters brought immense joy. Then tragedy struck. In 1873 the youngest girl died; in 1875 the older child, Katie, also died. The losses were so grievous to Ida's psyche that she suffered irreparable ''brain damage.'' Still in her twenties, she became a hopelessly chronic invalid for life. Her phlebitis scarcely allowed her to stand, let alone walk. Worse, she became an epileptic and was a victim of petit and grand mal attacks. The full extent of Ida's physical and mental disabilities has never been accurately treated by McKinley's biographers. It appears to have been far worse for her and for the Major than scholars have yet disclosed.

CONGRESSMAN McKINLEY: "THE NAPOLEON OF PROTECTION"

Quite soon after Ida's collapse, in 1876, he first ran for Congress. Indeed, many have speculated that he delved into national politics as therapy for his domestic worries. Skillfully using his affable personality, campaigning tirelessly, McKinley won an upset victory as a Republican in a Democratic working-class district. He was perceived as "a friend of labor" after having defended strikers in a famous trial. Elected seven times in all from his Canton district, McKinley served (with a brief interruption in 1884) until 1890, when he was narrowly defeated after a Democratic legislature gerrymandered the district.

The congressman specialized on tariff matters which, before he left the House, would give him a national image and make his name a household word. McKinley was long known as the leading protectionist on the Hill because of his detailed knowledge of tariff schedules and his support for high rates. He belonged to that wing of the Republican party which had inherited the old Whig doctrine of positive state; new Whigs felt, in Clinton Rossiter's view, that "tariffs, land grants, subsidies, lenient patent laws, hard currency laws, and other measures to business enterprises were promotions for the general welfare, . . . not special privileges."

He deliberately and eagerly chose to master the tariff with all its manifest publicity. Rightly or wrongly, from a modern economic point of view, protection was then widely viewed as the prime cause of a healthy post–Civil War economy. So intensely did the Major gauge public opinion that Congressman Joseph Cannon of Illinois, in an oft-quoted quip, charged that McKinley kept his head so close to the ground testing the tariff vibrations that his ear was full of grasshoppers.

Protection was an emotional, patriotic issue for McKinley and his brand of Republicanism, also an outgrowth of Whig ideology—a powerful nationalism. To many citizens, to be a Republican meant to be an ardent protectionist. It was a short intellectual leap from the tariff to being a loyal American! With his slogan, "America for Americans," he soon became known to House colleagues as "The Napoleon of Protection." (Indeed, his large head, beady eyes, subtle smile, and squat stature resembled the French emperor's likeness).[2]

McKinley became quite influential in national Republican councils. His party prestige and influence were largely acquired at the three presidential conventions of 1884, 1888, and 1892. Each time he played increasingly important roles; in the last two conventions, the Major himself became a credible dark horse candidate for both major nominations. He aligned himself with two power brokers in Ohio's factional strife, Senator John Sherman and Mark Hanna. A millionaire Cleveland businessman, Hanna busily promoted Sherman for the White House in 1884 and 1888. When the senator's "last hurrah" failed miserably at the 1888 convention, Hanna switched his support to McKinley in 1892. Eventually, McKinley and Hanna set their long-range sights on the 1896 election.

Hanna backed McKinley in a bold bid to become Speaker of the House in 1889, but Thomas Brackett Reed, a tough, wily politico from Maine, won the position. In a party unity gesture, Reed named "Napoleon" chairman of the Ways and Means Committee. McKinley reveled in the opportunity to do what he had always dreamed of doing—writing a major tariff act with his own stamp on it. The controversial McKinley Tariff of 1890 was heatedly debated and then finally signed by President Benjamin Harrison. McKinley became the best-known congressman in the nation. Sadly for him and the people, the economy hit a recession just at his great moment of triumph. More threatening, the Democrats took over the Ohio General Assembly and redrew the boundaries of his district. Thus his eighth straight canvass ended in ignoble defeat.

The newly deposed congressman surprised his friends by remaining optimistic about his political future. In 1891, again with Hanna's largesse, he ran for governor of Ohio and won an easy victory, even in a "Democratic year." He had campaigned on the *national* issues he knew so well—the tariff and "sound money." His slogan was "Protection Is Prosperity." As governor, he was chosen unanimously as permanent chairman of the 1892 National Convention in Minneapolis. Despite his insistence that he was not a candidate and that all delegates should renominate Harrison, McKinley did receive 182 votes, tying with James G. Blaine. Harrison took the nomination with 535 votes, and the stage was set for 1896. Now, it became apparent to everyone that Hanna was the Major's rich patron, as he had once been for Sherman.

A NEAR-BANKRUPT AS "THE ADVANCE AGENT OF PROSPERITY"

The 1891 campaign for governor and the 1892 convention bolstered McKinley's national standing far beyond his expectations. He campaigned vigorously for Harrison in the fall. Though the unpopular president was crushed by Cleveland, the Ohio governor made a host of out-of-state friends. Back in Columbus, McKinley—an executive for the first time—efficiently and honestly managed the state bureaucracy. Despite Ohio's chronic labor unrest, the governor maintained his appeal as "friend of the working man" by his evenhandedness in employer-employee disputes. In the Gilded Age, the governor's job held considerably less power than it does today, but even then it had immense prestige for advancement to the presidency.

In February 1893, at the very outset of the severe economic depression known as the Panic of '93, McKinley nearly had his own political ambitions (and those of Hanna) shattered permanently. Years earlier he had cosigned some business notes for an old Youngstown friend. The governor soon learned that the man had gone bankrupt. Tied to the same bad debts, McKinley faced an identical fate. Inevitable newspaper publicity made his dramatic plight front-page news from coast to coast, amid much conjecture over his future career. His first instinct was to resign, resume a private law practice, and pay off the huge debt totaling $130,000. In an example of pathetic bravery, Ida offered her substantial inheritance of $70,000 to help pay the bills. Mark Hanna would have none of this nonsense. As soon as he could think clearly and communicate with his wealthy friends, the businessman led a small committee that readily raised the money, saving not only the McKinleys' estate but also the dream of the presidency.

Publicly, the governor was highly embarrassed for having been so negligent in his financial affairs. Over 5,000 "common folk" mailed in small voluntary contributions; McKinley was most reluctant to accept such assistance, especially in hard times for most of his fellow citizens. Because it was impossible to return the many anonymous donations, they were added to the Hanna fund. As with other big setbacks in his life, Leech finds this "hard time only added luster to his name" and notes how the near-bankruptcy ironically enhanced the Major's image. Already an object of much sympathy for his exceptional husbandly dedication toward his ailing wife and for having been "cheated" out of his House seat in 1890, the governor was now widely admired as a generous friend who willingly had risked his own fortune to do a good deed. McKinley was applauded as an honest person of moderate wealth, and one who had not gorged at the public trough.

After the near-bankruptcy trauma, he returned to Columbus triumphant. In the fall of 1893, McKinley campaigned in eighty-six of the state's eighty-eight counties and was overwhelmingly reelected by a plurality of 80,000 votes—the most decisive gubernatorial victory in the state since the Civil War. About this time, much speculation occurred in the media about "McKinley for President." A *Cleveland Leader* cartoon showed Uncle Sam identifying the Major as "the rising sun" in what was labeled "the dawn of renewed prosperity." Hanna quickly saw the tremendous propaganda value in the idea as the nation struggled through the Panic of '93. According to Croly, "Thereafter a systematic attempt was made to impress McKinley *on the popular mind as the advance agent of prosperity.*"[3]

HANNA: SELLING OF THE PRESIDENCY, 1894–1896

Among numerous myths about McKinley, none has been more perverse or pervasive than those on his relationship with Mark Hanna. Eloquent critics have charged that the Major was simply a "puppet" cleverly manipulated by an evilminded, power-seeking plutocrat. For much of the twentieth century, much literature has implied that McKinley could scarcely have become president on his own initiative and his own resources. A prominent legend-maker was Homer Davenport. His brilliant but cruel, inaccurate cartoons appeared in William Randolph Hearst's *New York Journal*. Leech notes that Davenport and Hearst

made an unknown Ohio business man the most infamously caricatured figure in America. Hanna was depicted as a brutal, obese plutocrat, the symbol of sly malice and bloated greed, covered with moneybags and dollar signs. Behind the monster the little candidate cowered in his big Napoleonic hat. Hanna was the puppet-master who pulled McKinley's strings; the ventriloquist who spoke through the dummy, McKinley; the organ grinder for whom the monkey, McKinley, danced.

A less celebrated but distinctly more truthful view depicts McKinley as the stronger man in the relationship. Hanna genuinely loved McKinley and rarely opposed the latter's will. Hanna unfailingly deferred to one he considered his superior. There is no doubt McKinley liked Hanna, but it is equally plain that he pragmatically used his friend's organizational talents and access to wealth. Hanna had always been an independent power-broker in Ohio, but after 1896 most of his influence was derived directly from his close, subservient association with McKinley. Thus, despite Hanna's strategic benevolence, modern biographers feel that the Major had enough power, prestige, and resources to have become president without the businessman.

In any case, Hanna's "selling of the presidency" began in earnest by the fall of 1894, when the popular governor was sent out on an extensive stump tour, presenting over 400 addresses in thirteen states for local Republican congressional candidates. The GOP tide that year swept into office 117 House freshmen, dissolving the Democratic majority that had accompanied Grover Cleveland's landslide in 1892. The Cleveland administration and the Democratic Congress also badly bungled their effort to revise the McKinley Tariff. Unwittingly, the Democrats built up the one Republican candidate most likely to defeat the Democrats in 1896.

Hanna completely retired from his vast Cleveland business empire early in 1895 to devote full time to organizing the preconvention boom. From the outset of the 1896 race, McKinley was recognized as the party's front-runner. His strategic position as an established governor, long prominence in the Congress, service in the national party, far-flung network of influential friends and supporters, as well as the continued "Cleveland depression" and the growing perception that the McKinley Tariff and protection were what the country needed— all combined to renew national esteem for the Napoleon of Protection.

A half-dozen other potential GOP nominees began to stir in 1895, but only the Major's selection could be advertised, as Hanna did, as being "irresistible." Both the candidate and his manager sagaciously refused to discuss the troublesome and festering currency controversy. Though he had once favored silver, McKinley had touted his new reputation as a "bimetallist." Rejecting Hanna's wish to state a preference for gold, he wisely sought to avoid offending the western delegates who demanded silver currency as an inflationary scheme to aid the farmers, ranchers, and debtors. The eastern delegates, on the other hand, advocated gold, and pressure mounted from that side. To defuse the money issue, McKinley was determined to keep the focus on protection, where his expertise was unassailable.

Hanna proposed to assure the nomination by "deals" with the eastern party bosses in return for promised patronage. McKinley flatly declined. Indeed, Hanna later promoted the slogan, "McKinley Against the Bosses!" Following his careful game plan, Hanna purchased a plush vacation retreat in Thomasville, Georgia. Ida and the Major soon joined Gussie and Mark Hanna on what was described to the press as just an old-fashioned "vacation." Sipping lemonade in Mrs. Hanna's delightful sun parlor, the Major wooed scores of southern delegates. Later, in separate meetings without the candidate, Hanna did in fact strike some hard deals for convention votes in exchange for future patronage. Meanwhile, he and McKinley arranged to have a pro-McKinley Credentials Committee sent to the 1896 national meeting. As 1895 faded out, the manager increasingly took over more of the public compaign. Making no further speeches, the Major avoided the image of unseemly pushing of his own candidacy, allowing Hanna and the campaign to promote a "draft."

Hanna's organizational talents were unparalleled. Strict "business methods" and an efficient line-graph bureaucracy gave McKinley a jump on his competition. Hanna established major offices in Chicago, Cleveland, Boston, and Washington, D.C., for the boom. Speakers and personal emissaries, subsidized by the organization, went into enemy territory, touting the governor and winning delegates from other favorite sons. The *Cleveland Leader,* generously backed financially by Hanna for the duration, cranked out reams of complimentary copy which was sent to prospective supporters. "Copies of McKinley's speeches, printed at Hanna's expense, went across the land. McKinley badges, posters, and buttons flooded through the mails."

Hanna, a multimillionaire, refused to solicit donations for the boom; instead, he gave $100,000 of his own money to fund the delegate search. His wealth and connections to big business at once set him apart from the common run of bosses. Since the 1880s businessmen had escalated their participation in politics, but mainly at the local and state levels. Hanna (in 1895) was an entirely new phenomenon in creating for himself the role of a businessman as the first national boss. A man of strict ethics in business, Hanna became more pragmatic in politics. Croly observes, not unkindly, "When [Hanna] supped with the Devil, he fished with a long spoon." He believed that the Major's moral standards were higher than his. However, he knew that the candidate was a pragmatist, too, one who would politely look aside when necessity dictated that a deal be struck, patronage pledged, or boodle dispensed. For all the charges of corruption against Hanna, in the boom and afterwards, no one ever proved a wrongdoing by him.

By expensively nationalizing the selling of the presidency, Hanna and McKinley changed the preconvention delegate chase permanently. Yet, there were numerous high-minded souls who loudly echoed Theodore Roosevelt's rather self-righteous complaint about Hanna: "He has advertised McKinley as if he were a patent medicine!"[4]

ST. LOUIS: McKINLEY IS A "GOLDBUG"

The 1896 Republican Convention promised to be a lifeless affair, except, perhaps, for the nagging issue of money. Since no GOP incumbent sat in the White House to pull the strings on the National Committee, as morose Old Ben had done in 1892, Hanna's organization was able to capture the conclave's machinery, controlling the decisions on the format and seating. Keeping to tradition, McKinley, as an avowed candidate, discreetly remained in Canton (missing his first convention since 1884). It was apparent for some time that the overwhelming majority of delegates would favor a firm party stand on gold.

Refraining from pressures to declare prematurely for the yellow metal, McKinley kept his own counsel with Hanna and a few trusted friends. Secretly, he sent his manager to St. Louis with a rough draft of a hard money plank he could endorse. After much confusion and bickering over who actually wrote the plank, McKinley's version was finally adopted, but Hanna made it appear as if his candidate had been forced to accept the convention's will.

The Republican silverbugs were not appeased. When the platform was read by Ohio's Joseph Foraker, the western delegates mounted the podium dramatically in tearful protest, then stormed out of the hall en masse. Though McKinley regretted losing them, Hanna was confident that the nomination was safe. At that moment, the remaining delegates believed that the fall election could be won even if the western states failed to support the Republican candidate. Long anticipating such a confrontation on the floor, Hanna shrewdly minimized its negative impact on public opinion by scheduling the platform reading on the same day as the nomination balloting (in 1892 and 1900 they were on separate days). As he had foreseen, the lead stories in the major newspapers focused on McKinley's first-ballot nomination.

The actual voting for the nominee was anticlimactic. On the first ballot, McKinley received 661½ votes; Speaker Thomas Reed, a poor second, had only 84½, and three other boss-backed aspirants trailed way behind. The Major's placid friend, Garret Hobart of New Jersey, was rewarded for his help in the boom with the vice presidential nomination. An influential businessman, Hobart also was chosen because an easterner was needed to balance the ticket, and in 1896 it was doubtful if his state would vote Republican.

Meanwhile, back in Canton, the city erupted into wild celebration when the convention news from St. Louis flashed over the telegraph wires. McKinley listened anxiously to the convention proceedings over an open telephone line. The Major smiled as he listened to Ohio's forty-man delegation fittingly vote him over the top. That night in Canton, a torchlight parade of 50,000 Ohioans celebrated the nomination, complete with church bells, cannons, and fireworks.

In early July, the Democrats met and nominated William Jennings Bryan. That event was not totally unexpected, as myth has it; the "silver" craze (for inflationary money) had been building in agarian areas for a decade or so. Bryan's famous platform address, warning the enemy that it could not "crucify labor upon a cross of gold," electrified the delegates but was not the sole cause of his nomination. A week after the Democrats disbanded at Chicago, all bets were off on an easy GOP victory. The contest appeared even.

Hanna's task was no longer mainly to make a scapegoat out of President Cleveland.

The public opinion of the time, confused and ill-formed as it was, saw one truth very plainly, which was that the cause of the trouble (i.e., depression, unfair distribution of wealth) lay deeper than the administration of a Democratic president and the passing of the Wilson bill (the controversial tariff which replaced the McKinley Act).

The self-confidence of the Republican bosses was badly shaken by Bryan's sensational "Cross of Gold" speech, his subsequently startling nomination, and the positive public response to both events. When the Democratic nominee grandly announced that he intended to make an unprecedented "national campaign," Hanna kept his head: "the businessman in politics" hurriedly sought to reassemble his McKinley organization, which had self-confidently disbanded after the GOP St. Louis convention.

THE FRONT-PORCH CAMPAIGN

Perhaps the most unruffled Republican was the Major. Earlier he had announced that, like Harrison and most late nineteenth-century Republican presidential nominees, he intended to conduct a dignified "front-porch" canvass. Many twentieth-century critics have wrongly pointed to this tactic as proof of McKinley's "passive" nature. Nothing could be further from the truth. A lifetime stump politico, McKinley had no need to prove that he could blaze a campaign trail in 1896. Besides, the "front porch" allowed the nominee control over media access, which his opponent did not have. McKinley was accessible to those citizens who wished to journey to his home to see him in person.

The "front-porch" decision was a masterful stroke, and Bryan's novel coast-to-coast personal appearances ultimately became a fatal mistake. Remaining in Canton, the Major had ample opportunity to advertise his experience as a prudent, popular leader. At age fifty-three, he showed good sense in declining to match the physical exploits of his energetic opponent, seventeen years his junior. Initially, however, Hanna was not convinced on the wisdom of McKinley's resolve to stay home. In one of their few serious disagreements, Hanna sent Charles Dawes to Canton with yet another request that the candidate make his own personal tour. McKinley, unafraid to refute Hanna again, told Dawes:

Don't you remember I announced that I would not under any circumstances go on a speech-making tour? If I should do that now it would be an acknowledgement of my weakness. Moreover, I might just as well put up a trapeze on my front lawn and compete with some professional athlete as go out speaking against Bryan.[5]

Resigned to the decision, Hanna rebuilt his new organization accordingly. The main financial headquarters was set up in New York City to solicit huge contributions from the Wall Street crowd. Chicago became the central railroad hub for propaganda mailings and speaker corps; to match Bryan's challenge in touring 18,000 miles with some 570 speeches nationwide, Hanna's surrogates covered exactly the same territory, often simultaneously with the Democrat. McKinley kept in touch with Hanna almost daily by telephone; Boss Hanna handled details, but he still deferred to McKinley's approval on all large questions of strategy.

Spared the endless ordeal of a train schedule, McKinley kept well rested mentally and physically. As it was, he did deliver over 300 carefully prepared statements to visiting groups and a permanent press corps in Canton. While Bryan talked incessantly of silver ("That's where we've got the boy!" quipped Hanna) McKinley wisely gave protection and currency equal emphasis—or spoke in generalities.

The Major's tactful rhetoric was complemented by his manager's manipulation of the picturesque small-town setting. Canton offered the most ideal advertising as an "all-American" midwestern community. Conveniently, Canton had excellent railroad facilities extending in all directions. Rail magnates sympathetic to the Republicans offered low fares to see the candidate; "cheaper than staying home," complained disgruntled Democrats. In the early fall of 1896, the Hanna organization found lodging for the trainloads of visitors who came to see McKinley. Hanna's men carefully screened each delegation to include just the right cross-section of the general public.

Theodore Roosevelt claimed to be mystified that a presidential candidate could live in such a humble abode as the McKinley house on North Market Street. But the more than 700,000 Americans who visited Canton apparently were pleased to see that McKinley—sitting placidly in a rocker—dwelled in simple surroundings so much like their own.

Without fail, the Major (now retired as governor) was briefed in advance on which congregation was arriving at what time. He himself met privately with each group's spokesmen ahead of time and approved all the remarks they would make. Refusing to be interviewed (a practice that frustrated many newsmen, especially the eastern correspondents), he presented mostly short, memorized policy statements. His longer speeches, which he wrote himself—a testimony to his literary talents—were read verbatim. Out of context, these addresses appear monotonous. However, one must remember the man's "presence" in the flesh, his uncanny ability to fix an audience's attention by his logic, wit, charm, and Napoleonic countenance. Bryan, whose nickname was the "Great Commoner," had ample competition from McKinley for the label "Man of the People." In short order, McKinley's front lawn became a sea of mud beyond the porch steps. According to Morgan, "the front porch [itself] was splintered away by souvenir hunters." Estimates are that "between June 19 and November 2, McKinley spoke to 750,000 people in Canton from 30 states in over 300 delegations."

McKINLEY'S NEW VOTER COALITION OF 1896

As Richard Jensen cogently observes: "By election day the strategy was plain. [McKinley] was offering pluralism to the American people." His opponent, in effect, was "rejecting pluralism" with his narrow insistence on preaching "silver." Where the Major skillfully brought together a coalition of voters, the Democratic Commoner tended to alienate one social, ethnic, economic, and religious group after another, fracturing his potential constituency, even in states where the Democrats and Populists had the natural advantage. McKinley won this election because he unified the rich and poor, the farmers and the capitalists, the majority of ethnics, most major religious sects, and social groups of all political stripes. This Republican pluralist coalition dominated the presidency for the next thirty years (except for the Wilsonian years).

The key to the 1896 contest was which candidate could exert the most influence on the industrial workers. Bryan appealed to the emotions of the urban masses with inflammatory rhetoric. McKinley, on the other hand, bolstered his arguments with emotional patriotism, logically stating the case for an America where all could share the bounty. It was McKinley (and Hanna), *not* Bryan, who most clearly realized that industrial America had come of age.

Balancing the Silver Republicans who supported Bryan were the Democratic dissidents—Gold Democrats—or the disaffected Democrats who supported McKinley for his conservative stands on sound money and high tariffs. For the disaffected Democrats, the Major became a vehicle for sweet revenge. The Bryan silverites, the Gold Democrats felt, had stolen the convention and repudiated their man Cleveland. As a consequence, Boss Hanna had skillfully orchestrated "a classic counter-crusade" which had all the moral fervor of a born-again Christian camp rally. The silver-tongued Nebraskan was utterly denounced by Hanna's forces as "revolutionary," "anarchistic," and "subversive of the national honor" (to name a few of the milder anti-American epithets hurled his way).[6]

Workers, ethnics, and religious groups left the Democratic party in droves. All the big Republican newspapers, which had supported the Major before and after his nomination, remained loyal to him until the election; however, as the *New York Times* reported, as early as September most of the important Democratic dailies had long deserted the hapless Bryan.

On November 3, 1896, McKinley received 271 electoral votes to 176 for the Democrat/Populist Bryan. The popular vote was 7,108,480 (51.01 percent) to 6,511,495 (46.73 percent) in favor of the Republican standard-bearer. While this was not the biggest mandate in history, it was the first "convincing victory . . . of the Republican Party." McKinley's decisive win cemented the party realignment toward the GOP begun in 1894.

The new political reality was underscored by another stark fact—*money!* Though McKinley swept majorities of many pluralist groups, his huge campaign war chest was filled, as usual, by a mere handful of wealthy donors. The most conservative estimates show Hanna's organization spent an unprecedented $3.5 million to $4 million compared to estimates of $300,000 to $400,000 for Bryan's campaign. Wall Street was, by far, the biggest contributor to McKinley. The western silver-mine owners were the financial backbone for the Democracy. Yellow journalists attacked McKinley and Hanna for allegedly lavishing between $6 and $12 million to defeat Bryan, but those charges are unsubstantiated. Nevertheless, the most accurate estimate of Hanna's expenditures is still ten times what Bryan spent in 1896—and twice what the Republican incumbent Harrison spent in his losing bid in 1892.

AN ACTIVE-POSITIVE'S HONEYMOON—1897

The twenty-fifth president, William McKinley, entered the White House amid the usual high public expectations that the new man "would make things better." His front-porch rhetoric and Hanna's extensive advertising had fostered the believable image that he *was* really "the Advance Agent of Prosperity," a leader who could, at long last, end the devastating Panic of '93. It was in this optimistic atmosphere that McKinley began a honeymoon that was to last through most of his first year in office.

Likewise, McKinley ended the gloomy social atmosphere that had hung like a pall over the White House and all of official Washington after the last, for-tresslike days of the Cleveland administration. It was well understood in Washington society circles and among the general public that the First Lady was very much the invalid she had been since Congressman McKinley had come to the capital city in 1877. Ida's disability caused the Major and the White House staff innumerable difficulties of protocol initially until an ad hoc system could be worked out to accommodate her eccentricities. The president learned that he must always be near when his wife stood (or sat) in a receiving line or participated in a state dinner. An epileptic fit might seize her at any moment, in which case he would toss his handkerchief over her convulsed face and drooling lips, holding her gently in his arms until the fit had passed. Somehow, the president remained outwardly unnerved by these frightening experiences, and other startled guests often fought to retain their own composure. Gradually, Ida would regain her senses and the function would proceed as if nothing had happened.

McKinley truly enjoyed being president. A professional politico, he seemed born for the job as much as it seemed designed for his personality. Rarely did he complain, as so many presidents have, of the "tremendous burdens" that accompany the office. He had no formal label for his legislative program (like TR's "Square Deal"), but he knew from the beginning what he wished to accomplish. Right away he pushed through Congress a creditable new tariff bill, which stood for the next decade; he reformed civil service rules and seriously explored trade reciprocity and bimetallism with foreign powers.

He had a reputation as a hardworking president. In 1897 he began with a modest personal staff of six, the same number of aides assigned to Cleveland, but this was expanded to eighteen overworked assistants by 1901. McKinley was a restless president; he traveled by train far more than had any predecessor, making policy speeches and performing ceremonial functions as chief of state.

It was in his interpersonal relations with other politicos that McKinley proved positively brilliant. In the honeymoon, this was especially true with congressmen, whom he brought into his office singly and in small groups, for lessons in presidential consensus. His Napoleonic presence was enhanced by the great symbolic aura of the White House setting, and, of course, by his title, "Mr. President." It was absolutely apparent that here was no Hanna lackey in a moneybags livery. Elihu Root, later McKinley's secretary of war and a first-rate statesman, said of his patron; "He was a man of great power because he was absolutely indifferent to credit, *but McKinley always had his way.*"[7]

Thomas Bailey is explicit about how ex-congressman McKinley performed his role as chief legislator:

He was the *first* in a long succession to provide Congress with active and effective leadership. One has to go back to Andrew Jackson for a comparable performance; to Jefferson for as velvet-gloved a performance. In leading Congress, he served as a kind of half-way House—the last of the old-fashioned caretakers *and the first of the new-fashioned drivers.*

It is no accident that McKinley's name is linked with "prosperity." Public expectations in the honeymoon were well placed. The panic bottomed out just after his election; and, by the spring of 1897, a genuine recovery in the business cycle was under way. Before FDR's New Deal, the president had no statutory authority to enforce macroeconomic policies to stimulate aggregate demand. Even in an era of positive-state Republican government, national economic recovery had to occur strictly from the discretionary spending of individual investors, businessmen, farmers, and consumers. Government policies, like the tariff, could "protect" (and, hence, indirectly promote growth of) the productive sectors, but the government could not *initiate* the upward flow of goods and services, or what latter-day Keynesians called "expansionary fiscal policy," through more government spending and less taxation.

The key to such a hands-off economy was confidence. McKinley in no small way inspired this elusive quality in the private sector by his fiscal "soundness" on the currency and protection (never more appreciated by the investors than immediately following the bad scare of "Bryan revolution"). Unemployment dropped from an estimated 15 percent in 1897 to 10 percent by 1899. Businesses made huge new purchases to stock up depleted inventories and expand their capital plants and machinery. Confidence was further expressed when the stock market shot up in 1897, when farm prices rose at last, and exports expanded rapidly. In the span of McKinley's tenure (1897–1901) came the first of the three huge "merger movements" in the American economy; the muckrakers (with some justification) saw this as the beginning of an oligopolistic state. Despite some abuses, under McKinley's tenure there was formed the central corporation structure upon which the mighty twentieth-century national economy was built.

The biggest political flap early in the honeymoon concerned the president's relationship with Mark Hanna. Even before the inauguration, the manager had politely declined a cabinet job for himself as a reward for the success of the campaign. Instead, Hanna had informed McKinley of his long-held desire to serve in the Senate. The president-elect, believing that he was doing a wise and honorable thing, then offered Senator John Sherman the secretary of state portfolio. Sherman, up for reelection by the Ohio legislature in 1898 after having had a very close win in 1892, eagerly accepted the cabinet post. It seemed evident to many observers that Sherman was a bit senile; at the least he appeared incapable of assuming so important a post. Much embarrassing publicity ensued (for all concerned) about what was billed as a "cynical payoff." It seemed that a distinguished (if incompetent) public servant was being promoted simply to reward Hanna for the campaign. By then, Hanna already was pilloried in the media; when Sherman faltered on the job in his first foreign policy crisis, the criticism of Hanna (and the president) reached a crescendo.

Concerning Hanna's senatorial appointment in 1897, Ohio's governor, Asa Bushnell, procrastinated for five maddening weeks. (Bushnell was a member of the anti-Hanna Ohio faction.) Only direct pressure by the president-elect, and Hanna's own furious lobbying, finally brought forth the appointment at the eleventh hour, just before McKinley's inauguration, but just after Bushnell's ally Joseph Foraker had been sworn in, making Hanna Ohio's junior senator.[8]

After the election of 1896, a coolness developed between the president and Hanna. McKinley, ordinarily tolerant, even to unwarranted criticism as president, became obviously annoyed by the continuous insinuation in the yellow press that he was Hanna's puppet. Hanna was a most loyal and devoted friend, more emotionally attached to McKinley than vice versa; but Hanna was prone to give out the impression that he was more influential with the incoming administration than he actually was.

A PRESIDENT SEARCHES FOR PEACE

As memorable as the campaign of 1896 had been, it was mainly fought over domestic issues—sound money, the tariff, and the ending of the long economic depression. The new voter coalition which propelled McKinley into the White House had scarcely been concerned about foreign policy. Yet even before McKinley was sworn in, he (and the nation he was about to lead) became more aware each day of an irrepressible international crisis brewing off the Florida coast—Cuba!

The unpopular Wilson-Gorman Tariff, adopted by a Democratic Congress in Cleveland's last term (and which, as noted, had helped McKinley so much politically), blocked off sugar imports to the mainland, subsequently depressing Cuba's main crop; in turn, this exacerbated the existing but latent economic, social, and political tensions between the Cuban natives and their Spanish masters.

A bloody uprising, the second in twenty years, erupted in February 1895, almost two years before President Cleveland left office. Cleveland's sympathies had rested with Spain; he opposed armed U.S. intervention vigorously and more or less remained aloof from the growing conflict. Amid a festering clamor from Cuban nationals living in the United States, plus lurid reports in the sensational press on the newest insurrection, the presidential candidates in 1896 still largely ignored Cuba and focused on domestic issues. After the election, however, the problem had become so acute and well publicized that McKinley felt that he could no longer persist in a policy of American neutrality, actually the enforcement of Cleveland's pro-Spanish views. Complicating the crisis for the incoming chief executive was the substantial investment of $50 million which American businessmen previously had made in Cuba. Of course, real danger to the lives of hundreds of American citizens living on the island was an additional concern.

While moving ahead publicly and boldly with his new tariff, civil service reform, bimetallism, and reciprocity talks, McKinley stepped cautiously into the Cuban-Spanish conflict. His actions, and the alleged inactions that followed, were to have far larger expansionist consequences for the United States than anyone, including the president, ever could have imagined in 1897. The Spanish-American War would alter the entire country's destiny as have only a few other prior events, such as the American Revolution, the Louisiana Purchase, and the Mexican and Civil wars.

Lewis Gould critically noted that, since around 1920, McKinley's policies with respect to Spain and Cuba have received "almost uniform censure." The textbooks have informed generations of students that McKinley "gave in to jingoist pressure from a hysterical press and overheated public and therefore accepted war with a nation that had capitulated to American demands." Gould suggests that in the 1960s a more contemporary group of McKinley critics rejected the older view above (i.e., the image of McKinley the feckless leader who stumbled willy-nilly into war). The later version—equally erroneous, in Gould's opinion—portrays the president as "a Machiavellian and cunning executive" who had no heartfelt compassion for the long-suffering, freedom-seeking Cubans (and, later, Filipinos); McKinley's new critics argue that he was a lackey to the "business community" and (worse) deliberately provoked a war "when conditions were right for economic imperialism that relied on overseas markets."

Both criticisms can be refuted. Even before his inauguration, McKinley began to think about ways to encourage a peaceful, negotiated settlement between the rebels and the government in Madrid. McKinley did not share his thoughts publicly. Personally, he favored "nonintervention," having seen for himself in the Civil War the horrors of organized warfare. Emotionally, though, McKinley was distinctly more sympathetic to the Cubans' courageous quest for freedom. He rejected the Spanish claim of sovereignty for the island. On June 8, a spokesman for the president announced an official American protest over the Spanish policy of concentration camps to house native civilians being established by the odious Spanish commanding general, "Butcher" Weyler.

During the honeymoon, when public opinion on Cuba was yet relatively quiescent, the president had difficulty finding a capable and qualified diplomat who would accept "the thankless job of representing him in Madrid." Finally, General Stewart Woodford accepted the portfolio and sailed off to Spain, via other European capitals where he conferred with mainly pro-Spanish Continental leaders about the several options for negotiation. Ernest May believes that McKinley had no choice but to temporize on intervention during the honeymoon.

The president had not dealt long enough with the Cuban problem to chart any course other than to encourage negotiations. In 1897 neither the people nor the American economy were ready for war. Most certainly, McKinley was not ready for war! In his inaugural address, he characteristically had spoken to both sides; for the jingoes, he issued a warning to Spain that America would have "a firm and dignified foreign policy"; for those opposed to intervention, he said, "Peace is preferable to war in almost every contingency."[9]

From the first days of the administration, Secretary of State Sherman behaved publicly in an erratic and embarrassing manner unbecoming to subtle diplomacy. Obviously, the secretary could not be trusted to coordinate the delicate and complicated three-way negotiations among officials in Washington, Madrid, and Havana. To a large degree, McKinley was thus forced initially to become his own secretary of state. Fortunately, Sherman finally bowed to the inevitable and resigned on April 25. McKinley then named his close friend and assistant secretary of state, Judge William R. Day, to succeed Sherman.

Despite the backbiting and embarrassment from a bypassed and angry John Sherman, this ad hoc arrangement worked rather well. Day suffered from the same handicap as the president—a lack of extensive experience in foreign affairs—but both became astute self-taught diplomats under the rapidly escalating tension. (It was not until 1898, after the war, that McKinley appointed John Hay, his ambassador to Great Britain, to head the State Department. If the president had selected Hay, a superb expert in international relations, as his original choice at State, he would have saved himself enormous personal strain and trauma. But, then, he himself would not have become so skilled at diplomacy. Nor, with Sherman in the Senate, would Hanna have been rewarded.)

A new civil government came to power in Spain, and the official Spanish line was softened. But the president, wary from past disappointments, warned Madrid again that if it did not "face reality" (i.e., end the rebellion soon), he would be forced, against his will, to intervene. Meanwhile, threatening messages from Europe and Asia added to McKinley's resolve not to allow the Cuban war to go on indefinitely.

"REMEMBER THE *MAINE* AND TO HELL WITH SPAIN!"

Throughout the first fourteen months of the administration, ascending agitation for armed entrance into the Cuban rebellion arose from three levels. Emotion fueled all the sources, but the most rational dialogue emanated from an intellectual coterie in Washington which included Henry Cabot Lodge, Theodore Roosevelt, John Hay, and Captain Alfred R. Mahan, an American naval hero. They popularized a view that was at once practical and chauvinistic, namely, that the United States was now a truly great world power—and, to compete appropriately with its first-class rivals, the nation must unilaterally move the doctrine of Manifest Destiny forward toward the twentieth century, expanding to whatever foreign territories could be acquired before the Europeans, who had centuries of colonial mercantilism behind them, could deprive America of her rightful share of the underdeveloped world.

The second level of militarism was more of a mass sermon, preaching righteous indignation over the Spanish atrocities in Cuba. The catalyst for much of the outcry came from the yellow press, which (not incidentally) amassed big profits at the newsstands by sensationalizing the Caribbean rebellion. The same newspapers that had portrayed McKinley as Hanna's puppet now lambasted the president as a peacemonger, the insensitive dupe of Wall Street.

McKinley's third level of pressure came from Congress, building steadily from his inauguration until April 1898, when it reached the point where some jingoist representatives and senators threatened the new secretary of state (Day) that they would declare war without the president's approval. McKinley never panicked at so bold a threat to his presidential prerogatives; but he also was too wise a politico to ignore such powerful sentiment.

The most vociferous opponents to intervention were the influential big businessmen and conservative congressmen who felt, wrongly as it turned out, that American military involvement would destroy the long-awaited economic recovery from the Panic of '93. But many others were opposed to jingoism, too. After all, the United States had staunchly followed a policy of isolationism for over a century; many Americans sincerely believed that Cuba was not our responsibility. Millions thought war itself was immoral and should be avoided at all costs. McKinley was neither a pacifist nor a jingo. He just wanted to do what he perceived to be his and the country's moral obligation to humanity. During 1897 and into the new year, the conservative newspapers and the majority of public opinion (as far as it can be guessed) wavered on the Cuban issue. Most came to support intervention on both imperialistic and moralistic grounds.

In February 1898, two incidents set American public opinion ablaze. First, in December 1897, the Spanish minister to Washington, Dupuy deLôme, had written a letter to a Cuban friend describing the president as "weak and a bidder for the admiration of the crowd, besides being a would-be politician who tries to leave a door open behind him while keeping on good terms with the jingoes of his own party." The letter was stolen by pro-rebels and published in the New York *Journal* on February 9, 1898, under the headline: "Worst Insult to the United States in Its History." McKinley shrugged off the personal attacks. The true significance for him, he realized, would be that the deLôme letter proved once again the Spanish eagerness to stall further. Friends and foes alike were incensed over the alleged degradation to him and his office. To quiet the outrage and force Madrid's true intentions to public light, McKinley demanded an official apology. Typically, the Spanish procrastinated. Ambassador Woodford further strongly insisted upon a definite reply, which finally reached the White House a week later.

The deLôme letter was only a prelude to the more serious second event—the blowing up of the United States battleship, the *Maine*. This incident is forever welded in the American imagination as one of the major causes of the war. And, while it was, so to speak, the last straw, it was only one of numerous causes of the war. Shortly before publication of the deLôme "insult," McKinley had ordered the *Maine* to anchor in Havana Harbor, ostensibly "in an effort to alleviate tensions between the two countries and to show that neither feared the other." Actually, his experiment in fostering peaceful relations began well; then suddenly, on February 15, the warship mysteriously blew up while moored in the harbor, causing a tragic loss of life among the American seamen.

Domestic settlements were already at a fever pitch over the deLôme affair; millions of Americans now condemned the "treacherous" Spanish out of hand for the explosion. McKinley was obviously much shaken by this disaster. He called his cabinet together immediately to discuss the proper responses, then alerted Congress for action while simultaneously putting the armed forces on notice. However, he faced the crisis calmly and appealed to other American officials and the public to do likewise. He asked everyone to suspend judgment until the naval court of inquiry he had ordered could report back to him on the exact causes of the explosion. But the country was in no mood for patience. The president shuddered at the shocking national display of mass dissent—in street demonstrations, fiery speeches, and inflammatory headlines. The moralistic and imperialistic jingoes united behind the Hearst-inspired battlecry, "Remember the *Maine,* and to Hell with Spain!"

McKINLEY BITES THE BULLET FOR WAR

The deLôme letter and the sinking of the *Maine* convinced the jingoes that war was imminent. To their bitter frustration, the president said nothing officially to appease the people and the press, who were obsessed by intervention. In Congress only the Speaker, a few conservative House members, and the Republican leadership in the Senate stood loyally beside McKinley in the last grim days. Wayne Morgan argues:

Now was the time to break the long silence, to rally public opinion to his side by a firm declaration of his intentions, to repudiate the jingoes in public. But he remained inexplicably silent, the captive of caution, fearing that any statement would feed the jingo fire.[10]

Lewis Gould disagrees. What, he asks, were the advantages of the president abandoning his consistently quiet diplomacy at this point? The Spanish had yielded (albeit tardily and grudgingly) some concessions already; according to optimistic reports from Ambassador Woodford in Madrid, more progress was promised. McKinley stubbornly insisted on receiving the *Maine* naval inquiry before he acted. Declining passionate rhetoric—in which he easily could have engaged—the president chose to act with a quiet dramatic stroke. He requested a $50 million appropriation from Congress, which he could use for war if in his discretion it should be needed. The congressional jingoes passed the measure immediately. This was the first time that Congress had ever granted any president a huge, discretionary war appropriation in peacetime. Woodford reported that the sheer size of McKinley's military request "stunned" officials in Madrid. The Spanish had always perceived the United States as a second-class power; they could not imagine that America (or even a first-class power) would have reserve resources of such magnitude. The timing of this huge appropriation suggests, however, that by early March war was inevitable.

Events moved swiftly thereafter. On March 25, the president received the report on the *Maine*. It implied that the explosion had been "external" (and hence the Spanish were guilty). He sent the naval board's conclusions on to an enraged Congress, cautioning that a glimmer of hope remained for peace by negotiation. His final demand to Madrid was for an unconditional armistice, after which he hoped further negotiations could lead to a permanent peace and eventual Cuban independence. A flourish of last-minute diplomatic activities occurred among Secretary Day and the State Department in Washington, Lee in Havana, Pope Leo XIII and the European heads of state, and Woodford in Madrid with a Spanish cabinet.

Finally, on April 9, the Spanish would only consent to a proposed suspension of hostilities. McKinley's rejection of this latest "concession" led to war. Gould writes: "There is no better evidence, the President's attackers (historians, muck-rakers) charge, of his fecklessness, his weakness, his lack of courage. No in-cident, the indictment runs, better illustrates his ranking as a mediocre President." Likewise, the most recent critics take the same evidence to support their theory that Wall Street and McKinley's own imperialistic greed deliberately rejected Spain's reasonable capitulation. Either way, McKinley was portrayed as a dupe.

A frequent misperception of McKinley's critics is that Spain did submit to the will of the United States president. It is important for the record to understand why what *seemed* to be a Spanish capitulation, was, in fact, just the opposite. The difference between McKinley's demand for an armistice and Madrid's mere proposal to suspend hostilities is crucial. Moreover, the Spanish were well aware that their final offer failed to recognize the legitimacy of the rebel "govern-ment"—a major point in McKinley's last demand. He correctly interpreted Madrid's response as yet another deception, one more delay to gain additional support from the pro-Spanish European government. In the interlude, the pres-ident suspected that the military garrisons in Cuba would be reinforced to repel any American intervention. McKinley's central concerns (a permanent end to the killing, the independence of Cuba, and the role of the United States to act as a mediator in bringing about the first two items) were totally neglected.

He rejected outright the position of the noninterventionists, who argued that he should have accepted Spain's offer to suspend hostilities; once suspended, the pacifists argued, the civil war could not be resumed. In fact, McKinley was convinced that the Spanish would surely invent a flimsy pretext to continue the warfare and crush the rebels forever. McKinley was genuinely a man of peace, but he had to save his presidency. Spain left him no choice. At last, he asked

Congress for the declaration of war that he had earnestly avoided for over a year. The president was a political animal. His instincts were sure. He bit the bullet and went to war.

THE COMMANDER-IN-CHIEF COMES OF AGE

Professor Woodrow Wilson, then at Princeton, observed that President McKinley as a war leader had reversed the long post–Civil War trend of Congressional dominance over the executive branch. Ernest May contends, as well, that this "unprecedented" presidential use of military power was carried over into the postwar era by McKinley's firm governing of America's new colonial empire. The strength he derived from his war powers was also reflected in his vigorous domestic policies.

Not only was the "presidential office" per se strengthened by McKinley's role as commander-in-chief in the constitutional balance of powers, but his wartime experience (described below) enhanced the high self-esteem he already held. "In bearing and manner, in action and policy, he would," avers Gould, "become something of an imperial tutor to the American people." While he was alive, his positive public image soared. Even a scholar as unfriendly to the Major as Ernest May concludes that the Spanish conflict emboldened this president to demand the annexation of Hawaii (which Cleveland had forbidden) and resolutely to keep the newly acquired territories, that is, all of the Philippine archipelago, Puerto Rico, and Guam. (Cuba was promised a quick independence by McKinley.) "He seemed to have become an imperialist," May writes.[11]

McKinley's most valid claim as "the cutting edge of the modern presidency" is found in his role of commander-in-chief during the short war (and afterward in the controversial colonial period). Unlike Lincoln, who was restricted by the technology of the Civil War era, McKinley literally ran the Spanish-American War on a daily basis. Later, as military leader, the president decided entirely on his own initiative to acquire by force all of the Philippines and other Spanish possessions.

McKinley established a "War Room" on the second floor of the Executive Mansion and had special facilities installed for press briefings. Giant maps of the Caribbean and Asia adorned the War Room walls, and colored pins illustrated the deployment of both American and Spanish forces. The United States Signal Corps strung twenty telegraph wires to communicate with the American generals in Cuba. President McKinley pored over the maps daily and consulted with his military aides, often hourly. He sometimes directed field maneuvers himself as it was possible to reach Cuba by telephone in twenty minutes. The White House was connected by telephone to the president's eight cabinet departments to coordinate war-related activities for the duration. The "informational pressures of modern war" were well suited to McKinley's personality and political style, Lewis Gould believes. "The actual directive to attack the Spanish at Manila was based on McKinley's decision," Gould states. The president ordered the battle on April 21, but it was actually postponed until April 24. The naval engagement of Manila Bay was not fought for yet another week.

"NAPOLEON'S" SPLENDID LITTLE WAR AND MAGNIFICENT EMPIRE

The Spanish-American War, wrote Samuel Eliot Morison and Henry Steele Commager, was "emphatically a popular war." The fighting culminated in a colorfully patriotic celebration at home following awesome naval victories at Manila and Santiago bays and rapidly successful land engagements (with TR's "Rough Riders") on Cuban soil, where a numerically inferior volunteer American army overwhelmed professional Spanish troops. The latter lacked capable officers and the military morale needed to fight successfully. Never was a president so completely victorious in war as McKinley. What an irony that the "Napoleon of Protection's" greatest impact on the destiny of the United States would be achieved by warfare rather than with tariff schedules and tranquility.

Gould found the entire Spanish-American War was concluded in "ten glorious, dizzying weeks, with victories to fill every headline, slogans to suit every taste." The United States lost scarcely 5,500 men, of whom just 379 died in combat, the rest falling to disease and accidents. The 133 days it took to subdue Spain are best described by John Hay's famous one-liner: "A Splendid Little War!"

On August 12, 1898, the Spanish-American War ended with a signed protocol. The president was a great symbol of national unity at the time, more popular even than at the height of his presidential honeymoon in 1897.

Ernest May believes that McKinley only jumped on the imperialism bandwagon after it became publicly fashionable. However, McKinley never intended to give up the Philippine Islands after they were captured by Admiral George Dewey. Shortly after the stupendous naval victory, McKinley dispatched 20,000 troops to cement the American territorial claim in the Pacific. Both the Bryan and Cleveland wings of the Democratic party were opposed to this postwar "expansion." Nevertheless, the president was out in front of the anti-imperialists with the majority of public opinion. Among the nation's most prominent editorial writers, the most influential businessmen, and the religious sects eyeing missionary territory, McKinley had solid backing. The majority of Republicans, certainly including numerous jingoes, vocally supported the "Large Policy" of imperialism being advocated by the president after the war.[12]

In response, his "anti-imperialist" opponents helped to sell his expansionist peace treaty to the Senate. To an audience in the Chicago Auditorium on October 18, 1898, McKinley's message was clear as he spoke to great applause:

My countrymen, the currents of destiny flow through the hearts of the people. Who will check them? Who will divert them? Who will stop them? And the movements of men, planned and designated by the Master of men, will never be interrupted by the American people.

McKinley was careful in selecting the peace negotiators he sent to Paris. The Americans obtained nearly all of their president's demands; the Spanish felt much chagrin and humiliation, having lost their empire. McKinley agreed to pay Madrid $20 million for all of the Philippines. The vanquished also ceded to the United States the islands of Puerto Rico and Guam. Cuba was liberated, while Spain retained the island's large fiscal debt.

Arthur Schlesinger, Jr., was impressed by McKinley's "cunning" use of United States senators on the peace commission; Schlesinger noted how the president was equally adroit in leading the crucial treaty ratification process in Congress. The 1898 Treaty of Paris became the first major treaty approved by the Senate since 1871. At the time of the Senate vote, a Philippine native insurrection exploded, and the violence almost defeated the treaty. It was approved by only the slimmest of margins—one vote.

MINDING THE STORE: CIVIL RIGHTS, BIG BUSINESS MERGERS, CURRENCY

On the domestic front in 1898 and 1899, Negro Americans seemed particularly disappointed with McKinley's tenure. (Of course, blacks in the United States were unhappy with all American presidents' civil rights records up to Lyndon Johnson's programs in the Great Society of the 1960s.) McKinley had always had a compassionate, tolerant Christian view of Negroes so highly characteristic of white politicos in his time. White ethnic groups, especially Catholic workingmen, had always been important in the Major's electoral blocs. Despite opposition from Protestant supporters, McKinley appointed a Catholic, Joseph McKenna, as his first attorney general. Shortly thereafter, when the "Catholic seat" opened up on the Supreme Court, the president made McKenna his one and only appointment to the nation's highest bench.

Muckrakers (such as Matthew Josephson) promoted McKinley's image as a subservient lackey to big business. Admittedly, the Major admired businessmen and was ideologically dedicated to capitalism. Many of his friends and political supporters were men of substantial wealth. Mark Hanna was one of the greatest American success stories of Horatio Algerism. Yet, there is no evidence whatever that McKinley ever acted corruptly for anyone in big business.[13]

The president did not arouse much protest from social reformers. He explicitly endorsed the passive stance of both his first and second attorney general "toward the burgeoning force of business expansion." By the prosperous year of 1899, many had forgotten the lean era of business contraction earlier in the decade (1890–1897). McKinley's critics now focused on the record consolidation of small and medium-sized firms into large holding companies called trusts. There is distinct evidence that the president recognized the difference between "good" and "bad" trusts. Moreover, he realized that the states individually were unequal to the awesome prospect of regulating the most abusive giant business combinations. He informed his advisers that enforcement of the Sherman Antitrust Act of 1890 was a policy he must seriously consider in his second term.

Nelson has pointed out that McKinley plainly saw that the effects of mergers were not uniformly negative, McKinley understood that the conditions promoting growth of the trusts were more complicated than simple exploitation for big profits. The "economies of scale" in large-size production actually *can* lead to more efficient use of material resources, lower consumer prices, and better quality goods. In the McKinley years, there was an unusual excess of financial capital available for investment in trusts. Moreover, the stock market was peculiarly speculative following the long panic. Despite all the criticism that McKinley's reputation absorbed for not moving aggressively on an antitrust program, the first large merger movement in history (1897–1901), according to Nelson, *"laid the foundation for the industrial structure that has characterized most of American industry in the twentieth century."*

The Major (as noted earlier) had hoped to run on the issue of tariff revision in 1896—a plan aborted by the currency controversy "forced" upon him and Hanna by gold- and silverbugs from both parties. After a bimetallism resolution failed in his first term, he turned to a request for gold-standard legislation in his 1899 annual message to Congress. Such flexibility was consistent with his pragmatic, successful approach to politics. With the public focus mainly on imperialism and the preelection passion for "free silver" cooled, the measure for a gold currency passed easily under the conservative Republican leadership. On March 14, 1900, the president proudly signed his Gold Standard Act into law.

Historians and economists have noted that this particular action stimulated prosperity by increasing public confidence in the value of United States currency; the Gold Standard Act rapidly expanded the quantity of money in circulation and bolstered business transactions by quickly increasing the number of national and state banks then in existence. Barry Poulson says that during McKinley's first term New York City replaced London "as the major financial center of the world." Little wonder, then, that President McKinley believed the Gold Standard Act ranked among his most important accomplishments.

REELECTION: FRONT PORCH II

The enthusiasm and emotion that had gripped the electorate in 1896 was notably absent four years later. The urgency of the tariff and currency issues was resolved, at least for 1900. McKinley, a strong and popular war leader, established the foundation of what Schlesinger calls "the imperial presidency." The economy was relatively prosperous, and unemployment was down significantly. Again, McKinley's Democratic opponent was William Jennings Bryan, whose chances to win were slim. Mary Thurston Peck (who witnessed the 1900 contests) described Bryan's campaign as "forlorn."[14]

A curious aspect of the canvass was Mark Hanna's role. The senator tended to be bluntly impulsive when he spoke publicly on the issues, a trait that increasingly irritated the president, the man Hanna loved and served loyally. Still chairman of the Republican National Committee, Hanna suffered considerable anguish when McKinley "hesitated" on reappointing him as his manager for the 1900 campaign. In a fit of anxiety during the suspense, Hanna was stricken with a mild heart attack. While recovering, the senator threatened McKinley with his resignation from the National Committee. Unable to decide on a good alternative, the president casually renamed Hanna as his manager. If McKinley felt any guilt at all over his shabby treatment of Hanna, he never acknowledged it.

Because of McKinley's unassailable incumbency, Hanna needed to raise only $2.5 million ($1 million less than in 1896), and not even all this was actually spent. There was little need in 1900 for an extensive national organization, huge central control headquarters, a large staff of surrogate speakers and speechwriters, tons of literature and posters, and millions of lapel buttons. Hanna continued to dictate the daily operations and again faithfully kept in close touch with the Major. Again, the Republicans were able to cast McKinley as the epitome of patriotism and common sense. For the rest of his long career Bryan never lost his 1896 image as a fuzzy-minded radical and a politician who was somehow "un-American."

The comparatively dull campaign was not relieved by McKinley's decision (again wise from his strategical view) to conduct a second front-porch campaign in Canton. The city's celebrations and parades were minimal, the press corps almost nonexistent, and the imported delegations to see and hear the candidate few and far between. On Tuesday, November 6, it was over. McKinley surpassed his 1896 margin of victory. In 1900 he won 292 to 155 in the electoral college (21 votes more than in 1896). He received 7,218,039 (51.67 percent) popular votes to 6,358,345 (45.51 percent) for Bryan. His plurality in 1900 was 859,964 versus 596,985 four years earlier. Not an overwhelming victory (compared to subsequent ones), it was nonetheless an impressive mandate for him to continue his domestic and foreign policies another four years.

McKinley had procrastinated on the question of whom to choose as his next running mate. He was busy with affairs of state and, for once, badly neglected devoting time to a pressing political issue facing his own future. Many names surfaced for vice president, but none generated the enthusiasm and confidence of the delegates as that of the ex-Rough Rider Teddy Roosevelt, then governor of New York. Roosevelt had obvious presidential ambitions, yet wisely harbored no illusions about challenging the comparatively popular Republican incumbent.

Hanna, with prophetic vision, feared the possibility that the unpredictable TR might become president if tragedy struck McKinley. The president's manager fought hard to prevent Roosevelt's nomination. With uncharacteristic indifference to so weighty a political decision, McKinley rebuffed Hanna, announcing that he would abide by the will of the convention. The New York governor was then promptly nominated as the vice presidential candidate. "Whether by accident or prearrangement, McKinley allowed talent to enter his government in a way that improved the party he led,'' Lewis Gould argued in defense of the president. Though Hanna's self-esteem still smarted from being ''disciplined'' at the convention, he wrote to the president:

Well, it was a nice little scrap at Phila., not exactly to my liking with my hands tied behind me. However, we got through in good shape and the ticket is all right. Your *duty* to the country is to *live* for *four* years from next March. [Emphasis in original.]

TRAGEDY AT BUFFALO

In March 1901, the hyperactive Roosevelt was sworn in as vice president. Hanna snorted gloomily that the Rough Rider could never remain restrained throughout the second term, presiding over the Senate, waiting impatiently for his big chance in 1904.

When the Spanish-American War began, the number of threats against the president's life dramatically increased. Plots were uncovered, and several bombs were discovered in the White House mail. McKinley was probably among the most open of presidents. The job of protecting him was not easy. He steadfastly insisted on his long White House reception lines, mingling in crowds while campaigning, walking the streets of the capital city, and taking extended rail tours. Security was gradually increased by the Secret Service, but it remained inadequate, mostly because of McKinley's complacent attitude. His startling remark—''Who would want to shoot me?''—summed up the problem.

The Spanish-American War provided an ideal motivation for radicals of every stripe to attack the wealthy and public officials as exploiters of the underprivileged masses. By 1901 terrorists espousing anarchism had assassinated—or attempted to assassinate—a dozen renowned world leaders, and there was genuine fear in every country of this terrorist group. The yellow press in America sensationalized class distinctions. Any psychotic, many rational persons feared, might be inspired to take a shot at the president, the symbolic head of the great capitalist nation. One outrageous article in Hearst's *Journal* even implied that the president would be shot.[15]

Undaunted by any threats, the president serenely embarked on a long national tour soon after his second inauguration. An unusually large presidential party left the capital by train on April 29, 1901, swinging through the South, where McKinley presented a round of speeches. In Texas, however, Ida became seriously ill; later, the train was delayed in California for two weeks until the First Lady recovered enough to proceed. While on the West Coast, McKinley christened a new battleship, the *Ohio*. Ida recuperated enough to resume the tour, but the side trip to the northwestern states was cancelled, as was the final stop at Buffalo, where McKinley was to participate in ''President's Day'' at the Pan-American Exposition. Instead, the disappointed party escorted Ida directly back to Washington.

The McKinleys spent a restful, pleasant August at their home in Canton. The

Buffalo visit was rescheduled for September 5, 1901. On the way north, the presidential train stopped briefly in Cleveland, where McKinley conferred with Senator Hanna about the new departure in foreign trade policy that he was about to announce. Hanna, who was becoming more liberal in such matters himself, concurred with McKinley's message. At the Pan-American Exposition in Buffalo the next day, McKinley spoke to a huge crowd of 50,000 on the main plaza. He endorsed reciprocity and confidently predicted that his old pet policy of "exclusiveness" (high tariffs) was outdated.

On the day after his Buffalo speech, the president attended a reception at the Temple of Music on the exposition grounds. Security was unusually tight due to a premonition of danger held by his personal secretary, George B. Cortelyou. The president's own bodyguard of several Secret Service men, plus a few exposition detectives and a handful of soldiers, were nearby. At exactly 4:07 P.M., an anarchist named Leon F. Czolgosz stood immediately in front of the weary but smiling president. McKinley reached out to shake hands. Czolgosz thrust a hand forward, gripping a revolver concealed in a white handkerchief. He fired two shots at point-blank range; the first bullet lodged superficially in McKinley's chest, but the second burrowed dangerously deep into the victim's abdominal cavity. Chaos reigned in the Temple of Music as the gunman was subdued. McKinley was carried to a first-aid station on the grounds. An inexcusably amateurish operation was performed by a gynecologist who failed to locate the intestinal bullet. Fearing that to probe further would prove fatal, the doctors agreed to abandon the search for the second bullet and hope for the best.

Ida had accompanied her husband on the Buffalo trip. Exhausted from sightseeing at the exposition, however, she had avoided the Temple reception and had remained at a friend's mansion, where the presidential party was headquartered. After the surgery, McKinley was brought to this private home. In a day or so he rallied. His doctors issued optimistic bulletins about his expected recovery. Gangrene set in from the unremoved bullet; other complications followed and caused a sudden relapse. Eight days after he was shot, on September 14, 1901, William McKinley was dead.

When the president had rallied in the first few days, the government leaders who had rapidly gathered at his bedside gradually dispersed to their various posts. The grim news of the relapse brought most of them hurrying back to Buffalo in alarm. Hanna was among the first to return. "Although a self-contained man, he utterly broke down after the visit to the sick room and cried like a child," Moss and Cross report. The First Lady's grief was severe, but by some miracle she did not collapse entirely. Americans everywhere were shocked, as well as all the civilized world. "In an age unabashedly sentimental, McKinley's own countrymen, forgetful of his shortcomings and failures, wept openly in the streets as bells tolled the sad news across rivers, farmlands, mountains and prairies." The stock market plunged on Wall Street.

At his mountaintop retreat in upstate New York, a bewildered Theodore Roosevelt was informed that McKinley was near death. The vice president hardly digested the news before he dashed madly off to Buffalo. There he was sworn in as the twenty-sixth president.

Ida presided over calling hours at the White House. A state funeral was held at the Capitol. Then the presidential train, once festive in chugging for Buffalo, was now draped in black as it carried the casket and its sorrowful passengers from Washington to Ohio. As they had for Lincoln in 1865 and Garfield in 1881, Americans from all walks of life flocked to the railroad tracks to pay tribute as a slain president was carried home for the last time. In cities, towns, villages, at crossroads and in open fields—wherever they could catch a glimpse—McKinley's former constituents paid their last respects. At 3:30 P.M. on September 19, 1901, the body was placed in its temporary tomb.[16]

MODERN PRESIDENTIAL "ROLES" AND McKINLEY

In his classic study, *The American Presidency* (1960), the late Clinton Rossiter analyzes major roles of the "modern president." Some data presented on McKinley, namely, his performance as "Chief of State, Chief Executive, Commander-in-Chief, Chief Diplomat, Chief Legislator, and Party Chief," are applicable to Rossiter's criteria.

In the following cursory comparison of McKinley to the well-known taxonomy, no effort is made to be conclusive, nor is this an attempt to "prove" that the Major was the first "modern" president. Obviously, that is a subjective judgment, and the development of contemporary presidental prerogatives has been helter-skelter. Rossiter himself designated Theodore Roosevelt as the first modern president. However, a main purpose of this chapter has been to offer evidence to suggest that William McKinley has a more valid claim for that title.[17]

1. *Chief of State*. McKinley rose above partisan "politics" in 1897 as he encouraged the American economy out of the four-year-old depression. During the Spanish-American War, the president became a true symbol of national unity. Yet, it was following the conflict that he emerged as a lofty, "imperial" leader; McKinley clearly saw his function as a great educator on the issues. He was always conscious that his personal integrity served as a model of American conduct. He was the first president to realize fully the significance of the role of chief of state to foreign citizens. When he was assassinated, tears were shed around the world by thousands who knew nothing of his personal life, and millions of people abroad recognized the symbolic power which he alone had represented.

2. *Chief Executive*. Exercising his prerogative from the Constitution to execute the laws faithfully, McKinley was the first president to employ significant numbers of private sector professionals and academic experts on government commissions. They investigated such varied matters as charges of misconduct by the War Department in the Spanish-American War, adverse conditions in industrial workshops, options for an isthmian canal in Central America, and potential abuses of the trusts. Of course, he did not live to pursue or implement

most of the findings of his commissions, but they were influential in the reforms and achievements of the several presidents who followed. McKinley delegated executive authority well, letting the cabinet officers run the departments without undue interference.

3. *Commander-in-Chief*. It is in this role, more than the others, that McKinley's stature as a modern executive is most distinct. He was the first to conduct military operations in the field, and he did so personally from the White House. Unique in his time also was the huge discretionary war appropriation he received from Congress in peacetime. Later, in the Boxer Rebellion involving China, McKinley became the first president to order unilateral military action by the United States against a sovereign state without congressional approval or consultation. In the colonial administration of Puerto Rico, the Philippines, and Cuba, he distinctly set precedent by using his own military-civil authority to levy taxes and to regulate commerce at his discretion. Partly as a result of this role, McKinley was able to recapture the balance of power away from the legislative branch, where it had been since the days of Andrew Johnson.

4. *Chief Diplomat*. No president before McKinley had been faced with such a serious foreign policy crisis in his first year as that which existed with Spain in 1897. Saddled by his own admittedly poor selection of John Sherman for secretary of state, McKinley was literally forced to become a diplomatic expert in short order. That he failed to avoid war, as this chapter explains, was not due to his failure to pursue peace vigorously through diplomatic channels. The war was not waged from a lack of presidential courage. Rather, the conflict became inevitable and emanated from Spanish duplicity. In winning the war, the president demonstrated a unique talent for unifying American foreign policy. President Cleveland, after all, had not even attempted to settle the Cuban crisis; likewise, McKinley's predecessor had blocked the annexation of Hawaii. McKinley rejected both Cleveland policies. The composition of the peace commission he sent to Paris proved to be a master diplomatic stroke. His commissioners accomplished exactly what he wanted: an American empire. Any modern president would be proud of McKinley's list of diplomatic efforts: bimetallism, trade reciprocity, the Open Door Policy, an isthmian waterway, Anglo-American rapprochement.

5. *Chief Legislator*. Only two presidents prior to McKinley (Jefferson and Jackson) had as successful a relationship with Congress. It was McKinley who took the initiative away from the legislators with his tariffs, civil service, and currency reform measures, among others. He did not have a labeled legislative package (e.g., "Square Deal"), but the congressmen did look to him for leadership. Even when the Congress became consumed by prewar jingoism, he kept it on a tight string. The president received every military appropriation he requested. Many senators strongly opposed his imperialistic peace treaty, but he steered that through the upper house successfully, even if by a single vote. He cleverly employed his great popularity as chief of state to travel about the country widely, in the modern legislative role of the "lion," appealing directly to the

congressmen's constituents. In the contemporary guise of the "fox," McKinley had few peers—ever—in persuading a single legislator, or a small group of them, to see things his way. Legend has it that while McKinley's immediate predecessors could do a favor for a man, they would make an enemy; McKinley could refuse to grant a favor to an enemy and yet make a new friend. The thirteen years he spent in the House gave him great insight on the national legislative process.

6. *Party Chief*. Many presidents, especially those like McKinley who were reelected, have taken this role seriously. It has two aspects, understanding politics and control of the party machinery. As a lifelong politico, one who had held no other jobs in life (except briefly in the Union army and as a county prosecutor), the Major had a keen appreciation for the necessity of compromise and persuasion. He was essentially a man of consensus, but also one who forged and shaped that consensus. The Republican party's ideals of patriotism and protection were almost a religion with him. He was the epitome of party idealism when he was a congressman and governor, and most certainly when he was president. He had long service in the national party, at three national conventions, and as a popular stump speaker for other candidates. In ultimate control of Hanna's campaign organization, McKinley helped introduce businesslike efficiency into presidential politics. But, as president, there was never any doubt about who was in charge of the Republican party.

In retrospect, 1896 has been described as one of the few great "realigning elections" in the history of the American two-party system. McKinley also mastered Marcus Alonzo Hanna—and that was no mean accomplishment for any party chief in any era.

In sum: William McKinley can indeed be regarded as "the cutting edge of the modern Presidency." He will never have the lasting image of a "great" president like, say, Abraham Lincoln. There will be no state capital named after him, nor will he be enshrined by a fabulous marble memorial in Washington, D.C. The only single honor to McKinley was to name North America's tallest peak after him. However, even that may be revoked if Alaska's Athabaskan Indians succeed in renaming Mount McKinley Denalai. Whether the Indians have their way or not, historians and political scientists are gradually acquiring a renewed appreciation of McKinley's contributions to presidential prerogatives.

NOTES

This chapter was reviewed in progress by Professor Lewis L. Gould (Chairman, Department of History, University of Texas at Austin) and by Professor Robert E. Gilbert (Chairman, Department of Political Science, Northeastern University). I am grateful for their many insights and criticisms; most of their suggestions I have heeded. The full responsibility for any shortcomings, however, is mine alone. My sincere thanks, also, go to Marilyn Anobile, who proofread the manuscript, and to Theresa Graff, who typed the final draft.

1. The influence of the "muckrakers" (a term coined by Theodore Roosevelt) on McKinley's image is discussed in Richard H. Bradford, "Mask in the Pageant: William McKinley and American Historians," an unpublished manuscript furnished to me by Professor Gould. See Lewis L. Gould, "William McKinley and the Expansion of Presidential Power," *Ohio History*, 87, no. 1 (Winter 1978): 5, 6. Robert Gilbert suggests (in a letter to the author, June 16, 1982) that conservatives like McKinley (and Eisenhower) are being revised upward on performance less because of "new" evidence on these neglected presidents than because of changes in "scholarly views" on the presidency. James David Barber, *The Presidential Character*, 2nd. (Englewood Cliffs, N.J.: Prentice-Hall, 1977), contains low-level generalizations emanating from the neo-Freudian studies of the late psychoanalyst Karen Horney, particularly her *Neurosis and Human Growth* (New York: W. W. Norton, 1950). Elsewhere, using the Barber-Horney paradigm, I have argued to dispel the traditional view of McKinley as a "passive" and "average" character type. See John Latcham, "President McKinley's Active-Positive Character: A Comparative Revision with Barber's Typology," *Presidential Studies Quarterly*, 12, no. 4 (Fall 1982): 491–521.

2. McKinley's recent biographers (Gould, Morgan, and Leech) have devoted scant attention to his childhood and adolescence. Among more helpful earlier writers, see Charles S. Olcott, *The Life of William McKinley*, vols. 1 and 2 (Boston: Houghton Mifflin, 1916); Joseph G. Butler, Jr., *Presidents I Have Seen and Known* (Cleveland: Penton Press, 1910); and Charles H. Grosvenor, *William McKinley—His Life and Work* (New York: Trow Directory, 1901). Paul Glad, *McKinley, Bryan and the People* (Philadelphia: J. B. Lippincott, 1964), contains an excellent discussion of McKinley vis-à-vis myths about the "self-made man" and "rural virtue." Margaret Leech, *In the Days of McKinley* (New York: Harper and Brothers, 1959) (hereafter cited as Leech, *IDM),* and H. Wayne Morgan, *William McKinley and His America* (Syracuse, NY: Syracuse University Press, 1964) (hereafter cited as Morgan, *WMHA),* each offer thorough accounts of McKinley's early political career. For Ida Saxton McKinley's condition, see John Moss and Wilbur Cross, *Presidential Courage* (New York: W. W. Norton, 1980), and Leech, *IDM,* p. 34. On Whig ideology and Republicanism, see Clinton Rossiter, *Conservatism in America* (New York: Random House, 1962), pp. 130, 139, and Leech, *IDM,* pp. 34–37.

3. For a flavor of McKinley's image and the Republican national conventions, sample Herbert Croly, *Marcus Alonzo Hanna* (New York: Macmillan, 1912), pp. 122, 135–141, 166 (hereafter cited as Croly, *MAH).* Also see Leech, *IDM,* pp. 40, 41, 47–49, 55–57, 60; Morgan, *WMHA,* pp. 118–132, 155; and Croly, *MAH,* pp. 159, 160, 170, 171. Also see H. Wayne Morgan, "Governor McKinley's Misfortune: The Walker-McKinley Fund of 1893," *Ohio Historical Quarterly*, 59, no. 2 (April 1960): 103–120.

4. Leech, *IDM,* pp. 75, 76. While McKinley had always promoted a public image as "friend of the workingman," his partner Hanna was consistently vilified in the press as an enemy of organized labor. For refutation of this charge, see Gerald W. Wolff, "Mark Hanna's Goal: American Harmony," *Ohio History*, 79, no. 3–4 (1970): 138–151, and Morgan, *WMHA,* p. 148. Charles G. Dawes, a close friend of the Major's, stated, "The man did not live who dominated William McKinley." And that most certainly included Hanna. See Dawes, *A Journal of the McKinley Years* (New York: Lakeside Press, Donnelly and Sons, 1950), p. 368. Croly, *MAH,* p. 189, and Matthew Josephson, *The Politicos* (New York: Harcourt, Brace and World, 1963), p. 647, promote the popular myth that without Hanna's organizational talents and money, McKinley never could have become president. Morgan, *WMHA,* pp. 188–193, and Gould in private

correspondence with the author dispute this claim. See also Croly, *MAH*, pp. 176–185, and Stanley L. Jones, *The Presidential Election of 1896* (Madison: University of Wisconsin Press, 1964).

5. Jeffrey A. Nelson, "The Rhetoric of the 1896 and 1900 Republican Presidential Campaigns," Ph.D dissertation, University of Michigan, 1972, pp. 54–60; Croly, *MAH*, pp. 200–205, 209, 210; Leech, *IDM*, p. 81; Morgan, *WMHA*, pp. 223–226, 297, 310; Louis W. Koenig, *Bryan* (New York: Capricorn Books, G. P. Putnam's Sons, 1975), esp. pp. 174, 175. Remarks to Dawes cited in T. Bentley Mott, *Myron T. Herrick* (New York: Doubleday, Doran and Co., 1929), p. 64.

6. Morgan, *WMHA*, pp. 223–228; Richard Jensen, *The Winning of the Midwest: Social and Political Conflict, 1886–1896* (Chicago: University of Chicago Press, 1971), pp. 187–190, 291–308; Leech, *IDM*, pp. 88, 89; Nelson, "Rhetoric of the 1896 and 1900 Presidential Campaigns," pp. 124, 125. Jensen illustrates just how strong the Major was with ethnic voters in 1896 when he apparently won a majority of all groups but the Irish. After the Major's nearly disastrous brush with bankruptcy in 1893, both his and Ida's estates were managed for them by wealthy friends. See Glad, *McKinley, Bryan and the People,* chap. 1.

7. Jensen, *Winning of the Midwest,* pp. 271, 183, 290; *New York Times,* August 23, 1896; Lewis Gould, "Republicans' Search," in Morgan, *The Gilded Age.* On campaign revenues and expenditures, see Morgan, *WMHA,* pp. 227, 228; and Gould, *Presidency of William McKinley,* pp. 37, 38. (hereafter cited as Gould, *PWM.)* See also Morgan, *WMHA,* pp. 274, 304, 311, 317, 318, 321, 345; R. Hal Williams, *Years of Decision: American Politics in the 1890's* (New York: John Wiley and Sons, 1978), pp. 129, 130, 132–136; and H. Wayne Morgan, "William McKinley as a Political Leader, *Review of Politics,* 28 (1966): 422–430.

8. Thomas A. Bailey, *Presidential Greatness: The Image and the Man from George Washington to the Present* (New York: Appleton-Century, 1966), pp. 303–305 (emphasis added); Ralph L. Nelson, *Merger Movements in American Industry, 1896–1956* (Princeton, NJ: Princeton University Press, 1959), p. 5; Croly, *MAH,* pp. 236–238. Hanna's difficulty in being named by the Ohio General Assembly to the U.S. Senate is described in Gould, *PWM,* pp. 51, 56, 59, 60; Morgan, *WMHA,* pp. 250–251, 326–328; and Croly, *MAH,* pp. 228, 230–231.

9. Gould, *PWM,* p. 59; Ernest May, *Imperial Democracy: The Emergence of America as a Great Power* (New York: Harcourt, Brace and World, 1961), pp. 120, 121, 126–129.

10. Gould, *PWM,* pp. 63, 66, 73, 75, 76. Morgan, *WMHA,* pp. 330, 331, 354–370; James E. Pollard, *The Presidents and the Press* (New York: Macmillan, 1947), p. 559. Gould and Pollard agree that the influence of the yellow press as a cause of the Spanish-American War has been overblown in the textbooks. Note: As a leader with an active-positive character, McKinley was sure enough of his own self-esteem that he did not overreact to the personal insult in the deLôme letter. He was able, thus, to see the real danger—which was not a slur on his ego or office, but the continuation of a belligerent and insincere policy of Spanish stalling. Morgan, *WMHA,* pp. 359–361, 362. Gould explains: "The first modern study of the destruction of the *Maine* argues that it was caused accidentally by an internal explosion."

11. Gould, *PWM,* pp. 75, 76, 82–84, 121; Morgan, *WMHA,* p. 364. May, *Imperial Democracy,* p. 243. Gould's point on the Major's silence is well taken, but I tend to agree more with Morgan. The risk of antagonizing the Spanish seems minimal compared

to the rapidly deteriorating public approval toward the president's leadership on the Cuban issue.

12. Gould, *PWM,* pp. 91–93; Williams, *Years of Decision,* pp. 141, 142; Samuel Eliot Morison and Henry Steele Commager, *The Growth of the American Republic,* 2 vols., 4th ed. (New York: Oxford University Press, 1955), 2:143, 144; May, *Imperial Democracy,* p. 258; Gould, *PWM,* pp. 211, 97, 98.

13. William McKinley, *Speeches and Addresses: March 1 to May 30, 1900* (New York: Doubleday and McClure, 1900), p. 131; Arthur M. Schlesinger, Jr., *The Imperial Presidency* (Boston: Houghton Mifflin, 1973), p. 80; Morison and Commager, *American Republic,* 2:338; Gould, *PWM,* pp. 142–150, 153–159, 160–164; Henry J. Abraham, *Justice and Presidents* (Baltimore: Penguin Books, 1975), pp. 140–144. See Josephson, *The President Makers* (1940, Reprint. New York: Capricorn Books, G. P. Putnam's Sons, 1968), especially Chapter 1, "The Golden Years of McKinley and Hanna," for a muckraker's view of the Major and big business.

14. On the first U.S. corporate merger movement, see Nelson, *Merger Movements,* pp. 5, 104, 105; emphasis added. On McKinley-labor relations during his presidency, see Gould, *PWM,* pp. 164, 165, 214, 215, and Morgan, *WMHA,* p. 484. Barry Poulson in *Economic History of the United States* (New York: Macmillan, 1981) notes that under McKinley the federal Treasury in 1900 finally achieved a surplus after six years of deficits. See also Mary Thurston Peck, *Twenty Years of the Republic* (New York: Dodd, Mead, 1928), p. 641; Croly, *MAH,* pp. 320, 321.

15. Croley, *MAH,* pp. 322–333; Gould, *PWM,* pp. 228, 229, 215–218. The Populist party, which had conominated Bryan in 1896, ran a separate candidate in 1900 and received only 3.6 percent of the popular vote (50,340). Hanna to McKinley, June 25, 1900, McKinley Papers, Library of Congress, Washington, D.C. Gould believes that TR strengthened the party and was entirely qualified to be president himself. Morgan, *WHMA,* p. 510; A. Wesley Johns, *The Man Who Shot McKinley* (New York: A. S. Barnes and Co., 1970), pp. 16, 17.

16. Johns, *Man Who Shot McKinley,* pp. 27, 28, 92, 94; Croly, *MAH,* pp. 358, 259; Gould, *PWM,* pp. 250, 251; Johns, *Man Who Shot McKinley,* pp. 92, 94, 166, 167; Moss and Cross, *Presidential Courage,* p. 124; Morgan, *WMHA,* p. 525. Note: Even though McKinley's abdominal wound was critical, Moss and Cross conclude that his life could have been saved had he been taken to the Buffalo hospital where an X-ray machine and qualified surgeons were available.

17. See Clinton Rossiter, *The American Presidency,* rev. ed. (New York: Harcourt, Brace and World, 1960), Chapter 1, "The Powers of the Presidency." Gould is skeptical of Rossiter's obvious bias for TR as the first modern president. See Gould, "McKinley and the Expansion of Presidential Power," p. 5. Louis Koenig, in a review of Gould's *Presidency of William McKinley,* cites Rossiter's view and doubtless would have agreed with the criteria Gould applies—strength in office and impact on history—to reach that judgment (about McKinley's primacy). The best argument for Gould's thesis is in McKinley's "enlarged presidential influence" as commander-in-chief. (Review in *Presidential Studies Quarterly,* 12, no. 3 [Summer 1982]: 448–450.)

BIBLIOGRAPHIC ESSAY

The McKinley Papers in the Manuscripts Division of the Library of Congress represent the only significant collection of the twenty-fifth president's papers in existence. Ninety-eight reels of microfilm with a convenient index are available to various major libraries around the nation. The George B. Cortelyou Papers at the Library of Congress are also important. Cortelyou, President McKinley's private secretary, has left diaries and his own papers, which critically supplement the comparatively limited presidential collection. Because of gaps in the McKinley Papers, the Cortelyou Papers are essential for understanding the daily decision-making in the McKinley administration. In addition, the Library of Congress has papers of several dozen political contemporaries of McKinley that shed light on his career.

Several early biographies and campaign tracts offer some useful data on McKinley's childhood and adolescence that are not available elsewhere to current scholars interested in personality formation. Distinctly friendly to the subject, and frequently lacking objectivity, the early authors should be read cautiously. The best of the early group is Charles S. Olcott's *The Life of William McKinley,* 2 vols. (Boston: Houghton Mifflin, 1916). McKinley's boyhood companion, Joseph G. Butler, Jr., offers rare perspectives in *Presidents I Have Seen and Known* (Cleveland: Penton Press, 1910). Charles H. Grovenor, an Ohio congressman and longtime McKinley political associate, has helpful accounts in *William McKinley—His Life and Work* (New York: Trow Directory, 1901). McKinley's image suffered greatly at the hands of several generations of scholarly critics and professional muckrakers in the first half of the twentieth century. Much penetrating and persistent negativism can be found in writers such as the following: Mary Thurston Peck, *Twenty Years of the Republic* (New York: Dodd, Mead, 1906); William Allen White, *Masks in a Pageant* (New York: Macmillan, 1928); Charles and Mary Beard, *The Rise of American Civilization,* vol. 2 (New York: Macmillan, 1927); and Matthew Josephson's two works, *The Politicos* (New York: Harcourt, Brace and World, 1963) and *The President Makers* (New York: G. P. Putnam's Sons, 1940).

Since Olcott (1916), the first major contemporary revision of McKinley's image was accomplished by Margaret Leech's Pulitzer Prize-winning biography, *In the Days of McKinley* (New York: Harper Brothers, 1959). Leech presents a minute discussion of McKinley's personality, revising the traditional view of this president as weak, indecisive, and a cowardly leader. McKinley is shown by Leech to have been in complete charge of his own career and, certainly, his own presidential administration. The myth of Mark Hanna's alleged dominance over McKinley is demolished. The author heavily uses the McKinley Papers and the diary of his secretary, Cortelyou. Leech's study marks the turning point in the modern upgrading of McKinley's reputation; however, her work is objective and discusses the man's weaknesses as well as his strengths.

H. Wayne Morgan's *William McKinley and His America* (Syracuse: 1963) is an outstanding confirmation of Leech's thesis. Morgan likewise builds a strong case for McKinley as a twentieth-century type leader; yet he concludes somewhat ambiguously that this president was a "traditional" chief executive, found between the "old-fashioned" and the "modern" presidency. A controversial finding is that McKinley could not possibly have avoided the Spanish-American War, contrary to the conventional wisdom's image of him as a moral coward buckling under to jingoist war-fever. Morgan's well-received biography quickly surpassed Leech's and was the standard work on McKinley for two decades.

Lewis L. Gould has come to the fore in his *The Presidency of William McKinley* (Lawrence: American Presidency Series, Regents Press of Kansas, 1980). Gould's main thesis is clear from the outset: he argues that the evidence demonstrates conclusively that McKinley should be considered the *first* modern president. McKinley's establishment and elaboration of numerous presidential prerogatives are presented, particularly those dealing with the development of presidential press relations, traveling about as chief of state to sell his program to the electorate, and swinging the balance of federal power from Congress to the executive branch for the first time since Lincoln. McKinley's five years, Gould shows, were mainly consumed by foreign policy decisions. Using new data from the Cortelyou Papers (unavailable to Leech and Morgan), Gould fills in the gaps by explicitly reinforcing Morgan's contention that McKinley searched sincerely for peace, and then went to war only because it was inevitable.

Two important articles on McKinley are standard fare. The first, H. Wayne Morgan's "William McKinley as a Political Leader," *Review of Politics,* 28 (1966): 417–432, is a concise summary of the personality traits which the author presented in his earlier (1963) biography. This piece, which refutes critics who claim that McKinley was weak and pliable, takes a stronger stand on the president's claim on the modern era than was his position in the 1963 book. Morgan is convinced that McKinley was the right man at the right time; his achievements—especially in foreign policy—deserve much more recognition than they have received. The second article is by Lewis Gould. His "William McKinley and the Expansion of Presidential Power," *Ohio History,* 87, no. 1 (Winter 1978): 5–20, foreshadows many of his later arguments in his biography (1980). Gould, here, particularly debunks the myth of Theodore Roosevelt as the first modern president.

In John S. Latcham, "President McKinley's Active-Positive Character: A Comparative Revision with Barber's Typology," *Presidential Studies Quarterly,* 12, no. 4 (Fall 1982): 491–521, I have employed the well-known typology of the political scientist James David Barber (*The Presidential Character,* 1972) to analyze McKinley's personality and historical image. Using biographical data, I looked at Barber's constructs of childhood "character," adolescent "world view," and early adult "political style." My conclusion is that McKinley's traditional image as a "passive" personality is unfounded.

The standard for McKinley's landmark first election remains Stanley L. Jones, *The Presidential Election of 1896* (Madison: University of Wisconsin Press, 1964), which describes the effectiveness of the Hanna-McKinley campaign's organizational, business-like efficiency.

The spectacular performance of McKinley's 1896 campaign manager is well detailed in Herbert Croly, *Marcus Alonzo Hanna* (New York: Macmillan, 1912). Though far outdated, Croly still offers the closest insight into the character of the millionaire businessman who became McKinley's patron of many years and a political power in his own right. Unsurprisingly, Croly posits the once unchallenged argument that McKinley never could have become president without Hanna's financial support, influential friends, and organizational talents. The treatment of Hanna is sympathetic, but Croly readily discusses the (real and alleged) flaws in Hanna's personality which ultimately caused McKinley so much embarrassment in the presidential campaign and during the first term.

For a unique approach to the election of 1896, one should consult Paul Glad, *McKinley, Bryan and the People* (Philadelphia: J. B. Lippincott, 1964). Both candidates are analyzed as being economic "conservatives" for their era, and McKinley and Bryan are sensitively portrayed by Glad as the embodiment of the two great prevailing myths governing nineteenth-century American politics—the myth of "Horatio Algerism," which spurred the post–Civil War industrialism, and the Jeffersonian "myth of rural virtue."

For a broader political picture, an excellent source (rather critical of McKinley and Hanna) is Robert D. Marcus, *Grand Old Party: Political Structure in the Gilded Age* (New York: Oxford University Press, 1971). For a good account of how businesslike sales organizations became the party model replacing the military structure, see Richard Jensen's *The Winning of the Midwest: Social and Political Conflict, 1886–1896*. (Chicago: University of Chicago Press, 1971). Jensen emphasizes the critical role of "pluralism," which formed the core of the McKinley coalition that dominated American politics until the New Deal. Jensen's statistics, especially on the ethnic groups who supported McKinley in 1896, are revealing of the change this candidate made in the composition of the national electorate. Ernest R. May, in *Imperial Democracy: The Emergence of America as a Great Power* (New York: Harcourt, Brace and World, 1961), explains that McKinley's several options for Cuban "intervention" were constrained by the domestic politics of his 1897 honeymoon. May describes the intolerable pressure for American action on Cuba put upon the president by pro-Spanish Europeans with their own imperialist thrusts into Asia. Despite his own data supporting McKinley as a competent leader, May is highly critical of this president—e.g., May charges that McKinley only became an imperialist because it was politically expedient.

In his *America's Road to Empire: The War with Spain and Overseas Expansion* (New York: John Wiley and Sons, 1965), H. Wayne Morgan contends that the United States had a legal right to intervene in Cuba, and that it was distinctly in our own commercial interest to do so. Morgan sees the war policy set forth by McKinley as a prime example of American humanitarianism. For the two most recent books on McKinley's foreign policy, consult Davis Trask, *The War with Spain in 1898* (New York: Macmillan, 1982), and Lewis L. Gould, *The Spanish-American War and President McKinley* (Lawrence: University Press of Kansas, 1982).

8   THEODORE ROOSEVELT

David C. Roller

Jacob Riis, the premier investigative reporter of nineteenth-century New York's press corps, used to occupy an office on the second floor of the Mulberry Street police reporters' building. Often, while in this office and working on an article about health or housing or perhaps on parks and playgrounds, he would hear the shrill yell used by cowboys to round up stray steers: "Hi Yi Yi." The yells came not from prankish messenger boys outside his office, nor did they come from neighborhood children playing in the street below. The yell always came from across the street, from the second floor window in the office of New York's president of the Board of Police Commissioners. The gleefully delivered "Hi Yi Yi" would echo down the length of the Mulberry Street ravine, and Riis would rise from his desk to cross the street and call upon the commissioner of police. For this yell was the not-so-secret boyish code used to signal Riis by Theodore Roosevelt.[1]

"Jake" and TR enjoyed a special friendship. Both men approached life with apparently boundless energy. They shared a similar vision of what was unjust about contemporary society, a similar sense of duty to correct those injustices, and an unfaltering confidence in their abilities to bring about needed change. That two fast friends who worked together as pioneers of urban reform would share such playful banter as an innocent cowboy yell is not in itself remarkable. Yet this facet of their relationship is illustrative of several characteristics of one of this nation's more remarkable presidents.

Roosevelt's indifference to conventional amenities and formal protocol is legendary. Whether issuing cowboy yells, teaching the ambassador of France to perform cartwheels, or inventing his own spelling of the English language, TR always felt totally free to express the exuberant joy he found in life. If what was customary and expected could be amended or embellished, he would find a way to do that. But if what struck him as routine could not be altered, he would strike out to establish his own Rooseveltian mode of behavior.

The special relationship TR enjoyed with Riis also exemplifies the camaraderie he had with the press in general. Riis, Lincoln Steffens, and William Allen

White represent only the better known among the army of reporters summoned at one time or another to Roosevelt's home or office to hear him pontificate upon some subject he found important.

Roosevelt sought to dominate his meetings with the press in the same way he did in every social context. Occasionally he failed: Lincoln Steffens, for one, never yielded completely to the Roosevelt personality.

FAMILY AND CHILDHOOD BACKGROUND

The abundant energy and certain self-confidence of a Theodore Roosevelt can be learned and developed in a variety of ways. In his case it can almost be said to have been inherited. In those social circles where a Vanderlip is held in higher esteem than a Vanderbilt and where the name Auchincloss, Chew, Lowell, or Morris opens doors closed even to ordinary millionaires, no family's credentials are more impeccable than the Roosevelts'. Claes Martenzen van Rosenveldt's descendants might differ over the pronunciation of their illustrious surname (some prefer "Rose-e-velt," others "Rose-velt," and a few "Ruz-velt"). They might feel a closer affinity toward kin in the branch of the family popularly identified with Hyde Park on the Hudson River and FDR, the Democrat. Or they might identify more readily with relatives often represented as "the Oyster Bay Roosevelts." Nevertheless, they are Roosevelts. They are secure enough in their elite social status not to have to prove themselves to the world at large, and most have been wealthy enough for several generations not to concern themselves with the vulgar business of making a living. They belong to the American squirearchy, a class of gentry which often passes for an American aristocracy.[2]

Theodore Roosevelt, Jr., was born in 1858 in a substantial, if unpretentious, brownstone house on New York City's then fashionable East 20th Street. It was the family's gift to TR's mother and father shortly after their wedding. A house of their own, however, did not mean that the young couple was separated from relatives. His mother's mother and maiden sister moved from Georgia into the house next door. If this somehow was insufficient family, grandfather Cornelius van Schaak Roosevelt lived around the corner in a fine red brick residence which faced onto Union Square. TR would be born and reared surrounded by aunts, uncles, and cousins who were as socially and politically prominent as they were numerous.[3]

Grandfather Cornelius was a driving, determined, and energetic businessman who had dropped out of Columbia University to devote his considerable talents to the family hardware firm of Roosevelt & Son. He cornered a near monopoly on American imports of plate glass and founded the Chemical National Bank of New York. He also invested extensively in real estate: at the time of the Civil War his real property in New York City was valued at $1.5 million. Cornelius' brother James J. Roosevelt, meanwhile, dabbled at law, high society, and politics; he was elected to terms in the New York Assembly and the U.S. House of Representatives and was appointed a justice of the New York State Supreme Court.[4]

At least as prominent as grandfather Cornelius and great-uncle James, however, was Uncle Robert. Flamboyant, indefatigable, and even eccentric, Robert Roosevelt presaged many of his more famous nephew's accomplishments. He was the author of four books and the editor of the New York *Citizen,* a newspaper devoted to literature and reform politics. As a member of New York City's "Seventy Honest Men," he helped to topple William Tweed, the infamous "boss" of Tammany Hall. Robert served on the commission which oversaw construction of the Brooklyn Bridge, followed his uncle James to the U.S. House of Representatives, and represented the United States as its ambassador to the Netherlands. Yet his greatest, almost all-consuming passion was conservation. As the first chair of New York's Fish Commission, he restocked the state's lakes and rivers, publicized problems created by industrial waste and commercial fishing, and earned an international reputation in the conservation movement. His almost omnivorous enthusiasms placed him in correspondence with such diverse people as Oscar Wilde, Bret Harte, Horace Greeley, John Hay, Gilbert and Sullivan, and Admiral Dewey. House guests included the rich, the powerful, and the soon to be famous: the beautiful and talented Sarah Bernhardt as well as His Highness, the Prince of Wales.[5]

No member of the family was more admired and respected by TR, however, than his own father, Theodore Roosevelt, Sr. The elder Roosevelt was a warm and humorous man who regarded seriously the responsibilities and roles allotted a Victorian gentleman of his social standing. After seeing a shivering newspaper boy on New York's streets he founded a lodging home for news carriers and, thereafter, spent most Sunday evenings visiting his wards. He was among the founders of the Society for the Prevention of Cruelty to Animals, the Metropolitan Museum of Art, and the New York Museum of Natural History. And after physicians concluded that medical science was insufficient to correct the curvature of his eldest daughter's spine, he founded the New York Orthopedic Hospital. Attired in impeccably tailored clothes, he always was a model gentleman, completely at ease with himself and others. Whether chatting with street people or dining at the White House with his friend Mary Todd Lincoln, whether arguing politics with New York's Republican "Boss" Conkling or bartering with Berber tribesmen in Palestine, TR's father presented himself to the world—and to his son—with a self-confident grace, wit and charm worthy of emulation.[6]

Although TR deliberately made many of his father's attitudes and behaviors his own, there never was any likelihood of living up to his idealized vision of his father. For the elder Theodore was strong, tall, and handsome, while little "Teedie" (no one who really knew TR would have called him "Teddy" to his face at any time in his life) was a frail child trapped in a sickly body. Before he was one year old his family recognized a pattern of recurring attacks of asthma which became graver and more frightening with each passing year. Without benefit of twentieth-century medicine, the Roosevelts had no recourse but to pray and to drive a team of horses to dangerous speeds while someone held "Teedie" so as to force oxygen into his lungs. In addition to his asthma there was a continuing succession of colds, coughs, and fevers plus frequent attacks of gastrointestinal upset to cause the family immense concern. Physicians advised the family not to expect a long life for their eldest son, and when TR was twelve his father presented the situation to him as directly as possible. He would have to build a body for himself.[7]

The elder Theodore built an outdoor gymnasium onto the third floor of the 20th Street house and later moved the family to a West 57th Street residence so that "Teedie" could exercise in fresh and open air. A regime of gymnastics, hiking, and riding was established for him by his father, to which TR himself gradually added rowing, boxing, and even mountain climbing. The rigors of a period of such outdoor activities usually alleviated the youngster's asthma, but often they also left him exhausted and vulnerable to gastrointestinal inflammation. A sedentary period of rest, on the other hand, usually cured his diarrhea but threatened a recurrence of his asthma. During these strenuous periods of activity he learned, with his father's assistance, to marvel at the great outdoors. And during periods of enforced inactivity, also with his father's help, the precocious youngster developed a voracious appetite for the printed word, especially books about nature and history.[8]

It was not unusual in the nineteenth century for a young man of TR's social standing to be educated at home and not in school. In his case, however, TR's health mandated it. Although his mother or older sister usually oversaw his lessons, it was his father who set the gentle and genteel character of the curriculum. The elder Theodore would just happen to have a copy of *The Last of the Mohicans* to read by the campfire during a trip into the Adirondacks; during two family excursions to Europe the family carried a portable library of medieval history and Renaissance art; and on a father and son tour of the Holy Land they used the King James Version of the Old Testament as one of their guidebooks. The resulting education was extensive but uneven.[9]

As always, TR's health shaped his living patterns. The only available dormitory rooms at Harvard had been on the ground floor, so to escape the dampness which might aggravate his asthma he took a second-floor room two blocks off of Harvard Square. This location partly removed him from roguish fellows who used offensive language, but it also protected most of his classmates from the ever present smell of formaldehyde caused by his ornithological collection. His somewhat foppish dress, his more or less constant wheezing, and his righteous attitudes toward smoking, drinking, and swearing could have made him unpopular with many young men of his age. But at Harvard, Roosevelt was welcomed and, after years of being kept apart, he threw himself into the social as well as the academic whirl of college life.

He attended a constant string of teas, dances, poetry readings, plays, and dinners. Both of Harvard's two most exclusive clubs extended offers of membership (he elected to join the Porcellians, a club which a few years later would blackball his urbane and handsome cousin, FDR). He was editor of the *Advocate*, a secretary for the Hasty Pudding Club, and active in a half dozen assorted groups including, of course, the Natural History Society. Yet his diaries and letters record the habits of a student who was as self-disciplined as he was socially active. Despite having serious difficulty with French, he was elected to Phi Beta Kappa and was graduated twenty-first in a class of 177 classmates.[10]

Just prior to his graduation, TR underwent a routine physical examination. The physician informed him that, probably as a result of his rigorous regime of physical activity, he had developed a weakness of his heart. TR listened to the doctor's prescription of a less active life and then consciously rejected the advice. The lessons learned in his childhood were now part of the fiber of the man. He had lived with and overcome asthma and other disorders while traveling extensively over five continents and climbing several dangerous peaks. What was there he could not do? He could choose between a career in law, politics, or natural science without the necessity of supporting himself solely by such labor. With boundless energy and a consuming zest for life, he was ready to take on the world. He was, after all, a Roosevelt.

THE MEDIA DISCOVER ROOSEVELT

Radio and television would have been extremely unkind to Roosevelt. His double row of oversized teeth fixed in the frozen grin of a lifelong asthmatic gave him a less than photogenic smile. Set these below a pair of double-thick glasses and atop a chunky torso disproportionately short for the attached legs, and the result—by whatever name you call him or her—would be a video specialist's nightmare. And although radio embraced the idiosyncracies and the accent of Knickerbocker English when uttered in the modulated tones of FDR, that same accent and similar speech spoken in the shrill and sometimes falsetto voice of Theodore Roosevelt would be a wireless disaster. Yet it would be misleading to suggest that he was merely fortunate to have predated radio and television. For central to Roosevelt's rather considerable political successes was his remarkable ability to use and at times even to dominate the medium of his own era: the printed word.

A year and a half after being graduated from Harvard in 1880 (and only a few months after returning home from his European honeymoon), Roosevelt was serving his first of three terms in the New York State Assembly. His family's name and its political connections certainly helped his candidacy in the Twenty-first District, New York City's so-called silk stocking district. His meteoric career in Albany established his credentials among Republican party leaders as a hard-working "Young Turk." Yet it was the daily news coverage of his legislative comings and goings that established his public image as a vigorous reformer. And it was this public image that led New York City's Republicans to name Roosevelt (while still in his twenties) as their mayoral candidate in 1886. He ran a respectable, if unsuccessful, campaign which further enhanced his popular reputation as a man of integrity and energy.[11] Less than three years later, in 1889, President Benjamin Harrison appointed Roosevelt to the U.S. Civil Service Commission, in part because of TR's loyalty to the Republican party but also because of his reputation as a reformer. And when President Grover Cleveland wanted to demonstrate bipartisanship in the civil service system, he reappointed the Republican commissioner who, for the four previous years, had dominated press coverage of the commission: Theodore Roosevelt.[12]

Again and again along his path toward the presidency, Roosevelt's public image as a reformer preceded him and indeed helped to create political opportunities for him. In 1895, when New York City's scandal-ridden police department required a police commissioner with a popular reputation for absolute honesty and abundant energy, the appointment went, of course, to Roosevelt. And after brief—but highly publicized—periods of service as an assistant secretary of the navy (1897–1898) and a colonel of volunteers in Cuba (1898), Roosevelt was virtually drafted for governor of New York. Newspaper coverage of the scandals of the incumbent Republican governor had seriously embarrassed the state's G.O.P. A consensus of editorial opinion held that only a man of Roosevelt's integrity and with Roosevelt's popularity could win in 1898 on the Republican ticket. As only Roosevelt enjoyed both that reputation and that popularity, the press and the party were there to simultaneously offer him the gubernatorial nomination when he and his "Rough Riders" disembarked on their return from Cuba.[13] Long before he became governor, Roosevelt had developed a highly symbiotic relationship with the news media.

Journalism, like the nation, was undergoing profound and dramatic changes during the latter half of the nineteenth century. The development of pulp paper and mechanized typesetting made it economically feasible to publish inexpensive magazines and newspapers for mass circulation. But a mass readership is not the same audience as an elite one, and merely dropping the price of a magazine from thirty-five to fifteen cents or that of a newspaper from three cents to a penny never resulted automatically in mass sales. Well before the "muckraking" monthlies and the "yellow press" dailies of the turn of the century, publishers and journalists had begun a radical transformation of print media. Monthly periodicals like *McClure's* and *Munsey's* and the long-established *Saturday Evening Post,* a weekly magazine, watched their sales soar toward a million copies as they devoted more space to topical and human interest stories. Meanwhile, the more genteel and intellectual monthlies like *Harper's, Century,* and *Godey's Lady's Book* floundered or ceased publication. And daily newspapers that persisted in regarding schedules of arriving and departing ocean liners as front page copy were soon buried in metropolitan areas by competitors who successfully altered both their content and their format to appeal to a mass, daily readership.[14]

Roosevelt was not only a contemporary of these changes but a participant in them. Most of his biographers delight in recounting how, on the occasion in 1884 of his first visit to the Dakotas, Roosevelt invested $14,000 in the Maltese Cross Ranch. Fewer explain that he had made a prior investment of $20,000 in the publishing firm of G. P. Putnam's Sons. Although ranching proved to be a financial disaster for Roosevelt, writing—even writing about his ranching experiences—was a profitable and continuing activity of his.[15]

Some of Roosevelt's publications, especially those completed during the 1880s, never were intended to have popular appeal: his thoroughly researched and detailed history, *The Naval War of 1812* (1882), his vanity printing of 500 copies of *Hunting Trips of a Ranchman* (1885), and his semischolarly biography, *Thomas Hart Benton* (1887), were each elite publications of a kind. His four-volume history, *The Winning of the West* (1889, 1894, 1896), he wrote for a more broadly based audience; it is less scholarly, less technical, and less balanced than his naval history. Like the publishers of various journals of this time, Roosevelt gradually was altering his approach and style to better suit an emerging market of readers. By the 1890s, all of his major efforts had at least a semipopular aura about them. The grandson of Cornelius van Schaak Roosevelt never totally abandoned his ties with the gentry; he reviewed books for *Atlantic Monthly*, and he published his biography *Oliver Cromwell* (1900) in *Scribner's*, periodicals with a comparatively small and genteel readership. Yet well before riding with the Rough Riders in Cuba or serving as governor of New York, "Theodore Roosevelt" appeared as a not too infrequent by-line over articles in such popular periodicals as *Cosmopolitan, Independent,* and *Forum*.[16]

Roosevelt's postpresidential career as a contributing editor of *Outlook Magazine*, as a columnist for the *Kansas City Star*, and as the author of *African Game Trails* (1910) was founded only in part upon his status as a celebrity, a well-liked ex-president of the United States. It was also, in part, the resumption of an earlier vocation, one which the younger Roosevelt had pursued separate from but parallel with his political career. If people today recall that Roosevelt was once a cowboy, that he hunted big game in Africa, or that he led an exploration up an uncharted branch of the Amazon River, it is in large part because he himself published vivid journalistic accounts of these activities. Yet the parallel pursuit of these twin careers did not instantly bestow upon the younger Roosevelt full-fledged or even honorary membership in the brotherhood of newsmen. His interest in journalism may have heightened his awareness of the press. It also may have made him both more interesting to and interested in individual reporters. But it took him almost as long to earn his spurs as a politician with the press corps as it took him to hit his stride as a journalist.

In 1881, when the twenty-three-year-old Roosevelt first sought public office, the press paid him little attention. His race in the Twenty-first District for a seat in the New York State Assembly was only one among many. The Roosevelt family's various philanthropies to Columbia University may explain why that school's football squad, its baseball team, and most of its boxers and wrestlers volunteered to work on the campaign. Family friends such as Joseph H. Choate, Elihu Root, Chauncey Depew, and Theodore Dwight signed petitions in support of his candidacy. But the only significant attention paid Roosevelt by New York City's daily press was the editorial endorsement of the *New York Herald*. The editorial was written by Carl Schurz, a friend of TR's father, and it argued that Roosevelt had "hereditary claims to the confidence and hopefulness of the voters of this city."[17]

Although Roosevelt won election in this "silk stocking" district by almost double the normal Republican plurality, his arrival in Albany occasioned no particular press coverage. Yet the state's daily press continually needed fresh copy, and its reporters constantly sought quotable material from legislative proceedings. In the third week of the assembly's deliberation, Roosevelt delivered his maiden address. It was a satirical and partisan attack on the leadership of the Democratic majority. The *New York Herald, Times, Sun Tribune* and *Star* each reported his speech, with the Democratic *Sun* adding a few words to ridicule Roosevelt for his "quaint drawl" and his "English side-whiskers."[18] His either/ or approach to all political issues, his direct if intemperate speech, and even his personal idiosyncracies made him interesting copy. Yet even as a freshman assemblyman, Roosevelt found other uses for the press besides the publicity it could give him.

With some help from his Democratic uncle, Robert Barnwell Roosevelt, Theodore had been appointed to the Committee on Cities. This prestigious appointment placed Roosevelt at the center of discussions of issues vital to New York City, including a one-third reduction in the taxes assessed against Jay Gould's Manhattan Elevated Railway Company. Roosevelt's opposition to the measure added luster to his reputation as an honest and incorruptible legislator, but Gould's forces won with the combined support of the leadership of both Republican and Democratic parties. Roosevelt was stung by this taste of defeat. Then he recalled reading an article in the *New York Times* which had alleged corrupt and illegal dealings between Gould and New York State Supreme Court Justice Theodore Westbrook. With his inherited self-confidence and learned bravado, Roosevelt marched into the *Times'* office, asked to see the city editor, and insisted on seeing the newspaper's files. In those files he found enough evidence of collusion between Westbrook and Gould to manipulate the price of the Manhattan's stock that he introduced legislation to impeach Judge Westbrook.[19]

Roosevelt's bill of impeachment was a direct assault on Jay Gould, then one of the nation's wealthiest men and more notorious "robber barons." It also placed him in opposition to some of the Roosevelt family's more distinguished friends and to the leadership of the state's Republican party. Although the bill eventually was defeated, Roosevelt first managed to introduce most of his evidence and much of his argument against Gould and Westbrook in proceedings of the state assembly and, by that route, onto the pages of the state's daily newspapers. Westbrook died before a second bill of impeachment could be introduced, but Roosevelt's political career was launched.[20]

It would be misleading to imply that Roosevelt thereafter enjoyed nothing but plaudits from newsmen during the course of his political career. He often was the subject of criticism, even stinging rebukes, delivered by irate publishers or editors. Joseph Pulitizer's *New York World* editorials hounded Roosevelt for over thirty years.[21] Yet those same publishers and editors recognized Roosevelt as "newsworthy" copy; the *New York Tribune,* for example, assigned one reporter the full-time responsibility of covering the barely twenty-five-year-old assemblyman during his second term in Albany. The basic outlines of the mature Roosevelt's relationship with reporters—the people who write the daily news—already were evident.

Members of the working press corps always found him accessible. It was not merely that Roosevelt understood that impressions created by daily news accounts possessed a concrete quality that could not be shaken by an occasional editorial. Nor was it merely that Roosevelt grasped the political leverage attainable by having his version of any issue and his documentation in the minds and hands of those who wrote the news. Roosevelt genuinely enjoyed the company of newsmen. He liked to think of himself and them as fellow working journalists. Moreover, among the menagerie of continuing friendships sustained by Roosevelt, there were not only diplomats and scholars, poets and pugilists, painters and businessmen, but also always a number of reporters.

Roosevelt's special comradeship with Jacob Riis has already been noted and is probably the best known of his journalistic ties. The Danish immigrant had become by the mid-1890s one of the nation's more celebrated of a new generation of investigatory newsmen. He saw Roosevelt as a kindred spirit, and the two of them were close friends and mutual confidants. When Roosevelt as police commissioner needed hard information about housing for indigents in New York City he turned, not to his nonexistent staff, but to Riis. And when Roosevelt as governor encountered opposition from the state's pharmacists to a bill to reduce the workday of drug clerks he commissioned a survey of druggists' opinions done, not by nonexistent polling agencies, but by Riis. And when Riis believed that he had critical information or a workable reform to share with political leaders, he turned first to Commissioner Roosevelt and then to Governor Roosevelt.[22]

There is less familiarity with and less documentation for Roosevelt's friendships with Oscar K. Davis of the *New York Times,* Lyman Abbott of *Outlook Magazine,* David Barry of the *New York Sun,* and Joseph B. Bishop.[23] Though Bishop, for example, often found himself employed by papers that were editorially hostile to Roosevelt, the two enjoyed one another's mutual respect and friendship. While Governor Roosevelt sparred with the state legislature and the leadership of his own party over enactment of a comprehensive police reform bill, he shared his problems and perceptions of the unfolding battle with Bishop, both orally and in their personal correspondence. Years later, it was Bishop who would edit and publish the earliest edition of Roosevelt's letters.[24] And when Colonel Roosevelt of the Rough Riders found it inappropriate to campaign for the gubernatorial nomination while still on active duty, the campaign to "draft" Roosevelt was orchestrated in larger part by the chairman of the New York County Republicans, one Ely Quigg, a former reporter for the *New York Times* who knew and respected Roosevelt from his terms in the state assembly.[25]

Perhaps the best illustration from his early career of Roosevelt's special relationship with the press corps is an anecdote told in fullest detail by George
Spinney, a reporter who covered Roosevelt while in the New York legislature.
Spinney and others recalled the incident years after Roosevelt's presidency, and
the story may or may not be apocryphal. During one of Roosevelt's long strolls
across the countryside, walks that later would become famous, he stopped at a
roadhouse outside of Albany. One John Costello, a Tammany Hall Democrat,
was there drinking with a group of friends, and he began to taunt Roosevelt,
calling him a "damned little dude" and a "mamma's boy." As Spinney and
others recount, Roosevelt is supposed to have sent Costello and one of his friends
to the floor with rapid punches, to have sent the rest of Costello's friends running,
and then to have said: "When you are in the presence of gentlemen conduct
yourself like a gentleman." If the story is essentially true, it is noteworthy that
Spinney and other members of the Albany press corps chose not to file an account
of a roadhouse brawl between two members of the state assembly. If, on the
other hand, the story is merely a piece of Rooseveltian lore, it was one invented
or embellished by a newsman fondly recalling a very special friendship.[26]

THE ROOSEVELT TECHNIQUE: A CASE STUDY

In his relations with Congress, the Republican party, the nation, and the world
at large, Roosevelt often followed a complicated criss-cross of paths while simultaneously maintaining or even building upon the public image he most desired. He often provided vocal support for tariff reform and for a downward
revision of all schedules and rates. Yet he never wanted Congress to tackle that
politically divisive issue. He merely used the prospect of tariff reform to prod
Old Guard Republicans to approve railroad rate regulation. Meanwhile, he won
laurels for the Elkins Act and the Hepburn Act while enhancing his reputation
as an advocate of tariff reform.[27] During the Venezuelan crisis of 1902, the
public Roosevelt supported Germany's claims against President Cipriano Castro
with polite reminders to the Kaiser to respect the Monroe Doctrine. The semipublic Roosevelt ordered the U.S. fleet to gather off the coast of Puerto Rico.
The more secretive Roosevelt delivered to Ambassador Theodor von Holleben
an ultimatum: either Germany submitted its claims against Venezuela to binding
arbitration within ten days or Roosevelt would lead the United States into war.
After Germany bowed to Roosevelt's ultimatum and accepted arbitration, the
public and the semipublic Roosevelt was credited for having exercised balance
and restraint during a difficult diplomatic crisis. Not only could Roosevelt run
with the foxes and hunt with the hounds, he invariably ended the hunt with an
enhanced reputation. There is no better illustration of this than his handling of
racial politics.

When Roosevelt assumed the presidency, each of the southern states, through
some combination of devices, either had stripped blacks of the right to vote or
was about to do so. Yet few Americans were interested in a defense of the black

ballot. Most Republicans and northern "liberals" had abandoned the cause of Negro liberties. Numerous federal court decisions had made defense of any racial minority's rights difficult. And the nation's assumption of the "white man's burden" in Cuba and the Philippines had made professions of racial equality somewhat incongruous.[28]

For years a number of Republicans had dreamed of rebuilding the southern wing of the GOP with the support of that region's conservative white Democrats. Presidents Hayes, Arthur, and McKinley had tried to advance their party's fortunes with a "southern strategy" calculated to convert the business-oriented Bourbons of the South. Each had failed to circumvent the wall of white solidarity. With the disfranchisement of blacks, however, the bugbear of race might disappear. Instead the twin bogies of Bryan and Free Silver, frightening to many white Southern Democrats, might scare people into the Republican party. Disfranchisement might permit Roosevelt to succeed where his predecessors had failed. Yet Roosevelt, an accidental president, also needed to ensure his own nomination and election in 1904. If he flirted too overtly with white Southern Democrats, black and white Republicans in the South might throw their support and their convention delegates to Marcus Hanna or to some other candidate for the Republican nomination. And even if Roosevelt could ensure his own nomination, an overtly "lily-white" southern strategy might alienate the black vote in several pivotal states of the North.[29]

During the first twelve months of his administration, Roosevelt avoided a choice between alternative southern strategies. With the help of Booker T. Washington, he straddled the color line of southern politics and concentrated on securing control of the South's delegates to the next national convention. Most federal officeholders in the South who had been appointed by McKinley were Republicans of a lily-white persuasion. Incumbent postmasters, revenue agents, and marshals who could be convinced to support Roosevelt were reappointed. The others, still loyal to Hanna, had to be removed from federal office and replaced with appointees who would work for Roosevelt's renomination. When new appointments were to be made, however, Roosevelt sought to avoid a commitment to either the lily-white or to the so-called black and tan factions of the southern GOP.

To execute this delicate balancing act, Roosevelt made Washington his chief patronage referee for all federal appointments in the deep South. This bestowed unprecedented prominence upon a black Republican. It also undercut white Republican leaders loyal to Hanna in such states as Alabama, Louisiana, and Mississippi, and it cemented Roosevelt's ties with black and tan Republicans opposed to disfranchisement. Could political reporters then describe Roosevelt as a black and tan? Not while his new appointees tended to be conservative white Democrats. Not while Roosevelt was bragging about his Georgian uncles who had fought for the Confederacy. And not while he was using his "bully pulpit" to urge southern white businessmen to help build a new Republican party in their region. Could the White House press then say that Roosevelt, like

Hayes and McKinley before him, was pursuing a lily-white strategy in the South? Not while Roosevelt cleared the appointment of each white Southern Democrat with the president of Tuskegee Institute, Booker T. Washington.[30]

In the fall and winter of 1902, however, Roosevelt's delicate balance between alternative southern strategies was apparently upset. First the U.S. Senate refused to confirm Roosevelt's nominee as collector of the Port of Charleston, South Carolina. Roosevelt responded by renominating Dr. W. D. Crum, a black physician, and vowing to keep Crum in office if necessary through a series of renominations and interim appointments. Second, while Roosevelt warred with the Senate over the appointment of Crum, the white residents of Indianola, Mississippi, sought to rid themselves of the black postmistress holding federal appointment in their community. A succession of threats and insults convinced her that her life was in jeopardy. She fled town. Many whites in Indianola claimed that she had forfeited her appointment and asked Roosevelt to name a new postmaster, a white. Roosevelt's response was to close the post office and to deny mail service to the community until it could guarantee the safety of his appointee.[31]

Although Roosevelt's stalwart defense of Crum and his closing of the Indianola post office have been called the high point of his commitment to black rights, such a description of Roosevelt's actions is misleading. Roosevelt was an astute political thespian with a remarkable ability to project a self-selected public image. During and prior to this period, when he provided as vigorous a public defense of black rights as the country had witnessed since Reconstruction, Roosevelt was working just as vigorously but less publicly to remake the Republican party in the South on an all-white basis. His principal instrument in his first steps in this endeavor was Senator Jeter C. Pritchard of North Carolina.

Pritchard, a self-educated and walrus-bewhiskered Republican from the Appalachian Mountains, was the only Republican in the U.S. Senate from the South and the first elected since Reconstruction. During the 1890s he had forged in North Carolina a coalition or "fusion" of white and black Republicans with the state's white Populists. His "fusion tickets" had trounced Democrats in the elections of 1894 and 1896. But the Populist movement had run its course by 1902, and North Carolina's adoption of a black disfranchisement amendment in 1900 had erased half of Pritchard's Republican electorate.[32] Rather than accept a future of political impotence, Pritchard urged his fellow white Republicans to accept the fact of black disfranchisement but to build their party anew. He urged them to make room in an all-white GOP for conservative Democrats disenchanted with William Jennings Bryan, to solicit the support of North Carolina's growing business community, and to seek to become the state's "party of property and intelligence."[33] So extreme a reversal of political orientations might be anticipated from a political maverick, but Pritchard, throughout his public career, was a stalwart believer in party regularity. And to achieve his revolutionary remaking of the Republican party in North Carolina and throughout the South, he required the backing of the popular Roosevelt.

Several weeks prior to the August convention of North Carolina Republicans, Pritchard wrote Roosevelt: "There are some things I must talk with you about before our State Convention meets. In fact, my future course depends much upon what you have to say."[34] Eleven days later, Pritchard met with Roosevelt at the White House. The following day Pritchard followed the president to Oyster Bay, where the two men were joined by A. C. Lyon, state chairman of the Republican party in Texas. No announcements or press conferences followed Pritchard's and Lyon's meeting with the president, but Republicans and Democrats alike inferred what had transpired at Oyster Bay from the events of the North Carolina Republicans' August 28 state convention. Among the several hundreds of Republicans attending the convention, there were only a dozen black delegates, and Pritchard's credentials committee unseated all but one of these. When the sole remaining black delegate walked out of the convention, North Carolina's GOP was launched on its career as a white man's party.[35]

There was and there is no concrete, documentary evidence that Pritchard purged the black delegates at Roosevelt's behest or even with his approval. Yet only one week after North Carolina's lily-white Republican convention, the president interrupted one of his southern trips to stop in the small, out-of-the-way mountain hamlet of Madison, North Carolina, the home town of Senator Jeter Pritchard. There he praised Pritchard, his effort to build a strong Republican party, and his record as a U.S. senator. Five days later, the stalwart Pritchard boarded a train for Birmingham, Alabama. Although his own slim chances for reelection depended on the North Carolina campaign, although his wife had died of cancer less than two months before, and although his own health was doubtful, Pritchard went to Alabama to deliver the keynote address to the state's Republican convention. After a bitter floor fight and over the objections of the Republicans' state chairman, the convention unseated all but a single black delegate.[36]

Black leaders across the nation were outraged. Booker T. Washington complained to J. S. Clarkson, Roosevelt's chief lieutenant in charge of securing southern support for the 1904 nomination. Some black editors, like Thomas Fortune, tried to excuse Pritchard's behavior as actions ordered by the president. The black editor of the *Washington Bee* accepted no such excuses. The *Bee* had been distrustful of Roosevelt and of Booker T. Washington, but it had viewed Pritchard as a "good race man." "Et tu Brute," rasped the *Bee* after the North Carolina and Alabama conventions.[37]

J. C. Payne, Roosevelt's postmaster general and the national chairman of the Republican party, explained that the lily-white movement had been "a perversion of the fundamental principles of the Republican party." Then Roosevelt himself personally explained that he could not consent "to take the position that the door of hope—the door of opportunity—is to be shut upon any man, no matter how worthy, purely on grounds of color."[38]

If Pritchard had not been operating as Roosevelt's agent, then he was himself the leader of the lily-white movement. When, wondered the *New York Times,* would Roosevelt chastise Pritchard and the Republicans of North Carolina "where the white movement had its origin?" The *Washington Bee,* although pleased with the president's disavowal of lily-white Republicanism, remained suspicious and asked when Pritchard would be taught that he "was not the only bubble in the soda." When, indeed?[39]

A month after the elections Pritchard entered a Washington hospital for some badly needed surgery. For six weeks he remained in the hospital and out of the public eye. The holidays came and went. Congress recessed and reconvened. If Pritchard's illness had been only "diplomatic," it could not have been better timed, for the national debate over Roosevelt's southern racial policies soon centered on new and more acrimoniously debated issues and personalities.

On January 2, 1903, the president closed the Indianola, Mississippi, post office. He would not tolerate maltreatment of a federal official, and he would not be intimidated in his choice of federal appointments.[40] Three days later, on January 5, Roosevelt named W. D. Crum for reappointment as collector in Charleston. Suddenly Roosevelt looked very much like a "white knight" fighting to protect black political liberties.[41] No one accused him now of contemplating a lily-white southern strategy. And no one paid attention to an ailing, lame-duck senator from North Carolina when, late in January of the new year, Pritchard left the hospital. No one remembered, that is, except Roosevelt.

Roosevelt invited Pritchard to a family dinner at the White House. Within two months he appointed Pritchard to serve first as a justice on the Supreme Court of the District of Columbia and then as a justice on the bench of the Fourth U.S. Circuit Court of Appeals, one judicial step beneath the Supreme Court itself. Roosevelt also appointed one of Pritchard's chief allies in the North Carolina lily-white movement to serve as minister to Persia. And still in March 1903, Roosevelt removed from office the last remaining black to hold a federal appointment in North Carolina. To take his place Roosevelt nominated a white former Democrat who had been endorsed by Pritchard.[42]

After his nomination and election in 1904, Roosevelt resumed pursuit of a southern lily-white strategy. In 1905 and 1906 his courtship of conservative Southern Democrats became quite brazen; in 1907 he handled the Brownsville affair with casual injustice; and as the 'Bull Moose' candidate in 1912, he explicitly directed Southern Progressives to organize locally on an all-white basis. Yet more than eight years later he was remembered as he was regarded in 1903: as the president who refused to shut "the door of opportunity" on anyone "purely on grounds of color."

ROOSEVELT DISPENSES THE NEWS

Another piece of Rooseveltian lore, one of which at least some newspeople still are particularly fond, tells how Roosevelt institutionalized the White House press corps. As the story goes, the president was looking out his window one cold, wet, winter afternoon when he noticed the shivering figures of newsmen huddled outside the White House gate and waiting for a press handout. Roosevelt took pity. He invited them inside, assigned them their own headquarters room, and thereby created a permanent cadre of journalists at the White House.[43] Although TR did provide the press with its own quarters, and although he probably did more than any other president to create a separate and distinct cadre of newspeople assigned specifically to the White House, the institutionalization of these developments was neither so sudden nor so offhanded as this story suggests.

For many years, Washington reporters had made their daily rounds gathering enough copy to meet their assignments. Most stopped by daily at the Executive Mansion (when the president was in town) and at Capitol Hill (when Congress was in session), but the more enterprising would visit assorted agencies of the government: the Pension Office, the Bureau of Indian Affairs, the Treasury Department, or maybe even the Patent Office. Newsmen literally "gathered" the news. Only during the Civil War or in periods of an unfolding diplomatic crisis would they interrupt their rounds to remain at the Executive Mansion for the developments of any given day. The first newsman successfully departing from this pattern was William Price of the *Washington Evening Star*. In the fall of 1896, while the nation followed the campaigns of Bryan and McKinley, Price situated himself outside the offices of President Grover Cleveland and interviewed departing visitors. This simple strategy not only generated enough copy to please his editors but produced a by-lined column, "At the White House," which was syndicated across the nation for the next twenty years.[44]

President William McKinley inherited a small and growing army of reporters who sought to emulate Price's success. It was McKinley who invited the press into the Executive Mansion by offering them a reception room off the North Portico for their use as a combination cloakroom and waiting room. And it was McKinley who established daily, routine briefings for the press. Yet McKinley also insisted that a proper and seemly distance be maintained between the affairs of state and the needs of the press. Reporters met not with the president but with one of his secretaries, and all interviews with the president's guests had to be conducted outside the White House. These arrangements helped generate additional copy for the nation's highly competitive dailies. They also signaled the increased importance of the chief executive in government and of the news media in politics. Neither the press nor the presidency could be managed any longer as a "cottage industry." Indeed, by 1901 the situation was ripe for a president who would choose to bring about a political merger of these two public enterprises.[45]

Roosevelt not only knew the political advantages to be gained through a friendly relationship with the press, he was congenitally incapable of working in any other context. He liked the press. His uncle was a journalist and a newspaper editor. He was himself a practicing journalist who, at the time of McKinley's assassination, was awaiting the publication of one of his hunting stories.[46] The unfriendly attitude of Grover Cleveland toward the press was both politically and personally alien to Roosevelt. Nor could he observe the protocols with which McKinley had kept the press at arm's length. He always had enjoyed the company of a wide circle of close acquaintances. If Roosevelt as police commissioner had shared family dinners with Jacob Riis and while governor had delighted in hiking with Joseph Bishop, then Roosevelt the president would continue to dine and to walk with friends like Oscar Davis, Lincoln Steffens, and William Allen White. Moreover, his personal friendships with individual newsmen shaped and defined his relationship with the press as a whole. Roosevelt spoke with reporters as he would with any group of gentlemen: candidly, straightforwardly, and forthrightly. "It was all or nothing with him," recalled Oscar Davis. "He either talked with entire frankness and freedom, about anything and everything, or he didn't talk at all."[47]

Unlike the dialogues he shared with friends while walking or the freewheeling conversations he delighted in over dinner, however, his press conferences were more like sermonettes delivered to a passive and believing audience. Newsmen called them "seances."[48] Few inquiries were allowed, and no challenges or follow-up questions ever were permitted. He might summon the press into his office after a morning meeting of the cabinet or during his afternoon shave. Then, with a candor that stunned those who did not know him previously, he would deliver short or extended monologues on whatever topic or subjects interested him: Kaiser Wilhelm's Caribbean policy; the nesting habits of certain birds; the divorce rate; the arrogance of Standard Oil Corporation; the political ambitions of William Randolph Hearst; or the joys and woes of fatherhood.

Delivering these sermonettes and sustaining friendly relationships with reporters required that Roosevelt have regular and frequent access to newsmen. After their move into the new West Wing in October 1902, reporters almost always could be found just a few steps down the corridor from the president's own new Oval Office.[49] And when TR traveled, as he often did, he encouraged his friends to accompany him. The president's secretary could help make travel arrangements and ensure that the newsmen were included in all public events. After years of being restricted to the steps of the North Portico, there can be little wonder that some among the White House press corps thought of themselves almost as members of Roosevelt's cabinet.[50] Yet the cumulative effect of these arrangements was to facilitate Roosevelt's practice of those devices by which he shaped and even managed reporters' coverage of his presidency.

The most obvious and ingenuous of these devices was Roosevelt's approach to "human interest" stories. Presidents Harrison, Cleveland, and McKinley sought to keep a curtain drawn around their private lives, and Washington's newsmen understood that they never could feed their editors' voracious appetites for personal information about these public figures. Then Roosevelt became president. TR not only approved of stories about his personal life, he encouraged them. There was the Roosevelt who as a young boy had visited the Holy Land and had lived with Berber tribesmen. There was the Roosevelt who wrote histories and who rode with sheriff's posses. There was Roosevelt the big game hunter, Roosevelt the boxer, and Roosevelt the mountain climber. There was even the

Roosevelt who demonstrated for Thomas Edison's new moving picture camera the proper technique for taking a bath. The American newspaper and magazine public fell in love with the colorful and energetic Roosevelt in part because he was so colorful and so energetic, but also because he was the first president of the United States they felt they knew personally.[51]

By intertwining his private and his public lives, TR garnered from his personal popularity an additional degree of presidential authenticity and authority. He was, as president, particularly interested in a set of reforms intended to modernize the U.S. Army, including efforts to improve its physical fitness. Yet when, by executive order, he commanded senior officers to prove their fitness by riding ninety miles in three days on horseback, several members of Congress and some newspaper editors questioned the fairness of this particular test. The president's response was pure Roosevelt. One morning he departed on horseback from the White House stables, rode to Warrenton, Virginia, and then returned to Washington that same evening. He had completed a ninety-eight-mile round trip in seventeen hours and had done so in a blinding snowstorm. Not only had he dramatized the fairness of his fitness test, but he did so in a context that lent public credibility to his feat. A citizenry accustomed to reading about Roosevelt's physical feats saw nothing feigned or artificial about the president's ride.[52]

A second Rooseveltian device for managing his own public image, and one closely akin to his use of personal stories, was that of saturation. Roosevelt apparently believed that news about the president, almost any news, was better than no news. While governor of New York he had met with the press twice a day. While president he met with the press two or three times a day in addition to the private conversations and individual interviews he granted some journalists. He continued McKinley's practice of having his secretary provide daily briefings for the press (a practice already followed by Roosevelt while governor) and arranged for Mrs. Roosevelt's social secretary routinely to inform them about all social events.[53] "After years of reticence and starched dignity in the White House, reporters to their immense gratification discovered in Roosevelt almost more material than they could use."[54]

Not all of this great volume of copy gushed from mere exuberance. Roosevelt understood, for example, the special opportunities inherent in Monday morning editions of the daily press. Sundays were (and are) notoriously slow news days. By issuing a statement or report on Sunday evening, he usually could command more front page coverage than with the same statement if issued during the week. Nor was the timing of his 4:00 P.M. weekday "seances" entirely coincidental. If reporters were to meet the deadlines for that day's evening editions (5:00 P.M. Eastern Standard Time for East Coast papers and 6:00 P.M. for midwestern dailies), they had to use Roosevelt's story as he gave it to them or not at all. There simply was not time to interview people with a different or opposing viewpoint.[55] Once Roosevelt mastered the techniques for placing himself in the news, people came to expect news about Roosevelt. And once that was achieved, Roosevelt moved beyond image building to news management.

He had promised in 1904 that he would not seek reelection in 1908. Several members of TR's "official" family, including William Howard Taft, waited patiently for Roosevelt's blessing and with it almost certain nomination by the Republican party. Then Charles Evans Hughes, the Progressive Republican governor of New York, decided to initiate his own campaign for the nomination. He intended to launch his campaign with a major address on national issues of the day. Hughes was not in line for Roosevelt's blessing, but the president could not publicly oppose Hughes' candidacy or his bid for popular support. Instead, less than two hours before Hughes delivered his address, Roosevelt sent a Special Message to Congress. Both the House and the Senate had reacted with indifference to Roosevelt's State of the Union Message of the previous month, and the U.S. Supreme Court recently had overturned the Employer's Liability Act of 1906. Roosevelt wanted a new employer's liability and workmen's compensation law, legislation to curtail the use of injunctions in labor disputes, and comprehensive regulation of stock market speculation. Then Roosevelt threw a presidential "fit." He blamed the business community in general and Standard Oil Corporation in particular for bringing about the Panic of 1907 and denounced the "swollen pride" and "criminal misconduct" of "wealthy criminals" as a class. The next morning, Roosevelt and not Hughes dominated the front pages of the nation's dailies.[56] His Special Message was neither contrived nor trivial. It was a major presidential message, but its timing was deliberately calculated to minimize the attention given to Hughes. "If Hughes is going to play the game," TR is reported to have said, "he must learn the tricks."[57]

Other devices by which Roosevelt shaped his public image and partly managed the news were derived less from the media's hunger for copy than from TR's special, even confidential, relationship with newsmen. To speak candidly with the press is to court embarrassment and political ruin. So Roosevelt always insisted that his remarks be regarded as privileged conversations among friends. No correspondent ever was to quote him, whether while governor or while president, unless he had indicated specific authorization to do so.[58] Today such a posture toward the media would be naive, but that was not true at the turn of the century. Roosevelt was breaking precedent by speaking with the press as he did. Being a pioneer in presidential press relations, he enjoyed a unique opportunity to establish whatever rules he chose. And because reporters feared a return to the practices of Cleveland or to the protocols of McKinley, Roosevelt enjoyed a unique license to enforce the rules he had established. A reporter who disobeyed and quoted him without permission was, in Roosevelt's mind, not truly a gentleman. The president might publicly name the offending journalist "a liar" (no matter how accurate his story), and then he might bestow upon him a membership in the "Ananias Club" (TR's fictitious organization of lying and deceitful people). Worse yet, Roosevelt might refuse to speak to the press frankly or at all when in the presence of that correspondent.[59]

Confident that he would not be quoted, he could float "trial balloons" to test the political atmosphere prior to committing himself fully to a position. He would share an idea with the press, see it printed in the papers, and then gauge public opinion. If the suggestion met with public indifference or with exceptional hostility, he would claim that he had never even entertained such a thought. And any reporter who dared set straight the public record by naming Roosevelt as his source faced certain branding as a liar. To observe Roosevelt's prohibition against direct quotation and yet to publish the stories he gave them, newsmen simply attributed his expressed opinions as those of an unnamed "White House spokesman." This satisfied Roosevelt's sense of genteel discretion. It also released him to a considerable degree from the accountability to which a more independent press might have held him.[60]

Despite the opportunities they created for him to communicate with the nation, even the bans against direct quotation and attribution failed to provide Roosevelt with all of the confidentiality he desired. Some topics discussed by gentlemen, especially men who were true friends, required absolute or nearly absolute confidentiality. Thus much of what Roosevelt shared with correspondents was understood to be for "background" only or was designated as being entirely "off the record." When speaking with reporters in either of these modes, Roosevelt never expected to see this material in print. They allowed him to speak with utter candor. They ensured that even the most detached reporter, one fully immune to TR's personal magnetism, knew the reasons behind a presidential decision in greater depth and in greater detail than he was likely to discover about Roosevelt's critics. No doubt they also helped bond correspondents to Roosevelt personally.[61]

For individual reporters who adhered to his rules of discretion and confidentiality, Roosevelt gave additional treats in the form of deliberate "leaks." If Roosevelt had information he wished placed in circulation but with which, for whatever reason, he did not want to be associated, he shared it privately with a trusted friend among the White House press. "All things being equal, he preferred the stories to appear in opposition papers because the gambit was less transparent that way."[62] Sometimes, however, "Roosevelt had little purpose other than to reward or to support a reporter who had proved his friendship."[63]

"Backgrounders" given a group of correspondents and leaks shared with trusted individuals depended for their effectiveness upon absolute confidentiality. Breaking Roosevelt's rules governing one of these communications was deemed far more serious than the mere indiscretion of quoting a president who preferred anonymity. Accordingly, the punishments were more severe. The offending reporter "would be mercilessly cut off from further access to news," and the paper that published his story would be denied access to legitimate, governmental sources of news: one paper was even denied the reports of the U.S. Weather Bureau.[64]

A recent student of Roosevelt's relationship with the press concludes that "he upgraded the press corps at the price of corrupting it."[65] When TR was still the governor of New York, however, the *Brooklyn Eagle* reported on his practice of blending frank candor with discreet confidentiality. It commended him for his approach and believed that few reporters abused these "little innocent conspiracies against the public."[66] Undoubtedly Roosevelt would have agreed with the *Eagle,* adding emphatically that neither he nor the newsmen abused their special relationship. Of course his own work as a historian and journalist had taught him the importance of objectivity and independence. Yet before he became either a writer or a politician, he had been born a gentleman.

THEODORE ROOSEVELT'S LASTING IMAGE

Today the name Theodore Roosevelt still evokes in people recollections of strength, determination, patriotism, and boldness: all virtues praised by Roosevelt the journalist. We recall his interest in naval affairs and his enthusiasm for the environment and the frontier: favorite themes for many of his books and articles. We can see his face sculpted into the side of Mount Rushmore, but we forget that his three stone colleagues—Washington, Jefferson, and Lincoln—and the very environs of that monument once were subjects popularized by his pen. We are far too sophisticated a people to take literally the lore of his personal magnetism; we even smile somewhat skeptically at the thought that there ever could have been an age or an era named for someone so very eccentric. Yet we still send American children to bed with their Teddy Bears; we still dress young girls in the sailor suit jumpers made popular by his daughter; and we still market a color of paint known as "Princess Blue," named for Miss Alice, in stores across the nation. With less vivid detail and little understanding of why, we have essentially the same image of him as did people of his own time.

In the 1920s and the 1930s, after his death and during the presidency of his cousin Franklin, it was not uncommon for people to argue that the popular image of Roosevelt, both as a man and as president, was a mirage: an illusory phenomenon produced by a layer of hot air. Journalists vowed never again to succumb to the charms or the coercions of an American president, and they prided themselves on their professionalism and independence. One New York reporter, Henry F. Pringle, produced a Pulitzer Prize biography of Roosevelt that portrayed him as a childish and somewhat irresponsible eccentric who somehow conned people into believing that he had initiated many major reforms. We no longer feel the necessity of overturning a Rooseveltian yoke associated with Theodore. We no longer measure his achievements as a turn-of-the-century reformer against the social, economic, and political problems of the present. We have a more balanced, though dimmer and less vivid, image of him as president than did contemporaries who survived him. And despite his calculated efforts to manage the news and to project himself through the media onto the national consciousness, we remember the man—if not always his presidency—in terms similar to those used by "his" White House correspondents and in forms projected by his own journalistic pen. For, although Roosevelt sought to shape his image, he never attempted to create whole cloth out of thin air. The one element lacking today that was part of his image in his own lifetime is our remembrance of Roosevelt as a journalist.

After leaving the White House and during the final ten years of his life, Roosevelt resumed his career as an active journalist. Like most ex-presidents of his era, he required employment and he needed an income. *African Game Trails* (1910) earned him approximately $90,000 and it "contains some of the best writing he ever did and remains to this day a model of sporting reportage."[67] Then, in addition to his *Autobiography* (1913) and *Through the Brazilian Wilderness* (1914), he published two collections of essays: *History as Literature* (1913) and *A Book-lover's Holiday* (1916). Meanwhile he worked first as a contributing editor for *Outlook Magazine* and later as a columnist for William Rockhill Nelson's *Kansas City Star*. No one can or ever has challenged Roosevelt's reputation as a prolific writer. His last act in life may have been to proof copy for his newspaper column.

NOTES

1. Edith Patterson Meyer, *"Not Charity, but Justice": The Story of Jacob A. Riis* (New York: Vanguard, 1974), pp. 80–83.

2. Stephen Birmingham, *The Right People: A Portrait of the American Social Establishment* (Boston: Little, Brown, 1968), pp. 13, 46, 91, 327, 335; Carleton Putnam, *Theodore Roosevelt: The Formative Years* (New York: Charles Scribner's Sons, 1958), pp. 1–19.

3. Putnam, *TR: Formative Years,* pp. 20–22; Lillian Rixey, *Bamie: Theodore Roosevelt's Remarkable Sister* (New York: David McKay Co., 1963), pp. 5–9.

4. Allen Churchill, *The Roosevelts* (New York: Harper and Row, 1965), pp. 102–109; Putnam, *TR: Formative Years,* pp. 5–6.

5. Churchill, *The Roosevelts,* pp. 115–118.

6. Putnam, *TR: Formative Years,* pp. 34–54; David H. Burton, *Theodore Roosevelt: Confident Imperialist* (New York: Twayne, 1972), pp. 7–8; Churchill, *The Roosevelts,* pp. 118–123.

7. Putnam, *TR: Formative Years,* pp. 23, 25, 26, 32–33, 59, 62–65, 68–69, 71–73, 75–77; Churchill, *The Roosevelts,* pp. 125–126, 131–135; Rixey, *Bamie,* pp. 44, 89, 93.

8. Putnam, *TR: Formative Years,* pp. 116–128.

9. Ibid., pp. 81–101, 114.

10. Ibid., pp. 128, 135–142, 184.

11. Ibid., pp. 239–244, 247–249; William Henry Harbaugh, *Power and Responsibility: The Life and Times of Theodore Roosevelt* (New York: Farrar, Straus and Cudahy, 1971), pp. 17–23, 67–68.

12. Rixey, *Bamie,* pp. 60–62; Burton, *Roosevelt,* pp. 55–58; Harbaugh, *Power and Responsibility,* pp. 74–80.

13. Harbaugh, *Power and Responsibility,* pp. 81–90, 108–112; G. Wallace Chessman, *Governor Theodore Roosevelt: The Albany Apprenticeship, 1898–1900* (Cambridge, Mass.: Harvard University Press, 1965), pp. 25–49.

14. Kenneth B. Murdock, Arthur H. Quinn, Clarence Ghodes, and George Whicher, *The Literature of the American People* (New York: Appleton-Century-Crofts, 1951),

pp. 588–597; Sidney Kobre, *The Development of American Journalism* (Dubuque: W. C. Brown Co., 1969), pp. 336–339, 521–531.

15. Putnam, *TR: Formative Years*, pp. 313–346, 592–596: Rixey, *Bamie*, pp. 47–48; Burton, *Roosevelt*, pp. 33–44.

16. Roosevelt's books and most published articles are compiled in the twenty-four volume *The Works of Theodore Roosevelt*, ed. Herman Hagedorn (New York: C. Scribner's Sons, 1923).

17. *New York Herald*, November 1, 1881; Putnam, *TR: Formative Years*, pp. 238–249; Rixey, *Bamie*, pp. 34–35.

18. Putnam, *TR: Formative Years*, pp. 255–257.

19. Ibid., pp. 259–262.

20. Ibid., pp. 261–275.

21. George Juergens, *News from the White House: The Presidential-Press Relationship in the Progressive Era* (Chicago: University of Chicago Press, 1981), pp. 70–79; Chessman, *Governor Theodore Roosevelt*, pp. 55, 86, 110, 184–185, 246.

22. Jacob A. Riis, *The Making of an American* (New York: Macmillan Co., 1928), pp. 210–231; Meyer, *Not Charity, but Justice*, pp. 80–86, 93–94; Chessman, *Governor Theodore Roosevelt*, pp. 201–214.

23. Oscar King Davis, *Released for Publication: Some Inside Political History of Theodore Roosevelt and His Times, 1898–1918* (Boston: Houghton Mifflin, 1925), pp. 1–2, 29, 124, 135; Lawrence F. Abbot, *Impressions of Theodore Roosevelt* (New York: Doubleday, Page and Co., 1919), pp. 1–12.

24. Joseph Bucklin Bishop, *Theodore Roosevelt and His Time, Shown in His Own Letters*, 2 vols. (New York: Charles Scribner's Sons, 1920).

25. Chessman, *Governor Theodore Roosevelt*, pp. 20–30.

26. Putnam, *TR: Formative Years*, pp. 274–275.

27. C. Vann Woodward, *Origins of the New South, 1877–1913*, (Baton Rouge: Louisiana State University Press, 1951), pp. 321–349.

28. Ibid., p. 349.

29. Vincent P. De Santis, *Republicans Face the Southern Question, 1877–1897* (Baltimore: Johns Hopkins Press, 1959), pp. 32, 93, 135, 150; Seth Scheiner, "President Theodore Roosevelt and the Negro, 1901–1908," *Journal of Negro History*, 47 (July 1962): 169–182; Roosevelt to H. C. Payne, July 8, 1902, Theodore Roosevelt Papers, Library of Congress, Washington, D.C.

30. P. D. Barker to Marcus Hanna, August 7, 1901, and Hanna to William McKinley, August 10, 1901, William McKinley Papers, Series #3, Library of Congress; Williard B. Gatewood, *Theodore Roosevelt and the Art of Controversy* (Baton Rouge: Louisiana State University Press, 1970); Dewey W. Grantham, "Dinner at the White House: Theodore Roosevelt, Booker T. Washington, and the South," *Tennessee Historical Quarterly* 31 (June 1958): 112–113.

31. *New York Times*, January 3, 4, 5, 6, 1903.

32. Allen W. Trelease, "The Fusion Legislature of 1895 and 1897: A Rollcall Analysis of the North Carolina House of Representatives," *North Carolina Historical Review*, 57 (July 1980): 280–309.

33. Jeter C. Pritchard, "The Brightest Day of Republicanism: An Address Delivered Before the Republican State Convention at Greensboro, North Carolina, August 28, 1902."

34. Jeter C. Pritchard to Roosevelt, August 8, 1902, Theodore Roosevelt Papers.

35. *Raleigh Morning Post,* August 20, 21, 29, 1902; *Charlotte Daily Observer,* August 21, 29, 31, October 17, November 17, 1902; *New York Times,* October 20, 25, 1902.

36. *New York Times,* September 10, 12, 14, 17, 18, 20, October 20, 25, 1902: *New York Tribune,* September 19, 1902; *Raleigh Morning Post,* August 29, September 10, 11, 1902; *Charlotte Daily Observer,* September 16, 18, 1902; Jeter Pritchard to J. S. Clarkson, September 15, 1902, Theodore Roosevelt Papers.

37. Booker T. Washington to J. S. Clarkson, September 15, 1902, and J. S. Clarkson to Theodore Roosevelt, September 27, 1902, Theodore Roosevelt Papers; J. S. Clarkson to Booker T. Washington, September 17, 1902, File #223, Booker T. Washington Papers, Library of Congress; *Washington Bee,* September 6, 20, 1902.

38. *New York Times,* November 11, 28, 1902; Roosevelt to J. A. Smith (mayor of Charleston, South Carolina), November 26, 1902, Theodore Roosevelt Papers.

39. *New York Times,* November 11, 1902; *Washington Bee,* December 6, 1902.

40. *New York Times,* January 3, 4, 5, 6, 1903; Williard B. Gatewood, "Theodore Roosevelt and the Indianola Affair," *Journal of Negro History,* 53, no. 1 (January 1968): 48–69.

41. *New York Times,* January 4, 5, 6, 7, 1903; Roosevelt to Booker T. Washington, March 4, 1903, File #16, Booker T. Washington Papers; Williard B. Gatewood, "William D. Crum: A Negro in Politics," *Journal of Negro History* 53, no. 4 (October 1968): 301–320.

42. *Charlotte Daily Observer,* January 27, 29, March 6, 24, 27, 1903; *New York Times,* December 22, 28, 1902.

43. Juergens, *News from the White House,* p. 14.

44. F. B. Marbut, *News from the Capitol* (Carbondale: Southern Illinois University Press, 1971), p. 169; Juergens, *News from the White House,* pp. 14–15.

45. Lewis L. Gould, *The Presidency of William McKinley* (Lawrence: Regents Press of Kansas, 1980), pp. 38–39, 241; Juergens, *News from the White House,* pp. 5–6, 15.

46. Theodore Roosevelt, "With the Cougar Hounds," *Scribner's Magazine* (October 1901).

47. Davis, *Released for Publication,* p. 124.

48. Ibid., pp. 60–61.

49. Juergens, *News from the White House,* pp. 15–16, 65–66; Marbut, *News from the Capitol,* pp. 169–170.

50. Abbot, *Impressions of TR,* pp. 19–23.

51. Juergens, *News from the White House,* pp. 24–25.

52. Ibid., pp. 32–33.

53. Chessman, *Governor Theodore Roosevelt,* pp. 75–76; Juergens, *News from the White House,* pp. 16–18, 23–24, 45–50.

54. Juergens, *News from the White House,* pp. 24–25.

55. Abbot, *Impressions of TR,* p. 18; Juergens, *News from the White House,* p. 29.

56. *New York Times,* February 1, 1908; *Congressional Record,* 60th Congress, 1st Session, pp. 1340ff.; Juergens, *News from the White House,* pp. 42–43; Burton, *Theodore Roosevelt,* pp. 149–151; Harbaugh, *Power and Responsibility,* pp. 351–352; Davis, *Released for Publication,* pp. 64–72.

57. Harbaugh, *Power and Responsibility,* p. 336; Davis, *Released for Publication,* pp. 69–72.

58. Chessman, *Governor Theodore Roosevelt,* p. 75; Juergens, *News from the White House,* pp. 16–17, 20, 42; Davis, *Released for Publication,* pp. 61, 123–124.

59. Harbaugh, *Power and Responsibility*, pp. 250–251; Juergens, *News from the White House*, pp. 20, 41–42, 66–68.

60. Davis, *Released for Publication*, pp. 60–61, 123–124; Juergens, *News from the White House*, pp. 16–17, 41–42.

61. Davis, *Released for Publication*, p. 124.

62. Juergens, *News from the White House*, p. 44.

63. See, for example, Oscar Davis' reports of TR sharing evidence of William Randolph Hearst's collusion with E. H. Harriman and giving Davis and the *New York Times* an advance look at a report to Congress about the Panama Canal. Davis, *Released for Publication*, pp. 60–63, 122–124.

64. Juergens, *News from the White House*, pp. 17, 69.

65. Ibid., p. 66.

66. *Brooklyn Eagle*, January 14, 1899, as quoted in Chessman, *Governor Theodore Roosevelt*, p. 75.

67. Noel F. Busch, *T. R., the Story of Theodore Roosevelt and His Influence on Our Times* (New York: Reynal and Co., 1963), p. 223.

ANNOTATED BIBLIOGRAPHY

Blum, John Morton. *The Republican Roosevelt*. Cambridge, Mass.: Harvard University Press, 1954.
    A very well done biography which places emphasis on the White House years.
Burton, David Henry. *Theodore Roosevelt*. New York: Twayne Publishers, 1972.
Cadenhead, Ivie Edward. *Theodore Roosevelt*. Woodbury, N.Y.: Barron's Educational Series, 1974.
Feuerlicht, Robert Strauss. *Theodore Roosevelt*. New York: American ROM Corp., 1966.
Garraty, John Arthur. *Theodore Roosevelt*. New York: American Heritage Publishing Co./Harper and Row, 1967.
Gatewood, Williard B., Jr. *Theodore Roosevelt and the Art of Controversy*. Baton Rouge: Louisiana State University Press, 1970.
    Analysis of major issues of the Theodore Roosevelt era.
Grantham, Dewey W. *Theodore Roosevelt*. Englewood Cliffs, N.J.: Prentice-Hall, 1971.
Hagedorn, Hermann, ed., *The Works of Theodore Roosevelt*. 20 vols. New York: Charles Scribner's Sons, 1925.
    Roosevelt's own writings.
Hancock, Sibyl. *Theodore Roosevelt*. New York: Putnam, 1978.
Harbaugh, William Henry. *The Life and Times of Theodore Roosevelt*. New York: Farrar, Straus and Cudahy, 1963.
    A biography with analysis of the history of TR's active years.
Iglehart, Ferdinand Cowle. *Theodore Roosevelt: The Man As I Knew Him*. New York: Christian Herald, 1919.
    The account of a minister and reformer who closely followed TR's career.
Keller, Morton. *Theodore Roosevelt*. New York: Hill and Wang, 1967.
Lodge, Henry Cabot, ed., *Selections from the Correspondence of Theodore Roosevelt and Henry Cabot Lodge, 1884–1918*. New York: Charles Scribner's Sons, 1925.
    Correspondence with a close associate.
McCullough, David G. *The Pathway Between the Seas*. New York: Simon and Schuster, 1977.

A detailed account of the Panama Canal controversy with much material about Roosevelt's role in the building of the Canal.

————. *Mornings on Horseback*. New York: Simon and Schuster, 1982.

An account of Theodore Roosevelt's childhood and youth. Ends with the death of his first wife and his mother.

Morris, Edmund. *The Rise of Theodore Roosevelt*. New York: Simon and Schuster, 1982.

The Pulitizer Prize-winning account of the political career of Theodore Roosevelt up to his succession to the presidency in 1901.

Mowry, George E. *The Era of Theodore Roosevelt, 1900–1912*. New York: Harper, 1958.

The period during which Theodore Roosevelt was most heavily involved in national politics is analyzed; concludes with the Bull Moose campaign against Taft and Wilson.

Norton, Aloysius A. *Theodore Roosevelt*. Boston: Twayne, 1980.

Pinchot, Gifford. *Breaking New Ground*. New York: Harcourt, Brace, 1947.

Describes TR's major role in the conservation/environmental movement of the Progressive era.

Platt, Thomas Collier. *The Autobiography of Thomas Collier Platt*. Louis J. Lang, comp. and ed. New York: B. W. Dodge and Co. 1910.

A biography of the boss who set TR on the path to the vice presidency and the White House.

Pringle, Henry F. *Theodore Roosevelt: A Biography*. New York: Harcourt, Brace and Co., 1931.

Long considered the standard biography of Theodore Roosevelt.

————. *Theodore Roosevelt*. New York: Harcourt, Brace, 1956.

Riis, Jacob A. *Theodore Roosevelt the Citizen*. New York: Macmillan, 1904.

An admiring biography.

Robinson, Corrinne Roosevelt. *My Brother Theodore Roosevelt*. New York: Charles Scribner's Sons, 1921.

Intimate glimpses by TR's sister.

Roosevelt, Theodore. *Theodore Roosevelt: An Autobiography*. New York: Charles Scribner's Sons, 1913.

The remarkable career of Theodore Roosevelt described in his own words.

Schoch, Henry A. *Theodore Roosevelt*. Las Vegas, Nev.: KC Publications, 1974.

Steffens, Lincoln. *The Autobiography of Lincoln Steffens*. New York: Harcourt, Brace and Co., 1931.

Especially useful for an account of Theodore Roosevelt's nomination for governor in 1898.

9 WILLIAM HOWARD TAFT

Emil Dansker

William Howard Taft may have been the best prepared person ever to have assumed the presidency of the United States. After all, he had spent virtually all his adult life in public service.

He may have been the best liked. Theodore Roosevelt said of him that he had "the most lovable personality I have ever come into contact with," and Major Archie Butt, military aide to both men, described Taft's smile as one that would "deluge you like a huge pan of sweet milk."

And he may have had the fastest fall from public grace once in office and the quickest recouping once out. "We don't care how much Mr. Taft weighs," *Harper's Weekly* said. "He is a good man and will make as fine a President . . . as the country has ever had."

The *New York Times* described Taft as

a strong and healthy man, in the prime of life, of sound lineage, of best schooling, with a remarkable range of natural gifts in mind and character, developed and disciplined by varied and extensive experience in exacting posts of public and professional duty, in keen and active sympathy with the best spirit of his times and his nation.

The *Times* called him perhaps the best qualified and most fit candidate for the presidency at the time of his nomination since Washington. "He enters the White House today greatly admired," the *Toledo Blade* said on Taft's inauguration day in 1909. "When the hour comes for him to depart it is our faith that we shall be able to write in all truth that he leaves regretted."

It was not to be.

With hardly an ill-wisher when he took the oath—"there was not a more popular man in public life in the United States," wrote Edward G. Lowry of *Harper's*. His avowed distaste for the game of politics brought him an image of pliant bumbler so strong and pervasive that he was unable to shake it until after he left office and returned to law practice.

It was not so much that Taft was not a politician, Lowry wrote, but that he lacked "political sagacity [and] had no instinct for knowing what the people . . . are thinking, nor has he any sources of information; therefore he can neither guide, direct, nor control public opinion."

Taft's fall from popular favor began with his inept handling of the congressional fight over the Payne-Aldrich tariff bill at the opening of his administration—including his unfortunate praise of it as "the best tariff bill that has been passed at all"—in a Winona, Minnesota, speech during a 13,000–mile nationwide tour aimed, ironically, at countering criticism of the bill.

"GHOULISH DELIGHT" IN TRAVELING

Taft loved to travel—Archie Butt called it "almost freakish, the ghoulish delight he gets from traveling"—but the trip's purpose was to make speeches, something Taft did not relish and tended to put off.

This time, wrote Henry F. Pringle, "procrastination was to earn a bitter penalty," because, as the president told his audience, in order to have the speech ready for Winona, "I had to dictate it coming up from Chicago."[1]

The result was the ill-thought-out "best tariff bill" statement, a remark that brought down upon the Taftian head a crown of criticism, especially from his own party's insurgent-progressive wing—the *Blade* called Minnesota itself the hotbed of the movement—which had fought bitterly because the bill revised tariffs essentially upward despite the downward revision endorsed in the 1908 Republican platform in a break with GOP tradition.

So strong was the criticism that it festered and persisted despite the president's vow that his and the party's basic philosophy favored downward revision of tariffs where warranted, and his plea that keeping party support solidly behind the bill was better than no bill at all; thus, he appealed, "We ought to give it a chance."

He also was pleased "that a number of those who thought it their duty to vote against the bill insist that they are still Republicans and intend to carry on their battle" inside the party. He felt that this was much better than that they bolt to "another party which would probably not result in accomplishing anything more than merely in defeating our party and inviting in the opposing party."

Three years later he was to see it confirmed that this was precisely what such action would accomplish, whatever the reason.

(That the image of Taft and GOP concern for the effects of divisiveness persist is evidenced by a comment from conservative Republican Representative Newt Gingrich of Georgia, quoted December 27, 1984, in the *Christian Science Monitor* by historian Allan J. Lichtman, who wrote:

The near extinction of liberal Republicans has not united the party, only shifted rivalries to the right. Without Reagan to pull the Republicans together the question is when will the GOP's moderate, conservative and radical right factions begin squabbling over the post-Reagan succession.

Conservatives fired the first shot, wrote Lichtman, when Gingrich warned that "any attempt to compromise with Democrat House Speaker Tip O'Neill's liberal gang would split the GOP by Eastern and Western factions and mark Reagan as the William Howard Taft of the late 20th Century.")

Writer Ida M. Tarbell was among those who quickly perceived the negative impact of the Winona speech. Less than two weeks after the speech, on September 29, she wrote Kansas editor William Allen White that "Taft is done for. . . . I have failed yet to meet a single person in whom he had aroused the least interest. Not a man of discernment, but what shakes his head over him." O. K. Davis of the *New York Times* recalled that during the seventeen days he covered the tour "everywhere there was rage against Taft and the Republican party."

By 1911 the president had fallen so far that *Harper's* was asking: "Can Mr. Taft Be Saved?" Washington correspondent A. Maurice Low found that

Mr. Taft's bad luck has been phenomenal . . . not once has fortune smiled upon him. He has laughed and lost none of his courage, but fortune, like an acidulated virgin, has kept the corners of her mouth primly set and held him at her distance. Things done by other men that would have turned to their advantage have served only to emphasize the way fortune has jested with him. . . . His good deeds have been overlooked; his mistakes have blinded no one.

Mr. Taft is one of the unfortunates of history. A man whom all like for his engaging personal qualities, his courage, high purposes, and lofty ideals, he has been unable to make headway against the misfortunes that have been since entered into the Presidency.

But those same personal qualities began to make themselves better felt when he left the White House for the respected position of professor of law at Yale University, his alma mater; he began to recoup as an elder statesman, writing and speaking on constitutional government and continuing to promote arbitration as a means of solving conflict without war. Nine years later he achieved what had been his ambition all along: appointment as chief justice of the United States.

"The people did not appreciate him until he had been retired to private life," the *Boston Herald* wrote when he died in 1930. "He emerged from political disaster so upright, so undisturbed, so unresentful, that, when he finally became Chief Justice . . . there was a feeling that merit had been rewarded and justice done."

Wrote William Allen White: "The only ex-President ever to serve as Supreme Court Justice," he sat like "one of the high gods of the world, a smiling buddha, placid, wise, gentle, sweet."

HAND-PICKED SUCCESSOR

But speculation as to preparation, personality, and perception aside, there seems little doubt that Taft was Roosevelt's hand-picked successor in 1908 and even less doubt that the Republican party lost the White House four years later only because TR split the GOP when the two friends fell out and Roosevelt reneged on his oft-repeated vow that he would not seek another term and campaigned under the banner of the Progressive, or Bull Moose, party. "My hat is in the ring," Roosevelt declared. "The fight is on, and I am stripped to the buff."

The split may have been a long time a'brewing. It may have stirred not long after the elections of 1908 when Taft moved from the satisfaction of the returns into the beginnings of bitterness on the part of TR, who apparently felt that the president-elect was giving too much of the credit for his victory to his half-brother Charles.

Apparently? Judith Icke Anderson reports it as unmistakable in recalling Roosevelt's reaction to a letter from Taft in which the successful candidate wrote that he was "bound to say that I owe my election more to you than anybody else except my brother Charley."

With characteristic clenching of teeth, Roosevelt declared to Representative James Watson of Indiana:

He mentions his brother Charles in connection with me? Does he not know that I could have beaten him had I not been for him? Is he not aware of the fact that I would easily have taken that nomination myself? The idea of his putting his brother Charles alongside me in an expression of gratitude. . . . It is monstrous, I tell you.

Roosevelt had planned a year's hunting trip to Africa—with some hoping that the lions would win—and had written editor William Allen White even before election day that "my main reason . . . is so that I can get where no one can accuse me of running, nor do Taft the injustice of accusing him of permitting me to run, the job."[2]

But he did not leave for Africa until after the March 4 inauguration, of course, and already there were rumblings that Taft was being too independent in choosing his cabinet by dropping too many of the members who had served Roosevelt, as later there would be complaints from TR and others that he was breaking his promise to carry forward Roosevelt's policies.

Mrs. Douglas Robinson, Roosevelt's sister, told Archie Butt that her brother had told her he could never forgive Taft for having made him look foolish in an antitrust suit against the United States Steel Company in 1911 in which it appeared that TR had been deceived by the company as to its reasons for acquiring a Tennessee firm. That Taft had not been aware that Roosevelt had been mentioned by name did not help.

"Its effect on Roosevelt," wrote Erwin C. Hargrove, "was to hit his sensitive ego, drive him into a rage, and precipitate his candidacy."

Wrote historian Donald F. Anderson:

Whereas in November, 1910, Roosevelt had felt that Taft merely lacked "the gift of leadership," was "too easily influenced by the men around him" and did "not really grasp progressive principles," by December, 1911, Taft had become a "flubdub," "puzzle-witted," and a "floppy souled creature."

TR clearly was not happy. And, as in Greek tragedy, events moved on their inexorable course.

But it had not always been thus. The two men had been friends since the 1880s in Washington, when Taft was solicitor general of the United States and Roosevelt was a member of the Civil Service Commission. He had served TR in the Philippines and as secretary of war, functioning effectively as a trouble-shooter on several occasions.

GREAT REGARD FOR TAFT

So great was Roosevelt's regard for Taft that early on he had voiced the opinion that his friend was of presidential caliber. Three times he offered him appointment to the Supreme Court, his avowed goal as it was a dream of his father Alphonso.

Taft declined appointment out of a consummate sense of duty—also a legacy of his jurist father—that led him to see his work as governor-general of the Philippines through to what he felt was a logical point of departure. He found that point in 1904 when he agreed to join Roosevelt's cabinet as secretary of war because, wrote Paolo Coletta, "he still would be in charge of Filipino affairs, and because amoebic dysentery threatened to undermine his health."

Came consideration of a presidential candidate for 1908 and speculation continued—it had begun while he was in the Philippines—that Taft might be the man. So strong was this speculation that Taft wrote an old classmate, Judge Howard Hollister, from the Philippines:

I need not say to you that such reports do not set the bee buzzing in my bonnet, for to begin with, a presidential campaign has no attraction for me at all, but the anticipation simply produced a feeling of horror.... the office itself has not the slightest attraction for me, but of course why discuss it for it is nothing but a dull-seasoned joke.

As speculation continued and the need to make a choice grew more urgent, Roosevelt dabbled with dubbing Secretary of State Elihu Root as his successor but decided that he was too close to big business and lacked Taft's popularity.

"I would rather see Elihu Root in the White House than any other man possible," Roosevelt told Davis, but "there is too much opposition on account of his corporation connections."

He told Davis that he was afraid Taft might have trouble with the Republican Old Guard in Congress because he was not a fighter, even though he was an "able, upright man, a hard worker and a good administrator" and had shown courage as a judge and in the Philippines. "The controlling factor, ... " Roosevelt told Davis, "was that Taft was the only man who had made himself available ... by public endorsement of the Roosevelt policies." So the choices became clear.

To historian Sir George Otto Trevelyan, Roosevelt wrote that Taft "will carry on the work substantially as I have carried it on. His policies, purposes, principles, and ideals are the same as mine, and he is a strong, forceful, efficient man, absolutely upright, absolutely disinterested and fearless.''

"IN HEARTIEST AGREEMENT"

And to Conrad Kohrs of Montana he wrote:

For the last ten years, while I have been Governor of New York and President, I have been thrown into the closest intimacy with him, and he and I have on every essential point stood in heartiest agreement, shoulder to shoulder. We have the same views as to what is demanded by the National Interest and honor. . . . The policies for which I stand are his policies as much as mine.

There is irony in the Kohrs letter, however. It was written in 1908, all right, but it was inserted into the *Congressional Record* on June 24, 1912, by Representative Philip P. Campbell of Kansas to make a point at a time when Roosevelt was speaking quite differently of Taft.

Such were the new sentiments on both sides that *The World's Work* called the situation ''not only a national misfortune but a national disgrace'' in which ''the President and the former President have been engaged in a brawl, accusing one another of hypocrisy and falsification. Their 'debates' have not been about great principles nor important policies. It has been on the low level of personal attack and personal defense.''

''Worse yet,'' the magazine continued, ''the great office of President has been degraded in men's eyes. They have seen it handed over by one man to another and then treated by them as the prize of a personal combat to decide which of them shall *now* have it. This is a deep and lasting offense against the dignity of a great office.''[3]

Not that there had been no hints, at least, that the passage of presidential power between Taft and TR might not be simple.

White, the influential and perceptive editor of the *Emporia* (Kansas) *Gazette*, who was aligned with the progressive wing of the Republican party—the insurgents, who were challenging the conservative wing, which they felt was typified by Taft—while basically sympathetic to the president, had this to say of him:

I can see Taft now as we sat in the sunshine after lunch on an enclosed porch in the White House. He was a tall man and had accumulated a lot of fat on his long body. To me his legs seemed short for his torso. His face was full, long, florid; and he had a light blondish mustache, dark hair and a chuckling face which deceived many people into thinking he agreed with what they were saying. I am sure that Theodore Roosevelt had been completely fooled by Taft's amiable gurgling obbligato when they talked, and had really thought, when he left the White House, that Taft would carry out the Roosevelt policies. He did, but as Senator Dolliver remarked, ''on a shutter.''

It was on that day, White recalled, that he "realized how hopeless was the job of weaning him [Taft] away from the reactionary crowd that was surrounding him," recalling a further comment by Senator Jonathan P. Dolliver of Iowa that "Taft is an amiable island seen by men who knew exactly what they want."

The World's Work saw Taft as

by temperament not suited for sturdy executive duties, being too trustful of those near him and too accessible to those who speak plainly to him . . . patriotic but indecisive until driven to anger . . . an amiable and attractive man at close range, but an inept leader, not knowing the people; a man of policies rather than of fundamental convictions.

The president's grandson, former Senator Robert Taft, Jr., said that the president had a strong judicial temperament and tended to deal theoretically rather than in practical terms. "I fear the perception of my grandfather was not very accurate as to the kind of man he was," he told the author. "He was a very outgoing, gregarious person . . . and being as heavy as he was, he was thought of as being a fat, jolly guy. But while he was an amusing person, he was very dedicated, I think, to his work, and very serious-minded."

TOUGH ACT TO FOLLOW

The former senator, whose father, the late Senator Robert A. Taft, was the eldest of the president's three children, observed that Theodore Roosevelt would have been a tough act for anyone to follow, an opinion also expressed by others, including the president's youngest son, the late Charles P. Taft II, in an interview with the author before his death in June 1983.

Charles Taft—Uncle Charlie—said that he felt his father had been both misunderstood and underestimated as president because he was far from the big ol' happy guy many thought him to have been and because of such accomplishments as having improved the functioning of the federal court system, an achievement in which he recalled his father as having taken special pride. As president, William Howard Taft had filled five vacancies on the Supreme Court—virtually remaking that body—and had taken important steps in reducing the backlog of federal cases. He had achieved more success in persuading Congress to go along with him in this regard than in many other areas.

"There is a painting in the Taft museum . . . and he looks there like a happy, jolly old elf [but] he wasn't like that at all," Charles Taft told the author. "It's a complete misrepresentation. . . . He was not that kind of genial [person]. He had a good sense of humor. He had a collection of stories, many of which I have absorbed and stolen since then . . . and he told them often, and they were appreciated."

"His humor had a point to it all the time," he said, recalling, however, that often one person in an audience would laugh, and it started the whole audience laughing. "But that's not geniality, that's sense of humor."

Taft's brother Horace wrote that he had "always resented the picture of a smiling, good natured man, more or less negative," recalling that "the adjectives 'fat and lazy' were sometimes added to the picture." That his brother was fat was unquestioned, wrote Horace Taft—he weighed some 333 pounds at his inauguration but at times was able to diet and exercise himself to some 250 pounds—and that he was good-natured and charming was clear. "But positive force and courage were as prominent in his character as anything else," he continued, and he actually was capable of exerting great energy and vigor. He played thirty-eight holes of golf in winning a tournament when he was nearly seventy and still weighed 260 pounds.

He had become an avid golfer early on despite the concerns of some that it was bad for his image to play what was then seen as a rich man's game, and he certainly was energetic enough in 1910 to become the first president to throw out the first ball to begin a new baseball season.

The late Curtis D. MacDougall, emeritus professor of journalism at Northwestern University and himself a veteran of bitter political conflict as a candidate for Congress in 1948 on the Progressive party ticket with Henry A. Wallace, recalled for the author his impressions of Taft during the president's visit to MacDougall's home town of Fond du Lac, Wisconsin, in 1911 and later as a young reporter.

The visit to Fond du Lac had earned the community a place in history as the town that snubbed a president when the mayor withdrew an invitation after a promised visit was cut from three hours to a few minutes. "All arrangements . . . abandoned. Give all your time to Oshkosh and Appleton," Mayor Frank J. Wolff had wired Taft's secretary, Charles D. Hilles. But there had been second thoughts even before the snub had made news across the country, and the result was a renewal of the invitation. The president paid the city a visit of nearly two hours on October 26, 1911, and young MacDougall did not lose his chance to eye-witness history.

MacDougall recalled that the family was back at home after ceremonies during which students from each school in town sang a song they had practiced for weeks ("ours was 'Columbia the Gem of the Ocean' "), "and he drove by in his car, and so we got a wave from him for ourselves—my mother and my dog and me."

Later, as a reporter, MacDougall covered a Chautauqua talk by Taft after he had left the White House and recalled his quip after an introduction that made no reference to his having been president. He had learned something when he returned to Fond du Lac, he said: that it was possible for a man to have been president of the United States and have it forgotten in that short a time.

"And he chuckled," MacDougall recalled.

The characteristic of Taft was that he was a jolly fat man, and he would chuckle at his own jokes before he had told them. . . . He was a good joke teller, but he'd have you all laughing without you knowing what the hell you were laughing at.

Most people would do that and it would bore the crowd or kill the point of the joke, but not with Taft. He got 'em laughing before he told the joke, and they kept right on laughing. . . .

But he could be very dignified. I saw him when he was Chief Justice . . . when the Supreme Court was still in the Capitol building. . . . I saw Earl Warren preside in later years, and I saw Harlan Stone preside, and I would say that William Howard Taft was by far the most dignified.

"I think he was a great man," MacDougall said. "I realize now, studying his record, that he was not much of a President, but he had character, and he had courage—at least he created that impression."

William Howard Taft's roots go back nearly to the beginning of American history. The first Taft to settle in America was Robert, a carpenter from Weymouth, England, who settled in Braintree, Massachusetts, in the late 1670s.

It was Robert Taft's great-great-great grandson, Alphonso, who eventually left the home of his father Peter, in Vermont, to practice law in Cincinnati after becoming the first of the line to graduate from Yale. He did well, in one instance, for example, winning the case that led to the founding of the University of Cincinnati.

He also won landmark cases against the use of the Bible in the schools and made a ruling upholding the constitutionality of laws that allowed the city to build what became the Southern Railway. He later became a judge of the Superior Court and secretary of war to replace the impeached William W. Belknap, and then attorney general, both under President Ulysses S. Grant. Still later, he served as minister to Austria-Hungary and then to Russia.

Alphonso Taft apparently was an austere and disciplined man who drank little, considered smoking a wasteful habit, and urged his four sons to put good study habits above sports—a point especially apt in the case of young Will, who graduated second in his class of 132 at Yale, besides being a wrestler and a boxer and the strongest in his class at 225 pounds and six feet-plus.

ALPHONSO TAFT'S VIEW

In a foreshadowing of son Will's later passion, Alphonso Taft once wrote that "to be Chief Justice of the United States is more than to be President." He never received the appointment, nor did he live to see his son become the only person ever to have held both offices.

Will, known in his younger days as Big Lub and later as Big Bill, had been a hefty, healthy baby and became an outgoing and forceful young man to the point that he once slapped a contentious politician who later turned out to have had a pistol in his pocket, thrashed a Cincinnati editor he felt had insulted his father, and helped harassed police officers make arrests in a threatening crowd.

Still, there was a gentler side to Will's nature, and the future president enjoyed outings and cultural events in a circle that came to include Helen Herron—called

Nellie—whom he later married and to whom several observers ascribed the drive that led him to the White House.

After his graduation from Yale, Taft entered the Cincinnati Law School—now part of the University of Cincinnati and including a building named for his father—and worked as a reporter for the *Commercial,* a circumstance that apparently did nothing to alleviate the general strain on his relations with the press after he became president.

In 1880 he was named an assistant prosecutor in Hamilton County, where Cincinnati is located, thus beginning the lifelong career in public service that prepared him so well for the presidency, though he did enter private practice for a time with a former associate of his father.

This followed a few months as collector of internal revenue for the First District of Ohio, an appointment by President James A. Garfield. Taft resigned the post in part over his distaste for political patronage after he was criticized for party disloyalty for refusing to fire men he considered competent on the patronage request of a former congressman.

He was named assistant county solicitor in 1885 and attracted attention for his skill in arguing for the disbarment of Cincinnati criminal lawyer Thomas C. Campbell even though Campbell was exonerated on all but a minor charge. From there he was named to fill a vacancy on the Superior Court bench and in 1888 was elected to a full term—his only elective office before running successfully for president twenty years later.

The family's first tour of duty in Washington followed Taft's appointment as solicitor general, a position he held for only two years before returning to Cincinnati as a federal judge. But by 1901 he had, with great reluctance, left the bench to accept appointment as governor-general of the Philippines, first under President McKinley and then under Roosevelt after McKinley was assassinated.

He was, as has been indicated, a man of engaging personality who was almost impossible to dislike, and he tended to like and trust his fellow man almost to a fault, though Archie Butt recalled that one of his chief attributes was an ability to curse with the best of them. "I have found out three things he does well," wrote Butt. "He dances well, he curses well, and he laughs well."

"JUST LIKE THOSE FOLKS HE KNOWS OUT IN OHIO"

Mark Sullivan quotes an American correspondent in the Philippines as having written of Taft that

we ought to ship this splendid fellow back. It's a shame to spoil his illusion that folks the world over are just like the folks he knows out in Ohio. He makes me think of pies, hominy, fried chicken, big red apples, "Mr. Dooley," frosty mornings, oysters on the half shell, the oaks and the pines, New England town meetings, the little red schoolhouse, encyclopedias on the installment plan, the square deal, and a home run with the bases full—out here where a man wears his shirt outside his breeches to keep cool in mid winter, picks his dinner off a banana tree out of the window, conceals his bolo and his Mauser and his thoughts behind a smile of friendship varnished with Spanish manners, and is in the Four Hundred if he can sign his name in a scrawl. . . . Oh, but wasn't the Judge and his laugh good—and won't he be easy for them![4]

Taft's letters from Manila to his friend Judge Hollister describe conditions and people in the Islands in reports that counter this impression of naivete, but the picture persisted despite certain acknowledged accomplishments.

"An Englishman" wrote in *Harper's Weekly* in 1910 that he "would defy anyone to come across him privately without feeling drawn toward this good-humored, unconventional, rollicking giant, with his frank, free bearing, his massive look of power and adequacy, his radiating air of jollity and zest," adding that he himself had formed four distinct impressions of the then-presidential candidate: that he was "immensely likeable and trustworthy"; that, having seen him in the War Department as he "sat down, munched a sandwich, hoisted a huge leg over the arm of his chair, and relieved his waistcoat buttons of their normal functions . . . whatever might be his shortcomings, affectation, 'frills,' pretentiousness . . . were not among them" and that he had "an unhurried, ever-ready instinct and capacity for dealing with men and things that let him move like a smiling steam-roller through problems such as insurrection in the Philippines and the purchase from the Vatican of the lands of the friars there."

"He strikes me immediately," the Englishman wrote, "as having a peculiar gift of lubricating sagacity—and that kind of impersonal, disentangling mind which when united with a winning personality and a dependable character, makes its possessor a court of final appeal for private friends and public colleagues."

DISTASTE FOR POLITICS?

Taft may have professed a distaste for politics, and he may have lacked a degree of skill, but Charles L. Mee, Jr., points out that

the rewards for a political career in Ohio should be substantial . . . because Ohio was such a politically active, and corrupt, state—with such gutter fighters as Boss George Cox and Fire Engine Joe Foraker of Cincinnati; such hard money arm twisters as Mark Hanna, the Red Boss of Cleveland; and such snooty politicians as Charlie and William Howard Taft—that anyone who came up through Ohio politics was destined to have a first-rate education in the intricacies and pitfalls of forcing and scuttling legislation, manipulating conventions, rigging elections, securing campaign contributions from large and small corporations, disposing of public funds, and letting utility franchises, road contracts, permits, licenses, and jobs.

So well schooled were Ohio politicians that, in the same period, Ohio provided seven out of the twelve presidents of the United States—or every single Republican president except two, who succeeded to the job from the vice presidency. They said they were elected because Ohio was in the middle of the country, and because Ohio was the crossroads of the country. . . . But that was just convention blather. The truth was that Ohio politicians did well because the state weeded out all but the most ferocious survivors.

William Allen White wrote Taft in 1908 to ask whether it was the angels who had handed him his success, and he answered that "like every well trained Ohio man I always had my plate the right side up when offices were falling." Taft continued:

You ask me this—"Will you therefore tell me frankly and kindly where you got your political pull?" I got my political pull, first through the fact that I was hail-fellow-well-met with all the political people of the city convention going type. I also worked in my ward and sometimes succeeded in defeating the regular gang candidate by hustling around among good people to get them out. I didn't hesitate to attack the gang methods, but I always kept on good terms with them when I served on committee [sic] of credentials. My impression is that politicians do not care so much if you fight them, provided you get down on the floor with them and take part with them.

A month later Taft again wrote to White, this time enclosing a clipping of an item from the *New York Sun* that implied that he was ungrateful to Cox by seeking to disassociate himself from the Cincinnati boss after winning his support during the presidential campaign, and recalling an earlier Taft attack on the machine during a speech in Akron aimed at aiding Myron T. Herrick's campaign for governor of Ohio. Herrick lost, and there were those who charged that it was at least in part because of Taft's challenge to Cox at a time and place when he could have confined himself to statewide issues—another example, perhaps, of lack of political finesse.

"It is true," the *Sun* wrote, "that for many years Mr. Taft had been the beneficiary of the Cincinnati machine. Cox had put him in office and kept him there. In all human probability Mr. Taft would have been practising law in Cincinnati to this day but for George B. Cox and his disreputable understrappers."

COX SUPPORTED SUPERIOR COURT NOMINATION

Taft admitted that Cox had supported his nomination for election to the Superior Court after he had served a fourteen-month temporary appointment. But he said this came only at the urging of Governor Foraker and at a time when Cox was being opposed by the *Cincinnati Times-Star,* owned by Taft's brother, Charles P. Taft I.

"I was thankful to Cox for what he did, which was to throw his influence in the convention for me to nominate me," Taft wrote. "This was all that Cox ever did for me." Taft said that Cox's most recent support had come about "because . . . otherwise his machine would have been entirely broken up," adding, "I declined to go into the campaign except upon the assurance of my brother that he would make no bargain of any sort with Cox in my behalf and that is the situation today.''

One of the contrasts with which Taft had to deal in following Roosevelt was his reticence in dealing with the press relative to the latter's feel for the media. O. K. Davis wrote that Taft had been popular with the press despite his reputation for being unable to use it as TR had done, and while he was secretary of war correspondents often would ''go Tafting'' every afternoon for a half-hour or so of conversation that produced news.

Of those days, Davis wrote that

Mr. Taft exerted himself to get, and keep, on good terms with the newspapermen. He talked frankly about affairs in his own department, was much more communicative, as a rule, than other cabinet officers, and at times would even ''take assignments'' for the boys. . . . He seemed to accept the argument . . . that the Government business is public business, knowledge of which, in all but a few special cases, belongs, of right, to the public.

In fact, according to Davis, ''No man has ever been a candidate for the presidential nomination who had such a great body of voluntary newspaper support as Mr. Taft had.''

However, after Taft became president-elect, he responded with a clear chill to a call by Davis and others to pay respects and to offer congratulations. ''The old cordiality and friendliness [from] the days when he was Secretary of War and a candidate for the nomination was wholly gone,'' wrote Davis, ''and there was in its place a reserve that almost amounted to coldness.''

ESSARY HAS MORE POSITIVE VIEW OF PRESS RELATIONS

J. Frederick Essary of the *Baltimore Sun* had a more positive view of Taft's relations with the reporters, observing that he seemed to enjoy them even more than he had enjoyed the give-and-take during his days as Secretary of War.

Essary noted that Taft had only two special friends among the correspondents, William W. Price of the *Washington Star* and Gus J. Karger of the *Cincinnati Times-Star,* owned by the president's brother Charles. The Karger relationship was cited as so special that he had ready access to the president and to the White House mail and gave the news he gleaned to the reporters. Essary wrote:

He was an extremely valuable aide of Mr. Taft in getting the Taft viewpoint before the public without, in any sense, being a Presidential press agent. The wonder is still felt that in the successive changes in the secretaryship to the President—and there were five in four years—President Taft did not place Karger in that position. Things might have gone better if he had.[5]

James E. Pollard wrote that, as a result of his experience as a reporter, "Taft must have absorbed something of the atmosphere or viewpoint of the press," but that "time and events . . . were to suggest that the impression did not last."

He could become testy with reporters and irritated by what he read in the press, especially by what he and Nellie felt was undue attention to the least of their activities. Butt recalls this after-dinner exchange when Mrs. Taft handed the president a copy of the *New York World:*

"I don't want the *World,*" he said. "I have stopped reading it. It only makes me angry."

"But you used to like it very much," said Mrs. Taft.

"That was when it agreed with me, but it abuses me now, and so I don't want it."

"You will never know what the other side is doing if you only read the *Sun* and the *Tribune,*" said this wise woman.

"I don't care what the other side is doing," he answered with some irritation.

Wrote Butt: "He cannot brook criticism. But he has got to learn to put up with it, for it is going to come thick and fast."

Davis noted that access improved after Charles D. Norton replaced Fred W. Carpenter as his secretary, and Essary credits Taft with having been the first president to hold weekly press conferences.

Michael Medved and Archie Butt credited Norton with being responsible for at least a share of the negative image of the Taft administration. A successful insurance executive, he had joined the Treasury Department in order to do public service and had attracted the attention of the White House after changes that saved the government $2 million. He was, wrote Medved, just the sort of live wire, efficient and dynamic, to replace the timid and meticulous Fred Carpenter, who sought only to please the president and who trembled at his scowl. But Norton became even too close to the president, and, in fact, "buried . . . once and for all" any chance of a Taft-Roosevelt reconciliation after a meeting of the two in 1910 when it became impossible to ignore speculation that TR would seek a third term after all. Norton told reporters after the meeting that Roosevelt had begged for Taft's help in New York state politics. Roosevelt denied this and accused Norton, "and by implication the President . . . of duplicity and betrayal." Taft responded with what Archie Butt called unnatural laughter, "full of concern, as when one whistles in a graveyard." Norton eventually was replaced by Charles D. Hilles, "a competent if colorless administrator," who failed in trying to bring TR and the president together.

Elmer O. Cornwell, Jr., wrote that Roosevelt "elaborated a kind of 'model' for future executive exploitation of the mass media for opinion leadership" and that his successors added little to it except in terms of technology and scale. Roosevelt realized, as Cornwell put it,

that the journalistic fraternity, both the working press and the editors, therefore play the role of intermediary between the President and his audience. As a consequence, the

President is faced with a more complex problem than merely the phrasing and timing of announcements and appeals to the public. He must enlist the willing cooperation of the working press, in the first instance, or at the very least avoid alienating them. Hopefully, he will also have the sympathetic understanding of some of the owners, but whether he does or does not, he must weigh carefully the merits of front page coverage versus editorial support and favor. He must . . . become preoccupied with the mechanics of getting his utterance transmitted in an effective manner—without the power to *command* such cooperation. . . . The more sensitive an understanding he has of the publicist's art and the newspaper trade, the better off he will be.

Roosevelt had the knack.

Taft apparently didn't much care. And the result was a heightening of the appearance that he was doing little because the public hardly could escape recalling the idea that Roosevelt had done and was doing so much. As Mark Sullivan put it, "While he [Roosevelt] is in the neighborhood the public can no more look the other way than the small boy can turn his head away from a circus parade followed by a steam calliope."[6]

POIGNANT LEGACY FOR "SLOW MOVING" TAFT

So Roosevelt, according to Cornwell, "unquestionably left the office bigger and more important and more a focus of attention in the eyes of the public than it had been before him," which had

a particularly poignant meaning for his chosen heir, the affable and slow moving William Howard Taft. Throughout the latter's term . . . he was forced to live under the shadow of his predecessor. The public had become habituated to the activism and pyrotechnic displays of Roosevelt, and Taft either could not or would not *(probably both)* attempt to duplicate them. In short, there had to be a letdown.

Archie Butt expressed concern early in the Taft presidency for "all this newspaper notoriety" and pointed out that while Roosevelt "had the faculty of having things printed as he wanted them [Taft] does not understand the art of giving out news." Butt, with high regard for both men, said, "Mr. Roosevelt understood the necessity of guiding the press to suit one's own ends; President Taft has no conception of the press as an adjunct to his office."

Cornwell observed: "This was the matter in a nutshell. Taft was to this extent an anachronism in the office. Though miserable and out of place in the period 1908–1912, he might have ranked among the successful Presidents if he had had the good fortune to precede T.R. rather than to follow him."

SOUGHT TO MAKE INROADS IN SOLID SOUTH

Among the problems Taft inherited on taking office was that of trying to rebuild the strength of the Republican party in the Solid South; this meant dealing not only with a strong Democratic organization but with a black population increasingly skeptical of gaining satisfaction from their traditional commitment to the GOP.

One might have expected an enlightened outlook from a man whose state had, for example, enacted a strong public accommodations statute as early as 1884. But Taft was, in a way, a creature of his Jim Crow times as well as the protégé of a man—Roosevelt—who found himself in the paradoxical position of having had Booker T. Washington to dinner in the White House while also having ordered the dishonorable discharge of black troops allegedly involved in a shooting incident in Brownsville, Texas, in 1906.

Washington, himself criticized by some as too conciliatory to whites, was an adviser to Roosevelt on black affairs, including appointments—he continued the role with Taft—and it was in that capacity that he dined at the White House and not as a presidential statement on race relations. However, the incident drew bitter criticism in the South and expressions of satisfaction from some blacks who thought it showed that TR supported them. The *Washington Bee,* for example, front-paged the headline: "The Lie That He Is Opposed to the Negro."

Not long after, opinion began to shift back, and even the *Bee* came to feel that reliance upon TR was a waste of time, especially after the president signed and refused to reconsider the discharge of more than 160 black soldiers of the Twenty-fifth Regiment—including six Congressional Medal of Honor winners—after the Brownsville affair.

This incident, which left at least one man dead, developed out of a raid on the town by armed men after an alleged assault on a white woman by a black soldier. Even though the evidence was circumstantial and none of the soldiers went on trial, the discharge decision made its way up through channels to Secretary of War William Howard Taft. Taft never successfully purged himself of a share of the onus despite his role in investigations that led eventually to congressional creation of a board which passed upon applications for reenlistment of the discharged troops.

INAUGURAL WORDS ON RACE "UNINTENDED MOCKERY"

Nor did Taft succeed in escaping the overall onus laid upon him by much of the black community despite his likeable nature and his inaugural profession that "personally, I have not the slightest race prejudice or feeling."

Richard B. Sherman wrote:

In such an intensely race-conscious society his words were an unintended mockery; prejudice simply did not have the same meaning for Taft, or other white Americans . . . that it had for their Black countrymen. . . .

Predictably, some Negroes were skeptical about Taft's intentions. Pointing to his close association with Roosevelt's ill-regarded administration, they concluded long before his inauguration that his understanding of the race problem was limited. . . . [T]hey doubted that he was the man who could revive the Republican Party's ideals and lead a serious assault upon . . . discriminatory racial practices.[7]

He did not.

Despite expressions of support on education and the right to vote, Taft made it clear that federal appointees would have to be fully acceptable to the communities in which they would serve, virtually excluding blacks in the South, and he continued to support—or at least to fail to challenge—actions that failed to increase and often led to less black access to meaningful jobs, to promotion, to party power, and to the ballot.

He did make several of what Sherman calls "showcase appointments"—William H. Lewis in 1911 became an assistant United States attorney general, the highest federal post to that time held by a black—but his aim essentially was to build the party in the South, and this led to a catering to whites and to increasing disaffection among blacks, though they remained loyal to the GOP for lack of better alternatives.

Certainly one measure of anti-Taft feeling among blacks was the statement by seventy-five clergymen and several educators from eighteen states—thirteen northern and five southern—that "at no time, since the Negro has been a citizen, has he been so thoroughly ignored as a part and parcel of this great government, as he has been since William Howard Taft has been President," and asking support for Roosevelt, who, they said, should be given a chance to right Brownsville as a "hasty act."

W.E.B Du Bois, a founder of the influential Niagara movement that led to the founding of the National Association for the Advancement of Colored People, and an outspoken critic of Washington, decided to support Wilson on the grounds that the Democratic party was worth a try because it at least had shown itself supportive of black interests in much of the North.

In 1911 the Council of Confederated Negro Bishops, meeting in Mobile, Alabama, was sharply critical of Taft. Bishop B. F. Lee of Wilberforce, Ohio, declared that the president was no friend of the black community. Bishop H. M. Turner of Atlanta, Georgia, charged that the Negro had no rights and that "the so-called Supreme Court of the United States has always been robbing the Negro of his rights, and Congress and the President sit silently by without saying a word."

The result of such sentiment, according to Sherman, was that black opinion was divided as never before in a presidential election, with the result that more black voters than ever left the Republicans. In the end, however, the major concern for Taft and the GOP was that their southern strategy had failed and that 1912 saw the Republican vote in the South drop to an all-time low.

Coletta observed that there was no great scandal or corruption during the Taft presidency, "nor did he make any steps backward, yet he remains the gigantic symbol of standpattism—the champion of privilege, of property rights as the bulwark of civilization, and of status quo—and as the opponent of both direct and social democracy,'' an image Coletta regards as not quite fair, pointing to the accomplishments of Taft's administration:

He had undertaken the first tariff revision since 1897. The Payne-Aldrich tariff retained the Protective principle, yet its corporation tax feature was deemed to be "progressive." He had placed Roosevelt's conservation work on a legal basis and even improved upon it, made a real advance in railroad regulation, launched an antitrust crusade to which Roosevelt's paled in comparison, and nearly completed the Panama Canal. . . . his administration created postal savings banks and parcel post systems, added two states to the Union and two amendments to the Constitution, established a Department of Labor separate from Commerce, regulated corporate campaign contributions, provided a Children's Bureau, passed a White Slave Act, abolished the manufacture of phosphorus matches, limited work on federal projects to eight hours a day, and strengthened the Pure Food and Drug Act. Taft's appointments to the federal judicial systems . . . were excellent, and he made notable efficiency and economy in government and in suggesting the adoption of a federal budget.

PAYNE-ALDRICH ACT CREDITED FOR SURPLUS

Edward Howe Cotton wrote that one result of the Payne-Aldrich tariff was that "it reversed a deficit in the national treasury of $58 million to a surplus of $30 million in two years."

Under Taft, the State Department was reorganized and expanded and its merit professionalism enhanced by Secretary of State Philander C. Knox and his first assistant secretary, Francis M. Huntington Wilson, and a foreign policy was developed around defense of the Panama Canal, nonintervention in European affairs, and active support of overseas investments by the diplomatic and consular corps.[8]

"Not only would the investments earn profits," according to Coletta, "they would help to promote economic and social stability in the areas of investment and would promote peace. Here were the ingredients of dollar diplomacy as applied to Latin America and the Far East."

Coletta said that the policy in Latin America was based upon the idea that challenges to the Monroe Doctrine and to the strategic security of the United States could be avoided by arranging for American bankers to invest funds that the Latin nations could use to buy up their foreign debt.

As a result, wrote Coletta,

the American investor now would enjoy a practically monopolized investment market, cause for European intervention and economic competition would be removed, the more prosperous borrowers would move in the political and economic orbit of the United States, and peace and stability would be preserved. Economic, or "nonimperialistic" imperialism, would thus supplant territorial imperialism, and gold would replace guns. . . . Taft himself said that "the diplomacy of the present administration has sought to respond to the modern idea of commercial intercourse. This policy has been characterized as substituting dollars for bullets.''

MARINES DEPLOYED TO SUPPORT "DOLLAR DIPLOMACY"

So "dollar diplomacy" it became, and on went the attempt to extend American influence and foster commercial enterprise through expansion of trade and investments, backed by a readiness to deploy the fleet and even to send in the marines when such intervention appeared necessary to protect the national interest. Nor was the use of the marines necessarily a short-term approach. The last detachments of the 2,700 sent into Nicaragua in 1912 after a seizure of American property were not pulled out until 1933, wrote Coletta, who observed that "evidently, a President would be kept in power in Nicaragua only by the use of American Marines.''

Coletta found that this policy angered Latin Americans "by aggressively seeking commercial advantages particularly in Central America, in establishing financial protectorates, and in using . . . diplomatic and consular agents to find new fields for American enterprise.''

Some saw efforts to gain business for American shipyards as more like battleship diplomacy, and this led to such contrasts as that between the positive tone of a Taft message to Congress and the negative tone of a letter to the secretary of the navy from the Patriotic Order of the Sons of America.

Said Taft:

It gratifies me exceedingly to announce that the Argentine Republic some months ago placed with manufacturers a contract for the construction of two battleships and certain additional naval equipment. The extent of this work and its importance to the Argentine Republic make the placing of this bid an earnest of friendly feelings toward the United States.

The Sons of America, however, charged that what the government was doing by such sales was "peddling its naval secrets in an effort to boost the profits of the steel trust.''

There had been reports of Argentine displeasure over what that nation termed a lack of frankness and courtesy afforded officers invited to serve with the navy, but there also had been an advisory aimed at avoiding the appearance of concealment in allowing inspection of an otherwise closely guarded fire control system during a naval visit to Chile, a move seen as "a fair indication of the lengths to which the Taft Administration was willing to go to push its celebrated dollar diplomacy.''[9]

But, Coletta found,

American productivity and salesmanship rather than diplomatic dickerings caused foreign trade to increase during his term except, paradoxically, in China [and] the end result of

using the Department of State as field agency for commercial enterprise was failure—
failure either to earn profits for American bankers or to create the economic and political
stability needed to obtain peace in the countries to which it directed its attention.

"SHOPKEEPER" DIPLOMACY VIEWED AS RESENTED

Coletta also wrote that what he called Taft's "intrusive shopkeeper" diplomacy was

resented by such nations as Britain, Japan, and Russia, while his insistence upon keeping
rather than freeing the Filipinos appalled the anti-imperialists and liberals of his day. On
the other hand, he had settled by pacific means all important disputes with foreign countries
except the one with Great Britain over the Panama tolls, which he belatedly agreed to
arbitrate; the one with Colombia over Panama; and the one with Russia over the right of
Americans to freedom of travel.

In fact, he abrogated a long-standing treaty with Russia because that nation
refused to let Jews who were American citizens travel any more freely inside
that country than native Russian Jews.

Taft managed in 1911 to persuade Congress to ratify the treaty that embodied
one of his cherished goals, reciprocity—free trade—with Canada, only to see it
scuttled by Canadian and British concern over the possibility that it would lead
to an overwhelming extension of American influence and even economic control
over the Dominion.

Such fears hardly were allayed by awareness of such remarks as one by Taft
in a letter to Roosevelt stating that "one result of reciprocity would be such an
increase in trade that Canada would become only an adjunct of the United
States," and a statement by Democratic Representative Champ Clark of Missouri
that he looked forward to "the day when the American flag will float over every
square foot of the British North American possessions clear to the North Pole."
The result of such assertions and of fears based on long-standing concerns about
American expansionism was a reaction of Canadian voters that led to the death
of the treaty by the ouster of the Laurier government, which had negotiated it.

As has been seen, Taft himself was prone to making damaging remarks, such
as his "God knows" response to a reporter's question on the effect on the
ordinary citizen of the economic ills of 1907—it seemed not the substantive
response expected of a highly placed official. But he remained quietly judicious
in his response to attacks on his religious beliefs—he was a Unitarian who had
acknowledged that he did not believe in the divinity of Jesus Christ—so that the
matter did not become a major issue, for example, during the 1912 campaign.

ENVIRONMENTAL AND REGULATORY CONTROVERSIES

Two other controversies during the Taft administration which were costly to
the administration involved Chief Forester Gifford Pinchot, a Roosevelt favorite,

and Dr. Harvey W. Wiley, head of the Bureau of Chemistry in the Department of Agriculture, noted for strong handling of pure food and drug regulations.

O. K. Davis wrote that the Pinchot affair added to the insurgents' anger when tempers were already hot over the Payne-Aldrich tariff. The Progressives had wanted James A. Garfield, a Roosevelt man, as secretary of the interior, but Taft named Richard A. Ballinger; this aroused the suspicions of Pinchot, originator of Roosevelt's conservation policy, who charged that Ballinger had not been aggressive enough in dealing with Alaska coal lands that could fall into the hands of a monopoly, but Taft, instead of acting promptly, as "two or three of the hard-headed and cynical newspapermen advised . . . [crack] the heads of both . . . and throw them out of government service," sought to smooth over the situation, though he fired Pinchot even before the end of his first year as president, and retained Ballinger only after congressional hearings.

In the Wiley affair, the official committed a technical violation of the law with a salary arrangement that allowed retention of a highly regarded scientist, but Taft exonerated him.

Much of Taft's time between his presidential tenure and his Supreme Court appointment was spent working for world peace through collective international action—he supported the League of Nations idea—based on such earlier interest as his failed effort to win ratification of his cherished arbitration treaties.

He even achieved a reconciliation with Roosevelt in May 1918 when the two men accidentally found themselves at the Blackstone Hotel in Chicago at the same time. Taft had been on his way to his room when he heard that Roosevelt was in the dining room, Herbert S. Duffy related. He made his way to the table and the two clasped hands as though nothing had ever come between them.

"I NEVER WAS SO SURPRISED IN MY LIFE"

"By Godfrey, I never was so surprised in my life," Roosevelt told John Leary. "But wasn't it a gracious thing for him to do. . . . Jack, I don't mind telling you how delighted I am. I never felt happier over anything in my life. . . . It was splendid of Taft. . . . I've seen old Taft, and we're in perfect harmony on everything."[10]

"You may have seen that Roosevelt and I have been reconciled," Taft wrote family friend Mrs. Lucien Wulsin on July 16, 1918, at her home in Paris.

I don't know that he has changed his opinion on the issues of the past, but I think we're both glad to come into friendly relations again. Life is too short to cherish these resentments, and while one should not in future action ignore the lessons of the past, one may well forgive and forget, so far as associations are concerned. I have always admired many traits of Theodore Roosevelt. His besetting sin is his absorbing egotism that prevents his taking an interest in anything in which he is not the leader, and that makes him very unjust in dealing with those whom fortune has put on a level with him, and who independently mark out a policy for themselves to meet their responsibilities.

All in all, according to Paolo Coletta, Taft was "not a bad president but rather a good one," but he failed to achieve greatness because he was unable to practice the shrewd and hard-driving and explosive kind of politics played by his predecessor or to "mobilize power in the political system, to balance the advocates of reform against those of reaction."

Coletta wrote that "Mr. Taft did not fail as President, despite the popularly held notion." Instead, it was that "his activities were subjected to constant opposition and misrepresentation by insurgents in his own party, as well as by Democratic leaders who looked for control of the country at the next presidential election."

TWO OF ROSSITER'S ADMIRED TRAITS HELD BY TAFT

Taft had only two of the seven personal qualities cited by political scientist Clinton L. Rossiter as needed by a president: affability and a sense of humor. His lack of the other five—bounce, political skill, cunning, the newspaper habit, and a sense of history, led Coletta to see him as unable to thrive on the hard work of the presidency, to win support for his programs, and to deal with his rivals and with party interest groups, to know when to speak and when to be silent and when to lead and when to follow, and as unable to take criticism from the press to read the people's pulse.

He could be vigorous and unyielding in his likes and dislikes, but Coletta said that his basic response to attacks lay in that familiar quotation from Lincoln that he kept on his desk:

If I were to read, much less answer, all the attacks made on me, this shop might as well be closed for any other business. I do the very best I know how—the very best I can; and I mean to keep doing so to the end. If the end brings me out all right, what is said against me won't amount to anything. If the end brings me out wrong, ten angels swearing I was right would make no difference.

Donald F. Anderson wrote that, as a result, Taft naively "felt that his record would ultimately speak for itself and vindicate his strategy and that to actively use and manipulate the press of the country appeared almost Machiavellian to him."

"A Common Acquaintance" compared the 1912 candidates—Wilson, Taft, and Roosevelt—and wrote of Taft that he

not only lacks the instinct for publicity, but he has a contempt for it. I have heard him explain, "I don't want any forced or manufactured sentiment in my favor." It was in the White House, and a visitor was urging a campaign of press education, saying that all the country needed to bring it to the President's side was a better knowledge of his ideas and his aims; that Mr. Taft had only to open the sluices a little and to let out a few facts and his opponents would be silenced.

"I simply can't do that sort of thing," the President replied. "That isn't my method.

I must wait for time and the result of my labors to vindicate me naturally. I have profound faith in the people. Their final judgment will be right.'' But Mr. Taft will do nothing to help the people come to a judgment. If he is misjudged, he has himself to blame for it. No public man can afford to neglect the press.

PUBLIC RELATIONS EFFORTS ''TOO LITTLE TOO LATE''

He had some success in improving his public relations after the Democratic victories in the 1910 congressional elections, but his efforts were ''too little, too late,'' according to Anderson, who added:

Enlightenment had come too late. Taft's initial attitude had been appropriate for a federal judge with a lifetime tenure; it was highly inappropriate to the most vulnerable elected official in the United States. It is clear that Taft did learn, the hard way, what Roosevelt had earlier once tried to teach him—that it is not only necessary to do exactly what is right, but to do it so that the knaves cannot mislead the fool into believing it to be wrong. It is because Taft learned this lesson too late in his presidency that he became a one-term President. It is because he was not a skillful leader of public opinion that his remarkable knowledge of public affairs, his experience, his talents, and his integrity, in the end, produced a fascinating but disappointing Presidency.[11]

It seems clear that the Taft presidency cannot fully be assessed without noting the contrast between the high regard in which Taft was held when he took office and the then-unprecedented depths of his defeat—he received only 8 electoral votes as against 88 for Roosevelt and 435 for Wilson—when he sought reelection in 1912.

Polls perennially have ranked him as average. The recent Murray-Blessing survey drew a nearly 50 percent return from among 1,997 historians asked to respond to a nineteen-page instrument that took an average of two and a half hours to complete. The survey, aimed in part at a broader-scope sample of expert opinion than had been polled in earlier studies, ranked Taft nineteenth among the thirty-six presidents for whom responses were sought (W. H. Harrison, Garfield, and Reagan were not included).

Taft himself said of his presidency: ''It is a very humdrum, uninteresting administration, and it does not attract the attention or enthusiasm of anybody.'' The historian Pringle elaborated that ''if it was a humdrum and uninteresting administration, Taft had made it so by his inability to popularize or make exciting his accomplishments.''

Taft did say that he felt he had accomplished ''a great deal . . . which will be useful to the people in the future [which] is the only real satisfaction that one gets out of any public office.''

He concluded he had

held the office of President once, and that is more than most men have, so I am content to retire from it with a consciousness that I have done the best I could, and have accomplished a good deal in one way or another. I have strengthened the Supreme Court, have given them [the people] a great deal of new and valuable legislation, have not interfered with business, have kept the peace, and on the whole have enabled people to pursue their various occupations without interruption.

"DIFFICULT TO BE FAIR"

"It is difficult to be fair to Mr. Taft's administration," the *Times* of London declared on February 28, 1913.

Its failures have been spectacular and its achievements unsensational. Four years of Republican bickering, ending in the schism and defeat of the party—such is its political record. In foreign affairs its record is hardly happier. Nor has it been a question of pleasing the people at the expense of the party. In a period of restlessness and transition, probity and honest endeavor have failed as a substitute for popular leadership and ability to play the political game.

He was out of touch with the "spirit and needs of the times," the *Times* wrote, "and . . . the worst that can be said of him is that he has been a weak and unskillful politician who allowed himself to be identified with the wrong wing of a divided party."

Fortune smiled at William Howard Taft until the day he entered the White House as President. He had not wanted to be President and would have preferred an appointment to the Supreme Court. However, upon the urging of his wife and brother, who had political ambitions for him, he acceded to Roosevelt's willingness to secure the Republican nomination for him in 1908. In a sense, Roosevelt made Taft President. He also unmade him in 1912.

He was a man with a judicial mind at sea in a political job, and he had been successful in every major public position he had held except the Presidency. His other posts had been administrative or judicial. As Chief Justice . . . from 1921 to 1930 . . . he was strong and able. But he was not suited by personality for political leadership.

Erwin Hargrove wrote that he thought Taft's most serious weakness was his laziness, observing that

he ate too much, wanted to sleep too long, preferred bridge to work, and was always reluctant to leave the golf course. He would spend long hours in idle conversation with political visitors without any strategic end in view. He loved to travel because it got him out of Washington and away from problems but complained that he was expected to make speeches on his tours. He complained to Archie Butt that there was so much to do and so little time in which to do it, but it was his own fault. He did not really like doing many of the things a President must do and was not willing to work hard at the job.

William Allen White put it a bit differently, however, declaring that Taft was not lazy but rather that he was inclined to put things off and take the easiest course because of his desire for peace and comfort.

The New Republic commented after Taft's death in 1930:

If the success story is still the formula dearest to the American heart, the life of William Howard Taft should have been a pleasing one in a double sense for he had two careers. He rose by successive stages of a life mainly spent as government administrator to the President of the United States, and then, by being about as conservative as Calvin Coolidge, at a time when conservatism was less popular than it was from 1923 to 1928, he sank in the popular esteem until, running against Roosevelt and Wilson in 1912, he received the smallest number of votes ever recorded for a candidate of one of the major parties. No one would have ventured to predict that 18 years later he would have stood high in the affection of the American people. It was not so much that Taft changed during these 18 years, for he did not. It was partially that the United States reverted, after the war, to a frame of mind of which his own temperament was a better expression than before, and partially that, when his conservatism was an important matter to the whole country, it became possible to appraise at their true values his good humor, utter honesty and indefatigable devotion to his tasks.[12]

NOTES

1. Archibald Willingham Butt, *The Letters of Archie Butt* (Garden City, N. Y.: Doubleday, Page and Co., 1924), pp. 232, 233; *Harper's Weekly*, 54 (August 6, 1910), p. 15; *New York Times*, August 6, 1908; *Toledo Blade*, March 4, 1909, p. 4; *Winona (Minnesota) Republican-Herald*, September 19, 1909, p. 1; Archibald Willingham Butt, *Taft and Roosevelt: The Intimate Letters of Archie Butt, Military Aide*, 2 vols. (New York: Doubleday, Doran and Co., 1930), 1:316; Henry F. Pringle, *The Life and Times of William Howard Taft*, 2 vols. (New York: Farrar and Rinehart, 1939), 1:451; *Winona Republican-Herald*, September 19, 1909, p. 2.

2. *Winona Republican-Herald*, September 17, 1909, p. 3; letter from Ida M. Tarbell to William Allen White, September 29, 1909; Oscar King Davis, *Released for Publication* (Boston: Houghton Mifflin, 1925), p. 177; *Harper's Weekly*, December 30, 1911, p. 9; *Boston Herald*, quoted in *The Literary Digest*, 104, no. 12, (March 22, 1930): 15; William Allen White, *The Autobiography of William Allen White* (New York: Macmillan, 1946), p. 435; Judith Icke Anderson, *William Howard Taft: An Intimate History* (New York: W. W. Norton and Co., 1981), pp. 259, 224, 197–208; letter from Theodore Roosevelt to William Allen White, August 10, 1908, White Collection, Library of Congress, Washington, D.C.

3. Butt, *Letters*, 2:813; Erwin C. Hargrove, *Presidential Leadership* (New York: Macmillan, 1966), pp. 95, 96; Donald F. Anderson, *William Howard Taft: A Conservative's Conception of the Presidency* (Ithaca, N.Y.: Cornell University Press, 1973), p. 179; Paolo E. Coletta, *The Presidency of William Howard Taft* (Lawrence: University Press of Kansas, 1973), p. 5; Gary C. Ness, "Proving Ground for a President: William Howard Taft and the Philippines, 1900–1905," *Cincinnati Historical Society Bulletin*, 34, no. 3 (Fall 1976): 205–224; Davis, *Released for Publication*, p. 54; Herbert S. Duffy, *William Howard Taft* (New York: Minton, Balch and Co., 1930), p. 203; Davis, *Released for Publication*, p. 58; letter from Theodore Roosevelt to Sir George Otto Trevelyan, November 6, 1908, in *Theodore Roosevelt Cyclopedia* (New York: Roosevelt Memorial Association, 1941), p. 595; Rep. Philip P. Campbell, "Roosevelt on Taft," remarks of Hon. P. P. Campbell of Kansas reprinted from *Congressional Record*, June 24, 1912, including in full a letter from Theodore Roosevelt to Conrad Kohrs dated September 9, 1908, pp. 1–4; *The World's Work*, 24 no. 2 (June 1912): 128.

4. White, *Autobiography*, p. 426; *The World's Work* 24 (June 1912): 129; Robert Taft, Jr., to the author, Washington, D.C., June 29, 1982; Charles P. Taft II to author, Cincinnati, December 14, 1982; Horace Dutton Taft, *Memories and Opinions* (New York: Macmillan, 1942), p. 108; Stanley L. Gores, "Fond du Lac Snubs a President," *Wisconsin Magazine of History* (Winter 1963–64): 160–169; Curtis D. MacDougall to author, Evanston, Illinois, November 24, 1982; Butt, *Letters*, 1:21; Mark Sullivan, *Our Times: Pre-war America*, 4 vols. (New York: Scribner's, 1930), 3:4; Ness, "Proving Ground."

5. *Harper's Weekly*, 54 (August 6, 1910): p. 15; Charles L. Mee, Jr., *The Ohio Gang: The World of Warren G. Harding* (New York: M. Evans and Co., 1981), pp. 60, 61; letter from William Howard Taft to William Allen White, February 26, 1908; letter from the *New York Sun*, March 31, 1908; Davis, *Released for Publication*, pp. 95; 127; J. Frederick Essary, quoted in Michael Medved, *The Shadow Presidents* (New York: Times Books, 1979), pp. 89, 98.

6. James E. Pollard, *The Presidents and the Press* (New York: Macmillan, 1935), p. 601; Butt, *Letters*, 2:749, 750; Davis, *Released for Publication*, pp. 184, 185; Medved, *Shadow Presidents*, pp. 89, 124, 125, 131, 132; Elmer E. Cornwell, Jr., *Presidential Leadership of Public Opinion* (Bloomington: Indiana University Press, 1965), pp. 14, 15; (emphasis in original); Sullivan, *Our Times*, 1:15.

7. Cornwell, *Presidential Leadership*, p. 26 (emphasis in original); Butt, *Letters*, 1:29, 30; Cornwell, *Presidential Leadership*, p. 26; *Washington Bee*, October 19, 1901, p. 1, quoted in Richard B. Sherman, *The Republican Party in Black America* (Charlottesville: University Press of Virginia, 1973), pp. 28, 62, 54, 56.

8. Sherman, *Republican Party*, p. 82; David Charles Needham, "William Howard Taft, the Negro and the White South," Ph.D. dissertation, University of Georgia, 1970; Sherman, *Republican Party* pp. 92, 101, 93, 110, *New York Times*, February 2, 1911, p. 1; Sherman, *Republican Party*, p. 111; Coletta, *Presidency*, pp. 255, 256; Edward Howe Cotton, *William Howard Taft: A Character Study* (Boston: Beacon Press, 1932), p. 62.

9. Coletta, *Presidency*, pp. 183, 184, 185, 257, 189, 190; William Howard Taft, Annual Message to Congress, Papers Relating to the Messages of the President, *The Foreign Relations of the United States*, p. xv, The Annual Message of the President Transmitted to Congress, December 6, 1910 (Washington, D.C.: Government Printing Office, 1915); letter from the National Camp, Patriotic Order of the Sons of America, to the Secretary of the Navy, March 28, 1911, File 4793–38:31, O.S.N.; Seward W. Livermore, "Battleship Diplomacy in South America: 1905–1925," *Journal of Modern History*, 26 (March 12, 1944): 42.

10. Coletta, *Presidency*, p. 257; letter from Taft to Roosevelt, January 10, 1911, quoted in Pringle, *Life and Times*, 2:588; ibid., 2:589; Henry L. Stoddard, *As I Knew Them* (New York: Harper Brothers, 1927), pp. 375–76; Robert Bolt, "William Howard Taft: A Frustrated and Fretful Unitarian in the White House," *Queen City Heritage*, 42, no. 1 (Spring 1984): 39–48; Davis, *Released for Publication*, p. 180; Duffy, *William Howard Taft*, pp. 308, 309; John Leary, *Talks with T.R.* (Boston: Houghton Mifflin, 1920), quoted in Duffy, *William Howard Taft*, p. 309.

11. Gary Ness, "William Howard Taft and the Great War," *Cincinnati Historical Society Bulletin*, 34, no. 1 (Spring 1976): 7–23; Coletta, *Presidency*, p. 259; Cotton, *William Howard Taft*, p. 61; Clinton L. Rossiter, *The American Presidency* (New York: Harcourt, Brace and Co., 1956), pp. 135–137, quoted in Coletta, *Presidency*, pp. 264, 265; Cotton, *William Howard Taft*, p. 59; Donald F. Anderson, "The Legacy of William Howard Taft," *Presidential Studies Quarterly*, 12, no. 1 (Winter 1982): 32, 33; "A

Common Acquaintance," *The World's Work*, 24 (September 1912): 569–578; Anderson, "Legacy," p. 33.

12. Robert K. Murray and Tim H. Blessing, "The Presidential Performance Study: A Performance Report," *Journal of American History* 70 (December 1983): 535–555; William Howard Taft, *Presidential Addresses and State Papers* (New York: Doubleday, 1910); Pringle, *Life and Times*, vol. 2; *Times* (London), February 28, 1913; Erwin Hargrove, *The Power of the Modern Presidency* (Philadelphia: Temple University Press, 1974); White, *Autobiography*, p. 525; "Appraisal," *New Republic* 62 (March 10, 1930): 11.

ANNOTATED BIBLIOGRAPHY

Abraham, Henry J. *Justices and Presidents*. New York: Oxford University Press, 1974.
    Places a judicial perspective on the man who would rather have been chief justice than president and who, after having become the first and only man to come to hold both offices, rebounded from his failure to win reelection in 1912 to the earning of a warm and respected place in the affections of his fellow citizens.

Anderson, Donald F. *William Howard Taft: A Conservative's Conception of the Presidency*. Ithaca, N.Y.: Cornell University Press, 1973.
    Anderson writes of how Taft might have fared better in calmer times but suffered by comparison with his hard-driving predecessor, Theodore Roosevelt, and gradually lost the confidence of the public through the four uninspired years of his single term in the White House.

Anderson, Judith Icke. *William Howard Taft: An Intimate History*. New York: W. W. Norton, 1981.
    A psychodynamic study that deals in depth with apparent contradictions and conflicts in the life and career of a man who found himself suffering through an office he never really wanted, but who ended his life as one of the nation's most loved and respected public figures.

Baker, Ray Stannard. *American Chronicle*. New York: Charles Scribner's Sons, 1945.
    Baker's autobiography covers the career of one of the journalists tagged by Theodore Roosevelt as "the muckrakers" in reaction to their vigorous pursuit of corruption in business and politics, a pursuit that continued through and beyond the Taft administration.

Blum, John Morton. *The Republican Roosevelt*. New York: Atheneum, 1974.
    Blum cited this work as "intended to be neither a biography of Roosevelt nor a complete record of his public career, but an interpretation of the purposes and methods of that career." As such it offers an interesting background to the study of the presidency of William Howard Taft by offering insights into the mind of the man responsible for putting him into office.

Bowers, Claude G. *Beveridge and the Progressive Era*. New York: Literary Guild, 1932.
    Beveridge was another of the Republican senators often at odds with Taft.

Butt, Archibald Willingham. *The Letters of Archie Butt*. Edited by Lawrence F. Abbott. Garden City, N.Y.: Doubleday, Doran and Co., 1924.
    Taft was still alive at this first printing of the Butt correspondence, so the family of the late aide to both presidents withheld the letters from the Taft period. Nevertheless, this volume is of value if only because of the perspective offered in the editor's biographical introduction to a man torn by his loyalty to two men who came to be at odds.

————. *Taft and Roosevelt: The Intimate Letters of Archie Butt, Military Aide*. 2 vols. Garden City, N.Y.: Doubleday, Doran and Co., 1930.

An invaluable source of first-hand information about two presidents by a man who loved and was beloved of both and whose death in the sinking of the *Titanic* left Taft grieving as though he had lost a son.

Coletta, Paola E. *The Presidency of William Howard Taft*. Lawrence, Kans.: University Press of Kansas, 1973.

This volume in the American Presidency Series is perhaps the best sequel to Pringle in its detailed treatment of how the Taft administration coped—with changing times and with the whole host of complex and challenging personalities who appeared during that period.

Kelly, Frank K. *The Fight for the White House*. New York: Thomas Y. Crowell Co., 1961.

Covers details of the 1912 campaign between the Democrats and the doomed Republicans, split between the Taft and Bull Moose–Progressive Roosevelt factions.

Krock, Arthur. *Memoirs: Sixty Years on the Firing Line*. New York: Funk and Wagnalls, 1968.

Insight by a veteran Washington correspondent of the *New York Times* who was familiar with many of the personalities of the Taft era and well beyond.

Longworth, Alice Roosevelt. *Crowded Hours*. New York: Charles Scribner's Sons, 1933.

The irrepressible daughter of Theodore Roosevelt offers a first-hand look at the turbulent time of her father and the man he made and unmade as president.

Manners, William. *TR and Will: A Friendship That Split the Republican Party*. New York: Harcourt, Brace and World, 1969.

A comprehensive work that focuses on the most significant development in the relationship between Roosevelt and Taft, the breakup of their best-friend relationship—an event that changed the course of American history.

Pringle, Henry F. *The Life and Times of William Howard Taft*. 2 vols. New York: Farrar and Rinehart, 1939.

The result of early unrestricted access to the voluminous Taft papers in the Library of Congress, Pringle's work has been called the most definitive of the biographies of the twenty-seventh president. Charles P. Taft II, youngest of President Taft's three children, told the author before his death in 1983 of his high regard for the work in its treatment of his father.

Ross, Ishbel. *An American Family: The Tafts—1678 to 1964*. Cleveland: World Publishing Co., 1964.

Virtually all of this work is devoted to a respectful treatment of the most distinguished member of the family, the president, whose life is treated with enough attention to detail to render the book valuable as a reference.

Stephenson, Nathaniel Wright. *Nelson W. Aldrich: A Leader in American Politics*. New York: Charles Scribner's Sons, 1930.

One of the Senate's most powerful men, Aldrich was both a blessing and a millstone for Taft, who valued his ability to exert leadership but who was tarred by his association with a man for whom the Progressives had distrust and suspicion.

Taft, Helen Herron. *Recollections of Full Years*. New York: Dodd, Mead & Co., 1914.

President Taft's wife relates her story of the life of a singularly devoted couple— he wrote her every day when they were apart—through the failure of her husband to win reelection to an office that apparently meant far more to her than to him.

10 WOODROW WILSON

Marie D. Natoli

Two Democratic presidents led the United States into world conflict. One president was an arch-moralist; the other, an arch-pragmatist. A comparison of these men highlights the nature of America's World War I president. Many of their influences and circumstances bear striking similarity; they perhaps point to some inevitabilities of the "wartime" presidency. Woodrow Wilson's young naval undersecretary, Franklin D. Roosevelt, was heavily influenced by his predecessor's actions; he also built on these actions three decades later as the nation again prepared for war. The coming of World War II would lead to a reappraisal of Wilson, who had been so negatively viewed in the 1920s and 1930s. Thus, while the focus of this chapter is the wartime presidency of Woodrow Wilson, a contemporary view of Wilson requires a forward and comparative look at the Roosevelt wartime presidency.

CHARACTER AND EARLY INFLUENCES

"A boy never gets over his boyhood, and never can change those subtle influences which have become a part of him, that were bred in him when he was a child," Woodrow Wilson himself once observed. In reflecting upon the lives of great individuals, one has to observe particular caution not to overvalue early single events in their lives. Nonetheless, the broader environment of childhood influences provides a framework from which to understand later views and actions.

A child of neither poverty nor affluence, Wilson, the son of a Presbyterian minister, was born in an era of America moving toward war. Both the religious background that comprised his roots and the Civil War, the war among brothers that tore the nation apart and threatened to divide it forever, formed the essential elements of the environment that shaped Wilson's life and actions.

The young Tommy (Wilson did not drop his first name until he was twenty, speculating later that a "Woodrow" Wilson would go further) was greatly influenced by his stern and demanding father, Dr. Joseph Wilson, "a masterful

man" who was both "compelling in the pulpit and courtly in the parlor."
Woodrow Wilson would himself develop these qualities; his pulpit was at first
that of academe and then that of politics. Much literature has been written about
this father-son relationship—especially from a psychological perspective.[1] Suf-
fice it to say that what is important for the purposes of this study is that the
younger Wilson developed his world view—and his view of his role in that
world—from the elder Wilson. Actually, a long line of Wilson men ultimately
shaped the young man. Grandfather James Wilson had long advocated the pursuit
of "principles, not men," and the future president, soon realizing that men of
principle could become great leaders, studied the lives of men of greatness.

Wilson's maternal influences (his mother was a Woodrow, who came from a
family of ministers, writers, and intellectuals) reinforced the devotion to God
and family he learned from his father. Young Wilson "was often to acknowledge
the two strains that ran in his veins: that of the Woodrows, pure Scottish,
scholarly, tenacious, gentle, modest; and that of the Wilsons—Scotch-Irish,
boisterous, and mercurial, loving drama, applause, and exaggeration." Much
as FDR would be considered, Wilson recalled that he was "a laughed-at Mama's
boy until I was a great big fellow."

Wilson's religion gave him "the energy of a positive faith," as he himself
called it, and included a belief in service to the people. Wilson said of himself,
"I am a person, I am afraid, who observes no sort of moderation in anything,"
and certainly this character trait would at times drive him in his service to the
people but doom him as well.

Just as he was developing a profound and intense belief in God and morality,
he was also developing an intense reaction to the Civil War and its aftermath
which made up so much of his early environment. Biographer Arthur Walworth
recalls that as a three-year-old, Wilson's first recollection was standing in the
door of the Augusta, Georgia, manse and hearing a voice yell: "Mr. Lincoln's
elected. There'll be war." The experience of war and the years of Reconstruction
"ground into the boy's marrow a sympathy that was never to leave him,"[2] and
he developed an intense hatred for war that would surely influence his ambivalence toward world conflict prior to 1917. World War I left a similar imprint
on FDR.

Young Tommy developed in a world conditioned by his pervasive faith and
a sense of aloneness; insight and study were his keynotes. What he termed the
"driving power of religion" would be evident in his strident reform efforts on
the domestic level, his reaction as president to the coming of war, and his ill-
fated efforts for the League of Nations. Secretary of State Robert Lansing observed of the president: "Having convinced himself of the soundness of his own
opinion, he resented any implication that his opinion might be wrong. The result
was that his whole political philosophy was honeycombed with error."[3] In his
view, "God above, the people below, were joined by Woodrow Wilson."

Wilson's father was influential in the son's nurturing of a skill that would
become his most powerful political resource: oratory. Joseph Wilson told his

son: "Study manner, dearest Tommy, as much as matter" in encouraging the talent so useful to preachers. The young Wilson took heed. He soon learned that he had the power to persuade men with his words and style; and persuade he did. At Princeton he excelled in debate. In a *Princetonian* article, he wrote: "What is the object of oratory? Its object is persuasion and conviction—the control of minds by a strange personal influence and power." Wilson would come to exert that power over the minds of his people. Loner, moralizer, Messiah, man of conscience, he would bring to the presidency personal beliefs, traits of character, and a crusading spirit which would at once inspire and frustrate, lead him to greatness and to failure.

In contrast, Franklin Roosevelt, the pragmatist of these two wartime presidents, was described as "precious," but, as biographer Kenneth Davis notes, "Despite his shyness there was a strong will to power, an instinct for command, and an ardent, if often masked, competitiveness." FDR's parents sought to avoid spoiling him as a child, and "he was encouraged toward tactfulness and other pleasing qualities." As a five-year-old child, he accompanied his father, James, to visit President Grover Cleveland. The incumbent president told the child: "My little man, I am making a strange wish for you. It is that you may never be President of the United States."

Whereas Wilson had developed an introspective nature, young Franklin's "mental interests were turned almost wholly outward." But those mental interests were far-reaching, and he developed a mental dexterity that helped him matter-of-factly to absorb, synthesize, and utilize extraordinary bits and pieces of information.

Like Wilson, Roosevelt had faith in God—but not the all-absorbing kind that his predecessor had ingrained in him. Roosevelt's faith was a faith simply believed, simply followed, and "an effect of his faith was a profoundly optimistic attitude toward the world and its challenges." FDR developed consideration for others, a confidence in his own goals and ability to achieve them, and a profound courage to withstand pain.[4]

John G. Stoessinger's observation that Wilson was a crusader is aptly made. His background made him so. He believed that "power was never to be used without a moral purpose." On the other hand, FDR was *"both* a crusader and a pragmatist," and the ability to balance the two came largely out of "a childhood . . . secure [and] . . . serene . . . and the absence of early drama and upheaval."

THE PREPRESIDENTIAL YEARS

Prior to entering an active political life, Wilson had apprenticed himself in the practice of law with the early belief that law was the route to politics. However, within a year he despaired of the profession. He found it "dreadful drudgery" and took heart in his discovery that many of his models—Edmund

Burke, Sir Henry Maine, and Walter Bagehot—"trained as lawyers but found the legal profession unsatisfying."

Wilson's decision to abandon law practice and to pursue a Ph.D. at Johns Hopkins is crucial to his unfolding career, for he would now be free to continue his study of politics and history and to write on the themes he loved best. Characteristically, he endured the formal course work while placing most of his interests in his independent reading and writing. It was as a graduate student at Johns Hopkins that he wrote the evaluation of American governmental institutions that won him acclaim. *Congressional Government,* published in 1885 and reviewed in the *Nation,* was proclaimed "one of the most important books, dealing with political subjects, which [has] ever issued from the American press."

On completion of his studies, Wilson began a teaching career at Bryn Mawr. He found teaching women tedious and eventually moved on to Wesleyan, where he would be paid more and could teach men. In the intervening years, Wilson had been preparing a manuscript for a work entitled *The State,* dealing with the origins and development of democratic governments, which was published in 1889. His growing reputation as a teacher and scholar eventually gained him the offer of a position at Princeton in 1890. The Princeton years spanned two decades, including twelve as a professor and eight as the university's president. His teaching career there was brilliant. Arthur S. Link has said of Wilson's tenure as president of Princeton that it was "the microcosm of a later macrocosm." Much of his academic tenure credited him with greatness, just as would most of his presidency of the nation. In each instance Wilson undertook his job with characteristic zeal and energy. Curriculum reform, elevation of scholastic standards, and financial growth of the university were all early credits to the university president. Link cites, however, Wilson's "refusal to compromise (over the building and site determination of a graduate college)" as "almost Princeton's undoing" just as Wilson's "refusal to compromise in the fight in the Senate over the League of Nations was the nation's undoing." Wilson's early fanaticism on this academic issue overshadowed his later fanaticism as his presidency of the nation came to a close.

Following eight years as a university president, Wilson was courted as a political candidate. Ironically, a journalist (in fact, the editor of *Harper's Weekly,* George Harvey) saw a future president in Wilson. The irony lies in the fact that Harvey was close to political bosses and industrialists, both of whom Wilson would eventually spurn. Harvey's first attempts were toward getting Wilson a Democratic senatorial nomination (United States senators were then elected by state legislatures), and in effect Wilson was the bosses' candidate until he chose to withdraw his name, thus avoiding alienating the reform-minded Democrats. But Wilson was simultaneously pleasing conservative Democrats by uttering anti-Bryan statements. For example, in March 1908 Wilson publicly said of the progressive leader that he was "the most charming and lovable of men personally, but foolish and dangerous in his theoretical beliefs."

The more Wilson toyed with the possibility of a political career, the more it appealed to him. He wrote his dear friend Mary Hurlbert in September 1909, "My instinct all turns that way, and I sometimes feel rather impatiently the restraints of my academic position."[5]

Meanwhile, George Harvey pursued other political courses and in 1910 began positioning Wilson for a gubernatorial run in New Jersey, viewing this as a stepping stone to the presidency. The "moralist" seemed to be acting more the part of the "pragmatist" that his successor, FDR, would later play.

The nomination in hand, Wilson urged the Democratic party to serve as "the instrument of righteousness for the state and for the nation." Receiving a barrage of attacks from antiboss segments both in the party and among the electorate at large, Wilson astounded both boss and critic alike by clearly proclaiming his independence the night of his nomination at Trenton in 1909. Wilson asserted: "I did not seek this nomination. It has come to me absolutely unsolicited. . . . Not only have no pledges of any kind been given, but none have been proposed or desired."

With an almost uncanny understanding of the popular mood, Wilson—as Roosevelt did later—ran as a supporter of progressive proposals, winning the support of reformers of both parties. Employing his skillful oratory, Wilson won the gubernatorial election by a respectable plurality.

The former professor's two-year incumbency demonstrates political leadership skills. Noted one observer: "He did not harangue, though he occasionally indulged in a peroration. . . . Listeners were convinced that he was that very rare specimen: a completely frank candidate for office. He seemed to be thinking out loud in their presence."

Understanding public sentiment as he did, he could likewise shift his positions to maximize the moment. A shrewd and expedient politician, he shifted his image from that of a conservative to a liberal Democrat, taking on the bosses. Link says of this transformation:

Wilson wanted desperately to enter politics, to hold high office, and he must have recognized that the strength of the progressive movement, especially in New Jersey, was growing rapidly and that a continued adherence to his conservative creed would be almost certainly fatal to his political aspirations. After his nomination for governor, Wilson was forced to make a deliberate choice between conservatism and progressivism, and he knew that the outcome of the election depended upon his decision. The choice was inevitable— he finally capitulated to the progressives.[6]

Wilson's achievements as governor were astounding. Shortly after assuming office, for example, he set in motion a major reform working toward the direct election of U.S. senators—again conflicting with the bosses. As the "spokesman and adviser of the people," he explained, he felt morally obligated to increase direct democracy.

Wilson, much like FDR, seemed to possess an almost internalized understanding of the psychology of the people he was representing, and of the importance of "the cold bath of public opinion," as he was fond of calling it. He saw himself, he said, as having "new responsibilities as representative and champion of the common people against those who have been preying upon them." Wilson knew he could persuade the legislature by first creating a "popular backfire" on an issue. His incumbency can be credited with significant measures of electoral reform (a primary and direct election law) and a wide range of other progressive issues (an employer's liability law; the establishment of a strong public utilities commission with rate-setting powers; a corrupt practices act) because of his astute blending of understanding the people's mood and his ability to translate that mood into political power. Meteorically, he had become a national figure, even a popular hero. The *New York Times* credited him with "really very great" achievements, the *Washington Post* with being "a national rather than a purely local figure." By May 1912, the *New York World* editorialized: "Woodrow Wilson should be the Democratic candidate for president. . . . He would be a progressive constitutional President, whom the American people could trust and for whom they would never have cause to apologize."

Franklin Roosevelt, who used Wilson as a model, had difficulty with oratory in his early career. Ironically, however, this "seemed to endear him to many, who felt his difficulty their own, and to weight his words with persuasive earnestness and sincerity," [7] and Roosevelt won a handsome victory, far outrunning his party at the polls. FDR too took on the bosses and emulated Wilson and Theodore Roosevelt. As did Wilson, FDR too led a successful campaign for electoral reform. His early record on other reform issues, however, was more mixed.

As Wilson's growing stature as a national leader put him in the forefront of presidential eligibility, Democrats from all over the country paid personal homage to him. FDR was no exception, and the two future presidents met to discuss Wilson's potential support in New York. FDR threw himself into the Wilson campaign, buoyed by the disastrous Republican split. He won state senate re-election in 1912, only to be offered—and to accept—a position with the newly elected Wilson administration. On March 17, 1913, Franklin D. Roosevelt became the youngest assistant secretary of the navy in the nation's history, gaining an insider's perspective.

CAMPAIGN FOR THE PRESIDENCY

A coalition rapidly formed to promote Wilson as a reform candidate. Equally important was public reaction to the man, and "a ground swell of popular opinion . . . was being expressed in the liberal press and in the polling of state delegations." The *World,* for example, termed Wilson's nomination a "matter of Democratic life and death." In its May 30, 1912, editorial, it stated emphatically that "Woodrow Wilson should be the Democratic candidate for President. . . . The *World* believes that he would be a progressive constitutional President whom the American people could trust and for whom they would never have to apologize. . . . We appeal to Mr. Bryan to throw his great political influence upon the side of Mr. Wilson.''

Wilson's efforts to win the confidence of William Jennings Bryan—so crucial to any aspiring presidential candidate in 1912—represent a masterstroke. The Commoner had remained noncommittal throughout preconvention politicking, even though he had referred to Wilson's Jackson Day dinner remarks as "the greatest speech in American political history." Part of what bothered Bryan was the continued support Wilson received from the conservative *Harper's Weekly*. Following a discussion between *Harper's* editor George Harvey and Wilson, the publication played down its support of the New Jersey governor. For Wilson the situation was something of a "Catch-22" dilemma. Segments of the anti-Wilson press viewed the story as an example of Wilson's "ingratitude." The *Louisville Courier-Journal,* for example, said:

He who would show himself so disloyal to a private friendship cannot be trusted to be loyal to anything. Within a single year Governor Wilson's radical change of base, his realignments and readjustments, have been exactly concurrent with his selfish aims. There seems no abasement into which he is unwilling to descend with equal facility and grace. May God preserve Democracy from such a leader and such leadership!

Although such comments, at least initially, appeared damaging, the pro-Wilson press successfully managed to turn the story to the candidate's advantage, suggesting that Wilson's break with the editor of *Harper's Weekly* resulted from his refusal to accept a campaign contribution from a wealthy financier. The *World* commented:

Ingratitude is one of the rarest virtues of public life. "Gratitude" is responsible for many of our worst political abuses. Upon "gratitude" is built every corrupt political machine. . . . The great majority of the voices which are denouncing Wilson's ingratitude are the voices of machine politicians, chief among whose stock in trade is this "gratitude."

No, what we need in public life is a great deal more of discriminating ingratitude.

As the nomination battle raged, anti-Wilson forces searched his writing for viewpoints they could use against him. For example, from his *History of the American People,* they extracted statements that could be interpreted as negative regarding many immigrant groups, raising doubts about how he might handle their interests.

The exciting story of the 1912 Democratic presidential convention has been well recorded and need not be recapitulated here. Bryan's role was a prominent one, and when Wilson's major opponent for the nomination, Champ Clark, received the Tammany vote, the tide seemed to turn in Wilson's favor.

Public response to the nomination was extraordinary. One observer noted that "some ten thousand letters came in, more than half from people who said that they had *prayed* for the nomination of Wilson."[8] Wilson's acceptance speech reflected the political philosophy that had been growing in him as well as his keen understanding of the American people in 1912.

Wilson's "New Freedom" was devoted to the common man, although not the grand scale social welfare legislation being advocated by Theodore Roosevelt. In campaigning across the country, Wilson captured the imagination of the public. A contemporary noted:

His learning is precisely of the degree and the kind best calculated to impress the populace. He bears all the decorous marks of the scholar, fulfills the popular idea of a philosopher who confers honor upon the sordid concerns of political life by bringing to them the high thoughts and ideals amidst which he lived so long in cloistered contemplation above that which the vulgar are permitted or are fit to enjoy. On the other hand, his philosophy is not too high for human understanding, and is not withheld from the admiring multitude.

Wilson's view espoused "a freedom from fetters which business had placed [on the people]" but nonetheless the candidate's "whole program was a consistent emphasis upon moderation and morality." Wilson said, "Politics is a war of causes, a joust of principles," and this "morality" had its convincing impact on campaign audiences. One political scientist of the period suggested that Wilson "was extraordinarily gifted with hypnotic power of expression."

Besides his oratorical gifts, Wilson was abetted by the exciting Taft-Roosevelt split in the GOP. By 1916 Wilson had largely adopted the TR platform. Of the Progressive nominee, Wilson wrote: "Roosevelt . . . is a real vivid person whom [the public] have seen and shouted themselves hoarse over and voted for, millions strong; I am a vague, conjectural personality, more made up of opinions and academic prepossessions than of human traits and red corpuscles."

In the end, Wilson's persuasiveness contrasted with Roosevelt's tendency to "rush impetuously into details which might take the average man beyond his depth." Wilson "seemed *par excellence* the plain citizen, waiting calmly to learn whether the people wanted him for their servant."[9] This contributed to a Democratic victory, both in the White House and in the Congress.

Referring to a "vision of a new day," Wilson said in his inaugural:

This is not a day of triumph; it is a day of dedication. Here muster, not the forces of party, but the forces of humanity. Men's hearts wait upon us; men's lives hang in the balance; men's hopes call upon us to say what we will do. Who shall live up to the great trust? Who dares fail to try? I summon all honest men, all patriotic, all forward-looking men, to my side. God helping me, I will not fail them, if they will but counsel and sustain me!

As the crusade began, the *Cleveland Plain Dealer* said, "Not since Lincoln has there been a President so wonderfully gifted in the art of expression." Said the *New York World*. "Woodrow Wilson's inauguration as President marks the beginning of a political epoch. The United States has entered upon a new phase of popular government, and no man can foresee the outcome."

Wilson himself understood the merger of president and people. After the election he told a backer, "I wish it clearly understood that I owe you nothing. Remember that God ordained that I should be the next President of the United States." As it occurred in the 1930s, Wilson rode a tide of domestic reform that was later inundated by world war.

DOMESTIC REFORM, CONGRESS, AND THE PEOPLE

Woodrow Wilson had said prior to holding office: "We have enough heat; what we want is light. Anybody can stir up emotions, but who is master of men enough to take the saddle and guide those awakened emotions?" When Wilson entered the Oval Office, he did so with a clear vision of what Americans wanted and needed as well as a clear vision of where he could lead "those awakened emotions." He saw his *mission* as president to get his goals accomplished. Toward his progressive ends, he bent the newly elected Democratic Congress to his will—carving out a place for the presidency as the *people's* representative, a theme to be oft-repeated by Wilson's successors in the office—and entered the long-avoided valley of reform.

Wilson had spent a substantial part of his academic career studying institutions and power and the relationship between the two. Indeed, that early study itself had been toward the eventual aim of exercising political power himself one day. Wilson's initial views regarding the presidency were less than positive, but they slowly changed.

In his 1908 publication, *Constitutional Government in the United States,* Wilson's perception had come full circle to see the president as central in the scheme of American government. An earlier work, *Congressional Government,* published in 1885, had perceived Congress as the dominant force, suggesting of the presidency that it "has fallen from its first estate of dignity because its power has waned; and its power was waned because the power of the Congress has become predominant." In the earlier of the two works, Wilson had expressed an admiration for the British parliamentary system and the role of the prime minister, but as he moved toward the possibility of the White House rather than the U.S. Senate, he began to change his understanding of the office. The president, Wilson said in his later work, is free to be "as big a man as he can." Wilson's acute understanding of the underlying role of public opinion buttressed the guiding principles of his incumbency.

He can dominate his party by being spokesman for the real sentiment and purpose of the country, by giving direction to opinion, by giving the country at once the information and the statements of policy which will enable it to form its judgments alike of parties and men. . . .

Let him once win the admiration and confidence of the country, and no other single force can withstand him, no combination of forces will easily overpower him. He is the representative of no constituency, but of the whole people. When he speaks in his true character, he speaks for no special interest. If he rightly interprets the national thought and boldly insists upon it, he is irresistible.

Believing that the president could seize the moment of reform, Wilson symbolically shattered a century of precedent and journeyed in person to deliver his message on the tariff to Congress. "He literally dramatized the Presidential message to Congress," observed Wilfred Binkley.[10] "The present-day role of the President as policy determiner in the legislative field," E. S. Corwin later wrote, "is largely the creation of the two Roosevelts and Woodrow Wilson," and Wilson "boldly proclaimed his constitutional right and duty as executive to guide the legislative process."

Wilson had an astute understanding of the relationship between the president and the people's opinion. In discussing "Leaders of Men" in the 1890s, Wilson keenly observed, "The dynamics of leadership lie in persuasion." He told the National Press Club in 1914, "A great nation . . . is led by a man . . . in whose ears the voices of the nation do not sound . . . accidental and discordant . . . but . . . reveal to him a single vision . . . the common meaning of the common voice."

Wilson religiously—and the word is used decidedly here—strained to discern the direction of popular opinion and used that opinion to achieve his legislative ends. But that discernment was based more upon what Wilson himself *thought*—through his own intuition—the people's opinion was. "Nothing has to be explained to me in America," Wilson once proclaimed, "least of all the sentiment of the American people." This view, of course, would contribute to the president's obstinacy regarding his goals for those people, for, as he added, "The advantage of not having to have anything explained to you is that you recognize a wrong explanation when you hear it."

Nor would his perception of public opinion be gathered from the guardians in the media. Wilson rather candidly remarked in a Jackson Day address in January 1915: "With all due respect to editors of great newspapers, I have to say to them that I seldom take my opinion of the American people from their editorials."

Wilson *himself* would be the interpreter of the people; this was his service to them and his God. Commenting in a letter to a friend about press criticism of his domination of the Congress, Wilson said:

Do not believe anything you read in the newspapers. . . . Their lying is shameless and colossal! . . . They represent me . . . as . . . bending Congress to my indomitable individual will. That is, of course, silly. Congress is made up of thinking men . . . who wish to serve the country effectively and intelligently. [Congress] accept[s] my guidance because they see that I am attempting only to mediate their own thoughts and purposes. . . . They are using me; I am not driving them. . . . Why a man would wish to be the whole show and surround himself with weak men, I cannot imagine! How dull it would be! . . . Power consists in one's capacity to link his will with the purpose of others, to lead by reason and a gift for cooperation.

But later, when Wilson encountered difficulty with the Congress, he wrote to the same friend:

Why *should* public men, senators of the United States, have to be led and stimulated to what all the country knows to be their duty! Why should they see less clearly, apparently, than anyone else what the straight path of service is! To whom are they listening? Certainly not to the voice of the people, when they quibble and twist and hesitate.[11]

And he, for one, would listen to the people and their desire for progressive reform, for the president's ears "must ring with the voices of the people." The president must "serve the slow-paced daily need."

On the legislative front, Wilson seized the initiative and earned credit for considerable economic reform. He did so by carrying through with his interpretation that the president must also serve as the British prime minister does, that is, as a strong leader of his party. Wilson told a Jackson Day dinner audience in 1915 that only his party could institute progressive reforms wanted and needed by the people. Wilson "showed the people where their own best interests lay" and in him Greenback and Populist protesters had a spokesman solicitous of economic freedom. "Impulses that had agitated American society for decades were now mellowed, rationalized, and blessed in the person of the new President." In the first term Wilson continuously elevated his interpretation of the needs of the country above Congress' interpretation.

The outbreak of hostilities in Europe began to redirect the administration's attentions abroad; in early struggles with Congress Wilson focused on the war's impact on American industry and the American people. In urging Congress for a shipping bill—so that war-stymied trade and American access to shipping abroad could be smoothly continued—Wilson met recalcitrance. The year-long battle which Wilson won planted seeds of future animosity.

Wilson had once remarked that the presidency is "an office in which a man must put on his war paint." He often found himself pitted as the nation's "moral conscience" against an obstinate Congress. As tribune of the people, Wilson stated, "I cannot consent to any abridgment of the rights of American citizens. The honor and self-respect of the nation are involved." He felt that a ban on such rights would be "deep humiliation indeed." So strongly did the president stand on the issue that the Congress eventually backed down.

The Wilsonian impact may be seen by comparing him to FDR, who entered the White House without such a clear-cut vision of his presidency. Eric Goldman described Roosevelt as "the most complete devotee of playing by ear the White House had ever known." Roosevelt's flexibility enabled him to deal with issues and problems similar to but also different from those Wilson faced. Roosevelt could be pragmatic; for Wilson, problem solving would be considerably more difficult because of his inability to extricate himself from his view that he alone spoke for the nation.

THE COMING OF WAR: A PRESIDENT AND HIS PEOPLE

As Wilson waged a battle of reform at home, Germany, Great Britain, and France were moving toward a far more dramatic confrontation. Germany sought overseas territories—and, correspondingly, markets—that France and Britain dominated.

Wilson reflected the America of his times. It was an America unwilling to believe.[12] It was an America ruled by a hostility toward internationalism, particularly if it became imperialism. An idealism pervaded America: world involvement should come from moral goals, not narrow utilitarian ends. In this respect, the people could not have chosen a better president. Not only did Wilson *reflect* the prevailing moralistic mood in foreign (and domestic) affairs; he *reinforced* it. He would have the nation serve as the world's conscience, as "the nation which denies itself material advantage and seeks for those things which are of the spirit."

And so, Wilson remained more at home *at home*. His oratorical skills could guide the popular will. As Princeton president, Wilson had written: "One of the greatest of the President's powers is his control, which is very absolute, of the foreign relations of the nation. The initiation in foreign affairs, which the President possesses without any restriction whatever, is virtually the power to control them absolutely." Reluctant to enter the world arena, once in it he and his moralism would become the world's. Arthur Link commented that Wilson "shared a Calvinistic belief . . . in predestination—the absolute conviction that God had ordained the universe from the beginning, the faith that God used men for His own purposes. From such beliefs came a sure sense of destiny and a feeling of intimate connection with the sources of power."

Franklin Roosevelt the realist later saw Wilson as unwilling to accept the inevitable. And Wilson's key adviser, Colonel E. M. House—himself more of a realist—knew that the United States must play a role if war was to be averted. While on a European mission, House cautioned the president: "The situation is extraordinary. It is jingoism run stark mad. Unless someone acting for you can bring about a different understanding, there is someday to be awful cataclysm. No one in Europe can do it. There is too much hatred, too many jealousies."

Because House knew how the president perceived the world and America's place in it, the Colonel would more often characteristically play to Wilson's moral stance, as the president continued to equivocate between 1914 and 1917. These comments from House to Wilson are typical:

The world expects you to play the big part in this tragedy . . . for God has given you the power to see things as they are. . . . A great opportunity is yours, my friend—the greatest, perhaps, that has ever come to any man. . . . You have before you the biggest opportunity for service that was ever given to man, and I hope you will not risk failure.

On June 28, 1914, the murder of Archduke Franz Ferdinand, heir to the Austrian and Hungarian thrones, set off the powder keg. The murderer was a Serbian nationalist. With little American notice, the official declaration of war between Austria-Hungary and Serbia occurred July 28, 1914, and set off a chain reaction; within a week, most of Europe was at war.

As the war machinery churned, a shocked President Wilson saw personal crisis as well as world crisis. On August 6, the First Lady died.[13] The nation too was shocked by both events. Arthur Link found that "the coming of war was a shock of indescribable proportions" to inattentive Americans. Link said that "hopefully idealists . . . had been persuaded that western man had finally evolved beyond the barbarism of war."

It would be entirely too simple, as Link suggests, to dismiss the general mood of pro-Allied sympathy expressed in the press. This was exemplified by the *New York World*'s comment: "German autocracy has run amuck. . . . Either German autocracy must be crushed or European democracy will be obliterated." Another editorial found that the conflict was "not merely one of race against race. It is the war of a modern people against a mediaeval autocracy."

The true picture was a more complex one; Link notes that "reactions in the United States were as uniform and diverse and as naive and sophisticated as the American people themselves." He found this true of the administration as well as a composite of national opinion. Characteristic of a democratic state, public opinion in its intricacies "built the framework or set the limits in which President Wilson and his advisors had to operate in forming policies toward the belligerents." This was true in congressional voting and in the drafting of party platforms. "It helped determine the response that the government in Washington made to British and German efforts to control the seas."

Since Woodrow Wilson had sought to be spokesman for a united people, the division of public opinion was disconcerting. "Almost everyone agreed on neutrality; but when it was realized that, should America become involved, it would almost inevitably be on the side of the Entente, nearly all Americans more or less took sides with one of two groups . . . [between whom] a struggle of opinion soon flamed into passion."

Clearly, the majority of passions were pro-Allied, but as Link has suggested, this sentiment was further divided between moderates and extremists; the former constituted the overwhelming proportion. The moderates continued to support the Allies, but perceptions changed, and the view grew that *both sides* were responsible for the European conflict in all its perplexities. The German propaganda machine can be credited for some of this, and "the most important development in the American reaction to war before the spring of 1915, and probably afterward, was the dilution of pro-Allied sentiment." This brought more of a balance between pro-Allied and neutralist sentiment.

The extremist side of the pro-Allied sentiment, a minority, was "scattered throughout the country but concentrated in the East," and importantly, it had "strong individual spokesmen among the newspapers and magazines like the

New York *Tribune,* the New York *Times,* the Louisville *Courier-Journal, The Nation, Harper's Weekly,* and *Outlook,* and among a literary circle." With the exception of business and financial leaders among the extremists, whose concerns were primarily economic, extremists tended to feel that "the war was in essence a supreme battle between right and wrong . . . a conflict between democracy and autocracy, freedom and slavery, peace through international cooperation and terror through unrestrained militarism."[14] Less sympathetic toward—and sometimes opposed to—the Allies (especially Britain) were an odd mixture of "hyphenated Americans," immigrant groups such as the German-Americans, Irish-Americans, Swedish-Americans, and Jewish-Americans. By far, German-Americans were the most vocal and the most strongly pro–Central Powers of these hyphenated groups; German-Americans were very active in support of the Fatherland. As Bell has observed:

There was a certain element of humor in the make-up of this core [of hyphenated Americans]. It was rather amusing to see Irish and German hyphenates, very active and often noisy, as fellow workers with quiet Yankees. . . . Often distinct from, but working with, the Anglophobes, were isolationists and pacifists . . . and before long . . . this group was drawing influential allies from people of the farm belt and cotton-growing states, who saw their incomes dwindling, thanks to the British blockade,

and the combination of these forces "stood for peace at almost any price."

The important issue is why, with the majority of the public in support of the Allied cause, a prevailing atmosphere of neutrality lingered. Link offers four plausible explanations:

1. The assumption prevailed that the Allies would be victorious, even without American intervention.
2. The belief existed that the United States did not have enough of a vested interest—either economic or strategic—to warrant its involvement.
3. Idealism and pacifism extensively pervaded pro-Allied sentiment, for which the use of force was abhorrent.
4. Relatively little public expression of opinion existed on the part of the extremist political leadership of the country.

Link adds that there was a great proportion of the American people who were

on the whole neutral, that is, impartial, in their reactions and thinking, because they either did not care about the issues and outcome of the war, or were so mildly pro-Allied or pro-German as to be actually neutral insofar as policies towards the belligerents were concerned, or else made a conscious effort to follow the President's injunction to be impartial in thought as well as in deed.

Wilson felt a more kindred spirit with the Allied cause. He told the Associated Press in April 1915: "I am interested in neutrality because there is something so much greater to do than fight; there is a distinction waiting for this Nation that no nation has ever yet got. That is the distinction of absolute self-control and self-mastery.''

Later, responding to a public outcry over the sinking of the *Lusitania*, Wilson proclaimed, ''There is such a thing as a nation being so right that it does not need to convince others by force that it is right.''

Wilson's preference for aloofness from Europe's affairs brought this comment from Colonel House in the fall of 1914: ''I find the President singularly lacking in appreciation of the importance of this European crisis. He seems more interested in domestic affairs, and I find it difficult to get his attention centered on the one big question.'' Link, however, feels that the president had a different view which stressed the complexity of the situation. Link cites this excerpt from a White House interview with the *New York Times* in December 1914:

I think that the chances of a just and equitable peace and of the only possible peace that will be lasting, will be happiest if no nation gets the decision by arms; and the danger of an unjust peace . . . sure to invite further calamities, will be if some one nation or group of nations succeeds in enforcing its will upon the others.

Wilson warned against ''any nation imposing its governmental will upon alien peoples.''

Wilson's sense of destiny, morality, and determination clearly came across in public addresses. He said in Indianapolis:

Look abroad upon the troubled world. Only America at peace! . . . Only America saving her power for her own people. . . .

Do you not think it likely that the world will some time turn to America and say: ''You were right and we were wrong. You kept your heads when we lost ours. . . . Now, in your self-possession, in your coolness, may we not turn to you for counsel and assistance?

Think of the deep-wrought destruction of economic resources . . . in some parts of the world, and think of the reservoir of hope, the reservoir of energy, the reservoir of sustenance that there is in this great land of plenty. . . .

. . . I know the high principle with which the American people will respond to the call of the world for this service, and I thank God that those who believe in America, who try to serve her people, are likely to be also what America herself from the first intended to be—the servant of mankind.

Thus for three years the president walked this tightrope of neutrality. But beyond Wilson's admonition to ''be impartial in thought as well as action''[15]— beyond the rhetoric of neutrality—the United States engaged in policies supportive of the Allied cause. America's neutrality seemed to diminish as British mastery of the seas was exhibited. The president sought to deal with each episode as it arose. In a warning note to Germany, he stated:

If the commanders of the German vessels of war should act upon the presumption that the flag of the United States was not being used in good faith and should destroy on the

high seas an American vessel or the lives of American citizens, it would be difficult for
the government of the United States to view the act in any other light than as an indefensible
violation of neutral rights.

The president warned that the German government and its naval authorities would
be held to "a strict accountability" if "acknowledged rights on the high seas"
were violated. Questioned about his warning to Germany about the U-boats,
Wilson commented, "England's violation of neutral rights is different from
Germany's violation of the rights of humanity."

Within a prevailing framework of neutrality, then, the United States moved
steadily toward war. The president, meanwhile, loathing war and still believing
in the divinely ordained role of the United States in keeping the peace, tried to
play the mediator. Wilson acquiesced to a plan, largely conceived by Colonel
House, to bring the warring sides to a peace table to seek a *negotiated* peace.
This plan was rejected by the belligerents. Part of the plan dealt with working
out a postwar security system.

Despite the failure of the House plan, Wilson was determined to bring peace
to the world. After his reelection in 1916, Wilson issued a public letter to all
warring nations, urging their peoples to sit down at a peace table. On January
22, 1917, Wilson told the Senate in a speech he was "for the *people* of the
countries now at war," and that his goal was a "peace without victory." He
offered his first hint at the League of Nations and suggested that "only a peace
among equals can last." To the bitter end, Wilson sought to save the world from
itself; but as he led the nation into the inevitable war, Wilson would also lead
and shape American public opinion.

WAGING WAR AND PEACE

Elected because "He Kept Us Out of War" in 1916, Wilson faced a test of
how closely he was in touch with the nation. Ironically, considerable domestic
focus in 1916 by Wilson had spotlighted non–foreign policy issues. Blum stated:

Charmed by peace and progressivism, rural Americans voted for Wilson. So, by and
large, did labor, the liberals, the intellectuals—enough to provide, in spite of defections
by urban Democrats, the margin of narrow triumph.

Wilson couched American policy in terms of moral principle, lecturing the belligerents
on their responsibilities as civilized nations.

He began to receive domestic criticism from Theodore Roosevelt, leader of a
preparedness movement.

The sweep of events pushed Wilson nearer the brink. In succession, there
came the German invasion of Belgium; the Zimmerman Affair involving Mexico;
and the sinking of the *Falaba, Gulflight, Lusitania,* and *Sussex* by U-boats with
loss of American lives.[16] None of these events in itself was enough to provoke

the American people or their president to war; but *cumulatively* they had an impact. Wilson wrote to Senator Stone: "If the clear rights of American citizens should ever unhappily be abridged or denied . . . we should have in honor no choice as to what our course should be. . . . I cannot consent to any abridgment of the rights of American citizens. . . . The honor and self-respect of the nation is involved."

Ultimately, Wilson's decision to ask Congress to declare war was based upon two contentions: that a German victory would not be in the interests of the United States, and that entering the war would be the only certain way he would be able to hold a seat at the peace table—where he hoped to be able to forge the moral tenor of the world's future. Ironically, the moral crusader entered the world conflict out of a pragmatic consideration, but nonetheless his ultimate goals were moral ones. Despite the domestic impact of war, America would not only make the world safe for democracy; the peace America helped forge would have to *keep* it safe. And so, in April 1917, the president delivered his war message to the Congress, proclaiming, "We will not choose the path of submission."

Opposition to the war came from Senators George Norris and Robert La Follette, who argued that the call for war was being made by "munition manufacturers, stockbrokers, and bond dealers" wanting enormous profits from the conflict; La Follette said that only a popular referendum could justify the war. Eric Goldman underscores the "pro-German, anti-English tone of much of 1917 progressivism" that was incorporated in La Follette's rhetoric.[17] Reformers were concerned that interventionism would doom domestic reform; moreover, among many progressives there was a profound respect for the German nation's socialist achievements. Reformers were split into contending factions with "an important minority continuing a stubborn, dramatic isolationism." Outspoken leaders of this group were Secretary of State William Jennings Bryan, social worker Jane Addams, and industrialist Henry Ford; Addams had organized a Woman's Peace party. Goldman notes Theodore Roosevelt's approval of the decision to fight. Other prominent progressive internationalists included Albert Beveridge and Herbert Croly of the *New Republic*, who wrote, "The isolationism which has meant so much to the United States, and still means so much, cannot persist in its present form."

That Wilson had held such a hatred of war made him well suited to persuade the nation of the necessity of war. The key progressive journal of the day, the *New Republic*, moved with Wilson's twofold rationale. Just days after his war message to Congress, Wilson urged that the American people "all speak, act, and serve together." Richard Hofstadter noted that Wilson urged his people to be "citizens of the world."[18]

Both Congress and the public responded well to the president's war speech. "People who had deplored Wilson's cautious hesitancy and the lack of consistency or realism in some of his policies as long as we remained neutral, were pleasantly surprised when he turned out to be a very good war President."

Wilson seemed changed overnight, and "in the war fervor that took hold of the nation, the President seemed more than ever The Leader, the 'common voice.' " Like Lincoln before him, Wilson realized the need for crisis government. He described the war effort as a "people's war" and added, "Woe be to the man or group of men that seeks to stand in our way." Wilson led the American people to see themselves as a "chosen people among all the belligerent nations."

Rallying public opinion, too, was a special Committee on Public Information, chaired by journalist George Creel. Creel himself—criticized by others for having fed war hysteria—boasted after the war that the committee was involved in a "fight for the minds of men, for the 'conquest of their convictions.' " Some congressmen saw him as Wilson's "personal press agent." Pamphlets, speaking appearances, posters, the press, and the motion picture industry all joined in the information effort.

As the nation was being rallied behind the war effort, its president was looking ahead to the peace. Indeed, the president's peace initiatives themselves, as embodied in the Fourteen Points, "were all designed to serve their propaganda purpose . . . and proved one of the most effective subjects of propaganda in modern history."[19] Perhaps the most important aspect of his appeal was his inclusion of the League of Nations as the basis for a lasting peace, but his Fourteen Points, enunciated on January 8, 1918, also included an appeal for freedom of the seas, open diplomacy, a reduction of armaments, a peace of moderation, and the right to self-determination.

As the war drew to a close, Wilson looked forward to the Paris Peace Conference. He surprised the nation with his announcement that he would personally attend. Omission of prominent Republicans from the delegation helped lay the groundwork for the rejection of his Fourteen Points, for the Republican party he was ignoring had just ridden to a comfortable congressional victory in the 1918 election. The struggle over the League and the peace treaty—well chronicled elsewhere—bears no need for repetition here, except for a few comments on public opinion. By the time Wilson's opponents in the Senate had their say— couched in frightening and propagandistic rhetoric—"American public sentiment, insofar as it really rejected the provision of the Covenant, did so mainly for non-existent reasons." Nor was the Senate alone in spreading an image of the peace being negotiated. Bell says, "Distortions, perversions, and misstatements were soon spreading out and out—carried, not only by the lower type and anti-League and anti-Wilson newspapers, but sometimes, innocently enough, by papers not endorsing them, but alert for 'snappy' headlines and readable copy." And Wilson could assert that his opponents had "poisoned the wells of public opinion." The vocal opposition was more than the relatively silent supporters of the League could sustain. Barraged, too, by previous Wilson supporters such as the *New Republic,* as well as by other publications such as the *Nation, Reconstruction,* and *Century,* Wilson's great plan for the instrument of a lasting peace was in trouble. The *Nation,* for example, entitled one of its articles on the League "A Colossal Humbug"; in another, it proclaimed "Mr. Wilson Rants."

The president had invited this opposition with his selection of the delegation and his own behavior. For example, when asked at a press conference about the possibility of Senate reservations on the treaty, Wilson snapped: "I do not think hypothetical questions are concerned. The Senate is going to ratify the treaty."

Prominent among the Senate opponents was Senator Henry Cabot Lodge, who took his arguments on a nationwide tour. Arguing that if involved in the League, America would no longer be free of entanglements abroad and that Americans would be ordered to fight for foreign causes, Lodge and his supporters managed to frighten and confuse the American people. The Senate opponents were solidified by a renewed spirit of isolationism and the increasing perception of the League's antipatriotic consequences. The League, it was charged, would allow other nations to interfere in the internal affairs of the United States. Prophetically, Edward Corwin had written two years before the League defeat that "the ultimate viability of an executive policy in [the foreign policy field] will depend upon the backing of public opinion as reflected in the Congress or in the Senate."

Resorting to the intimate forum of a president communing with his people, Wilson hoped to place his case before the public. "Things get very lonely in Washington sometimes," Wilson had once said. "The real voice of the great people of America sometimes sounds faint and distant in that strange city." As a three-week whirlwind tour ended in Wilson's collapse, the president allowed himself to fall victim to what Hughes would later term "the presidential loss of a sense of proportion." This same hubris was to inflict FDR on the Supreme Court issue, Lyndon Johnson on Vietnam, Richard Nixon on Watergate, Ronald Reagan on tax policy.

As always, in moving about the country, Wilson felt *he* best knew the public mood. In speech after speech, he entreated his audiences. Tirelessly, he strove to convince them of the inherent moral role of America in shaping the world's destiny. In the end, his own destiny was that of a bitter, defeated man. Refusing to lessen his pace, Wilson suffered a stroke in Pueblo which resulted in partial paralysis. He never recovered, although he did survive his full second term. Without Wilson's full thrust behind the treaty battle, the treaty and the League failed. In the final analysis, Wilson did not heed his own understanding of power. "Power," he had said, "consists in one's capacity to link his will with the purpose of others, to lead by reason and a gift for cooperation."[20]

POSTSCRIPT: THE WARTIME PRESIDENCY

In his First Inaugural Address, President Abraham Lincoln had asserted: "The Chief Magistrate derives all his power from the people. . . . In *your* hands, my dissatisfied fellow countrymen, and not in *mine,* is the momentous issue of civil war." Lincoln's nineteenth-century handling of the domestic strife which so poignantly influenced Wilson as a boy also set the precedent for the wartime presidencies of the twentieth century. Lincoln's virtually unilateral handling of the crisis and his often dictatorial measures formed the basis upon which both

Wilson and later Franklin Roosevelt would build. In this regard, the wartime presidency must be seen as *evolutionary*. That is, each succeeding president has built upon what his predecessor had viewed as necessary behavior in the handling of the then-pressing problems confronting the nation.

By the time Woodrow Wilson faced the moral and practical dilemmas confronting the nation and the world, it was painfully evident that wartime brings with it the deprivation of civil liberties and that crisis government is essentially strong government. Poignantly, Wilson's own evolving philosophy regarding the presidential role aptly suited the twist of events with which he would have to deal. Elected on a platform of domestic reform, Wilson faced his greatest dilemmas in the foreign policy arena. Wilson had earlier observed that "the President is at liberty, both in law and conscience, to be as big a man as he can." His virtually dictatorial handling of the war crisis naturally evolved from both that perception of the president's role and existing circumstances.

Wilson's heir to the wartime presidency, Franklin D. Roosevelt, carried the Lincolnian and Wilsonian precedents even further. Ironically, the pragmatist Roosevelt had pronounced the presidency "a place of moral leadership," and that sense of morality extended to the essential and inevitable role to be played by the president during wartime. In his "Message to the Congress on Wartime Stabilization," for example, FDR proclaimed: "The responsibilities of the President in wartime to protect the nation are very grave. This total war, with our fighting fronts all over the world, makes the use of executive power far more essential than in any previous war." Lincoln, Wilson, and Franklin Roosevelt each set precedents to underscore this essential nature of the wartime presidency and its relationship to the people in a democracy.

NOTES

1. Ray Stannard Baker, *Woodrow Wilson: Life and Letters,* 8 vols. (Garden City, N.Y.: Doubleday, Page and Co., 1927, 1931, 1935, 1937, 1939), 1:49, 50.

2. Arthur Walworth, *Woodrow Wilson,* 3 vols. (New York: W. W. Norton and Co., 1958, 1965, 1978), 1:4, 19, 6, 68, 193, 7, 8 (hereafter cited as Walworth, *WW*). Wilson letter to Ellen Axson Wilson, April 9, 1888, from Baker, *Life and Letters,* 1:35.

3. Arthur S. Link, "The Higher Realism of Woodrow Wilson," *Journal of Presbyterian History,* 41, no. 1 (March 1963); John Morton Blum, *Woodrow Wilson and the Politics of Morality* (Boston: Little, Brown, 1956), cited by John Braeman, ed., *Wilson* (Englewood Cliffs, N.J.: Prentice-Hall, 1972), p. 155; James David Barber, *The Presidential Character,* 2nd ed. (Englewood Cliffs, N.J.: Prentice-Hall, 1977), p. 63; Braeman, *Wilson,* p. 88; Barber, *Presidential Character,* p. 64; Walworth, *WW,* 1:18; Baker, *Life and Letters,* 1:92, 93.

4. Kenneth S. Davis, *FDR: The Beckoning of Destiny,* (New York: Putnam, 1971), pp. 67, 73, 63, 83, 84.

5. John G. Stoessinger, *Crusaders and Pragmatists* (New York: Norton, 1979), pp. 11, 36; Baker, *Life and Letters,* 1:152, 154, 223; Arthur S. Link, *The Road to the White House* (Princeton: Princeton University Press, 1947), p. 90; James Kerney, *The*

Political Education of Woodrow Wilson (New York: Century Co., 1926), pp. 32, 33; James David Barber, *The Pulse of Politics* (New York: Norton, 1980), p. 122; Baker, *Life and Letters,* 3:47.

6. Baker, *Life and Letters,* 3:53; Kerney, *Political Education,* p. 26; Barber, *Pulse,* p. 37; Baker, *Life and Letters,* 3:78; Walworth, *WW,* 1:163; Link, *Road,* p. 123.

7. Walworth, *WW,* 1:175, 177, 181, 178, 183, 200, 189; Editorial, *New York World,* May 30, 1912; Davis, *Beckoning,* pp. 239, 240.

8. *New York Times,* January 22, 1911; Ernest K. Lindley, *Franklin D. Roosevelt: A Career in Progressive Democracy* (New York; 1932), as cited in Davis, *Beckoning,* p. 270; Walworth, *WW,* 1:231, 233; Editorial, *New York World* May 30, 1912; Baker, *Life and Letters,* 3:265, 266, 246–255; Link, *Road,* pp. 372, 384–387; Walworth, *WW,* 1:235.

9. William Bayard Hale, *The Story of a Style* (New York: B. W. Huebsch, 1920), p. 246; H.C.F. Bell, *Woodrow Wilson and the People* (Hamden, Conn. Archon, 1968), p. 120; Walworth, *WW,* 1:147; Charles W. Merriam, *Four American Party Leaders* (New York: Macmillan, 1926), p. 86; Woodrow Wilson, "What Is a College For?" *Scribner's Magazine,* 46, no. 5 (November 1909): 574–77; Bell, *WW and People,* pp. 80, 82, 83, 87.

10. Baker, *Life and Letters,* 4:11; Editorial, *Cleveland Plain Dealer,* March 5, 1913, cited in Baker, *Life and Letters,* 4:10; Editorial, *New York World,* March 13, 1913; Barber, *Presidential Character,* p. 62; Eric Goldman, *Rendezvous with Destiny* (New York: Vintage Books, 1956), p. 250; Walworth, *WW,* 1:49; Woodrow Wilson, *Congressional Government* (Boston: Houghton Mifflin, 1885), pp. 79, 68; Wilfred E. Binkley, *The Man in the White House* (Baltimore: Johns Hopkins University Press, 1959), p. 166.

11. Edward S. Corwin, *The President: Office and Powers,* (New York: New York University Press, 1957), pp. 267, 268; Robert J. Sickels, *Presidential Transitions* (Englewood Cliffs, N.J.: Prentice-Hall, 1974), p. 115; Walworth, *WW,* 1:146; Wilson speech at Trenton, New Jersey, January 13, 1913, cited in Baker, *Life and Letters,* 3:434; ibid. 4:235; Sickels, *Transitions,* p. 16; Wilson statement on "sentiment of people" in New York, March 4, 1919, cited in Ray Stannard Baker and William Edward Dodd, eds., *The Public Papers of Woodrow Wilson,* 6 vols. (New York: Harper and Brothers, 1925–1927), 1:453 (hereafter cited as *WW, Public Papers*); Baker, *Life and Letters,* 5:124, 183, 184.

12. Walworth, *WW,* 1:287, 149, 259–60; Baker, *Life and Letters,* 5:122–124; Walworth, *WW,* 1:289; *New York Times,* February 25, 1916; Davis, *Beckoning,* p. 380.

13. WW, Public Papers, 2:81; Wilson, *Congressional Government,* p. 138; Arthur S. Link, *Wilson: The New Freedom* (Princeton: Princeton University Press, 1956), p. 64; Davis, *Beckoning,* p. 449; E. M. House, letter to Wilson, May 29, 1914, cited in Arthur S. Link, *Wilson: The Struggle for Neutrality* (Princeton: Princeton University Press, 1960), p. 2; House to Wilson, January 18, 1914, cited in Charles Seymour, ed. *The Intimate Papers of Colonel House,* 4 vols. (Boston and New York: Houghton Mifflin, 1926, 1928), 1:324, 325; House to Wilson, February 9, 1916, and November 30, 1916, cited in ibid, 1:165, 195; Link, *Struggle for Neutrality,* p. 2; Davis comments in *Beckoning* (p. 382): "Wilson's necessity of dealing with the height of the Presidency perhaps saved him a breakdown over his wife's death." Tom Schactman, *Edith and Woodrow* (New York: G.P. Putnam's Sons, 1981), pp. 19–66.

14. Link, *Struggle for Neutrality,* p. 7; "Blaming Germany for the War," *Literary Digest,* 49 (August 22, 1914): 292–295; "The Real Crime Against Germany," *New York*

World, 99 (August 13, 1914): 181, 182; Link, *Struggle for Neutrality*, p. 8; Bell, *WW and People*, p. 166; Link, *Struggle for Neutrality*, pp. 9, 10, 12; Davis, *Beckoning*, p. 402; Link, *Struggle for Neutrality*, pp. 12, 13.

15. Bell, *WW and People*, p. 166; Link, *Struggle for Neutrality*, pp. 18, 19, 25, 31; *WW, Public Papers*, 1:315, 321; House Diary, October 22, 1914, cited in Link, *Struggle for Neutrality*, p. 52; H.B. Brougham, "Memorandum of Interview with the President, Dec. 14, 1914," in F. Fraser Bond, *Mr. Miller of "The Times,"* cited in Link, *Struggle for Neutrality*, p. 53; Wilson address at Indianapolis, *New York Times*, January 9, 1915; *New York Times*, August 19, 1914.

16. James W. Gerard, instructions as ambassador to Germany from Wilson, February 10, 1915, in *WW, Public Papers*, 3:280–283; Wilson to Secretary of State William Jennings Bryan, June 2, 1915, U.S. State Department, Papers Relating to the Foreign Relations of the United States: The Lansing Papers, 1914–1920 (Washington, D.C.: Government Printing Office, 1939, 1940), p. 421, cited in Braeman, *Wilson*, p. 61; Seymour, *Intimate Papers*, vol. 2, chapters 4–7; Arthur S. Link, *Woodrow Wilson and the Progressive Era, 1910–1917* (Princeton: Princeton University Press, 1957), chapter 8; U.S. Note, December 24, 1916, Papers Relating to the Foreign Relations of the United States, 1916, p. 112, quoted in Baker, *Life and Letters*, 6:406, 407; Stoessinger, *Crusaders*, p. 14; Blum, *Politics of Morality*, p. 125; Stoessinger, *Crusaders*, p. 13; Davis, *Beckoning*, for discussion of preparedness movement; ibid., p. 383.

17. Patrick Devlin, *Too Proud to Fight: Woodrow Wilson's Neutrality* (New York: Oxford University Press, 1975), pp. 648, 649; Walworth, *WW*, 1:19, 20; Devlin, *Too Proud*, pp. 676, 440, 441; Davis, *Beckoning*, p. 453; Walworth, *WW*, 1:148, especially the comment: "Though Wilson's mind accepted the strengthening of the Presidency as a historical fact, his conscience was troubled by the threat to constitutional processes"; Goldman, *Rendezvous*, pp. 201, 184, 185.

18. Goldman, *Rendezvous*, pp. 180, 181, 183, 184, 188, 193, 194 (especially on Wilson–*New Republic* relationship); Davis, *Beckoning*, p. 504; Bell, *WW and People*, p. 224; Richard Hofstadter, *The Age of Reform* (New York: Vintage Books, 1955), p. 279.

19. Bell, *WW and People*, pp. 218, 219, 220, 221, 222; Davis, *Beckoning*, p. 509; Braeman, *Wilson*, p. 11; Stanley Coben, *Reform, War and Reaction, 1912–1932* (New York: Harper and Row, 1972), p. 91; Davis, *Beckoning*, pp. 590–591; William L. Langer, "From Isolation to Mediation," quoted in Arthur P. Dudden, *Woodrow Wilson and the World of Today* (Philadelphia: University of Pennsylvania Press, 1957), p. 73.

20. Braeman, *Wilson*, p. 12 ("By going to Paris he lost his unique position above the battle, while depriving the country of badly needed leadership at home"); Bell, *WW and People*, pp. 323, 324, 327, 328; "A Colossal Humbug", *The Nation*, September 27, 1919; "Mr. Wilson Rants," *The Nation*, October 4, 1919; Thomas Andrew Bailey, *Woodrow Wilson and the Great Betrayal* (New York: Macmillan, 1945), p. 9; Corwin, *Office and Powers*, p. 126; "Things get very lonely . . . " cited in Richard Harris, *The Real Voice* (New York: Macmillan, 1964), frontispiece; Emmet John Hughes, *The Living Presidency* (Baltimore: Penguin Books, 1972), pp. 180, 109; Walworth, *WW*, 3:315.

ANNOTATED BIBLIOGRAPHY

Books

Annin, R. E. *Woodrow Wilson: A Character Study*. New York: Dodd, Mead, 1925.
    An early biography.

Aron, Raymond. *The Century of Total War*. Boston: Beacon, 1954.

A French observer's view of global conflict.

Bailey, Thomas Andrew. *Woodrow Wilson and the Great Betrayal*. New York: Macmillan, 1945.

Post–World War II study of the Senate intrigues that defeated Wilson's League proposal.

Baker, Ray Stannard. *Woodrow Wilson: Life and Letters*. 8 vols. Garden City: Doubleday, Page and Co., 1927, 1931, 1935, 1937, 1939.

Perhaps the earliest "standard biography."

Baker, Ray Stannard and William E. Dodd, eds. *The Public Papers of Woodrow Wilson*. 6 vols. New York: Harper and Brothers, 1925–1927.

Wilson's edited documents.

Barber, James David. *The Presidential Character*. 2nd ed. Englewood Cliffs, N.J.: Prentice-Hall, 1977.

This revision categorizes the Wilson of the League fight in the active-negative category.

———. *The Pulse of Politics*. New York: Norton, 1980.

A cyclical theory of presidential elections which includes media analysis.

Bell, H.C.F. *Woodrow Wilson and the People*. Hamden, Ct.: Archon, 1968.

A prime source for understanding Wilson's public image.

Beschloss, Michael R. *Kennedy and Roosevelt: The Uneasy Alliance*. New York: Norton, 1980.

Profiles of FDR and his ambassador to London; much about inter-war diplomacy.

Binkley, Wilfred. *The Man in the White House*. Baltimore: John Hopkins University Press, 1959.

A general study which places Wilson in context.

Blum, John Morton. *Woodrow Wilson and the Politics of Morality*. Boston: Little, Brown, 1956.

Wilson's early formulation of human rights and domestic reform positions.

———. *The Progressive Presidents: Theodore Roosevelt, Woodrow Wilson, Franklin D. Roosevelt, Lyndon B. Johnson*. New York: Norton, 1980.

A comparative study embracing Wilson.

Braeman, John. *Wilson: Great Lives Observed*. Englewood Cliffs, N.J.: Prentice-Hall, 1972.

A biography drawing on recent sources.

Bragdon, H. W. *Woodrow Wilson: The Academic Years*. Cambridge: Belknap Press, 1967.

The formative and academic period of Wilson's life; ends with Princeton presidency.

Buehrig, Edward H. *Woodrow Wilson and the Balance of Power*. Bloomington: Indiana University Press, 1955.

A diplomatic study.

Burns, James MacGregor. *Roosevelt: The Lion and the Fox*. New York: Harcourt, Brace, 1956, and *Roosevelt: The Soldier of Freedom*. New York: Harcourt, Brace, Jovanovich, 1970.

The two-volume biography of FDR which is both commendatory and critical and reflects his Wilsonian legacy.

Campbell, Bruce A. *The American Electorate: Attitude and Action*. New York: Holt,

Rinehart, Winston, 1979.

A public opinion study.

Cantrill, Hadley, ed. *Public Opinion, 1935–1946*. Princeton: Princeton University Press, 1951.

Opinion analysis—FDR's second term to the early Fair Deal.

Carr, E. H. *The Twenty Years' Crisis, 1919–1939*. New York: Harper, 1939.

Analysis of interwar diplomacy.

Churchill, Winston S. *The Gathering Storm*. Boston: Houghton Mifflin, 1948.

The British leader's view of how ultranationalism at Versailles brought on World War II.

Cohen, Stanley. *Reform, War and Reaction, 1912–1932*. New York: Harper and Row, 1972.

Places Wilson in context of the early 20th century political cycle.

Corwin, E. S. *The President: Office and Powers*. New York: New York University Press, 1957.

A classic constitutional analysis by a political scientist who traces the growth of the war powers.

Craig, Gordon, and Felix Gilbert, eds. *The Diplomats, 1919–1939*. Princeton: Princeton University Press, 1949.

An analysis of Wilson's League failure and its impact on interwar diplomacy.

Dallek, Robert. *Franklin D. Roosevelt and American Foreign Policy, 1932–1945*. Oxford: Oxford University Press, 1979.

FDR diplomacy from the London Economic Conference to Yalta.

Davis, Kenneth S. *FDR: The Beckoning of Destiny*. New York: Putnam, 1971.

Good material on FDR's apprenticeship under Wilson.

Devlin, Patrick. *Too Proud to Fight: Woodrow Wilson's Neutrality*. Oxford: Oxford University Press, 1975.

Diplomacy of the *Lusitania* period.

DiClerico, Robert E. *The American President*. Englewood Cliffs, N.J.: Prentice-Hall, 1979.

A general text including Wilson references.

Divine, Robert A. *Roosevelt and World War II*. Baltimore: Penguin Books, 1971, 1972.

A recent account of the war presidency under FDR.

Dudden, Arthur P. *Woodrow Wilson and the World of Today*. Philadelphia: University of Pennsylvania Press, 1957.

The legacy of Wilson viewed from an era of greater conservatism.

Ellul, Jacques. *Propaganda: The Formation of Men's Attitudes*. New York: Vintage Books, 1972.

A general but useful study.

Everson, David H. *Public Opinion and Interest Groups in American Politics*. New York: Franklin Watts, 1982.

A contemporary analysis of opinion dynamics.

Faulkner, Harold U. *From Versailles to the New Deal*. New Haven: Yale University Press, 1950.

A study of the interwar period.

Foley, Hamilton. *Woodrow Wilson's Case for the League of Nations*. Princeton: Princeton University Press, 1923.

An early defense of the Wilson stance.

Freidel, Frank. *Franklin D. Roosevelt: The Apprenticeship*. Boston: Little, Brown, 1952, and *FDR: The Ordeal*. Boston: Little Brown, 1954.

The first two volumes of the detailed study deal with FDR's service under Wilson in the Navy Department and relations between Wilson and the 1920 Democratic ticket.

Gelfand, Lawrence E. *The Inquiry: American Preparations for Peace, 1917–1919*. New Haven: Yale University Press, 1963.

The diplomacy of House and other associates in preparing for the Versailles Conference.

George, Alexander L. and Juliette L. George. *Woodrow Wilson and Colonel House*. New York: John Day, 1956.

A pioneering psychological study with heavy emphasis on the House Diaries.

Goldman, Eric F. *Rendezvous with Destiny*. New York: Vintage Books, 1956.

FDR and the influence of Wilson.

Grayson, Cary T. *Woodrow Wilson: An Intimate Memoir*. New York: Holt, Rinehart, Winston, 1960.

An admiring view by a naval aide.

Grew, J. C. *Turbulent Era*. London: Hammond, 1953.

A diplomat's view.

Gunther, John. *Roosevelt in Retrospect*. New York: Pyramid Books, 1962.

A free-lance journalist's view.

Hale, William Bayard. *The Story of a Style*. New York: B. W. Huebesch, 1920.

An early analysis of Wilson's leadership style.

Hofstadter, Richard. *The Age of Reform: From Bryan to F.D.R*. New York: Vintage Books, 1955.

Wilson in the context of reform movements.

————. *The American Political Tradition*. New York: Vintage, 1974.

A comparative study which places Wilson in long-term context.

House, Edward M., and Charles Seymour, eds. *What Really Happened at Paris: The Story of the Paris Peace Conference, 1918–1919*. New York: Harcourt, Brace, 1921.

An early account of the postwar peace conference published by Wilson's chief aide and a collaborator.

Hughes, Emmet John. *The Living Presidency*. Baltimore: Penguin Books, 1972.

A more general study which compares Wilson mainly with his successors.

Kennan, George F. *The Decision to Intervene*. Princeton: Princeton University Press, 1956.

An exploration of Wilsonian diplomacy in the period of the post-Revolution upheaval in the Soviet Union.

Kerney, James. *The Political Education of Woodrow Wilson*. New York and London: The Century Co., 1926.

An early study of Wilson's pre-presidential years.

Latham, Earl, ed., *The Philosophy and Politics of Woodrow Wilson*. Chicago: University of Chicago Press, 1958.

An anthology dealing with thought and action.

Levin, N. Gorden, Jr. *Woodrow Wilson and World Politics: America's Response to War and Revolution*. New York: Oxford University Press, 1968.

A fresh interpretation of Wilsonian diplomacy.

Lindley, Ernest K. *The Roosevelt Revolution*. New York: Viking, 1934.
> The journalist who became a *Newsweek* columnist chronicles the rise of a Wilson disciple.

Link, Arthur S. *The Road to the White House*. Princeton, Princeton University Press, 1947.
> The Progressive Era and Wilson's achievement of national power.

———. *Wilson: The New Freedom*. Princeton: Princeton University Press, 1956.
> Programmatic analysis of the early Wilson era.

———. *Woodrow Wilson and the Progressive Era, 1910–1917*. Princeton: Princeton University Press, 1956.
> Wilson as governor and president in context.

———. *Wilson the Diplomatist*. Baltimore: Johns Hopkins University Press, 1957.
> An analysis of the president who wrote diplomatic notes on the famous white typewriter.

———. *Wilson, the Struggle for Neutrality*. Princeton: Princeton University Press, 1960.
> A detailed analysis of the diplomatic struggle which involved a balancing act between Britain and Germany.

Link, Arthur S., and William M. Leary, Jr. "Election of 1916." In Arthur M. Schlesinger, Jr., ed. *The Coming to Power*. New York: Chelsea House, 1971.
> An essay on an election whose closeness is comparable to those of 1948, 1960 and 1976.

Lipset, Seymour Martin. *Party Coalitions in the 1980's*. San Francisco: Institute for Contemporary Studies, 1981.
> Includes material tracing party coalitions.

Lodge, Henry Cabot. *The Senate and the League of Nations*. New York: Charles Scribner, 1925.
> The original "scholar in politics" and grandfather of the Vietnam-era U.S. Ambassador to Saigon presents the anti-League case.

May, E. R. *The World War and American Isolation*. Cambridge: Harvard University Press, 1959.
> The development of isolation from a historian's view.

Mayer, Arno J. *Politics and Diplomacy of Peacemaking: Containment and Counterrevolution at Versailles, 1918–1919*. New York: Knopf, 1967.
> A recent interpretation of Versailles.

Merriam, Charles W. *Four American Party Leaders*. New York: Macmillan, 1926.
> A study of Wilson and three others as party leaders in the pretelevision era.

Morrison, Elting E., ed. *The Letters of Theodore Roosevelt*. Cambridge, Mass.: Harvard University Press, 1954.
> A basic source on a leading rival of Wilson.

Myers, William Starr, ed. *Woodrow Wilson: Some Princeton Memoirs*. Princeton: Princeton University Press, 1946.
> Memoirs of the academic years.

Rubin, Richard L. *Press, Party and Presidency*. New York: Norton, 1981.
> A linkage analysis of these major institutions.

Schactman, Tom. *Edith and Woodrow: A Presidential Romance*. New York: G. P. Putnam's Sons, 1981.
> This study contains material on Edith Bolling Galt Wilson's relationship to her

husband, her role as confidante, and the controversial regency following the president's stroke while touring in Colorado.

Schlesinger, Arthur M., Jr., *The Age of Roosevelt:* Vol. 1, *The Crisis of the Old Order;* Vol. 2, *The Coming of the New Deal;* Vol. 3, *The Politics of Upheaval.* Boston: Houghton Mifflin, 1957, 1959, 1960.

A colorfully written beginning of a multivolume series. A fourth volume has been in preparation.

Seymour, Charles. *The Intimate Papers of Colonel House.* 4 vols. Boston and New York: Houghton Mifflin, 1926, 1928.

Behind-the-scenes correspondence of the Texan who was a senior Wilson aide.

Sickels, Robert J. *Presidential Transactions.* Englewood Cliffs, N.J.: Prentice-Hall, 1974.

This study adapts transactional analysis to the study of the presidency; includes Wilson examples.

Smith, Gaddis. *American Diplomacy During the Second World War.* New York: John Wiley, 1965.

Roosevelt era wartime diplomacy.

Smith, Gene. *The Shattered Dream.* New York: Morrow, 1970.

A popular historian's account of the League defeat. Also dealt with in Herbert Hoover's *The Ordeal Of Woodrow Wilson.*

Stoessinger, John G. *Crusaders and Pragmatists.* New York: Norton, 1979.

Comparative case studies including a Wilson profile.

Tugwell, Rexford G. *The Enlargement of the Presidency.* Garden City, N.Y.: Doubleday, 1960.

A political and administrative study which parallels Corwin's constitutional analysis.

———. *The Democratic Roosevelt.* Baltimore: Penguin Books, 1969.

An aide's view.

Walworth, Arthur. *Woodrow Wilson.* 3 vols. New York: Norton, 1958, 1965, 1978.

A multivolume study which stresses Wilson's prophetic role in leadership.

Williams, William Appleman. *The Tragedy of American Diplomacy.* New York: Dell, 1962.

Wilson as viewed from the modern left.

Wilson, Woodrow. *Congressional Government: A Study in American Politics.* Boston: Houghton Mifflin, 1885.

Wilson's Johns Hopkins doctoral thesis, this is termed a classic in political science literature, a cogent analysis of legislative-executive relations in an era of caretaker national government.

———. *Constitutional Government in the United States.* New York: Macmillan, 1908.

As a more mature scholar and president of Princeton, Wilson as author of this work concluded that there was greater potential for executive leadership in the American system than he had believed in 1885.

———. *Leaders of Men.* Princeton: Princeton University Press, 1952.

A posthumous edition of Wilson's leadership study.

Articles

Link, Arthur S. "The Higher Realism of Woodrow Wilson." *Journal of Presbyterian History,* 41, no. 1 (March 1963): 4–13.

Wilson, Woodrow. "What Is a College For?" *Scribner's Magazine,* 46, No. 5 (November
    1909): 574–577.

Documents

Papers of Franklin D. Roosevelt. Franklin D. Roosevelt Library, Hyde Park, New York.
Papers of Woodrow Wilson. 12 vols. Ed. Arthur S. Link. Princeton, N.J.: Princeton
    University Press, 1966.
Papers of Woodrow Wilson. Library of Congress, Washington, D.C.
Papers Relating to the Foreign Relations of the United States. Washington, D.C.: Gov-
    ernment Printing Office, Supplements 1914, 1915, 1916, 1917 (2 vols.).
Seymour, Charles. *The Intimate Papers of Colonel House.* 4 vols. Boston and New York:
    Houghton Mifflin, 1926, 1928.

Periodicals

Literary Digest
New York Nation
New York Outlook
New York Times
New York World
Scribner's Magazine

Documentary Records

Harris, Julie, Hal Holbrook, Kevin McCarthy, and Edward Woodward. *The White House
    Saga.* Caedmon Records stereo production TC 11945.
        Based on Nanette Kutner book of same name. Includes Julie Harris portrayal of
    Edith Bolling Galt Wilson; jacket diagram shows location of president's sickroom
    during League debate.
Murrow Edward R., with Fred Friendly. *I Can Hear It Now,* Vol. 2, 1919–1932. CBS
    News, Columbia Special Products.
        Includes cuts on League debate and 1920 campaign.

Motion Picture

Wilson. Produced by Darryl F. Zanuck for Twentieth-Century Fox, 1944. (Mentioned in
    Robert Sobel, *The Manipulators: America in the Media Age* [Garden City, N.Y.:
    Anchor Press/Doubleday, 1976], p. 210.)

11 WARREN GAMALIEL HARDING

David H. Jennings

The *Marion Star* of March 2, 1921, has a nostalgic picture of President-elect Warren Gamaliel Harding standing with his wife on the rear platform of their departing Washington-bound train and waving to their fellow townsmen even as the home folks are singing "God Be with You Till We Meet Again." The hymn was appropriate to the occasion. The prior ceremonies had been full of McGuffeyism, Methodism, and McKinleyism, with much of the Horatio Alger theme thrown in for good measure. Looking at the picture, the viewer catches the figure of a knickered lad of about twelve years sitting on top of a railroad car and gazing with awestruck eyes upon the scene. One wonders what happened to that boy of yesteryear. How often did he tell his children, grandchildren, and friends about the scene? Of the youth, nothing is known; of the object of his hero worship, much is known. Yet even today, the researcher finds significant gaps, especially in the relationship to and the influence of Harding's wife, the Progressives, and several of his cabinet members and his diplomatic corps.

The much known about Warren G. Harding, twenty-ninth president of the United States, should carry a "handle with care" warning to persons seeking the truth—that is, the agreement of ideas with realities—about the man and his administration. A cautious approach to such "facts" and judgments is necessary because three widely differing versions of this Ohioan and his administration have been given by writers.

Harding's first biographers wrote in praise of him for political or personal purposes. In 1920 Joe Mitchell Chapple extolled him in *Warren G. Harding: The Man,* and C. D. Philbrick wrote *What a Country Boy Did with 200 Pounds of Type* in order to promote their hero's presidential campaign. In 1922 S. A. Cuneo traced the incumbent's life in *From Printer to President.* "My Boy Warren," in the March 1921 issue of *McClure's,* was based on an aged father's memories. In most cases, save for the researcher, these mainly hagiographic works deserve the oblivion to which they have been assigned.

The full revelations of the "Harding Scandals" soon after his death essentially put an end to the first school of historiography. In place of the admirers came the debunkers, a coterie of writers—sales-minded journalists, alienated former associates—whose views on "WG" are still probably the most commonly accepted ones. The composite picture presented was that of a lazy youth, a small-town newspaper editor dominated by his wife, a "bloviating" or boasting do-nothing Ohio politician, a roll call missing senator introducing vote bait bills on the occasions he showed up, and an insecure president whose responsibilities were beyond his capacities. Only by immoral compromising and vicious flag waving did he stay in power. Sex, public scandals, and whispered claims of Negro blood dominated the stories.

The above view of Warren Harding has come under severe—even if only partly successful—attack since 1964. In that year, more than 800 boxes of Harding papers were given by the Harding Memorial Association to the Ohio Historical Society. Accompanying these papers in the society's archives are valuable collections of several close friends of the Marion man who were co-workers or in frequent contact with him. These new sources have furnished extensive material for a truer portrait as attempted by several writers. Several scholarly historians did attempt prior to the release of the papers to give an accurate accounting of the era.

The post–Harding Papers era, the third school of historiography, was launched when the Ohio Historical Society published a special Spring-Summer Harding edition of *Ohio History*. This had revisionist articles based upon research into the new materials. Soon thereafter two hastily researched books came out. One was *The Available Man* by Andrew Sinclair. While his research should have been more extensive and his judgments (made on inadequate evidence) are doubtful in some instances, his data do undermine certain prevailing myths. While committing the unpardonable sin for a researcher of not footnoting his findings, Francis Russell in his *Shadow of Blooming Grove* wrote a fascinating biography dispelling the myth of Negro blood in Harding's ancestry and adding a new "Harding woman," Mrs. Carrie Phillips. Russell, however, fully pursued the sex and scandal formula of the debunker writers. Ironically, it was the considerable fear that exploiters would make quicker and fuller use of the papers than scholars that for many years kept the trustees of the Harding Memorial Association from releasing his papers to the public.

DOWNES AND MURRAY'S VIEWS

However, the prediction of persuasive Archives Committee members of the Ohio Academy of History that scholarly works would result from the release of the Harding Papers came true when Randolph C. Downes and Robert Murray wrote *The Rise of Warren Gamaliel Harding, 1865–1920* and *The Harding Era, 1921–1923: Warren G. Harding and His Administration*, respectively, becoming the leaders of the third school of Harding historiography. Downes' lengthy book is loaded with effective rebuttals to some old myths created by the debunkers. Significantly, the editor-researcher-professor, who ended up after years of study on his subject as no admirer of Harding, was able to dismiss some earlier negative interpretations of the Ohio politician as almost pure fables, especially these: the lazy youth and adult theory; the Harding ancestry blood theory; Harry Daugherty's domination of Harding; the thesis of Harding's insecurity in public office and politics.

In his well-received major work, *The Harding Era,* Robert Murray depicts the Ohioan as neither a poor nor a great president but a solid one. Murray thus challenges the usual estimation of scholars that Warren G. Harding was among the worst or the worst, as Thomas A. Bailey insisted. From the new data, Murray destroyed the debunkers' accounts of the president's selection of his cabinet. For example, Secretary of State Charles Evans Hughes, so the story went, had been offered the State position late in February 1921, after acquaintances of the president-elect, especially George Harvey, had turned it down. Actually, Murray proved that Hughes had been the first person approached and that he accepted the job a few days after the November 1920 election but joined with Harding in postponing the announcement until February 1921.

There was fear that a fourth school of Harding historiography might unfold, depicting the man as a great leader and president. Even the scholarly Murray took the role of advocate when he suggested that Harding won the campaign of 1920 and was an effective president because he told and gave the people what they wanted to hear and obtain. Such a criterion obviously defines the successful politician. It does not move a president into the statesman niche. In a democracy, a statesman must know where the people are in order to bring them to where he believes the society should go.

In *The Conciliator,* primarily an analysis of Harding's speeches and oratorical techniques, Dale Cottrill, a speech professor, verifies Harding's ability as an orator and harmonizer but does not emphasize his narrow range of topics before the 1920 Presidential campaign and his scanty knowledge of issues, in some important fields even afterwards.

As true of the earlier schools of theory, the post–Harding Papers era writers also have their defects even though the new sources may well have placed them nearer to the truth. Yet insights may also be gained from the debunkers. Actually, the most accurate profile of Warren G. Harding and his presidency will emerge only as the new historiography is joined with a modification, not a negation, of the older views. This image analysis, based on the study all these schools of writers and especially the new materials available since 1964, represents an effort to accomplish this task.

HARDING'S FORMATIVE YEARS

The first thirty-three years of Warren Gamaliel Harding's life and career were the developmental years spent in Blooming Grove, Caledonia, and Marion, Ohio, from 1865 to 1898. In a farmhouse near the village of Blooming Grove on the Mansfield-Marion pike, Warren was born on November 2, 1865, to George

Tyson and Phoebe Dickenson Harding. Extensive research has been done on Harding's English and Dutch ancestry, and the claim of Negro blood in his ancestry seems totally false. Even so, Harding had to face this allegation from the time he was a youth. Harding's mother, a devout Christian, brought "Winnie" fundamentalist morals and ideas. By 1873 his country doctor father was lured to Caledonia, hoping that it would become a thriving railroad center. There Warren attended school, church, and prayer meetings and befriended Jack Warick. The tall, mischievous lad was by no means the lazy youth depicted by the debunker school. Its members found him so lazy that he quit a well-paying farm job a few hours after he took it. Warren acquired sympathy for farmers but no love for their occupation. The capacity for physical labor, however, was not matched by a zeal for intellectual life. Warren's father had brought a printer to Caledonia to start a weekly paper, and Warren and Jack were trained by him in "ink." They dreamed of someday owning a newspaper.[1] At Ohio Central College at Iberia six miles away, Warren, with little zeal for books or courses, worked his way through college and devoted much time to extracurricular activities. His real efforts at Iberia were put into editing six editions of a college newspaper.

In 1882 his father, disappointed at the railroad's bypassing Caledonia, took his family to live in Marion, a "three-railroad" town. Warren, after an unhappy term teaching school, followed his family to Marion. Dr. Harding had set up a medical practice, but Warren had no interest in medicine. His father advised him to try law; Warren studied in a friend's office but found Blackstone heavy and boring. Warren and Jack (on a visit from Kansas) met afterwards and discussed their Caledonian dream. The two and another friend put in a third of the cost each to buy the decrepit, unwanted, laughed-at newspaper, the *Star*. Warren's father contributed a few hundred dollars for Warren's share. The third youth missed the outdoor life he was used to and soon quit. Later, Jack, in debt and frightened by the risks Warren was proposing in getting new equipment by large loans, sold out his third to WG (as he was known in the *Star* office), but remained as an employee.

He and Jack worked long hours side by side to keep the *Star* from folding. The young editor was patient and sympathetic with his employees, often reporter tramps. Between 1884 and 1890, together they turned the dilapidated newspaper from a weekly paper into a daily urban journal.[2] By the time of his courtship and marriage to Florence Kling De Wolfe in 1891, WG was clearly in control of his newspaper household, and the basis for success had been laid. Evidence indicates that Florence Harding aided her husband but did not run the newspaper, as debunkers claimed. Detractors were quite correct, however, when they said that editor Harding viciously engaged in squabbles over advertising with rival editors.

THE *STAR*'S EDITORIAL POLICIES

Harding's major energies as editor, however, were not devoted primarily to mud-slinging but rather to the *Star*'s success and town building. Projects pushed in the editorial pages and special columns of the renamed *Marion Star* included creation of a coal-hauling ''Black Diamond Railroad''; oil drilling in Marion County with the hope that drillers would strike it rich as in Findlay; building a local opera house at public expense, if necessary; laying additional street car track; and paving of streets. In endeavors such as these, the editor's aim was to turn Marion from an essentially rural-oriented village to a modern industrial city.

The leader of the Realtors-Small Town enthusiasts was Amos H. Kling, the wealthiest man in town and its largest property holder, which included one-third ownership of the attractive Marion Hotel built in 1883. Kling regarded the group led by Warren G. Harding as people who sought to destroy beautiful Marion— and his wealth.

Warren brought about expansion, then gained a second win over the realtor when he married Kling's only daughter. Florence, like Kling, was high-spirited and wanted her own way. If Amos Kling had earlier disapproved of his daughter's youthful marriage to drinking Peter De Wolfe, he fought Harding so hard that the young couple conducted their courtship clandestinely, but not secretly enough that gossips missed their meetings. Only after fourteen years did she and her father become reconciled.[3]

In the early newspaper years, WG was not as partisan publicly as in the 1890s. Then he began to express more boldly his conservative Republican leanings on state, national, and international issues. If, as Randolph C. Downes stressed, these views neatly coincided with those of most Central Ohioans, it is likewise true that Warren Harding also believed in them.

In his *Marion Star,* Warren G. Harding editorialized on the relationship of capital and labor. Unfortunately, he projected the favorable local economic situation of a labor shortage to the entire nation, even though he admitted that he knew little about large cities. He opposed unions and saw businessmen as the real architects of American prosperity and political life. Workers could become good citizens by their own efforts.

BREAKING INTO OHIO POLITICS

The trouble with the Ohio Republican party for a young hopeful was that it was controlled by an aging leadership dominated by U.S. Senator John Sherman who, in 1892, won a sixth term from the state legislature. For Harding to have joined the Old Guard would have been to have assigned himself the role of a cheerleader, not a player, in the political game. And the latter Harding more and more wanted to be.

Harding adopted two strategies against the Old Guard domination of the Ohio Republican political scene directed from Washington. The first was using the pages of his newspaper constantly to demand a youth movement in the party. The second was the promotion of a leader eventually to replace John Sherman. Harding was a militant patriot in the *Star* during the short Spanish-American War and started a wire service to keep up to the minute on the happenings.

In 1899 it was Marion County's turn to select the state senate candidate for the Marion-Logan-Union counties district. Though the city of Marion was Democratic, and WG had been defeated earlier for auditor, the Thirteenth District had a Republican majority. Encouraged by Governor Asa S. Bushnell's secretary, WG announced his bid for the state senate nomination. Marion Hannaites backed another Marion young enthusiast, Grant Mouser. Harding won by one vote, and Mouser pledged his support. After a rousing unity speech at the district convention, Harding was nominated, then gave his first oratorical demonstration of how to defeat Democrats; he won the election.

In his two terms as state senator, 1895–1903, Harding demonstrated the approach to political life that he maintained through his election to the presidency. He had two aims. One was to please the people. The second was to satisfy those leaders whose support was vital to his career.

"PARTY UNITY" OVER "CONSCIENCE"

Chairing the Municipal Government Committee, Harding could promote the urban reform movement sweeping Ohio and the nation. Often he acted like a Progressive, but no significant legislation resulted. Speeches about battling the "interests" pleased the people; his actions pleased politicians upon whom his future in politics depended.

Harding's transition from a freshman politician to an Ohio leader of oratorical and political maneuvering skills occurred around the turn of the century. The state senator was a congenial and friendly colleague to fellow legislators and ingratiating to his constituents. Many did call him a friend. Later there would be those "friends" who would take advantage of his friendship and hurt his reputation. The group of friends and promoters of Harding called later by name "the Ohio Gang" was not a gang in the sense of a well-organized group planning malicious schemes but merely a small number of political and personal friends impressed by him in his Ohio political career who gradually, in the years following his state senatorship, worked on behalf of his rise, sometimes unskillfully and amorally but, as history proves, skillfully enough to gain him the presidency. The bosses of Ohio at the time Harding's rise began either died, as Marcus Hanna did in 1904, or lost power, as George (Boss) Cox, Joseph Foraker, Charles Dick, and several Ohio governors did before the 1920 election.

As a spellbinding speaker at Republican rallies to gain office for his fellow partisan leaders even before his own state senatorship, and especially as a faithful party worker to keep together the weak linkage of various party factions, Harding was outstanding.

Though Harding has been accused of mainly sponsoring petty measures and straddling serious issues, especially Prohibition and woman suffrage, early in his political career, he undertook the leadership of the Republican conservative George K. Nash policy program against Tom Johnson, the Democratic progressive leader considered by conservative Republicans as a radical. The harmonizer saved the program.

When the Municipal Code Act passed in Harding's first term, the political situation required skillful handling. The Republican Committee, with Nicholas Longworth, who later introduced Harding to Washington circles, prepared the Board Plan, which allowed bosses easily to control cities. The Democrats proposed the Federal Plan. The big issue was the length of franchises. Nash and Harding favored a twenty-five year one. Pressure from "Mighty Marcus" and corporate entertaining of key senators, including Harding, resulted in a move to form a bipartisan study commission and ultimately in another Republican victory for bossism. Harding had become the party bosses' reliable man, and the Democrats' Federal Plan was defeated.

SLATED FOR LIEUTENANT GOVERNOR

In 1903, whether to support Hanna, Foraker, or Theodore Roosevelt for president in 1904 disunified the party again. However, both Hanna and Foraker persuaded Nash to back Myron T. Herrick, a Hanna man and Cleveland industrialist, as candidate for governor, instead of Harding. The harmonizer's acceptance of this decision and Boss Cox's support for Harding for lieutenant governor resulted in the "inner circle" selection for the post. In the campaign, Harding's speeches rather than Herrick's were show stealers. The slogan "Hanna, Herrick, Harding and Harmony" and prosperity produced an easy Republican victory over Tom Johnson. When, in February 1904, Hanna died, the Ohio Republican party became more divided than previously. Fear of Harding's rise by former Hannaites resulted in the legislature refusing to approve Governor Herrick's taking Hanna's U.S. Senate seat. Charles Dick, chairman of the State Executive Committee, was appointed instead.

Harding again promoted harmony by his "Deference and Devotion" speech at the Ohio Republican Convention in May 1904 and succeeded in getting the new Republican "Big Four," Herrick, Dick, Cox, and Foraker, to back "Teddy" for president. The National Campaign Committee asked the harmonizer to speak on Roosevelt's behalf in Indiana, Michigan, and New York as well as Ohio. Harding was beginning to make national leaders aware of him.

By 1905 Herrick had alienated one set of Republicans after another, especially the racetrack fans, the farmers, and the Prohibition supporters. Throughout the state there was talk of booming Harding for governor. Herrick, aware of this, "railroaded" the old Hanna supporters into endorsing his reelection, according to Downes. Herrick's strong tactics worked with both Foraker and Cox.

His term ended, Harding returned to Marion and the *Star* and devoted some time to trying to reunify the party. He traveled to Europe three times with the now reconciled Amos Kling.

Unrealistically, he tried to mend a feud between Senator Foraker and President Roosevelt over the regulation of the railroads in the Hepburn bill. At the Dayton

State Convention in 1906, Harding, as platform committee chairman, developed a compromise, with Senator Dick reelected as State Executive Committee chairman and a platform adopted that was acceptable both to the Old Guard and to the insurgent Daugherty-Burton-Herrick group.

THE *STAR* ENDORSES TAFT

Senator Foraker broke with President Roosevelt over the Brownsville Affair. Roosevelt endorsed Ohioan William Howard Taft, his secretary of war, to be his successor in 1908. Harry Daugherty, influential since the 1980s, and the scholarly Theodore Burton of Cleveland aligned themselves to the Taft organization, led by Arthur Vorys in Ohio, continuing to oppose Dick and Foraker. Ohio Progressive leaders and press supported Taft and attacked the Old Guard, including Harding. At the midwinter party primary convention the Ohio Central Committee, prodded by Taft supporters, had to choose between Foraker and Taft delegates to the state convention. Harding continued to support Foraker, but by January 20, 1908, the filing deadline, he realized that Foraker had lost his power. On January 22 a *Star* editorial, "Foraker Is Defeated and Ohio Is for Taft," endorsed the Cincinnatian. Harding, who agonized over deserting an old political friend, wrote him to explain why. He thus kept Foraker and his friends on a friendly basis while gaining the warm welcome of Taft-Roosevelt supporters.

Harding, after Taft's nomination in Chicago, stumped for four weeks. He spoke on national issues, especially the tariff, accompanying Governor Andrew L. Harris of Eaton, up for reelection. Although the Democrats lost the state to Taft, scandals in the Treasurer's and auditor's offices caused Harris' loss to Judson Harmon, a conservative reformer of great competence and prestige.

In 1910 defeat for Buckeye Republicans seemed inevitable. Harding and others were reluctant to run, but he did modify his views on the tariff. He kept himself available but did not seek the gubernatorial nomination. But he won it on the third ballot at the convention after Boss Cox shifted support to him from a Dayton candidate. Governor Harmon made scandals and "boss control" campaign issues. Harding fought back but equivocated on Prohibition.

DEFENDS TAFT AGAINST PROGRESSIVES

Despite an endorsement speech for Harding by former President Roosevelt, Harding was overwhelmingly defeated. This time he had failed to harmonize the factions. However, his loyalty to Taft later brought some rewards. He had words of encouragement from then-Congressman Frank Willis. He made a European cruise with Jim and Carrie Phillips, then devoted his time to the *Star* and the Chautauqua circuit.

After his "flirtation" with progressivism in 1910, he returned publicly to conservatism. In an April 1912 address to the Cleveland Tippecanoe Club he claimed that Taft carried out the "Square Deal." He was disgusted by the way the Progressives treated Taft and considered Gifford Pinchot a troublemaker and Robert Ballinger businesslike. The *Star* continued to praise party loyalty. It referred to the direct primary, initiative, and referendum rule by the mob, not representative government. Harding barely got elected as a delegate-at-large to the National Convention in Chicago in 1912. He was asked to put Taft's name in nomination at the convention, but the Ohio Progressive League had enlisted thirty-five delegates for Roosevelt while Taft had only eight.[4]

ASSOCIATION WITH DAUGHERTY

Harding and Harry Daugherty first worked together in 1912. Daugherty had been state executive chairman in the early 1890s but lost that post to Charles Dick in 1899. Until 1910, however, Daugherty was a lawyer and lobbyist and had become controversial over efforts to influence President Taft in the Morse Case. Both he and Harding were compatible with Taft's conservative views and policies. Before April 1912, Arthur Vorys and Daugherty were two of only a few Ohioans working to reelect Taft. In May Daugherty told a Taft caucus that there was as much difference between the principles of Taft and Roosevelt as between the American and Red flags. On May 14 Taft began a seven-day Ohio campaign. The next day, Roosevelt followed on a campaign trip by private train that, sad to say, resulted in an exchange of abuse between the two leaders. Daugherty joined Taft on May 18 at Lima and spoke for him. But Daugherty was not a vote getter or orator of Harding's caliber.

Harding, according to Alice Roosevelt Longworth's *Crowded Hours,* came to the gallery where she and her husband sat and offered Nicholas Longworth the governorship of Ohio. Haughty Alice told him, "We do not accept favors from crooks." In 1914, when Harding came to Washington as senator, the Longworths welcomed the Hardings by entertaining them in their home, but Alice would never visit the Hardings' Wyoming Avenue home.

After the split, Harding worked for unity in the Ohio Republican party and for Taft's reelection. He won the Ohio State convention's endorsement of Taft in July after a masterful unity speech. Harding discouraged overtures for another race for governor for himself. After Progressive defections and a purge by Daugherty, Taft ran second instead of third to Woodrow Wilson in Ohio. While Harding was more popular, a better speaker, and more persuasive with voters and party leaders, Daugherty was a more skillful administrator and boss.

Harding, depressed after the Wilson victory, failed to get a diplomatic post as a reward for his work for Taft. With Wilson in the White House, Dayton newspaper editor James Cox in the statehouse, and Democrat Attlee Pomerene as the legislature's choice for United States senator, no political office at the time seemed attainable. His *Marion Star* editorials predicted a major depression resulting from President Wilson's support of the Underwood Tariff with its low rates.[5]

This severe gloom did not prevent Harding from planning a political comeback.

Unlike Daugherty, the harmonizer believed that dissidents should be appeased, not threatened. He was tolerant of Progressives as well as fellow conservatives.

HARDING STAGES A COMEBACK

By 1914 progressivism was losing its attraction. Voters appeared tired of reform. To take advantage of the new mood, a reunion banquet was planned by both factions of the Ohio Republican party in February. Harding and Daugherty represented the Regulars and Dan Hanna and David Massie the Progressives on the reception committee.

Harding's comeback strategy was to await the party leaders' call to become sole Republican nominee for the 1914 senate race. But Senator Burton and former Senator Foraker threatened this "above-the-fray" stance. Harding, in an editorial, termed Burton a "scholarly, Christian man," but said that he "does not appeal to popular acclaim." Both factions opposed Burton because of his support for the Payne-Aldrich Tariff and for President Wilson in the Panama Canal Tolls controversy. Burton offered to step aside. Daugherty, notified of this, alerted Harding, but Foraker, still hoping to vindicate himself, could not be persuaded to withdraw. Party leaders, afraid that Foraker would win in the primaries, called Harding to Cleveland. Harding had kept hoping that Foraker would come to his senses and realize that his record would defeat him in November and therefore withdraw from the race. In Cleveland, the Big Four of 1914, Burton, Hanna, Daugherty, and Maurice Maschke, convinced Harding that he must enter the race. After the votes were counted, leaders were impressed that Harding not only won but made a good showing all over the state.

THE SENATOR FROM OHIO

In 1915 the freshman senator from Ohio was determined to keep his position secure both in Ohio and Washington. Only thus would still another term and perhaps the presidency become available. Harding's strategy was to exchange favors with his colleagues, to be genial and friendly to them and others, to use "glittering generalities" in his public speeches, and, as usual, to promote harmony and to keep in constant contact with his political sponsors, helpers, and voters. The man may not have been deeply informed about national issues, but he was a real pro in the game of politics.

Writers have cited Senator Harding's rather barren legislative record between 1914 and 1920. Frederick Lewis Allen noted "pure vote bait bills" sponsored to please constituents and said that such bills were far more frequently introduced by Harding than were prospective measures for the "public good." Despite his mediocre Senate record, Harding enjoyed his years there. What he later called the White House—that is, "a prison"—he never would have called the Senate. Samuel Hopkins Adams described Harding's reaction to entering "the goodly fellowship of the Senate":

Sunny days now dawned for Warren G. Harding. The Senatorship answered his every ambition, every hope. Had he been permitted to retain this status following election with re-election, with his beloved Marion *Star* to retire to eventually, he would have been as fortunate and blessed an Ohioan as ever rose above his capacities or expectations. . . . Warren G. Harding would have lived and died, unnoted, leaving just another group of entries as just another senator in the forgotten pages of . . . the *Congressional Record.*[6]

However, fate decreed otherwise. War had broken out in Europe and there was revolution in Mexico. Next to Harding in the United States Senate sat Republican Albert Fall. A colorful Westerner elected in 1912 after New Mexico became a state, Fall had prospected in his youth, later become a rancher and "gunfighter politician," and had invested in mines in Mexico and studied Mexican law. Though Harding knew little about mines, both were disturbed by American investments being confiscated by revolutionaries. Fall impressed Harding as well as other senators.

After the 1914 campaign, Harding visited his friend Frank Edgar Scobey in Texas, the West Coast, and Hawaii. In Hawaii he met and was shown around the islands by naval officer Charles Forbes, who gave the Hardings a jolly good time. Unfortunately, Harding did not size up either Forbes' or Fall's characters. They later were among friends in Harding's administration who "let him down."

THE GOP UNIFIES BEHIND HUGHES

In April 1916 Harding was chosen to serve as keynote speaker and chairman of the 1916 National Convention to be held in June. His role was to promote unity between Regulars and Progressives. The Progressive party was holding its convention in Chicago; Harding played a conciliatory role as both the GOP and Progressives negotiated. The Regulars nominated Charles Evans Hughes, former governor of New York and justice of the United States Supreme Court. Hughes, once opposed by Theodore Roosevelt, won his support after the convention and had been in the "Wisconsin Idea" movement. The Progressives, on hearing of Roosevelt's refusal to run, "licked their wounds" and returned to the fold and the campaign for Hughes.

After the convention, Harding wrote TR applauding his support of Hughes. Roosevelt's reply included an invitation to visit him at Oyster Bay. Harding was impressed, on that visit, with his understanding of the members of the Senate and came away feeling that TR hoped to run in 1920.

Harding felt that Wilson's endorsement of the eight-hour day was an important factor in his carrying Ohio. He wrote Scobey that he meant to translate the people's wish for an eight-hour day into reality but was still disturbed by "labor agitators."

Harding's convention prominence and wide campaigning in 1916 had made him recognized in Republican circles as "a big Republican." He was viewed as less rigid than Hughes; handsome Harding looked like a president, voters felt, but he acted like a human being and fellow Republican. He was being promoted as a future presidential candidate as early as 1914 by a neighbor, George Christian, Sr., as well as by other Ohio notables such as Malcolm Jennings and Harry Daugherty.

Ohio has a large German-American segment, especially in Cincinnati. Harding had soft-pedaled the European war and courted the German-American voters. His friend Carrie Phillips had undiplomatically championed Germany after a trip abroad. Though locally there was some gossip in Marion about the Harding-Phillips relationship, they kept their affair secret enough so that it was not revealed publicly until many years after his death when her letters were found. However, there can be no doubt that her devotion to Germany and the Ohio German-American voters influenced Harding's thinking on the war.

Harding felt that Wilson was a hypocrite, and the senator viewed American entry into the war as a fight for American rights rather than a war for world democracy. He viewed Wilson's Fourteen Points proposal for lowering tariffs as an attack on Americanism, socialistic, and therefore anarchistic. Harding called Wilson a "Presbyterian Priest" who saw morality first and America as its servant.

REACTION TO U-BOAT OFFENSIVE

Harding's war position was more representative of the views of the average American in 1918. Only when U-boats attacked American ships did Harding and most Americans opt for war. Then he considered the national honor was at stake and voted for war so that the "maddened power seeking to dominate the earth" might be destroyed.

Harding supported Roosevelt's wish to lead an American division in Europe by proposing an amendment to the Senate army bill allowing him to raise a division. The bill was amended to give the president this authority; Wilson of course, never allowed it, but TR was grateful.

All his life, according to Downes, Harding believed Democrats to be bunglers, depression creators, demagogues, place hunters, and incapable of living up to the responsibilities of power. He found the Republican senators united, patriotic, capable, and businesslike. As a Commerce Committee member he demanded an inquiry into the Shipping Board to find reasons for the lack of necessary ships and other alleged inefficiencies. In an influential speech in 1918 to the National Security League, he found America "adrift to a socialist state" and warned, "Bolsheviki are getting stronger in America every day."

By 1917 Harding found it necessary to mend fences in Ohio, particularly regarding the Prohibition Amendment. He sought to buttress party support in Ohio by following the pattern of Will Hays, National Committee chairman in 1918, who had developed county and congressional district advisory committees. Harding and Daugherty differed on tactics to reconcile "wets" and "drys" in the party as well as on the woman suffrage plank. But Daugherty felt that victories achieved at the August 1918 state convention and in the November elections had cleared the way for support for harmonizer Harding to run for president in 1920.[7]

Harding was upset by Daugherty's convention tactics and by the end of 1918 had temporarily given up his push for an active advisory committee. War problems in the Senate had changed to those of peace after the November 11, 1918, armistice.

While the war was in progress, Harding was involved in another "illicit" romance. A young Marion doctor's daughter, Nan Britton, who had a high school girl's crush on the handsome Marion editor, in 1917 wrote the senator asking for a recommendation for a secretarial job. He, remembering her beauty, suggested a New York City meeting. The story of their romance is told, as Nan viewed it, in *The President's Daughter*, published in 1927.

TR'S DEATH CHANGES OUTLOOK

In 1918, in Ohio, even Old Guard Republicans talked of TR for president and Harding for vice president in 1920. Again fate suddenly changed the planning. On January 6, 1919, the beloved Progressive leader and former Rough Rider died. Immediately there was talk of Harding or General Leonard Wood for the presidency in 1920. Harding's harmonizer role was beginning to pay off. All factions of the party felt that he was straight on the leading issues, Prohibition and woman suffrage. At the January 15 State Central Committee meeting, Harding finally got the advisory committee revived, and Daugherty acquiesced and was given a place on it. George Clark was appointed chairman. Harding and Clark got Dan Hanna's support. Daugherty and Harding became a team. Daugherty was the astute politician; Clark the glad hander; Harding the masterminder. During most of 1919, however, Harding did not intend to run for the presidency. He enjoyed being a senator too much, and the strain and worries of the presidential office did not appeal to the poker-playing, golf-playing, playing-around-with-Nan man. After the Toledo Lincoln Day banquet, he told Charles E. Hard on the train that he was not a candidate; Hard argued that Harding "owed it to the State and party." Mrs. Harding was against his running because of his health. She felt that it would be a tragedy for both of them.[8]

"In the summer of 1919," Daugherty wrote in his *Inside Tragedy,* he believed "the hour had struck" and he "should at once enter the race and we should organize our forces." He met in Washington with Mrs. Harding, who noted the impact of the presidency on Wilson. "The office is killing him," she said. "I've a presentiment against this thing. Don't ask him to run." Daugherty continued:

I spent three days in Washington talking with Harding and his friends. He received an invitation to speak to the Ohio Society in New York. I saw an opportunity for him to test his strength. I suggested before he made a decision on running to make several speeches in Ohio. He did. Then he came to my house in Columbus and we talked for six hours. . . . I felt neither Wood nor Lowden could win. "The people are sick of war and won't vote for a General and Lowden's a nice man but he's too rich, married to Pullman's daughter." "They'll fight each other to a deadlock. Hiram Johnson hasn't been forgiven for Hughes' defeat in California." Harding asked if he was "big enough." I told him "every day garden variety of man is the prime force that makes our nation great," "truest greatness lies in being kind." He said "you know better than any man in the world." I told him "I'm not presuming to decide—it's up to you but I believe we can win the nomination. They must name a candidate who can carry Ohio. This year, our state will be the battleground. Governor Cox is a formidable candidate for the Democratic nomination. You can beat him." Harding was silent a long time, "had a gift of silence and used it often." Then, "all right, I'll make the race," he said.

In the Senate Harding blasted Wilson's Fourteen Points, said that Wilson betrayed the war-built Merchant Marine, criticized Wilson's secrecy at the Paris Peace Conference, and in March signed a round robin statement of thirty-three Republican senators opposing the League Covenant. He saw the League as a war promoter, not a war preventer. Harding's feelings of political nationalism were stronger than his feelings of moral responsibility. He soon approved of Elihu Root's plan for a League with reservations and was chosen by Senator Henry Cabot Lodge to take part in the Foreign Relations Committee's hearings on the Wilson League. He could only see the League as a patriot, as an America Firster.

Harding's most significant part in the committee hearings occurred in an encounter with Wilson in the White House conference over the question of the moral nature of the League's influence. Harding asked, "If the League is nothing more than a moral obligation, what avails Articles 10 and 11?" Wilson, shocked, replied, "If we understand an obligation we are bound . . . to carry it out." Harding was silent. His role in shaping the Lodge reservations was minor, but his role in publicizing them was major. He was the keynote speaker in Senate consideration of the League with the Lodge reservations. The substance of his speech was: without reservations, the League was "unthinkable"; with them, it would be a framework on which to build intelligent cooperation; the president had made mistakes at Paris. By November 19, both the Wilson League and the League with reservations were defeated in the Senate. Harding saw this action as overthrowing the president's "dictatorship."

The Harding team's strategy back in Ohio, meanwhile, was to promote Harding as a leading second choice candidate at the convention and first choice of the Ohio delegation. Daugherty's strategy was to start the boom slowly and increase it with publicity to reach the pinnacle just before the convention. He felt that General Wood had "peaked" his campaign too soon. Wood disregarded custom and entered the Ohio primary, winning eight delegates. In the meantime, Senator William E. Borah, an ally, had begun a Senate investigation of Wood's and Lowden's campaign finances.

On the verge of defeat in the Indiana primary, the only one he had entered, Harding was about to pick up the phone and announce his withdrawal when his strong-willed wife, who originally had to be persuaded by Daugherty to consent to her husband's entering the race, grabbed the phone and said something to the effect that "you cannot let your friends down now after all they have done."[9]

Although Harding was not nationally known by the common people at the time the convention in Chicago opened, as a result of his summer Chautauqua speeches, his Senate term, his nomination of Taft in 1912, and his 1916 keynote speech, he was acquainted with many people outside Ohio and with business, newspaper, and political leaders. Thus he was considered more than the usual "favorite son" candidate.

Daugherty angled for second choice pledges and sometimes third or fourth choice pledges from delegates. He foresaw a deadlock between Wood and Lowden; his strategy worked. His astute planning before and during the convention, rather than the much publicized "smoke filled room" myth, accounts for Harding's being chosen by the hot, weary delegates.

On May 14, Harding gave his famous "Back to Normal" speech:

America's present need is not heroics, but healing; not nostrums, but normalcy; not revolution, but restoration; not agitation, but adjustment; not revolution, but restoration; not surgery, but serenity; not the dramatic, but the dispassionate; not experiment, but equipoise; not submergence in nationality, but sustainment in triumphant nationality.

Lowden's and Harding's managers coordinated strategy. Daugherty's plan was to loan Lowden some of his pledges until Lowden passed Wood in the balloting. Then, as loaned pledges were called in, Harding's strength would rise and, it was hoped, Wood delegates would change to Harding instead of Lowden. In a speech to Johnson delegates, Borah denounced Wood's and Lowden's use of money in the primaries, and fear developed of another Republican split occurring if either Wood or Lowden were nominated.[10]

The scandal-scared delegates did not move toward the deadlocked contenders. That Friday evening, in the Hays–George Harvey suite of the Blackstone Hotel, Room 404, senators came and went and discussed the situation without agreement. No doubt before 2:11 A.M. the room was filled with smoke and there was talk of the chances of the candidates' being nominated. Harding's speaking and harmonizing ability as well as his party faithfulness over the years may have been weighed; Harvey may have heard rumors about Carrie and Nan and even possibly Elizabeth Ann (the alleged daughter of Harding and Nan Britton) and may have asked Harding if there was anything in his past to prevent his accepting the nomination, but no consensus was reached and no plan for nominating him was formulated.

Daugherty had one fear constantly on his mind—treachery from the Cincinnati organization. Harding refused to believe that the Cincinnati boss, Richard (Rud) Hynicka, would let him down, but he did not have enough faith in his winning to let the Senate filing deadline pass without filing for reelection. That night, late, he called in his intention to seek his Senate seat again. Daugherty kept his promise not to withdraw his loaned pledges, and on the fifth ballot Lowden passed Wood.

The betrayal did materialize, but it boomeranged and strengthened Harding with the other delegates. By the seventh ballot, Harding's total was 100. Missouri switched its vote to Harding, and he now passed Hiram Johnson. The Wood forces, seeing the lead slip away, panicked. The time had come to draw in all the pledged votes, which Daugherty proceeded to do. Alvin Hert of Kentucky, Lowden's floor manager, realized that a stop-Harding move was necessary and moved for a recess until 4 o'clock. The Harding forces did not want a recess. Delegate Frank B. Willis ran to the platform protesting when Lodge declared that a voice vote of the delegates carried. Daugherty shouted at Lodge: "You can't beat this man by any such tactics. You ought to be ashamed of yourself. This is an outrage." Herrick also protested. Lodge said that a recess might be beneficial to Harding. Daugherty did not think so, but he sent his forces to the delegates to urge them to vote for Harding on the next ballot. Lodge told Daugherty before he left the hall that they were planning on offering Johnson the vice presidency and swinging his stubborn followers over to Harding in order to obtain a unified party. Daugherty warned Lodge that Johnson would insult the messengers. During the recess, Boise Penrose, from his sickbed in Philadelphia, called and told Daugherty he was going to come out in favor of Harding. Daugherty, fearing that the press would headline the message "Boss Nominates Harding" and ruin Harding's chances, told Penrose that he had taken down the message and would release it when it seemed the right time. He kept the message until after Harding was nominated.

During the recess, Lowden and Wood took a taxi ride, and each tried to persuade the other to withdraw in return for getting the nomination for vice president. Neither would give in, and all they could agree on was to try to get an adjournment until Monday. During the discussion, Lowden revealed to Wood that it had been arranged that if he lost he would throw his support to Harding. Later, Will Hays came to Lowden's room, and there was talk of throwing their joint support to Hays. George Harvey then got J. Henry Rorabeck and James Walsh of Connecticut to come to Room 404 and told them that 600 delegates had been pledged to Hays, and therefore Harvey wanted Rorabeck to get his Connecticut delegates to switch and start a stampede for Hays. Rorabeck said that he had to refuse, as Harding was Connecticut's pledged second choice. It had been arranged for Lowden and Harding to meet, but when Daugherty got to Lowden's headquarters, Lowden had left for the coliseum to withdraw his name while he was still ahead, and Harding had not arrived. Daugherty talked to a Lowden assistant who said, "We had played the game with them and they would play square with us." Daugherty then sent word to Lodge that he would be late and requested the courtesy of delaying the reconvening until he could arrive, as he was confident Harding would be nominated. Lodge delayed, though the delegates were getting restless, while Daugherty found Harding and they found Lowden. Lowden told them he had released his delegates and congratulated Harding on his coming nomination.

As the balloting moved to a climax, Daugherty, realizing that Mrs. Harding had a weak heart and, feeling that she ought to be prepared for the outcome, went up to her in the gallery and told her to expect her husband to be nominated on the next ballot. She had her hat pins in her hand and in her excitement jabbed them into Daugherty. He thought his lung was punctured, left her, and listened in a daze to the roll call of the tenth ballot. In the moment of victory for which he had worked so long, he thought he was bleeding to death. He discovered later that he was just perspiring from the shock and Harding had won by 692½ votes. Calvin Coolidge was quickly nominated for vice president, a surprise even to the leaders who had contacted Irvine Lenroot of Wisconsin.

FRONT PORCH TACTICS PLANNED

Although Robert La Follette had refused to make Harding's nomination unanimous, and a small group of Progressive leaders had talked sadly together after the convention about their waning cause, the Progressives did not bolt.

Harding's acceptance, following Lodge's notification speech on July 22, was basically filled with the same viewpoints he had given many, many times. He declared, "We stabilize and strive for normalcy." He concluded eloquently: "Have confidence in the Republic! America will go on."

By various pamphlets, newspaper articles, pictures, and billboards, Harding's handsome appearance and affability were emphasized and contrasted to Wilson's austerity and remoteness. The campaign strategy was to associate Progressive governor James Cox, also from Ohio and nominated by the Democrats two weeks after Harding, with idealistic and autocratic Wilson and his unrealistic League. Judson Welliver depicted Cox as a "puppet" of Wilson and a "boss," while cartoonist Charles A. Reid identified him as a "bogeyman." To enhance Harding's folksy image, his hometown Marion, his Mt. Vernon Avenue home, his neighbors and town folk, and his wife and father were publicized. Harding masterfully evaded specifics on issues.

Henry C. Wallace, editor of *Wallace's Farmer*, had been suggested as knowing the farm situation. Harding depended on him and Hubert Work of the National Committee's farm division for statements on farm problems. Harding was familiar with family farming in Ohio, of course, but knew little about problems of the farm belt related to conversion from war to peace. Harding needed no image build-up as a friend of business and management, but this was not true regarding the laboring man. The unions, especially the American Federation of Labor, opposed the businessman's "darling." Harding seemed oppressed with suspicion and distrust of the labor movements. The antiforeign, "red scare" atmosphere of 1919 and 1920 affected his thinking. More than half of his front-porch Acceptance Address was devoted to words of calm and assurance for the

American economy. He aimed to harmonize capital and labor by promoting mutual understanding of the problems of each. He emphasized the Esch-Cummins Act as labor's "Bill of Rights" and used his Tariff Americanism. Labor must accompany an increase in wages with an increase of production. Harding differed with the platform's internationalist trade provisions. In response to the American Tariff League, by the end of the campaign he had committed his party to restoring high tariffs. Downes felt that Harding's tariff views set the pace for a superprotective pattern of legislation for the entire decade. Harding must therefore be given a large share of the blame for the domestic and European financial collapse of 1929. To combat Harding's efforts to build a prolabor image for him, the newly created National Non-Partisan Political Campaign Committee of Samuel Gompers and the American Federation of Labor attacked the Republican platform, Harding, and the Esch-Cummins Act with its antistrike implications. Conservatives in the business world liked Harding's bearing down hard on the excess-profits tax, his support of a national budget bureau, and advocacy of businesslike reorganization of federal administrative machinery.

Herbert Hoover, shocked by Harding's failure to contradict Hiram Johnson's isolationism, wrote Harding that the "majority of Californians are for 'a' League and unless Johnson's interpretations are rejected, many will vote for Cox."

JOHNSON STIRS CONTROVERSY

Johnson then ruffled the waters with an eastern "anti–any-League" tour; internationalists, including Hoover, Henry Stimson, and Speaker Frederick Gillett, became alarmed that liberal Republicans would vote for Cox. On October 5, Elihu Root's "Appeal of the 31 Eminent Americans" was released and promptly denounced by Johnson. Hays' advisory committee, however, revised the platform plank to word it more strongly. Arthur Brisbane and future Secretary of Labor James Davis did not calm the waters by their rather crude anti-League material. Harding, however, was able to.

At a Colored Voters Day at Marion on September 10 General John Pershing praised the Negroes for their wartime service and Mrs. Lethia Fleming of Ohio spoke for the Negro women. Then, in fatherly fashion, Harding praised them for their restraint under provocation and cited their great gains, but said that continued progress was possible only in a "land of ordered freedom and opportunity such as in America." On October 9, in Oklahoma City, Harding was asked for his views on segregation. He answered that he favored "race equality before the law." He added, "I do not mean white people and black people shall be forced to associate together." The Southerners were pleased but not the militant leaders. Democrats charged that the Republicans were endangering "white supremacy."

In the last week of the campaign, anonymous circulars by the millions charged that there was Negro blood in Harding's ancestry. A family tree, researched by Wooster College history professor William Chancellor, was in the circulars.

Both parties denied the charges, but newspapers headlined it; Harding publicly ignored it. Daugherty said that Harding was furious with him after seeing a copy of Cox's journal with a front page denial of the slander. Harding thought that Daugherty had ordered this printed and felt that the denial would only bring the slander to the attention of more people. Later Daugherty, in no way responsible but concerned, told an angry Edward McLean, a Washington and Cincinnati publisher, that he expected that the charge would boomerang and Harding would win handily. He did. He won 60 percent of the popular vote and 404 of the electoral votes.

Up to Harding's presidency, there is no evidence of his being involved in corruption except for the collusion of Marion editors in upping "the cost of printing and dividing the profit." Daugherty indicated that Harding liked to bet with friends and accepted the established boss system, but there is no evidence that Harding ever bought votes or took money from corporations at any stage of his career.

NARROW BRUSH WITH DEATH

Election day had been a memorable one. After golfing in Columbus, having a near miss with death when returning to Marion as his chauffeured car slipped on the rain-slick road and nearly overturned, and sharing his fifty-fifth birthday with his father, wife and Daugherty, Harding received wired reports in the George Christian home nearby of his election as president. He had been chosen by a vote of 16,189,289 to 9,141,750 for Cox.[11] From little Blooming Grove to the White House! Horatio Alger couldn't top this!

Harding and his wife went on a postcampaign vacation trip to visit friends Scobey and Fall in the Southwest and tour Panama. Returning on December 5 to Marion, as he had proclaimed he would, Harding consulted "the best minds" of his party on cabinet selection. The president-elect announced these criteria:

Three things are to be considered. . . . First, there is the man's qualifications for public service. That is the most important consideration of all. Second, there is the attitude of the public concerning the man under consideration. Third, there is the political consideration. As to that—well. This is going to be a Republican Cabinet.

A great deluge of politicians, including hopefuls for appointment, visited the Mt. Vernon Avenue home. Reporters termed Marion the "Great Listening Post." Harding, with some trepidation and awe from his youth about the presidency, sifted the opinions of Old Guard pros, his Senate cronies, his National Advisory Committee, the returned Progressives, and even the visiting Democrats. At times his close advisers, Daugherty, Charles Hilles, and Senators Joseph Freelinghuysen, Harry New, and Frank Brandegee were asked to screen potential candidates. Although he consulted with his running mate, Harding found that "Silent Cal" was of only "minimal help." The president-elect rapidly discovered differences over cabinet choices among the "best minds" but, worse yet, he came to realize that "intrigues and cabals designed to sway him" were operating.

Murray feels that Harding soon was convinced that (1) "the Secretary of State had to be a man universally respected by the country, yet able to work with all elements in Congress"—Hughes was chosen. (2) "The Secretary of Agriculture should be a practical farmer and not merely a professor of farming or an agricultural lobbyist"—Wallace, who had only farmed five years but had taught and was a nationally recognized farm editor and expert, was chosen. (3) "The Labor post should go to someone identified with labor, possibly a union member, but not of the radical element." After "adverse reports" about T. V. O'Connor, organized labor's choice, and James Duncan, favored by Sam Gompers, Harding finally chose lodge brother James Davis, who was anti-Gompers, a hard working party man, and a staunch backer. (4) The Treasury position should be filled from the Middle West and not New York or the Northeast—Harding wanted McKinleyite Charles Dawes, American Expeditionary Force commander and Chicago financier; but to still the Old Guard opposition to having Hoover in the cabinet, he compromised on Andrew Mellon, a wealthy man but of high integrity, though backed by Penrose and Philander Knox. Hoover then was offered his desired position—Commerce. Dawes later became budget director.

Harding also thought that "one or two" places should be given "to his friends" as a source of personal advice and loyalty. The irony is that they, not the other members, let him down. Despite opposition to Daugherty, Harding in gratitude appointed him attorney general. The Interior post traditionally went to a Westerner. Westerners were known for being anti-conservation. Harding no doubt had some idea of Fall's views on private and public land use. He admired Fall's vibrant personality and his knowledge of the Southwest and Mexico. So did most senators.

As usual, the chairman of the National Committee was offered the postmaster generalship, and Hays accepted it. Former Senator John Weeks, championed by Lodge for the cabinet, was offered the War post. Both Weeks and Lowden had suggested former serviceman Edwin Denby for Navy. Denby had gone to Detroit and made millions in autos. When Harding, at the last minute, offered him the post, he was amazed, but accepted.

Although Harding's friend Scobey became director of the Mint; neighbor George Christian, Jr., his personal secretary; his former missionary brother-in-law Heber Votaw, Superintendent of Prisons; Mrs. Harding's doctor, Charles Sawyer, White House physician; and Caledonian "chum," Marion lawyer, and local Democratic politician Daniel Crissinger, Comptroller of the Currency, no taint of corruption, only charges of lack of skill, fell on them.

NOT USED TO NATIONAL AFFAIRS

Not only overworked legalist Daugherty, but also the overworked chief executive should have checked more on the people serving under them. The pressure of Ohioans made Daugherty call his Washington Court House helper and book-keeper, Jess Smith, to his aid in dealing with the less influential seekers. Much of the scandal, except for the Charles R. Forbes and Fall actions, was caused by lack of skill and judgment rather than intentional wrongdoing. Harding, his cabinet, his ambassadors, and their assistants were accustomed to dealing with specific local, district, party, and state problems; they were not trained in exe-cuting national or international affairs, and with the massive problems suddenly thrust upon them they found themselves in too deep water in the "big league" arena of sophisticated Washington.

As Harding took the oath of office on March 4, 1921, his hand was on the Bible, opened to his favorite passage: "What doth the Lord require of thee but to do justly, to love mercy and to walk humbly with thy God." How differently the president's life and, indeed, American history would have been if he had taken this passage and not only the "faith of our fathers" but also of his beloved mother more seriously.

In his inaugural, Harding said, "We have seen a world passion spend its fury but we contemplate our Republic unshaken." "We crave friendship and harbor no hate." Even so, he declared, "America can enter into no political commit-ments." While not mentioning the League of Nations, he said, "We are ready to associate ourselves with the nations of the world . . . for conferences, for counsel . . . to recommend a way to approximate disarmament . . . suggesting plans for mediation, conciliation and arbitration" and to "establish a world court for the disposition of . . . justiciable questions."[12]

In his last speech, handed to the press two days before his death, the president declared that his administration had always sought to achieve four goals in foreign policy:

First—the re-establishment of peace with the Central Powers, and the orderly settlement of those after problems of war which directly involved the United States. Second—the protection and promotion, amid the conflict of national interests, of the just rights of the United States and the legitimate interests of American citizens. Third—the creation of an international situation, so far as the United States might contribute thereto, which would give the best assurances of peace for the future. Fourth—the pursuit of the traditional American policy of friendly cooperation with our sister republics of the Western Hem-isphere.

To go "from destruction to production" was more on the newly inaugurated president's mind than his proclaimed "association of nations." He declared, "We can reduce the abnormal expenditures and we will. . . . Our most dangerous tendency is to expect too much of government and at the same time to do for it too little." John F. Kennedy, a serious student of history, conveyed a similar thought in the familiar line, "Ask not what your country can do for you but what you can do for your country."

The really catchy domestic phrases in Harding's address were: "Strive for normalcy to reach stability . . . trade restoration . . . administrative efficiency . . . lightened tax burdens . . . industrial peace . . . sound commercial practices and adequate credit facilities'' and ''common welfare and service.''

After the inauguration, pressure by the ''Irreconcilables'' continued. Harding, to divert attention from rumors that he would send Root to Europe on a mission to lay groundwork for his pledged ''Association,'' announced that the March 18 cabinet meeting had dealt with pressing domestic problems. A French mission to Washington, prompted by disappointment at Harding's not mentioning the Allies in his inaugural, was promised by Harding that the Knox resolution for a separate peace with Germany would not be pushed. Hughes announced that America deplored German defiance of the Treaty of Versailles, but the mission was clearly told that an ''Association'' was not in the immediate offing.

The March Senate debates were so anti-League that Harding was emboldened to declare to the Special Session of Congress in April that ''in the existing League . . . this Republic will have no part.'' But, he said, ''we pledge our efforts'' toward an ''Association,'' and ''the pledge will be faithfully kept.'' He rejected the Knox resolution, suggesting a settlement by working with the Allies through the Treaty of Versailles minus the League covenant. The Irreconcilables were bothered by this last statement and by the appointment of Americans to the Allied Peace Council, the Council of Ambassadors, and the Reparation Commission. On May 19 George Harvey, ambassador to England, declared at the Pilgrim's Day dinner that Americans wanted nothing to do with the League and told his audience, including the British prime minister, that America had sent its manhood to Europe solely to save the United States.[13] Hughes was dismayed, but Harding privately and publicly praised his speech.

A study of the Harding Papers reveals the almost step-by-step influence that Hughes exercised on Harding—first, silence toward the League; next, cautious probing followed by open contact with it; then the proposals for the Washington Naval Conference, an Association of Nations, and finally the World Court. Harding's awe of Hughes changed to friendship as a result of their working together on world issues. His personal world views were modified not only by Hughes but also by the internationally minded Hoover. They were not, however, altered significantly.

In July Congress cancelled the Declaration of War of 1917. Harding created an uproar when he signed the joint resolution between rounds of golf.

Borah had resolved that a disarmament conference be held. Hoover in May had brought up the idea in the cabinet; Harding, though a big navy man, realized the strength of the sentiment for disarmament around the country and also that the Anglo-Japanese Alliance would soon be up for renewal. Since disarmament was historically accepted and the League was not, nor had his pledged ''Association'' been, Harding and Hughes decided before naval rivalry began in earnest to call a disarmament conference in Washington. Preliminary planning with world leaders started in the summer.

On November 12, 1921, Harding, deeply moved by the burial of the Unknown Soldier at Arlington the day before, opened the Naval Conference thus:

Here in the United States we are but freshly turned from the burial of an unknown American soldier, when a nation sorrowed while paying him tribute. Whether it was spoken or not, a hundred million of our people were summarizing the inexcusable causes, the incalculable cost, the unspeakable sacrifices, and the unutterable sorrows, and there was the ever impelling question: How can humanity justify or God forgive? Human hate demands no such toll; ambition and greed must be denied it. If misunderstanding must take the blame, then let us banish it.

Enthusiastic applause by the audience and approving handshakes of the delegates followed. Historically, this seems to be Harding's "finest hour."

Next Hughes shocked the delegates by his proposal of a world moratorium on naval ship building. From November to February, delegates worked on disarmament, ratios of comparative naval strength, and Pacific and Far Eastern problems. At Harding's suggestion that "secret diplomacy" be avoided, seven public sessions were held. Three treaties resulted. The Five Power Treaty with a ratio of 5:5:3:1.75:1.75 gave the United States parity with Great Britain provided for scrapping vessels down to the ratio, and a ten-year moratorium on capital ship building. The Four Power Treaty supplanted the Anglo-Japanese Alliance; it bound the Pacific powers to respect each other's rights and to adjust differences. The Nine Power Treaty approved of the Chinese "Open Door" policy. With Lodge, having been a delegate, backing the treaties in the Senate, all three were ratified after considerable opposition from the isolationists.[14] No "Association," as hoped for by many pro-Leaguers, however, materialized.

Harding, though abiding by the treaties he had supported, with the backing of Denby, Theodore Roosevelt, Jr., and Sinclair Weeks, resisted huge military cuts and advocated air power and a Pacific Fleet with a strong storage base at Pearl Harbor.

As the research into Harding's foreign policy progressed from postwar problems to Hemispheric ones, especially the results of the Mexican Revolution and the recognition issue, the idea occurred to this researcher that there was a link between Harding's continuing Wilson's nonrecognition policy and the later "oil" scandals. Further research links Fall's need for more funds to his losses in investments in Mexico as a result of the confiscation, by the revolutionary government, of foreign investors' lands, and also widens Edwin Doheny's involvement. Doheny held oil reserves not only in the United States but also in Mexican lands by his Palomas Land and Cattle company, for which he testified that he, according to his memory, paid William McAdoo $250,000 to represent his interests. Much has been made of how his testimony spoiled Wilson's son-in-law's chances for the Democratic presidential nomination in 1924, but little has been said of how his testimony showed a reason for Fall's opposition to the recognition of Mexico without American investors getting compensation for their investments there.

The youthful prospecting together of Fall and Doheny may account for Doheny having been willing to loan Fall $100,000 to pay his back taxes and buy a neighbor's ranch to get the source of Three Rivers' water for his stock. Friendship may even explain why Fall gave him preferential rights in the naval oil reserve in Elk Hills, partly in July 1921, and more later. Why Fall, unless he feared public criticism, or felt guilty, kept the leases secret and lied—saying in the investigation that he had gotten a loan from Ned McLean (which Thomas Walsh, chief Senate investigator, found to be untrue after going all the way to Florida for an interview with the ailing McLean) and putting his personal aggrandizement above his character and his public services—is not clear. Wealth and power seem to have engulfed him. Harry Sinclair's and Doheny's successes loomed before him, and "Seward's Icebox" beckoned him so much that he kept trying to influence Harding to consider the bountiful resources of forest, coal, and oil in Alaska.

It seems now that Harding's trip there, which had been postponed from the summer of 1922 because of the railroad strike, may originally have been planned as a result of Fall's wanting private development of Alaska. A controversy arose over conserving or using resources; Fall wanted the Division of Forestry transferred to his Department of the Interior, and Wallace threatened to resign if that happened.

Denby, not as alert as Wallace, had unwittingly consented to having the naval oil reserves transferred to Fall's department.[15] Wallace's, and Hughes' growing influence on Harding and public pressure for the recognition of Mexico resulted in Fall's decline in influence in the cabinet and perhaps his resignation, and Harding's suggestion to Hughes that negotiations for Mexican recognition be started. The United States and Mexico were in the midst of conferring at the time of Harding's death.

That Theodore Roosevelt, Jr., took the conference result to Harding for the transfer of the naval oil reserves to former Rough Rider Fall's department may have been the reason the president saw no need to consult Daugherty about the transfer's legality (later questioned). That TR, Jr., also defended Fall before Harry A. Slattery seeking information on the rumors that the Forest Service was going to be transferred seems to indicate that the son absorbed the father's military love but not TR's "saving the forest" dedication.

Harding's awe for "great personages" and their families, for "magnates" of business as well as for "great minds," influenced many of his actions. Neither the personages nor the magnates and only to a small degree the great minds understood the complexities of the tremendous economic and moral world problems. Small wonder they failed to cope with them.

The awe he felt for the presidency was only great enough to make him try to be the "best loved" president, not to make him try to be a shining example to his countrymen. Having chosen the great minds, he considered them the experts, listened to their reports and suggestions, and usually approved their actions. When the great minds did not agree and infighting developed, as especially in the Hoover-Wallace jurisdictional dispute, Harding, failing sometimes to restore harmony by his friendly, conciliatory manner, at least succeeded in cooling their tempers and keeping them working.

NARROWNESS UNDERMINES HARDING

Narrowness of purpose, selfishness, and greed undermined not only the Harding administration but the whole Republican decade. Wallace, although a dedicated worker, was almost solely concerned with the farmers' welfare. Mellon, although the Prohibition Bureau and the Veterans' Bureau were also under his jurisdiction, concentrated mainly on tax cuts, tariffs adjustment, and high finance. Dawes, appointed director of the new Republican-created Budget Bureau, proceeded to cut the fat from expenditures, not always to the liking of the department heads, but left the bureau to an assistant after a year.

The ire of farmers, labor, and veterans was felt at the polls in the midterm 1922 election. The Republican majorities dwindled in both houses. Harding's pet project, a Merchant Marine subsidy, was defeated soon after. Representative Oscar E. Kellar, Republican of Minnesota, brought fourteen charges, including the "strong arm tactics" of FBI head William Burns, Jr., against Daugherty's administration. The investigation, because of lack of evidence, was dropped.

Harding paid lip service to the enforcement of the Eighteenth Amendment and had appointed Wayne Wheeler's choice as head of the Prohibition Bureau, but liquor permits were easily obtained, with bootlegging widespread. Neither the White House nor Washington society obeyed the law.

By January 1923, the dispensing of patronage by Daugherty, Jess Smith and Howard Mannington and the "comings and goings" in the Little House on H Street and the Manningtons' house on K Street aroused suspicion.

The strain of office and mounting criticism caused Daugherty to have a nervous breakdown and Harding to recover only slowly from a January flu attack. In February Daugherty told Harding that Dr. Sawyer had discovered that Forbes was selling government property below cost as "damaged." Harding, disbelieving, investigated and found it to be true. Daugherty said that "nothing hurt Harding so much." Harding asked "Charlie" to resign but kept his misdoings quiet. Charles Carmer, his assistant, fearful, committed suicide.

On February 24, Harding sent a message to the Senate requesting its adherence to permit the United States to join the Permanent Court of International Justice. He included a letter from Hughes containing four "reservations" in hopes of getting Senate support. Both Hughes and Harding felt the proposal to be feasible, but it revived the anti-involvement sentiment of 1919. Harding began to realize that compromise was necessary.[16]

Daugherty, recuperating, embarrassed his chief by announcing that Harding would run in 1924. A "Voyage of Understanding" was being planned for June to try to regain the confidence of the American people, but a nonpartisan tone was desired. Despite the embarrassment caused by Daugherty's announcement, Harding remained supportive of Harry.

Reports reached Harding about Jess Smith's "reputation about town." On Daugherty's return to Washington, the boss told him to get Jess out of town and that Jess could not go on the Alaskan tour as planned. Rejected, diabetic, and not fully recovered from earlier surgery, and perhaps fearful of investigation into his shady dealings, in late May he burned his papers and committed suicide. Daugherty grieved for his closest friend except Harding, and Harding felt bad about the tragedy.

As Harding left on the "Voyage," he was tense and worried, and his blood pressure was high. How much he knew or guessed about the coming oil scandal, Alien Property Custodian Thomas Miller's acceptance of bribes, and possible Smith-Daugherty profiting from dealings has not been discovered. That he was personally involved in financial wrongdoings of any great magnitude is doubtful.

In St. Louis, where intense heat exhausted him, he spoke on the World Court. He told William Allen White that "his enemies gave him little trouble. His chief worry was his friends." As the trip progressed, more speeches were added; he had trouble sleeping and relaxing; the chill of Alaska contrasted with the heat of the forty-eight states; a possible heart attack on the golf links in British Columbia was kept secret. In hot Tacoma, he felt that he could not disappoint the crowds so, though unwell, gave his speech. The ordeal was too much. Though he survived an attack and pneumonia, in the evening of August 2 in San Francisco, after Mrs. Harding finished reading him a favorable article about himself, his heart stopped. Gaston Means' book suggesting that his wife murdered him has been thoroughly discredited, and no evidence has been found to justify his charge.

The tour had heightened his popularity, and as the funeral cortege wended its way across the countryside he was truly mourned. The "great minds" had gained more influence over him the last year than the "lesser ones," but in less than a year the misdoings of the latter became public, and investigations and trials continued through the decade. Fall, Miller, and Forbes were imprisoned. Daugherty was acquitted by only one vote. Sinclair was charged only with contempt of Congress. The oil leases were finally cancelled.[17] The skill of lawyers and the views taken by juries, rather than evidence, seem to account for the different decisions.

Despite the scandals, the policies of the Harding era continued as the "great minds" became even more powerful in the Coolidge-Hoover years. Harding's image, however, was tarnished.

This researcher, in seeking the image of Harding and his administration, has combined the various schools of thought on the man, his colleagues, and his era. Despite various authors' conflicting views and lack of evidence about certain events and characters, especially his wife, it is hoped that a more perceptive and truthful image has been portrayed.

NOTES

1. Robert K. Murray, *The Harding Era 1921–1923: Warren G. Harding and His Administration* (Minneapolis: University of Minnesota Press, 1969), p. 5; Randolph C. Downes, *The Rise of Warren Gamaliel Harding, 1865–1920* (Columbus: Ohio State University Press, 1970), pp. 4–6; Francis Russell, *The Shadow of Blooming Grove* (New York: McGraw-Hill, 1968), p. 40; Murray, *The Harding Era*, p. 6; Jack Warick, *Growing Up with Warren Harding*, excerpts reprinted from his *All in a Lifetime* (1938), p. 5; Samuel Hopkins Adams, *Incredible Era* (Boston: Houghton Mifflin, 1939), p. 5; Warick, *Growing Up*, pp. 4–9; Downes, *The Rise*, p. 7; Warick, *Growing Up*, pp. 3, 4, 2.

2. Downes, *The Rise*, p. 38; Warick, *Growing Up*, pp. 29–34; Adams, *Incredible Era*, p. 35; Warick, *Growing Up*, p. 34; Adams, *Incredible Era*, pp. 11–15; Downes, *The Rise*, pp. 19–33; Warick, *Growing Up*, pp. 29–32.

3. Downes, *The Rise*, pp. 112–133. Downes' chapter agrees with this researcher's notes from the George Nash Papers, Ohio Historical Society. Downes, *The Rise*, pp. 112–117. A check of the Harding Ohio appointees of his administration reveals that the majority of them were personal and political friends, mostly hardworking and well-meaning, not used to complex problems and pressures but not malicious. Ibid. pp. 134–154; Herrick Papers, Ohio Historical Society, agree. Cottrill, *The Conciliator*, pp. 19, 20; Downes, *The Rise*, pp. 156, 157; James N. Giglio, *H. M. Daugherty and the Politics of Expediency* (Kent, Ohio: Kent State University Press, 1978), p. 34; Downes, *The Rise*, p. 167.

4. Downes, *The Rise*, pp. 162–173; Cottrill, *The Conciliator*, p. 23; Downes, *The Rise*, p. 173; Cottrill, *The Conciliator*, p. 24; Russell, *The Shadow*, p. 195; Cottrill, *The Conciliator*, p. 25; Downes, *The Rise*, pp. 174, 175–178, 179–182.

5. Giglio, *H. M. Daugherty*, pp. 42–54. The Morse Case in which Daugherty succeeded in pressuring President Taft for the pardon of convicted criminal Charles W. Morse on the untrue grounds that he was dying (Morse had convinced Daugherty and the warden of this) haunted Daugherty all of his political life. Ibid. pp. 55–60; Downes, *The Rise*, pp. 182–184, 65; Russell, *The Shadow*, p. 260; Downes, *The Rise*, pp. 186–191; Giglio, *H. M. Daugherty*, pp. 55–68; Downes, *The Rise*, p. 192; Cottrill, *The Conciliator*, p. 29; Downes, *The Rise*, pp. 192–194.

6. Cottrill, *The Conciliator*, p. 30; Downes, *The Rise*, pp. 196–211; Harlow Lindley, *Ohio in the Twentieth Century, 1900–1938*, vol. 4 of *History of the State of Ohio* (Columbus: Ohio State Archaeological and Historical Society, 1942), p. 364; Downes, *The Rise*, pp. 212–215; Adams, *Incredible Era*, pp. 86, 82.

7. Burt Noggle, *Teapot Dome* (New York: W. W. Norton and Co., 1962), pp. 8–11; Russell, *The Shadow*, pp. 255, 256; Downes, *The Rise*, pp. 217, 134, 241–247; William Henry Harbaugh, *The Life and Times of Theodore Roosevelt* (New York: Collier Books, 1961), pp. 332, 333, 456–465; Downes, *The Rise*. pp. 247–250; Russell, *The Shadow*, pp. 167–363; Downes, *The Rise*, pp. 254–276, 283–292; Daugherty, *Inside Tragedy*, pp. 10–12; Giglio, *H. M. Daugherty*, pp. 86–89.

8. Downes, *The Rise*, pp. 291–293; Russell, *The Shadow*, pp. 215, 216, 287, 288, 254, 289, 631–632, 642; Murray, *The Harding Era*, pp. 487–490. Whether Harding ever really believed the baby born to Nan in late 1919 was his (especially since Florence and he had no children, though she had a son by her first marriage and Harding was thought by physicians to be sterile) is not recorded. Though Nan lost the case to gain part of Harding's estate for her child and despite Daugherty and Scobey not believing her story,

historians as well as debunkers feel that there is enough evidence to prove that an affair somewhat similar to Nan's revelations did occur between her and Harding. (See Russell, *The Shadow*, p. 323; Murray, *The Harding Era*. pp. 489, 390; Daugherty, *Inside Tragedy*, pp. 248–251.) Russell, by the Carrie Phillips letters, proves Harding's unfaithfulness to his wife very conclusively. The fact that there are similar expressions in Nan's book, as well as the Harding family's, forcing the deletion of certain parts of Carrie's letters and allowing other parts to be printed, points to an affair.

9. Downes, *The Rise*, pp. 294–300; Daugherty, *Inside Tragedy*, pp. 130–138; Downes, *The Rise*, pp. 315–344, 345, 373–385; Daugherty, *Inside Tragedy*, pp. 20, 21; Downes, *The Rise*, pp. 346–352; Giglio, *H. M. Daugherty*, pp. 54–116; Daugherty, *Inside Tragedy*, p. 28; Downes, *The Rise*, pp. 352, 353; Daugherty, *Inside Tragedy*, pp. 26–28. Downes differs with Daugherty on who was responsible for the Borah resolution; *The Rise*, p. 407. Daugherty, *Inside Tragedy*, p. 13; Giglio, *H. M. Daugherty*, p. 103.

10. Downes, *The Rise*, pp. 355, 361–376. Since the able and respected Hughes had declined to run again when a Republican delegation asked him soon after the death of his daughter from the flu, the "Old Pros" were divided on whom to support. Hughes' loss of California and Ohio in 1916 made it more important to please those states' voters in 1920 in order to achieve victory. Russell, *The Shadow*, p. 352; Downes, *The Rise*, pp. 372–373, 412–414, 419–422, 411, 416, 108, 109, 417; Daugherty, *Inside Tragedy*, pp. 29–39.

11. Downes, *The Rise*, pp. 418, 419, 415, 416; Daugherty, *Inside Tragedy*, pp. 40–43; Downes, *The Rise*, pp. 419–422; Daugherty, *Inside Tragedy*, p. 51; Downes, *The Rise*, pp. 457–475, 475–486, 496–531, 562–598, 535–559; Daugherty, *Inside Tragedy*, pp. 51–58; Downes, *The Rise*, p. 632; Murray, *The Harding Era*, p. 66; Adams, *Incredible Era*, p. 33; Daugherty, *Inside Tragedy*, pp. 8, 61, 62; Murray, *The Harding Era*, p. 66.

12. Robert K. Murray, "President Harding and His Cabinet," *Ohio History* 75 (Spring-Summer 1966): 109, 110, 111, 112–116, 118–120; Giglio, *H. M. Daugherty*, pp. 116–122; Murray, "President Harding," p. 121; Giglio, *H. M. Daugherty*, pp. 122, 123; Murray, "President Harding," pp. 122, 117, 118, 120, 121; Murray, *The Harding Era*, pp. 134, 229–301; Daugherty, *Inside Tragedy*, pp. 63, 64; Murray, *The Harding Era*, p. 111; Inaugural Address, March 4, 1921, quoted in Cottrill, *The Conciliator*, pp. 160–162.

13. *Literary Digest* (August 11, 1923): 9; Inaugural Address, quoted in Cottrill, *The Conciliator*, pp. 114, 115; Inaugural Address of John F. Kennedy, January 20, 1961; Inaugural Address, quoted in Cottrill, *The Conciliator*, pp. 164–167; *New York Times*, March 19, 1921. In the *Times*, see March 3–April 4 issues of the pro-League newspaper for French Mission Reception. President Warren G. Harding, "Messages of the President of the United States to Congress, April 12, 1921," *Foreign Relations of the United States* (Washington D.C.: U.S. Government Printing Office, 1921), 11: xvii–xx; "Workability of the Harding Peace Plans," *Literary Digest* 69 (April 23, 1921): 5, 6; "Mr. Harding's New Foreign Entanglements," *Literary Digest* 69 (May 28, 1921): 10; *New York Times*, May 20, 1921. See also "Harveyized Diplomacy," *Literary Digest* 69 (June 18, 1921): 10.

14. *New York Times*, June 26, 1921. See also Harding to Harvey, June 3, 1921, Box 697, Harding Papers. For Harding's speech, see *New York Times*, May 30, 1921. David J. Hill to Charles Evans Hughes, June 22, 1921, Harding Papers, Box 42. Nicholas

Murray Butler to Harding, August 31, 1921, Box 693. Perhaps nowhere better than in a Boston speech, October 30, 1922, did Hughes pull together his thinking on the subject, *Harding Papers*, Box 44. See also *The Memoirs of Herbert Hoover*, 3 vols. (New York: Macmillan, 1951–1952), 2:36, 37, and Merlo J. Pusey, *Charles Evans Hughes*, 2 vols. (New York: Macmillan, 1951), 2:432. Hughes to Harding, October 26, 1921; December 7, 1921, and August 28, 1922, Box 45, Harding Papers. Papers in Box 171 of the Hughes Papers also help explain the Hughes approach. "The Peace of Raritan—and After," *Literary Digest* 69 (July 16, 1921): 12; John Chalmers Vinson, *William E. Borah and the Outlawry of War* (Athens: University of Georgia Press, 1957), pp. 31–47; Murray, *The Harding Era*, pp. 140–150; Cottrill, *The Conciliator*, p. 192; Murray, *The Harding Era*, pp. 151–164. Also see *A Diplomatic History of the American People*, 10th ed. (Englewood Cliffs, N.J.: Prentice-Hall, 1980), pp. 638–648.

15. Hamilton Holt, "Future of the Conference Idea," *The Independent*, April 25, 1921; Murray, *The Harding Era*, pp. 164, 165; Russell, *The Shadow*, pp. 264–266, 491; John Shover, ed., *Politics of the Nineteen Twenties* (Waltham, Mass.: Ginn-Blaisdell, 1970); U.S. Congress, Senate Hearings, 68th Congress, Part 7, 1939–1940, pp. 54, 55; Murray, *The Harding Era*, pp. 492–494; Noggle, *Teapot Dome*, p. 38; Shover, *Politics;* Thomas J. Walsh, "True Victory of Teapot Dome," *The Forum*, 72 (July 1924): 1–12, 43–54; Noggle, *Teapot Dome*, pp. 22, 23, 26–30, 19.

16. Daugherty, *Inside Tragedy*, pp. 115–145; Giglio, *H. M. Daugherty*, pp. 146–155; Murray, *The Harding Era*, pp. 314–326, 427; Daugherty, *Inside Tragedy*, pp. 147–160; Murray, *The Harding Era*, pp. 403–407, 431–433; Adams, *Incredible Era*, pp. 44, 45; Giglio, *H. M. Daugherty*, pp. 155, 156, on Daugherty's breakdown; Murray, *The Harding Era*, pp. 423, 438, 439, on Harding's poor health; Daugherty, *Inside Tragedy*, pp. 170–176; Murray, *The Harding Era*, pp. 429, 430; David H. Jennings, "President Harding and International Organization," *Ohio History* 75 (Spring-Summer 1966): 161–165.

17. Murray, *The Harding Era*, pp. 425, 439, 440, 421; Daugherty, *Inside Tragedy*, pp. 229–245; Murray, *The Harding Era*, pp. 430–437; Daugherty, *Inside Tragedy*, p. 253; Murray, *The Harding Era*, pp. 441, 480, 481; Giglio, *H. M. Daugherty*, pp. 180–192; Cottrill, *The Conciliator*, pp. 208, 209; William Allen White, *A Puritan in Babylon* (New York: Macmillan, 1938), p. 239; Cottrill, *The Conciliator*, pp. 208–220; Murray, *The Harding Era*, pp. 441–450, 490, 491, 451–455, 423, 472, 473.

ANNOTATED BIBLIOGRAPHY

A fuller discussion of Harding historiography is contained in the opening section of this chapter. Some key sources are listed here.

Adams, Samuel Hopkins. *Incredible Era*. Boston: Houghton Mifflin, 1939.
    Another popular history with some details about the "Ohio Gang."
Allen, Frederick Lewis. *Only Yesterday*. New York: Bantam Books, 1946.
    This popular journalistic history (first published in 1931) contains background material.
Downes, Randolph C. *The Rise of Warren Gamaliel Harding, 1865–1920*. Columbus: Ohio State University Press, 1970.
    A Toledo historian's account of the prepresidential years. Not a muckraking study.

Murray, Robert K. *The Harding Era 1921–1923: Warren G. Harding and his Admin-istration*. Minneapolis: University of Minnesota Press, 1969.
    An effort to put the scandals in context; more on Harding's achievements.
Russell, Francis. *The Shadow of Blooming Grove* New York: McGraw-Hill, 1968.
    Unfortunately, the controversy over the Carrie Phillips correspondence oversha-dowed the new research contained in this volume.

12 CALVIN COOLIDGE

Malcolm Lee Cross

Calvin Coolidge, president of the United States from 1923 to 1929, is held in low esteem by American scholars. Relatively little has been written about him, and much of the published material is critical of him and his administration.

Scholars consider Coolidge to have been a weak and ineffective president. They believe that he almost totally lacked energy, initiative, imagination, or leadership. They charge him with encouraging and condoning the frenzied stock market speculation of the 1920s, while failing to foresee the resulting collapse of the market and the onset of the Great Depression.

In 1948 historian Arthur Schlesinger, Sr., polled fifty-five experts on the American presidency—mostly historians—to determine their views on the relative effectiveness of the American presidents to date. The respondents rated Coolidge "below average." When Schlesinger conducted a similar poll among seventy-five experts in 1962, he discovered that the experts continued to downgrade Coolidge. They continued to rate him below average. Indeed, they believed that out of the thirty-one presidents they considered, only four—Franklin Pierce, James Buchanan, Ulysses S. Grant, and Warren G. Harding—were worse presidents than Calvin Coolidge.

Coolidge's reputation has not fared much better in the modern American press. He was briefly the object of renewed attention when Ronald Reagan was first elected president because Reagan had announced that he was an admirer of Coolidge's efforts to cut taxes and government expenditures in the 1920s. A major national news magazine periodically publishes Coolidge's sayings to illustrate his basic common sense. But most of the comment on Coolidge is in the form of anecdotes—real or apocryphal—printed to fill up the white space at the end of newspaper stories of awkward length. If Coolidge is not the hero of American scholars, he is at least the hero of American newspaper fillers.

The fillers' hero is Silent Cal, the Vermont backwoodsman, whose refusal to say anything unless absolutely necessary always baffles all who meet him. For example:

In 1919, when Silent Cal was governor of Massachusetts, he had to play host

to the governors of the other five New England states as they watched a parade
of World War I soldiers who had just returned to Boston from France. The
parade lasted for over five hours. But as the six governors stood in the reviewing
stand watching it go by, the only comment their host made was a single sentence
explaining how they could all stand at attention without letting their feet get too
tired.

In another instance, Silent Cal had been entertaining another politician at his
home in Northampton, Massachusetts. When it was time for the other man to
leave, he escorted his guest outside and stood with him while the visitor's
chauffeur brought his car around to the front door. The chauffeur was late, and
an uncomfortable silence developed as Silent Cal resolutely refused to make any
conversation with his guest. When, after a long delay, the chauffeur had come
and the visitor had left, Mrs. Coolidge asked her husband why he had not said
anything. Silent Cal explained, "I had already said good-bye before we came
outside."

But in the fillers, Silent Cal's silence frequently masks an acid wit and a sharp
tongue which enabled him to get to the heart of any matter or puncture the ego
of any city slicker or pompous society matron who tangled with him. For example:

Once, when Silent Cal had just returned from church service, someone asked
him to explain the topic of the minister's sermon.

"Sin," said Silent Cal, lapsing back into silence.

"But what did the minister say?" asked the exasperated questioner.

"He said he was agin it."

On another occasion, when Silent Cal was vice president in the Harding
administration, he was dining at a banquet. A rich, pushy society woman observed that he was not enjoying himself and asked him why, if he detested
banquets, he attended so many.

Said Silent Cal: "Gotta eat somewhere!"

Another wealthy, pompous woman prominent in Washington social circles
was sitting next to Silent Cal at yet another banquet and attempted to engage
him in conversation.

"Oh, Mr. Vice President!" she gushed. "You must speak to me! I have a
bet that I can get you to speak at least three words!"

Snapped Silent Cal, as he turned away: "You lose!"

In a lonely little valley in the Green Mountains of Vermont, one can find the
President Calvin Coolidge Homestead at Plymouth Notch, where he was born
on July 4, 1872. A visitor can see the farmhouse where Coolidge lived as a boy,
where his mother and sister died, where he learned of Warren Harding's death,
and where his father swore him in as thirtieth president of the United States in
the early hours of August 3, 1923. Just down the road is the family cemetery,
where Coolidge was buried following his own death on January 5, 1933.

The state of Vermont maintains the homestead for tourists, but it is no shoddy,
gaudy tourist trap. The buildings are clean and well-kept. The few souvenirs for

sale—mainly postcards and books about Coolidge—are invariably in good taste. The attendants take real pride in their work and show genuine friendliness and courtesy to all visitors who come.

And the visitors do come. If one inspects the guest book, one will see that hundreds come each year, from all parts of the United States and from many foreign nations as well. The homestead is not visible from any major highway, but people seek it out.

The popularity of the homestead is an echo of the popularity Calvin Coolidge himself once enjoyed. As governor of Massachusetts in 1919, he won national acclaim for his perceived role in suppressing the Boston police strike, and once he won the public's adoration, he kept it for the rest of his life.

Calvin Coolidge was one of the most successful vote-getters ever to enter the White House. He won his last election to a full term as president in 1924—in a landslide. Over 15 million Americans voted for Coolidge, while only 8 million voted for Democratic nominee John W. Davis and 4 million voted for Wisconsin Senator Robert M. La Follette, the nominee of the Progressive party. Coolidge's share of the total popular vote—over 54 percent—was greater than any won by Woodrow Wilson, Harry S Truman, or Jimmy Carter. Even Franklin D. Roosevelt, running for a fourth term as president in 1944 during World War II, was not able to win as large a percentage of the popular vote as Calvin Coolidge won in 1924.[1]

Coolidge was able to retire voluntarily from the presidency in 1929 with his popularity as great as ever. Editors and publishers were willing to pay up to $3 a word for his writings. His popular newspaper column was syndicated in papers from coast to coast. He probably could have easily won reelection to the presidency in 1928 had he chosen to run. There was widespread hope that he would run for president in 1932 as the Republican nominee instead of the unpopular Herbert Hoover. After Hoover's defeat by Roosevelt that year, talk began of nominating Coolidge for president in 1936. Calvin Coolidge may be an object of low esteem and a figure of fun today, but when he died, he was one of the most beloved and respected men in America.

What hold did Calvin Coolidge have over the collective American imagination in the 1920s? Why did the public find him so attractive? What qualities of his did the American people worship, and why? What did he do to earn the enormous esteem in which he was held?

Calvin Coolidge lived, worked, and died before the development of modern techniques for measuring public opinion. There are no formal, scientifically conducted polls on his administration. The election returns attest to his popularity but do not really explain it. Therefore, precise answers to these questions may never be fully known.

But books, newspaper articles, and magazine stories from and about the 1920s exist in abundance. From these sources it is possible to learn about the image Calvin Coolidge projected. Since he was so popular, it is reasonable to infer that the American people liked what they saw—or what they thought they saw.

The image Calvin Coolidge projected was complex. The most striking thing about him, to the American people of the 1920s, was that he was not just another politician—at least he did not seem to be. Most politicians were congenial, outgoing, hand-shaking, knee-slapping back thumpers who talked a mile a minute and never said anything. Calvin Coolidge was curt, aloof, and austere—a man who kept to himself and who never said anything unless he had something to say. In the wake of the scandals of the Harding administration, the contrast between Calvin Coolidge and the typical politician was definitely in Coolidge's favor.

But if Calvin Coolidge was not just another politician, then what was he? His perceived role in the Boston police strike and his notable emotional reserve made him appear to be a strong, thoughtful leader. More important, his Vermont boyhood and his middle-class lifestyle made him seem to be an average American, but an idealized average American, the embodiment of traditional American values and a reminder of a simpler America for which the people were nostalgic in the years following World War I. In essence, therefore, Calvin Coolidge seemed to be a strong leader who derived his strength from his all-American roots, and whose very presence in the White House reassured the American people that the traditional America of their dreams had not really disappeared forever—that it could, and did, live on even in the frantic 1920s.

The image of Calvin Coolidge, the way he projected it, and the reasons for his popularity are the major subjects of this chapter. But because Calvin Coolidge first became famous for his perceived role in the Boston police strike, it is necessary to review his career before the strike, to examine the strike itself and his own role in it, and to see how and why he emerged so triumphantly from such a tragic event.

IMPACT OF THE POLICE STRIKE

The Boston police strike began on September 9, 1919. Five days later it was all over, and Calvin Coolidge was America's newest hero. The White House was just around the corner.

The strike was to have three effects on Coolidge's image. First, it was to focus national attention on Calvin Coolidge. Second, it was to help forge the concept that Calvin Coolidge was a strong leader. Third, it was to help forge the linkage between Calvin Coolidge and traditional American values.

At the time of the Boston police strike, Calvin Coolidge was forty-seven years old. He was a lawyer by training, but he had been in politics for over twenty years. He was married and had two sons.

Coolidge possessed a variety of characteristics resulting from his Vermont upbringing. His most unusual trait—since he was a professional politician—was his emotional reserve. Calvin Coolidge was not without emotions. On the one hand, he had an explosive temper, allegedly worse than that of Theodore Roosevelt. On the other hand, Coolidge felt a genuinely deep love for his friends and family. But he always kept his emotions in check.

One of the reasons for his reserve was his Vermont heritage. The people of rural Vermont were typically sober, industrious, and self-reliant—they had to be if they were to support themselves in a bleak environment. They had no time for the frivolity or idle chatter at which Coolidge himself was so poor. He was raised in their tradition and taught to suppress his emotions regardless of circumstances.

But Calvin Coolidge was shy even by the standards of his region. His boyhood was marked by more loneliness and tragedy than was typical. The two worst events were the deaths of his mother and his sister while he was still a boy. He never fully recovered from their deaths.

Furthermore, Coolidge's grandmother discouraged him from dating, dancing, and party-going. His father sent him to a private boarding school when he had completed the nine years of education available to children in the Plymouth Notch public school. These actions served to increase his loneliness and his subsequent discomfort in the presence of others.

But Coolidge was never one to wallow in self-pity. He believed that, given his family's principles and circumstances, he had the best boyhood possible. He knew that his father had given him more than shyness. He had instilled the principles of industry, of thrift, of integrity. But above all, Coolidge's father had given him an intense interest in public affairs and a devout love of politics.

Coolidge's father was Colonel John C. Coolidge. He was a most remarkable man. With no resources other than ability, integrity, and hard work, he had become a prosperous farmer and storekeeper. But he had also held numerous local public offices, had served in both houses of the Vermont State Legislature, and had been an administrative assistant to a Vermont governor. He was an honorary colonel in the Vermont National Guard. Calvin Coolidge worshipped his father and wanted to follow in his footsteps.[2]

The Colonel sent young Calvin to prestigious Amherst College in western Massachusetts, from which he graduated in 1895. Calvin thereupon decided to study law in nearby Northampton. He was admitted to the bar and certified to practice law in 1897, but decided to devote a major portion of his time to politics and the Republican party.

Coolidge's decision to enter politics might have been unusual, given his introverted nature. Yet his integrity and his ability made him inherently respectable and more than compensated for his shyness. Indeed, his shyness was an asset. By following his taciturn instincts he was able to avoid saying things that otherwise might have created controversies and enemies. As he frequently liked to say, "I have never been hurt by what I have not said."

Consequently, Coolidge's climb up the political ladder was all the smoother. He was elected to the Northampton City Council in 1899. Thereafter, he served successively as city attorney, clerk of the local courts, state representative, mayor, state senator, president of the Senate, and lieutenant governor.

Calvin Coolidge was elected to a one-year term as governor of Massachusetts in 1918. He hoped to win reelection in 1919, and then to retire from politics at the end of his second term in January 1921. He planned to spend the rest of his life practicing law to support his wife, Grace Goodhue, whom he married in 1905, and his two sons, John and Calvin.

Coolidge was unknown beyond the borders of his adopted state, but his reputation within Massachusetts was solid. He was an able, industrious public servant of impeccable personal integrity. If he was more aloof than the typical politician, he nevertheless treated everyone, regardless of race, sex, class, or party affiliation, with honesty and fairness.

Coolidge was basically conservative. He favored economy in government and a balanced budget. He was skeptical of the ability of the state to eliminate society's problems through legislation. He believed that economic and social justice could be best achieved if business and industry were permitted to operate with only a minimum degree of government regulation. He wanted to rely on the American free enterprise system to generate and redistribute wealth, and assumed that the result would be reasonably equitable: everyone would get what he earned—no more and no less.

But Coolidge moderated his conservatism with a willingness, on occasion, to support government action to rectify problems for which capitalism offered no adequate solution. In the course of his career in state government, he worked for female suffrage and the direct election of United States senators. He supported and enforced legislation to strengthen pension plans, to promote safety in the factory, to limit monopolistic practices, to protect tenants' rights against landlords, and to limit the number of hours wage-earners—especially women and children—had to work. Hence, if Coolidge was conservative, he was also human, enlightened, and compassionate for his time.

The Boston police strike was essentially a local matter, but it was the subject of intense nationwide public interest. In September 1919, the United States was in the grip of the Great Red Scare. The 1917 communist seizure of power in Russia, the continuing communist agitation for world revolution, and the political turmoil in Europe following World War I frightened the American people.

Their fears were increased by the conduct of radicals at home. American communists and socialists tried to stir up labor unrest and demanded the violent overthrow of the United States government. Some planted bombs or sent them through the mail. One exploded near the home of Attorney General A. Mitchell Palmer.

Palmer himself was contributing to the hysteria. Justice Department agents under his command were relentlessly arresting radicals or suspected radicals, often without just cause. The rhetoric and conduct of radical anticommunists such as Palmer served only to inflame further the climate of fear. It was this atmosphere that led many to believe erroneously that the Boston police strike was part of a communist plot to overthrow the government of the United States.[3]

According to legend, the Boston police strike began when irresponsible, sub-versive policemen deserted their posts and surrendered the city to the forces of terrorism and anarchy. Coolidge, then governor, put down the strike by calling out the Massachusetts National Guard to restore order and by firing the deserters. When Samuel Gompers, president of the American Federation of Labor (AFL), attempted to pressure Coolidge into rehiring the mutinous policemen, Coolidge stopped him dead in his tracks with a telegram stating that "there is no right to strike against the public safety by anybody, anywhere, anytime." In reality, the events surrounding the strike were much more complicated, and the role played by Coolidge was much more ambiguous.

The Boston police were, of course, employees of the city of Boston, but were under the command of a commissioner who, according to Massachusetts law, was an appointee of the governor of the state rather than of the city. In 1919 the commissioner was Edwin U. Curtis, whom Coolidge's predecessor had ap-pointed.[4]

The strike had nothing whatever to do with communism. The strikers were reacting to low wages, bad working conditions, and lack of civil service regu-lations governing duties and promotions. They wished to join the American Federation of Labor and use the collective bargaining process to rectify their problems.

Coolidge considered the policemen's grievances to be legitimate, and he pri-vately urged Commissioner Curtis to do what he could to satisfy them. But both Coolidge and Curtis believed that the police had no right to unionize: they owed absolute loyalty to the city of Boston, and that loyalty would be compromised if they joined the AFL. Coolidge and Curtis further believed that the police had no right to strike: they were the equivalent of soldiers in the war against crime. To strike would be to desert.

Nevertheless, the police voted on August 15, 1919, to join the AFL. Curtis' response was to announce, on September 8, the suspension from the force of nineteen leaders of the unionization movement. The police protested by going on strike. On Tuesday, September 9, 117 police (out of a total of 1,544) left their jobs. Curtis thereupon fired them.

Curtis had thought that he could maintain law and order with the policemen who had not struck, with the police of neighboring jurisdictions, and with vol-unteers. He was wrong. On the night of September 9, looting, vandalism, and robbery broke out. The disorders worsened as the criminal elements learned that Curtis' forces were inadequate to maintain law and order. They terrorized the city until dawn.

The following morning, Boston Mayor John J. Peters, a Democrat, took action. Invoking an obscure Massachusetts law, he called out the elements of the Mas-sachusetts National Guard stationed in Boston and appointed General John N. Cole to the command of a joint force of guardsmen and loyal policemen. The effect of this act was to eliminate Curtis' authority. When rioting erupted that night, Peters' forces were ready. With rifle fire and cavalry charges they suppressed the violence. Three lives were lost, but by the morning of Thursday, September 11, order had been restored in Boston.

Throughout these events, Calvin Coolidge had taken no action other than to keep himself fully informed. But he was concerned that Peters might attempt to reinstate the striking policemen. As much as Coolidge sympathized with their plight, he did not think that they were entitled to have their old jobs back. As he put it, "To place the maintenance of the public security in the hands of a body of men who have attempted to destroy it would be to flaunt the sovereignty of the laws the people have made."

Therefore, to prevent Peters from reinstating the strikers, Coolidge mobilized the entire National Guard and assumed command himself. He sent additional troops to Boston, restored Curtis to command of the police, and allowed him to secure the permanent dismissal of the strikers.

But Samuel Gompers, the president of the AFL, with which the striking policemen had wanted to affiliate, attempted to intervene on their behalf. He telegraphed Coolidge on Friday, September 12, urging him to reinstate the fired policemen.

Coolidge attempted to turn Gompers aside with a soft answer. He replied that the policemen were under the command of Curtis, that Curtis had decided to dismiss the strikers, and that he, Coolidge, had "no authority to interfere" under the state law.

But Gompers was unwilling to accept Coolidge's answer as the final word. He reiterated his belief that Curtis had been wrong to dismiss the strikers and urged Coolidge to reinstate them. On Sunday, September 14, Coolidge issued the well-publicized, definitive reply which would shortly earn him the vice presidency and the presidency of the United States. His telegram said, in part:

The right of the police of Boston has always been questioned, never granted, is now prohibited. . . . Your assertion that the Commissioner was wrong cannot justify the wrong of leaving the city unguarded. That furnished the opportunity, the criminal element furnished the action. There is no right to strike against the public safety by anybody, anywhere, anytime.

To this telegram Gompers made no reply. The fired policemen were not reinstated. Curtis was free to rebuild the Boston police force. Calvin Coolidge was famous.

In one sense it is ironic that Calvin Coolidge should have become the hero of the Boston police strike. It had been Mayor Peters who had restored order and Commissioner Curtis who had fired the policemen.

Yet it was Coolidge whom the press and the public chose to lionize. He had been the senior official involved, and he had taken the last actions in the drama, by mobilizing the entire National Guard, by restoring Curtis to his command, and above all, by sending the famous second telegram to Gompers.

It was the second telegram itself which won Coolidge the most fame. Of the principal actors—Coolidge, Curtis, and Peters—only Coolidge had been able and willing to defend his actions in direct language understandable to everyone. The telegram was a stylistic masterpiece. Its most famous sentence—"There is no right to strike against the public safety . . . "—perfectly summarized the beliefs of the overwhelming majority of the American people, while simultaneously providing them with a powerful, concise slogan to adhere to during the turmoil and confusion of the Great Red Scare. By standing up to Gompers, and by explaining his stand in terms of a traditional value—law and order—against a background of suspected Communist subversion, Calvin Coolidge was able to project the image of a strong All-American leader defending traditional values in the face of foreign attack. Coolidge could not possibly have coined a better phrase. In the opinion of much of the press and the public, it was the final word.

It was also the final word from Calvin Coolidge on the subject. He thereafter rarely discussed the Boston police strike in public. He refused to write any articles on the matter despite the enormous fees he was offered. He never announced his own humanitarian efforts to secure jobs for the fired policemen—whom, after all, he had believed to have some justifiable grievances in the first place. He simply accepted the glory he received.

And receive it he did. Coolidge had acted to enforce his principles, and he had feared that he would be defeated for reelection. Yet in 1919 he was reelected governor in a landslide.

SUCCESSOR TO HARDING

Coolidge's popularity outside Massachusetts grew too. The intense media coverage of the strike made him a national figure; his conduct—or at least the public perception of his conduct—made him a national hero. Newspapers across the country proclaimed him the new champion of the people who, with courage, common sense, and good old-fashioned Americanism, defeated the forces of subversion and anarchy. The next year, the delegates to the Republican National Convention, acting against the instructions of their leaders, nominated Coolidge for the vice presidency of the United States. The Harding-Coolidge ticket won overwhelmingly in November. Warren Harding died in August 1923. Calvin Coolidge was president of the United States.

The worship of Calvin Coolidge never stopped in his lifetime. For the rest of his life the American people would regard him as the strong, thoughtful leader who represented the best aspects of the American heritage. Their perceptions, and what he did to shape them, must now be discussed.

According to students of the 1920s, Calvin Coolidge became president at a time when most Americans regarded the years before World War I with intense nostalgia. The years of the Great War, as it was then called, had left them emotionally exhausted. They had been worn out by the idealism and activism the war had inspired. They had been made cynical by the politics of the postwar peace process.

Their cynicism had been reinforced by the scandals of the Harding administration. Although President Harding himself had been personally honest, several of his appointees and closest associates had used their official positions to profit personally at the public expense. Teapot Dome—wherein Harding's secretary of the interior leased public lands to oil companies in exchange for loans and bribes—was the most notorious scandal, and Teapot Dome became synonymous with the entire range of graft and corruption that permeated the Harding administration.

Millions of Americans felt not only cynicism but uncertainty. The postwar years were ones not only of political disillusionment, but of economic and social upheaval as well, of which the Red Scare was symptomatic. Recessions, strikes, and unemployment, which had quickly followed the war as the country tried to adjust to peace, frightened people. The novelists, playwrights, poets, and journalists who called into question basic American values increased the public's uncertainty about itself and its values.

The American people longed for the "good old days," the days of a simpler America, when life was slower, when values were more certain, when betrayal was not just around the corner. They wanted to return to the days when direct democracy, and prosperity for everyone who worked hard, saved what he earned, and trusted God were not merely phrases in civics books but ideals which were considered valuable and attainable. They wanted strong leaders who did not merely play politics-as-usual, but who came from the people, shared their ideals, and could lead them through the troubled times.

Whether or not such an America ever really existed is a question beyond the scope of this work. What is important is that to many millions of citizens in the 1920s, that America had once existed, and they wanted it back. The presence of Calvin Coolidge in the White House told them that their dreams could become reality.

SUSTAINING THE "COOL" IMAGE

Although the image of Calvin Coolidge as the strong, all-American leader first took shape following the Boston police strike, it was sustained by four other factors: his perceived silence, his Vermont heritage, his middleclass lifestyle, and his own public relations techniques.

Of these four factors, the most important was the set of tactics Coolidge used to affect media coverage of his image. Naturally, his tactics would help shape the public perception of his silence, background, and lifestyle.

But Coolidge's set of tactics is also the most difficult factor to discuss. Calvin Coolidge never explicitly acknowledged that he was attempting to shape his media coverage. Nor is there any concrete evidence—no secret report, for example—that Coolidge had a detailed blueprint for the maintenance of the image he had won in the Boston police strike. Nevertheless, Coolidge frequently acted as though he used a variety of tactics to shape media coverage and preserve his image.

Some of his tactics were so subtle as to be almost undetectable. Calvin Coolidge was no hypocrite. He had too much personal integrity ever to pretend to be anything other than himself. Furthermore, he was genuinely proud of who he was, where he came from, and how he lived. He made no deliberate attempt actively to conceal anything from the press or the public. Yet he frequently acted as though he were trying to call attention to certain aspects of himself and his life which the public considered especially attractive, and his subtlety was so great that nobody could ever really be sure when he was passively allowing reporters to collect facts and when he was actively trying to influence their efforts and interpretations.

Calvin Coolidge's most subtle tactic was silence at appropriate times. It has already been noted that he had used silence to avoid controversy while climbing the ladder in Massachusetts politics. Yet Coolidge also used silence if he discovered that the press and the public were interpreting the facts of a situation in a manner favorable to him, even if the interpretation was not altogether justified.

The classic example is Coolidge's reaction to the media coverage of the Boston police strike and his own role in it. He knew that the strike was not part of a communist plot, that the policemen had had at least some justifiable grievances, that it had been Curtis who had first stood up to the strikers, and that it had been Peters who had first restored order. Yet by remaining silent, Coolidge could accept credit for the strike's resolution without actively taking away credit from anyone else. Since the public thought that the police were being manipulated by the communists and that their grievances were unjustified anyway, Coolidge could also avoid the unpopularity he might otherwise have earned if he had voiced his true opinions to the contrary. Coolidge could win popularity for appearing to defeat the policemen while secretly following his humanitarian impulses and helping them find new jobs at the same time.

By using silence as a political tactic, Coolidge could also project the image of being a basically silent man. Indeed, his perceived silence was itself his most famous and popular trait. His nickname—Silent Cal—was a sign of the affection and respect with which he was held in his lifetime.

Calvin Coolidge was never really as silent as his reputation indicated. Sometimes he could be depressed, moody, and uncommunicative for hours. But Coolidge could also be candid and open with friends of long standing. He gave more press conferences than any of his predecessors or most of his successors, and he made numerous speeches and public statements.

But Coolidge's inability to engage in small talk with strangers, his tactical refusal to discuss politics in public, and his continuing iron control over his emotions made him seem less talkative than the average politician. It was not difficult for the trait to become exaggerated in the public mind.

In the public mind, Coolidge's perceived silence set him apart from other politicians, and especially from his outgoing predecessor, the tragic Warren Harding. In much the same way that Howard Hughes' penchant for privacy was merely to attract more attention, Calvin Coolidge's reserve generated for him the publicity most politicians crave.

Coolidge's silence made him seem enigmatic. One prominent reporter, Edward G. Lowry, in a magazine article published in 1921, said:

The election of 1920 imported in the City of Conversation, as one of its necessary consequences, perhaps the oddest and most singular apparition this vocal and articulate settlement has ever known: A politician who does not, who will not, who seemingly cannot talk. A well of silence. A centre of stillness.

According to Lowry, neither Washington nor Massachusetts had ever "seen a man prominent in public life like him."[5]

Another prominent commentator, Forrest Crissey, in writing about Coolidge, said:

It is the fewness of his words which makes him a political mystery. That a man in public life can be so saving of words and still have a full working equipment of human feelings is not readily understandable to men and women who are at no more pains to conceal their emotions than their clothes.

But though the Coolidge reserve set him off from others, it did so to his advantage, as Bruce Bliven noted in *The New Republic,* a journal normally opposed to the Coolidge administration's policies: Coolidge's "taciturnity has become famous in a country whose public men all suffer from a nervous flow of words." In the stories of other journalists, Coolidge became known as the man who "does not talk until he has something to say."

Coolidge seemed not only different, but more thoughtful as well. It was simply assumed that because Coolidge spent relatively little time talking, he must have been spending more time thinking about weighty issues than most politicians did.

Coolidge contributed to this attitude by showing reporters his personal library with its extensive collection of books on law, economics, and politics. They concluded that he was so serious that he had no time for any frivolous pastimes. They were partly correct. Coolidge had little interest in opera, the theater, or popular music and literature. But he enjoyed reading Shakespeare, and one of his few hobbies was translating Dante's *Inferno* from Italian to English and back to Italian. He simply remained silent to avoid spoiling the effect that the examination of his public affairs library had made.

Coolidge further contributed to this part of his image by remaining silent when one of his employees and admirers, Bascomb Slemp, published a book entitled *The Mind of the President,* which came out in 1926. In it Slemp said that Coolidge "concentrates more intensely than any man I have ever known." Coolidge was always "thinking, and thinking, and thinking."

Coolidge knew that the public was making too much of his alleged silence, and he could make gentle fun at the public's attitude in private. For example, Coolidge once took some visitors for a cruise on the presidential yacht *Mayflower*. As they were going down the Potomac River, Coolidge allowed his guests to see him standing alone by the rail, staring intently over the water, and looking serious and lost in thought. When one of his guests began to speculate on what great thoughts were going through the mind of the world's most powerful leader, Coolidge turned and said: "See that sea gull over there? Been watching it for twenty minutes. Hasn't moved. I think he's dead!"

But Coolidge remained silent about his perceived silence in public. He allowed his image of thoughtfulness to merge with the image of strength he had won following the Boston police strike. He was not about to confess that he owed his reputation for silence simply to being too shy to make small talk and too sly to discuss politics. He was too crafty to spoil a good thing.

Since the public also considered Coolidge's perceived silence to be an extreme instance of Yankee reserve, Coolidge, by simply saying nothing, was able to keep everyone aware of his Vermont heritage. But to publicize his heritage even more effectively, he also took steps—or at least he acted as though he were taking steps—to keep Vermont in the public eye.

REMINDER OF EARLY AMERICA

It would be wrong to say that rural Vermont in the 1870s and 1880s was truly representative of the United States in the 1920s. Certainly Coolidge's homeland had little in common with the great American cities, with the farmlands and prairies of the Midwest, with the mountains and deserts of the West. The values and lifestyles of the people with whom Coolidge grew up were different—to put it mildly—from those of the immigrants from eastern Europe, of the impoverished of America's cities, of the farmers, of the businessmen throughout the nation.

Yet to millions of Americans in the 1920s, Calvin Coolidge's Vermont reminded them of the principles of patriotism, democracy, individualism, and universal prosperity which seemed so typically American. Since Coolidge came from that region, he was a constant reminder of the ideal America, as many considered Vermont to be.

The one event that more than anything else helped remind the public of Calvin Coolidge's Vermont heritage was totally unplanned. Coolidge had been visiting his father in Plymouth Notch when President Harding died on August 2, 1923. The Coolidges were truly shocked and saddened when they learned the news shortly after midnight on August 3. Since Coolidge's father, the Colonel, was a certified notary public, Coolidge had him administer the presidential oath of office. The ceremony was conducted with the family Bible, in the living room of the Colonel's simple farmhouse, by the light of a kerosene lamp, in the small hours of the morning of August 3. The simplicity of both the setting of the ceremony and the ceremony itself conveyed a sense of quiet drama which could not have been artificially created. Throughout the remainder of Coolidge's administration, the press wrote of his first inaugural, thereby helping to keep Coolidge's Vermont heritage constantly in the public mind. Coolidge himself apparently had some doubts about the legality of his first inaugural, since the Colonel had been a state officer. To alleviate those doubts, Coolidge arranged to have himself sworn in a second time in 1923 by a federal judge. However, he kept his second inaugural a secret, thus avoiding hurting his father, and perhaps straining the Vermont connection.

Coolidge also actively promoted the Vermont connection by frequently returning to Plymouth Notch. His main reason for going back was his genuine love for Vermont and for everything in it. He loved his native state. He loved his home town. He loved the people. Above all, he loved his father. Had Coolidge's feelings not been genuine, he would never have tried to publicize his Vermont heritage. But by being perfectly true to his feelings, he could satisfy his emotional needs while reaping good publicity at the same time.

To this latter end, Calvin Coolidge allowed himself to be photographed doing chores on his father's farm. The pictures look stilted today. The sight of the president of the United States working in the fields or around the barnyard while dressed in a business suit would seem highly unusual, at least. Yet in the 1920s the gimmick worked. Calvin Coolidge could relax and have a good time while simultaneously advertising his Vermont roots. If the public forgot that he had been a professional politician for most of his life, and that he had risen to the governorship of one of the most populous, socially diverse, and industrialized states in the nation, Calvin Coolidge was not hurt.

THE PRESIDENT'S FATHER

In calling attention to his Vermont heritage, Coolidge had an able assistant in his father. Colonel Coolidge was probably one of the most colorful and popular figures on the American scene in the 1920's, until his death in January 1926. Despite his success in business and politics, he liked to play the role of the shrewd Yankee farmer, especially when tourists and reporters came to visit. In interviews with the press, the Colonel would indicate ignorance of "modern" child-rearing techniques and the permissiveness they frequently involved. He would emphasize that in the 1870s and 1880s, when most Americans had lived on farms, he had made sure that his famous son had had a normal farm boy's upbringing, with all the chores and hard work that this involved. The Colonel rarely mentioned, however, that unlike most farm boys of that period, his son had gone to boarding school, to college, and to legal training. He made no deliberate effort to suppress the truth. But since nobody ever asked him about his son's advanced education, he remained silent.[6]

Calvin Coolidge's small-town, middle-class lifestyle in Northampton also endeared him to the public. What captured the public's imagination was how typical his lifestyle seemed to be of that of the "Average American," the descendant of the New England Yankee, who still worshipped the old values of thrift, self-reliance, and success through hard work.

In shaping his lifestyle, Calvin Coolidge had had three goals. First, he wanted to provide a comfortable home for his wife and children. Second, Coolidge had also wanted to live in a Republican part of town, so that it would be easier to be elected to local office.

Finally, Coolidge had always wanted to live within his means. He wanted to maintain a home and support his family only on money honestly earned as a lawyer and politician. To meet the standards of his own conscience and to preserve his independence as a politician, he wanted to avoid totally the money readily available to politicians in the form of easy loans, consultants' fees, and other payments tantamount to bribes.

Since Coolidge's income was never especially great, his lifestyle had to be modest. From 1906—the year after his marriage—to 1921, when he was inaugurated vice president, Coolidge lived in one-half of a duplex in a middle-class Republican section of Northampton. His monthly rent was $27.

Coolidge had not deliberately set out in 1906 to fashion a lifestyle which would seem so middle-class, and hence seem so popular, in the 1920s. Yet had he chosen to do so, he could not have been more effective. His house at 21 Massassoit Street quickly became "the most famous address in America" as the public read more about it. The simplicity of his life, the utter lack of anything to distinguish it from that of any other "Average American," captured the public imagination and added to his image as the exemplar of Americanism. Coolidge was perfectly willing to show reporters his home, to let them write about its modesty, and to spread the word that he lived just like everyone else. He even continued to pay rent on his Northampton home while president, since his announced intention was to return there after his retirement. Actually, when Coolidge retired, he bought a larger, secluded home to avoid curious sightseers, but by continuing to pay the rent on the duplex during his term in the White House, he had at least succeeded in calling continuous attention to his middle-class lifestyle, even if that had not been his original intention.

Coolidge's use of silence and his emphasis on his background were his most subtle tactics, but they were not his only ones. He was also good at making symbolic gestures to emphasize himself and his ideas. For example, in an era when most politicians wore formal long frock coats in public, Calvin Coolidge wore a regular business suit. His choice of clothing thus served to further emphasize that he was less like the typical politician and more like the average middle-class American.

Coolidge also used public relations stunts and gimmicks to underscore his devotion to Yankee thrift in government. For example, in one instance, he arranged to have a "21 tree salute," rather than the 21 gun salute normally accorded presidents. Twenty-one trees were dynamited for Coolidge. The act

simultaneously produced lumber and saved the government money on ammu-
nition.

Coolidge frequently used bill-signing ceremonies for another unusual gimmick. It was customary at such a ceremony for a president to sign his name with
several pens, using each pen to write a letter or part of a letter in his name. He
would then give each pen to a guest. However, Coolidge frequently used one
pen with interchangeable points and gave each guest only a pen point. He was
thereby able to save the government money on pens.

Coolidge's most famous trick was to travel as a regular passenger on a train
from Washington to Chicago, when he could have had a private railroad car like
other presidents. The press noted with admiration that Coolidge had saved the
government several hundred dollars it would otherwise have paid the railroad
for a private car.

TERSE SPEAKING STYLE

But Calvin Coolidge used no device more often or more effectively than the
speech or public statement. Strangely enough, if his silence was his most popular
and famous trait—and tactic—his statements and speeches were his most frequently used tactics.

Coolidge had long been interested in public speaking. He had been on his
college's debating team. He was well aware of the importance of a good speech
in politics, and he would spend many hours writing and revising each speech
he had to give to make certain it would have the precise effect he wanted. As
a result, his statements were noted for their unusual style, delivery, and content.

The style of Coolidge's public statements was so simple that many observers
thought that he had no style. Actually, the simplicity of his statements was a
distinct style itself. Coolidge's writing style stood out because it was so terse
and concise. He avoided the long-winded pomposity so much favored by other
politicians in his day. His phraseology reinforced the impression of strength,
seriousness, reliability, and detachment from politics created by his perceived
silence.

Coolidge's statements were dominated by short, simple, declarative sentences,
with relatively few longer, more complex sentences among them. A good example is the opening paragraph of the speech Coolidge made following his
election as president of the Massachusetts State Senate. He said:

This Commonwealth is one. We are all members of one body. The welfare of the weakest
and the welfare of the most powerful are inseparably bound together. Industry cannot
flourish if labor languish. Transportation cannot prosper if manufactures decline. The
general welfare cannot be provided for in any one act, but it is well to remember that
the benefit of one is the benefit of all, and the neglect of one is the neglect of all. The
suspension of one man's dividends is the suspension of another man's pay envelope.[7]

Coolidge phrased many of his sentences as aphorisms: concise statements of principle and terse formulations of apparently self-evident truths, easy to remember. His most famous aphorism, of course, was his "no right to strike against the public safety" statement. But his speeches were notable for numerous other aphorisms as well: For example, speaking on patriotism and citizenship, Coolidge said:

We are citizens before we are partisans.

Partisanship should stop at the boundary line, but patriotism should begin there.

When you substitute patronage for patriotism, administration breaks down.

On good government, Coolidge said:

Good government can not be found on the bargain counter.

In office holding only the man of broad sympathy and deep understanding of his fellow man can meet with much success.

We need more of the office desks and less of the show window in politics.

Let there be a purpose in all legislation to recognize the right of man to be well born, well nurtured, well educated, well employed, and well paid.

Laws must rest upon the eternal foundations of righteousness.

Men do not make laws, but discover them.

Laws do not make reforms, but reforms make laws.

Coolidge's sayings on higher education included:

Our public schools have made education possible for all and ignorance a disgrace.

Education must give not only power but direction; it must minister to the whole man or it fails.

The profession of teaching has come down to us with a sanction of antiquity greater than all else.

The power to think is the most practical thing in the world.

If knowledge be wrongly used, civilization commits suicide.

It may not be so important to determine just where we are, but it is of the utmost importance to determine whither we are going.

Even when Coolidge used longer sentences, he made them as simple and as easy to understand as possible. For example, in the speech he gave at his 1925 presidential inauguration, he said:

Here stands our country, an example of tranquility at home, a patron of tranquility abroad. Here stands its government, aware of its might but obedient to its conscience. Here it will continue to stand, seeking peace and prosperity, solicitous for the welfare of the wage-earner, promoting enterprise, developing waterways and natural resources, attentive to the intuitive counsels of womanhood, encouraging education, desiring the advancement of religion, supporting the cause of justice and honor among the nations. America seeks no earthly empire built on blood and force. No ambition, no temptation, lures her to thought of foreign dominion. The legions which she sends forth are armed not with the sword, but with the cross. The high state to which she seeks the allegiance of all mankind is not of human, but of divine origin. She cherishes no purpose save to merit the favor of Almighty God.

A passage from another speech—Coolidge's famous "Business of America Is Business" speech—illustrates the same point:

After all, the chief business of the American people is business. They are profoundly concerned with producing, buying, selling, investing and prospering in the world. I am strongly of the opinion that the great majority of people will always find these are moving impulses of our life. . . . Wealth is the product of industry, ambition, character and untiring effort. In all experience, the accumulation of wealth means the multiplication of schools, the increase of knowledge, the dissemination of intelligence, the encouragement of science, the broadening of outlook, the expansion of liberties, the widening of culture. Of course, the accumulation of wealth cannot be justified as the chief end of existence. But we are compelled to recognize [that] it is a means to well-nigh every desirable achievement. So long as wealth is made the means and not the end, we need not greatly fear it.

If Coolidge's writing style was distinctive, so too was his style of delivery. He normally spoke in a relatively high-pitched nasal monotone. He used little change of inflection and few gestures to underscore his points. His style was the exact opposite of the bombastic rhetorical overkill, accompanied by frantic shouting and arm-waving, so favored by other politicians of his era, notably his predecessor, Warren G. Harding.

Coolidge occasionally bored audiences with his calmness. But more often than not he impressed his listeners as being—for a politician—unusually straightforward, matter-of-fact, businesslike, and serious. His demeanor reinforced the impression that he was not just another politician; that he was, rather, a stronger, more thoughtful, more serious leader.

The aphorisms and the passages from Coolidge's speeches also illustrate the typical content of a Coolidge utterance. In keeping with his tactical use of silence to avoid controversy, Coolidge rarely discussed public issues in detail. He usually confined himself to the discussion of nonpartisan topics and traditional values such as good government, citizenship, patriotism, democracy, education, and religion. He tried to speak in terms with which nobody could disagree.

The public was not disappointed. Its nostalgia for a simpler America and its cynicism with politics-as-usual made it especially responsive to Coolidge's messages. The virtues Coolidge discussed, and the way he discussed them, were precisely what the public wanted to hear.

Hence Coolidge's choice of speech topics worked to his advantage. His emphasis on traditional values reinforced his identification with those values; his silence on politics reinforced his detachment from politics and augmented his reputation for strength and thoughtfulness.

Coolidge made no cynical effort merely to tell the American people what he thought they wanted to hear. He honestly believed every word he spoke, and he honestly believed that it was more important to repeat the traditional American values than to discuss specific details of public policy.

But Coolidge did make every feasible effort to reach the widest possible audience with his views. To do so, he gave an inordinately large number of speeches. He spoke before as many different types of audiences as possible, and he fully exploited the radio to his enormous advantage.

Given Calvin Coolidge's reputation for silence, the sheer quantity of speeches he made is amazing. One prominent reporter of the 1920s, Charles Merze, calculated that Coolidge gave a speech or issued a public statement at least three days out of every four. Despite his reputation for silence, he spoke more frequently and at greater length than most of his predecessors. For example, Woodrow Wilson, a former college professor and indisputably a man of letters, gave an average of seventeen major addresses a year. Coolidge gave twenty-eight and issued scores of statements. In fact, his speeches and statements were collected and published in several large volumes, including *Have Faith in Massachusetts, The Foundations of the Republic,* and *The Price of Freedom.*

Especially amazing was the diversity of the audiences Coolidge chose. Merze, in his study, reported that Coolidge made a real effort to speak before as wide a range of groups as possible:

He chooses audiences for his more ambitious efforts with a catholicity of taste which is remarkable.... Not with a pair of calipers could Mr. Coolidge parcel out his time more carefully between different races, different creeds and different occupations.

Calvin Coolidge became president just as the American people were turning to the radio as a major source of information and entertainment. Probably no politician of the 1920s had a better understanding of the importance of radio as a mass medium than Coolidge. He was well aware of his own superior skills as a radio speaker. As he told another politician,

I am very fortunate that I came in with the radio. I can't make an engaging, rousing, or oratorical speech to a crowd as you can, ... but I have a good radio voice, and now I can get my messages across to them without acquainting them with my lack of oratorical ability.

Coolidge was right. He was a much better radio speaker than the politicians who used the ranting, raving, bombast, and arm-waving so much in vogue. His dry, nasal monotone carried especially well over the air. The *Literary Digest,* one of the most important and popular journals of the 1920s, reported that

Coolidge's voice sounded "clear, natural, well modulated, [and] was easily heard and every word understood. It carried a suggestion of restraint and rang with conviction and common sense; to the average citizen listening to him over the radio it mirrored accurately the man behind the voice."

According to Elmer Cornwell, an eminent political scientist and expert on mass media and the American presidency, Coolidge's use of radio was "highly imaginative" and "highly successful." Coolidge read his first State of the Union Message, in December 1923, on a nationwide radio broadcast. Thereafter, he broadcast about one speech a month over the new medium. The novelty of the radio, the desire of the people to hear their president's voice, and Coolidge's skills as a speaker were enough to provide him with huge audiences.[8]

Calvin Coolidge's tactics frustrated his opponents. The fact that he was the president of the United States was enough to make him the dominant political figure of the 1920s. But the sheer quantity of speeches he made, his success in reaching numerous different types of interest groups, and his success in using the radio dramatically strengthened his domination. His opponents likened him to a great fog: Coolidge seemed to be everywhere. He permeated and covered all parts of the political landscape. From Calvin Coolidge there was no escape.

Yet, also like a fog, Coolidge seemed insubstantial, intangible. His refusal to discuss specific issues in concrete terms deprived his opponents of openings for attacks. He reduced them to political shadow boxers, unable to challenge the image he projected.

POPULARITY SIMILAR TO FDR'S

Calvin Coolidge might not have been so successful if he had had a hostile press. But throughout his presidency he maintained friendly relations with the reporters assigned to cover him. His personal popularity with the White House press corps was probably as great as the popularity enjoyed by media masters such as Franklin D. Roosevelt.

Coolidge's popularity was no accident. He treated the press with the same creativity and imagination that had made him a radio star. He was the first president to meet with the press on a regular basis, although he did not invent the press conference. Several of his predecessors, notably Wilson and Harding, had attempted to hold regular press conferences. But Wilson's impatience with the press, his preoccupation with World War I, and his postwar physical collapse forced him to abandon press conferences. Harding soon realized that his inability to discuss issues intelligently with reporters made press conferences unwise— for him, at least.

But Coolidge not only established a regular schedule for press conferences; he stuck to it throughout his entire term. He met with the White House press corps each Tuesday and Friday. Reporters who regularly attended his conferences said that Coolidge created a pleasant atmosphere: he was relaxed, informal, and talkative. Both Coolidge and the press enjoyed the conferences.

Coolidge also wielded iron control over the conduct of the press conference. He insisted that the reporters' questions be submitted in writing. He apparently did not read them in advance, but if he encountered a question he did not want to answer, he simply ignored it. In one instance, the members of the press corps all wanted to ask Coolidge about plans he did not want to discuss. They all conspired to submit the same question to him. Standing before the corps, Coolidge silently read each slip of paper on which the question was written, and then proceeded to make up his own question, which he answered. In another instance, he read through all the questions, apparently failed to find a single question of which he approved, and terminated the conference.

But Coolidge was usually more candid. Transcripts of his conferences show that he was both willing and able to discuss a wide range of issues—provided that he was never directly quoted.

Calvin Coolidge followed examples of his predecessors and prohibited the press from quoting him directly. His public explanation was that "the words of the President have enormous weight and ought not to be used indiscriminately." But he also knew that if the press did not quote him, it would be more difficult for anyone to link him with controversial matters, or at least he acted as though he knew. He could maintain his separation from politicians as a class, and he could avoid the possibility of controversy tarnishing his image.

The members of the White House press corps cooperated with Coolidge. They agreed to attribute Coolidge's ideas and beliefs to a "White House spokesman" or a "source close to the president." Most sophisticated Americans could probably guess the true identity of the spokesman and the source, but the fictions helped Coolidge discuss controversial matters without risking the disadvantages of being controversial.

There are probably many reasons for the reporters' acceptance of Coolidge's terms for press conferences. The institution of the press conference was still in its infancy, and the current adversarial tactics so much in evidence in modern press conferences had not yet evolved. Most newspapers, perhaps because they were businesses, supported Coolidge's probusiness policies. The reporters were genuinely grateful for Coolidge's news morsels.

Yet is must also be noted that Coolidge was unusually concerned for the personal comfort and convenience of the reporters assigned to cover him. Whenever he traveled—and he did travel extensively—he did his best to make sure that the reporters had convenient travel arrangements, decent accommodations, and adequate communication facilities. Theodore H. White, in *The Making of the President 1960,* noted that John F. Kennedy was exceptionally popular with the reporters covering him, while Richard Nixon was generally disliked by his own press corps. One of the reasons was that Kennedy acted as though he was much more interested than Nixon in the welfare of the reporters assigned to travel with him, and provided them with much better accommodations and facilities.[9]

PRESIDENT BEHIND THE IMAGE

Two questions arise: How true was the Coolidge image to reality, and how much did the Coolidge image contribute to his popularity? Precise answers cannot be given, but a few generalities can be offered.

The image of Calvin Coolidge as both a strong leader and an average American was rooted, to a certain extent, in reality, but it was not the whole story.

Calvin Coolidge was a strong person. He had to be to withstand the temptations available to politicians in his time and to cope with the tragedy that cast shadows over his personal life while he was in the public eye. Not only had he lost his mother and sister in childhood; he had to withstand the deaths of his stepmother in 1920, of his younger son, Calvin, in 1924, and of his father, the Colonel, in 1926. He had felt each death keenly, but he had never permitted his personal tragedy to deter him from giving unstinting devotion to his country.

Yet Calvin Coolidge was not a strong leader, as scholars on the presidency understand the concept today. He declined to take the active role in government that has characterized the administrations of most presidents since his time.

Coolidge apparently interpreted literally the sections of the Constitution dealing with the powers of the president and the separation of powers between the president and Congress. The failure of the Constitution explicitly to authorize the president to exert leadership in the legislative process seems to have made Coolidge reluctant to attempt to persuade members of Congress to support his ideas. The few efforts he made were normally ineffective. As a result, he had to endure the rejection by the Senate of several of his appointments—including his nominee for attorney general. He had to suffer defeat on various legislative issues as well. Coolidge's inability to cope with Congress led the Omaha *World-Herald* to remark, shortly after the adjournment of the Congress in 1924, that "a Republican Congress has devoted itself to bloodying the President's nose, boxing his ears, and otherwise maltreating him."

Nor did Coolidge really attempt to dominate the executive branch of the government, of which he was head. He once said that "the only way to succeed is when there is a job to be done, to look around and find the best man to do it and let him do it." This was not necessarily a bad approach, since Coolidge was perfectly capable of making excellent appointments. Yet his statement reflected his unwillingness to assert himself beyond the making of the initial appointment.

Actually, Coolidge frequently permitted the federal bureaucracy to dominate him. He saw himself as its *representative* and not necessarily as its leader: "When technical matters come up," he said, "I feel called on to refer them to the proper department of the government which has some information about them and then, unless there is some good reason, I use this information as a basis for whatever

I have to say." Regardless of the benefits of that sort of decentralization, the fact remains that by promoting it, Coolidge voluntarily weakened his own position and allowed his conduct to be guided by the information supplied by his subordinates.

Nor can it be said that Calvin Coolidge was really a typical American. He never misrepresented his lifestyle as a boy or as a mature adult, and it is true that his way of life was more or less typical of that of millions of his countrymen. But Coolidge had qualities that were not typical: keen ambition, shrewd judgment, a devout love of politics, a phenomenal genius for self-advertisement, and a remarkable ability to establish a rapport with the public while remaining totally true to himself. The typical American does not become president of the United States. Calvin Coolidge did.

Coolidge's image contributed to his popularity, but it was not the only reason for it. Perhaps the 1920s are best known for the Big Bull Market—the unprecedented stock market speculation which culminated in the Great Crash of 1929. The American people believed that the boom in the market would lead to unprecedented prosperity, created by business and destined to last forever.

The range of economic policies pursued by Calvin Coolidge and his administration are beyond the scope of this work. Yet the fact remains that his administration did not take effective action to check the speculation. To the contrary, in speeches like his previously quoted "Business of America Is Business" speech, Coolidge exalted the role of business in society, thereby associating himself and the Republican party with its activities. Coolidge's public support for business made it easier for the Republican party to take credit for the temporary prosperity of the 1920s, and the popularity of both Coolidge and the party soared.

The onset of the Great Depression in October 1929—eight months after Coolidge retired from the presidency—did nothing to diminish his popularity. To the extent that he was blamed at all, he was blamed for *not* being in the White House, coping with the problems which seemed to be defeating his successor, Herbert Hoover.[10] To the American people, Calvin Coolidge remained the man who had come from the people, and who still had the unique ability to lead them through the troubles they faced. When he died in January 1933, economic recovery was years away. The country would, of course, revive and prosper, but millions of Americans did not know that. They looked not to the future for comfort, but to the past—to the memory of Calvin Coolidge.

NOTES

1. Calvin Coolidge's full name was John Calvin Coolidge, Jr., but his parents always called him Calvin, and as an adult he never used his first name, according to Donald R. McCoy, *Calvin Coolidge: The Quiet President* (New York: Macmillan, 1967), p. 7. See also William Allen White, *A Puritan in Babylon: The Story of Calvin Coolidge* (New York: Capricorn Books, 1965), p. 11, and Claude R. Fuess, (*Calvin Coolidge: The Man*

from Vermont (Hamden, Conn. Archon Books, 1965), p. 22. The general consensus is summarized in Thomas A. Bailey, *Presidential Greatness: The Image and the Men from George Washington to the Present* (New York: Appleton-Century, 1966), pp. 315–317. This writer used the summary of Schlesinger's methodology and results for each poll presented in Bailey, *Presidential Greatness,* pp. 23–25. The Calvin Coolidge Memorial Foundation, Inc., has distributed reprints of various newspaper articles illustrating the limited current interest in Coolidge. Reprints used by this writer include Haynes Johnson, "The Second Coming of Calvin Coolidge," San Francisco *Chronicle,* June 30, 1981, and Marvin Stone, "The Good Sense of 'Silent Cal,' " *U.S. News & World Report,* July 6, 1981, p. 72. Parade anecdote in W.A. White, *Puritan in Babylon,* p. 142. Departing guest anecdote was described in a filler in a recent issue of the *St. Louis Post-Dispatch,* page and date unknown. The sermon anecdote has cropped up in many books about Coolidge, including Paul F. Boller, Jr., *Presidential Anecdotes* (New York: Penguin Books, 1981), pp. 241, 242, which contains stories about all presidents since Washington, and in Edward Connery Lathem, ed., *Meet Calvin Coolidge* (Brattleboro, Vt.: Stephen Greene Press, 1960), p. 151. These books have many other Coolidge anecdotes as well. The banquet anecdotes are from Irving Stone, "Calvin Coolidge: A Study in Inertia," in Isabel Leighton, ed., *The Aspirin Age 1919–1941* (New York: Simon and Schuster, 1949), p. 144. The description of the homestead and its staff is based on the observations of this writer, made when he visited the homestead in August 1982. The raw data on elections were taken from Hanna Umlauf Lane, ed., *The World Almanac and Book of Facts 1983* (New York: Newspaper Enterprise Association, 1981), p. 297. This writer made the association and comparisons.

2. Edward Connery Lathem, ed., *Calvin Coolidge Says* (Plymouth, Vt.: Calvin Coolidge Memorial Foundation, 1971), p. 22. This volume is a collection of Coolidge's newspaper columns, published daily, except on Sunday, from July 1, 1930, through June 30, 1931. Lathem reports that Coolidge was paid $3,000 a week, which works out to about $3 a word. The probability that Coolidge could have been reelected in 1928 is mentioned in Bailey, *Presidential Greatness,* p. 257. Talk of renominating Coolidge in 1936 is discussed in Henry L. Stoddard, "I No Longer Fit In," in Lathem, *Meet Calvin Coolidge,* pp. 214, 215. Coolidge told Stoddard, a reporter, that under no circumstances would he run for president in 1936. This chapter's discussion of the Boston police strike is based on material in McCoy, *The Quiet President,* pp. 83–94; W.A. White, *Puritan in Babylon,* pp. 149–167; and Richard L. Lyons, "The Boston Police Strike of 1919, *New England Quarterly,* 20 (June 1947): 147–168. Biographical material on Coolidge comes from McCoy, *The Quiet President,* pp. 1–153, and Calvin Coolidge, *The Autobiography of Calvin Coolidge* (New York: Cosmopolitan Book Corp., 1929), pp. 2–168. "Silent Cal," *New Republic* 177 (August 6 and 13, 1977): 45. There is unanimous agreement on Coolidge's deep sentimental strain and his constant effort to keep his emotions in check. The point is discussed exceptionally well in W.A. White, *Puritan in Babylon,* p. xiii. Coolidge's Vermont heritage is discussed in all the major biographies, including Fuess, *The Man from Vermont,* pp. 3–19; and McCoy, *The Quiet President,* pp. 1–3, 7–22. Family deaths discussed in W.A. White, *Puritan in Babylon,* p. 29. The best discussion of the reasons for Coolidge's shyness is in McCoy, *The Quiet President,* pp. 8, 9. Coolidge's shyness at school is also discussed in ibid., p. 29. John Coolidge's background and career are discussed in ibid., pp. 5, 6. McCoy also advances the idea that Coolidge may have inherited some of his desire for success and advancement beyond Vermont from his mother.

3. Career decision in Coolidge, *Autobiography*, pp. 84–86. Shyness noted in Edward G. Lowry, "Calvin the Silent," *New Republic* (September 28, 1921): 131. Advancement described in Coolidge, *Autobiography*, pp. 86–116. Postgubernatorial plans in ibid., p. 124. Coolidge asserted, "I was quite content to finish my career as Governor of Massachusetts." It is noted in McCoy, *The Quiet President*, p. 59, that Coolidge as president of the Massachusetts Senate was open-minded. There is no evidence anywhere that Coolidge tried to be less than honest and fair while he was in state government. In ibid., p. 56, it is noted that Coolidge believed in the "trickle-down" theory of economics. Additional comments can be found in "Mr. Coolidge's Paradise; Message to Congress," *New Republic*, 51 (December 12, 1928): 82, 83. The most comprehensible discussion of Coolidge's moderately conservative policies in state government is in McCoy, *The Quiet President*, pp. 44–82. Also see W.A. White, *Puritan in Babylon*, pp. 97–176. The Great Red Scare is discussed in a wide variety of works on post–World War I America. This writer has relied on Frederick Lewis Allen, *Only Yesterday: An Informal History of the 1920's* (New York: Harper and Row, 1964), pp. 38–62.

4. The legend about the Gompers telegram was summarized and criticized in "Calvin Coolidge: Made by a Myth," *The Nation* 117 (August 15, 1923): 153. On legal status of police and negotiations, see Lyons, "The Boston Police Strike," pp. 147–149, 151. Coolidge-Curtis consultation in White, *Puritan in Babylon*, p. 156. Details in Lyons, "The Boston Police Strike," pp. 160–163. Also see McCoy, *The Quiet President*, p. 91. Coolidge's role in ibid., p. 96. Outcome of strike in W.A. White, *Puritan in Babylon*, p. 165.

5. Legal view in McCoy, *The Quiet President*, p. 93. See this source for statement, and also Calvin Coolidge, *Have Faith in Massachusetts* (Boston and New York: Houghton Mifflin Co., 1919), pp. 222, 223. Silence on strike noted in L. Brentano, "He Did Not Choose to Write," *Forum* 93 (February 1935): 100, 101. Quiet efforts for fired police noted in W.A. White, *Puritan in Babylon*, p. 165. For example of media comment, see "Coolidge's Victory for Law and Order," *Literary Digest* 63 (November 15, 1919): 14, 15. Rise related in W.A. White, *Puritan in Babylon*, pp. 213–215, 241. The nostalgic picture of post–World War I America is an obvious oversimplification. Several works, including Allen, *Only Yesterday*, and John D. Hicks, *Republican Ascendancy 1921–1933* (New York: Harper and Row, 1963), will offer the reader an excellent understanding of this era. Coolidge's "strategy of studied paradox" and its subtlety are discussed in Arthur Krock, *Memoirs: Sixty Years on the Firing Line* (New York: Popular Library, 1968), pp. 116–118. On vice presidential image, see Lowry, "Calvin the Silent," pp. 128, 131.

6. On "political mystery" see Forrest Crissey, "They Call Him Cal," *Saturday Evening Post* 197 (October 25, 1924): 8. Laconic style in Bruce Bliven, "Two Presidents," *New Republic* 35 (August 15, 1923): 322. Also see Samuel G. Blythe, "New President," *Saturday Evening Post* 196 (October 20, 1923): 3, and "Coolidge's Chances for the Nomination," *Literary Digest* 79 (December 22, 1923): 3–5. Hobbies and interests in White, *Puritan in Babylon*, p. 64; also see "Books the President Reads," *Literary Digest* 78 (September 1, 1923): 33. Myth of concentration in W. A. White, *Puritan in Babylon*, pp. 276–277. Sea gull anecdote in Krock, *Memoirs*, p. 117. The nature of Vermont at the time of Coolidge's birth is discussed in W. A. White, *Puritan in Babylon*, pp. 7–22; Fuess, *The Man from Vermont*, pp. 5–11; and McCoy, *The Quiet President*, pp. 1–4. The identification of Coolidge with Vermont is discussed elsewhere in W. Hard, "Coolidge's Country," *The Nation* 117 (October 10, 1923): 381; George Harvey, "Calvin Coolidge," *North American Review* 219 (June 1924): 723–727; K. L. Roberts, "Con-

centrated New England," *Saturday Evening Post* 196 (May 31, 1924): 10; A. Shaw, "Character and Services of Calvin Coolidge," *Review of Reviews* 87 (February 1933): 17; John Spargo, "Coolidge in Spite of Himself," *North American Review* 224 (September 1927): 338; "Quiet but Convincing Cal Coolidge," *Literary Digest* 63 (November 19, 1919): 46. Succession described in McCoy, *The Quiet President,* pp. 150, 151. The extent to which Coolidge was willing to allow himself to be photographed for publicity purposes is discussed in John T. Blair, "Coolidge the Image-Maker: The President and the Press, 1923–1929," *New England Quarterly,* 46 (December 1973): 504. Typical comments about Coolidge's upbringing under his father's supervision include an interview with Colonel John C. Coolidge, "I Didn't Raise My Boy to Be a President," *Literary Digest,* 86 (September 5, 1925): 41, 42; and E. G. Lowry, "Coolidge in the Scales," *New Republic,* 38 (February 27, 1924): 16.

7. The averageness of Calvin Coolidge's middle-class lifestyle is discussed in W. A. White, *Puritan in Babylon,* pp. 83, 145, 146. The attractiveness of his lifestyle to the general public is mentioned in many articles, including R. R. Child, "President," *Saturday Evening Post* 198 (April 17, 1926): 4; A. R. Pinci, "Coolidge: Political Mystery," *Saturday Evening Post* 193 (October 23, 1920): 82; "Calvin Coolidge as the Victory Maker," *Literary Digest* 80 (November 15, 1924): 7; "Profile," *Literary Digest* 106 (November 29, 1929): 47; "More Myth Than Man," *New Republic,* December 7, 1927): 59; Heywood Broun, "It Seems to Heywood Broun," *The Nation* 126 (January 11, 1928): 36. Simplicity of dress noted in Roberts, "Concentrated New England," p. 11. "Twenty-one tree salute" in "The Coolidge Week," *Time* (August 22, 1927): 7; (February 25, 1929): 11. Travel on regular train in "Coolidge out to Save Money and Cut Our Taxes," *Literary Digest* 80 (December 13, 1924): 5–7. Debate experience in McCoy, *The Quiet President,* p. 19. Efforts on speeches in Roberts, "Concentrated New England," p. 141. Lack of pomposity in "Profile," p. 47. State senate speech in Coolidge, *Have Faith in Massachusetts,* pp. 3, 4.

8. These aphorisms on patriotism, good government, and higher education are from Arthur MacDonald, comp., "Coolidge Aphorisms," *North American Review* 219 (June 1924): 742–745. Inaugural in W. A. White, *Puritan in Babylon,* p. 315. Speech on business in Thomas B. Silver, "Coolidge and the Historian," *American Scholar,* 50 (August 1981): 509. Deadpan style in "The Message," *Time,* (December 17, 1923): 1. Mention is made of the fact that Coolidge could be more convincing than dynamic orators in W. A. White, *Puritan in Babylon,* p. 123. Frequency of speeches and variety of audiences in Charles Merze, "The Silent Mr. Coolidge," *New Republic* 47 (June 2, 1926): 51, 52. Use of radio noted in Elmer E. Cornwell, Jr., "Coolidge and Presidential Leadership," *Public Opinion Quarterly,* 21 (Summer 1957): 270. "Was Coolidge Elected by Radio?" *Literary Digest* 84 (January 10, 1925): 62. Cornwell, "Presidential Leadership," p. 269.

9. On ubiquity see W. Hard, "Johnson Chases Coolidge," *The Nation* 118 (January 16, 1924): 59. Coolidge's enormous popularity with the press and the frequency and nature of his conferences are detailed in numerous articles, including Cornwell, "Coolidge and Presidential Leadership," pp. 270–274; Blair, "Coolidge the Image Maker," p. 501; Frank R. Kent, "The Press and Mr. Coolidge," *New Republic* 142 (June 13, 1960): 13, 14; David Lawrence, "The President and the Press," *Saturday Evening Post* 200 (August 27, 1927): 27ff. Predecessors' news conferences in Lawrence, "The President and the Press," p. 27. News conference description in Maitland A. Edey, ed., *Time Capsule/ 1923* (New York: Time-Life Books, 1967), p. 17. Accounts of Coolidge's press con-

ferences with edited transcripts can be found in Howard F. Quint and Robert H. Ferell, eds., *The Talkative President: The Off-the-Record Press Conferences of Calvin Coolidge* (Amherst, Mass.: 1964). On "spokesman" see Blair, "Coolidge the Image-Maker," p. 508. "A White House spokesman" was the preferred phrase. The press stopped using "a source close to the president" in 1924. On travel with press, see ibid., pp. 504–506, and Lawrence, "The President and the Press," p. 117. For Kennedy impressions, see Theodore H. White, *The Making of the President 1960* (New York: Atheneum, 1961), pp. 333–338.

   10. On stoicism, see W. A. White, *Puritan in Babylon,* p. 444. Congressional relations in "Coolidge as Leader," *Literary Digest* (May 24, 1924): 10. On personnel choice, see W. A. White, *Puritan in Babylon,* pp. 370, 391. The concept of "Coolidge Prosperity" is discussed in detail in Allen, *Only Yesterday,* pp. 132–154. Postpresidential image in McCoy, *The Quiet President,* p. 418. Of course, as McCoy notes, Coolidge was eventually blamed for his policies anyway: "Coolidge was doubly blamed. . . . He was reproached for pursuing the domestic policies he did and for not pursuing them for four more years."

ANNOTATED BIBLIOGRAPHY

Books

Fuess, Claude R. *Calvin Coolidge: The Man from Vermont.* Hamden, Conn.: Archon Books, 1965.
    An excellent profile of the man.
Lathem, Edward Connery, ed. *Meet Calvin Coolidge.* Brattleboro, Vt.: Stephen Greene Press, 1960.
    This anthology captures the flavor of the man and his times.
———, ed., *Calvin Coolidge Says.* Plymouth, Vt.: Calvin Coolidge Memorial Foundation, 1972.
    This is a collection of the newspaper columns written by President Coolidge between July 1, 1930, and June 20, 1931.
McCoy, Donald R. *Calvin Coolidge: The Quiet President.* New York: Macmillan, 1967.
    The work of a historian, this biographical analysis seeks to portray Ronald Reagan's "favorite President" in a balanced fashion.
White, William Allen. *A Puritan in Babylon: The Story of Calvin Coolidge.* New York: Capricorn Books, 1965.
    In this reprint, White's contemporary account, written in the late 1920s, is made available again. It was widely viewed as the best profile from that era.

Articles

Crissey, Forrest. "They Call Him Cal." *Saturday Evening Post* (October 25, 1924): 8.
Johnson, Haynes. "The Second Coming of Calvin Coolidge." *San Francisco Chronicle,* June 30, 1981.
Lowry, Edward G. "Calvin the Silent." *New Republic* (September 28, 1921): 131.
Lyons, Richard L. "The Boston Police Strike of 1919." *New England Quarterly,* 20 (June 1947): 147–168.

Shaw, A. "Character and Services of Calvin Coolidge." *Review of Reviews* (February 1933): 17.

"Silent Cal." *New Republic* (August 6 and 13, 1977): 45.

Stone, Marvin. "The Good Sense of 'Silent Cal.'" *U.S. News & World Report,* July 6, 1981, p. 72.

Documentary Records

Carradine, John, narrator. *If I'm Elected: The Actual Voices of Our Presidents and Their Opponents.* Audio Archives Enterprises, 1951.

This record of actualities contains a cut of Coolidge speaking in the 1924 campaign against John W. Davis.

Murrow, Edward R. with Fred Friendly. *I Can Hear It Now,* vol. 2. Columbia Records Special Products, 1949.

This contains cuts of the "business is business" and "they hired the money" speeches and the oath-taking by kerosene lamp in Vermont.

Voices of the Presidents. EAV Lexington, Educational Audio Visual, Inc., Pleasantville, N.Y., 1967.

This collection of actualities contains a cut made at the time of the Lindbergh reception in 1927 following the "Lone Eagle's" return from Paris.

13 HERBERT HOOVER

William C. Spragens and Linda J. Lear

> Slow and painful though progress was, popular government had functions, even against political sabotage. The fundamental moral strength of the people was greater than that of debilitating political tactics.
>
> —Herbert Hoover, *Memoirs*

Herbert Clark Hoover was born in West Branch, Iowa, in 1874. Prior to his service in high federal positions, culminating in his presidency, he had a distinguished career as a mining engineer.

Hoover, who served as the thirty-first president and was a Republican, was a son of Jesse Clark Hoover, a blacksmith, and Hulda Randall Minthorn Hoover. After his birth in Iowa, Hoover grew up in Indian Territory (now the state of Oklahoma) and in Oregon.

He was graduated from Stanford University, Palo Alto, California, with an A.B. in engineering in 1891. He worked briefly with the U.S. Geological Survey and then was employed in western mines. After this service in the United States, he worked as a mining engineer in the United States and around the world, including Australia and countries in Asia, Europe, and Africa. While a relatively young man in his thirties, he had already become a multimillionaire.

HOOVER'S EARLY PUBLIC SERVICE CAREER

In 1900, as chief engineer for the imperial mines in China, Hoover directed food relief for the Boxer Rebellion victims and thus gained experience valuable to him when he was asked by the American government to provide similar services during and after World War I.

After the Boxer Rebellion, Hoover continued his career as a mining engineer. During World War I, however, he was called on several occasions for public service leadership. The first occasion came in London prior to the American entry into the war. During 1914 and 1915, he directed the American relief committee in London. As the war continued, in 1915, he was named director of the U.S. Commission for Relief in Belgium, a post he held for four years. After American entry into the war, President Wilson appointed him as U.S. food administrator; he served until 1919. He popularized ''meatless Tuesdays'' and other government-sponsored campaigns to promote food resource conservation as a wartime measure.

After World War I, Hoover was American relief administrator in Europe from 1919 to 1923, and in this position he was responsible for feeding children in the defeated nations. After the Soviet Revolution and during the Russian Civil War, he managed Russian relief from 1918 to 1923.

Hoover was appointed by President Harding as secretary of commerce in 1921; he served until 1928, when he received the Republican presidential nomination. A major activity in which Hoover engaged at the Department of Commerce was the guidance of the fledgling radio industry into a pattern of government regulation. The shape of such regulation was gradually devised during annual conferences from 1922 through 1925. The first conference dealt with wave-length allocation, but there was still very little government-imposed regulation in the industry. Successive conferences dealt with further efforts to bring order out of chaos, as the radio broadcasting industry had mushroomed in a very short time without any real guidelines for growth. As secretary of commerce, Hoover led in organizing the First International Radio Conference in 1927. He also was instrumental in securing passage of the Federal Radio Act in 1927, which established the Federal Radio Commission and launched a rudimentary form of regulation. This legislation was later supplanted by the Federal Communications Act of 1934, which remains in force in its major provisions.

The Department of Commerce, already awarding licenses under the radio law of 1912, designed for wireless, had not had to deal with the problem of broadcasting on frequencies until the 1920s. During 1922 alone some 500 radio stations rushed to get on the air. By 1922, according to Eric Barnouw, Americans were spending $60 million on radio receiving equipment, of which $11 million worth was built by the RCA group, the first radio equipment manufacturing venture. Secretary Hoover stated that the radio boom, which was generating many applications for broadcasting licenses, was created by ''the genius of the American boy.''

Regarding Hoover's prepresidential career, Peri E. Arnold summarized recent scholarship, which has focused on ''an examination of Herbert Hoover's policy initiatives in the various public posts he held between 1917 and 1932.'' The main thrust of this revisionist view is to see Hoover's policy innovations as entailing intervention in the economy, thus marking a sharp break with the laissez-faire tradition. In this view, Hoover's public policies had more in common with the general level of governmental activities post-1932 than they had with a nineteenth-century laissez-faire tradition. The revisionists concur in seeing Hoover's policy contributions to American politics as essentially modernist and not traditional, ''far more like Franklin Roosevelt than Calvin Coolidge.'' Still,

Arnold finds that Hoover remains "an elusive figure" and suggests that "much of his character and work retains a traditionalist character." He terms Hoover "essentially a precocious traditional politician."

Arnold suggests that Hoover sought to separate administration from politics in the narrow partisan sense, and that this view of administration was followed by Hoover as secretary of commerce. Arnold concludes that

Secretary Hoover's administrative reforms at Commerce had three different aspects. They are: (1) a fundamental reorganization of the department's functional relationship to business; (2) a rationalization of central management in the department and an attempt to impose overall goals on the programs of various agencies; (3) a departmental public relations program which gave it great capacity to reach its constituency while it added to the department's public visibility and political strength.[1]

THE NOMINATION CAMPAIGN OF 1928

Because of his activities as secretary of commerce, as well as the Belgian and other food relief campaigns, Hoover had become a renowned and popular public figure. In the political environment of the day, he was deemed a progressive leader. In the summer of 1927, President Calvin Coolidge issued his statement that "I do not choose to run in 1928." Because of Hoover's widespread popularity, not only within the Republican party but also nationwide, the Coolidge statement prompted a presidential boom for Hoover for the 1928 GOP nomination. As considerable support developed for Hoover, those who wanted to promote a "draft" for President Coolidge were soon in a distinct minority.

Some observers thought that President Coolidge had hoped that a movement for Hoover would be opposed and that the resulting deadlock might cause a draft movement for Coolidge. Others argued that the president did not really want to run again and attributed to Grace Coolidge the remark, "Papa says there's going to be a depression."

The first Coolidge announcement of August 2, 1927, was not particularly clarified when in December 1927, at a White House meeting attended by members of the Republican National Committee, he said, "My decision will be respected." The president, however, did not elaborate. Pro-Hoover factions in the party went to work. Senator Robert M. La Follette, Jr., of Wisconsin aided the anti-Coolidge Republicans by introducing a resolution that endorsed the tradition that no president should serve for more than two terms, and complimented Coolidge for adhering to the custom. A leader of the draft-Coolidge forces, Senator Simeon D. Fess of Ohio, moved that the reference to the two-term tradition be deleted. His motion brought this response from Senator George W. Norris of Nebraska:

Here is a resolution to be passed by this high legislative body in which we directly commend the President for a patriotic act that he did. . . . Then here come a few earnest, perhaps honest, perhaps ill-advised insurgents and they insist that we shall insult the

President of the United States, that at least we shall not commend him for following in the footsteps of Washington.[2]

Hoover's opponents for the nomination included Governor Frank Lowden of Illinois, Senator Charles Curtis (minority floor leader from Kansas), Senator Frank B. Willis of Ohio, and James Watson of Indiana.

By the time the gavel fell to begin the Republican National Convention in Kansas City in June 1928, Hoover's nomination appeared almost certain. The platform favored high tariffs, economy, and tax reduction, as well as the enforcement of the Eighteenth (Prohibition) Amendment. It also spoke of international cooperation, but did not endorse American participation in the League of Nations.

Hoover was nominated by an overwhelming majority on the first ballot at Kansas City. Because of his strong farm following and his record of party regularity in the Senate, Senator Charles Curtis of Kansas was named as Hoover's running mate. The Republican campaign made Prohibition and farm policy key issues. Hoover was still riding on the crest of a wave of popularity as the election campaign approached.[3]

THE CONTEST AGAINST AL SMITH

At the Democratic National Convention held in Houston in the summer of 1928, the party out of power chose Governor Alfred E. Smith of New York, a man with a progressive record, as Herbert Hoover's opponent for the presidency. The Democrats came closer to having a harmonious convention than had been the case in 1924, when John W. Davis was nominated in New York City on the 103rd ballot.

Although regional conflicts, wet versus dry, and Klan versus anti-Klan controversies were still in evidence at Houston, the Democratic contest was affected by an announcement in 1927 by William Gibbs McAdoo, who ran in 1924, that in the interest of party unity he would not oppose Smith. The withdrawal of Smith's most prominent contender made it all but certain beforehand that Smith would be the nominee at Houston. For the third time in eight years, Franklin D. Roosevelt placed Smith's name in nomination, commending the "Happy Warrior."

Al Smith ran on a platform which charged that the Republican party had left American industry depressed and had prostrated agriculture. It advocated farm-relief measures, tariff reform, and a "constructive" foreign policy, without mentioning the League of Nations and the World Court, both still controversial in 1928. The Prohibition plank merely pledged "an honest effort" to enforce the Eighteenth Amendment and cited the Republican party's failure to endorse the amendment.

Although Smith was the favorite, nine other persons were placed in nomination, the most prominent of which were Senator James A. Reed of Missouri,

Representative Cordell Hull of Tennessee, Jesse Jones of Texas, and Senator Walter F. George of Georgia (Hull was later secretary of state). As Smith's running mate, the delegates made another first ballot nomination, this time for Senator Joseph T. Robinson of Arkansas, a strong Prohibitionist and a southern Protestant.

The Republicans had already nominated Hoover and, as in 1924, their greatest asset in terms of domestic issues was the economic prosperity that prevailed. In his acceptance speech, Hoover stated: "We in America today are nearer to the final triumph over poverty than ever before in the history of the land. The poorhouse is vanishing from among us."

Despite the platform statements, Prohibition became an issue in the fall campaign because of the candidates' views. Hoover came out strongly for full enforcement and described Prohibition as "a great social and economic experiment." Smith, however, favored a modification of the Prohibition laws.

Behind the scenes, largely in the form of a "whispering campaign," Smith's Catholic religion also became a factor in the campaign, if not an overt issue. Herbert Hoover denounced appeals to bigotry and stated that they "give violence to every instinct I possess," but it cannot be doubted that some of Hoover's support came from persons who took seriously campaign charges that Smith would be dominated by the Vatican if elected. Much derogatory propaganda against Smith was circulated, although this was usually not done in a highly visible fashion.

Smith conducted an aggressive and active campaign. While his campaign was somewhat more restrained than Smith's, Hoover did carry on a more active campaign than Coolidge had conducted in 1924. Hoover spurned several challenges from Smith to engage in a public debate, and indeed managed to conduct the entire campaign without mentioning Smith by name even once. Both parties openly courted the support of large corporate interests, then at one of the peaks of their popularity in modern times. It was estimated that campaign expenditures for the Republicans totalled nearly $9.5 million and for the Democrats more than $7 million. These sums were triple the amount spent by each party in previous presidential campaigns.

In the election, Hoover was victorious. He took forty states, including Smith's own New York State as well as five states in what had previously been the Democratic "Solid South." The popular vote result was 21,392,190 for Hoover and 15,016,443 for Smith. In the Electoral College Hoover gained 444 votes to 87 for Smith. The remaining months prior to Hoover's inauguration were relatively peaceful and uneventful, and Coolidge continued to provide the quiet—even taciturn—leadership identified with him.[4]

HOOVER AS PRESIDENT: FOREIGN POLICY

Herbert Hoover took the oath of office as president on March 4, 1929, and he had to deal with the usual run of foreign policy problems. One issue he had to grapple with was the implementation of the Kellogg-Briand Pact of August 27, 1928, negotiated by the Coolidge administration. This was in effect a treaty to outlaw war, but it was not very effective because not all nations had chosen to join the League of Nations to make it an instrument to preserve the peace. One of these nonmembers was the United States. Foreign economic problems in the wake of the Great Depression presented another serious policy issue for Hoover.

There was continuing pacifist sentiment, and when in 1931 the Japanese Empire invaded Manchuria, Hoover had Secretary of State Henry L. Stimson send a note of protest to Tokyo, but the note was rejected. All during this period the expansionist and imperialistic policies of Japan in the Far East were a concern for the State Department, but the simplistic popular feeling for pacifism limited the Hoover administration in taking stronger countermeasures.

A greater preoccupation than peacekeeping on the other side of the globe was perhaps the development of tariff barriers against other nations, an outgrowth of the economic distress that eventually resulted in the Great Depression beginning in October 1929. Reacting to the difficulties in international trade, the Congress adopted (with more or less support from the administration) the Smoot-Hawley tariff schedule.

HOOVER AS PRESIDENT: DOMESTIC POLICY

George H. Mayer says in *The Republican Party: 1854–1966*:

All three postwar Republican Presidents believed in a general way that the national government ought to promote prosperity without infringing on the freedom of the individual or stifling the initiative of local governmental units. With Harding and Coolidge this outlook was instinctive. They would have been hard-pressed to formulate it in theoretical terms and would not have worried unduly about vacillations that suited the interests of their political supporters. Hoover, on the other hand, knew exactly what he believed and why. His program was predicated on basic doctrines about the nature of man and his institutions. Urgent practical problems never tempted Hoover to deviate consciously from his philosophy. When the lines of demarcation which he had drawn between spheres of individual and institutional activity grew blurred, Hoover invoked principles as a guide to action, although occasionally he might have made unconscious rationalizations in line with his wishes.[5]

The foregoing may provide some understanding of the popular image of Herbert Hoover as the president who kept adhering to the principles of "rugged individualism" in the face of the stock market crash, an image so well known that it will not be repeated here. But Hoover's reaction was to speak immediately of efforts to "restore confidence" in the economy. "Prosperity is just around the corner" became the watchword of the new administration. And the campaign slogan of "two chickens in every pot, two cars in every garage" took on an ironic ring as the economy began its dizzying slump. At the nadir of the Depression one out of every four Americans was out of work. Villages set up by hoboes (unemployed men who rode the rails and foraged for food wherever they could find it) came to be known as "Hoovervilles." Had Hoover been less steadfast in his belief in rugged individualism, had the circumstances been different, his dogged persistence in the creed of individual responsibility might not have been so damaging to his image, nor would it have so greatly undermined the public's confidence in him as a leader. Hoover stuck to the philosophy of rugged individualism, but he did bend sufficiently in the last part of his administration to allow the establishment of an agency known as the Reconstruction Finance Corporation (RFC), which was intended to help corporations by making government loans. But he continued to resist direct aid to needy individuals as a move that was contrary to his own tenaciously held beliefs.

THE CAMPAIGN AGAINST GOVERNOR ROOSEVELT

Although President Hoover signed the RFC enabling legislation in January 1932, it was already late in his term. He would soon have to defend the record of his four years in office before the voters.

Stefan Lorant has written of the Hoover administration and its period in office:

Looking back at the Hoover Administration, the four years seem to fall into five markedly different periods. The first phase lasted from inauguration day until the crash in October (1929). During these months prosperity was on the upgrade and the President's popularity peaked. The second phase extended from the crash until early 1930, when Hoover battled manfully against the disaster without realizing its gravity. Its third phase lasted from March 1930 until June 1931, a period of despair. It was during this time that the President's attitude underwent a marked change. He now declared the Depression was part of the international economic debacle and advised America to free itself "of world influences and make a large measure of independent recovery." During the fourth period—from June to October 1931—the administration held that the German economic crisis had a retarding effect on American recovery, and the President, declaring a moratorium on war debts, bluntly admitted the seriousness of the crisis. From then on until the end of his term—the fifth period—Hoover faced the problems which confronted the nation more realistically.[6]

While some Republicans urged Hoover not to seek another term in 1932, the Progressive Republicans' efforts in this direction and toward establishing a third-party movement were unsuccessful. Hiram Johnson and Gifford Pinchot were asked to run, but they did not seem to have sufficient grass-roots support.

The Republican National Convention of 1932 met in Chicago. Regulars in the Republican party made no real effort to find a new candidate, so Hoover's managers continued to get delegate commitments without serious hindrance despite the gloomy economic situation. On June 14, 1932, the Republicans opened their Chicago convention. There was little enthusiasm until a strong attack was delivered against the Democrats by the permanent chairman, Bertrand Snell of

New York State. A former senator from Maryland, Dr. Joseph D. France, was the president's only open rival for the nomination. When he sought to withdraw his name and asked the delegates to support former President Coolidge, one account says that he was removed from the platform by Hoover supporters and not allowed to speak.

The Republican platform, a general defense of Hoover's policies, was passed without much dispute. In 8,500 words it defended Hoover's record but did not offer many constructive suggestions for new action. A few vague phrases dealt with the nation's economic problems. Concerning Prohibition, the compromise written into the platform suggested that Congress should submit to state conventions—not to the legislatures—a proposed new amendment governing the liquor traffic, and these conventions should decide whether liquor could be manufactured and sold within each state's borders.

When the Democratic National Convention met in Chicago on June 22, a much more enthusiastic atmosphere prevailed than had been the case during the Republican convention two weeks earlier. Democrats believed that the twelve long years of Republican administrations were nearing and end, and the resulting optimism brought a large number of candidates to Chicago in search of the nomination. Al Smith, former governor of New York and the previous nominee, felt that he deserved another chance to defeat Hoover. Speaker John Nance Garner of Texas sought the nomination as a reward for the leadership role he had played in the Seventy-second Congress. Besides numerous favorite sons, Governor Franklin D. Roosevelt of New York had entered the convention with a clear majority of delegates but well short of the two-thirds needed for nomination.

The favorites were clearly Roosevelt and Smith. A "stop Roosevelt" coalition denied him the nomination for three ballots, but then a deal was struck with the Texas delegation, and on the fourth ballot Garner switched sufficient delegates to FDR to put him over in exchange for being selected as the vice presidential running mate. After the Texas switch, William McAdoo of the California delegation threw an additional bloc of delegates to FDR. Roosevelt finally received 945 delegate votes to 190¼ for Smith.

FDR shattered all precedents by taking a plane to Chicago to accept the nomination at the convention itself. Previous nominees had awaited a formal notification ceremony, but FDR made a memorable speech to the convention in which he promised a "new deal" for the "forgotten man" hard hit by the Depression.

During the 1932 election campaign, two innovations were introduced into the image-building process for the candidates. First, professional public relations experts rather than organization politicians performed the public relations task of the campaign. Second, extensive use was made of radio broadcasting during the campaign. In the election campaign FDR traveled about 17,000 miles, and this was long before the age of the jet plane.

It was reported by a cabinet member to Paul W. Anderson of *The Nation* that the Republican party developed a strategy. One element was to attack Speaker Garner as "unsound" and "radical," along with the suggestion that Roosevelt's poor health would force him to turn over the presidency to Garner within a year or two; the second phase of the strategy was to attack Roosevelt as a radical on the issue of electric power generation and to point to his reference in his acceptance speech to a new deal for the forgotten man; a third theme was a "whispering campaign" against Roosevelt targeted toward his Catholic supporters, suggesting that FDR instigated anti-Catholic propaganda against Al Smith during the nomination campaign. James A. Farley denied various stories about Roosevelt's health and stated that FDR was recently permitted to take out a $500,000 life insurance policy with the Warm Springs Foundation—which treated polio—as a beneficiary.

Roosevelt campaigned actively with twenty-seven major addresses and thirty-two shorter speeches, and in general he impressed his audiences with his magnetism.

In contrast to FDR, President Hoover delivered ten major speeches, each quite similar to the others. He defended his antidepression measures and again blamed the Depression on overseas economic ills. Hoover frequently looked harassed and preoccupied, and his platform manner contrasted poorly with the magnetism exhibited by Roosevelt. In his final speech, Hoover said: "The campaign is more than a contest between two men. It is a contest between two philosophies of government." He said that the people must choose between individualism and regimentation. "You cannot extend the mastery of government over the daily life of a people without somewhere making it a master of people's souls and thought."

The election resulted in a landslide victory for Roosevelt. FDR carried forty-two states and Hoover only six. FDR's electoral vote was 472 to Hoover's 59, and his popular vote was 22,821,857 to 15,761,841 for Hoover.

HOOVER'S POSTPRESIDENTIAL CAREER

Upon his retirement from the White House in 1933, Hoover had not yet reached the age of sixty. He was one of those presidents who was blessed with additional years to perform public service in retirement; he also lived to see some restoration of his reputation, badly tarnished when he left office. Hoover, who eventually took up residence in the Waldorf Astoria Towers in New York, lived to the age of ninety; he died in 1964, the same year as another noted conservative, General Douglas MacArthur.

Between 1933 and 1946, Hoover was active in speech-making. He also regularly attended Republican conventions; his name during this time became almost synonymous with the concept of reform and efficiency in government. The Hoovers also maintained a home in Palo Alto, California. Here is an explanation of why they spent so much time in New York, in the late president's own words:

In the years after leaving Washington, my various activities in many benevolent institutions, crusading against the New Deal and advocating national policies, kept me constantly traveling. In 1934, Mrs. Hoover and I found that we must spend much of the
time in the East and, therefore, we took an apartment in New York City where we spent
a good part of the fall and winter months over many years.

New York is the place from where a large part of America's intellectual life is transmitted. Here centers the control of much of the magazine, the book, and the radio world.
Some of its daily papers spread into every other newspaper office in the country. The
control of many charitable and educational institutions is centered here because of the
closeness to "big money." A multitude of political, social, economic, and propaganda
organizations spread out or infiltrate into the whole of American life from this great city.
When one is interested also in the promulgation of ideas, it is more effective to be at the
distributing point than at the receiving end.[7]

Former President Hoover's conservative speeches and his viewpoints as expressed in public utterances were published in a series of volumes entitled *Addresses upon the American Road*. Six of these volumes had been published when
the final volume of his memoirs appeared.

The former president viewed the progressive experimentation of the Roosevelt
years as inimical to the ideal of freedom as he saw it in the preceding years. He
wrote:

The period from 1933 to 1941 may be viewed from two angles: first, as an attempt to
revolutionize the American system of life, and second, as a mere continuation of the
Great Depression into its sixth phase by inept economic action. It was, in fact, both—
the first being largely the cause of the second. My interest in my country could not be
ended by an election, especially as I knew the character and purposes of the men coming
into power were not those of traditional America. . . .

What had been, up to the election, an ideological debate was now transformed into a
reality of national experience. In adopting the New Deal, most of the American people
did not realize that they had departed from the road of free men.[8]

Hoover, though critical of the New Deal and its underlying philosophy, did
find some worthwhile reforms among its programs. These included giving further
authority to the RFC, which had originated in his term, and the expansion of
activities of the Home Loan Banks and the Federal Farm Banks. He noted that
his own administration had urged stock exchange reforms and the regulation of
electric power companies. Hoover was critical of direct action through federal
agencies, noting that his own administration preferred to act through existing
financial or other institutions. He found that many New Deal measures constituted
the kind of "collectivism" to which he was unalterably opposed. He was particularly critical of the Roosevelt administration for recognizing the Soviet Union
on November 16, 1933, and he felt that this action would long be regretted.

Through the next twelve years Hoover as an opposition spokesman continued
to have a loyal following within the Republican party. But he did not return to
public service in any formal capacity until after the death of President Roosevelt

in 1945. Ironically, President Truman, Roosevelt's Democratic successor, appointed Hoover as chief of a study group on governmental efficiency and reform that was to become known as the First Hoover Commission.

In 1947, the year of the Truman Doctrine and the Marshall Plan, President Truman had named Hoover honorary chairman of the Famine Emergency Committee. Hoover went abroad to survey conditions in Europe, and the committee asked Americans to eat 25 percent less wheat and published thirty nine ways to conserve food.

In 1949, after the First Hoover Commission had issued its report, President Truman designated his appointment secretary, Matthew J. Connelly, and another staff aide to have responsibility for its congressional liaison. The First Hoover Commission functioned from 1947 to 1949. Its work included that of the Task Force on National Security Organization, launched in June 1948. Task force recommendations became the basis for the 1949 amendments to the National Security Act and closely followed Defense Secretary James Forrestal's recommendations. When assistant secretaries of defense were designated, these 1949 recommendations called for a comptroller for the Department of Defense and for each of the three subunits of the military establishment which it embraced.

In 1953 President Dwight D. Eisenhower appointed the Second Hoover Commission, which continued the work begun by the first commission under President Truman. One of its important achievements was Reorganization Plan Number Six of 1953, which strengthened the role of the secretary of defense in relation to the Joint Chiefs of Staff and the service secretaries in the National Security Act of 1947, which had established the National Security Council. In presenting the amendment to Congress, President Eisenhower advocated the elimination of waste and duplication of services, strengthening civilian control with clearer lines of responsibility, better administrative procedures within the Department of Defense, and an improved mechanism for strategic planning.[9]

Peri E. Arnold in an enlightening analysis about the work of the First Hoover Commission suggests that it provided the means for developing bipartisan support for the concept of the modern managerial presidency and suggests that it built on the beginnings made by the Brownlow Commission during the Roosevelt administration. President Truman's desire to strengthen the institutionalized presidency overrode any partisan doubts he may have had about the Hoover Commission, in Arnold's view. Budget Director James Webb is seen as one of those who sought to strengthen Hoover's support for the institutionalized presidency. As Arnold writes:

Webb explained [to President Truman]:

Based on my relations with Mr. Hoover, as your liaison representative, I believe there is now a possibility of getting the last Republican President to urge you to accept an implementation of and organization for executive responsibility that the Republican Party has historically denied to Presidents. If that can be managed, you will undoubtedly be able to achieve—with at least a show of bipartisan agreement—a new level of Presidential leadership and effectively discharged responsibility for administration unknown in our history.[10]

Webb's plan promised far more advantage for President Truman than he could ever obtain by denouncing the Hoover Commission. For over a year, Truman had lived with its political ambivalence while he offered co-operation and support. Now his benign stand would pay off, both for himself and the managerial Presidency.

Webb's advice rested on his accurate insight into former President Hoover. On the face of the matter it would have seemed that Hoover's view of the expanded Presidency would be inextricably tied to his view of the expansion of government under the New Deal. But Webb understood that he was ready to be sold the contemporary Presidency.

Herbert Hoover's readiness to accept the Truman-Webb view of the Presidency did not mark a political about face between the 1930's and the 1940's. There is a distinct thread (which Webb sensed) in Hoover's career that prepared him to favor the mechanisms of the expanded, institutionalized Presidency. Hoover's public career, from the days of the U.S. Food Administration during World War I, through his tenure as Secretary of Commerce, to the Presidency, had been closely tied to interests in management of bureaucratic organizations. He was a mining engineer become politician who viewed organizations in mechanistic terms, believed in orthodox administrative doctrines, and felt that responsibility in official roles should be matched by a like and corresponding amount of authority.

Every phase of Herbert Hoover's public career demonstrates an abiding concern with administrative reorganization. At the Department of Commerce, from 1921 to 1927, he completely reorganized the internal arrangements of the agency and then sought a number of interdepartmental reorganizations to join like functions together with Commerce. He became the strongest supporter in the Harding Cabinet for the work and recommendations of the Joint Committee on Reorganization which reported to Congress in 1923. Hoover's interest in reorganization continued into the White House, and he was the first President to propose that Congress grant him reorganization powers subject to legislative veto. In his first State of the Union message, Hoover enunciated the principles of proper organization which would still guide him two decades later when he approached the problems of the Presidency in the Hoover Commission report. He stated:

It seems to me that the essential principles of reorganization are two in number. First, all administrative activities of the same major purpose should be placed in groups under single-headed responsibility; second, all executive and administrative functions should be separated from boards and commissions and placed under individual responsibility. Indeed, these are the fundamental principles upon which our Government was founded and they are the principles which have been adhered to in the development of our business structure, and they are the distillation of the common sense of generations.[11]

The Hoover Commission recommendations relating to the Presidency represent Hoover's solutions to the problems of an expanded government and Presidency. These solutions spoke to the contemporary Presidency, but with a sympathy and understanding which Hoover had developed for the office many years before. These recommendations were his own. In the words of Herbert Emmerich, "He constituted himself the task force for the treatment of the Presidency." . . .

Perhaps the final irony of the Hoover Commission's work on the Presidency is that after the Commission's "liberals" taught Chairman Hoover the importance of providing flexible staff aid to the President they themselves were caught in their own orthodoxy.

In the Commission's report, Herbert Hoover accepts the basic logic of the presidential secretariat position, but refuses to limit the President within a particular organizational form. The report on the executive office recommends increased support for staff along with complete presidential discretion over how that staff will be used. The case is clear; Hoover first learned to move beyond his own administrative orthodoxy and then moved beyond the orthodoxy of his teachers.[12]

COMMENTS OF HOOVER'S CONTEMPORARIES

Conservative publications of his time spoke highly of Hoover as a great humanitarian and a great engineer. But he had his critics too. Comments from his critics have been drawn from various editorials found in the *New Republic* in 1928 and 1932. For example, in August 1928 this publication was commenting editorially:

Mr. Herbert Hoover's speech accepting the nomination of the Republican Party for the Presidency is not a distinguished or an important expression of political conviction. On the surface it is little more than an awkward, confused procession of Republican commonplaces. It is not easy for Mr. Hoover to find an individual and appropriate verbal equivalent for his living feelings and ideas. He is a plain, shy, moody, sensitive man of action. Effective public speaking implies the playing of a part, and this he cannot do. . . . Certainly Mr. Hoover's economic and political doctrine appears to endorse all of the President's most dreary Coolidgisms. It flourishes the same misleading claims. . . .

The preceding estimate of Mr. Hoover's speech of acceptance would, however, if he were left alone, convey a wholly false report both of the speech and of the quality of his mind. Conventional as it is in intellectual substance and jerky and tense as it is in form, it is in the quality of its feeling almost pathetically sincere. Mr. Hoover's formulation of public policy does not apparently differ from that of Mr. Coolidge, but he nonetheless means something different by what he says. . . . From Mr. Coolidge's point of view, America is a finished Utopia, which, like one of Mr. Ziegfeld's show girls, requires only to be exposed in order to be glorified. From Mr. Hoover's point of view, America is also a Utopia, but a Utopia still in the making. . . .

Mr. Hoover, consequently, displays in his speech the conscience, if not of a liberated political thinker, at least of a good professional engineer. Engineers are essentially innovators who are making the world over according to preconceived and accepted patterns and ideas. . . . Mr. Hoover is in a sense a typical engineer in politics. He takes for granted, just as Calvin Coolidge and Alfred Smith do, without examination and without inquiry, the traditional plan, organization and ideal outlook of American social and economic life. He considers it his business to examine the working of the mechanism and to propose and execute desirable improvement therein. It is not a very lofty and far-reaching aim, but it is different from that of his chief, and it is better. . . .

"Our purpose is," says Mr. Hoover, "to build in this nation a human society, not an economic system." Yet throughout the whole of his address the materials out of which he proposes to build a human society are the selfish economic motives of individuals and the satisfaction of their cravings for possessions and power plus a smoke screen of pious discourse about the beauty of public spirit and constructive service. It is the old story of the silk purse and the sow's ear.[13]

The *New Republic* editorial from 1928 conveys a sense that Hoover was considered more progressive than his predecessor in the White House, if not very imaginative in his public statements. Four years later the same publication was more critical of President Hoover in dealing with the issue of the bonus marchers, as the following selected comments indicate: In a John Dos Passos comment:

The arrival of the Bonus Army seems to be the first event to give the inhabitants of Washington any inkling that something is happening in the world outside their drowsy sun parlor. Maybe it's the federal pay cuts that have made them take notice. In the Anacostia street car two mail carriers and the conductor started to talk about it. "Well, they say they'll stay here till they get the bonus if they have to stay till 1945. . . . I guess they ought to get it, all right, but how'll that help all the others out of work? . . . Terrible to think of men, women and children starvin' and havin' to get charity relief with all the stuff there is going to waste in this country. Why up home . . . "

If the BEF [Bonus Expeditionary Force] fails, it'll be because they've asked for too little, not because they've asked too much.[14]

In an essay by Malcolm Cowley and Slater Brown:

Their shanties and tents had been burned, their personal property destroyed, except for the few belongings they could carry on their backs; many of their families were separated, wives from husbands, children from parents. . . . When threatened with forcible eviction, they answered that no American soldier would touch them: hadn't a detachment of Marines (consisting, some said, of 25 or 30 men, though others claimed there were two whole companies) thrown down its arms and refused to march against them? But the infantry, last night, had driven them out like so many vermin. Mr. Hoover had announced that "after months of patient indulgence, the government met overt lawlessness as it always must be met if the cherished processes of self-government are to be preserved." Mr. Hoover and his subordinates, in their eagerness to justify his action, were about to claim that the veterans were Red radicals, that they were the dregs of the population, that most of them had criminal records and, as a final insult, that half of them weren't veterans at all. . . .

A haggard face—eyes bloodshot, skin pasty white under three days' beard—suddenly appeared at the window of our car. "Hoover must die," said the face ominously. "You know what this means?" a man shouted from the other side. "This means revolution." "Yes, you're damned right it means revolution."

But a thousand homeless veterans, or fifty thousand, don't make a revolution. This threat would pass and be forgotten. . . . No, if any revolution results from the flight of the Bonus Army, it will come from a different source, from the government itself. The army in time of peace, at the national capital, has been used against unarmed citizens— and this, with all it threatens for the future, is a revolution in itself.[15]

Regarding Mr. Hoover's 1932 acceptance speech:

Mr. Hoover's acceptance speech carries a burden of genuine emotion which has been lacking in other documents of the campaign. One gets the sense that the author has lived and suffered, that he is speaking out of his heart. He is deeply convinced of something, and for that reason what he says commands a kind of respect that would not be accorded to a mere exercise in logic, to a superficial appeal for voters. The speech is perhaps better material for the psychologist or the novelist than for the political scientist.

And as one reads the acceptance with imaginative sympathy, the faith that Mr. Hoover has, and the effect which it has exerted on his policy, become clear. He is living in the American fairy tale which nurtured his youth and which offers the whole justification for his life. . . . [Here the editorialist recites the free enterprise creed of individualism.]

Once upon a time, also, in the golden age of Coolidge, this nation approached the height of ambition. Nearly everyone was rich and happy. The doctrine of individualism had almost done its work. And then something strange happened. The dragon of depression thrust its ugly head into the idyl. Mr. Hoover plainly resents it bitterly; he must find ways of explaining this dragon which challenges his faith, ways of slaying it. . . . To Mr. Hoover, it is the dream which is real, not the dragon. For a long time he just shut his eyes, so that he would not see the depression. Even yet he does not believe it to be genuine. . . .

But why continue with the recital of facts known to everyone who is not lulled to sleep by the Hoover bedtime story? Mr. Hoover and his adherents may go on dreaming for some time yet. Too many of them have lived the dream. Have they not seized opportunity, become rich and secure? Is it not to their interest that the government stay out of business? Does it not comfort them to think that all the misery in the world arises from the incompetence and wickedness of others? Why does not the whole people become as they are? For them to acknowledge that they are mistaken would undermine the dignity, the meaning of their entire lives. The whole power of Herbert Hoover's personality, rising from the unplumbed depths of his being, rises to resist the challenge to his faith which he discerns on the horizon. That is what gives his speech its vibrancy. Conservatism is putting on its armor. It will resist change to the death.[16]

In the wake of the Roosevelt election victory:

Although no Republican candidate for President has ever been so overwhelmingly defeated as Hoover, except Taft, when his own party was split, the result should occasion no surprise. Indeed, the reaction of the American people to the calamities which have befallen them is astonishingly mild, when we remember that many nations have had revolutions. . . . The proportion of our working population which has been unemployed is larger than in any other great industrial nation except Germany, and our farmers are carrying as heavy a burden of deflation as any farmers in the world. The contrast between the conditions prevailing when Hoover entered office and those existing at present is so striking, and the failure of the Republicans to carry out their promises is so dramatic, that anything less than a landslide against them could be accounted for only by immeasurable stupidity and sluggishness of the electorate.[17]

Ronald Steel, biographer of Walter Lippmann, the *New York World* editor and later a renowned columnist, notes how the pundit viewed the Hoover administration:

"It is a marvel, looking back on it now," Lippmann wrote in his first column for the *Tribune* on September 8, 1931, "that we could ever have so completely thought that a boom under such treacherous conditions was permanent." "In other periods of depression it has always been possible to see some things which were solid and upon which you could base hope," Calvin Coolidge said just a few days before his death in January 1933. "But as I look about, I now see nothing to give ground for hope, nothing of man."

Such pessimism would have been inconceivable only a few years earlier. When Herbert Hoover took office as President in March 1929 it seemed as though the key to peace and prosperity had at last been found. The boom rolled on, world trade was at an all-time high, the war debts-reparation snarl had been largely resolved, moderates ruled in Tokyo and democrats in Weimar, and war had been outlawed. Within six months it all came apart. . . .

"Today we know that we have not yet made peace and that nothing is really got for nothing," Lippmann wrote on New Year's Day, 1931. "We begin to know that we do not know. We begin to see that we are not guaranteed an unending good fortune. . . . There are no phrases to save us. There are no miracles. There is only the courage to be intelligent and sober."

Hoover, the great engineer, the organizing genius of Belgian relief and European postwar reconstruction, seemed incapable of coming to grips with the emergency. Although a man of decent instincts and great administrative talents, he could not modify the faith in self-reliance and voluntary cooperation he had inherited from more tranquil times. Yet he was not a reactionary. He used the powers of government to an unprecedented degree to compensate for the failure of local and private initiative. He authorized public works projects, set up a system of home-loan banks, encouraged farm cooperatives, created the Reconstruction Finance Corporation to lend money to ailing businesses and banks, and made the federal government ultimately responsible for relief when local sources proved inadequate. In an unplanned manner he adopted most of the principles that were later implemented in the early years of the New Deal. His "historic position as a radical innovator has been greatly underestimated and . . . Mr. Roosevelt's pioneering has been greatly exaggerated," Lippmann later wrote. "It was Mr. Hoover who abandoned the principles of laissez faire in relation to the business cycle, established the conviction that prosperity and depression can be publicly controlled by political action, and drove out of the public consciousness the old idea that depressions must be overcome by private adjustment."

Hoover's foreign policy record—so overwhelmed by the domestic crisis that defeated him—seemed a model of enlightened restraint. He opposed Wilson's intervention against the Bolsheviks, worked for Russian relief, sought international arms agreements, withdrew the marines from Nicaragua, tried to ban foreign loans to Latin America for military purposes, and opposed economic warfare against Japan during the Manchurian crisis. Hoover, Lippmann wrote appreciatively three decades later during the Vietnam War, "never believed in America as a global power with military and political commitments in every continent. He was an isolationist and, insofar as his beliefs could be reconciled with his duties as president and commander-in-chief, he was a conscientious objector."

Hoover's faults were in part a magnification of his virtues. . . . With his dour personality and his homilies about prosperity being just around the corner, he won a deserved reputation for political rigidity.

The defeatism that marked the last two years of his term could not have been foreseen at the time of the election, when the nation was still riding high with the Coolidge boom. Lippmann was not alone in feeling that Hoover, as he wrote just before the 1928 election, was a "reformer who is probably more vividly conscious of the defects of American capitalism than any man in public life today." If Hoover had his way, Lippmann predicted, he would "purify capitalism of its predatoriness, its commercialism, its waste, and its squalor, and infuse it with a very large measure of democratic consent under highly trained professional leadership."[18]

CATEGORIZATION BY BARBER AS ACTIVE-NEGATIVE

In recent assessments of the presidency and its modern incumbents, the style analysis of presidential leadership developed by James David Barber suggests two dimensions for describing style. One of these is the degree of activism: Did the president take an active or a passive attitude toward his leadership task and role performance? The other measure is one of whether the president had positive or negative feelings toward his office and his role in it. Combining these two sets of categories, Barber determined that a president might be considered active-positive, active-negative, passive-positive, or passive-negative. In analyzing the Hoover administration, it was Barber's view that Herbert Hoover could be categorized as an active-negative president (suggesting at least some contrast to Ronald Steel's view). Other modern presidents who were placed in this category by Barber included Woodrow Wilson and Lyndon Johnson.[19]

Other analysts of the presidency such as Alexander George have raised questions about this categorization of Hoover's presidency, but there are some pieces of evidence to support it. It is generally known that Hoover's rise to public attention coincided with his work in various international relief efforts, and Barber suggests that expansion of the role of the mass media of the day, including newspapers and radio, brought this record of Hoover's more forcefully to the nation's attention. Barber found that Hoover took "discomfort in his public performances" and that he had an inherent shyness. In the White House, says Barber, Hoover "transmuted all adventure into business."[20]

In many places in the literature, Hoover's background as an engineer is cited in explaining his approach to the problems of government. He shied away from the arts of showmanship associated with relatively successful presidents—successful in the art of communication, at least—such as Franklin Roosevelt and Ronald Reagan.

It was clear that Hoover had the capability to generate much loyalty in those who worked for him, and prior to the Depression he was the object of much public adulation in appreciation of his accomplishments, not only as a relief director but also as a leading spokesman in the Harding and Coolidge cabinets.

Hoover had a preference, in making his public statements, for using "facts and reason" rather than dramatics, according to Barber's diagnosis. Thus it was clear that what was in actuality shyness on Hoover's part should be interpreted by the unknowing public as casual or careless indifference. In other words, to some extent, Hoover's public image suffered from the nature of his personality. The modesty and avoidance of bombast that might have been attractive in a private person were a detriment to a public leader.

Hoover can be viewed as the antithesis of Franklin D. Roosevelt in both personality and policy terms, but it is sometimes forgotten that Roosevelt in the 1932 campaign ran on a platform which called for a balanced budget and accused the Hoover administration of extravagant spending.

CONCLUSIONS ABOUT HERBERT HOOVER'S IMAGE

It is important to compare the views about Hoover held by his contemporaries with those of the present generation who can recall the postpresidential service of his retirement years. Gene Smith saw Hoover as a tragic figure who could come to be better understood with the passage of time:

Hoover was the finest flower of our system. It was bewildering, phenomenally so, to look at him on March 4, 1933, and see him as the discredited leader whose name would be poison in the mouths of millions for decades to come.

What happened?

There was something in Hoover himself that caused it. That something was his fate and the country's fate. Perhaps he was, as Franklin Roosevelt thought, not what he seemed. Or that in any other time he would have served eight glorious years and gone out of office covered with laurels.

There are those who feel Hoover can be characterized by the words "dogmatic," "inflexible," "unintelligent." His inadequacies, they say, were far deeper than a mere lack of spirit and of fire; it was that he misunderstood the situation, not that he was a poor performer. To those who see him this way, he will always be the unimaginative President whose methods and beliefs, put to the test, failed.

There are those who see him as having been crucified because he was too pure—and that this pureness, this idealism, was the something that brought him low. America's democracy brought him to high position; and America's democracy brought him down because democracy gives every man a vote. And every man is selfish, not faultless, as Hoover thought the Americans were. . . .

. . . He remained throughout an American patriot.

Why, then, did he not bring an end to the suffering of the American people as he had alleviated the hunger of the Europeans during and after the War? Why did he not rise out of himself, throw aside the Quaker gray cloak and lead a revolution in American ways?

These questions resolve themselves into two issues.

First, could he look like he was curing the Depression? The answer is that he could not. . . . Deep in Hoover's feeling for Americans was his thought that they were better than the Europeans. On a local level, personal charity could be endured because it was a matter of human kindness between individuals and families. But it could not be made a national, institutionalized way of life, because it was impersonal, degrading and in the end futile.

The other question is whether in fact he had cured the Depression, as he thought he had. In later years he used to say that in retrospect he could have done better. But that is true of everything we all do. Hoover was infuriatingly stubborn in the eyes of his subordinates. He could not bend his principles. . . .

There are many "ifs" with Hoover. Could he but have raised his voice? Might he not have unbalanced the budget and gone for deficit spending—as every one of his successors did? His supporters answer that flamboyance is not achievement; and that unbalanced budgets lead to welfare states and welfare catastrophes and postponed disasters.

He remains an enigma. William Allen White said it would take decades for history to render judgment on him. Decades have come and gone, but the judgment is still hanging in the balance.[21]

Martin Fausold's 1985 study differs with this view. Fausold comments:

It has often been said that the jury on the Hoover Presidency is still out—that scholars who seek to assess American Presidents react differently depending upon their sources of information, their times, and their values. In fact, however, the jury on the Hoover Presidency is in, with a verdict that is compelling enough to make it unlikely that it will ever be overturned. The jury consists of three important constituencies: Hoover's close associates of high stature at the close of his Presidency; the majority of Americans throughout the half-century following his Presidency; and historians at the half-century mark after his Presidency. The constituencies agree that the Hoover Presidency was a failed one. They do so notwithstanding three arguments in defense of the Administration: that its goals and antidepression efforts were in many respects without precedent; that it was surely as much failed by American capital as by presidential leadership; and that probably no American elected in 1928 could have survived the nation's greatest depression. Ironically, Herbert Hoover's very success in pursuing his goals and antidepression efforts [was] probably paramount in creating the misfortunes of his Presidency. His unalterable commitment to ordered freedom as a canopy for solutions to the depression proved to be more telling to this jury than did either the inequities of capital or the seeming facileness of his political opponents. Of course, Hoover's friends of eminence saw the many magnificent qualities of the whole life of Hoover, if not of his singular Presidency; and increasing numbers of historians . . . see them now. It is regrettable that as the Twentieth Century nears its end, many of the nation's citizens continue to see in the man Herbert Hoover what he himself frequently saw in his own Presidency—"the dark side first." Given the emphasis that is placed on the Presidency in American public affairs, it is improbable that this assessment will ever change.[22]

Eugene Lyons said of Hoover: "Herbert Hoover is a great monolithic figure. Time is rapidly washing off the mud with which he has been bespattered. The granite of integrity underneath is becoming obvious even to the less perceptive of his countrymen."[23]

It is something of a commentary on the nonpartisan underlying cement that binds together American hopes and aspirations that a Democratic president with a somewhat different philosophy, Harry Truman, saw and respected Hoover's basic integrity and tapped him to perform useful government service with the First Hoover Commission. This was a noteworthy contribution and an important precedent.

NOTES

1. These comments are abstracted from Peri E. Arnold, "The 'Great Engineer' as Administrator: Herbert Hoover and the Modern Bureaucracy," *Review of Politics*, 42, no. 3 (July 1980): 329–348.

2. Stefan Lorant, *The Presidency: A Pictorial History of Presidential Elections from Washington to Truman* (New York: Macmillan, 1951), pp. 565–575.

3. Ibid.

4. Ibid.

5. George H. Mayer, *The Republican Party: 1854–1966*, 2nd ed. (London: Oxford University Press, 1967), p. 410.

6. Lorant, *The Presidency*, p. 582.

7. Herbert C. Hoover, *The Memoirs of Herbert Hoover, 1929–1941: Vol. 3: The Great Depression* (New York: Macmillan, 1952), pp. 346, 347.

8. Ibid., p. 351.

9. See R. Gordon Hoxie, *Command Decision and the Presidency* (New York: Reader's Digest Press, 1977), p. 196.

10. Memorandum, Webb to President Truman, November 5, 1948, Papers of James E. Webb, Harry S Truman Library, Independence, Mo.

11. Herbert Hoover, First Annual Message on the State of the Union, December 3, 1929, *Congressional Record* 72, Part 1, 71st Congress, 2nd Session.

12. Peri E. Arnold, "The First Hoover Commission and the Managerial Presidency," *Journal of Politics*, 38, no. 1, (February 1976): 46–70.

13. "Herbert Hoover's Great Illusion," *New Republic*, 56, no. 716 (August 28, 1928): 3–5.

14. John Dos Passos, "Washington and Chicago: I. The Veterans Come Home to Roost," *New Republic*, 71 (June 29, 1932): 177, 178.

15. Malcolm Cowley and Slater Brown, "The Flight of the Bonus Army," *New Republic*, 72 (August 17, 1932): 13–15.

16. "Hoover's Fairy Tale," *New Republic*, 72 (August 24, 1932): 30–31.

17. "The Week," *New Republic*, 73, no. 937 (November 16, 1932): 1–4.

18. Ronald Steel, *Walter Lippmann and the American Century* (Boston: Little, Brown, Atlantic Monthly Press Book, 1980), pp. 285–287.

19. James David Barber, *The Presidential Character* (Englewood Cliffs, N.J.: Prentice-Hall, 1972). See especially Chapter 3, "The Active-Negative Presidents," pp. 58–98, and in particular pp. 68–78.

20. Ibid., p. 60.

21. Gene Smith, *The Shattered Dream: Herbert Hoover and the Great Depression* (New York: William Morrow and Co., 1970), pp. 237–239.

22. Martin L. Fausold, *The Presidency of Herbert C. Hoover* (Lawrence: University Press of Kansas, 1985), pp. 245, 246. For further comments see the author's review of Fausold in *Presidential Studies Quarterly*, 16, no. 1 (Winter 1986): 131, 132.

23. Eugene Lyons, *Our Unknown Ex-President: A Portrait of Herbert Hoover* (Garden City, N.Y.: Doubleday, 1948), p. 29.

BIBLIOGRAPHIC ESSAY

David Hinshaw, *Herbert Hoover: American Quaker* (New York: Farrar, Straus, 1950), stresses President Hoover's spiritual, moral, and intellectual qualities. The Quaker author was for thirty-five years an associate and friend of Hoover.

Alexander De Conde, *Herbert Hoover's Latin American Policy* (Stanford, Calif.: Stanford University Press, 1951), updates the Hoover Latin American policy through use of *Foreign Relations* volumes and with access to the Hoover Papers.

Eugene Lyons, *The Herbert Hoover Story* (Washington, D.C.: Human Events, 1959) originally carried the title *Our Unknown Ex-President,* but this edition includes a final chapter, "Postscript—1959," with an interpretation of Hoover's life, including his upbringing, his childhood, the presidency, and his retirement.

Louis P. Lochner, *Herbert Hoover and Germany* (New York: Macmillan, 1960), marshals facts in an effort to clarify Hoover's relationship to imperial, republican, National Socialist, and postwar federal Germany and its people.

Joseph Brandes, *Herbert Hoover and Economic Diplomacy* (Pittsburgh: University of Pittsburgh Press, 1962), analyzes the development and motivation of Hoover's economic policies as a major factor shaping American post–World War I positions.

Jordan A. Schwarz, *The Interregnum of Despair: Hoover, Congress and the Depression* (Urbana, Ill.: University of Illinois Press, 1970), analyzes congressional response to the Great Depression. The author examines congressional attitudes and actions on major pre-1933 economic and social problems; accordingly, the president becomes somewhat secondary in the narrative.

Craig Lloyd, *Aggressive Introvert: A Study of Herbert Hoover and Public Relations Management (1912–1932)* (Columbus: Ohio State University Press, 1972), seeks to fill a gap in historical literature in focusing on one major facet of Hoover's life and career, his development and use of an administrative style that relied heavily on public relations techniques and was closely tied to a complex personality and deeply held philosophical commitments.

Martin L. Fausold and George T. Mazuzan, *The Hoover Presidency: A Reappraisal* (Albany, N.Y.: State University of New York Press, 1974), includes several new interpretations of the Hoover presidency. Though inexperienced and unhappy about electoral politics, Hoover is found to have conducted a superb presidential campaign in 1928. The authors say that two inimical themes dominated the Hoover presidency—a vision of an Americanized corporatism and a commitment to nonelectoral politics.

Donald J. Lisio, *The President and Protest: Hoover, Conspiracy, and the Bonus Riot* (Columbia, Mo.: University of Missouri Press, 1974), is not intended as a full-scale review of the Hoover administration, but should correct some misconceptions about the president, while recognizing the shortcomings of his handling of the 1932 Bonus crisis.

Francis William O'Brien, ed., *The Hoover-Wilson Wartime Correspondence: September 24, 1914, to November 11, 1918* (Ames, Ia.: Iowa State University Press, 1974), embodies correspondence between President Wilson and the food administrator during the above period. Letters portray relationships and nuances of feeling between the two officials.

Benjamin H. Weissman, *Herbert Hoover and Famine Relief in Soviet Russia: 1921–1923* (Stanford, Calif.: Hoover Institution Press, 1974), deals with a moment in history when millions of lives depended on men's ability to transcend political animosity in a common interest. The author analyzes problems that arise when leaders of antagonistic countries decide to collaborate on a great humanitarian undertaking.

Gary Dean Best, *The Politics of American Individualism: Herbert Hoover in Transition, 1918–1921* (Ames, Ia.: Iowa State University Press, 1974), is a study of the relationship between Hoover's programs during this political interlude in the name of American individualism, and political decisions made then, providing an image of Hoover quite at variance with portraits of him commonly painted since the Depression.

Robert Sobel, *Herbert Hoover at the Onset of the Great Depression, 1929–1930* (Philadelphia: Lippincott, 1975), is an attempt to understand Hoover's actions in the context of his own times. To do so one must understand basic assumptions and views of humankind and society that Hoover carried into office, in the author's view.

Joan Hoff Wilson, *Herbert Hoover: Forgotten Progressive* (Boston: Little, Brown, 1975), an important book, may throw light on Hoover's career and the changing nation which rejected him. With heavy emphasis on the prepresidential years, the book puts Hoover in a different light than the common public view and stresses his progressive reputation in his earlier career.

James Stuart Olson, *Herbert Hoover and the Reconstruction Finance Corporation, 1931–1933* (Ames, Ia.: Iowa State University Press, 1977), evaluates Hoover's administration through the RFC. The author reviews current scholarship on President Hoover's political philosophy. He concludes that the administration played only a minor role in the RFC's failure to revive the economy, and portrays the relationship between the Hoover administration and the New Deal as a transition rather than a watershed.

David Burner, *Herbert Hoover, a Public Life* (New York: Knopf, 1979), is considered a major work, a good piece of scholarship, and a necessary revision, emphasizing Hoover's "virtues of self-control, persistence, workmanship, and . . . conscience."

Philip T. Rosen, *The Modern Stentors: Radio Broadcasters and the Federal Government, 1920–1934* (Westport, Conn.: Greenwood Press, 1980), is an analysis of pioneer broadcasting interest groups, with perhaps the most complete account of the contributions of Hoover as secretary of commerce to the early development of communications regulation.

Gary Dean Best, *Herbert Hoover: The Postpresidential Years, 1933–1964*, 2 vols. (Stanford, Calif.: Hoover Institution Press, 1983), deals in the first volume with Hoover's period as titular GOP leader, his abortive campaign for the 1936 nomination, his isolationist fight against intervention in World War II, and his wartime role as opposition leader, and in the second volume with the constructive work of the first and second Hoover commissions and his final years.

George H. Nash, *The Life of Herbert Hoover: The Engineer, 1874–1914* (New York: W. W. Norton, 1983), is the first of a multivolume biography and carries Hoover through his early years and education, his mining career in Australia, China, and elsewhere around the globe, and his work as a financier and business leader which preceded his philanthropic and public service. It is sensitively written and thoroughly researched.

14 FRANKLIN DELANO ROOSEVELT

Robert E. Gilbert

During 1982 the United States commemorated the one hundredth anniversary of the birth of Franklin Delano Roosevelt. He had emerged from a life of personal wealth and affluence to lead the nation as president during times of widespread economic collapse and worldwide warfare. Forsaking the two-term tradition observed by his predecessors, Franklin Roosevelt was elected four times to the office of president and only death, in April 1945, limited him to the twelve years during which he occupied the oval office. In fact, it was largely in reaction to Roosevelt's lengthy presidential tenure that Congress, a few years after his death, pushed to enact the Twenty-second Amendment to the Constitution, which stipulates that

no person shall be elected to the office of the President more than twice, and no person who has held the office of President, or acted as President for more than two years of a term to which some other person was elected President shall be elected to the office of President more than once.

As a result of this amendment, and unless and until it is repealed, Roosevelt's record of longevity as president will never be equalled or surpassed. For that alone he is distinct among American presidents. But Franklin Roosevelt is distinct for many other reasons as well.

It is not surprising that innumerable myths should spring up and surround a man who had served during times of domestic and international crisis for so many years. Some of those myths surrounded Roosevelt during his presidency, and some remain all too prevalent even today. The myths, of course, distorted the popular image of Roosevelt among his own contemporaries and continue to fuel aspects of the Roosevelt legend in the 1980s. In light of the fact that more than forty years have passed since Roosevelt's death, another attempt should be made to penetrate the myths and clarify the image of one of America's greatest presidents.

THE EARLY YEARS

Franklin D. Roosevelt was born at Hyde Park, New York, on January 30, 1882. The only child of James and Sara Roosevelt, Franklin led a well provided for and somewhat cloistered life on his parents' Hyde Park estate. As a child, he traveled extensively in Europe and spent summers at Campobello, New Brunswick, where he developed a deep love for the sea. Young Franklin was close to his parents, both of whom were from socially prominent families. His mother doted on him both as a child and later as a man, and was a powerful presence in his life. His father, although fifty-four at the time of Franklin's birth, was a solicitous companion to his son and passed on to him his affiliation, unusual for someone of his social class, with the Democratic party.

When he was fourteen, Franklin left home for Groton Academy, a preparatory school in Massachusetts for wealthy boys. Although it was difficult for him to be separated from his parents, just as it was difficult for them to be separated from him, young Franklin was able to adjust well to the Groton school routine. His record there was a good but not an outstanding one, but he further developed his interest in history by reading "historical works that would have bored most his age." Also at Groton, Franklin joined clubs that were directed toward helping the poor. Later, one of his own sons suggested that these activities constituted the future president's introduction to public service.

Upon leaving Groton, FDR entered Harvard University, where he became involved in a number of social and extracurricular activities, the most notable perhaps being the editorship of the Harvard student newspaper. It was during his college years that his father died at the age of seventy-two, an event that allowed his mother to move to Boston to be close to her son. It was also during his college years that his cousin Theodore became president of the United States, an event that undoubtedly whetted Franklin's appetite for a career in politics and public service.

Soon after leaving Harvard, Franklin married his fifth cousin, Anna Eleanor Roosevelt. He did this over the strong objections of his mother, who felt that the quiet, rather homely Eleanor, whose father had been an alcoholic, was not "good enough" for her son. At their wedding, the bride was given away by her uncle, President Theodore Roosevelt—a fact that did little to diminish the dismay of the groom's mother over the marriage. Sara would do all she could to dominate and control her son and his wife, even going so far as furnishing their first home for them and building their second home right next to hers with several connecting doorways and a common vestibule. According to one report, when Franklin came home for the first time to his newly built home, he found Eleanor in tears. " 'This was not her house,' she sobbed. 'She had not helped plan it and this wasn't the way she wanted to live.' "

POLITICAL BEGINNINGS

In 1910 young Franklin decided to enter politics. Blessed with a magnetic and famous name, he was elected state senator in a district which had not elected a Democrat in fifty years. Once in the New York State legislature, he became a member of the progressive reform Democrats but never a member of the "inner club." One observer described him as

tall and slender, very active and alert, moving around the floor, going in and out of Committee rooms, rarely talking with the members, who more or less avoided him, not particularly charming, . . . artificially serious of face . . . with an unfortunate habit—so natural that he was unaware of it—of throwing his head up. This, coupled with his pince-nez and great height, gave him the appearance of looking down his nose at most people.

In 1913 President Woodrow Wilson appointed Roosevelt assistant secretary of the navy, a position once held by his cousin, Theodore. For seven years, Franklin held that post—a natural one for someone who loved the sea—and acquired much useful administrative experience in the process.

In 1920 the Democratic National Convention chose James M. Cox as its presidential nominee. For reasons of geographical balance as well as in recognition of the work he had done in the Navy Department, Franklin D. Roosevelt was nominated as the Democratic party's vice presidential standard-bearer. Despite his vigorous campaigning, the Democratic ticket was buried on election day under a Republican avalanche.

This defeat was followed soon after by a personal crisis of even deeper proportions. In 1921 Franklin Roosevelt was stricken with polio and permanently lost the use of his legs as a result. His long bout with this serious illness interrupted the future president's political career but probably served to strengthen his character, soften his personality, and give him greater empathy toward those suffering affliction of various kinds.

In 1928 Roosevelt was elected governor of New York at the same time that his party was losing the presidency to Herbert Hoover in a landslide. The practical consequence of these companion events was that the new governor of New York immediately emerged as a leading contender for the 1932 presidential nomination of the Democratic party. This prospect was not unappealing to Roosevelt. Soon after his election to the New York governorship, he contacted party leaders across the country, suggesting that "it is the time for putting into effect a permanent working organization . . . which would help in the 1930 congressional campaign and serve to educate the public continuously." Whatever else this communication was meant to achieve, it served to make party leaders aware of the fact that Franklin Roosevelt was now governor of New York and that they might think of him as a future presidential nominee. Many party leaders responded to Roosevelt's communication by indicating their support for his nomination in 1932. Southern party leaders were perhaps especially enthusiastic. Though Roosevelt was governor of New York, he was looked upon as an adopted son of Georgia because of all the time he had spent at Warm Springs, trying to overcome his physical affliction. Also, Southerners felt that Roosevelt represented their best hope of uniting "with their agrarian brethren in the West to overcome the influence of the party's wet, urban, Catholic wing in the North."

The Democratic presidential nomination of 1932 was a prize sought after by a wide variety of candidates. The country had been plunged into a catastrophic depression in 1929, and the Republicans, under President Herbert Hoover, were blamed widely. A Democratic victory seemed inevitable—even to Republicans. On the first ballot at the Democratic National Convention, Roosevelt won the support of every southern state except Virginia (which had a favorite son candidate) and enjoyed widespread support in the states west of the Mississippi, with the two major exceptions of Texas and California. However, former New York governor and 1928 standard-bearer Al Smith, an urban, anti-Prohibition, Catholic Democrat, carried substantial support in the East and prevented Roosevelt from winning the two-thirds vote required for nomination on the first three ballots. Displaying the pragmatism that characterized his political career, Roosevelt nailed down delegate support in Texas and California by offering the vice presidential nomination to John Nance Garner of Texas. Roosevelt's nomination was now secure, and it came to him on the fourth ballot. Breaking with tradition, the New York governor flew to Chicago to personally accept his nomination and in his speech to the convention uttered the words that immediately became indelible in the American political lexicon—"I pledge you, I pledge myself to a new deal for the American people." He continued, "Let us all here assembled constitute ourselves prophets of a new order of competence and courage. This is more than a political campaign; it is a call to arms. Give me your help, not to win votes alone but to win in this crusade to restore America to its own people."

Despite Roosevelt's political strengths, he conducted an undistinguished campaign. He seemed to promise all things to all men, holding out the illusory hope that he could lead the nation out of the Depression while cutting government expenditures and balancing the federal budget. In some of his campaign pronouncements, Roosevelt sounded much like future president Ronald Reagan. He attacked President Hoover for "reckless and extravagant spending" and for "thinking that we ought to center everything in Washington as rapidly as possible." He complained also of government deficits, remarking that the current deficit was large enough to "make us catch our breath."

While today's popular image of Roosevelt is that of a firm believer in government intervention in the economy, that image certainly did not shine through in the Democratic campaign of 1932. Roosevelt's running mate even attacked Hoover for "leading the country down the path to socialism."[1] Somewhat ironically, perhaps, FDR lambasted the Republicans for having "piled bureau on bureau, commission on commission . . . and for having lent money to backward and crippled countries." Roosevelt's public statements and campaign pronouncements led one respected journalist to write:

Franklin Roosevelt is no crusader. He is no tribune of the people. He is no enemy of entrenched privilege. He is a pleasant man who, without any important qualifications for the office, would very much like to be President.

On election day, Roosevelt achieved that goal. He captured 57 percent of the popular vote and carried forty-two of the forty-eight states. The electoral vote count represented a landslide Roosevelt victory, with the New York governor winning 472 votes to Hoover's 59. At the same time, Democrats swept the congressional elections, giving them 310 seats in the House to the Republicans' 117, and 60 seats in the Senate to 35 for the Republicans. The Franklin Roosevelt era had begun, and it would transform American politics for decades to come.

THE PRESIDENTIAL YEARS

Roosevelt began his presidency at a time of severe economic distress. A quarter of the nation's work force was unemployed. In some places, 50 percent or more were jobless. More than a million of the unemployed traveled around the country living the life of hoboes. Hunger was so widespread that crowds each evening fought over the garbage discarded by restaurants. Large numbers of people suffered from malnutrition; according to one report, more than a quarter of school children in Pennsylvania alone were so afflicted. Disease resulted from the persistent malnutrition in many communities across the country. Homeless people lived under bridges and railroad trestles, and some built shacks in parks to provide shelter from the elements. Clusters of those shacks which dotted the landscape became known as Hoovervilles—an eloquent tribute to the public derision heaped on Roosevelt's discredited predecessor. The economic severity of the Depression was so pronounced that there was even talk of revolution in the streets.

In his Inaugural Address, the new president struck a confident and even an electrifying note. He proclaimed that there was "nothing to fear but fear itself" and promised that he would seek a "broad Executive Power to wage a war against the emergency as great as the power that would be given to me if we were, in fact, invaded by a foreign foe."

At the outset of his administration, the new president acted boldly to meet the economic crisis. This period is often referred to as the "Hundred Days" since so much executive activity occurred then. To forestall further bank failures (almost 5,000 banks had failed since the beginning of 1930), FDR declared a banking holiday that closed all banks, some for months. In this instance, the president used an expedient utilized in several states and cities even before his inauguration. To further protect depositors, he secured the passage of the Glass-Steagall Act, which established a federal guarantee for bank deposits under $5,000.

Roosevelt also signed into law the National Industrial Recovery Act (NIRA), which provided for codes of fair industrial competition, minimum wages and maximum hours, and collective bargaining for workers. This law, described by the president as "perhaps the most important and far reaching legislation ever enacted by the American Congress," tried to achieve fair profits for industry and living wages for labor. Another early feature of the New Deal was the Agricultural Adjustment Act, which sought to control the prices of farm products by regulating their production. Farmers were asked to advance agricultural recovery by reducing the number of acres planted, and they received cash payments from the government in return.

The Agricultural Adjustment Act and the National Industrial Recovery Act represented "an extraordinary new departure for the U.S. national government which abandoned its previous stance of minimal interference in the domestic market economy in favor of comprehensive attempts at administrative intervention." Despite FDR's earlier attacks against Hoover for piling "bureau on bureau, commission on commission," the National Industrial Recovery Act called for the creation of the National Recovery Administration (NRA), and the Agricultural Adjustment Act mandated the establishment of the Agricultural Adjustment Administration (AAA). These new administrative bodies acquired the power to plan and regulate economic functions that previously had been subject to the forces of the open market.

Although it achieved considerable notoriety, the NRA proved largely ineffective in accomplishing its objectives. In a recent study, Theda Skocpol and Kenneth Finegold judged that over time, it became "increasingly unwieldy, conflict-ridden and uncertain about its basic goals and preferred means for achieving them." These authors concluded that "the apparent opportunity offered by the National Industrial Recovery Act's extraordinary peacetime grant of economic authority to the U.S. government was lost." The AAA, on the other hand, operated more successfully. It "sorted out its priorities, resolved a major internal contradiction of programs and personnel, streamlined its organizational structure and launched ambitious new plans for the future."[2]

It is important to note that during much of his first term in office, Roosevelt proved to be a cautious, if not conservative, leader. Not only did he truly believe in balanced budgets, he tried strenuously to hold the country together and to prevent serious clashes between the few haves and the many have-nots. If any overriding theme emerged during these early months, it was that of mutual cooperation. At one point in 1933, he asked, "Must we go on in many groping, disorganized, separate units to defeat or shall we move as one great team to victory?" This father of the modern Democratic party was so intent on national unity that in 1934 he refused to participate in Jefferson Day celebrations for fear his participation would appear to be too partisan.

In 1933 Roosevelt set up the Civil Works Administration (CWA) as a mechanism for utilizing the half billion dollar relief appropriation made available by Congress. By January 1934, the CWA put some 4.2 million workers on the federal payroll and set them to work repairing roads, refurbishing schools, and doing various other types of construction work across the country. Roosevelt, however, was concerned about the great cost of the program and feared that he would never be able to get these new workers off the government payroll. At the end of the winter of 1934, he brought the CWA to an end, demonstrating both caution and conservatism in his approach toward the problem of unemployment.

These same traits were also visible in the Social Security program that the president proposed to Congress and then signed into law in 1935. President Roosevelt did not look upon this program as a panacea. What he said about it was that it "gives at least some protection to thirty million of our citizens."

As governor of New York, Roosevelt had urged unsuccessfully a mandatory old-age pension law for workers. As president, he showed continued interest in some form of social insurance but did not make any specific recommendations on a program of social security until June 1934. The plan finally submitted to Congress was a relatively moderate federal-state cooperative arrangement. It provided insurance for loss of income due to old age or unemployment and protection for families in case of the death of wage earners. The unemployment insurance provisions were to be administered under a joint federal-state plan. Also, federal-state cooperation in providing aid to the blind and to dependent children was called for by the legislation. Ironically, the program led a number of states to enact regressive tax legislation in order to meet the program's cost.

The old-age insurance provisions were to be administered by the federal government. Benefits were modest and were to come from a fund contributed by both workers and their employers. Thus, Social Security was to be a contributory program rather than one funded from general tax revenues. Rexford Tugwell, a member of Roosevelt's staff, tells us that "Roosevelt . . . was . . . determined that social insurance should actually be insurance—that is, paid for directly by those who were to receive the benefits. They should be deductions from, not additions to, wages." When a number of liberals suggested that the federal role in this partnership should increase, FDR snapped, "Not one nickel more. Not one solitary nickel. Once you get off the . . . matching basis, the sky's the limit, and before you know it, we'll be paying the entire bill."

Some critics have argued that the contributions made by employers under this plan were simply passed on to consumers and that workers essentially were funding the Social Security program in its entirety. G. William Domhoff has written that the Social Security system "put a floor under consumer demand, raised people's expectations for the future and directed political energies back into conventional channels." Domhoff continues:

The difference between what could be and what is remained very, very large for the poor, the sick and the aged. The wealth distribution did not change, decision-making power remained in the hands of upper-class leaders.

While Americans of the post-Roosevelt era might believe that the New Deal consisted of a number of coherent and integrated programs and that Roosevelt, the master planner, had a specific game plan in mind to overcome the Great Depression, in fact nothing could be further from the truth. The president often showed no commitment to specific lines of action and his cabinet and "kitchen cabinet" often were divided over the course of action that the administration should follow. Indeed, in monetary matters, the president's behavior has been termed "baffling." One State Department economist has noted that it was difficult to tell what the president wanted since "his ideas veered and waffled."

One reason for the president's confusion and for the conflict among members of his staff has obvious roots in the nature of the economic crisis confronting the nation. Unprecedented misery was widespread, and it was not clear what approach would be effective in producing a national recovery. A second reason is found in the fact that New Deal programs did not work immediate wonders in curing the Depression. Unemployment remained unacceptably high throughout much of Roosevelt's first two terms in the White House, and the real cure for this malady occurred in the early 1940s when the United States entered World War II.

It was largely the slowness of the economic recovery that led to a major change in direction during Roosevelt's first term. At the outset of his administration, he sought consensus and unity. But midway through his first term there was a noticeable shift in New Deal policy and the rationale behind it, and a "second New Deal" was initiated. Rather than unity and consensus, the second New Deal was aimed at a redistribution of wealth that would benefit the "common man."[3] The change in emphasis clearly is reflected in FDR's speech accepting his presidential renomination in 1936. In that address, he referred to "economic royalists," "economic tyranny," and "economic slavery," and he announced that "our allegiance to American institutions requires the overthrow of this kind of power."

Recognizing that unemployment was still prohibitively high in the mid-1930s, Roosevelt established the Works Progress Administration (WPA) to disburse the relief funds provided by Congress for the unemployed. Ironically, this was a larger-scale version of the Civil Works Administration, which he had terminated earlier because he felt that it was too expensive and would make workers too dependent on the federal government. During the first three years of its existence, the WPA provided public works jobs to as many as 3 million of the unemployed annually and spent almost $10 billion. Critics complained that the public works jobs were of the dead-end variety and that the WPA was little more than an attempt to buy the votes of the poor. One prominent critic called the WPA "a scab army of a scab President." Another claimed that it was the "greatest financial boon which ever came to the Communists in the United States."

As Roosevelt began to champion the unemployed and the poor more forcefully and as public revenue began to be used on a broad scale to help the disadvantaged, the president found himself attacked by a wide variety of critics. In his own party, Al Smith criticized the administration by saying, "I have known both parties to fail to carry out some of the planks of their platform, but this is the first time that I have known a party, upon such a large scale, not only not to carry out the planks but to do directly the opposite thing to what they promised." The governor of Montana, a Democrat, wrote that "it does seem to me that some departments of the Administration are catering too much to the 'Red' element," while his gubernatorial counterpart in Oregon, also a Democrat, complained that New Deal relief policies were "creating a nation of softies." The upper class became thoroughly hostile to Roosevelt, and their hostility at times reached fever pitch. Indicative of these hostile feelings, Geoffrey Smith writes:

In bank offices, country-club locker rooms, and lawyers' chambers, apocrypha-become-truth was the order of the day. The President was "an inveterate liar, immoral, . . . a tool of Negroes and Jews, a madman given to unbroken gales of immoderate laughter, an alcoholic, a megalomaniac dreaming his dreams of dictatorship."

To much of the nation, however, Franklin Roosevelt remained a savior and a miracle worker. He projected confidence and self-assurance, and the intensity of his administration's actions in proposing new programs and establishing new agencies created the impression that the economic ills associated with the Depression were being cured. As he shifted gears and tried new approaches, Roosevelt appeared innovative rather than uncertain. So bold was the image Roosevelt projected that toward the end of his second term in office, almost 40 percent of the nation considered him to be a radical and only 1 percent regarded him as conservative. The remainder believed him to be a liberal in political philosophy.

ROOSEVELT AND CONGRESS

Many contemporary Americans, frustrated by the endless tangling between the executive and legislative branches and hearing of Franklin Roosevelt's greatness, undoubtedly believe that FDR either dominated or enjoyed enormous rapport with Congress. The image of executive-legislative harmony during the Roosevelt years, however, has been distorted by the passage of time. Perhaps, surprisingly, it was even somewhat distorted during Roosevelt's own era.

Franklin Roosevelt enjoyed his greatest successes as a legislative leader in the early years of his administration when he worked hard to cement relations with Congress. He spoke to Congress in person and consulted frequently with congressional leaders, committee chairmen, and other members of the House and Senate. To be sure, Roosevelt was able to sign into law an impressive number of major proposals which Congress had enacted with considerable speed. Indeed, Roosevelt's first hundred days in office were so filled with legislative accomplishments that the legislative accomplishments of his successors are often measured against the experience of 1933.

However, a closer analysis would indicate that relations between Congress and the White House were not entirely harmonious. Liberals in the legislative branch were impatient with Roosevelt's moderation and caution. Senator Huey Long, a Populist Democrat from Louisiana, attacked Roosevelt for standing on Herbert Hoover's policies and for failing to "guarantee something for every family." Long was not alone in his criticism. Desperate to help their constituents, many members of Congress were noticeably more liberal than the president, and some were clearly radical in their approach to the problems of the Great Depression. Because of this climate of impatience, the president sometimes needed the support of Republicans to keep Congress on a moderate course of program-building. For example, it clearly took Republican support to have the Economy Act of 1933 passed over the objections of some liberal Democrats.[4]

Roosevelt's early proposals were so moderate in tone that all but a small handful of them enjoyed the support of the majority of Republicans. The vote that passed the Social Security Act approached unanimity—372–33 in the House and 76–6 in the Senate. This lopsided vote, however, and the apparent Republican cooperation with the administration should not be allowed to mask the deep conflicts that existed between Democrats and Republicans, liberals and conservatives, and Congress and the president. In its approach to handling inflation, mortgage refinancing, silver, spending, and labor, the bulk of Congress was to the left of the president. Even as early as 1935, it took enormous effort on Roosevelt's part to get what he wanted from the legislature. Frank Freidel summarized the situation by writing that Congress clearly "demonstrated that when it wished it could effectively check the powers of even a President as popular as Roosevelt."

Perhaps nowhere was the tension between the executive and legislative branches more pronounced than in the area of labor legislation. Attacked at one point by United Mine Workers President John L. Lewis as an aristocrat "born to the purple," Roosevelt clearly was interested in getting the unemployed back to work. But while he was sympathetic toward labor, he was not a supporter of a militant labor movement.

Although the National Recovery Administration asserted labor's right to organize, it did not require employers to bargain collectively with unions, and it did not prevent company unions from being formed as competitors of worker-formed organizations. The disputes that arose between labor and management were many and severe. Supposedly handling these disputes was the National Labor Board (NLB), an impotent agency headed by Senator Robert Wagner of New York, which could only make recommendations and hope that the recommendations would be observed. In fact, many large-scale corporations rejected the NLB's "rulings," and the board had no real recourse against them.

In the face of these difficulties, Senator Wagner recognized that further congressional action was necessary. He introduced, first in 1934 and then again in 1935, new legislation which protected the right of labor to organize, and which made unlawful the denial of the right to bargain collectively. It also set up an independent government agency, the National Labor Relations Board, and gave it the power to investigate charges of unfair labor practices, to supervise union elections among workers, and to enforce its decisions in labor disputes.

Roosevelt's role in the passage of Senator Wagner's National Labor Relations Act was one of hesitation and ambivalence. It became law in 1935 with his consent but not with his active endorsement. Undoubtedly the president was reluctant at that point to break with conservative business interests whose support and good will he was still trying to cultivate. Congress, however, was considerably less reluctant to act and the president could do little but follow its lead.

Despite the president's lack of enthusiasm for a militant labor movement, he was widely believed to be a strong friend of labor. In September 1937, 45 percent of Americans believed that the Roosevelt administration was too friendly toward labor, while 41 percent believed that the attitude of the administration toward labor unions was "just about right." Only 14 percent believed that it was not friendly enough.

In 1936 Roosevelt was reelected in a landslide victory and led his party to even bigger majorities in both houses of Congress. The Democratic victory was so massive that only sixteen Republicans remained in the Senate and only eighty-nine sat in the House. Ironically, Roosevelt's relations with Congress soured in his second term, and after 1938 no major piece of domestic legislation was enacted. Most dangerously, perhaps, Congress chose to ignore Roosevelt's requests for increased military spending even though the flames of war were being fanned throughout Europe and the Far East.

So unhappy was the president with the level of support he was receiving from some members of his own party that in 1938 he launched his ill-fated attempt to interfere in primary elections and bring about the defeat of a number of prominent Democratic conservatives. Roosevelt openly opposed the renomination of Senators Walter George of Georgia, Millard Tydings of Maryland, and "Cotton Ed" Smith of South Carolina, and Representative John O'Connor of New York, Chairman of the House Rules Committee. With the exception of O'Connor, each of these Roosevelt foes was renominated by Democratic primary voters and reelected to office in the November elections. The results were not particularly surprising. A poll taken in September 1938 had disclosed that 61 percent of all Democrats and 66 percent of Southern Democrats opposed the purge attempt.

The country, therefore, witnessed the spectacle of a president who in 1936 had captured 87 percent of the popular vote in Georgia, 62 percent in Maryland, and almost 99 percent in South Carolina seeing his own personally endorsed candidates defeated by Democratic voters in these same states just two years later. The president who contributed so greatly toward an expansion of the power of the national government learned to his dismay that in the matter of state elections, the American political system was still very much decentralized.

World War II would mute much of the hostility between the executive and legislative branches as the country became united in the fight against the Axis powers. But it is interesting to note that despite the view that Congress was a rubber stamp for Roosevelt's legislative desires, Franklin Roosevelt established a record during the first eight years of his presidency in his exercise of the veto power—"not a record in the quantity of measures disapproved, but a record in the wide range of subjects drawing his attention and his adverse action. The Roosevelt disapprovals represent over 30 percent of the total measures disapproved since 1792, when the veto was first used."

ROOSEVELT AND THE NEWS MEDIA

Regardless of the depth of their knowledge of American history, probably few Americans have not heard something about Franklin Roosevelt's relationship with the mass media. To many he has become the prototype of what a president should be as a leader of public opinion and as the nation's foremost media celebrity.

Undoubtedly, the most famous aspect of Roosevelt's media usage revolves around his masterful appearances on radio. Blessed with a strong, clear, and confident voice, Roosevelt used radio to establish an intimate bond between the president and his constituents throughout the country. Daniel Boorstin wrote:

By the time that Franklin D. Roosevelt came into office on March 4, 1933, technological and institutional innovations had in many ways prepared the way for a transformation of the relations between President and people. Communications from the President to the reading or listening public, which formerly had been ceremonial, infrequent, and addressed to small audiences, could now be constant, spontaneous and directed to all who could read or hear (sometimes whether they wished to or not).

Ironically, at the outset of his national political career, Roosevelt's closest advisers were concerned that his voice, inflection, and speaking style might go over badly on the electronic medium. They worried that Roosevelt's radio personality might conjure up the image of an aristocrat at a time when so many of the people were suffering the effects of economic collapse. In point of fact, however, the president's radio personality came to electrify much of the nation.

The medium of radio enabled Roosevelt to enter people's homes not only as president but as a friend. During his famous fireside chats, he spoke in intimate terms to members of his audience, using language and analogies that they could easily understand. The response was almost always positive, with thousands of ordinary citizens writing the White House and/or Congress, indicating their support for the president's programs. It was not uncommon for the president to refer in his speeches to the volume of his mail and even occasionally to read from individual letters so that those who did not support him would realize that they were out of step with most of the American people.[5]

Contrary to widespread opinion, however, Roosevelt did not conduct frequent fireside chats despite their great success. In the many years of his presidency, only about twenty-eight radio chats were broadcast, and the president staunchly resisted taking to the airwaves too frequently. At one point he explained that "the public psychology and for that matter individual psychology cannot because of human weakness, be attuned for long periods of time to a constant repetition of the highest note in the scale." Roosevelt was so concerned that he might become too familiar to his audience that the White House asked a popular radio program of the time to end its practice of having its announcer imitate the president's voice.

While the mood of his fireside chats was relaxed, informal, and intimate, those radio appearances were planned rather carefully by the White House. Typically they were broadcast on one of the first three evenings of the week, when audience interest would likely be strongest. Their usual length was thirty minutes, since after that time attention might wander and interest lag. In all, Roosevelt's fireside chats and other radio speeches became important sources of presidential power, enabling him to achieve a strong national identity and to heighten public morale at a time of great economic distress.

So strong was the hold that Roosevelt achieved through his radio appearances that on his death, a poet wrote:

I never saw him—
But I knew him. Can you have forgotten
How, with his voice, he came into our house,
The President of the United States
Calling us friends . . .

Roosevelt's reputation as a leader of public opinion is not confined to his usage of radio. He is also renowned for his lively and effective interaction with representatives of the print media. Roosevelt was interested intensely in press coverage of his activities and utilized the services of a clipping agency which reviewed the treatment accorded his administration by 350 newspapers and 43 magazines. Unlike many other presidents, Roosevelt seemed genuinely to like members of the press and enjoyed meeting with them. He showed his trust and good will toward the working press by allowing spontaneous questions and answers at press conferences rather than insisting on the written questions required by his three immediate predecessors, and allowed himself to be identified as the source of news stories rather than having stories attributed to an anonymous "White House spokesman."

Few presidents have gone so far to cultivate journalists. Roosevelt knew, of course, that newspaper publishers and editors were often extremely critical of his administration. Opposition to his election in 1932, 1936, 1940, and 1944 was found on the editorial pages of a large majority of the nation's newspapers, and similar editorial opposition was focused on many aspects of the New Deal. In an effort to counteract this editorial hostility, Roosevelt tried to captivate members of the working press. He befriended some of their number, called them by their first names, regularly invited them to informal Sunday night suppers and teas at the White House, and provided them with a degree of accessibility that was unusually large.

In terms of formal meetings with the press, FDR's conferences were lively, informative, and frequent. Leo C. Rosten wrote that when the oral questioning began, the president demonstrated his full virtuosity.

Cigarette-holder in mouth at a jaunty angle, he met reporters on their own ground. His answers were swift, positive, illuminating. He had an astonishing amount of exact information at his fingertips. He showed an impressive understanding of public problems and administrative methods. . . . He indulged in humor and laughed at reportorial quips. He was thoroughly at ease: poised, confident, indicating his pleasure at the give and take of the press conference.

During Roosevelt's first administration, he conducted 329 formal meetings with the press, an average of about 82 a year. His second administration saw 369 press conferences; his third, the period during which World War II was fought, 276; and the few months of his fourth administration saw 25 press conferences conducted before his death on April 12. This is a record unparalleled in presidential history. Perhaps the dimensions of Roosevelt's press conference activity can be best seen by comparing it with the press conference activity of more recent presidents. Overall, Roosevelt held approximately 83 press conferences annually. In sharp contrast, Ronald Reagan has conducted 7 press conferences a year, Jimmy Carter 22, Gerald Ford 16, Richard Nixon 6, Lyndon Johnson 27, and John Kennedy 23. Undoubtedly and understandably, live television has operated to reduce the frequency of presidential press conferences, but the dimensions of Roosevelt's efforts in this area are most impressive nonetheless.

It would be erroneous, however, to assume that Roosevelt's interaction with the media was without flaw and/or conflict. Almost from the start of his presidency, he complained from time to time about the coverage being accorded his administration by some segments of the press. He even went so far as to mention publicly belligerent newspapers and reporters who he felt were guilty of inaccuracies of various sorts. For example, he remarked in late 1934:

The number of people who have come to me . . . and said—readers of these papers— "Why are people trying to destroy the credit of our Government?" It is a bit like the front page of the *Sun* that came out two weeks ago Saturday and that I wrote Will Dewart [*New York Sun*] about.

The president's unhappiness with the press increased sharply around the midpoint of his first administration. During 1935 the journalists' "honeymoon" with Roosevelt came to an end and press coverage began to become more critical and less deferential. Roosevelt responded by aiming more frequent criticism not only at newspaper editors (the Hearst press, the eastern managing editors, etc.) but also at reporters, headline writers, and other members of the working press. He was angered by "fool stories in the fool press," by "cuckoo stories" in the press, by reportorial inaccuracy, by misleading headlines, and by speculative stories. He complained of having his remarks misquoted and misinterpreted and at one point warned reporters not to draw unwarranted inferences from his failure to comment on certain topics "since 80 percent of such conjectures were incorrect."[6] Presidential anger began to rise to the surface at press conferences— at one conference, Roosevelt snapped at a persistent reporter, "This isn't a cross-examination."

The president's criticism of reporters' work had the effect of further alienating them. Attendance at press conferences began to decline after the middle of 1935. Ironically, some of the very traits that drew members of the press toward Roosevelt in 1933 and 1934 drove some of them away from him as the months of his administration rolled by. Again, Rosten's remarks are illuminating:

Many newspapermen began to feel that the exercise of presidential wit to evade a question was less a novelty than an irritant. The use of correspondents' first names was resented by some as a form of psychological bribery. . . . The Roosevelt smile was maliciously likened to a faucet, turned on and off with calculated purpose. . . . One heard repeated displeasure over Mr. Roosevelt's facial gestures ("mugging").

As he encountered a more antagonistic press, Franklin Roosevelt looked to radio increasingly as a means of reaching the public without having his message filtered through and distorted by second and third parties. As previously noted, Roosevelt was a superb radio personality, the first to show how powerful a weapon the electronic media could be in the hands of a mediagenic chief executive. However, even here he was not always able to achieve his objectives. A case in point involves his attack on the Supreme Court in 1937 and his attempt to initiate judicial "reform."

Angered by Court decisions that nullified various parts of the New Deal, Roosevelt sent a controversial piece of legislation to Congress in February 1937. The most significant aspect of that legislation allowed a president to appoint an additional justice to the Supreme Court, up to a maximum of six, for every sitting justice who did not retire at the age of seventy. Thus, the size of the Court would vary between nine and fifteen depending on the ages of its members. The proposal would have enabled Roosevelt to add six liberals to the Court since, at that time, six sitting justices were older than seventy.

The "court-packing" bill caused much controversy both in Congress and throughout the country. Urged by one of his advisers to "take the country to school" on this issue, Roosevelt took to the airwaves, seeking public support. In his fireside chat broadcast on March 9, 1937, Roosevelt told the nation that because of the advanced age of some of its members, the Supreme Court could not keep up with its workload. He wanted to add younger members, he explained, so that the Court's efficiency would be enhanced. Also, he said that younger members would modernize the thinking of the Court by bringing it into close contact "with modern facts and circumstances under which average men have to live and work."

It was common knowledge that Roosevelt's move against the Court had been precipitated by the Court's decisions undermining the New Deal. When the president took to the airwaves to attribute his action, in part, to judicial inefficiency, he damaged his own credibility and standing even with his own followers. According to public opinion polls taken at the time, the public did not rally to the president's support in his battle with the Court—even after his radio address on the subject. In fact, a majority consistently opposed his court-packing plan, frightened that he was trying to make the judicial branch into an arm of the executive and angered that he had lied to the country in the process. The greatest support ever enjoyed by the president on this issue was the 47 percent in favor in February 1937. After that time popular support for the plan steadily declined.

A few weeks before Roosevelt initiated his move against the Court, a Gallup poll revealed that almost 60 percent of the people opposed any constitutional amendment curbing the Court's power to declare acts of Congress unconstitutional. The president should have read these poll results with greater care. For even the most effective radio president who ever sat in the White House could not mobilize public support on this issue, one of the most important and one of the most divisive of his second term.

It is clear that Franklin Roosevelt possessed rather pronounced media skills and that those skills extended to both print media and radio. Through his generally adroit use of the media, Roosevelt augmented executive power, boosted his programs, and established a linkage with the public that was, in some respects, remarkable. Fred I. Greenstein writes that "when President Roosevelt died, a number of psychoanalysts reported that their patients responded to his death in ways which indicated that they symbolically equated the President with one or both of their parents."

Nevertheless, Roosevelt was not always able to mobilize public opinion through his use of the media and occasionally suffered a backlash effect when he was thought to be misusing it. Also, his relationship with the working press, which began on such a high note in 1933, became a source of frequent anger, frustration, and disappointment only two years into his lengthy term of office.

This president's experience serves as a reminder of both the opportunities and dangers that result from the symbiotic relationship existing between the president and the news media. It is a relationship with striking ebbs and flows, and those ebbs and flows affected Franklin Roosevelt in much the same way that they have affected all presidents. At the outset of his administration, the press hero-worshipped the new and dynamic leader. His initial actions drew favorable journalistic attention, and his cultivation of the working press proved most successful. After only two years, however, as conflicts with Congress grew and as attacks by his enemies intensified, the press moved away from its hero-worshipping phase and into more open criticism of the now more familiar chief executive. A consequence of the more aggressive press coverage was a subtle but clear change in Roosevelt's political image. No longer treated as a hero easily able to conquer economic ills or a god able to work national and international miracles, Roosevelt became more of a mortal, and his presidential style, once it had become familiar, began to be covered in a more measured and skeptical way. This had an impact on popular support for the president. In January 1937, 67 percent of adult Americans opposed a third term for Roosevelt, and in April 1939, 51 percent favored a Republican victory in the presidential election of 1940. (See Figure 14.1 for FDR approval ratings between 1938 and 1943.)

Figure 14.1
Approval Ratings for Franklin Delano Roosevelt

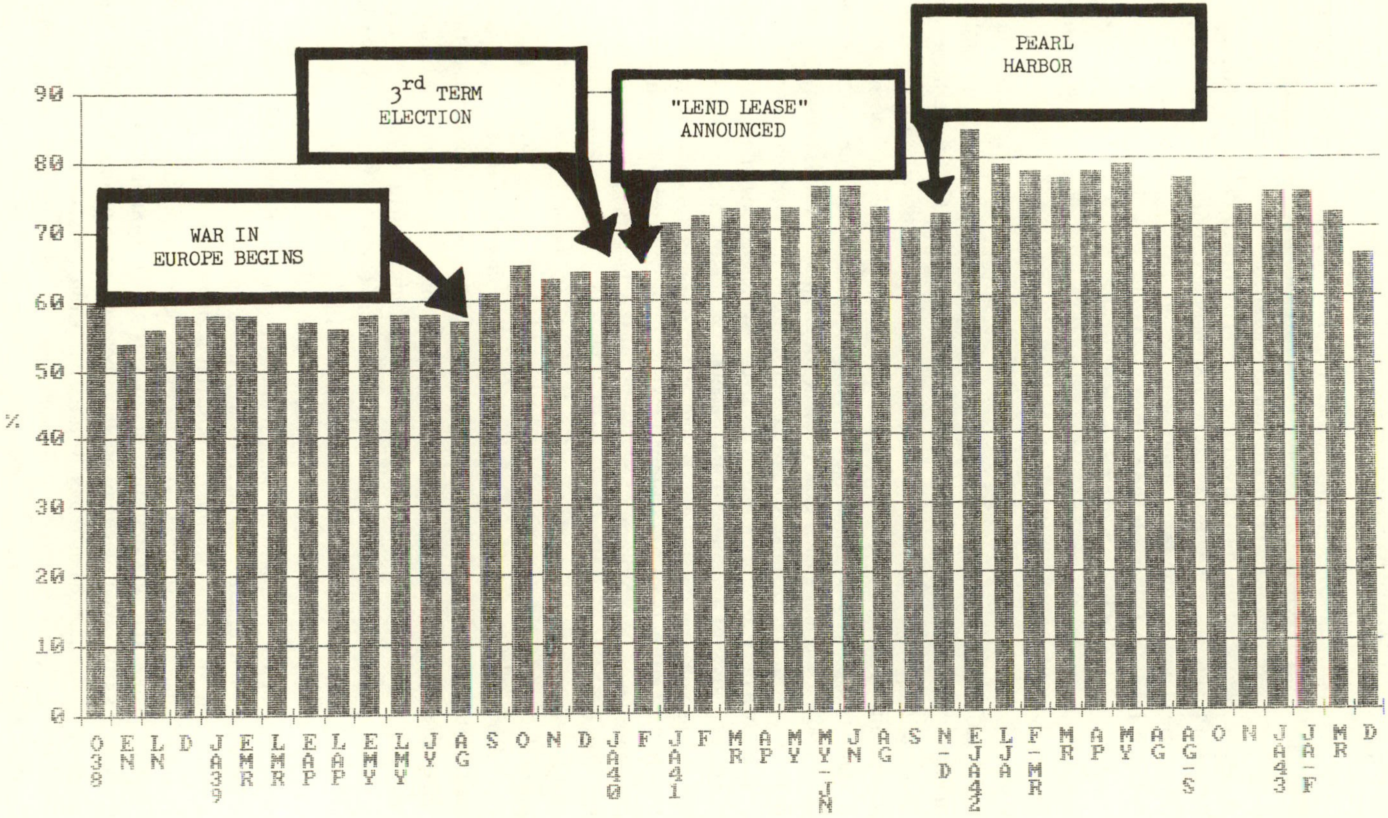

Source: Gallup Opinion Index, September-October 1980.

ROOSEVELT AND THE COURT

As previously noted, Franklin Roosevelt in 1937 sought to alter the composition and independence of the Supreme Court. This effort constituted the sharpest dispute between the executive and judicial branches in American history and proved to be one of the most divisive conflicts of the Roosevelt presidency. The nature of that conflict, however, has been subject to considerable misunderstanding, a misunderstanding that should be dispelled.

When Franklin Roosevelt took office in March 1933, he faced a rather formidable and forbidding Court. On it sat four justices sometimes referred to as the Four Horsemen of Conservatism (Justices Pierce Butler, James McReynolds, George Sutherland, and Willis Van Devanter), three liberals (Justices Louis D. Brandeis, Benjamin Cardozo, and Harlan Stone), and two moderates (Justice Owen Roberts and Chief Justice Charles Evans Hughes). Since a number of these men were elderly, Roosevelt expected that during his first term he would have the opportunity to appoint at least some new justices. By the end of his first administration, however, not even one Court vacancy had occurred.

During the early years of Roosevelt's first term, the Court upheld some aspects of the New Deal and struck down others. Beginning in 1935, however, the Supreme Court moved against Roosevelt's programs with renewed vigor. In 1935 it struck down the National Industrial Recovery Act and ruled unconstitutional Roosevelt's removal of a member of the Federal Trade Commission (FTC).[7] In 1936 it invalidated the processing tax created by the Agricultural Adjustment Act, ruled invalid the Guffey Coal Act and the Frazier-Lemke Act, and struck down a state minimum wage law. Within a few months of this latter action, and shortly after his 1936 landslide reelection victory, Roosevelt initiated his court-packing plan.

It is generally imagined that the Court's invalidation of parts of the New Deal pitted the conservative justices against their liberal brethren. Against this backdrop, Roosevelt would appear to have moved against the conservative wing of the Court in his court-packing proposal. However, some of the most significant judicial rebukes to the New Deal came at the hands of a *unanimous* Court. All nine justices voted to invalidate the National Industrial Recovery Act, and all nine ruled against Frazier-Lemke. A unanimous Court also struck down Roosevelt's controversial removal of a federal trade commissioner. To be sure, a number of decisions saw the Court divide along liberal-conservative lines and/ or by 5–4 or 6–3 majorities. But some of the judicial decisions that most disappointed and irritated Franklin Roosevelt saw a unanimous Court take a position against him. With this in mind, Roosevelt's attribution of his reform proposal to the advanced age of the Court's members becomes perhaps somewhat more plausible since the oldest justice of all was Louis Brandeis, a liberal. Also, Roosevelt's true objectives may not have been to move against the conservative majority of the Court but rather to force the Court to accept its "proper" role in society by ratifying the New Deal policies which were emanating from the "political" branches of the government.

In any event, it is important to note that, contrary to a frequently held opinion, Roosevelt experienced serious difficulty in a number of policy areas, not only with the conservative members of the Court but with the moderates and liberals as well. The breadth of judicial opposition to parts of the New Deal led Roosevelt to try to capture control of the Supreme Court by means of an overt assault on it. The president was so angered by the Court's behavior that he refused any compromise in his battle to "reform" it. At one point, congressional leaders indicated that the size of the Court might be increased to eleven in return for the withdrawal by the president of his controversial court-packing bill. Additionally, the president was told that one of the conservative justices could be persuaded to resign from the Court at the same time that Justice Van Devanter, who had already announced his retirement, would vacate his seat. By accepting this compromise the president would have secured the opportunity to name four new justices to the Court within a matter of a few months—enough to change its philosophical composition. Roosevelt, however, refused to give in and stood instead on his controversial plan, demonstrating an unusual degree of political ineptness for a man widely regarded as a master politician.

Ironically, while the specific court-packing plan endorsed by the president was not enacted by Congress, the effort at reform probably produced the result Roosevelt most wanted. During early 1937, the Court became more sympathetic toward New Deal–type programs. In fact, in March of that year, while Congress was debating the president's proposal, the high court upheld by a 5–4 majority a minimum wage law very similar to the one it had struck down by an identical majority just a few months earlier. Also, it affirmed the Social Security Act, the Wagner Labor Relations Act, the Farm Mortgage Act, and the Railway Labor Act between March and June 1937. Justice Roberts, and to some extent Chief Justice Hughes, began to vote with the liberal justices, in a judicial maneuver that is sometimes called "the switch in time that saved nine."

Also, the end of the 1937 term ushered in a period of large-scale turnover in Court personnel that eventually enabled Roosevelt to name eight new justices to the high bench. However, FDR's conflict with the judicial branch was one instance when the public felt it understood the president's true intentions and was repelled by them. While Roosevelt ultimately gained his objectives, the fight with the Court weakened his credibility with much of the country and soured his relationship with both liberals and conservatives in Congress. It also further alienated important segments of the press which aggressively reported about a president who was attempting to violate the separation of powers principle of the Constitution and the doctrine of judicial independence.

ROOSEVELT'S HEALTH: APPEARANCE AND REALITY

When one thinks today of Franklin D. Roosevelt, the image of optimism and persistent buoyancy springs to the forefront. During much of the Roosevelt era, his contemporaries also thought of him as a resilient, spirited, dynamic leader, a man who symbolized the very soul of a young nation. Roosevelt's voice and his physical demeanor radiated supreme self-confidence and told a suffering nation that all would be well.

Certain aspects of Roosevelt's life, however, were kept from his constituents and from the world by conscious design of the White House. The photographs that appeared in the newspapers and newsmagazines of the day generally showed a smiling president, head thrown back in delight, as he waged war against the ills associated with the Great Depression. He was even photographed standing at the rear of railway cars, speaking and waving to cheering crowds. Then, as now, the image of Roosevelt that radiated through the media was that of a man who had conquered the physical afflictions of polio by dint of his strong will and then gone on to lead the nation for a longer time than any other president in American history. Even today, there is much surprise when the truth becomes known.

In point of fact, Roosevelt had not really conquered polio or escaped its ravages. He had lost the use of his legs in the early 1920s and was confined to a wheelchair for the rest of his life. The White House was concerned that the image of a crippled president trying to lead a crippled nation was a thoroughly inappropriate one for the times. They feared that psychological damage would result from public knowledge of Roosevelt's severe physical disability and determined to prevent that public knowledge from becoming realized.

Radio and print journalists were asked never to report, write about, or publish pictures of the president being lifted into or out of his limousine or being carried or otherwise heavily assisted up flights of stairs. It is remarkable that this request was honored so completely and for so long. In the television age, of course, this ruse would not have been possible, but secrets were easier to keep then. So completely was Roosevelt's image controlled that even the chief usher at the White House reported that he was shocked when he first saw this president. He wrote:

On my second day in the White House, Charles Claunch, the usher on duty, took me on the elevator to the second floor. The door opened, and the Secret Service guard wheeled in the President of the United States. Startled, I looked down at him. It was only then that I realized that Franklin D. Roosevelt was really paralyzed. Immediately I understood why this fact had been kept so secret. Everybody knew that the President had been stricken with infantile paralysis, and his recovery was legend but few people were aware how completely the disease had handicapped him.[8]

In addition to securing the cooperation of news photographers, the White House took other calculated steps to control the president's physical image. At state dinners, for example, the president was wheeled into the dining room and seated first, before other guests were admitted. The wheelchair would then be removed from the scene before the dining room doors were opened. More elaborate steps were taken at formal receptions. White House gardeners would set up a wall of ferns at one end of the reception room and a special seat would be placed among and concealed by the ferns, on which the president would sit while appearing to be standing. At some formal ceremonies, aides would close the double doors of the reception room after all the guests had entered. The president would then ride to the closed doors in his wheelchair and be assisted to his feet. Then the doors would be thrown open dramatically and the president, on the arm of an aide, would swing his legs two or three steps to the podium which he would grasp for support as he spoke. These entrances were interpreted as presidential dramatics rather than as what they really were—attempts to camouflage the president's severe physical limitations. So successful were these efforts at image management that one prominent writer recalled that "during the 1930's when I lived in Europe I repeatedly met men in important positions who had no idea that the President was disabled."

It is interesting to note that Franklin D. Roosevelt's physical ailments were not confined to his legs. Despite his long tenure in office and despite the image of vigor and sturdiness that he projected, Roosevelt suffered from cardiovascular disease long before a stroke ended his life in April 1945. Roosevelt's postmaster general has said that he found indications of poor health as early as 1937. There is one report that in 1938 President Roosevelt suffered a dizzy spell and showed several symptoms that were later diagnosed as the first of a series of little strokes.

During his third term, Roosevelt's physical condition deteriorated and his appearance clearly began to show the strain of the past ten years. Scant news of this fact ever reached the public. World War II was being fought then, and it was felt that the commander-in-chief had to project a hale and hearty image.

In 1943 Roosevelt reportedly suffered an attack of heart failure. By 1944 his voice had grown so weak that he could not always be heard at press conferences. The president appeared so tired and emaciated by the summer of 1944 that many Democratic party leaders felt that he could not survive another term in the White House. Because of their concern, great attention was focused on the choice of his vice presidential running mate. Incumbent Vice President Henry Wallace, who appeared too left-wing for many party leaders, was replaced on the 1944 ticket with Missouri senator Harry Truman, a more moderate Democrat.

Despite the president's deteriorating physical appearance, concerted efforts were made to downplay the issue of his health. Roosevelt campaigned for a fourth term vigorously, at one point riding in an open car through a driving rain for several hours in New York City. Such campaign appearances reinforced public confidence in his well-being, but they undoubtedly took their toll on the weakened and ill president. One observer commented that "the strain of campaigning showed on the President's face."

Another remarked that "he was shocked in Roosevelt's physical appearance on election night. . . . He looked older than ever before and his remarks contained many irrelevancies."

Reelected in 1944 to a fourth term, Roosevelt delivered his Inaugural Address at the White House rather than at the Capitol, and all inaugural festivities were kept to a minimum. The toned-down inauguration ceremonies were attributed to the war effort. Little was said of the president's poor health at the time. Robert Dallek wrote:

At his Inaugural on January 20, he seemed to tremble all over. "It was not just his hands that shook, [Secretary of State] Stettinius remarked, but his whole body as well." [Secretary of Labor] Frances Perkins also found him looking "very badly!" His deep-gray color, expressionless eyes, and shaking hands persuaded her that he had been ill for a long time.[9]

Harry Truman later said that he saw expressions of pain on Roosevelt's face as he spoke that day.

When he delivered his last address to Congress on March 1, 1945, the president made no effort to hide his exhaustion or his physical disability. Publicly seated in his wheelchair for the first time, Roosevelt said:

I hope you will pardon me for the unusual posture of sitting down during the presentation of what I want to say, but I know that you will realize it makes it a lot easier for me in not having to carry about ten pounds of steel around on the bottom of my legs.

This was Roosevelt's first public reference to his physical condition, and the photographs that captured the moment were the first ever taken of the president seated in the wheelchair that had been his constant companion for more than twenty years. The president's appearance that day shocked many in his audience. His physical condition had deteriorated markedly. He "spoke haltingly, slurring some of his words and stumbling over part of his text; his right hand trembled, and he awkwardly turned the pages of his speech with his left hand."

On March 30, Roosevelt left for a vacation in Warm Springs, Georgia. As the days passed at Warm Springs, his condition seemed to improve. However, on April 12, while posing for a portrait, Roosevelt complained of a headache, collapsed, and died two hours later of a massive stroke. The nation was unprepared for the news of his death. There had been rumors of the president's weakening condition but little public discussion and no official confirmation. The public outpouring of emotion was great. Many people reacted to his death as they would to the loss of a parent—a parent whose terminal illness had not been disclosed to them. The extent of the president's physical deterioration was so severe that funeral directors experienced great difficulty in preparing his body for lying in state. His arteries had become so clogged that embalming fluid could not be injected into them in the normal way. Instead, the undertakers had to use individual syringe injections in many parts of his body. Clearly, the president had suffered from cardiovascular disease for some time, and it had apparently affected all of his arteries. Winston Churchill's doctor, on seeing Roosevelt shortly before he died, told a member of the president's cabinet that FDR "has all the symptoms of hardening of the arteries of the brain in an advanced stage,'' and added, "I give him only a few months to live." The public, however, was left in the dark as to the nature and seriousness of the president's condition.

It is a tribute to the image-makers of that time that even today, over forty years after Roosevelt's death, much of the public still does not know that this great leader was confined to a wheelchair throughout his long presidency. Also, few realize that he suffered from serious arterial disease for a considerable period of time before the stroke that ended his life. The "sudden" death that had so stunned the nation and the world in April 1945, and that still today is sometimes portrayed as an unexpected tragedy, was no surprise to White House insiders and Democratic party leaders at the time, who knew that the only president ever elected four times to office would almost certainly not survive his last term as the nation's leader.

ROOSEVELT: COMMANDER-IN-CHIEF DURING WORLD WAR II

During his long tenure as president, Franklin D. Roosevelt had to face not only the crisis of worldwide economic depression but also the tragedy of world war. The same boldness that characterized his leadership in domestic affairs— and even greater steadiness—can be seen in his actions as commander-in-chief, both before and after Congress declared war on the Axis powers in December 1941. However, the image of the commander-in-chief leading a united nation toward preparedness and into battle as soon as the foreign threat became visible is one not based on fact. Instead it exaggerates Roosevelt's success in managing the events of the day.

In preparing the nation for war Roosevelt experienced great difficulty. The forces of American isolationism were still very powerful during the 1930s and were united in their attempts to prevent American involvement in the affairs of other nations. Roosevelt clearly saw the storm clouds gathering over Germany. Whereas many *heard* Hitler's voice, Roosevelt was one of those who *listened* to the German chancellor's words, and he became alarmed. At the same time, he watched Japanese activities in the Far East with dismay and foreboding. During the late 1930s, the president began urging a dramatic increase in military spending, but isolationist leaders across the country warned that this would draw the United States into conflict with foreign powers. Charles Lindbergh, for example, warned that "American frontiers did not lie in Europe; American destiny would not be decided on foreign soil." He added that it "was the President, and not Hitler, who sought world domination."

Some of the most powerful and prominent members of the legislature were part of the isolationist establishment and broke sharply with the president as he tried to arm the nation. As an example, Senator Carter Glass of Virginia wrote, "I am afraid that the 'war scare' is to be used as a red herring across the spendthrift record of the Administration to divert attention from the reckless expenditures that have already bankrupted the nation.'' One Senator, Josiah Bailey of North Carolina, went so far as to charge that Roosevelt's talk of war was "aimed at winning the vote of the Jews in New York City." Much of the public shared the view that Roosevelt's warnings of German aggression were exaggerated. In October 1939, 52 percent of Americans believed that the United States would never again have to go to war against Germany, and 54 percent felt that the United States would be able to stay out of war in Europe.[10] Even more striking, as late as April 1940, 96 percent of Americans opposed American military action against Germany.

Despite public apathy, Roosevelt realized that victory for Hitler's Germany throughout Europe would be a disaster for the world and tried to provide material assistance to Great Britain and France so that they could withstand the German onslaught. Various pieces of Neutrality and Arms Embargo legislation made it extremely difficult for him to do so, but Congress rebuffed Roosevelt's initial attempts to revise these laws. In order to secure the revision that he sought, the president began to woo Southern Democrats, infuriated by his 1938 attempt to unseat some of their number, back to his banner. He met with Senator Glass to discuss the appointment of Virginia judges, invited Senator Bailey to the White House for a friendly chat, and made a number of appointments designed to please conservative members of Congress. One student of the Roosevelt presidency wrote that "while Roosevelt's affability was by no means the only reason for the return of conservative Democrats to the fold, it certainly contributed materially to the smoothness and rapidity with which it came about.'' The conservatives began to support the president in his moves against the Axis powers, specifically, his plan to allow cash sales of weapons to Great Britain and France. Public support also shifted toward support of the president's position. Whereas in September 1938, only 34 percent of Americans supported the sale of war materials to England and France in case of war, by April 1939, 57 percent favored such a policy.

Anticipating possible defeat in Congress, Roosevelt had already developed contingency plans that would allow him to aid the British and French. When France requested American planes, Roosevelt replied that he was trying to have repealed the arms embargo, which prevented him from sending the French these machines of war. If Congress did not cooperate, he proposed to circumvent the embargo, which forbade flying planes out of American airfields to any combatant nation, by having the planes pushed across the border into Canada and delivered to France from Canadian airfields.

The fall of France in 1940 jolted the nation. As the threat of Adolf Hitler grew more and more obvious, the hold of the isolationists began to crumble. By the end of the year, "the national consensus had shifted from intransigent neutralism to an elastic nonbelligerence." In June, 80 percent of the nation favored aid to those fighting Hitler, and 20 percent urged an immediate declaration of war. Public opinion was beginning to respond more realistically to international events and to the president's urging.

Capitalizing on the changing public mood, Roosevelt asked Congress for substantial arms production and received an $8 billion appropriation in response. American industry began to mobilize for the war effort and turned out planes, tanks, guns, and ammunition on a broad scale. This high productivity would persist throughout the war years. The production of planes serves as an example. In 1940 the United States produced 3,800 planes. In 1941 the number grew to 19,400; in 1942 to 47,800; in 1943 to 85,900; in 1944 to 96,300.

During the period immediately preceding American entry into the war, Roosevelt displayed the same pragmatism in foreign policy that he displayed at home. He worked to keep Spain neutral by agreeing to purchase Spanish exports and by providing Spain with petroleum supplies. He promoted Portuguese neutrality by pledging economic assistance in exchange for bases in the Azores and Canary Islands. To forestall the Vichy government in France from signing over the French fleet to Germany, Roosevelt recognized the government of Marshall Petain and offered it aid. Although the president incurred the deep hostility of Charles de Gaulle, leader of Free French forces, through these actions, he succeeded in preventing Nazi expansion in French North Africa.

It may well have been that the international situation persuaded Roosevelt to break with the tradition that had been observed by every president since Washington by seeking a third term. A number of Roosevelt aides believed that he would retire from the White House in 1941. Apparently he had told at least one member of his cabinet that "of course I will not run for a third term. Now I don't want you to pass this on to anyone because it would make my role difficult if the decision were known prematurely."[11] Interestingly, on January 20, 1940, the president had entered into an agreement with the Crowell-Collier Publishing Company under which he was to be employed as one of that company's contributing editors, effective January 20, 1941.

The war in Europe surely gave the president cause for rethinking his decision to leave office. His efforts to move public opinion away from the isolationist camp were beginning to be effective. He could see no truly national figure in the Democratic party who might succeed him at this time of peril, and the prospects of a Republican victory were undoubtedly disturbing to him. He had no interest in seeing a resurgence of isolationism that might follow a Republican victory. Such concerns may well have led Roosevelt to the decision to seek a third term as president.

At the Democratic Convention, Roosevelt swept to renomination with ease, and in the November elections he defeated his Republican opponent, Wendell Willkie, by a comfortable margin. The victory margin, however, was not as great as in 1936. This time his opponent carried ten rather than two states and captured 45 percent of the popular vote. The president's electoral vote victory was a solid 449 to 82, an impressive showing but nowhere near the dimensions of his 523–8 avalanche of 1936.

Despite the fact that his victory margin was narrower, Roosevelt interpreted the vote as a mandate to continue his war policies. The Democratic slogan, after all, had been "Don't change horses in the middle of the stream," and once reelected, the president had no intentions of changing policies in midstream either. His comfortable victory margin, despite the loss of many Italo-American and German-American votes, reinforced his determination to do everything he reasonably could to stop the Axis powers.

Long before a congressional declaration of war, Franklin Roosevelt took a series of bold steps, as commander-in-chief, which put the United States on a collision course with Germany and its allies. In 1938 he issued an executive order that instructed "the Army to turn back older weapons to private contractors, who would then be free to dispose of them abroad, while replacing them with newer weapons for the Army." In 1940 he entered into an executive agreement under which the United States provided fifty American destroyers to Great Britain in return for the lease of a number of sites for naval bases in the British West Atlantic. This action, in a very real sense, brought to an end even the illusion of American neutrality. One member of the Senate termed this executive agreement "an act of belligerency and war." Interestingly, Roosevelt had consulted his attorney general on the constitutionality of such an agreement only *after* he had concluded it.

In March 1941, in an effort to bolster the British war effort, Congress enacted the Lend-Lease Act. This legislation empowered the president to issue authorizations for the manufacture or procurement of defense articles and "to sell, transfer title to, exchange, lease, lend or otherwise dispose of these materials to the government of a country whose defense the President deems vital to the defense of the United States." In passing the Lend-Lease Act, Congress came very close to recognizing the existence of a state of war.

Three months before Pearl Harbor, Roosevelt responded forcefully to a German submarine attack on an American destroyer by ordering American air and naval crews to shoot first at German and Italian warships found in U.S. defensive waters. Roosevelt explained that "when you see a rattlesnake poised to strike, you do not wait until he has struck before you crush him. The Nazi submarines and raiders are the rattlesnakes of the Atlantic. They are a challenge to our sovereignty." The president's "Shoot on sight" order excited the nation with its bold assertion of American rights. It also effectively brought the United States into the war.

At the same time that the United States and Germany moved onto a collision course, American relations with Japan also became increasingly tense. In July 1941, reacting to Japanese troop movement into southern Indochina, the United States froze Japanese assets, thereby bringing economic relations between the two countries to an abrupt halt. So strained did American relations with Japan become that Roosevelt and his secretary of state rejected, in August 1941, a Japanese invitation to meet with the premier of Japan to discuss and try to iron out mutual problems. Instead, the American government indicated that a prior agreement in principle had to be in place on the major points of contention between the two nations before such a conference could be convened.

On Sunday, December 7, 1941, Japan launched a surprise attack against American forces at Pearl Harbor. It was an eminently successful military operation since it destroyed much of the U.S. Pacific Fleet. American defense analysts had been monitoring Japanese troop movements and believed that an attack was likely somewhere in the Pacific, possibly the Philippines or Borneo. But Pearl Harbor was not considered a likely target and military forces there had not been put on a full alert.

On the day following the Japanese attack, Franklin Roosevelt appeared before a Joint Session of Congress and, in ringing tones, proclaimed, "I ask that the Congress declare that since the unprovoked and dastardly attack by Japan . . . a state of war has existed between the United States and the Japanese empire." Congress gave the president the declaration of war he sought, and three days later made similar declarations against Germany and Italy.

To effectuate his war-related policies, Roosevelt moved to harness American activity in many areas. The agencies created to combat the domestic crisis were multiplied many times over by this president as commander-in-chief. He set up the War Production Board to oversee production and distribution of industrial products, the War Manpower Commission to manage employment in war industries, the Office of Price Administration to regulate wartime prices, the Office of Economic Stabilization to control supplies of steel, copper and aluminum, the Office of Scientific Research and Development to foster scientific research, the Office of Strategic Services to gather intelligence for government use, the Office of Censorship to oversee the communication and transmission of war news, and the Office of War Information to disseminate war-related facts and figures. By 1942 he had established approximately thirty-five such bodies.

Roosevelt's actions in setting up these agencies and in delegating to them broad grants of power raise a number of constitutional questions. However, his actions did convey to the country and to the world the image of an aggressive leader, determined to take all steps necessary to win the war. Roosevelt went so far as to say, in 1942, that the powers under which he acted came to him not solely from the Constitution but from the people themselves. He told Congress:

The American people can . . . be sure that I shall not hesitate to use every power vested in me to accomplish the defeat of our enemies in any part of the world where our own safety demands such defeat. When the war is won, the powers under which I act automatically revert to the people—to whom they belong.[12]

The creation of a large number of agencies to supervise particular segments of the war effort necessarily led to some bureaucratic tensions. However, the overriding interest in winning the war kept those tensions generally subdued and under control. It was Roosevelt's administrative style to create deliberately overlapping functions and jurisdictions among agencies so that he would be exposed to different viewpoints on the same policy questions. He did not believe in an administrative structure characterized by neat lines of responsibility and clear-cut points of authority. During his presidency, he presided over what has been called "planned chaos" by organizing and reorganizing numerous agencies so that they would compete against each other and provide him with alternative sources of information.

In the conduct of World War II, Roosevelt kept "White House decision making intimate, personalized, ad hoc, 'disorderly,' and in his hands." He used the agencies and commissions which he appointed as a means whereby he could personally handle affairs of state and influence the conduct of the war. This practice, as might be expected, caused considerable unhappiness in the State Department and at the Pentagon. Secretary of War Henry Stimson once said, "The President is the poorest administrator I have ever worked under in respect to the ordinary procedure and routine of his performance. He is not a good chooser of men and he does not know how to use them in co-ordination." A contemporary student of the Roosevelt presidency tells us that "testimony upon Mr. Roosevelt as administrator is practically unanimous to the effect that he was not efficient or effective."

Regardless of his administrative style, Roosevelt's shadow fell heavily across strategic wartime planning. At state dinners, he even preferred to be introduced as commander-in-chief of the armed forces rather than as president of the United States. He felt sufficiently confident in 1942 to ignore the advice of most of his military commanders, who urged greater stress on the campaign against Japan, and ordered instead major U.S. involvement in the invasion of North Africa. He came into some conflict with British prime minister Winston Churchill when he endorsed the opening of a second front in France rather than endorsing Churchill's preference for a major campaign in the Balkans. Also, Roosevelt staunchly insisted on an unconditional surrender by the Axis nations even though this insistence caused some concern that the war would be prolonged because of it.

To successfully prosecute the war, Roosevelt was convinced that his powers as commander-in-chief extended to internal or domestic matters which conceivably could have an effect on the war effort. He seized private property both before and after Congress declared war in an effort to prevent labor unrest or even inefficient management from impacting negatively on the military effort. In one striking move he asked Congress, in September 1942, to repeal a section of the Emergency Price Control Act by October 1, saying rather ominously that inaction "on your part by that date will leave me with an inescapable responsibility to the people of this country to see to it that the war effort is no longer imperiled by the threat of economic chaos." The president warned that in "the event that Congress should fail to act, and act adequately, I shall accept the responsibility, and I will act." The nation, then, was confronted by a commander-in-chief who publicly asserted his right, in the face of a world war, to usurp the legislative prerogatives of Congress.

Perhaps, however, the most famous and controversial use of Roosevelt's "war powers" within the United States came in his February 1942 order authorizing the secretary of war, and the military commanders designated by him, to establish "military areas" wherever deemed appropriate, "from which any or all persons may be excluded" and concerning which "the right of any person to enter, remain in, or leave shall be subject to whatever restriction the Secretary of War or the appropriate military commander may impose in his discretion."

The practical result of this order was the removal of more than 110,000 persons of Japanese ancestry who resided in western states from their homes and jobs and their placement in relocation centers in Arizona, Utah, Idaho, Colorado, and Wyoming and other remote places away from the West Coast. This action was taken because of the fear that these persons might assist Japan if it attempted to invade American territory. The fact that most of the people placed in relocation centers were native-born Americans who theoretically enjoyed the same constitutional rights as all other Americans did not prevent this extreme action from being taken. As testimony to the war hysteria of the day, the Supreme Court upheld the validity of the action.

The press, of course, gave heavy coverage to many of Roosevelt's war-related activities. The image that was projected so widely was that of a determined and bold commander-in-chief taking actions that were both constitutional and extra-constitutional in an effort to win military victory. The fact that some of those actions may perhaps have been unconstitutional received scant attention. After Pearl Harbor, the nation was united, fully committed to the military effort, and supportive of Roosevelt's war leadership. Ironically, perhaps, it was only after the United States began to mobilize and equip its military forces that the army of the unemployed, still formidable in 1941, finally disappeared.

So involved did Roosevelt become in efforts to win the war that in 1944 he accepted still another presidential renomination by the Democratic party without hesitation or indecision. Facing his most formidable opponent in the Republican governor of New York, Thomas E. Dewey, Roosevelt was elected to his fourth term. Capturing 53 percent of the popular vote and carrying thirty-six states with 432 electoral votes, Roosevelt won a convincing but not an overwhelming victory. At the same time, Democratic majorities in both Houses of Congress were reduced.

Roosevelt, of course, would be dead less than six months after his fourth presidential victory and would not see the war brought to a successful conclusion. However, in his final weeks as president, he engaged in a major conference with allied leaders at Yalta, and that conference has served as the focal point for rumors about Franklin Roosevelt's diplomatic performance that began to circulate shortly after his death and that remain prevalent even today.

Reduced to their most common denominator, the rumors center on the impact of Roosevelt's deteriorating health on his effectiveness at the Yalta negotiating table. Typical is this assessment of Roosevelt's behavior:

Even Churchill did not seem able to make him understand that Stalin was deliberately playing them against each other, attempting to split them in order to achieve his own ends. Again and again the President seems to have fallen into traps set by Stalin—and to some extent even by Churchill—losing points that he never would have conceded had he been in good health and with his earlier ability to control situations.

Because of his weakened state of health, Roosevelt has been described as finding it difficult to concentrate for too long on any subject by 1945 and as being increasingly reluctant to engage in argument. The Yalta Conference was certainly not an appropriate place for such traits to be on display, especially since the other wartime leaders did not share them. While the image of a dying president being manipulated and outmaneuvered at the conference table is rather commonplace, it is not necessarily accurate.

One recent analysis of the Yalta Conference assures us that those closest to Roosevelt at Yalta thought that the president performed effectively. They found him to be mentally fit and able to deal well with each problem as it arose. A British official at the conference felt that the president's declining health did not alter his judgment.[13] These positive assessments of Roosevelt's performance are borne out by an analysis of several of the agreements reached at Yalta. Dallek writes:

On all the central issues—the United Nations, Germany, Poland, Eastern Europe and the Far East—Roosevelt largely followed through on earlier plans and gained most of what he wished: the world body, the division of Germany, the pronouncement on Poland, and the Declaration on Liberated Europe promised to encourage American involvement abroad and possible long-term accommodation with the U.S.S.R.; similarly, the Far East agreement promised to save American lives and hold China together to play a part in helping the United States preserve postwar peace.

Probably the two most important American objectives at Yalta were the entry of the Soviet Union into the war against Japan and the advancement of the idea of a United Nations. At the negotiating table, Stalin agreed to enter the Pacific war within three months after the German defeat and promised to commit a substantial portion of Russian forces to the battle with Japan. With respect to the United Nations, the Soviets agreed that France would become a permanent member of the UN Security Council and that only two—rather than sixteen—Soviet republics would have voting rights in the UN General Assembly.

Stalin also agreed to sign a treaty of friendship with Nationalist China and to recognize Chinese authority over Manchuria. In return, the Soviets were given sovereignty over a portion of Japanese owned islands, acquired certain rights to a Manchurian port, and secured a degree of control over the Manchurian railway.

Probably the greatest and most specific stream of criticism aimed at Roosevelt surrounds his apparent acquiescence in Soviet control of Poland. Although President Roosevelt was unhappy with the fact that Soviet troops were in Poland, he realized that they could not be dislodged easily. The American people were war-weary and wanted the troops to come home soon. They would find it difficult, after securing the defeat of the Axis powers, to begin a new military campaign, this one against the Soviet Union. Consequently, Roosevelt simply accepted the facts of political life—both those prevalent in the United States and those in Eastern Europe—by not forcing a showdown with Stalin over this issue. He very much hoped that postwar American-Soviet friendship would ensure a lasting peace.

The president was aware that the outcome of the Yalta Conference was not completely satisfactory in all respects. He admitted to Assistant Secretary of State Adolf Berle, "I didn't say the result was good, Adolf, I said it was the best I could do." Despite Roosevelt's misgivings, however, and despite his state of health at the time, he seems to have performed creditably at Yalta. Available evidence indicates that he was "an alert and aggressive bargainer at these sessions who gave up no more than he got back in the high-stakes give and take."

Critics sometimes are prone to forget that international conferences owe their success to the final willingness of the participants to strike reasonable compromises. The Yalta Conference was no different. The fact that Roosevelt did not get everything that he wanted does not necessarily mean that he "sold out" to the Russians. After all, Stalin failed to get everything that he wanted, too. In point of fact, just as Roosevelt had to face the reality of American isolationism as he tried to prepare the nation for war, so did he have to confront the fact of American war-weariness when he met with his allied counterparts at Yalta. Always a pragmatist, Franklin Roosevelt worked to achieve realistic objectives at the Yalta Conference and refrained from allowing visions of a perfect world to divert his attention and energies to unrealizable goals. However, it is important to note that despite the interpretation of Roosevelt's performance at Yalta that is often bandied about, the president managed to achieve at that conference perhaps his greatest single vision—a permanent end to American isolationism and the beginning of a new era of internationalism for the United States.

CONCLUSIONS

Franklin D. Roosevelt commonly is rated one of the nation's most effective presidents. The Schlesinger polls of 1948 and 1962 rank him among the top three in presidential greatness. Perhaps it is axiomatic of great men that myths come to surround them, both in life and in death. Some of the Roosevelt myths persist even today, more than forty years after the end of his presidency.

Franklin D. Roosevelt was not universally popular while he sat in the White House, even though he sat there so many years. Contrary to popular belief, he experienced severe difficulty not only with important segments of the public but also with both conservatives and liberals in Congress and on the Supreme Court. The dominant impression created by his presidential performance, however, was that he was a crusading leader, bent on social reform, committed to social welfare programs, and dedicated to bringing to an end the Great Depression.

Undoubtedly Roosevelt worked hard to alleviate the economic distress of the times. But, in reality, his attempts to do so were moderate in scope, generally cautious, and highly eclectic. Far from steering a steady and consistent course, Roosevelt sometimes veered about erratically, trying to find policies that would prove effective for curing the nation's economic ills. Never completely comfortable with unbalanced budgets and a government that was too interventionist, Roosevelt was an experimenter whose domestic New Deal programs never really restored the nation to full prosperity. Interestingly, his experimentation sometimes resurrected and/or expanded programs discussed or initiated before he came to office. Portions of his New Deal agricultural programs had been discussed as early as Calvin Coolidge's administration, and it was Herbert Hoover who initiated a limited public works program to provide jobs for the unemployed. It is to Roosevelt's credit, however, that he was neither afraid nor reluctant to experiment with both old and new ideas in an effort to end the Depression. This was, after all, the president who at one point exclaimed, "Above all, try something."

As the president in office immediately before and then during World War II, Roosevelt's image as diplomatist and commander-in-chief was and continues to be subject to some distortion. Portrayed by much of the press and by any number of prominent isolationist leaders as a warmonger and an imperialist, Roosevelt was unable, during the 1930s, to ready his nation for the coming firestorm. In December 1941, when Japan attacked Pearl Harbor, the United States was largely unprepared for war.

As commander-in-chief, Franklin Roosevelt again projected the image of confident optimism and self-assurance. He resorted to all constitutional and extra-constitutional means of securing victory, and he served as an effective spearhead for an unparalleled mobilization of national war effort against the Axis powers. The unconstitutionality of and the violation of civil liberties inherent in some of his war-related activities received little notice from a nation gripped by war fever. It was not until 1983, for example, that a government-sponsored commission blamed President Roosevelt in particular for the "failure of political leadership" that had allowed the grave injustice associated with the wartime relocation and internment of more than 100,000 persons of Japanese ancestry.[14]

It is not surprising that the image of dynamic determination that Roosevelt projected was in no way undermined by his severe physical afflictions, since the public remained blissfully unaware of those afflictions. Because of the cooperation of the press, the topic of his crippled legs simply did not reach the public domain. Also, the severe arterial deterioration that finally ended his life in 1945 came as a surprise to much of the nation, which almost believed that he would be on the scene forever.

As with all presidents, the image of Franklin D. Roosevelt occasionally diverged from the reality. This fact, however, should not be allowed to cloud his greatness. Roosevelt ushered in the era of American internationalism, taught the nation that government had a proper role to play in managing the economy, served as the father of the modern Democratic party, strengthened the presidency, and stood as a symbol of national stability during times of severe crisis. In a very real sense, Franklin D. Roosevelt transformed his nation and left an indelible mark on the world.

NOTES

1. On FDR Groton record, see Kenneth S. Davis, *F.D.R.: The Beckoning of Destiny, 1882–1928* (New York: G. P. Putnam's Sons, 1972), p. 82. On clubs for poor, see Karl Helicker, "The Education of Franklin D. Roosevelt," *Presidential Studies Quarterly,* 12 (Winter 1982): 51. On Eleanor's reaction to new home, see Joseph Lash, *Eleanor and Franklin* (New York: W. W. Norton, 1971), pp. 161, 162. On FDR as state senator, see Gerald D. Nash, *Franklin D. Roosevelt* (Englewood Cliffs, N.J.: Prentice-Hall, 1967), p. 80. On FDR's national organizing efforts, see Earland I. Carlson, "Franklin D. Roosevelt's Post-mortem of the 1928 Election," *Midwest Journal of Political Science,* 8 (1964): 300, 301. On FDR's support in South, see ibid., p. 298. For 1932 acceptance, see Samuel I. Rosenman, ed., *The Public Papers and Addresses of Franklin D. Roosevelt,* 13 vols. (New York: Russell, 1930–1939), 1:659 (hereafter cited as Rosenman, *Public Papers, FDR).* For FDR attack on waste, see *Time,* February 1, 1942, p. 21. FDR attack on deficit in Richard Hofstadter, *The American Political Tradition and the Men Who Made It* (New York: Knopf, 1967), p. 325. Garner attack on Hoover "socialism" in *Time,* February 1, 1982, p. 22.

2. Attack on FDR extravagance in Harris G. Warren, *FDR, Hoover and the Great Depression* (New York: W. W. Norton, 1967), pp. 260–262 (hereafter cited as Warren, *HH and Depression).* Walter Lippman critique of Roosevelt in Nash, *FDR,* p. 88. For a detailed discussion of the Great Depression, see John Kenneth Galbraith, *The Great Crash, 1929,* 3rd ed. (Boston: Houghton Mifflin, 1972). On malnutrition see Warren, *HH and Depression,* p. 277. FDR First Inaugural in Rosenman, *Public Papers, FDR,* 2:11, 16. Bank holiday cited in Warren, *HH and Depression,* p. 285. NIRA message in Rosenman, *Public Papers, FDR,* 2:246. AAA and NIRA policy departure noted in Theda Skocpol and Kenneth Finegold, "State Capacity and Economic Intervention in the Early New Deal," *Political Science Quarterly,* 97 (Summer 1982): 255. Conflict in NRA cited in ibid., p. 257. "Lost opportunity" cited in ibid., p. 278. Success of AAA noted in ibid., p. 257.

3. On FDR's caution as leader, see Nash, *FDR,* p. 40. Fear of partisanship noted in James M. Burns, *Roosevelt: The Lion and the Fox* (New York: Harcourt, Brace, 1956), p. 185. Concern about CWA cost cited in William E. Leuchtenberg, *Franklin D. Roosevelt and the New Deal 1932–1940* (New York: Harper and Row, 1963), p. 122. View on Social Security in Nash, *FDR,* p. 47. Social insurance view in Rexford G. Tugwell, *In Search of Roosevelt* (Cambridge, Mass.: Harvard University Press, 1972), p. 160. FDR retort to liberals in James T. Patterson, *The New Deal and the States* (Westport, Conn.: Greenwood Press, 1969), p. 93. View of elitist control in G. William Domhoff, *The Higher Circles* (New York: Vintage Books, 1970), p. 218. On FDR unpredictability, see Elmus Wicker, "Roosevelt's Monetary Experiment," *Journal of American History,* 55, (March 1971): 873. Redistributionist policies noted in Alonzo L. Hamby, "Sixty Million Jobs and the People's Revolution: The Liberals, the New Deal and World War II," *The Historian,* 30 (1967–1968): 578.

4. "Economic Royalists" attack quoted in Burns, *The Lion and the Fox,* p. 274. Early WPA record in Patterson, *The New Deal and the States,* p. 74. "Scab army" attack

in Charles J. Tull, *Father Coughlin and the New Deal* (New York: Syracuse University Press, 1965), p. 160. "Boon to Communists" charge in Richard Polenberg, "Franklin Roosevelt and Civil Liberties: The Case of the Dies Committee," *The Historian*, 30 (1967–1968): 166. Al Smith attack in Nash, *FDR*, p. 106. "Nation of softies" attack in Patterson, *The New Deal and the States*, pp. 154, 155. Upper-class vitriol cited in Geoffrey S. Smith, *To Save a Nation* (New York: Basic Books, 1973), p. 78. Image of FDR as radical in George Gallup and Saul F. Rae, *The Pulse of Democracy* (Westport, Conn.: Greenwood Press, 1968), p. 294. Huey Long attack recorded in *U.S. Congressional Record*, 74th Congress, 1st Session, 1935, vol. 79, p. 3437. Republican help for FDR noted in Robert E. Burke, "The Roosevelt Administration," *Current History*, 38–39 (1960): 223.

5. On radicalism in Congress, see Burns, *The Lion and the Fox*, p. 185. Congress' restraint on popular presidents noted in Frank Freidel, *Franklin D. Roosevelt* (Boston: Little, Brown, 1973), p. 452. On FDR's role in labor legislation, see Domhoff, *The Higher Circles*, p. 240. Perceptions of FDR's attitudes toward labor in Gallup and Rae, *Pulse of Democracy*, p. 307. Speaking in Georgia with Senator George beside him, Roosevelt told his audience that he considered Georgia his second home and that if he could vote there, he would cast his ballot against Senator George because the senator had opposed much of his program; see Booth Moody, *Roosevelt and Rayburn* (Philadelphia: J. P. Lippincott, 1971), p. 117. On Democrats' attitudes toward purge, see Gallup and Rae, *Pulse of Democracy*, p. 297. On ratio of FDR vetoes to total, see George C. Robinson, "The Veto Record of Franklin D. Roosevelt," *American Political Science Review*, (February 1942): 75. On modern communications advances, see Daniel Boorstin, "Selling the President to the People," in *The American Presidency: Vital Center*, ed. Elmer E. Cornwell (Glenview, Ill.: Scott, Foresman, 1966), p. 119. On fears about FDR's radio personality, see Edward W. Chester, *Radio, Television and American Politics* (New York: Sheed and Ward, 1969), p. 94. FDR's letter-reading on fireside chats in Richard W. Steele, "The Pulse of the People: Franklin D. Roosevelt and the Gauging of American Public Opinion," *Journal of Contemporary History*, 9, no. 4 (October 1974): 202.

6. On overexposure, see Chester, *Radio, Television and American Politics*, p. 95. Poet's view of FDR from Carl Carmer, quoted in Walter Johnson, *1600 Pennsylvania Avenue* (Boston: Little, Brown, 1960), p. 195. On FDR's press analysis, see Steele, "The Pulse of the People," p. 197. FDR technique with press in Elmer Cornwell, *Presidential Leadership of Public Opinion* (Bloomington: Indiana University Press, 1965), p. 143. News conference description in Leo C. Rosten, "President Roosevelt and the Washington Correspondents," *Public Opinion Quarterly*, 1 (January 1937): 38. Frequency of news conferences in B. H. Winfield, "Franklin D. Roosevelt's Efforts to Influence the News During His First Term Press Conferences," *Presidential Studies Quarterly*, (Spring 1981): 189. Successors' news conference frequency noted in Robert E. Gilbert, "Television and Political Power," *Journal of Social, Political and Economic Studies*, (Spring 1981): 81. Letter to *Sun* correspondent in Winfield, "FDR's Efforts to Influence the News," p. 195. "Cuckoo stories" reference in ibid. On misquotation, see Rosten, "Roosevelt and Correspondents," p. 43.

7. "Cross-examination" in Rosten, "Roosevelt and Correspondents," p. 44. Criticism of "mugging" in ibid., pp. 44, 45. On court-packing bill, see Max Freedman, ed., *Roosevelt and Frankfurter* (Boston: Little, Brown, 1967), p. 390. On court modernization, see *New York Times*, March 10, 1937, p. 15. On peak FDR "packing" support

see Gallup and Rae, *Pulse of Democracy*, p. 85. On opposition to restricting Court, see ibid. p. 129. On reaction to FDR death see Fred Greenstein, "The Psychological Functions of the Presidency for Citizens," in Cornwell, *American Presidency*, p. 35. Opposition to third term cited in Gallup and Rae, *Pulse of Democracy*, p. 293. NIRA killed in *Schecter Poultry Corp.* v. *United States* (295 U.S. 495, 1935). FTC dismissal voided in *Humphrey's Executor* v. *United States* (295 U.S. 602, 1935).

8. AAA tax voided in *United States v. Butler* (297 U.S. 1, 1936). Guffey Coal Act nullified in *Carter* v. *Carter Coal Co.* (298 U.S. 238, 1936). Frazier-Lemke Act struck down in *Louisville Joint Stock Land Bank* v. *Radford* (295 U.S. 555, 1935). Minimum wage law killed in *Morehead* v. *New York ex rel. Tipaldo* (298 U.S. 587, 1936). Speculation on FDR motivation in Freedman, *Roosevelt and Frankfurter*, p. 381. Proposal for Court enlargement in Robert Scigliano, *The Supreme Court and the Presidency* (New York: Free Press, 1971), p. 47. On conservative resignations, see ibid. Minimum wage law upheld in *West Coast Hotel Co.* v. *Parrish* (300 U.S. 379, 1937). Restrictions on FDR photos cited in Michael B. Grossman and Martha J. Kumar, *Portraying the President* (Baltimore: Johns Hopkins Press, 1981), pp. 27, 28. On FDR physical disability, see J. B. West, *Upstairs at the White House* (New York: Coward, McCann, and Geoghegan, 1973), p. 17.

9. Seat among ferns noted in West, *Upstairs*, p. 18. FDR entrance described in ibid. Ignorance of FDR's disability noted in John B. Moses and Wilber Cross, *Presidential Courage* (New York: W. W. Norton, 1980), p. 137. Farley's observation of poor health in Herbert E. Bateman, "Observations on President Roosevelt's Health During World War II," *Mississippi Valley Historical Review*, 42, (June 1956): 85. Dizzy spell in 1938 in Moses and Cross, *Courage*, p. 200. Heart failure cited in Jim Bishop, *FDR's Last Year* (New York: William Morrow, 1974), p. 295. Weak voice noted in Bateman, "Observations on President Roosevelt's Health," p. 91. Strain of campaigning in West, *Upstairs*, p. 46. Election night fatigue cited in Merriman Smith, *Thank You, Mr. President* (New York: Harper, 1946), pp. 158, 159. Cabinet members' observations in Robert Dallek, *Franklin D. Roosevelt and American Foreign Policy* (New York: Oxford University Press, 1979), p. 519.

10. Observation of pain on FDR's face in Harry S Truman, *Memoirs: Year of Decision*, 2 vols. (New York: Doubleday, 1955), 1:2. Post-Yalta report in *New York Times*, March 2, 1945, p. 13. See also Geoffrey Perrett, *Days of Sadness, Years of Triumph* (New York: Coward, McCann and Geoghegan, 1973), p. 288. Slurring of words noted in Dallek, *FDR and Foreign Policy*, p. 520. Deterioration cited in Bishop, *FDR's Last Year*, p. 620. Effect of disease noted in Bernard Asbell, *When FDR Died* (New York: Holt, Rinehart and Winston, 1961), p. 128. Churchill physician's prognosis in Bishop, *FDR's Last Year*, p. 294. Lindbergh attack on FDR in Geoffrey Smith, *To Save a Nation*, p. 178. Senator Glass on "war scare" in James T. Patterson, "Eating Humble Pie: A Note on Roosevelt, Congress and Neutrality Revision in 1939," *The Historian*, 31 (1968–1969): 408. Senator Bailey's charge in ibid. Poll on prospect of war in Gallup and Rae, *Pulse of Democracy*, pp. 315, 319.

11. Opposition to intervention cited in Gallup and Rae, *Pulse of Democracy*, p. 320. Rebuff on neutrality repeal cited in Robert A. Devine, "Franklin D. Roosevelt and Collective Security, 1933," *Mississippi Valley Historical Review*, 48 (April 1939): 43. Reconciliation with conservatives in Patterson, "Eating Humble Pie," p. 413. Shift in opinion on aid in Gallup and Rae, *Pulse of Democracy*, pp. 204, 316. Circumvention of embargo in John McVickar Haight, Jr., "Roosevelt as a Friend of France," *Foreign*

Affairs, 44 (January 1966): 518. Reaction to fall of France in Cabell Phillips, *The 1940's: Decade of Triumph and Trouble* (New York: Macmillan, 1975), p. 8. Opinion on aid to allies in John A. Woods, *Roosevelt and Modern America* (New York: Macmillan, 1959), p. 134. Plane production cited in Gerald D. Nash, *The Great Depression and World War II* (New York: St. Martin's Press, 1979), p. 135. Vichy policy in ibid., p. 123. FDR private intent on third term in Moody, *Roosevelt and Rayburn,* p. 117.

12. FDR writing contract noted in Paul H. Appleby, "Roosevelt's Third-Term Decision," *American Political Science Review,* 55 (September 1952): 756. On surplus weapons disposition, see Edward S. Corwin, *The President: Office and Powers* (New York: New York University Press, 1957), p. 288. Destroyers-for-bases deal in Sidney Warren, *The President as World Leader* (New York: McGraw-Hill, 1964), p. 212. Opinion on bases deal cited in Martin S. Sheffer, "The Attorney General and Presidential Power," *Presidential Studies Quarterly,* 12 (Winter 1982): 57. Lend-Lease Act, Act of March 11, 1941, Chap. 11, *55 Stat. 31.* "Shoot on sight" order in *New York Times,* September 12, 1941, p. 6. On undeclared war see Robert E. Gilbert, "The President's Power to Make War," *UMKC Law Review,* (Winter 1973): 169. Bargaining with Japan in R.J.C. Butow, "Backdoor Diplomacy in the Pacific: The Proposal for a Konoye-Roosevelt Meeting, 1941," *Journal of American History,* (June 1972): 50. Pearl Harbor speech in Rosenman, *Public Papers, FDR,* 10:514. FDR on prerogative doctrine in Edward S. Corwin, "The War and the Constitution: President and Congress," *American Political Science Review,* 37 (1943): 18.

13. On FDR administrative style, see Richard E. Neustadt, "Approaches to Staffing the Presidency: Notes on FDR and JFK," *American Political Science Review,* 77 (December 1963): 860. Stimson view of FDR in Nash, *Franklin D. Roosevelt,* p. 123. On FDR inefficiency, see Burns, *The Lion and the Fox,* p. 153. Unconditional surrender policy in Nash, *Depression and War,* p. 117. Vow to act in *New York Times,* September 8, 1942, p. 1. On Japanese-American "internment camps," see Executive Order 9066, 7 *Fed-Reg.* 1407. Court opinions on internments in *Hirabavashi* v. *United States* (320 U.S. 81, 1943); *Korematsu* v. *United States* (323 U.S. 214, 1944). View of FDR as dupe of Stalin in Moses and Cross, *Courage,* p. 209. On FDR impatience with argument, see Gaddis Smith, *American Diplomacy During the Second World War, 1941–1945* (New York: John Wiley, 1965), p. 131. On FDR alertness at Yalta, see Dallek, *FDR and Foreign Policy,* p. 519.

14. FDR achievements at Yalta cited in Dallek, *FDR and Foreign Policy,* p. 519. Yalta objectives cited in Phillips, *The 1940's,* p. 225. Soviet concessions at Yalta in ibid., p. 223. FDR, Poland, and Eastern Europe in ibid., p. 225. Remark to Berle in Dallek, *FDR and Foreign Policy,* p. 520. "Alert bargainer" in Phillips, *The 1940's,* p. 223. FDR as an experimenter in Dexter Perkins, *The New Age of Franklin Roosevelt* (Chicago: University of Chicago Press, 1957), p. 71. Hoover pioneering in public works noted in Rexford G. Tugwell, *FDR: Architect of an Era* (New York: Macmillan, 1967), p. 71. Experimental attitude cited in Arthur M. Schlesinger, Jr., *The Crisis of the Old Order* (Vol. 1 in *The Age of Roosevelt* series) (Boston: Houghton Mifflin, 1957), p. 289. In February 1983 the Commission on Wartime Relocation and Internment of Civilians concluded that the relocation and internment of persons of Japanese ancestry during World War II was a "grave injustice" motivated by "racial prejudice, war hysteria and failure of political leadership." The Commission's report also blamed President Roosevelt for delaying the release of these persons from internment camps until after the 1944 election for "political reasons" *(New York Times,* February 25, 1983, p. 1).

ANNOTATED BIBLIOGRAPHY

Books

Beschloss, Michael R. *Kennedy and Roosevelt*. New York: Norton, 1980.
    A detailed study of FDR's relationship with Joseph P. Kennedy.
Burns, James MacGregor. *Roosevelt*. 2 vols. New York: Harcourt Brace, 1956, 1970.
    A prize-winning pair of biographies, this set includes *Roosevelt: The Lion and the Fox* (1956), covering the pre-war New Deal, and *Roosevelt: The Soldier of Freedom* (1970), covering the World War II era.
Davis, Kenneth S. *F.D.R.: The Beckoning of Destiny, 1882–1928*. New York: Putnam, 1972.
    A biography of the years preceding the New York governorship; good account of the battle with polio.
Einaudi, Mario. *The Roosevelt Revolution*. New York: Harcourt, 1957.
    A European perspective on the FDR era.
Freidel, Frank. *Franklin D. Roosevelt*. Boston: Little, Brown, 1952–73.
    This continuing series so far has included the Harvard historian's *FDR: The Apprenticeship* (1952); *FDR: The Ordeal* (1954); *FDR: The Triumph* (1956), and *FDR: Launching the New Deal* (1973).
Lash, Joseph. *Eleanor and Franklin*. New York: W.W. Norton, 1971.
    A sympathetic study of the First Lady's own political career as well as her marriage. Written by a veteran of the 1930s youth movement.
Lindley, Ernest K. *The Roosevelt Revolution*. New York: Viking, 1933.
    A columnist-journalist's account of the New Deal's emergence.
Miller, Nathan. *FDR: An Intimate History*. Garden City, N.Y.: Doubleday, 1983.
    A well-written biography, incorporating newly discovered material.
Rollins, Alfred B., Jr. *Roosevelt and Howe*. New York: Knopf, 1962.
    A more recent account of FDR's relationship with his prepresidential and early New Deal adviser.
Roosevelt, Eleanor. *This Is My Story*. New York: Harper, 1937.
    The First Lady's account of the early New Deal.
——. *This I Remember*. New York: Harper, 1949.
    An autobiographical account of the entire FDR era.
Roosevelt, Elliott, ed. *F.D.R.: His Personal Letters, 1928–1945*. 4 vols. New York: Duell, 1947–1950.
    The FDR correspondence, edited by the president's son.
Rosenman, Samuel I. *Working with Roosevelt*. New York: Harper, 1952.
    The senior aide's memoirs.
——, ed. *The Public Papers and Addresses of Franklin D. Roosevelt*. 13 vols. New York: Russell, 1930–39.
    Documents edited by a senior speechwriter for FDR.
Schlesinger, Arthur M., Jr. *The Age of Roosevelt*. 3 vols. Boston: Houghton Mifflin, 1957–1960.
    A fourth volume of this series in preparation by the chronicler of the Kennedy brothers. Works thus far published have included *The Crisis of the Old Order, The Coming of the New Deal*, and *The Politics of Upheaval*.

Sherwood, Robert E. *Roosevelt and Hopkins: An Intimate History*. New York: Harper, 1948.
>   Playwright and FDR's wartime speechwriter, Sherwood provides an account of FDR's collaboration with a principal aide.

Stewart, William J., comp. *The Era of Franklin D. Roosevelt*. Hyde Park, N.Y.: Franklin D. Roosevelt Library, 1974.
>   A good recent bibliography.

Stiles, Lela. *The Man Behind Roosevelt*. New York: World Publishers, 1954.
>   The first complete biography of mentor Louis McHenry Howe.

White, Graham J. *F.D.R. and the Press*. Chicago: University of Chicago Press, 1979.
>   An excellent account of FDR's media relations in the heyday of the daily newspaper; some details of cartoons and fireside chats as well.

Pamphlet

Molella, Arthur P., and Elsa M. Bruton. *FDR: The Intimate Presidency: Franklin D. Roosevelt, Communication, and the Mass Media in the 1930's*. Washington, D.C.: National Museum of American History, Smithsonian Institution, 1982.
>   An illustrated study of FDR's media relations, timed to coincide with the 1982 observance of the centennial of his birth.

Document

President's Committee on Administrative Management. *Report with Special Studies*. Washington, D.C.: U.S. Government Printing Office, 1937.
>   This is the famous Brownlow Commission Report, which many scholars say marked the launching of the modern presidency.

Documentary Records

F.D.R. Speaks. Authorized edition of speeches, 1933 to 1945. Introduction by Mrs. Eleanor Roosevelt. Edited by Henry Steele Commager. Washington Records, 1960.
>   Excerpts from fireside chats, campaign speeches, and public addresses. Commentary by Charles Wood of Radio Station WGMS, Washington, D.C.

The Great Depression: A Radiosound Portrait of Hard Times in the 1930's. Radiola Actuality Series No. 6, Release No. 120, 1980.
>   Background of the FDR era.

I Can Hear It Now. Vol. 1 (1933–1945). Columbia Special Recordings, 1948.
>   The Roosevelt Years described by Edward R. Murrow in collaboration with Fred Friendly. First of a series of three records narrated by the pioneer broadcast journalist. Contains commentary as well as actualities.

"Mr. President": From FDR to Eisenhower. James Fleming of NBC, narrator. RCA Victor Red Seal, 1954.
>   Includes,material on FDR campaigns, wartime speeches.

The Voice of FDR: Excerpts of His Speeches During the Presidential Years (1932–1945).
>   Special narration by Quentin Reynolds, the journalist; written foreword by Robert

E. Sherwood; written and produced by Arthur Lane. Decca Records, 1946.
A memorial album.

Voices of the Presidents. Lexington Educational Audio Visual, 1967.
FDR Speech "On the Broader Definition of Liberty," 1936, on Band 7.

15 HARRY TRUMAN

Bernard Sternsher

A glance at Figure 15.1 reveals a definite sequence in the general or overall Gallup poll approval rating of President Harry S Truman's performance (Do you approve or disapprove of the way Harry Truman is handling his job as President? Approve, Disapprove, No Opinion): brief *honeymoon,* precipitous *decline* in 1946, *postelection comeback* in early 1947, *decline* in 1947 and 1948, *post-election comeback* in early 1949, and *decline* through the second term. Truman began with the highest Gallup poll approval rating and ended his first year with the lowest among presidents in the period 1945–1970:[1]

	First Measurement	After One Year
Truman	87%	50%
Eisenhower	68	71
Kennedy	72	77
Johnson	79	69
Nixon	59	61

Pollster Elmo Roper accounts for the honeymoon Truman enjoyed during his first six months in office, observing that the public was "inclined to make the largest allowances in judging his performance . . . at the end of his first summer in office, with their original expectations of their new President low, and their elation over the end of the war high, the people's appraisal of his administration was extremely favorable."[2]

Truman's approval rating in the Gallup poll published on July 1 (interviewing dates 6/1–5/45)—Approve 87 percent, Disapprove 3 percent, No opinion 10 percent—declined only slightly in the poll of November 2 (interviewing dates 10/5–10/45)—Approve 82 percent, Disapprove 9 percent, No opinion 9 percent.[3] From late 1945 to early 1946, however, his approval rating suffered a substantial decline. In the Gallup poll of February 1, 1946 (interviewing dates 1/5–10/46), it fell 19 points to 63 percent (Disapprove 22 percent, No opinion 15 percent).[4]

Figure 15.1
Approval Ratings for Harry Truman

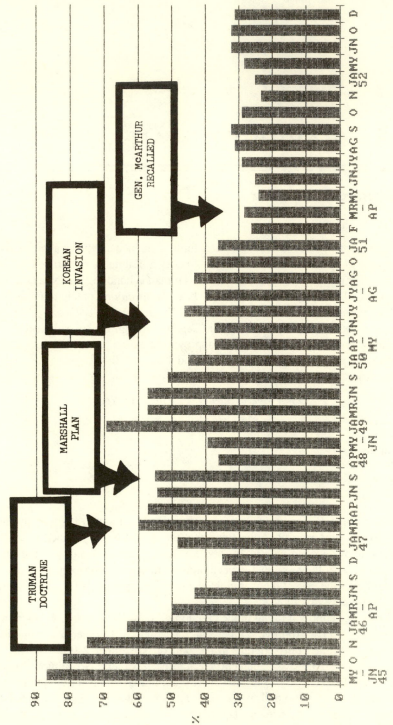

Source: Gallup Opinion Index, September-October 1980.

It is apparent that sometime soon after the polls of November 1945, the end of the honeymoon began.

Roper emphasizes the importance of an earlier development—Truman's address of September 6 in which he presented a twenty-one-point reconversion program to Congress. "The change," Roper writes, "began with his message to Congress on September 6, 1945. This message spelled out his allegiance to the government-guaranteed securities of the New Deal."[5] Now, Roper comments, "conservative hopes that he would be a 'safe,' moderate President who would not attempt to force his will on Congress began to decline." At the same time, Truman's reaffirmation of his loyalty to the New Deal failed to satisfy many liberals because, in a word, he was not Roosevelt.[6] Robert J. Donovan refers to the unfavorable response to the "vintage New Deal" message of September 6 on the part of Southern Democrats, who had supported Truman for the vice presidential nomination because they "wanted to get away from the New Deal" and on the part of Republicans, noting that "Truman's honeymoon with Congress began to sour."[7] One wonders, however, whether the public's response was as quick and as sharp as the congressional reaction in view of Truman's receiving, as noted above, an 82 percent approval rating in the Gallup poll of November 2.

Meanwhile, the events that had the most immediate disturbing impact on the public occurred in the field of labor relations. In 1945 and early 1946 there were major strikes by workers in meat-packing (265,000), electrical manufacturing (200,000), transportation (50,000), communications (7,000), autos (320,000 at General Motors alone), steel (750,000), and various other enterprises (80,000). On April 1, 400,000 soft-coal miners walked off the job, staying out until May 29, when a contract was signed after Truman, on May 22, had ordered the secretary of the interior to seize the mines.

These developments undoubtedly related to the decline in Truman's Gallup poll approval rating from 82 percent on November 2, 1945, to 63 percent on February 1, 1946, since the public's desire for peaceful labor-management relations was evident in a Gallup poll of January 6, 1946 (interviewing dates 12/7–12/45): Truman's proposal of a law requiring a thirty-day cooling-off period before a strike could start, during which time a fact-finding committee would prepare a report, was favored by 78 percent.[8] In a Gallup poll of February 2 (interviewing dates 1/5–10/46), respondents were asked: "Which one thing do you like least/best about the way Harry Truman is handling his job?"

Items were listed according to frequency of mention:[9]

Least	Best
The way he is handling the labor problem	His honesty, sincerity, and friendliness
His lack of leadership	The fact that he is doing the best he can under present circumstances
The fact that he is too easily influenced, too easily led	His carrying on of Roosevelt policies

His playing of politics and taking care of his friends in his appointments

His inability to get along with Congress

His foreign policy—loans to Britain and Russia

His failure to take his job seriously enough

His handling of demobilization

His poor advisers

His lack of experience and stature for the job

His handling of foreign affairs

His interest in the general welfare and in the common man

His handling of strikes and labor difficulties

The rapidity of demobilization

His continued attempts to get Congress' co-operation

His willingness to take sound advice

His essential independence of attitude

A Gallup poll in March (interviewing dates 3/15–20/46) found 70 percent in favor of congressional action concerning strikes,[10] while another poll (interviewing dates 3/29–4/3/46) found 70 percent agreeing with Bernard Baruch's suggestion that all strikes and lockouts be called off for a year.[11]

But short-run factors—that is, events—were probably no more contributory to the decline in Truman's approval rating from November 1945 to February 1946 than a long-run factor—that is, Truman's relationship in voters' eyes to Roosevelt. The perception of FDR as a commanding leader, according to Roper, worked in Truman's favor at first in the form of sympathy for an ordinary man in a giant's shoes; but as problems mounted, the giant was increasingly missed.[12] This apparently logical sequence becomes less tidy, however, when one considers evidence that the public, while at first recognizing that Truman was not FDR and thus offering sympathy to the new president, did not want Truman to be like Roosevelt. A Gallup poll of May 13, 1945 (interviewing dates 4/20–25/45), asked: "Some writers believe that with Harry Truman as President, Congress will have more importance and power than it had under Franklin Roosevelt. Do you think this would be a good thing or a bad thing for the country?" The responses were: Good thing 65 percent, Bad thing 16 percent, No opinion 19 percent.[13] This initial contradiction was apparently resolved in time by the impact of events and the consequent felt need for the giant. A Gallup poll of November 25, 1945 (interviewing dates 11/2–7/45), asked: "Do you think President Truman should take a stronger stand in trying to get Congress to carry out his recommendations for things that need to be done in this country?" The answers were: Yes 52 percent, No 21 percent, No opinion 27 percent.[14]

These shifts in opinion as to whether Truman should or should not have been like FDR are subsumed in the context of considerable evidence over an extended period that the public, to the extent that it regretted the absence of Roosevelt, would have preferred him without the New Deal or, more precisely, without any extension of the New Deal into new areas. This theme of retention (of existing programs such as Social Security) without extension (into new areas such as health insurance) goes back at least to 1936, when it appeared in one of the earliest election polls ever taken, a Roper poll of October. It was evident again in Roper polls in January and September 1939.[15] Nor did the elections of 1938, when the Republicans gained eighty-one seats in the House and seven in the Senate, represent repudiation of the New Deal, although, John Allswang concludes, "the anti-New Dealers jumped to that conclusion."[16]

The theme of retention without extension of the New Deal also accords with the results of the Gallup polls of September 2, 1945 (interviewing dates 8/10–15/45), and February 4, 1946 (interviewing dates 12/21–26/45):[17]

Which of these three policies would you like to have President Truman follow: (1) Go more to the left by following more of the views of labor and other liberal groups, (2) Go more to the right by following more of the views of business and conservative groups, or (3) Follow a middle-of-the-road policy?

	September 2	February 4
Go to the left	16%	18%
Go to the right	18	21
Stay middle-of-the road	55	52
No opinion	11	9

A second question asked in connection with these polls suggests the possible importance of Truman's twenty-one-point message of September 6. The question was: "Which of these policies do you think the Truman Administration has been following?"

The responses were:[18]

	September 2	February 4
Going left	10%	44%
Going right	17	13
Middle road	54	27
No opinion	19	16

The impact of Truman's message of September 6, as noted above, was not evident in his Gallup approval of November, but the increase from August to December (interviewing dates) in the percentage of respondents who thought he was going left and the decrease in the percentage of those who thought his policy was middle-of-the road were substantial. These results accord with his decline from 82 percent approval in the Gallup poll of November to 63 percent approval in the Gallup poll of February. When Truman declared his allegiance to the New Deal, his approval rating was bound to fall.

The majority preference for retention without extension of the New Deal indicates that the continuing decline in Truman's approval ratings through 1946 was caused by short-term (or non-anti–New Deal) factors rather than a widespread desire to repeal the New Deal. This was also true of his poor showing in the pollsters' presidential trial heats in 1948 in view of his so-called incredible victory over Governor Thomas E. Dewey of New York in that year—a triumph Truman owed to voters who wished to preserve the New Deal or, in any case, remained loyal to the party of the New Deal.[19]

Another longer-run perspective on voter attitudes during the Truman administration is afforded when one notes that from June 1938, when Congress passed the Fair Labor Standards Act (or wages-and-hours law), until Lyndon Johnson's Great Society legislation of 1964–1965, no significant innovative domestic measures were enacted. William E. Leuchtenberg, referring to this "politics of dead center," remarks that most of the voters were satisfied with it[20]—another illustration of the theme of retention without extension of the New Deal (as well as a reminder that public images of Roosevelt as a giant overlooked his inability to gain congressional approval of New Deal–type measures after 1938). Accordingly, Truman's declining approval rating, after a brief postelection comeback in early 1949, was not the result of disapproval of the New Deal.

Having considered the longer-run context of voters' attitudes toward Truman, we may return to consideration of them in some detail. Truman's Gallup poll approval rating, as noted above, fell from 82 percent in November 1945 to 63 percent in February 1946. It then fell to 43 percent in July 1946 (interviewing dates 6/14–19/46) and to 32 percent in October (interviewing dates 9/13–18/46).[21] On election day, November 5, the Republicans gained control of the House, 246 to 188, and of the Senate, 51 to 45. "In 1946," Roper writes, "whatever Truman did seemed to make him new enemies. He gave the impression of a man who was being pulled in conflicting directions and did not himself know which way to go."[22]

As in the case of the period late 1945–early 1946, in the remainder of 1946 domestic developments had the greatest adverse impact on Truman's popularity. Labor unrest continued with a strike by 300,000 railroad trainmen and engineers, marked by Truman's seizure of the railroads on May 17, the day before the strike was scheduled to begin, and the end of a two-day strike on May 25, ten minutes before the president asked Congress for emergency authority to end the walkout. At the end of May, hard-coal miners began a nine-day strike. Gallup polls of May 29 (interviewing date not indicated) and June 14, 1946 (interviewing dates 6/1–6/46), showed that a solid majority of respondents expressing an opinion approved of Truman's proposals that "employers and employees be compelled to run strike-bound essential industries that Government has taken over" and that "employers and employees who refuse to run strike-bound essential industries taken over by the Government be drafted into the armed forces and sent back to their jobs."[23]

As in early 1946, however, agreement with Truman's proposals did not mean that the public was undisturbed by the strikes that had taken or were then taking place. In a Gallup poll of November 10 (interviewing dates 10/12–17/46) on the question whether Congress should pass new laws to control unions, 66 percent said yes, 22 percent said no, and 12 percent were undecided.[24] A week later (interviewing dates 10/18–23/46), 50 percent favored a law forbidding all strikes and lockouts for a year, 41 percent were opposed, and 9 percent were undecided.[25]

Meanwhile, in a Gallup poll (interviewing dates 6/1–6/46), 33 percent thought the Democrats and 41 percent thought the Republicans could best handle the labor problem, with 26 percent feeling that it made no difference;[26] and a Gallup poll of July 10 (interviewing dates 6/14–19/46) found 36 percent approving and 49 percent disapproving of the way Truman was handling the strike problem.[27]

Developments in 1946 with respect to price controls adversely affected Truman's popularity. On June 28, two days before the Office of Price Administration (OPA) was to expire, Congress extended it for a year, but the president, who had requested a simple extension, vetoed a measure that substantially reduced OPA's authority. On July 1 the nation was without price controls for the first time since 1942. A compromise extension bill of July 25 extended OPA until June 30, 1947, transferring much of its authority to a three-member Decontrol Board to be appointed by the president, while providing that controls on livestock could not be reimposed until August 20.

A Gallup poll of March 4, 1946 (interviewing dates 1/25–30/46), asked whether the price ceiling law should be allowed to end in June or should be continued; 73 percent wanted it continued and 21 percent wanted it to end (6 percent had no opinion).[28] A Gallup poll of May 24, 1946 (interviewing dates 4/16–5/1/46), asked whether OPA price ceilings should be kept on or taken off certain items for the next year:[29]

	Keep	Remove	No Opinion
Food	75%	21%	4%
Rent	78	17	5
Clothing	70	26	4
Manufactured Goods	66	27	7

Another poll of the same date asked whether prices would be lower a year later if OPA ceilings were eliminated or continued; 21 percent specified "done away with" and 68 percent "kept on" (11 percent had no opinion).[30] At the same time, 51 percent thought OPA ceilings made it impossible for manufacturers to make a profit and 9 percent did not think so (14 percent had no opinion).[31] The only other Gallup poll on price controls in 1946, a poll of October 5 (interviewing dates 9/13–18/46), asked whether price ceilings should be kept on or taken off certain items:[32]

	Kept On	Taken Off	No Opinion
Meats	42%	53%	5%
Other foods	42	51	7
Clothing	49	44	7
Manufactured goods	45	46	9
Rents	67	27	6

Except in the case of rents, the support for price controls declined substantially from May to October. As for meats, a separate item only in the October 5 poll, the majority's preference, noted above, was implemented. Meat prices soared from July 1 until August 20, when the Decontrol Board restored the ceilings as of June 30. Livestock raisers simply kept their cattle on the farm, causing a severe meat shortage. In a radio address of October 14, Truman announced the end of all livestock and meat controls. "Miraculously the next day the wholesale and retail markets throughout the land were suddenly filled with all kinds of meat, but at prices as much as 50 percent higher than the OPA ceilings of the previous 24 hours."[33]

Robert J. Donovan entitles a chapter "The Beefsteak Election of 1946."[34] This underlining of an immediate grievance accords with John W. Jeffries' conclusions, in his intensive study of Connecticut politics, concerning the 1946 elections. Despite a booming economy, Jeffries notes, 1946 was a year of "pessimistic prosperity" and "uneasy peace" marked by growing anti-Russian sentiment, anxiety about internal communism, and concern over labor unrest, a housing shortage, price controls and inflation (an 18 percent increase during the year in the cost of living compared to a 13 percent increase in factory wages), and the meat shortage. Democratic losses in Connecticut and the nation were the result of "the resentments and irritations of the electorate . . . the troubled domestic scene . . . the general sense of malaise about the Truman Administration."[35] The Republican majorities did not "indicate quite the reaffirmation of conservatism that some perceived . . . as in 1942, the Democratic decline reflected a protest vote against specific ills, not a call to restore the pre-New Deal political economy."[36]

Truman's approval rating in the Gallup poll of January 8, 1947 (interviewing dates 12/13–18/46), was 35 percent.[37] Then it climbed to 48 percent in the poll of February 2 (interviewing dates 1/17–22/47);[38] and 60 percent in the poll of March 30 (interviewing dates 3/14–19/47);[39] holding at 57 percent in the poll of June 2 (interviewing dates 4/25–30/47);[40] and 55 percent in the poll of October 19 (interviewing dates 9/12–17/47).[41]

Accounting for the rise in Truman's popularity from rock-bottom in early 1947 to a respectable level by March and its persistence at this level at least through September is not a simple matter, as consideration of Roper's commentary reveals. "Up until November, 1946," he writes, "Truman had been, in effect, running against the memory of a dynamic and popular leader. But now he was running against a Republican-controlled Congress. . . . it provided the springboard for his return to public favor."[42] In this connection, Roper cites the rise in prices after the lifting of OPA controls, the scuttling of Wilson Wyatt's housing plan, the failure to deliver a promised tax reduction, the "star-chamber" hearings of the House Un-American Activities Committee (HUAC), and the passage over Truman's veto of the Taft-Hartley labor bill.

In fact, on November 9, 1946, before the Eightieth Congress met, Truman issued an executive order ending controls on prices and wages except for sugar (until June 11, 1947) and rents (until March 1, 1948). This action did not represent

Truman's preference but, rather, was his response to the public's apparent wish as expressed in the elections of November 5. If, as Roper states, the public's resentment at rising prices in 1947 contributed to condemnation of the Eightieth Congress, people shifted the blame from themselves to the legislators, although voters, no doubt, did not look at it this way. As for the housing shortage, in December 1946 Wilson Wyatt had resigned in disgust at the fate of legislation in the Seventy-ninth, not the Eightieth, Congress, although it is true that dissatisfaction with the housing situation persisted after Wyatt's resignation. After the Eightieth Congress convened, it was Truman who, in June, vetoed two versions of the Knutson bill calling for a tax reduction of $3.8 billion. To be sure, Truman said that the Knutson cuts would benefit only those with high incomes, but he opposed tax reductions in general as inflationary given high business profits and personal income. As for the HUAC hearings, it is doubtful that they harmed the public standing of the Eightieth Congress since, as Roper notes, in 1947 Americans displayed "near hysteria over domestic communism."[43]

The anticommunist feelings that Roper cites were persistent throughout Truman's presidency and worked to his disadvantage despite his issuing an executive order in March 1947 providing for checkups on the loyalty of federal employees and job applicants. A Gallup poll of July 6, 1946 (interviewing dates 6/14–19/46), asked what should be done about communists in this country, and the responses were: kill or imprison 36 percent; curb, make inactive 16 percent; watch carefully 7 percent; do nothing 16 percent; no opinion 25 percent.[44] Four years later, a Gallup poll of August 21, 1950 (interviewing dates 7/30–8/4/50), asked what should be done with Communist party members in event of war with Russia, and the responses were: place in internment camps 22 percent; imprison 18 percent; deport 15 percent; send to Russia 13 percent; shoot or hang 13 percent; watch them and make them register 4 percent; nothing 1 percent; miscellaneous 9 percent; no opinion 10 percent.[45] In Gallup polls of March and October 1947 and May and August 1948, from 16 percent to 23 percent thought Communist party members were loyal to the United States, while 56 percent to 61 percent thought they were loyal to Russia, with 19 percent to 29 percent expressing no opinion.[46] In a Gallup poll of August 15, 1948 (interviewing dates 7/30–8/4/48), 8 percent thought Communist party members would help the United States in a war with Russia, and 73 percent thought they would help the Soviet Union.[47] In Gallup polls of May and July 1948, March 1949, and March and July 1950, 67 percent to 83 percent thought Communist party members should register with the Department of Justice, 9 percent to 20 percent thought they should not, and 8 percent to 15 percent had no opinion.[48] In Gallup polls of August 26, 1946 (interviewing dates 7/26–31/46), and April 18, 1947 (interviewing dates 3/28–4/2/47), 69 percent and 67 percent, respectively, thought Communists should not be allowed to hold civil service jobs, while 17 percent and 19 percent, respectively, thought they should.[49] Among the 64 percent who had heard of the House Un-American Activities Committee in a Gallup poll of

January 31, 1949 (interviewing dates 1/7–12/49), 41 percent preferred to continue it, 11 percent to abolish it, and 12 percent had no opinion.[50] In a Gallup poll of April 27, 1949 (interviewing dates 3/19–24/49), 80 percent approved of requiring union officers to take a noncommunist oath, 10 percent disapproved, and 10 percent had no opinion.[51] Finally, among the 78 percent, in a poll of July 7, 1950 (interviewing dates 6/4–9/50), who had heard of Senator Joseph McCarthy's charges that there were communists in the State Department, 31 percent approved of or believed in the charges, 10 percent expressed qualified approval, 20 percent disapproved or disbelieved, 6 percent thought he was sometimes right and sometimes wrong, and 11 percent had no opinion.[52]

Similarly, the Taft-Hartley Act was, as Roper notes, "keyed to the public's mood."[53] In June 1947, Truman's veto was overridden by a vote of 331 to 89 in the House and 68 to 25 in the Senate. That the public was ready for the Taft-Hartley Act was evident in Gallup polls in late 1946 and early 1947. A poll of January 10, 1947 (interviewing dates 11/29–12/4/46), on the Wagner Act yielded these responses: leave as is 36 percent, change it 53 percent, do away with it 11 percent.[54] In another poll of the same date, 8 percent favored a closed shop, 18 percent a union shop, and 66 percent an open shop, with 8 percent having no opinion.[55] A Gallup poll of February 12, 1947 (interviewing dates 1/17–22/47), and two polls of April 7, 1947 (interviewing dates 3/14–19/47), showed that the public favored the banning of jurisdictional strikes, strikes by government workers, and strikes by workers in public service industries by 2–to–1 or 3–to–1 margins.[56] Unaccountably, the first Gallup poll on the Taft-Hartley Act after its enactment, published on August 10, 1947 (interviewing dates 7/4–9/47), showed 33 percent approving, 39 percent disapproving, with 28 percent having no opinion;[57] but in Gallup polls of October 1947, February and June 1948, and May and July 1949, among those having an opinion, the combined percentage for those preferring to leave the act as it was or to revise it in order to afford stricter control of unions was far greater than the percentage for those favoring repeal.[58] In a poll of June 7, 1948 (interviewing dates 5/7–12/48), regarding strictness of the act, the responses were: too strict 18 percent, about right 22 percent, not strict enough 42 percent, no opinion 18 percent.[59] A poll of April 13, 1949 (interviewing dates 3/19–24/49), called for agreement or disagreement with Truman's claim that the act was unfair to labor: 35 percent agreed, 49 percent disagreed, and 16 percent had no opinion.[60] Finally, in four polls from November 1949 to July 1952, which offered choices between repealing or keeping the law, or favoring or opposing it, among those expressing an opinion, opposition to the act was in the range of 20 percent to 30 percent, while support for it ran from 36 percent to 46 percent.[61]

It is difficult to see how the Taft-Hartley issue could have contributed to a rise in Truman's popularity and a decline in that of the Eightieth Congress. In any event, Roper offers other, more persuasive arguments concerning Truman's political comeback in 1947. He stresses Truman's shaking off the shadow of Roosevelt and his emergence as a stronger figure, especially after the departure in 1947 of James F. Byrnes, who was replaced as secretary of state by George Marshall. The president "began increasingly to follow his own convictions, his own judgment in preference to that of the rather hastily assembled brain trust he had previously followed. . . . In the spring an aggressive, coherent foreign policy emerged."[62]

The centerpieces of American foreign policy were the Truman Doctrine and the Marshall Plan. Historians have stressed Senator Arthur H. Vandenberg's advice to Truman that the president, in his Truman Doctrine address of March 12, frighten the American people,[63] and Alonzo L. Hamby states that "the growing anti-Communist hysteria that was sweeping the country . . . was stimulated by the enunciation of the Truman Doctrine."[64] A recent study of public opinion concludes that the American people did not clamor for the tough policy Truman laid down in March 1947,[65] but another inquiry holds that Soviet behavior, anti-Soviet images in the press, and private organizations' anticommunist campaigns by themselves generated anticommunist attitudes among Americans, and that presidential rhetoric struck a responsive chord.[66] In any event, a Roper poll in March 1947 revealed substantial suppport for the Truman Doctrine, and five Gallup polls from July 1947 to November 1948 reported Marshall Plan approval ratings ranging from 47 percent to 67 percent, with disapproval ratings ranging from 13 percent to 18 percent.[67] With respect to the purposes of the Marshall Plan that respondents most often specified, a Gallup poll of February 9, 1948 (interviewing dates 1/23–28/48), produced these results: to help Europe 56 percent, to curb communism 8 percent, other 10 percent, no opinion 26 percent.[68] Noting that humanitarian motives and a desire for international stability worked for the Marshall Plan, while a "hard-headed approach to financial problems" characterized the opposition, Roper found it significant that Americans rejected left-wing arguments that the plan would increase the likelihood of war with Russia and the right-wing contention that it would strengthen socialist governments.[69]

Truman signed the Greek-Turkish Aid bill on May 22, 1947, but the European Recovery Program remained on the congressional agenda until April 2, 1948, when the Economic Cooperation bill passed the Senate by voice vote and the House by 318 to 75. The president signed it the next day. Meanwhile, whatever benefit Truman had derived, with respect to his popularity, from his two central foreign policy measures had faded. His approval rating declined from 55 percent in the Gallup poll of October 19, 1947 (interviewing dates 9/12–17/47), to 36 percent in the Gallup poll of April 23, 1948 (interviewing dates 4/9–14/48).[70] In the Gallup poll of June 11 (interviewing dates 5/28–6/2/48), his approval rating was 39 percent.[71] No additional approval ratings were solicited until January 1949. Instead, the Gallup organization conducted presidential trial heats in which Truman fared badly.

Accounting for the plunge in Truman's approval rating from October 1947 (55 percent) to April 1948 (36 percent) is not an easy task. After discussing the rise in Truman's rating in the first part of 1947, Roper comments:

But 1947 was a troubled year. It was a year of mounting tension over the course of international relations, over the future of prosperity at home, over the threat of Communism at home and abroad, and over the 1948 presidential election. . . . The worry that hit closest to home for most people was rising prices. Times continued good. But high prices dampened enthusiasm over wage increases. The job market seemed to be tightening up, and expenditures for amusements were down. The economic mood was one of caution.

It was against this backdrop that the presidential campaign of 1948 would be fought.[72]

Surely Truman's position on civil rights did not enhance his popularity. In October 1947, the President's Advisory Committee on Civil Rights, which had been appointed in December 1946, submitted its report, *To Secure These Rights*. On February 1, 1948, Truman responded to this report, submitting a ten-point program to Congress, but no action on his proposals was taken. Gallup polls of July 25, 1948 (interviewing dates 3/5–10/48), showed condemnation of poll taxes—65 percent to 24 percent (11 percent no opinion)—but there was a closer division of opinion on giving the federal government the right to step in on lynching cases or leaving them to the states—48 percent for federal intervention and 41 percent for state jurisdiction (11 percent no opinion)—and on requiring blacks to sit in a separate part of a train or bus—42 percent for and 49 percent against (9 percent no opinion).[73] In a Gallup poll of January 17, 1948 (interviewing dates 11/26–12/1/48), among the 64 percent who had heard of Truman's civil rights program, 27 percent favored it and 22 percent opposed it (15 percent no opinion).[74] Truman's persistent advocacy of his civil rights program would help spur the formation of the Dixiecrat party and cost him the thirty-nine electoral votes received by J. Strom Thurmond in 1948.

The approval rating of June 11 (interviewing dates 5/8–6/2/48) in which Truman's score was 39 percent, was, as noted above, the last before the election on November 2, and that of January 21, 1949 (interviewing dates 1/7–12/49), was the first after the election. This gap is filled by the presidential trial heats published from July 28, 1947, to November 1, 1948. The apparent decline in Truman's prospects in the period before the nominations of the candidates was evident in early 1948. From July 28, 1947, to February 16, 1948, Truman led all the possible Republican candidates except Eisenhower. On April 11, he fell behind Dewey (whom he had led 46–41 on January 23) 39 to 47 and on May 10 behind Harold Stassen (whom he had led 45–41 on February 16) 33 to 56. On May 19, he trailed Vandenberg 39 to 45, and on July 18 he trailed Dewey 38 to 49 in the last prenomination trial heat. He lost to Dewey in all nine postnomination trial heats from August 2 to November 1. The most striking change in this phase of the trial heats was the shrinkage of Dewey's lead over Truman from 17 percentage points on October 16 (interviewing dates 9/23–28/48) to 5 on November 1 (interviewing dates 10/15–25/48).[75] In the actual election, Truman received 49.6 percent and Dewey 45.1 percent of the total vote.

In 1948, in the area of foreign relations, Israel declared its independence in May, and Truman extended de facto recognition. When the Arabs attacked Israel, the administration helped neither side. Both political parties, however, favored an Israeli victory (soon after his inauguration in 1949, Truman granted de jure recognition to Israel). Truman's action accorded with public opinion as expressed in a Gallup poll of November 19, 1947 (interviewing dates 10/24–29/47), in which 65 percent were favorable, 10 percent opposed, and 25 percent had no opinion regarding a proposal to create two states, Arab and Jewish, in Palestine and admit to the latter 150,000 Jews. At the same time, 65 percent preferred that United Nations troops and only 3 percent preferred that American troops be employed if it were necessary to send a military force in order to maintain order in Palestine.[76]

In response to the Berlin blockade crisis which began on June 25, Dewey decided, in July, to refrain from criticizing Truman's foreign policy, and the campaign revolved primarily around domestic issues. This is not to imply that Americans considered foreign policy unimportant. On the contrary, in a Gallup poll of July 14, 1948 (interviewing dates 6/18–23/48), 44 percent designated foreign policy as the most important problem facing the nation; in second place was the high cost of living at 23 percent. Nor can it be assumed that Dewey would have benefited by making an issue of foreign policy. Another Gallup poll of July 14 (interviewing dates 6/18–23/48) asked respondents to indicate which party they thought could do a better job of handling the problem they specified as the most important; 52 percent said the Democratic and 48 percent the Republican party.[77]

A main reason for the outcome of the election, Roper stated, was that "to a great many people Dewey simply was not very likeable as a person." An even more important factor in Dewey's defeat was his "lack of a clear stand on a number of issues." In the case of issues on which the public was divided, Dewey seemed, intentionally or otherwise, to be "a man who was all things to all voters."[78] Unlike Dewey, Truman took definite stands on most of the issues. In some cases, such as the Taft-Hartley Act, his position differed from that of the majority of voters. Truman had been able "to convince people of his determined loyalty to the New Deal tradition." Whether the public agreed or disagreed with his various positions, "they knew where Harry Truman stood, and on the balance a majority decided that he was for the things they wanted." Still, Roper concluded, Truman, "who had spelled out a program that came straight out of the New Deal tradition . . . did not win the election simply by the stands he took." If, in July, "the emphasis was not on Truman the man but on what he represented," his "give 'em hell" campaign against the "good for nothing," "do nothing" Eightieth Congress "made the difference."[79]

Truman's approval rating of January 21, 1949 (interviewing dates 1/7–12/49), was 69 percent.[80] It declined to 57 percent on March 30 (interviewing dates 3/6–11/49)[81] and held at that level on July 20 (interviewing dates 6/11–16/49).[82] Then it fell to 51 percent on October 21 (interviewing dates 9/25–30/49),[83] to 45 percent on February 17, 1950 (interviewing dates 1/8–13/50),[84] to 37 percent on April 12 (interviewing dates 2/26–3/3/50).[85] After rising to 43 percent on

September 25 (interviewing dates 8/20–25/50),[86] it declined to 36 percent on January 10 (interviewing dates 1/1–5/51)[87] and registered in the 20s or 30s throughout 1951 and 1952.

Truman's approval rating of 69 percent soon after the election may have represented the voters' ex post facto ratification of their decision. Irwin Ross observes:

In the retrospective wave of admiration for Truman that followed his victory, his zest, combativeness, and informality were favorably contrasted with Dewey's somewhat prim dignity and aloofness; a temporary amnesia seemed to overtake the country in regard to those other qualities of Truman (such as his lack of dignity or seeming lack of competence) which had formerly brought him disparagement.[88]

Admiration, however, did not preclude a lack of confidence.[89] A glance at Figure 15.1 underlines the validity of Elmer Davis' comment on Truman's second term: "It was roses, roses all the way for Harry Truman when he rode in the bright sunlight to be inaugurated. But a good deal of the rest of the way . . . was poison ivy."[90]

Truman's declining standing with the public during the last three years of his second term is also evident in presidential trial heats revealing his losses (3 to 8 percentage points) to Robert A. Taft, his substantial losses (18 to 23 percentage points) to Earl Warren and Harold Stassen, and his enormous losses (29 to 37 percentage points) to Eisenhower. Three trial heats in April 1952 suggest the main reason the Republicans nominated Eisenhower: he defeated Estes Kefauver handily, while Taft lost to the senator from Tennessee.[91]

In 1949, Roper writes, "the anxieties of the American people were the same ones, but they were more intense."[92] In the area of subversion, in January 1949 the trial of the eleven highest American communist leaders, who were accused of conspiring to overthrow the government, began; it lasted until October 14, producing a verdict of guilty (which was upheld by the Supreme Court on June 4, 1951). In March, Judith Coplon, already indicted in Washington for allegedly having passed classified Justice Department documents to Soviet agents, was arrested in New York. She was found guilty in Washington while awaiting her trial in New York, where, in the spring of 1950, she was also found guilty (in both cases higher courts eventually ordered retrials, but they did not take place). In May the trial of Alger Hiss on charges of perjury began. It ended in a hung jury, and a second trial began in November. In January 1950, Hiss was found guilty of perjury on two counts; he served a prison term from March 1951 to November 1954.

In domestic affairs in 1949, Congress ignored Truman's call for compulsory health insurance. This neglect was in keeping with public opinion as expressed in a Gallup poll of April 6, 1949 (interviewing dates 3/6–11/49), in which 33 percent favored the Truman Plan, 47 percent the American Medical Association

Plan, 7 percent neither plan, with 13 percent having no opinion;[93] and a Gallup poll of January 30, 1950 (interviewing dates 11/27–12/2/49), in which 22 percent favored the Truman Plan, 31 percent opposed it, and 13 percent had no opinion.[94] In the area of civil rights, the Senate killed two bills providing for the elimination of the poll tax as a requirement for voting—while a Gallup poll of April 29, 1949 (interviewing dates 3/19–24/49), found 67 percent for abolishing poll taxes, 22 percent for retaining them, and 11 percent with no opinion[95]—a Senate committee quashed an anti-lynching bill, and the House defeated a bill to give the vote and self-government to residents of the District of Columbia.

In the summer of 1949, evidence of corruption in the Truman administration was revealed by a special Senate subcommittee which reported that several persons close to the administration were "influence peddlers" in obtaining government contracts or loans. General Harry Vaughan, Truman's military aide, was implicated, and John Maragon, a friend of Vaughan, was found guilty of perjury. Truman retained Vaughan, and the "mess in Washington" politically damaged him and his party.

Two of the three components of the Republicans' 1952 campaign slogan, K1C2—Korea, Communism, and Corruption—were evident in 1949. Further developments in the area of subversion occurred in 1950 and 1951. In February 1950, Klaus Fuchs, who had worked in America's atomic Manhattan Project, was arrested in Britain for allegedly providing Soviet agents with atomic secrets. He confessed and was sentenced on March 1 to fourteen years in prison. On February 12, in Wheeling, West Virginia, Senator Joseph R. McCarthy of Wisconsin delivered his widely reported speech charging that fifty-seven Communist party members or communist sympathizers helped determine American foreign policy. In the summer of 1950, a special Senate subcommittee chaired by Millard Tydings of Maryland declared that McCarthy's charges were "a fraud and a hoax" (in November, McCarthy helped to defeat Tydings' bid for reelection). The summer of 1950 also saw the arrest of Julius and Ethel Rosenberg and Morton Sobell for allegedly giving atomic secrets to Soviet agents, and this case remained on the public mind until the Rosenbergs were executed, on June 19, 1953, and beyond. In August 1950, Congress extended Truman's executive order on loyalty of March 1947 to cover "security risks," and in September Congress passed the McCarran Internal Security bill, which, among a number of other things, required all communist-action and communist-front organizations to register with the attorney general. Truman's veto of this act was overwhelmingly overridden in both houses. In 1952 Congress also easily overrode Truman's veto of the McCarran-Walter bill, which authorized the attorney general to deport immigrants associated with communists or communist-front organizations even if they had become citizens.

The issue of corruption remained in the headlines in 1951 when the Senate Subcommittee on Banking investigated irregularities in the Reconstruction Finance Corporation, and a House Ways and Means subcommittee followed up similar allegations with respect to the Internal Revenue Bureau (IRB). As a result of the IRB investigation, 38 officials and about 200 employees resigned or were dismissed, and the agency was reorganized.

The third component of K1C2 materialized when North Korea invaded South Korea on June 24, 1950. Seizing on an opportunity provided by the Korean War, the President, in December 1951, appointed a committee that acted more or less as a wartime Fair Employment Practices Commission. That Truman took this action only in an emergency is understandable in view of public opinion as registered in a Gallup poll of January 9, 1950 (interviewing dates 11/27–12/2/ 49): asked how far the federal government should go with respect to fair employment practices, 34 percent said all the way, 14 percent said part of the way, and 41 percent preferred no federal action (11 percent had no opinion).[96]

The Korean War occasioned the extension of the draft, tax increases, and wage, price, and rent controls. Despite these controls, the Consumer Price Index rose from 177.8 in June 1950 to 191.1 in September 1952. During the war there were numerous strikes—more in 1952 than in any previous year—including major ones in railroads (under government seizure from December 1950 until May 1952) and steel (after seizure on April 8, 1952, was disallowed by the Supreme Court on June 2); in a Gallup poll of May 28, 1952 (interviewing dates 4/27–5/2/52), 43 percent disapproved of the seizure, 35 percent approved, and 22 percent had no opinion.[97]

In a Roper poll of August 1950, 73 percent of the respondents agreed with the statement that Truman did the right thing in sending American troops into Korea, and only 15 percent disagreed.[98] Truman's Gallup poll approval rating rose to 43 percent on September 25 (interviewing dates 8/20–25/50).[99] In a Gallup poll of January 10, 1951 (interviewing dates 1/1–5/51), however, Truman's approval rating was 36 percent;[100] and in a poll of March 14 (interviewing dates 1/4–9/51) 26 percent.[101] In fourteen Gallup polls from April 18, 1951, to November 12, 1952, Truman's approval ratings fell into a range of 23 percent to 32 percent.[102] A Roper poll of August 1951 showed that many people, 42 percent, had lost confidence in Truman, while only 18 percent expressed confidence in him.[103]

The frustration of the American people with pursuit of a "limited" war was evident in Gallup polls. In a poll of July 29, 1950 (interviewing dates 7/9–14/ 50), 67 percent and in a poll of October 4, 1950 (interviewing dates 9/17–22/ 50), 70 percent thought the war would end in a year or less,[104] an expectation that, needless to say, was not fulfilled. In a poll of October 13, 1950 (interviewing dates 9/17–22/50), 64 percent thought the United States should continue fighting until the enemy surrendered and 27 percent thought we should stop fighting when the North Koreans had been pushed back over the line from where they started (9 percent had no opinion).[105] In a poll of March 5, 1951 (interviewing dates 2/ 4–9/51), however, 73 percent thought we should and 16 percent thought we should not stop at the 38th Parallel if we reached it and the Communist Chinese, who had entered the war on October 30, and the North Koreans were willing to stop fighting;[106] and in a poll of March 28, 1951 (interviewing dates 3/4–9/51), 43 percent approved and 36 percent disapproved of dividing Korea at the 38th Parallel if Communist China and North Korea agreed to stop fighting (21 percent had no opinion).[107] In regard to widening the war theater, in a poll of December 4, 1950 (interviewing dates 11/12–17/50), 46 percent thought we should fight in Korea only and 39 percent thought we should invade China if the Chinese kept on fighting (15 percent had no opinion).[108] In a poll of January 22, 1951 (interviewing dates 1/1–5/51), "now that Communist China has entered the war in Korea with forces far outnumbering the United Nations troops there," 66 percent thought we should pull out and 25 percent thought we should stay "to fight these larger forces" (9 percent had no opinion). Yet, in a poll of May 3, 1951 (interviewing dates 4/16–21/51), 66 percent disapproved and 25 percent approved of Truman's dismissal in April of General Douglas MacArthur, who favored widening the war theater; presumably some respondents' admiration for MacArthur was not accompanied by knowledge of the military strategy he advocated.[109] In a poll of March 2, 1951 (interviewing dates 2/4–9/51), 50 percent thought the United States had made a mistake in going into Korea and 39 percent did not think so (11 percent had no opinion).[110] In a poll of November 5, 1951 (interviewing dates 10/14–19/51), 56 percent agreed with a senator that the Korean war was "a useless war" and 33 percent disagreed (11 percent had no opinion).[111] Finally, in a poll of April 2, 1952 (interviewing dates 2/28–3/5/52), 51 percent thought the United States had made a mistake going into Korea and 35 percent did not think so (14 percent had no opinion).[112]

A Roper poll of August 1952 showed that the Korean War was not the only factor inflicting political damage on Truman and his party. There was considerable anxiety over the Truman administration as high spenders, "just a bunch of politicians," second-rate in ability, and prone to corruption.[113] Three polls of August 1952 on corruption in government led Roper to conclude that there was "a widespread feeling that a certain amount of corruption would inevitably accumulate when a party—any party—had been in power as long as the Democrats.[114] Although only 2 percent saw softness on communism in the Truman administration, this issue, Roper notes, would also eventually cost the Democrats votes.[115]

Other poll data for 1952 show that Truman, like Adlai Stevenson, had no chance to defeat Eisenhower. In a Roper poll of August 1952, respondents were asked to name two or three things that they thought were most important for the next administration to do. "End the war in Korea," "Keep prices from going any higher," "Keep Communists out of government jobs," and "Prevent dishonesty and corruption among government officials" were the first four, three of them being signified in the Republicans' K1C2 campaign slogan.[116] Other polls in August show that the public thought that of the two parties, the Republican party would be more effective in dealing with communists in government

(45 percent to 13 percent for the Democrats), with prices (36 percent to 22 percent for the Democrats), and with Korea (43 percent to 14 percent for the Democrats).[117]

The corruption issue, Roper states, had "nothing to do with attitudes toward the New Deal,"[118] and poll data caution against concluding that Eisenhower was elected to undo the New Deal. A Roper poll of June 1952, for example, found that 87 percent thought Social Security laws were a "Good Thing" and only 3 percent thought they were a "Mistake,"[119] and in the same month Roper found the normal party affiliation of voters to be Democrat 50 percent, Republican 34 percent, Independent 16 percent.[120] Finally, during the campaign, Eisenhower was very hazy about the New Deal,[121] and in a Roper poll of December 1952 respondents were more uncertain about what Eisenhower would do with the New Deal than they were about his probable course of action with respect to seven of eight other matters.[122]

The decline in Truman's popularity during his second term appears to have derived not from dissatisfaction regarding ideology and policy but from discontent with "management." As a manager, Truman found himself in a no-win situation. For example, it is a commonplace that the Korean settlement Eisenhower obtained would not have been politically acceptable if Truman had arranged it. Truman was handicapped by a Rooseveltian legacy of stalemate on domestic legislation after 1938 and Republican frustration, especially after 1948, at having lost five presidential elections in a row with "me too" candidates. The Korean War saw the emergence of additional frustration among the citizenry. Finally, McCarthyism, with its anti-Rooseveltian origins, created a climate of opinion that made it extremely difficult for Truman to enjoy a fair hearing for his proposals or a judicious appraisal of his performance. Thus, in 1948 the Roosevelt coalition saved Truman for a bout with poison ivy.

NOTES

Oscar T. Barck, Jr., *A History of the United States Since 1945* (New York: Dell Publishing Co., 1965), is the source of narratives of events in this essay. George H. Gallup, *The Gallup Poll: Public Opinion 1935–1971*, 3 vols. (New York: Random House, 1972), is cited hereafter as Gallup. Elmo Roper, *You and Your Leaders: Their Actions and Your Reactions 1936–1945* (New York: William Morrow, 1957), is cited hereafter as Roper.

1. Gallup, 3:2234.
2. Roper, p. 123.
3. Gallup, 1:512, 537.
4. Ibid., 1:557.
5. Roper, p. 126.
6. Ibid.
7. Robert J. Donovan, *Conflict and Crisis: The Presidency of Harry S Truman, 1945–1948* (New York: W. W. Norton, 1977), p. 114.
8. Gallup, 1:553.

9. Ibid.

10. Ibid., 1:567, 568.

11. Ibid., 1:573.

12. Roper, p. 126.

13. Gallup, 1:503.

14. Ibid., 1:542.

15. Roper, pp. 28, 30, 39.

16. John M. Allswang, *The New Deal and American Politics* (New York: John Wiley and Sons, 1978), p. 127.

17. Gallup, 1:523, 558.

18. Ibid.

19. Everett Carll Ladd, Jr., with Charles D. Hadley, *Transformations of the American Party System: Political Coalitions from the New Deal to the 1970's,* 2nd ed. (New York: W. W. Norton, 1978), pp. 73, 108–110; Irwin Ross, *The Loneliest Campaign: The Truman Victory of 1948* (New York: New American Library, 1968), pp. 237, 240.

20. William E. Leuchtenberg, "The Pattern of Modern American National Politics," in Stephen E. Ambrose, ed., *Institutions in Modern America: Innovation in Structure and Process* (Baltimore: Johns Hopkins Press, 1967), pp. 55, 62.

21. Gallup, 1:587, 604.

22. Roper, p. 127.

23. Gallup, 1:580, 583.

24. Ibid., 1:606.

25. Ibid., 1:608.

26. Ibid., 1:585.

27. Ibid., 1:588.

28. Ibid., 1:561.

29. Ibid., 1:579.

30. Ibid.

31. Ibid.

32. Ibid., 1:602.

33. Barck, *History*, pp. 48, 49.

34. Donovan, *Conflict and Crisis,* pp. 229–238.

35. John W. Jeffries, *Testing the Roosevelt Coalition: Connecticut Society and Politics in the Era of World War II* (Knoxville: University of Tennessee Press, 1979), pp. 242, 243.

36. Ibid., p. 243.

37. Gallup, 1:617.

38. Ibid., 1:623.

39. Ibid., 1:636.

40. Ibid., 1:650.

41. Ibid., 1:680.

42. Roper, pp. 129, 130.

43. Ibid., p. 131.

44. Gallup, 1:587.

45. Ibid., 1:934.

46. Ibid., 1:639, 690, 736, 752.

47. Ibid., 1:752.

48. Ibid., 1:736, 751; 2:808, 910, 911, 934.

49. Ibid., 1:594, 640.

50. Ibid., 2:787.

51. Ibid., 2:809.

52. Ibid., 2:924.

53. Roper, p. 196.

54. Gallup, 1:618.

55. Ibid., 1:621.

56. Ibid., 1:626, 638.

57. Ibid., 1:664.

58. Ibid., 1:676, 711, 738; 2:814, 829.

59. Ibid., 1:738.

60. Ibid., 2:805.

61. Ibid., 2:870, 882, 908, 1078.

62. Roper, p. 131.

63. Donovan, *Conflict and Crisis,* p. 281.

64. Alonzo L. Hamby, *Beyond the New Deal: Harry Truman and American Liberalism* (New York: Columbia University Press, 1973), p. 170.

65. George H. Quester, "Origins of the Cold War: Some Clues from Public Opinion," *Political Science Quarterly,* 93 (1978–1979): 656–660.

66. Dale Sorensen, "The Language of a Cold Warrior: A Content Analysis of Harry Truman's Public Statements," *Social Science History,* 3 (1979): 171–186.

67. Roper, p. 177; Gallup, 1:661, 683, 691, 715, 770, 771.

68. Gallup, 1:708.

69. Roper, pp. 180, 181.

70. Gallup, 1:727.

71. Ibid., 1:739.

72. Roper, pp. 131, 132.

73. Gallup, 1:747, 748.

74. Ibid., 1:782.

75. Gallup published presidential trial heats on 7/28/47, 9/28/47, 10/5/47, 1/4/48, 1/23/48, 2/16/48, 4/11/48, 5/10/48, 5/19/48, 7/18/48, 8/2/48, 8/11/48, 8/22/48, 9/8/48, 9/24/48, 10/2/48, 10/16/48, and 11/1/48. These polls are readily located without page citations since polls are presented, regardless of subject, in chronological order.

76. Gallup, 1:686.

77. Ibid., 1:744. Foreign policy ([1] preventing war, [2] helping Europe, [3] atomic bomb, [4] international relations, [5] China, [6] Russia, [7] Marshall Plan, [8] future of United Nations, [9] German problem, [10] Palestine, [11] Korea, [12] military preparedness) was always a concern in Gallup polls published under the heading "Most Important Problem" on 10/22/45, 1/31/47, 8/17/47, 9/15/47, 2/13/48, 4/19/48, 7/14/48, 12/17/48, 10/10/49, 11/25/49, 5/5/50, 6/28/50, 10/31/51, 12/15/52, placing in these polls, respectively, numbers 4—2—2, 3, 6, 8—2—2, 3, 5, 8—1, 2, 8, 9—1, 7—3, 5, 7—1, 4—2, 5, 8, 10—1, 5—1, 2—1, 5-1 or, with respect to highest placement only, 4–2–2–2–2–1–1–3–1–2–1–1–1–1. A corollary of this development was the good economic health of the nation during the Truman years: the annual average rate for unemployment was 4 percent, for economic growth almost 5 percent, and for inflation 3 percent; there was one recession, 1948–1949. See Francis H. Heller, ed., *Economics and the Truman Administration* (Lawrence: University Press of Kansas, 1981). This condition no doubt contributed to the public's assigning greater relative importance to foreign than to domestic

policy, although on the latter public opinion apparently came to be affected by a general discontent since, as we shall see, polls in August 1952 showed substantially greater confidence in the ability of the Republican party than in that of the Democratic party to deal with both domestic and foreign matters.

78. Roper, p. 113.

79. Ibid., pp. 111, 136–142, 196. Although analysis of the polls' error in 1948—their prediction of a Dewey victory—is beyond the scope of this essay, one finding should be mentioned. In a Gallup poll of April 23, 1948 (interviewing dates 4/9–14/48), Democrats gave Truman an approval rating of 50 percent, while in a Gallup poll of June 4 (interviewing dates 5/7–12/48), 76 percent of the Democrats preferred Truman as their party's candidate. Gallup, 1:727, 738. This gap may have indicated that the approval rating represented chastisement rather than abandonment of the Democratic president.

80. Gallup, 2:784.

81. Ibid., 2:800.

82. Ibid., 2:834.

83. Ibid., 2:860.

84. Ibid., 2:890.

85. Ibid., 2:903.

86. Ibid., 2:939.

87. Ibid., 2:958.

88. Ross, *The Loneliest Campaign*, p. 244.

89. Roper, p. 143.

90. Quoted in Barck, *History*, p. 87.

91. Gallup published trial heats on 4/24/50, 1/15/51, 1/17/51, 4/20/51, 7/16/51, 6/18/51, 7/20/51, 11/16/51, 11/17/51, 11/19/51, 2/4/52, 4/13/52, and 4/18/52.

92. Roper, p. 142.

93. Gallup, 2:802.

94. Ibid., 2:886.

95. Ibid., 2:810.

96. Ibid., 2:880.

97. Ibid., 2:1065.

98. Roper, p. 145.

99. Gallup, 2:939.

100. Ibid., 2:958.

101. Ibid., 2:970.

102. Ibid., 2:977, 989, 995, 999, 1007, 1015, 1020, 1032, 1040, 1046, 1050, 1062, 1071, 1102.

103. Roper, p. 148.

104. Gallup, 2:928, 942.

105. Ibid., 2:943.

106. Ibid., 2:969.

107. Ibid., 2:972.

108. Ibid., 2:950.

109. Ibid., 2:960, 961, 981.

110. Ibid., 2:968.

111. Ibid., 2:1019.

112. Ibid., 2:1052.

113. Roper, p. 149.

114. Ibid., p. 147.
115. Ibid., p. 255.
116. Ibid., p. 249.
117. Ibid., pp. 250–253.
118. Ibid., p. 254.
119. Ibid., p. 247.
120. Ibid.
121. Gary W. Reichard, *The Reaffirmation of Republicanism: Eisenhower and the Eighty-Third Congress* (Knoxville: University of Tennessee Press, 1975), pp. 87, 88, 95; Dean Albertson, ed., *Eisenhower as President* (New York: Hill and Wang, 1963), p. xiii.
122. Roper, p. 259.

BIBLIOGRAPHIC ESSAY

Books and Articles

Robert H. Ferrell, *Harry S Truman and the Modern American Presidency* (Boston: Little, Brown, 1983), pp. 193–209, provides a comprehensive annotated bibliography. Ferrell has edited *Off the Record: The Private Papers of Harry S Truman* (New York: Harper and Row, 1980), and *The Autobiography of Harry S Truman* (Boulder, Colo: Colorado Associated University Press, 1980). Formal writings by the president are *Memoirs by Harry S Truman: Year of Decisions* [1945], and *Memoirs by Harry S Truman: Years of Trial and Hope* [1946–1952] (Garden City, N.Y.: Doubleday, 1955, 1956). The president's daughter has provided *Souvenir: Margaret Truman's Own Story,* with Margaret Cousins (New York: McGraw-Hill, 1956), and *Harry S Truman* (New York: William Morrow, 1973). She has also edited *Letters from Father: The Truman Family's Personal Correspondence* (New York: Arbor House, 1981). Additional informal writings by the president are presented in Monty M. Peon, ed., *Strictly Personal and Confidential: The Unmailed Letters of Harry Truman* (Boston: Little, Brown, 1982).

Jonathan Daniels, *The Man from Independence* (Philadelphia: J. B. Lippincott, 1950), is informative on Truman's early life. On the presidency, see Alfred Steinberg, *Man from Missouri: The Life and Times of Harry S Truman* (New York: Putnam, 1962); Cabell Phillips, *The Truman Presidency: The History of a Triumphant Succession* (New York: Macmillan, 1966); Bert Cochran, *Harry Truman and the Crisis Presidency* (New York: Funk and Wagnalls, 1973); Robert J. Donovan, *Conflict and Crisis: The Presidency of Harry S Truman, 1945–1948* and *Tumultuous Years: The Presidency of Harry S Truman, 1949–1953* (New York: W. W. Norton, 1977, 1982); Harold F. Gosnell, *Truman's Crises: A Political Biography of Harry S Truman* (Westport, Conn.: Greenwood Press, 1980); and John Hersey, *Aspects of the Presidency* (New Haven and New York: Ticknor and Fields, 1980).

Research and historiography are treated in Richard S. Kirkendall, ed., *The Truman Period as a Research Field: A Reappraisal, 1972* (Columbia, Mo.: University of Missouri Press, 1967, 1974). See also Robert Griffith, "Truman and the Historians: The Reconstruction of Postwar American History," *Wisconsin Magazine of History,* 59 (Autumn 1975): 20–50; Daniel Yergin, "Harry Truman—Revived and Revised," *New York Times Magazine,* October 24, 1976, pp. 40, 41, 83–93; and Donald R. McCoy, "Trends in Viewing Herbert Hoover, Franklin D. Roosevelt, Harry S Truman and Dwight D. Eisenhower,'' *Midwest Quarterly,* 20 (Winter 1979): 126–130. On special topics see the items cited by Ferrell in *Harry S Truman and the Modern Presidency,* pp. 202–209. See also the bibliography in Francis H. Heller, ed., *Economics and the Truman Administration* (Lawrence: University Press of Kansas, 1981), pp. 143–186.

Documentary Records

Bob Hope, *Not So Long Ago* (RCA Victor, 1953), depicts both cultural and political events between VE Day and the Korean invasion of 1950—all part of the Truman era. Edward R. Murrow with Fred W. Friendly, *I Can Hear It Now,* Vol. 2, 1945–1949 (Columbia Special Products, 1954), focuses on the first portion of the Truman era in sound. James Fleming, narrator, *"Mr. President" from FDR to Eisenhower* (RCA Victor, 1955), is narrated by the poineer news editor of NBC's ''Today'' and contains cuts of actualities from the Truman period. Sidney Shalett, narrator, *"Veep": Alben W. Barkley Tells His Own Story* (Folkways Records and Service Corp., 1957), presents a detailed interview with Harry Truman's vice president in the second term. *Voices of the Presidents* (EAV Lexington, Educational Audio Visual, Pleasantville, N.Y., 1967) has a cut which contains the 1949 inaugural in which Truman proposed the Point Four program to aid less developed countries.

Television Program

James Whitmore, "Give 'Em Hell, Harry," CBS-TV, is a one-man show in which the noted actor gives his impressions of Harry Truman the man. The president is also depicted in the motion picture *MacArthur* with Gregory Peck.

16 DWIGHT D. EISENHOWER

R. Gordon Hoxie

THE ULTIMATE YARDSTICK

What determines greatness in the presidential office? Do historians and political scientists view it in the same terms as the American people? And how do those closest to the president perceive it? Professor Richard E. Neustadt, who served with Presidents Truman, Kennedy, and Johnson, in 1960 measured presidential success in terms of the ability to persuade. In 1982 Edwin Meese III, then counsellor to President Reagan, suggested another measure of both the president *and* the presidency as an institution: the quality of leadership. Meese perceives leadership as "an evolving thing, changing with time, responding to events." As such, the Eisenhower presidency should be measured in terms of the conditions and needs of the 1950s.

Since the 1930s demands on the presidency have become so complex as to require an effective institutionalization of the office. Dwight D. Eisenhower, principal architect of the modern institutional presidency, made an impossible task appear easy, through three basic functional bodies: cabinet, National Security Council (NSC), and the Office of Budget. He emphasized the National Security Council, creating the NSC Planning Board for policy inputs and the Operations Coordinating Board for policy implementation. In 1954 he created a cabinet secretariat and made the Bureau of the Budget for the first time the coordinator of all legislative proposals. For more effective coordination with the Congress, he created the Office of Legislative Liaison. While he created a strong chief of staff, to whom he delegated authority, as with department heads, there was never any doubt as to who was in charge: the president.

Eisenhower did all this, so matter of factly, based upon both his experiences as a military organizer and planner and his observations of the White House. In his view,

For years I had been in frequent contact with the Executive Office of the White House and I had certain ideas about the system, or lack of system, under which it operated. With my training in problems involving organization it was inconceivable to me that the work of the White House could not be better systemized than had been the case during the years I observed it.

Historians and political scientists who have equated greatness with personal presidential activism have not entirely appreciated the significance of the Eisenhower presidency and the Eisenhower institutional legacy. Effective instruments for policy determination, enunciation, and implementation, absolute integrity, and trust and confidence of the American people—such characteristics of the Eisenhower presidency combine to form what Meese terms "the ultimate yardstick by which our chief executives can be measured and 'greatness' apportioned."

By these standards Eisenhower may well emerge as one of our "great" presidents. A skilled administrator, effective in employing cabinet and staff, Eisenhower led with no emphasis on the first person singular pronoun, thus for two decades gathered little appreciation from historians or political scientists. The 1962 Schlesinger poll placed him near the bottom of the medicre presidents, just ahead of maladroit Andrew Johnson. A few journalists and scholars did suggest otherwise. As early as 1955 Arthur Krock of the *New York Times* admired Eisenhower's political skills and his "good statesmanship." After observing Eisenhower's press conferences for more than four years, Krock concluded, conventional wisdom to the contrary, that "the President's mental process is penetrating and alert." Journalist Murray Kempton in 1967 found Eisenhower not as guileless as he appeared. As Kempton put it, it had taken him all those years to discover that the famous Eisenhower "smile was always a grin." In 1972 Herbert Parmet's landmark revisionist volume, *Eisenhower and the American Crusades,* had appeared. Two years later this author in a CBS telecast asserted that "history inevitably is going to bring Dwight Eisenhower a considerably higher mark than he has received to date."[1](Approval ratings for Eisenhower between 1953 and 1960 and found in Figure 16.1.)

Still, it was not until 1977 that a major reappraisal began in earnest. That year, former President Ford observed of Eisenhower that for too long it had appeared that "only his public admired his performance in office." Then, in 1982, political scientist Fred I. Greenstein's persuasive volume, *The Hidden-Hand Presidency: Eisenhower as Leader,* noted, "The public saw a folksy, common-sense replica of the man on the street." However, this was not the whole story. Greenstein found "a man with extraordinary capacities for detached, orderly examination of problems and personalities. . . . His ability to win friends and influence people—both face to face and in the mass—seemed to result from the magnetism of his sunny personality. But," Greenstein concludes, Eisenhower "worked at his apparent artlessness, consciously choosing strategies that made people want to support him." Finding "Eisenhower a far more effective leader than many realized," Greenstein assessed Eisenhower as "not a political genius."

Perhaps "genius" is too strong a word. But, as Herbert Parmet recently observed, "Any man who could become Supreme Commander of Allied Forces

Figure 16.1
Approval Ratings for Dwight D. Eisenhower

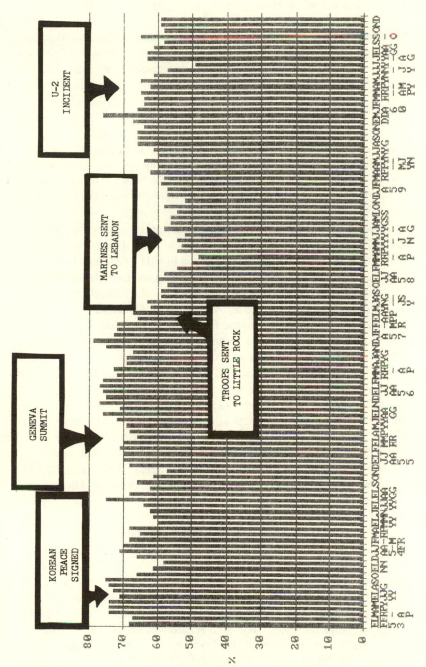

Source: Gallup Opinion Index, September–October 1980.

in Europe, lead NATO, get himself installed as president of a major university, and go on to the White House, had to be a pretty good politician.''

Why does the appraisal come so surprisingly, almost begrudgingly? Why was Eisenhower charged with inability for sharply focused, sustained leadership? Why does it take someone like former President Ford to say, "Criticism of the Eisenhower years as being a time of unfocused leadership was—and still is—a mistake in assessment of both the man and the era." As Ford perceptively points out:

Another source of misunderstanding that few of his critics realized was that the habit of a lifetime in the military had given President Eisenhower a military concept of organization. He used it extensively. He delegated authority and trusted the judgment of his subordinates—leaving him precious time to scan the broader horizons of national and international policy, to look further down the road, to think, to plan, to lead.

The mark of a good mind, good communications ability, and political skills had long been there. A graduate of the Class of 1915 at the United States Military Academy, he married Mamie Geneva Doud in 1916. Ten years later, Eisenhower graduated first in a class of 275 at the Command and General Staff School. From 1933 to 1940, Eisenhower was General Douglas MacArthur's assistant—no easy task unto itself. MacArthur was army chief of staff when Eisenhower joined him and two years later took him to the Philippines. To President Manuel Quezon's disappointment, Eisenhower, a lieutenant colonel, returned to the United States in 1940. He was still a lieutenant colonel on March 10, 1941. Twenty-three months later, in a scarcely paralleled record, he was a full general. Recognizing Eisenhower's skills in dealing with people, President Roosevelt personally selected Eisenhower, with General George C. Marshall's recommendation, over more senior generals as supreme allied commander. In that post and, at war's end, as army chief of staff until early 1948, then until late 1950 as Columbia University's president, on leave until the summer of 1952 as NATO's first supreme commander, Eisenhower, without a break in between, had exercised leadership in complex, demanding assignments. Drew Middleton, *New York Times* military correspondent, found that Eisenhower possessed "great organizational and political talents."

Quite apart from the historians, political scientists, and journalists, the American people themselves had long since made up their minds with regard to both the goodness and greatness of Dwight D. Eisenhower. This high regard they continued to hold for him throughout his eight years as president. Moreover, this was a view shared by peoples throughout the world. Indeed, the much traveled president was quite universally regarded as the leader of the free world.

Yet during his presidency this high regard was not shared by many members of the intellectual community. Typical was the 1960 expression by the then Harvard associate professor of political science, Henry Kissinger, deploring Eisenhower's traveling diplomacy. Kissinger, who a decade later began setting new records for such travel, had in 1960 found Eisenhower's style suitable only for "a state which wishes to demoralize its opponent by confusing all issues."

By contrast with the turbulent years of war abroad and demonstration at home that preceded and followed, the eight Eisenhower years appeared placid and relatively quiet. Yet nothing could be further from the truth. Eisenhower's skillful termination of the Korean War was followed by numerous testing points for the president dedicated to waging peace: Berlin, Iran, Lebanon, Guatemala, Vietnam, Taiwan, Suez, the Congo, the U-2 and RB-47 incidents, and the aborted Paris summit conference.

At home the eight years were characterized by remarkably balanced or nearly balanced budgets and by little inflation. There was also relatively little civil strife. Although the Republicans had congressional control for only two of the eight years, Eisenhower got along so well with the Democratic leaders of both the House, Sam Rayburn, and the Senate, Lyndon Johnson, as to be an embarrassment to the Democratic party.

Eisenhower simply made being president appear so easy that there seemed little to be concerned about. To his intellectual critics the record number of times he played golf seemed more impressive than the record number of times he presided at National Security Council meetings (339). The polls indicated that the American people believed Ike had every right to play golf; still, to be on the safe side, his remarkable press secretary, James C. Hagerty, portrayed Eisenhower as making momentous decisions when on the golf links.

In the last year of his life, even after Richard Nixon's 1968 election victory, Eisenhower was still regarded by the American people as their most respected countryman. However, as a student of history and political science and as a former university head, he continued to be troubled by the lack of regard of the intellectual community. In a personal letter to Jim Hagerty, written October 18, 1966, at a time when both the Truman and Kennedy presidencies were rated above his own by scholars, he confided his distress with those who "equate an individual's strength of dedication with oratorical bombast; determination, with public repetition of a catchy phrase; achievement, with the exaggerated use of the vertical pronoun." He concluded: "To them record means little. Manner and method are vital."

By 1982 twenty-nine historians and political scientists had elevated Eisenhower to a ranking among the top ten American presidents. In this poll, conducted by Steve Neal for the Chicago *Tribune,* evaluations were made of "leadership qualities; accomplishments and crisis management; political skills; recruitment and appointments, and character and integrity." Still, forty-one others, perhaps recognizing Neal as an Eisenhower biographer, declined to participate.[2]

CONSIDERATIONS OF BECOMING A CANDIDATE: EISENHOWER A MODERN WASHINGTON?

What moved Dwight Eisenhower to seek the presidency of the United States? When he completed his term as army chief of staff in 1948 and became president of Columbia University, he looked to this assignment as the completion of his career. So likewise when he and Mamie, from the proceeds of his highly successful book *Crusade in Europe*, bought their own first home, a 190–acre farm near Gettysburg, Pennsylvania, they looked yearningly to retiring there. But circumstances dictated otherwise, not unlike the instance of another general who became the first president of the United States.

The distinguished American historian Curtis P. Nettels has drawn an interesting parallel between Washington and Eisenhower:

1. Each was born in a rural setting and grew up in a countryside environment.

2. At the end of the period of youth, each entered upon military activities.

3. During the stage of young manhood each was engaged in public service.

4. Each served as the chief commander of a large multinational military force in a successful war that had great significance in world history and that served a good cause.

5. During a postwar period of six or seven years, each was active in various forms of public service.

Like Washington, Eisenhower was for a time deemed apolitical. Both necessarily came to be identified with a particular party, Federalist and Republican. Both found especial interest in reading *The Federalist* essays.

EISENHOWER AT COLUMBIA UNIVERSITY

Eisenhower had enjoyed a cordial relationship with President Truman, who chose him as army chief of staff in November 1945. After Eisenhower accepted the Columbia University presidency in the spring of 1948, there had been both Republican and Democratic overtures for his candidacy. At the instigation of radio columnist Walter Winchell, the Columbia president was soon besieged with approximately 20,000 letters, postcards, and telegrams urging him to run for the presidency. Eisenhower turned them over to the Columbia University Bureau of Applied Social Research, providing the opportunity for a fascinating psychological study on mass political interests. The study, headed by the bureau's associate director, sociologist Robert Merton, revealed that Eisenhower was perceived as a humane, sincere person who, while a great military leader, had led a crusade for peace and human dignity. As such he was deemed well suited for civil leadership. People viewed him as a "born leader." Eisenhower took keen interest in the report and discussed it several times with Merton.

Still, Eisenhower, despite both Democratic and Republican overtures, had felt compelled to write a statement which Bob Harron, the university's director of public relations, distributed to the press. The message concluded, "I . . . could not accept nomination for any public office or participate in a partisan political contest."

Inevitably, however, events were drawing Eisenhower back into public life. The intense interservice rivalry and the tense relationships with the Soviet Union had prompted President Truman early in 1949 to name Eisenhower as his principal military adviser and informal chairman of the Joint Chiefs of Staff. Hence, the Columbia president was making frequent trips to Washington until the naming, late that year, of Omar Bradley as the first designated chairman of the Joint Chiefs of Staff.

Dewey's defeat by Truman in the 1948 election prompted progressive Republicans, including Paul Hoffman, an industrialist who in 1950 became president of the Ford Foundation; Helen Rogers Reid, publisher of the *New York Herald Tribune;* and Arthur Hays Sulzberger, Columbia trustee and publisher of the *New York Times,* to promote an Eisenhower candidacy.

Observing these events from afar, General MacArthur, in the famous Wake Island Conference of October 15, 1950, had told President Truman, "If you have any general running against you, his name will be Eisenhower, not MacArthur."

EISENHOWER AT NATO

Meeting in Brussels in December 1950, representatives of the member nations of the North Atlantic Treaty Organization unanimously nominated Eisenhower as NATO's first supreme allied commander, Europe (SACEUR). Recognizing the peril of Soviet expansionism, Eisenhower accepted the assignment and was granted a leave of absence by the Columbia trustees.

Eisenhower was a strong believer in the interdependence of the West as a bastion against further invasions by the Soviet Union. Eisenhower's views on the subject were more advanced than most Europeans'. In a notable July 4, 1951, address at a dinner of the English Speaking Union in London, Eisenhower had declared a primary goal of "achieving political unity in Europe." Former Office of Strategic Services (OSS) head William J. Donovan recalled, "Those who were at that dinner and listened were struck by the force with which it was delivered and the coolness with which it was received." General Donovan, who headed the American Committee on United Europe, became convinced that the United States, more than his alma mater, Columbia, needed Eisenhower as president.

Such sentiments increasingly persuaded Eisenhower of the need for a candidate as an alternative to the more conservative, isolationist wing of the Republican party, which continued to advocate a fortress America concept. For his part Eisenhower argued that a military build-up of the eleven NATO nations was the best means to persuade the Soviet Union to consider general disarmament.

Of all those who communicated with Eisenhower to persuade him to come home, Henry Cabot Lodge, in a September 4, 1951, visit perhaps set forth the most telling argument. Lodge warned of the consequences of right-wing control of the Republican party. "You," Lodge contended, "are the only one who can be elected by the Republicans to the Presidency. You must permit the use of your name in the upcoming primaries.''

THE CALL TO COME HOME

It was the American people themselves who really persuaded Eisenhower to come home and become the alternative to this more conservative wing of the Republican party. Minnesota has long been a home to more liberal Republicanism. On March 18, 1952, in the Republican primary, more than 100,000 Minnesotans wrote in Eisenhower's name on their ballots. Two days later, Sulzberger's *New York Times* inquired, ''What does it all mean?'' Editorially, it responded:

It means . . . that the American people have an instinctive trust in Eisenhower, that he is the kind of man they want for President, and that they will go to great lengths to vote for him. Though he has not participated directly in this campaign, Americans feel they know enough about him to be sure of his integrity, his wisdom and his ability.

Following the Minnesota primary, Eisenhower needed little more persuasion to come home. Harry A. Bullis put it well when on April 25, 1952, he wrote Eisenhower: ''The people want another George Washington. They really think of you as a modern George Washington. To them you are the man who can help them keep their liberty and their freedom.''

Eisenhower found himself reading Washington's letter of May 5, 1789, setting forth his concern as he was about ''to embark again on the tempestuous and uncertain Ocean of public life. . . . So much is expected, so many untoward circumstances may intervene in such a new and critical situation, that I feel an insuperable diffidence in my own abilities.''

So Eisenhower accepted the call to come home, to resign in July 1952 as a five-star general of the army, with its salary and perquisites, to challenge Senator Robert A. Taft for the Republican nomination for president. In the first balloting in the July Republican Convention in Chicago, Eisenhower had 595 votes and Taft 500. Then Minnesota changed its vote from its favorite son, Harold Stassen, to Eisenhower, and it was all over. Paul Hoffman wrote: ''We have a new kind of candidate. . . . I think he is going to put 'new heart' in the Republican Party and recast it in the image of Abraham Lincoln. We can use a party which takes its orders neither from the N.A.M. nor the C.I.O.''[3]

THE PRESIDENT: 1952 ELECTION

Eisenhower campaigned skillfully for the presidency against both a talented opponent, Governor Adlai E. Stevenson of Illinois, and the maladroit incumbent, President Truman. The latter, more to the discomfiture of Stevenson than Eisenhower, sought to portray the general as politically inept: ''Now when you

take a man who has spent his whole life in the Army and put him in politics,''
Truman lamented, ''he's just like a fish out of water. . . . I think he is an amateur
in politics.''

Eisenhower had no easy task. The nation enjoyed record prosperity. Not since
Hoover in 1928 had a Republican been elected president. Hoover and the Republicans were still being painted as the party of the Great Depression. Moreover,
not since 1852, exactly a century before, had the party of the incumbent president
been ousted from the White House during a period of prosperity. Stevenson,
Truman, and Eisenhower all campaigned vigorously. Candidate Eisenhower trav-
ersed 51,376 miles by rail and plane through forty-five states, with stops at 232
towns and cities. He emphasized both ''the mess'' in Washington and the need
to end the Korean War. In his October 24 address in Detroit, he promised, if
elected president, to go to Korea; this particularly infuriated Truman; the address
doubtless contributed to Eisenhower's election victory. He received a record
33,824,000 popular votes, and his Electoral College victory was also impressive:
442 to 89. For the first time since 1928 the Republicans had broken into the
Solid South.

THE PRESIDENT: KOREA

True to his promise, the president-elect journeyed to Korea. During his seventy-two hours there he visited both the troops and the military commanders.
En route home on the cruiser *Helena,* Eisenhower, assisted by press aide Jim
Hagerty, sent a dramatic message to General of the Army Douglas MacArthur,
broadcast throughout the world, asking the outspoken advocate of military victory
to meet him at the president's residence at Columbia University to discuss
measures for ending the Korean War. Whatever the two old soldiers talked
about, it conjured up unleashing nuclear arms. Thus, even before his inauguration, with the aid of Hagerty and also C. D. Jackson, publisher of *Life,*
Eisenhower began his psychological warfare on the Chinese and Soviet masters
of the North Koreans. As Robert Leckie pointed out, many persons began to
realize that Eisenhower was far more skillful than ''the amateur politician he
professed himself to be.''

Eisenhower the politician and the strategic planner did persuade the North
Koreans to sign, on June 18, 1953, an armistice to end the fighting. Eisenhower
the statesman realized that this was something less than peace. He stated, ''We
have won an armistice on a single battlefield—not peace in the world.''

THE PRESIDENT: BRICKER AMENDMENT

The end of the Korean War was only one early testing of Eisenhower the
politician and statesman. Another was the so-called Bricker Amendment. This
would have empowered Congress ''to regulate all executive and other agreements
with any foreign power or international organization.'' The measure had been

introduced by conservative Republicans who had found Roosevelt's Yalta agreement an especial anathema.

Senator John Bricker of Ohio, a Republican, meeting Eisenhower on March 18, 1953, told the president that the measure was not aimed at him personally. Neither to Bricker nor to the press did Eisenhower confide the depth of his feelings on this subject. Eisenhower recognized the mood of the Congress which, after experience with both Roosevelt and Truman, was seeking to curb the presidency. He perceived that the measure had the support of as much as two-thirds of the Senate. In a press conference the day after his meeting with Bricker, Eisenhower adroitly observed "that a man has two ears and one tongue" and that he would not speak out on the issue. But he found "a little bit of an anomaly" in the position of those senators who would amend the Constitution "in order to show that it is going to remain the same."

While posing as noncommittal, Eisenhower without delay posed a plan of action. The West Point graduate from Abilene sent for his Brahmin Princetonian secretary of state, John Foster Dulles, who had not yet had an opportunity to fully measure the president. After asking Dulles for his views, which seemingly were not strongly opposed to the proposed amendment, Eisenhower told Dulles that he was going to do some reading and ponder the issue. The following day Eisenhower again sent for Dulles. To the latter's amazement, Eisenhower advised that his reading the previous evening had been from *The Federalist,* that he had been rereading the views of Hamilton, Madison, and Jay, particularly Hamilton's No. 15 and Jay's No. 64.

This would have come as no surprise to Columbia University historians, including Harry J. Carman, John Krout, and Robert Livingston Schuyler, with whom Eisenhower, during his Columbia presidency, had discussed the writings of Columbia's distinguished alumni, Jay and Hamilton. Indeed, Schuyler's most notable graduate seminar on historiography in 1948 had been with Eisenhower as the guest lecturer. Still and all, it came as a revelation in 1953 to Dulles when the president succinctly made the case that the proposed amendment would "put us back" into the weak kind of government of the Articles of Confederation which had preceded the Constitution. Dulles suddenly realized that the man from Abilene was his intellectual peer and could only stammer: "Mr. President, you don't need a lawyer. You can handle this by yourself." The incident and the discussion of *The Federalist* contributed to the deep personal respect that developed between Eisenhower and Dulles. Admiringly, Eisenhower observed of Dulles, "He talked about *The Federalist Papers* as though he had begun their study in kindergarten."

On the Bricker proposal Eisenhower made Dulles the lightning rod for conservative opposition, while he himself worked quietly with Democrats who opposed the amendment. This technique of letting his cabinet members and senior staff take the public flack was used frequently. His "Man Friday," as he referred to his highly regarded press secretary, Jim Hagerty, clearly recalled the strategy. Having a nineteen-year difference in age, they enjoyed almost a father-son relationship. As Hagerty recalled:

Many times, after he sought my personal opinion . . . President Eisenhower would say, "Do it this way." I would say, "If I go to that press conference and say what you want me to say, I would get hell." With that, he would smile, get up and walk around the desk, pat me on the back and say, "My boy, better you than me."

Eisenhower gradually became more openly assertive. On January 8, 1954, Hagerty recorded in his diary that Eisenhower vowed to " 'fight to the last ditch' any amendment seeking to usurp or cancel out presidential powers." Subsequently, Eisenhower avowed, "I'll go into every state to fight it." He termed the Bricker movement "stupid, blind violation of [the] Constitution by stupid, blind isolationists." To Eisenhower's disgust the amendment fell only one vote short (60–31) of the two-thirds majority needed in the Senate.

THE PRESIDENT: McCARTHYISM

Eisenhower's handling of Senator Joseph R. McCarthy revealed both the depths of the president's feeling and his skillful strategy. McCarthy's investigating committee on communism and subversion had caused President Truman considerable discomfiture. In January 1953, when Eisenhower became president, McCarthy was riding high. His first test of strength with the new president came two months later, when he challenged Eisenhower's nomination of Charles E. Bohlen as Ambassador to Russia. McCarthy told the Senate on March 25: "The mere fact that Dwight Eisenhower nominates Bohlen does not, to me, mean that we should blindly confirm the nomination."

Eisenhower, with Hagerty's help, the following day praised Bohlen at a press conference. Bohlen, confirmed by the Senate, subsequently indicated that Eisenhower had been his strongest administration supporter during the hearings. Then, in June 1953, Eisenhower further undermined McCarthy by warning the Dartmouth graduating class against "the book burners." But it was the army-McCarthy hearings that brought Eisenhower to encourage McCarthy's destruction. When Ike learned of McCarthy's harassment of Army Secretary Robert T. Stevens, he avowed: "This guy McCarthy is going to get in trouble over this. I'm not going to take this one lying down."[4] Far more skilled than Truman, who had sought to combat McCarthy directly, Eisenhower used his lieutenants, especially Hagerty and Vice President Nixon, and quietly backed Senators Ralph E. Flanders and Arthur F. Watkins' censure move on McCarthy. On December 2 the Senate, by a 67–22 vote, "condemned" McCarthy's conduct. Hagerty publicized Eisenhower's congratulations of Watkins, and McCarthy was finished. As Allen Yarnell concluded, "While there is still much to learn about the strategy, when we think that McCarthy was a major force in American politics in January 1953 and was finished by December 1954, some credit must go to the President." Eisenhower, who came from this two years of McCarthyism to abhor the extreme right wing of his own party, confided to Hagerty, "This party of ours has got to realize that they won't exist unless they become a party of progressive moderates."

THE CABINET AND THE INSTITUTIONALIZED PRESIDENCY

More than any other modern president, Eisenhower achieved cabinet collegiality. He asserted, "The history of past administrations . . . recorded much Cabinet bickering, personality conflicts, and end running, tale bearing, and throat cutting." This, to a great degree, he eliminated, both by organization and by the quality of his leadership and his appointments, making team players of his associates. Fred I. Greenstein concluded: "I have had conversations with associates of all nine of the modern presidents from Roosevelt to Reagan. None of the nine groups is more unified than Eisenhower's in its admiration of its leader." From the outset of his administration, the cabinet met regularly. During his first eighty days in office the cabinet had 10 meetings (compared to 3 for his successor). During his eight years in the presidency, the cabinet had 34 meetings annually. The National Security Council met even more often: 51 times the first year and 366 times over the eight years.

Based upon his experience in military staffing, in 1954 he created a cabinet secretariat charged with developing relevant agendas, meaningful presentations, and options for decision-making. This was the first cabinet secretariat in the history of the presidency. Moreover, he enlarged the cabinet to about two dozen members, including key presidential assistants, directors of important government agencies such as the Bureau of Budget, and the ambassador to the United Nations.

Eisenhower also proposed the creation of the first new cabinet department in forty years. From a hodgepodge of bureaus, he established in 1953 the Department of Health, Education and Welfare (HEW). Furthermore, believing in cultural exchange overseas and a strong broadcasting voice of freedom, he founded in 1953 the United States Information Agency (USIA).

The institutionalizing of the cabinet was somewhat mixed in terms of the significance of the agendas. The meetings involved philosophical discussions, as, for example, on the merit of federal aid to education, as well as specific programming proposals. Richard F. Fenno, Jr., concluded in his classic study, *The President's Cabinet,* that the Eisenhower cabinet developed "a relatively high degree of coherence, the highest perhaps. " Thomas Cronin concluded that of all presidential cabinets through Carter, "the Eisenhower Cabinet . . . came about as close to the ideal of an upgraded or European style of Cabinet as we have witnessed in the United States."

THE NATIONAL SECURITY COUNCIL

Eisenhower likewise institutionalized other policy formulating bodies, notably the National Security Council, which he viewed as "correlative in importance with the Cabinet." The cabinet was his principal advisory body "for domestic affairs" and the NSC "for all matters pertaining to the nation's security." Believing financial strength to be basic in national security, after March 23, 1953, he had Secretary of the Treasury George Humphrey participate in NSC meetings. Record reductions were made in the defense budget in the "New Look" emphasizing air and long-range nuclear strike forces. Eisenhower also emphasized internal security and psychological factors as national security policy elements. Hence (for internal security affairs) Attorney General Herbert Brownell, as well as (for external security affairs) Central Intelligence Agency Director Allen Dulles and (for psychological affairs) Special Assistant to the President C. D. Jackson, each had a significant role in NSC meetings.

DECISION-MAKING AND STAFFING

Gordon Gray, special assistant for national security affairs during the final three Eisenhower years, contrasted the structured decision-making of the Eisenhower years with the rather informal methods of the Roosevelt and Truman administrations. He concluded, under Eisenhower, "You don't have this kind of ad hoc piecemeal business of arriving at a decision."

Personally and politically free from anxieties, Eisenhower attracted and welcomed strong colleagues. Both in the cabinet and the NSC he encouraged frank expressions of differences of opinion.

Like all presidents since 1940, Eisenhower found foreign policy and fiscal matters occupying more than two-thirds of his time. Dulles at State and Humphrey at Treasury were his towering cabinet members during the first Eisenhower administration, not unlike their forbears, Jefferson and Hamilton, in the first presidential cabinet. In the second term, Humphrey's successor at the Treasury, Robert B. Anderson, likewise played a leading role. Dulles continued his own strong role until February 1959, when he stepped down during his terminal illness. Eisenhower was the first president to elevate significantly the role of the vice president. He was the first president to have the vice president participate in all cabinet meetings and to formulate a plan for the vice president to serve as acting president during the incapacity of the president (an arrangement formalized by the Twenty-fifth Amendment, ratified in 1967).

COMMAND ESTABLISHMENT

The president, who had stood with firmness against Britain, France, and Israel in the Suez crisis, and who had enforced the court orders against Governor Orval Faubus of Arkansas in the Little Rock crisis, was equally firm and tenacious in reorganizing the defense establishment. He found the chain of command through the service secretaries diffused. He would enhance the roles of the secretary of defense and the Joint Chiefs, and he would create a system of unified commands. Eisenhower would establish a direct command channel from the secretary of defense through the Joint Chiefs to the unified commands. The service secretaries would be clearly subordinate to the secretary of defense and a new high-level post would be created, director of defense research and engineering. Opposition was intense in the services and in Congress. Eisenhower was condemned as imperialistic and intrusive. "I am intrigued with, but not convinced by, the argument that the Congress ought to resolve all its troubles," Senator Richard Russell complained, "by just delegating all its powers to the executive branch." Similarly, Congressman "Uncle Carl" Vinson charged that Eisenhower's proposal smacked of a "Prussian style general staff."

With a fight on his hands in a field to which he had devoted his career, Eisenhower asked Hagerty both to convene a series of press conferences and to feature the president's address to the American Society of Newspaper Editors. He told the editors that his conclusions were based upon "all the years since 1911 when I entered military service." He assured them that "each service will remain intact" and that there would be no "Prussian general staff," no "czar" secretary of defense; no usurping of congressional authority.

With the media's support, he put the case to the Congress. With encouragement from Hagerty, and also Bryce Harlow, he wrote to hundreds of friends throughout the nation, asking them, in turn, to convey their views to their friends as well as to the Congress. One business leader alone wrote 20,000 letters in support of Eisenhower's reforms. Members of Congress lamented that the president was "going over the heads of Congress." The president found this "most welcome," indicative that he was getting results.

By such means Eisenhower triumphed over the long entrenched, parochial service views. On August 6, 1958, he signed into law what has since been the basic Department of Defense organization and United States worldwide military command organization and command channels. "It was," as this author wrote, "largely a personal accomplishment of President Eisenhower, both in its authorship and enactment." Having for several years invited others to make the reforms, the old soldier did it himself.

Beyond effective organization, Eisenhower recognized the basic elements of national strength, economic, moral, and spiritual, as well as effective armed services. Disarmament remained his steadfast goal. Negotiations with the Soviets could only be successful when dealing from positions of economic and military strength. And yet there were inherent dangers in a powerful business-military relationship. Hence, in his farewell address to the American people, Eisenhower warned that "in the councils of government we must guard against the acquisition of unwarranted influence, whether sought or unsought, by the military-industrial complex." The old soldier concluded in this farewell address in these last days in presidential office that "only an alert and knowledgeable citizenry" could guarantee that "security and liberty may prosper together."

ASSESSMENT AND SUMMING UP

Conservative? Liberal? Active? Passive? Students of the presidency have, until recent date, had difficulty categorizing and classifying Eisenhower. He was far more liberal than most students have recognized. Indeed, his progressiveness in foreign policy, as an active internationalist in an interdependent world, opposed to isolationists and "fortress America" advocates, caused him to make a run for the presidency. Believing in economy in government and in fiscal restraint, his efforts were rewarded by eight years with virtually no inflation and general economic vigor, with only one short-lived recession of mild character.[5]

FOREIGN POLICY LEADERSHIP

Eisenhower did *not* serve passively in placid times. There was no doubt in his cabinet and staff whence leadership stemmed. With the experience of leadership in the world's largest and most complex military command, he understood the vital importance of consultation, decision-making, and policy direction. Accordingly, he always worked with and through the Congress and, with the tragic exception of Suez, for which he had no alternative, with the concurrence and support of principal allies. His methods in that exception bear examination. He believed that unless the Anglo-French and Israeli invasion at Suez were checked, the Russians, already in Egypt, would emerge as the protectors of the oil-rich Arab states and that the whole Third World would turn against the West. Russian control of Middle East oil would endanger the very survival of Britain and France. When the Senate resisted Eisenhower's efforts to apply sanctions to the Israelis to force them out of the Gaza strip, as in so many of his battles, he went to the media and to the people. The Israelis' supporters in the Senate backed down, the Israelis withdrew, the Suez Canal reopened, and the vital oil flow resumed. To this day many American Jews have never forgiven Eisenhower and have misconstrued and misunderstood his motives.

Suez had been followed by the Eisenhower Doctrine and the landing of 14,000 troops in Lebanon. Eisenhower's incisive action in that instance is illustrative, conventional wisdom to the contrary, that Eisenhower, not Secretary Dulles, was in charge. When Dulles demurred in an NSC meeting, Eisenhower tersely interrupted, "Foster, I've already made up my mind. We're going in." So likewise in the first Quemoy-Matsu crisis of 1954, Eisenhower had rebuked his own Senate majority leader, William Knowland, who was demanding a blockade of mainland China. Likewise he countered the 1954 demands of his then chairman of the Joint Chiefs of Staff, Admiral Arthur Radford, who was urging American intervention in Vietnam.

As the very title of Eisenhower's reminiscences, *Waging Peace,* implies, his great quest was for world peace. With the pretext of the U-2 incident, Nikita Khrushchev had walked out of the 1960 summit and eliminated Eisenhower's hope to visit the Soviet Union in his last year in office.

Eisenhower equated peace with social justice at home and abroad. In his final press conference, with Jim Hagerty at his side, he confided, "The big disappointment . . . was that we could not in those years get to the place where we could say it now looks as if permanent peace with justice is now in sight." This abortive effort perhaps spelled the difference in the closely contested 1960 election.

DOMESTIC POLICY

In domestic policies he was again far more liberal than his detractors realized. His closest counselor, his brother, Dr. Milton S. Eisenhower, the popular and respected president of Kansas State University from 1945 to 1950 and of Pennsylvania State University until 1956, and thereafter president of Johns Hopkins University, has usually been regarded as more liberal than his elder brother. Yet, Dr. Eisenhower has confided, "I, if I differed with my brother at all, was more conservative than he on economic and fiscal policy. We never differed," Milton concluded, "on matters of human values and human welfare."[6]

Conventional wisdom to the contrary, Eisenhower was a moderate civil rights activist. Believing in human dignity and in the equal protection of the laws, he fought for the first civil rights act in more than four score years, initially opposed by such "liberals" as John F. Kennedy and Lyndon Johnson. However, he realized and sought to soften a white backlash, which those less sensitive to southern prejudices would have ignited. Again, conventional wisdom to the contrary, Eisenhower never equivocated, never hesitated to use force where needed, as in Little Rock to break segregation.

Eisenhower's views on Chief Justice Earl Warren and the Supreme Court have been misconstrued. The famed desegregation decision of 1954 was not a Warren decision. It was the *unanimous* decision of the Court. Moreover, Eisenhower gets highest marks for his appointments to all the federal courts. Indeed, his southern appointees were always the most progressive on civil rights. "It always amazes me," a Democratic lawyer in Washington declared, "but you look back and the Eisenhower appointments are clearly the best."

Believing strongly in the services of the church, the home, and the school, he believed that neighbors could better minister to local needs than the Washington bureaucracy. Yet, as the organizer of HEW, he saw the necessity for federal planning. Furthermore, he saw the necessity for federal funds, as, for example, in his National Defense Education Act as well as in his enormous interstate highway program and the St. Lawrence Seaway. Eisenhower, like Lincoln, was something of an old-fashioned Whig. Philosophically, he wondered whether we were inevitably and irrevocably destined to move toward more socialism. As he expressed it in a 1959 cabinet meeting, "Perhaps we are like the armed guard with rusty armor and a broken sword, standing at the bridge and trying to stop progress."

LEADERSHIP

Activist-prone historians and political scientists have never fully appreciated Eisenhower's style of leadership. The Latin motto on his desk, so much more subtle than Truman's "The Buck Stops Here," sums up Eisenhower's style: *Suaviter in modo, fortiter in re* (Gently in manner, strong in deed). His critics likewise have not grasped his highly successful leadership style, which in World War II could make such egocentrics as Bernard Montgomery and George Patton effective members in a winning team. Ike himself put it this way:

Leadership is a word and a concept that has been more argued about than almost any other I know. I am not one of the desk-pounding type that likes to stick out his jaw and look like he is bossing the show. I would far rather get behind and, recognizing the frailties and the requirements of human nature, I would rather try to persuade a man to go along—because once I have persuaded him he will stick. If I scare him, he will stay just as long as he is scared, and then he is gone.

Presidential Counselor Edwin Meese III, attorney general in the second Reagan term, has invited attention to a small brass plaque on President Reagan's desk, which states, "There's no limit to what one man can accomplish, as long as he's willing to let someone else have the credit." Counselor Meese concludes: "To a striking degree, Eisenhower's presidency was a reflection of that sentiment. Eisenhower abhorred the use of the first person [singular] pronoun."

EXPOSITORY POWER

Those who worked with Eisenhower appreciated not only his leadership style, but also his organizational ability, his decision-making processes, and his expository style. John J. McCloy, who was closely associated with FDR, Truman, and Eisenhower, has compared their style and their substance. Roosevelt made decisions on feelings, hunches, and personal assessments. Although McCloy found Roosevelt inconsistent, and superficial in his decision processes, he admired his mastery. He observed that Roosevelt could not organize his ideas in an essay or a speech. However, if that speech were written by someone else, Roosevelt could deliver it with a charm and persuasion rarely matched. By contrast, as McCloy has pointed out, Eisenhower had great powers of exposition. Theodore White, like so many other students of the presidency, once viewed Ike as "a simple man." But, White concluded, "Gradually . . . I found his mind was tough." As a writer, White admired how Ike, "disciplined by his own pencil," produced "clean hard prose."

He could plan his own ideas on paper with brilliance, charm, clarity, cogency, depth, and succinctness. Yet, when he came to read those words aloud or otherwise orally discourse, he often stumbled over his own syntax. On occasion, as he admitted to Hagerty, this was by design, to confuse potential adversaries on a controversial issue. This contrast contributed directly to Roosevelt's high marks and Eisenhower's low.

POLITICAL SKILL

Eisenhower, as Roosevelt recognized, had great political skill. Again, part of it was his disarming, often seemingly simplistic manner. Again, this was often by design. Only in retrospect did many skilled politicians recognize their master was among them, calling the best from them. Recalling in 1970 the long hours in the 1950s of working for Eisenhower programs, which they believed were their own, George E. Reedy, Jr., staff director, majority party committee (with Senate Majority Leader Lyndon B. Johnson), concluded that Eisenhower "was a master politician. I did not think so at the time. . . . Lord, it is funny," Reedy concluded, "how different things look a few years later." Reedy put his finger on a part of the Eisenhower genius, the ability to give others a sense of accomplishment, and the disarming act of giving the impression that he knew less than he really did.

RELATIONS WITH CONGRESS

Eisenhower was masterful in dealing with the Congress. In the eight years of his presidency his own party had control of the Congress in only two years, and then by the narrowest of margins. But this never proved an impediment to his legislative program, though on occasion, as with the Defense Reorganization Act of 1958, he had to make a major counterappeal to editors and publishers and even organize a letter writing campaign. To get the Civil Rights Act adopted, he had to compromise and conciliate. He also exercised the veto 181 times with great skill.

President Carter was asked by members of the press how he accounted for Eisenhower's success in working with the Congress, and particularly his skill with the opposition leaders, Lyndon Johnson and Sam Rayburn. According to James Reston of the *New York Times,* Carter responded, "I wish I could have experienced that; it must have been a delightful atmosphere." What Carter failed to grasp is that Eisenhower *created* a splendid working relationship. He did *not* inherit it. His predecessor, Truman, had severe problems with the Congress.

Eisenhower was a master of the art of consultation, and the Congress loved him for it. For example, early in 1955, when he asked the Congress, should occasion arise, for permission to come to the aid of Taiwan, an inspired Speaker Rayburn avowed, "If the President had done what is proposed here without consulting Congress, he would have had no criticism from me." Arthur Krock of the *New York Times,* termed Eisenhower's consultation "good statesmanship." Krock, a veteran observer of the Washington scene, added, "In the highest sense of the word, it was good politics too."[7]

RANKING AND ACCOMPLISHMENTS

Because of scholarship utilizing recently released papers at the Eisenhower Presidential Library in Abilene, Kansas, and the travails of the post-Eisenhower presidencies, it is understandable how, late in the decade of the eighties, the Eisenhower presidency has come to be viewed as the most effective since Truman, and by some scholars as the most effective since FDR. In the 1982 Neal poll, Eisenhower was rated among the top ten presidents, by contrast with the 1962 Schlesinger poll, which placed him among the mediocre, just above Andrew Johnson, the only president ever actually tried for impeachment.

It is understandable that Eisenhower, who never lived to view this recent appraisal, felt bad about the mediocrity rating historians and political scientists gave him during his lifetime. In a personal letter to Jim Hagerty, October 18, 1966, he confided his distress at the low marks his administration had received. With no view of its ever being published, Eisenhower countered in this letter with twenty-three principal accomplishments of a "team effort." As Hagerty later observed, "It is quite interesting that he did not refer to *my* administrations." Eisenhower's points ranged from the "first civil rights laws in [over] eighty years" and "desegregation in Washington, D.C., and the Armed Forces without laws," to "slowing up, and practical elimination of inflation" and "fighting for responsible fiscal and financial policies throughout eight years." He noted Alaskan and Hawaiian statehood, the St. Lawrence Seaway, the interstate highway system, the establishment of HEW (he might have added the National Aeronautics and Space Administration, the Federal Aviation Administration, and USIA), "intelligent application of federal aid to education," substantial extension of the old age insurance and "the largest reduction of taxes to this time."

In the area of national security Eisenhower offered these ten points:

End of Korean War (thereafter no American killed in combat)

Prevention of Communist efforts to dominate Iran, Guatemala, Lebanon, Formosa, and South Vietnam

Reorganization of the Department of Defense

Initiation of a space program which successfully orbited within three years, after starting from scratch

Initiating a strong ballistic missile program

Conceiving and building the Polaris submarine program, with ships operating at sea, within a single administration

Preservation, for the first time in American history, of adequate military establishment after the cessation of war

Goodwill journeys to more than a score of nations in Europe, Asia, South Pacific, and the Pacific

Initiation of plans for social progress in Latin America after obtaining necessary authorization from the Congress

"Atoms for Peace" proposal

Eisenhower might have added his judicious restraint in Indochina, Suez, and Berlin, and his termination of atmospheric nuclear explosions. Robert Divine recently observed, "Tested by a world as dangerous as any American leader has ever faced, Eisenhower used his sound judgment and instinctive common sense to guide the nation safely through the first decade of the thermonuclear age."

CONCLUDING PERCEPTIONS

Clearly Eisenhower was far more than the folk hero he so well portrayed; he was *not* the head of state who was above politics. What he did so well was to combine the roles of chief of state and chief of party, without making these roles contradictory. He was extremely skilled politically, the most skilled politically of the modern presidents with the possible exception of FDR. He had an amazing ability to make friends, to influence people. He was a careful, discerning planner. Unlike his two immediate predecessors, he did not "shoot from the hip." Rather he exercised great restraint. A part of that restraint was in keeping the volcano of his own temper in check. The golf course became his release, and the American people did not begrudge him for it.

SPIRITUAL LEADERSHIP

With the exception of Lincoln, more perhaps than any other president, Eisenhower conveyed his views in moral and spiritual terms. The first of the modern presidents to do so, he added a moral and spiritual dimension to presidential leadership roles.

From his earliest youth, Eisenhower had been inspired with a sense of faith by his mother, Ida Stover Eisenhower. But the religious, the spiritual, had not always shown through. "Why, dammit, I am a religious man!" he protested one day to his World War II aide, Harry C. Butcher.

It was as president that Eisenhower especially emphasized the importance of spiritual leadership. Mamie had been a Presbyterian since she was a child. After his election as president, he became a member of the National Presbyterian Church, where Dr. Edward L.R. Elson was the pastor. There, on the morning of his inaugural, January 20, 1953, Eisenhower took Communion with his family. "Believing we were getting too secular," after the service, he wrote his own inaugural prayer. He began, "Almighty God, as we stand here . . . especially we pray that our concern shall be for all the people, regardless of station, race, or calling."

In his second inaugural prayer, the president concluded, "May we, in our dealings with all peoples of the earth, ever speak truth and serve justice." Our most traveled president conveyed these views in his journeys to Europe, the Middle East, South Asia, the Americas, and the Far East. He reached the hearts and minds of peoples worldwide to a degree only matched in the twentieth century by Churchill, Wilson, and the two Roosevelts. More even than they he did so in terms of moral and spiritual purpose.

Here at home he sought to mobilize a "spiritual crusade" in terms "the fellow planting a row of corn or driving a taxi" could feel a part of. Dr. Elson asserted that Eisenhower became "the focal point of a moral resurgence and spiritual awakening of national proportions."[8] James David Fairbanks concludes, "The language Eisenhower used was simple but it was effective in reaffirming for the large majority of the country the great truths underlying the nation's liberal democratic tradition." He could do this, where others might be charged with hypocrisy, because, as William Lee Miller expressed it, "he was not only a good man; he was a man whose goodness . . . [did] not have to be proven."

Eisenhower would have dismissed this view of his personal goodness as generous hyperbole. Yet, like but few other presidents, by his deeds, by his faith, and by his person, Eisenhower had contributed to a conception of national purpose which so many of his countrymen came to share. His concern was for human dignity and its moral and spiritual foundations. He earnestly believed, as he expressed it, that "America is not good because it is great. America is great because it is good."[9]

NOTES

1. Richard E. Neustadt, *Presidential Power* (New York: Wiley, 1980); Edwin Meese III, "The Institutional Presidency: The Cabinet, the Staff, and the Vice Presidency," *Presidential Studies Quarterly*, 13, no. 2 (Spring 1983): 192; Robert J. Spitzer, *The Presidency and Public Policy* (University, Ala.: University of Alabama Press, 1983), p. 5; Dwight D. Eisenhower, *The White House Years: Mandate for Change, 1953–1956* (Garden City, N.Y.: Doubleday, 1963), p. 87; Meese, "Institutional Presidency," p. 197; *New York Times*, January 25, 1955; Arthur Krock, "Impressions of the President and the Man," *New York Times Magazine*, June 23, 1957, pp. 5ff.; Murray Kempton, "The Underestimation of Dwight D. Eisenhower," *Esquire*, 63 (September 1967): 156; Herbert S. Parmet, *Eisenhower and the American Crusades* (New York: Macmillan, 1972); R. Gordon Hoxie, "Presidential Greatness," in Philip C. Dolce and George H. Skau, eds., *Power and the Presidency* (New York: Scribner's, 1976), pp. 261–268.

2. Gerald R. Ford in "Foreword" to R. Gordon Hoxie, *Command Decision and the Presidency* (New York: Reader's Digest Press, 1977), p. xvi; Fred I. Greenstein, *The Hidden-Hand Presidency: Eisenhower as Leader* (New York: Basic Books, 1982), pp. 53, 248; Herbert Parmet, "Why We Liked Ike," *The New Leader*, December 12, 1982, p. 13; Ford, "Foreword," pp. xvi–xvii; John Gunther, *Eisenhower: The Man and the Symbol* (New York: Harper and Row, 1952), p. 65; *New York Times*, October 12, 1981; Henry A. Kissinger, *The Necessity for Choice: Prospects of American Foreign Policy*

(New York: Harper and Brothers, 1961), pp. 189, 343; Hoxie, *Command Decision,* p. 245; Thomas E. Cronin, "News Notes," *Presidential Studies Quarterly,* 12, no. 2 (Spring 1982): 291–293.

3. Curtis P. Nettels, "Washington and Eisenhower," manuscript in Center for the Study of the Presidency, New York, N.Y.; Greenstein, *Hidden-Hand Presidency,* p. 96; Eisenhower, *Mandate,* p. 10; Douglas MacArthur, *Reminiscences* (New York: McGraw-Hill, 1964), pp. 362, 363; R. Gordon Hoxie, ed., *Frontiers of Freedom* (Denver: University of Denver Press, 1952), p. 171; Eisenhower, *Mandate,* p. 18; Philip A. Grant, Jr., "The 1952 Minnesota Republican Primary and the Eisenhower Candidacy," *Presidential Studies Quarterly,* 9, no. 3 (Summer 1979): 311, 313; Parmet, *Eisenhower and the American Crusades,* p. 42; Eisenhower, *Mandate,* p. 25.

4. Harry S Truman, *Public Papers of the Presidents of the United States, 1952–53* (Washington, D.C.: U.S. Government Printing Office, 1966), p. 842; Robert Leckie, *Conflict: The History of the Korean War, 1950–1953* (New York: G. P. Putnam's Sons, 1962), pp. 370, 371; Eisenhower, *Mandate,* p. 191; Arthur M. Schlesinger, Jr., "Congress and the Making of Foreign Policy," in Rexford G. Tugwell and Thomas E. Cronin, eds., *The Presidency Reappraised* (New York: Praeger Publishers, 1974), pp. 83–116; Dwight D. Eisenhower, *Public Papers of the Presidents of the United States, 1953* (Washington, D.C.: U.S. Government Printing Office, 1960), pp. 109, 110. The anecdote about the Dulles conversation is based upon several sources including the author's conversations with President Eisenhower, James C. Hagerty, and Professor Robert Livingston Schuyler. Also Parmet, *Eisenhower and the American Crusades,* pp. 309–312; Eisenhower, *Waging Peace,* p. 372; and Robert H. Ferrell, ed., *The Diary of James C. Hagerty* (Bloomington: Indiana University Press, 1983), pp. 4–14, 20, 24, 46, 157, 159. R. Gordon Hoxie, ed., *The White House: Organization and Operations* (New York: Center for the Study of the Presidency, 1971), p. 4; Ferrell, *Hagerty Diary,* pp. 5, 6; Allen Yarnell, "Eisenhower and McCarthy: An Appraisal of Presidential Strategy," *Presidential Studies Quarterly,* 9, no. 1 (Winter 1980): 93; Ferrell, *Hagerty Diary,* p. 20.

5. Yarnell, "Eisenhower and McCarthy," p. 96; Ferrell, *Hagerty Diary,* p. 129; Eisenhower, *Mandate for Change,* p. 134; Greenstein, *Hidden-Hand Presidency,* p. ix; Richard F. Fenno, Jr., *The President's Cabinet* (Cambridge, Mass.: Harvard University Press, 1959), pp. 109, 110; Thomas E. Cronin, *The State of the Presidency,* 2nd ed. (Boston: Little, Brown, 1980), p. 271; Hoxie, *Command Decision,* p. 201; Dwight D. Eisenhower, *The White House Years: Waging Peace, 1956–1961* (Garden City, N.Y.: Doubleday, 1965), p. 633; Hoxie, *White House,* p. 119.

6. Hoxie, *Command Decision,* pp. 217, 218, 221, 222, 226, 259; Robert A. Divine, *Eisenhower and the Cold War* (New York: Oxford University Press, 1981), pp. 21, 99, 33, 57, 58; Hoxie, *Command Decision,* pp. 205, 206, 259; Milton Eisenhower, *The President Is Calling* (Garden City, N.Y.: Doubleday, 1974), p. 66.

7. Ronald Stidham, Robert A. Carp, and C. K. Rowland, "Patterns of Presidential Influence in the Federal District Courts: An Analysis of the Appointment Process," *Presidential Studies Quarterly* 14 (Fall 1984): 548–560; James C. Durbin, " 'A Good Growl': The Eisenhower Cabinet's January 16, 1959, Discussion of Federal Aid to Education," *Presidential Studies Quarterly,* 8, no. 4 (Fall 1978): 441; Hoxie, *Command Decision,* pp. xvi–xvii; Meese, "Institutional Presidency," p. 193; Theodore H. White, *In Search of History: A Personal Adventure* (New York: Harper and Row, 1978), p. 347; Hoxie, *Presidency of the 1970's,* p. 10; Hoxie, *Command Decision,* p. 246; *New York Times,* January 17, 1979, p. A23; R. Gordon Hoxie, "Presidential Leadership and Amer-

ican Foreign Policy,'' *Presidential Studies Quarterly,* 9, no. 2 (Spring 1979): 136; Hoxie, "Presidential Leadership,'' pp. 136, 137.

8. Hoxie, *Command Decision,* p. 18; Thomas E. Cronin, "News Notes,'' *Presidential Studies Quarterly,* 12, no. 2 (Spring 1982): p. 293; Hoxie, *Command Decision,* pp. 245, 246; Divine, *Cold War,* pp. viii, 154, 155; Harry C. Butcher, *My Three Years with Eisenhower* (New York: Simon and Schuster, 1946), p. 438; Eisenhower, *Mandate for Change,* p. 100; Dwight D. Eisenhower, *Public Papers of the Presidents, 1957* (Washington, D.C.: U.S. Government Printing Office, 1958), p. 61; Peter Lyon, *Eisenhower: Portrait of the Hero* (Boston: Little, Brown, 1974), pp. 473, 477.

9. James David Fairbanks, "Religious Dimensions of Presidential Leadership: The Case of Dwight D. Eisenhower,'' *Presidential Studies Quarterly,* 12, no. 2 (Spring 1982): p. 266; William Lee Miller, *Piety Along the Potomac* (Boston: Houghton Mifflin, 1974), p. 20; Eisenhower, *Public Papers of the Presidents, 1961,* p. 1040; Ford, "Foreword,'' p. xix.

ANNOTATED BIBLIOGRAPHY

Books

Alexander, Charles. *Holding the Line: The Eisenhower Era, 1952–1961.* Bloomington: Indiana University Press, 1975.

A review and analysis of Eisenhower as a president who was a consolidator.

Ambrose, Stephen E. *Ike's Spies: Eisenhower and the Espionage Establishment.* Garden City, N.Y.: Doubleday, 1981.

An analysis of espionage in the Eisenhower era, including a discussion of the U-2 crisis.

Butcher, Harry C. *My Three Years with Eisenhower.* New York: Simon and Schuster, 1946.

A World War II aide's memoirs of service with General Eisenhower.

Cutler, Robert. *No Time for Rest.* Boston: Little, Brown, 1965, 1966.

A staff aide's recollections of work in the Eisenhower White House.

Divine, Robert A. *Eisenhower and the Cold War.* New York: Oxford University Press, 1981.

An analysis of Eisenhower diplomacy at the peak of the Cold War.

Eisenhower, Dwight D. *Public Papers of the Presidents.* 8 vols. Washington, D.C.: U.S. Government Printing Office, 1958–1961.

The official record of all Dwight Eisenhower's public papers, addresses, and news conferences.

———. *The White House Years. Vol. 1, Mandate for Change, 1953–1956.* Garden City, N.Y.: Doubleday, 1963. Vol. 2, *Waging Peace, 1956–1961.* Garden City, N.Y.: Doubleday, 1965.

This two-volume autobiography gives Eisenhower's personal view of his two administrations.

Eisenhower, John S.D. *Strictly Personal.* Garden City, N.Y.: Doubleday, 1974.

A memoir by the son of President Eisenhower, a former army officer.

Eisenhower, Milton S. *The President Is Calling.* Garden City, N.Y.: Doubleday, 1974.

A memoir of the Eisenhower presidency by the president's brother.

Ewald, William B., Jr. *Eisenhower the President: Crucial Days, 1951–1960*. Englewood
    Cliffs, N.J.: Prentice-Hall, 1981.
    An analysis of crisis decision-making under Eisenhower.
Fenno, Richard F., Jr., *The President's Cabinet*. Cambridge, Mass.: Harvard University
    Press, 1959.
    An analysis of cabinet politics with emphasis on the FDR, Truman, and Eisenhower
    administrations.
Ferrell, Robert H., ed. *The Eisenhower Diaries*. New York: Norton, 1981.
    An edited version of the diaries kept by President Eisenhower, with behind-the-
    scenes views of major events.
Greenstein, Fred I. *The Hidden-Hand Presidency: Eisenhower as Leader*. New York:
    Basic Books, 1982.
    A noted political scientist's view of Eisenhower's administrative and political
    leadership techniques; could be termed a revisionist study; upgrades the assessment
    of Eisenhower's leadership.
Gunther, John. *Eisenhower: The Man and the Symbol*. New York: Harper and Row,
    1952.
    A campaign biography with an analysis of Eisenhower's personality.
Hoxie, R. Gordon. *A History of the Faculty of Political Science, Columbia University*.
    New York: Columbia University Press, 1955.
    Eisenhower's service at Columbia University in context.
————. *Command Decision and the Presidency*. New York: Reader's Digest Press,
    1977.
    A thorough analysis of the president's commander-in-chief role. Carries a foreword
    by former President Gerald R. Ford.
————, ed. *Frontiers of Freedom*. Denver: University of Denver Press, 1952.
    An anthology of essays including material on Eisenhower.
————, ed. *The White House: Organization and Operations*. New York: Center for the
    Study of the Presidency, 1971.
    Proceedings of the Montauk leadership conference of the Center (including remarks
    by press secretaries Herb Klein, George Reedy, and James Hagerty).
————, ed. *The Presidency of the 1970's*. New York: Center for the Study of the
    Presidency, 1972.
    Proceedings from a Center leadership conference.
Hughes, Emmet John. *The Ordeal of Power*. New York: Atheneum, 1963.
    The memoirs of an Eisenhower aide and speech-writer. Puts White House service
    into context.
Larson, Arthur. *Eisenhower: The President Nobody Knows*. New York: Scribner's, 1968.
    An effort to explore the reserve and dignity behind the famous Eisenhower grin.
Leckie, Robert. *Conflict: The History of the Korean War, 1950–1953*. New York: G. P.
    Putnam's Sons, 1962.
    One of the first one-volume analyses of the war in Korea.
Lyon, Peter. *Eisenhower: Portrait of the Hero*. Boston: Little, Brown, 1974.
    An analysis that focuses on the aspects of Eisenhower's personality that made
    him a hero to the American public.
MacArthur, Douglas. *Reminiscences*. New York: McGraw-Hill, 1964.
    General MacArthur's own personal memoir of his military career and retirement.

Miller, William Lee. *Piety Along the Potomac*. Boston: Houghton Mifflin, 1974.
    A study of religious and spiritual aspects of Washington life.
Neustadt, Richard E. *Presidential Power*. New York: Wiley, 1980.
    A reputational analysis of presidents from FDR to Carter; upgrades assessment
    of Eisenhower.
Parmet, Herbert S. *Eisenhower and the American Crusades*. New York: Macmillan,
    1972.
    One of the first revisionist views of Eisenhower as president.
Reichard, Gary W. *The Reaffirmation of Republicanism: Eisenhower and the Eighty-third
    Congress*. Knoxville: University of Tennessee Press, 1975.
    An analysis of the role of President Eisenhower in reviving Republican party
    support.
Richardson, Elmo. *The Presidency of Dwight D. Eisenhower*. Lawrence, Kans.: Regents
    Press of Kansas, 1979.
    An analysis of the Eisenhower administration which is part of a series of such
    histories.
Spitzer, Robert J. *The Presidency and Public Policy*. University, Ala.: University of
    Alabama Press, 1983.
    A study which includes analyses of Eisenhower and the public policy-making
    process.
White, Theodore, H. *In Search of History: A Personal Adventure*. New York: Harper
    and Row, 1978.
    A personal memoir which includes White's reminiscences about Eisenhower and
    why he was a major hero.

Documents

Letters of Dwight D. Eisenhower and Milton S. Eisenhower, at Center for the Study of
    the Presidency, New York, N.Y.
Letters of James C. Hagerty and Curtis P. Nettels, at Center for the Study of the Pres-
    idency, New York, N.Y.

Documentary Records, Tapes, and Videotapes

Considine, Bob, narrator. *Eisenhower—Volume I* and *Eisenhower—Volume II*. Audio
    set. Superscope, E-103, E-104, Superscope Educational Products, San Fernando,
    Calif. Produced by Caedmon Records, New York.
    Includes material on D-Day, victory in Europe, the transition from 1945 to 1952,
    the 1953 inauguration, the first Eisenhower administration, satellite insurrections,
    second campaign and inauguration, and race into space, including the 1959 Camp
    David summit.
Fleming, James, narrator. *"Mr. President"; From FDR to Eisenhower*. Record. RCA
    Victor Red Seal Records, LM 1753, 1953.
    Actualities from the Eisenhower 1952 campaign are included in material narrated
    by James Fleming, news editor of NBC's *Today* in 1953.
Lamar, Howard and Charles Blitzer, eds. *Campaign '56: Sounds of an Election Year*.
    Record. Folkways Records, FH 5505, 1961.

Actualities from the 1956 Eisenhower-Stevenson campaign. Edited by a Yale historian and political scientist and produced by Douglas R. Daniels.

Middleton, Drew, narrator. *Eisenhower: Years of Caution*. Video. Learning Corporation of America, Deerfield, Ill., LEP023.

Analysis of the Eisenhower campaigns and administrations by a *New York Times journalist*.

Voices of the Presidents. Record. EAV Lexington, Educational Audio Visual, Inc., Pleasantville, N.Y., LE 7711, 1967.

The second side of this record contains a cut from the Eisenhower First Inaugural Address in 1953.

17   JOHN F. KENNEDY

William C. Spragens

> Updike of Oxford or Harvard says "I die for England" or "I die for America"—not me. I'm too Irish for that—I may get killed for America—but I'm going to die for myself.[1]
>
> F. Scott Fitzgerald
> Letter to Mrs. Richard Taylor
> Princeton, New Jersey
> June 10, 1917

CAMELOT TWO DECADES LATER

November 22, 1983, marked the twentieth anniversary of the assassination of John F. Kennedy. Looking at the early 1960s in retrospect two decades later, the single outstanding feature of Kennedy's presidency appears to be the "Camelot Myth." This myth, which some say originated with an essay written by Theodore H. White and published in *Life* magazine after an interview by White with Jacqueline Kennedy, revolves around images of President Kennedy that grew up and developed in the wake of the Dallas tragedy. This chapter's purpose is to pierce the superficial images of the Camelot Myth to determine the underlying images of President Kennedy held by the American public and the nation's elites, including those close to Kennedy and both contemporary and recent historians, as they appear to us today.

First, popular images of JFK will be explored as they are conveyed in polling and survey data of his own era. Popular images of John F. Kennedy through polling data indicate that he maintained a high level of personal popularity, even when his programs enjoyed less popularity than he held personally.[2]

In many instances, JFK was viewed as a charismatic leader, with a personalized leadership style—appealing to his supporters across partisan lines. His style was to take a detached attitude toward critical issues. Though for his time he was ideologically left of center, his administration was generally considered as only moderately liberal, chiefly as a projection of JFK's own personality.

A second intent of this chapter is to explore popular images of JFK as presented to the public in the media. Kennedy's era saw the rise of television, and his administration was the first to permit live TV broadcasts of White House news conferences. Both Kennedy and members of his family were widely photographed; the visual image of JFK was that of a young, virile president, active and involved. Besides the visual appeal of his young children, Mrs. Kennedy was a refreshingly youthful First Lady. She conducted a television tour of the White House, advertised as the first of its kind.

A third intent of this chapter is to explore popular images of John F. Kennedy through the views of contemporaries from his own White House staff, including Arthur Schlesinger, Jr., Theodore C. Sorensen, and Pierre Salinger, as well as through the views of political scientists such as James MacGregor Burns and Richard Neustadt.

Finally, popular images of JFK as reflected in the views of revisionist writers such as Bruce Miroff, Richard Walton, and Herbert S. Parmet will be examined. In the 1960s most biographical writings were positive, in the 1970s they tended to be more highly critical, and some of those appearing in the 1980s for the first time appeared to be seeking a balance between the two views.

THE JFK CAMPAIGN ANALYZES THE AMERICAN PUBLIC

This chapter also will probe the Camelot Myth by looking at how the 1960 Kennedy presidential campaign staff assessed the American public in the management of the campaign.

While both the Kennedy and Nixon campaigns conducted a research operation, the Kennedy campaign developed a team which drew on the circle of advisers Kennedy called on as a senator—the so-called Cambridge Group—later enlarged to include broader origins of public policy advice. A media plan was established for minority media, including Spanish language and black periodicals. The Kennedy campaign of 1960 targeted ethnic appeals; $22,400 was spent for black radio spot commercials in major metropolitan areas.[3] Other targeting was directed at swing states in the election.[4]

Besides media contacts, Kennedy relied on the advice of a number of academic experts; despite the "ivory tower" reputation of academics, one finds in these documents from experts no lack of pragmatic interest in the campaign. Academic expertise was melded with practical campaign experience in one important phase of the campaign, the "Simulmatics" experiment (to be described later).[5]

The 1960 Kennedy campaign saw the American public through the eyes of public opinion analysts, but it also received many letters written with suggestions for strategy. These letters indicate a widespread response from partisans and supporters of Senator Kennedy at the same time the campaign was analyzing public opinion data. Evidence indicates how the 1960 campaign made a broad effort to reflect, as well as to lead, public opinion.

There will follow an examination of how the Kennedy administration, once elected, assessed the public reaction to itself. Source materials for this analysis include commissioned Harris polls, the *Gallup Opinion Index,* and a White House study of right-wing activities.[6]

Finally, tentative conclusions can be based on the available analysis. One is that the Kennedy campaign was reaching out to the public, particularly its core constituencies, to seek to develop new ideas and approaches. The campaign also displayed JFK as a candidate who was beginning to emerge with a flair for style, taste, and the right touch for effective interaction. Elements of this appeal were supported by survey research, widespread correspondence between the campaign and the public, and a professional campaign.

POPULAR IMAGES OF JFK IN POLLING DATA

Popular images of JFK indicated in the polling data of the 1960s reflect public perception of him as a young, virile, aggressive leader willing to tackle difficult problems. His approval rating, like President Eisenhower's, was on the whole higher than the approval ratings of recent presidents, both in his own commissioned surveys and in published surveys.

These data indicate a much higher degree of personal popularity for him than was true for many of his programs, which encountered difficulties in a Congress not yet impacted by either reapportionment or the rise of the subcommittee system. This pattern appeared to persist throughout his administration, although a source at the Democratic National Committee told the author that toward the end of his tenure, Kennedy was much concerned about his decline in popularity after the 1962 midterm elections.

While popularity fluctuations in public opinion measurements of Kennedy's approval ratings with the voting public show that he ranks slightly below Eisenhower and the early period of Franklin D. Roosevelt, JFK maintains a respectable level in comparison with all his successors.

As Paul C. Light has noted in suggesting the concept of the "no win presidency," the presidency of the 1980s is quite different from the presidency of the 1960s despite superficial similarities.[7]

Nonetheless, the average popularity rating of President Kennedy was 70 percent. One can recall that this was the pre-Watergate presidency, but when seven out of ten Americans look favorably on the president, that is a good showing. Comparisons are made difficult by the fact that the assassination in large measure probably eliminated what might have been the downside of JFK's popularity curve.

The Gallup data show that the high point for JFK was reached in April-May 1961, just after the Bay of Pigs failure, when his approval rating reached 83 percent. His low point, in September 1963, just after the civil rights March on Washington, was 56 percent. A more detailed breakdown is given in the accompanying Figure 17.1.

Files at the Kennedy Library indicated that commissioned White House surveys

Figure 17.1
Approval Ratings for John F. Kennedy

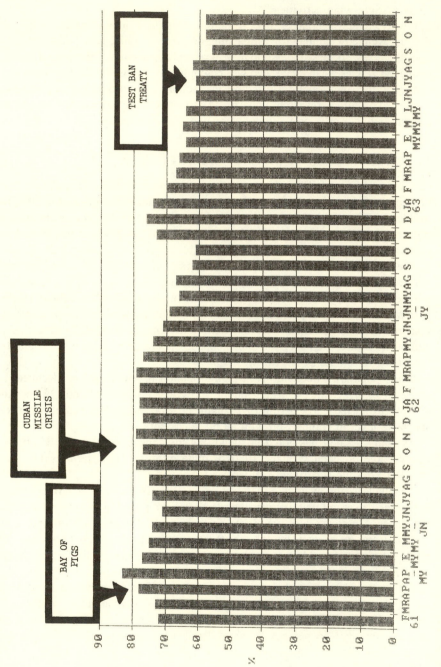

Source: Gallup Opinion Index, September–October 1980.

pinpointed traditional Democratic constituencies; findings of these surveys tended to parallel the Gallup reports.

JFK AS VIEWED BY CONTEMPORARY MAGAZINES

Popular images of JFK as presented in the news media of the time stressed his youthfulness, a leadership style that emphasized grace and poise as well as self-assurance, and other characteristics associated with a successful leader. While his opponents had derogatory things to say about him while he was in office, as in Victor Lasky's *JFK: The Man and the Myth,* most of the publicity about JFK and his family was overwhelmingly positive. Looked at in the light of the 1980s it is likely that Kennedy's positive image could not have been as strong were he an incumbent today.

A term frequently used by President Kennedy in referring to his administration's aims was "vigor." In his inaugural address JFK stressed the theme of a new generation of leadership, and he sought to approach the problems of his term in a systematic, determined way. His philosophy of leadership was an activist one, reaching out for problems to solve. He had a considerable personal involvement in the handling of issues that came to the Kennedy White House. According to staff members working in the Kennedy White House, his technique was to work with a small staff of generalists. He sought to maintain open access to his own office, especially for his principal staff people. Several members of his staff spoke of the president's personal magnetism and his ability to put people at ease.

To provide an idea of what contemporary periodicals were saying about President Kennedy from the time of the 1960 election to the assassination in 1963, some excerpts have been culled from magazine files which will give the flavor of the kind of media comments Kennedy had as president and president-elect prior to his inauguration.

Time described JFK on election night:

Before the moment of victory Jack Kennedy allowed himself to doubt that he might make it. In the final swing of the campaign, the Kennedy troupe was showing the frazzled edges of fatigue, even unaccustomed confusion. . . .

Slowly, as the Election Day sun rose off the horizon, Jack Kennedy's old cool confidence reasserted itself. . . .

In terms of the popular vote accorded Kennedy, the U.S. electorate withheld the resounding mandate that it gave Dwight Eisenhower in 1952 and 1956. But . . . he had stirred sufficient numbers of voters to take him and his New Frontier on faith. Kennedy's challenge had been accepted.[8]

TRB commented in *The New Republic* after the 1960 election:

A few days more and Republicans will convince themselves they won the election. No doubt about it, Kennedy would be in a stronger position if he had won by a 1932 landslide. He didn't, and it's worth analyzing the result.

This was a wonderfully close election, a difference of some 300,000 popular votes out of 67 million. A couple of Republicans named Hayes and Harrison back in 1876 and 1888 won the Presidency on electoral votes alone and overcame the handicap. Republicans see the situation hopefully. It will be, they say, like the 1958 Democratic victory that turned out to be a terrible dud.

How much substance is there in this? Some, we think, but not much. A huge majority seemed developing on that strange, unforgettable election night but it melted away like a snowball after 12. Now the GOP would like to discredit the new Administration entirely and argue it has no mandate at all.

This is silly. To begin with this isn't 1958. The problem then was Eisenhower's veto, requiring an unobtainable two-thirds vote in the Congress. That is gone for keeps. . . .

A point to remember, we think, is that the religious issue is deflated. The wonder is not that a Catholic was elected by a close vote, but that he was elected at all. . . .

There is one more thing. It is our estimate of Kennedy. We have hardly dared to mention it, it is so high. Maybe we are wrong, but we think you may be seeing the beginning of an important political personality. Certainly, at 43 he should be around for a good while. . . .

The friendly but businesslike press offered Kennedy every opportunity to stub his toe, every chance to fall into a pit. Reporters are not hostile, they like him, but it is their job to spread bait for the unwary. For example, did he consider the election a "repudiation" of Eisenhower? Quite skillfully and with poise and dignity Kennedy refused the bait. "Repudiation?" Certainly not that word. And he sent a tactful message to the hero-President.

What happens now to Nixon? If Republicans want to run him in 1964 as some backers hope, it will be all right by us. We still think Rockfeller could have beat Kennedy in 1960, but four years hence nobody will beat him.[9]

In an editorial titled "Who Lost the Election?" the conservative *National Review* commented:

Richard Nixon chose to fight his campaign as a practical politician, a technician. This [was] presaged by his handling of the nominating convention, and was made clearer each week of the campaign itself. The first television debate fixed the pattern: not one but half a dozen times Mr. Nixon assured Senator Kennedy, and through him the TV audience— that is, the voters—that they shared the same goals, sought the same things, differed not on ends but, in some degree, on method. This was equivalent to saying that there were no deep issues at stake, that the decision would be reached by the electorate on the basis of, 1) the voters' estimate of the candidates' personal qualifications, and 2) the candidates' respective organizational tactics and skill in exploiting the electoral process.

Whenever an issue raised a sharp point, Mr. Nixon was concerned only to blunt it. . . .

Now purely technical, practical politics is sometimes justified, even for a candidate who is himself a man of profound principle. It is the necessary aim of candidates, in elections, to get elected, and sometimes this is best assured by a careful smothering of issues for the duration. But though such a kind of practical politics is sometimes justified, it is justified by one fact only: by success. . . .

That is why Mr. Nixon's defeat, though by so minute a mathematical margin, is nevertheless total.[10]

Concerning the Kennedy inauguration, *Newsweek* stated:

When John Fitzgerald Kennedy spoke his first words as the 35th President of the United States, his mind was on all the manifold dangers of the booby-trapped world around us. The world had eagerly awaited to hear what he had to say—and statesmen nearly everywhere agreed the words had been worth waiting for.

Speaking as the new leader of 180 million Americans, and addressing himself to every human on earth, the young President gave a solemn pledge that America would "never negotiate from fear, but let us never fear to negotiate." And turning to the perils and problems that any President must confront, Mr. Kennedy said: "Let us begin anew."

Thus, he swung wide the door for negotiations to lift the ever-present danger of atomic war. And his move came none too soon. . . .

. . . Answering Khrushchev's congratulations on his inauguration, he declared himself "ready and anxious to cooperate with all who are prepared to join in genuine dedication to the assurance of a peaceful and more fruitful life for all mankind." . . .

At 10 a.m. the President received the first White House visitor: Former President Harry S Truman, who had casually mentioned the day before that he would like to see the changes since his occupancy. Tears in his eyes, Mr. Truman told an aide: "Isn't it nice of him to want to bother with an old farmer like me on his first day?"[11]

This was the *National Review's* view of the JFK inaugural:

It's clear—even now—that Kennedy's Washington will be different: vastly different from the Washington of the Eisenhower years, the Truman years or the Roosevelt years. Many of the men moving into positions of power, with Kennedy, like Kennedy, are young, from the new generation that fought the Second World War as junior, not general, officers. Democratic faithfuls and Democratic lame ducks, a handful of tame businessmen—these are included—but the tone, the coloration of the new Administration may be set by the heavy influx of intellectuals: college professors, directors of the big foundations, economists, the Left-ideologues, among them Harvard's finest—Arthur Schlesinger Jr., who helped polish (or did he write?) the Inaugural Address; John Galbraith who hopes to remold America into a society more affluently to his liking; McGeorge Bundy, and the rest. Washington will hum with big-name intellectuals, an often unstable breed that welcomes the chance to use the United States as a Social Science laboratory; able verbalizers, most of them who have popularized their notions as FDR's brain trust was never able to do.

Gone, from Kennedy's Washington, the staid businessmen and army cronies who were, more and more, Eisenhower's intimates in his final years in office; gone the political hacks, the pokerplaying, Bourbon-drinking friends of the Truman era. Jack Kennedy and his wife expect to bring more glitter to their capital city.[12]

One of the first foreign policy crises of the Kennedy administration was the Bay of Pigs invasion, which failed in Cuba in April 1961. Regarding this, *Time* wrote:

Great nations are always criticized when they appear aggressive. They are despised when they seem weak. By backing an inadequate and mismanaged invasion attempt, President

Kennedy achieved the unhappy feat of making the U.S. seem both aggressive and weak at the same time.[13]

In October 1962 came the Cuban missile crisis. Concerning this significant event, the *National Review* commented:

It goes without saying that we support every firm and positive action the President has taken, and will take, in the Cuban crisis. Mr. Kennedy was in good form when he spoke to the nation and the world last Monday evening. There was little of the overblown rhetoric that in some of his earlier declarations—on Laos, for example, or the Berlin Wall—substituted for action that never came. This time action in a vast if still unfocused scale preceded and thus gave weight to the words. His manner was restrained and serious; his explanations were straightforward.

An act that was so long overdue, and the President's initiation of the selective sea-air blockade brought a response that must have surprised Chester Bowles and Adlai Stevenson: this symptom of firmness *in action* at once won enthusiastic support from virtually all Latin America—Yankee-baiting Mexico and Brazil included—support or acceptance from our allies and near-allies, and from nearly every citizen except the pacifists, cranks and collaborators.

We must be united, then, in strength for the action ahead. But it would be no service to the nation if all questions concerning the past and future conduct of our Cuban policy were now to be dissolved in a misty feeling of "national unity".

1) The abruptness of the President's turn is both puzzling and disturbing. A few weeks ago he assured us that Cuba "does not constitute a threat to any other part of this Hemisphere," and less than a fortnight before imposing the blockage he bitterly denounced Senator [Homer E.] Capehart, who has been demanding action on Cuba, as one of the "self-appointed generals and admirals who want to send someone else's sons to war" (a phrase that Mr. Kennedy must now find bitter on his tongue). What could have changed him so completely so quickly? . . .

2) Many of those who have been criticizing the President's post-Bay of Pigs lethargy on Cuba view his present steps as "too little"; and this is of course true at this point. But it is obvious that the President cannot stop here even if he would, though we do not know how far ahead he sees the road. The present inadequacy is both military and political. It is hard to grasp just how this selective blockade, or quarantine, limited to "offensive arms", can be carried out even from a narrowly technical standpoint. . . .

3) It is even more persuasively argued that the present action is "too late". It is indeed too late to avoid the dangerous action that we now confront. But it is not too late for victory.[14]

In *The New Republic,* which was editorially more dubious of the president's action, columnist TRB wrote:

Khrushchev tried a power grab in Cuba and America clapped him down. As this is written, the great event is still developing but, so far, Khrushchev's reaction to Kennedy has been nothing worse than noise and bluster.

Is this explanation too pat and simple? Maybe. But after one of our grimmest weeks in Washington the simple explanation seems to fit the facts better than infinitely more ingenious and cynical theories which are flooding the capital like Los Angeles smog.

After repeatedly hearing President Kennedy (at press conferences), and State Department officials (at off-the-record briefings), insist that minute study of the Soviet buildup in Cuba convinced them it was "defensive," this reporter reached the conclusion that the officials might be wrong but that they were sincere. They showed a startling familiarity with what was going on in and around Cuba. The Administration refrained from interference at some political cost although (again using a personal judgment) Cuba did not seem to be a very threatening issue during a dull and apathetic midterm election.

Then one Tuesday morning (October 16) the President got new information. It was like a physician discovering malignancy under his microscope. The evidence was not conclusive; Kennedy made—and cut short—his Chicago political trip. New pictures showed a startling speed of development. Russians like Gromyko assured Kennedy there were no offensive nuclear installations. U.S. aerial cameras—which can spot a golf ball on a putting green—showed something else. Some flashed by at 500 feet and came back with pictures that convinced the technicians. Suddenly erected installations were in an advanced state of completion.

This was a power grab in the international crisis game. At the rate the sites were growing, Washington appeared to have only a week or two to react. Unless checked it seemed that Moscow would nearly double its nuclear striking capability against the U.S.A. and would shake up the whole balance of power, perhaps knocking over a chessman or two. Operating within an area so fuzzy that nobody can strictly define "offensive weapon", "quarantine" or even "war" anymore, Kennedy launched his own melodrama. As by-products he produced a stock-market commotion and a gratifying unanimity of support from Latin American OAS countries; he also knocked an election off the front page in its final weeks and produced ulcers in 998 reporters on the Washington scene. . . .

There was a memorable little scene two hours before Kennedy spoke. He came out onto the driveway of the west wing to say goodbye in person to Uganda's intelligent, coal-black young premier. Cameramen and newshawks drooled for information; Kennedy seemed absolutely unflustered and unconcerned. He smiled to his guest with courteous dignity and saw him into his beflagged Cadillac; then he turned, smiled aloofly (but pleasantly) at the unhappy press, and moved swiftly back through the doorway—immaculately dressed, brown-haired, quietly reserved. A *very* tough young man.[15]

A major highlight in the Kennedy administration occurred in June 1963, when the president made major addresses on civil rights and the test ban treaty, as reported in *Newsweek:*

As a senator seeking the Presidency, John F. Kennedy said in 1960: "The White House is not only the center of political leadership, it must be the center of moral leadership—a 'bully pulpit' as Theodore Roosevelt described it." For a long time, many Americans have wondered when President Kennedy would demonstrate what Teddy Roosevelt had in mind.

In two remarkable, historic speeches last week, Mr. Kennedy stepped into the bully pulpit to speak out on two overriding issues. One speech was the most forthright appeal any President has made for coexistence in the world power struggle. The other was an unprecedented plea for a basic change in American society itself.

On the world scene, the President urged that the outworn rhetoric of the cold war be abandoned and a fresh start be made in the dialogue on "the most important topic on earth: world peace." As a beginning, he announced the U.S. would suspend nuclear testing in the atmosphere and, with the British, would undertake new high-level test-ban negotiations in Moscow. . . .

The address, at American University's commencement in Washington, was notable for its confidence, magnanimity, and lack of cant. It was greeted enthusiastically abroad and printed in full in Moscow papers.

"Let us not be blind to our differences," said the President, "but let us also direct attention to our common interests and the means by which those differences can be resolved. . . . For us to seek a relaxing of tensions without relaxing our guard, confident and unafraid, we labor on—not toward a strategy of annihilation but toward a strategy of peace." When he said that "no government or social system is so evil that its people must be considered as lacking in virtue," President Kennedy seemed to be taking a cue from Pope John XXIII's "Pacem in Terris". As one observer put it: "Pope John opened the door, and Kennedy stepped through."

The next evening, the President went before the television cameras to deal with the nation's worsening racial situation. Long awaited and much postponed as it was, the speech rose eloquently to the challenge. Mr. Kennedy threw the full weight of his prestige and power behind the Negro's struggle for equality of opportunity. He made his case not merely in terms of obedience to the law, or maintenance of civil peace, but as a matter of human principle in meeting "a moral crisis."[16]

Newsweek questioned whether the timing of the JFK civil rights speech was soon enough, and added:

The President counseled that law alone was not the answer. The issue, he said, was moral—not only for national policy but in the personal conduct of every American. . . .

Toward the end, he . . . ad-libbed the last four minutes. The right to equal opportunity, he said, was what had made America one country. "We cannot say to 10 percent of the population that 'you can't have that right. Your children can't have the chance to develop whatever talents they have, that the only way that they're going to get their rights is to go in the street and demonstrate.' "

"I think we owe them—and we owe ourselves—a better country than that."[17]

Within months of those two major policy speeches of the summer of 1963, the voice that delivered them was permanently stilled. The tragedy of Dallas left the country in shock, as can be seen from published comments after the assassination. First, this one from the *National Review*, under the heading "R.I.P.":

In the Middle Ages, before men turned introspective from brooding on Copernican astronomy, tragedy was straightforwardly defined as "a fall from high to low estate". The tragic essence, that is to say, was felt to lie, not in the soul and character of the protagonist, as came to be the post-Hamlet intuition, but in the structure of the world and the universe. The fall of the great ones of the earth—all the more when sudden and seemingly arbitrary—showed men how ephemeral are the triumphs—or defeats—in this valley of the shadows, how little the weight of even the mightiest in the hand of nature and nature's God. . . .

The editors of *National Review* judged John Fitzgerald Kennedy to be a consummate politician of mass politics. His programs and policies—often chosen, by the evidence, in opportunistic furtherance of technical manipulations—we judged to be, for the most part, dangerous to the nation's well-being and security, and to the survival of our perilously threatened Western civilization. Neither his death nor the fearful manner of it provides any reason to change these judgments. At the same time they do not in any way lessen the sharpness with which we have shared the nearly universal sense of ineluctable tragedy beyond the dimension of individual men.[18]

From a different viewpoint, *The New Republic* said:

It comes over us now how seldom, these past three years, we admitted to ourselves how heavily our hopes were riding on one man. This journal was a devoted critic of John F. Kennedy. It spoke for his nomination as the Democratic candidate in 1960, admired his restraint, respected his intellect, regretted the evasions and hesitations that political realities seemed to command, and hoped for his re-election and a new Congress more hospitable to his program. . . .

. . . The few on whom the burden of tragedy was heaviest never for one moment faltered. Nothing became the Kennedy Administration more than the dignity of its last weekend.[19]

THE NEW FRONTIER LEADERSHIP STYLE

JFK approached both foreign and domestic policy issues with which he had to deal in an activist style. This was noticeable in his handling of the 1961 crisis in West Berlin, and again in his handling of the Cuban missile crisis of 1962. Even in the case of the abortive invasion of the Bay of Pigs, Kennedy reacted to the failure of this military action by launching a detailed investigation into what went wrong.[20]

On the domestic front between 1961 and 1963, his major policy initiative included two important moves—one to deal with aid to economically depressed areas, another to deal with the rising civil rights movement. Here again, his was an activist approach in which he dealt with unemployment and other difficult problems in "pockets of poverty" with a specific program. The coal miner in West Virginia with a picture of JFK on the wall (sometimes alongside a picture of FDR) is a familiar image which grew out of Kennedy's interest in depressed areas legislation. On the civil rights issue, Kennedy sought to balance the slowly awakening response of the nation at large with pressures from the freedom movement in the South. Because of his narrow mandate in 1960 and the pivotal character of southern support in the Congress, he first proceeded cautiously, but it could be argued that he sought to step up his response as events such as the Birmingham riots and the Ole Miss crisis heightened public awareness. Unlike his younger brother Robert, who moved to respond to more urgent pressures in his 1968 presidential candidacy, JFK sought to proceed cautiously to prevent the issue from being divisive within the party. He apparently was always weighing what he considered to be the necessity for civil rights action against the need for adopting other programs. He apparently believed that the difficulty of achieving passage of the rest of his program could be exacerbated if civil rights advances were made so rapidly as to alienate southern and moderate supporters within Congress.[21]

Kennedy has been described by Arthur Schlesinger, Jr., as a chief executive of great magnetism.[22] Other staff aides have described him as a man possessing the kind of leadership skills that facilitated good interpersonal working relationships.[23] Although by current standards his staff was relatively small, President Kennedy managed to maintain a high degree of esprit de corps and supportive morale. Contemporary historians who observed him at close hand gave him high marks for leadership, as exemplified in accounts of the Cuban missile crisis and the civil rights turmoil of the 1960s. He was seen by some as a strong leader in his dealings with the Soviet Union, especially after the missile crisis. Even the action he took did not satisfy hard-line critics.[24] These observers, recalling the Bay of Pigs and early events of the Kennedy administration, including erection of the Berlin Wall and the Vienna summit, felt that his leadership was not strong enough. Later in this chapter, we will review the leadership image of JFK as perceived by more adulatory writers of the 1960s, particularly members of his own staff; some revisionist historians of the 1970s who showed the impact of the anti-Vietnam feeling of that period; and some of the 1980s historians now seeking to balance positive and critical comments in an effort to achieve greater equilibrium.

THE 1960 KENNEDY CAMPAIGN FOR THE WHITE HOUSE

A crucial factor in determining the public images of John F. Kennedy was the 1960 campaign. It is possible two decades later to observe underlying trends reflected in that campaign.

One of those trends was that a generation born in the twentieth century was coming to power and that it had different ideas than its predecessors about priorities and about how the country should be run. While Kennedy was essentially a political moderate, he felt that more should be done for the deprived and underprivileged, and he also felt that more should be done to protect freedom around the world. He did not look at the latter issue through the prism of disillusionment that came to surround Vietnam because that whole experience had not yet colored American thinking about foreign policy.

The Kennedy team sought to move away from some of the emphases of President Eisenhower. Kennedy and his supporters felt that while some of Eisenhower's goals might be worthy ones, JFK's immediate predecessor lacked a sense of urgency about doing more for the poor and about defense. This author's opinion is that Kennedy made a better record in implementing a policy of humaneness on domestic issues than in exploiting American impulses of spreading democratic ideals throughout the world (despite the Peace Corps, Alliance for Progress, and other initiatives). But this insight is gained with the passage of two decades of history, and it must be acknowledged that he commanded sufficient public support for his policies to win an election. How did he do it?

Because Kennedy had to attract the attention of his party constituency over the opposition of established leaders who frankly viewed him as something of a young upstart, he had to stake out positions that were advanced—but not too advanced. He had to be a centrist liberal. No Democrat in 1960 could win the party's nomination without being at least a moderate liberal, but neither could any Democrat in 1960 win an election by scaring an essentially moderately conservative electorate. So Kennedy had to follow a moderate liberal line—apparently in accord with his own cast of thought.

Thus, we get a picture of a young senator awakening the American public from a kind of complacency which some people associated with the Eisenhower years—granting that the Eisenhower administration gave the American people a much-desired opportunity for consolidation and the restoration of some conservative values. Kennedy felt that the status quo was not enough, and that in order to preserve the best in American democracy, some advanced positions must be taken. But he sought to move with the times.

Since no one can win an American presidential election without a supporting coalition of established interests or without forging a new coalition to replace it, Kennedy in the real world of politics had to look for hard support from existing interests in the political arena.

Despite his obvious appeal to America's youth, which helped give ''Camelot'' an idealistic cast, as symbolized by the Peace Corps and other programs, JFK had to turn to more established power brokers.

As a graduate student in East Lansing, the author heard JFK appeal to American youth to support the concept of a volunteer service organization to go overseas on invitation, but on the same platform with Kennedy when he made this appeal were Senator Pat McNamara of Michigan, a member of the Plumbers and Pipefitters Union of the AFL-CIO and a typical old-style Democrat, as well as Governor G. Mennen (Soapy) Williams, the multiterm governor of Michigan who had a loyal and devoted progressive following.

One could suggest that Kennedy sought to shape the issues that helped develop his public image along class-based, ethnic, and occupational lines. Let's examine them.

JFK had to mobilize lower-middle-class support and the support of poor people while retaining a smattering of upper-middle-class support from noblesse oblige–oriented privileged groups. This he could do best with a moderate liberal program.

The depressed areas initiative that sought to alleviate poverty in Appalachia was one part of this thrust. Some of the drive for alleviating urban poverty was supplied by Lyndon Johnson, but JFK had read Michael Harrington's book, *The*

Other America, which had an activist orientation. He also had visited West Virginia coal mines and midwestern farms during the primary campaigns. While he did not gather the same degree of support in the traditionally Republican Midwest as in New England, Kennedy did gain some support there, and he gained much gratitude for his help to the deprived areas of Appalachia, which came to symbolize the deprived of America.

For JFK, the 1960 campaign was more than simply dealing with calculations of delegates and the like. While those were important, the campaign itself was an important learning experience. JFK turned forty-three in May of the primary season. Remember also that the primary season focused on fewer states then than it did more than twenty years later. Even though seasoned reporters would start to pack their typewriters when Kennedy reached that standard part of his speech in which he said "give me your hearts, your votes, your hands," it never failed to stir enthusiastic audiences impressed by his youth and his *caring* attitude. He was influenced by the tradition of Roosevelt and Truman, but also here was a young senator who had dedicated his life to public service when he could have been idling away his time. So the attacks and cynicisms of twenty years and more must be stripped away to grasp how the American public—at least American progressives looking for an answer—interacted with JFK in that year. But since Adlai Stevenson, the 1956 Democratic nominee, had been a favorite of liberals, it was still an uphill climb for JFK. So he sought the support of the longtime progressives, but he also sought the support of blue-collar America—a bigger slice of the electorate then than now.

A marked section of blue-collar America was ethnic in nature. Today we would think of this voting bloc as "older ethnics" in that established ethnic groups such as those of Eastern and Southern European extraction would be included. But JFK also had to seek the support of black Americans and other ethnics such as Hispanics in newly emerging groups. The black people never gave Kennedy full support in his lifetime, for the most part, because there was a wide cultural gap. Also, there had been suspicions about Kennedy not only among blacks but among other liberals as well, including Jewish voters, partly because of the well-known conservatism of JFK's father, Ambassador Joseph P. Kennedy, on many social issues. The same rapport that was extended later to Robert and Ted Kennedy by black voters was not given quite so freely to JFK. And yet, what he was doing was similar to, if less spectacular than, what RFK attempted to do in 1968. JFK sought to get across the common denominator that united blacks, Irish-Americans, and the other ethnics—that they had gone through deprivation and struggle in an effort to find a place in the United States, and that this struggle was far from over. So the ethnics were a major target, and it is clear that he could not have won without them. They were no longer quite so heavily Catholic, but this was another point of identity with some of them that JFK could establish.

And while JFK appealed to the youth, to the deprived, and to the ethnic voters, he had to base yet another appeal on essentially occupational lines. Store clerks, intellectuals, both blue-collar and white-collar voters who sought more attention from Washington, appeared to be his natural constituency. In seeking their support, he also tried to retain what he could of the southern base of the Democratic party. The choice of Lyndon Johnson as his running mate indicated this. The authors of *The American Voter* speak of "the collective memory," and it was to this that Kennedy appealed.

One final matter should be discussed in relation to JFK's campaign image: his Catholicism. He felt that Al Smith, who was defeated partly because of this identity in 1928, did not deal with it properly. A whispering campaign about Kennedy's religion could best be dealt with by making the issue highly visible. In the opinion of most observers, JFK acquitted himself well in the confrontation and debate before the Houston Ministerial Association. He may not have won a lot of converts from the Nixon side in the campaign, but he established a right to have American voters consider his merits on the basis of fairness and common decency. So it was not surprising that in his own time he was a target of the political right despite his Catholicism.

It is hard to recall today that before JFK broke the barrier of religious prejudice, no Catholic had ever served in the White House. Even today no Jew has been elected, nor has a woman. And, of course, inevitably some nervous individuals in his own campaign wished that Kennedy would say less about his religion. Kennedy put it this way: he was the nominee of the Democratic party who happened to be a Catholic. He was not "the Catholic candidate for president." While his Catholicism is believed to have hurt him and to have held down his margin in the election, he cannot be blamed in retrospect for airing his appeal to the fairness of the American voters.

Having constructed this base for coalition support, how did JFK identify it? He had the assistance of the Simulmatics Corporation, itself an interesting and important phenomenon. Ithiel de Sola Pool and his colleagues at the Massachusetts Institute of Technology (MIT) developed the project and worked on it under the direction of Robert Kennedy, his brother's campaign director. Their relationship with RFK was a consulting one; they set up a computer program which synthesized a demographic cross-section of some 1,600 American voters. The survey analysts then extrapolated from the data concerning past political behavior of this voter sample how voters with such characteristics were likely to react to campaign issues. RFK and the strategists took this into account and decided that they would devise appeals to the profiled voters in some cases. In other cases, they did not, but they always had the benefit of knowing what the likely response would be.

Simulmatics was used in the campaign of Senator Barry Goldwater in 1964 and proved effective in helping Goldwater gain the Republican nomination. It opened the door to the later direct-mail solicitations of campaign support, such as that devised by Morris Dees for George McGovern in 1972 and by Richard Viguerie for Ronald Reagan in 1980.

With Simulmatics put into historical context, let's examine excerpts from a series of the Simulmatics reports as they appear in the files of the John F. Kennedy Presidential Library in Boston.

A memo explains the functioning of the project: It made use of (1) computer technology; (2) a process known as simulation; (3) a survey bank with a great variety of polling data and historical voting data, which could procure answers to salient questions within twenty-four hours and through use of sampling procedures made possible the analysis of small but typical segments of the electorate; and (4) objective, creative judgment.[25]

Simulmatics Report No. 1, dated May 15, 1960, was titled "Negro Voters in Northern Cities":

1. In the campaign ahead the Negro vote will be of great strategic importance.

Over 5 million Negroes live in the Northern portion of the United States, most of them in the largest cities.

They are concentrated in States having a high percentage of electoral votes. In eight Northern states sharing a total of 210 electoral votes, non-whites comprise over 6 percent of the population. These are:

State	Electoral Votes
New York	45
Pennsylvania	32
California	32
Illinois	27
Ohio	25
Michigan	20
New Jersey	16
Missouri	13
	210

269 votes constitute a majority in the Electoral College. The above eight states fall short of this majority by only 59 votes.

2. In the past the Northern Negro vote has been a great reservoir of Democratic strength. We entered the Eisenhower era with this vote three to one Democratic.

3. In the elections of 1956 and 1958 a small but significant shift to the Republicans occurred among Northern Negroes which cost the Democrats about one percent of the total vote in the eight key states listed above.

a) In those years the Democratic Party loss to the Republican Party was about 7 percent of the Northern Negro vote—enough to cause a 1/2 percent loss in the *total* popular vote in the eight key states.

b) In addition, among Northern Negro independents only about 1/4 actually voted Republican in 1952 but about 1/2 voted Republican in 1956—enough of a shift to cause an additional loss of a little less than 1/2 percent in the total popular vote in the eight key states.

4. The shift against the Democrats is somewhat more marked among the opinion-leading middle class Negroes than among lower income Negroes.

5. The most important single issue to Northern Negroes is civil rights. They are also

concerned with liberal social and economic policies. For example, both middle class and working class Negroes are more pro-labor than comparable groups of Northern urban whites.

6. Anti-Catholicism is less prevalent among Negroes than among Northern urban Protestant whites.

7. *The most significant point of all is the fact that the shift is not an "Ike" shift: it is a Republican Party shift.*

It affects Congressional votes as much as Presidential votes.

Those Negroes who defected to the Republicans will *not* swing back just because "Ike" is out of the picture. They will return to the Democratic fold *only* when the Democrats present them with an image of the Party that will restore their confidence in its being the party that best serves their interests.

8. There is no sharp difference between Negroes and comparable whites in their feelings about Nixon. At this point both groups see him neither as hero nor as villain exclusively.

The crucial question is whether the erosion of Democratic strength among Northern Negroes will continue up to November. The recent trend is clear, but frequent polls are needed to keep check on its course and development.

This trend, because it is fundamentally determined by party-image and is not just a reflection of Eisenhower's personal popularity, may be expected to continue unless the Democratic Party, through its leaders, its convention and its candidate, is able to create a counter-image of itself as the party which best serves Negro interests and aspirations.[26]

Simulmatics Report No. 2, dated August 25, 1960, was titled "Kennedy Before Labor Day" and was based on a sample of 1,817 voters interviewed August 13–18. It found that Kennedy's personal image was somewhat more favorable than Nixon's, that people regarded him as "more friendly" than Nixon. It also found the following: Neither Kennedy nor Nixon had the image of a hero. Nixon, not Kennedy, had more popularity with women voters; Kennedy was more popular among men. Although personality would not be a decisive influence, Kennedy *could* be hurt if his campaign style did not capitalize on his personal assets. *The key determinants of voting behavior at the time of the survey were religion, party, and foreign affairs.* The religious issue could be turned to Kennedy's greater advantage. The party issue was JFK's greatest source of strength, foreign affairs his greatest weakness. Despite Kennedy's Catholicism, *Republican Catholics were staying Republican. Should Kennedy make an issue of anti-Catholicism and religious prejudice, he would lose some reluctant Protestant votes but he would gain more Catholic votes in the exchange. It was axiomatic that Kennedy gained votes as partisan feeling in the country increased.* Kennedy had not yet mobilized his supporters, and indecision and hesitation were more frequent among Democrats than Republicans. Domestic issues were not stirring voters; Kennedy was *not* doing very well among Negroes, better among farmers, and quite well among Jews, though they were unenthusiastic. Kennedy was weak by historic standards in both the South and the border states. A Kennedy campaign stressing bread-and-butter issues and aggressively, partisanly identifying Nixon with the Republican party at every opportunity would improve his chances in that he would halt potential defections and minimize the strong points in Nixon's image. Kennedy's weakness was offset by the fact that 23 percent of voters were still undecided pending further campaign developments.[27]

To put the Simulmatics reports into context, the voting literature shows that Republicans are more dependable voters (partly because of higher socioeconomic status). Also, the recent swing vote embracing shifters is important. The chief difference between the Kennedy and Reagan eras seems to be not that the swing voters have lost importance, but that many of them have moved to the Republican-tending Sun Belt. The rising level of affluence has tended to make more voters "have" voters who look with a more kindly eye on the Republican party.

Besides the scientifically documented voter surveys, discussed in some detail, some features of the 1960 campaign gave it a special flavor. Newspaper correspondents noted, for example, the phenomenon of the "jumpers" in the campaign—the women in campaign audiences who would jump as high as they could to get a glimpse of JFK's motorcade. This phenomenon was commented on widely then and afterward. Because of this it is surprising to find in the Simulmatics reports that Nixon outpaced Kennedy in support from women.

There also was a kind of Hollywood glamour aura over the campaign. The senator's father was quoted as suggesting that some of this grew out of the family's celebrity status. The elder Kennedy was a bank president at age twenty-five and had been U.S. ambassador to London. The senator's eldest brother, Joe, had been lost at sea on a daring drone-bomber mission over the English Channel aimed at Nazi buzz-bomb sites. The senator himself as a young naval officer had been a survivor of the ramming of his tiny torpedo boat, PT-109.

Another significant aspect of the image-building was a legacy from the 1952 and 1956 Adlai Stevenson campaigns. Stevenson had a following among intellectuals and the literary set. Out of this following grew a loose collection of volunteer speechwriters and researchers who came to be known as the New York Writers Group. This group operated as a research team and compiled drafts of material growing out of political research. These would often be fragmentary drafts laying out a position on an issue. The chief coordinator was Harvard law professor Archibald Cox (later a prominent figure in the "Saturday Night Massacre" of October 1973), whose job was to channel suggestions for speeches to Theodore C. Sorensen, JFK's principal speechwriter.[28]

The chief effect of the New York Writers Group on JFK's image apparently was that it kept him in close touch with the public and the issues and it gave him the image of one who had knowledge in depth on current issues. Also, JFK, who had taken a speed-reading course as a senator, had been a voracious newspaper reader, and for a short time had been a journalist himself. He thus sought, through his own extensive reading and the work of his staff, to keep in touch with political developments and to assess the public pulse.

Letters to the candidate were scanned for ideas, Kennedy himself seeing many of them. In addition, the candidate held strategy sessions with his brother Robert. The primary campaign was a learning experience regarding the state of public opinion, and he continued the effort to keep in touch with trends of public thinking during the fall campaign.

Kennedy also got advice from seasoned campaign counselors, including his father, and all this added to his image as a responsive, caring candidate who was seeking the best solutions to the American people's problems.

Kennedy's interaction with his potential followers in 1960 followed the axiom of James MacGregor Burns: "Leadership, unlike naked power wielding, is . . . inseparable from followers' needs and goals."[29]

BEGINNING OF CAMELOT: JFK AS PRESIDENT (1961–1963)

An understanding of how John F. Kennedy became president, what concerned him, and what his purposes were is essential to an understanding of what the Kennedy administration represented and the images it projected.

Kennedy, as president, for the most part continued his rapport with the news media. There were episodes such as the effort to have the *New York Times* reassign Saigon correspondent David Halberstam, who was filing negative reports about the war in Vietnam, and the petulant order to the White House staff to discontinue the president's subscriptions to the *New York Herald-Tribune*. But these were exceptions. Pierre Salinger, ABC News Paris bureau chief and former press secretary to JFK, told the author that if President Kennedy had had the time, he could have been his own press secretary.[30] Not only was JFK a former journalist, but he knew many people in the Washington press corps from his own years of service in the Congress, and he had a natural interest in the work of journalists. While he sometimes risked the wrath of journalists by giving exclusive interviews to their competitors, there were enough of these interviews to allow newspaper correspondents who lost a beat to feel that there were other opportunities to get the ear of the president and to get interviews of their own.

What is sometimes lost sight of in the relationship between presidents and the news media is that the communications process is a two-way business. While presidents channel their views and interpretations of major events of the day to the public through correspondents, they learn from correspondents how the latter view the state of public thinking. This is invaluable to any president, and there is evidence that JFK understood the importance of this kind of information.

Kennedy also pioneered some new forms of traveling appearances. Although the tours may not have been as orchestrated as those later taken by Richard Nixon or the "town meetings" of Jimmy Carter, Kennedy understood the need to "get out to the public," and he did this whenever possible. Jet transportation was just coming into its own at this time, and he used Air Force One for this purpose.

Although the late Peter Lisagor, an old-line correspondent, described them as too theatrical,[31] JFK's set-piece news conferences—usually held in the State Department auditorium—were quite effective as a means of communicating with the public. A former congressman told the author that it was common for Capitol Hill legislators either to view the televised news conferences or to look in on them with special passes. It should be remembered that no president prior to President Kennedy had ever gone live on camera, so there was a good deal of novelty to the whole procedure as well as a feeling that this was the kind of activity at which the president excelled.

It has become a commonplace for briefings to occur prior to such news conferences. Kennedy was not the first president to have systematic briefings—Eisenhower did it too—but he seemed to have a flair for public relations, and this was reflected in his conduct.

Public reaction to President Kennedy, as is true of each president, was mixed. He seemed more controversial then some but less controversial than others. It could be argued that presidents bringing gradual, incremental change have roiled the waters much less than presidents who sought major changes. By this measurement, Kennedy was less of an innovator than either FDR or Ronald Reagan, but he was not a status quo president.

Admirers of President Kennedy most obviously included members of the coalition that helped elect him. Toward the end of his administration he seemed to be developing better rapport with blacks and other minority groups, who gradually came to feel that he was a friend. He drew support from most of the voting blocs that had been active in the Democratic party, and yet his coalition differed somewhat from that of Franklin D. Roosevelt, even as FDR's coalition had differed from that of Woodrow Wilson.

Detractors and critics of President Kennedy, in the sense of those who gave more serious than friendly criticism, included such writers as Victor Lasky, author of *JFK—The Man and the Myth*. This group also included members of right-wing organizations as well as less rigid conservatives who opposed organized labor and some of JFK's other allies. There were critics from among fundamentalist religious organizations, allies of the far right who were concerned about JFK's Catholicism.

However, distinctions can be made between popular criticism and adulation of JFK and support by elite groups. The electorate of the 1960s was perhaps somewhat less sophisticated than the modern electorate, although more so than those of earlier years.

The living JFK was seen by his contemporaries as a very human president with both shortcomings and achievements. Certain policies and program initiatives, as well as certain international crises, came to be identified symbolically with him. In view of the doubts of minorities about JFK during the 1960 campaign, he ironically became identified—partly through the force of events in places such as Birmingham, Alabama, and Oxford, Mississippi—with movements in the field of civil rights. A weak bill had been sent to Congress before the Birmingham riots, and JFK immediately sought stiffer action, as noted in the discussion above of his June 1963 civil rights speech. One must remember that many of JFK's other initiatives depended on the support of southern congressmen in his own party, and JFK was obliged to weigh carefully one legislative goal against another. In addition to this, the conservative coalition had considerable influence in Congress.

President Kennedy also was identified with the tax cut bill. The inflation rate was 3 to 4 percent, and the administartion felt that a tax cut was needed to stimulate and revitalize the economy. In a widely noted 1962 commencement address at Yale University, the president sought to explain in lay terms the need for his economic program—an approach later viewed as "jawboning."

He also had a symbolic confrontation with the business community when he used a public relations campaign to bring about a rollback in steel prices after U.S. Steel board chairman Roger Blough had announced a major price increase in the spring of 1962.

Some beginning was made in the field of regulatory reform, to work toward making federal regulatory agencies, including the Federal Communications Commission, Interstate Commerce Commission, Federal Reserve Board, and others more responsive toward the needs of consumers.

In foreign policy, JFK was associated with the establishment of the Peace Corps as a volunteer agency for overseas service in a follow-up on a campaign pledge made in 1960 at the University of Michigan. JFK was also identified with the space program. His diplomacy contributed to the treaty banning the atmospheric testing of nuclear weapons, and he was closely identified with the crises over the building of the Berlin Wall and the 1962 Soviet efforts to install offensive missiles in Cuba.

It is difficult to recreate the public mood toward JFK that existed in the pre-Dallas period of 1963. The glamour aura of the campaign remained, but he also was a typical leader reflecting the Cold War experiences of his early political career. His Vienna summit with Khrushchev in 1961 brought about gloomy political pronouncements. After the Cuban missile crisis, both the West and the Soviet bloc cooperated toward the test ban treaty. Some critics feel that JFK's preoccupation with European and Caribbean matters allowed things to go from bad to worse in Vietnam; JFK obviously shares the blame for Vietnam with presidents from Truman through Ford.

CONTEMPORARY VIEWS OF KENNEDY

The journalist Joe McCarthy, in a campaign biography of JFK written while Kennedy was still a senator, observed:

Trying to pin down the quality in Jack Kennedy that makes him seem so different from other Irish American politicians, William V. Shannon, political columnist of the ultra-liberal New York *Post,* and no great advocate of the senator, has decided that Kennedy's career, supported as it is by family wealth and family prestige, follows more of a British upper-class parliament member's pattern than that of an American Democrat. Kennedy's return to run for office in 1946 in the Boston area congressional district of his family ancestors reminds Shannon of the Oxford-educated scion of English nobility who leaves his London club life to try for the House of Commons from a remote constituency in Yorkshire where his name is well known but where he, himself, is a stranger. . . . [32]

. . . Few Washington leaders work as intensively at their politics as he does; in the past four years, he has taken only one vacation that lasted for two consecutive weeks. One day before his spinal injury's pain was eased by operations and a series of novocaine injections, Jack made his way on crutches to Cleveland to speak at a luncheon, hurried back to Washington in the afternoon to vote on a bill in the Senate and flew to Cleveland again in the evening to appear at a political dinner. [33]

One of the major domestic policy crises of JFK's term is described by con-temporaries. Roy Hoopes, a magazine journalist, commented of JFK's contest with the steel industry in the pricing controversy of 1962:

The President continues to maintain that he would not have reacted to the steel price increase in the way he did if his leadership had not been challenged. "The steel situation won't happen again," he has said. "That was a personal thing."
  And this is the essence of the steel crisis. The most serious miscalculation on the part of U.S. Steel was a simple one and one that big business is often guilty of making: Roger Blough and his executives seemed to overlook the obvious fact that the President of the United States is still a human being, and no human being enjoys a public affront. "U.S. Steel picked the wrong President to double-cross," said one White House aide. But to paraphrase Roger Blough's comment about the right time to raise prices, one can only ask: Who is the right President of the United States to double-cross? From George Washington to Dwight Eisenhower, any President would have reacted pretty much the same as Kennedy—although some with more vigor than others. . . . Despite all the howling about the "demagogic tactics" displayed by the White House during the steel crisis, the President's reaction was a very human one, and it was not the first time—and it will probably not be the last—that our giant corporations have demonstrated their inability to understand human emotions. [34]

Concerning the steel pricing crisis, Grant McConnell said:

Power is not solely a grant of authority under a constitutional provision. It is also a capacity for action which rests upon intangibles of previous history, public confidence, and prestige. These elements of power are fundamental to the modern Presidency. If they are weak, the Presidency is diminished and the republic is endangered.
  The affair of steel in 1962 poses this problem. The hasty judgement of some who were themselves involved in that affair and of others who only noted the tenor of the language of the presidential response was that the President wielded a gross excess of power. This judgement was correct only in that it touched on the central issue, power. Otherwise it was mistaken. The President did oppose the price increase announced by United States Steel, and the price increase was rescinded. The sequence, however, did not represent cause and effect. For this one time at least, the frequent contention of steel-industry leaders that strong competitive market forces were at work in the industry was correct. These forces were much more important in bringing about abandonment of the price increase than the actions of the President. Those actions showed weakness, not power.

On the large issue, the affair was ominous. Whatever the intentions of Mr. Blough and his associates in United States Steel, the announcement of the price increase amounted to a direct challenge of the Presidency. If the action by Big Steel had been successful, the power of the Presidency could only have been diminished. The ultimate results of such success are unfathomable, but it is not unthinkable that they would have been felt in Europe and in the Caribbean. If United States Steel should not have placed the President in such a situation, perhaps the President should not have made himself open to such a challenge. The danger implicit in such a bargain as was attempted, an exchange of support in achieving a labor settlement in return for price stability, was that its terms would not be kept and that the government would be left without recourse. In the event, the danger became reality. President Kennedy gave a virtuoso performance of simulating action and the situation was successfully disguised. Perhaps his greatest achievement lay in holding the diverse elements of his administration together and creating a facade of unity in government. This required intense effort and much skill, but it could not have continued for long. Events rescued the President. Nevertheless, the administration's venture came perilously close to an exposure of impotence.[35]

In a 1962 magazine article, Joseph Kraft, the columnist, wrote of the Kennedy White House:

Nine months before he entered the White House, John F. Kennedy said that as President he would want to be "in the thick of things." It is the supreme achievement of the White House staff that it has helped keep the President—perhaps more than any of his recent predecessors—right there. From the Cuban invasion to the Cuba quarantine, from the steel case to the refusal to go for a tax cut last July, every major decision has been made by the President. At times, as in the case of James Meredith and the University of Mississippi, the White House has been transformed into a command post, issuing detailed orders direct to the field. When the Medicare proposal was up before the Senate, the President personally—and unsuccessfully, as it turned out—was in touch with the key senator, Jennings Randolph of West Virginia. When the Tax Bill was before the House, the President personally—and as it turned out, successfully—was in touch with Representative Wilbur Mills. When newspaper stories satisfy or displease the Administration, it is often the President himself who lets reporters know his views.[36]

In a discussion of "Myth and Symbol" relating to the modern presidency, Grant McConnell commented:

The Presidency is the highest office in the land. Yet the office is not a given quantity and never a known factor in any political equation. Its character varies with the character, activities and views of the man who is President. Perhaps this quality was nowhere better put than in a statement of Woodrow Wilson before he came President, "The President is at liberty both in law and conscience to be as big a man as he can." Yet it is not true that the Presidency is a developing office in any strictly cumulative sense; one President may greatly enlarge it during his tenure, but his successor has no assurance of being able to exercise the newly added powers. The most that may be said is that here is an office of great latency; the Presidency is what the Presidents have made of it.

It is also true that to a great degree the President is what the office makes of him. . . .

Neither John Kennedy nor Lyndon Johnson exhibited any doubt as to the nature of the Presidency; in their hands it has been unambiguously a position of leadership to be used to the fullest extent. Yet each has followed Franklin Roosevelt in relying heavily on congressional approval. On the essential issue, however, both agreed that initiative in the American system lies with the President.[37]

THE ASSASSINATION AND THE CAMELOT LEGACY

The image of John F. Kennedy was forever changed on Friday, November 22, 1963, when the assassination in Dallas struck him down just as some of his most promising policy initiatives were nearing fruition. The assassination also spared him from having to confront the very difficult decisions in Vietnam which Lyndon Johnson had to cope with in the mid-sixties. It also tended to romanticize the public's view of JFK in ways that probably would have been uncongenial to him. He always had a wry, self-deprecatory approach to politics and the responsibility of governing.

The reaction to the assassination was an outpouring of genuine grief. For four days—from the Friday of the event until the Monday of the funeral services— the nation's attention was focused on the sequence of events that constituted the first phase of the transition. It was not until Thanksgiving week, when President Johnson addressed the Congress, that full attention seemed to be focused on LBJ.

Unlike the death of Franklin D. Roosevelt in 1945, which was covered by radio, the Kennedy assassination was followed by four days of intensive television coverage. This appeared to provide a unique opportunity for unifying the nation in grief over the loss of a president with whom many differed greatly, but whose loss was the loss of a symbol. And so Kennedy's name was added to the list—Harrison, Taylor, Lincoln, Garfield, McKinley, Harding, and Franklin Roosevelt—who died in office. His was the fourth assassination of an incumbent president, but it was the first instance in which the public could participate vicariously through the means of television in all the events surrounding the period of mourning. Studies indicated that for some Americans, it was a traumatic experience—like losing a member of the family.[38]

Almost immediately the image of President Kennedy was transformed from that of a flesh-and-blood politician struggling to keep the focus on his programs at the beginning of a midterm slump in his popularity while preparing a reelection campaign into a historical figure who reflected the poignancy of speculation about what might have been. One commentator said of the timing of Kennedy's death that it was as though Lincoln had been killed at the time of Gettysburg. Because JFK was killed earlier in his term than Lincoln and McKinley, questions arose. Would he have succeeded in pushing his civil rights and tax bill initiatives through Congress? Would his foreign policy initiatives toward reconciliation with the Soviet Union and a moderation of the Cold War have succeeded? Would he have avoided a deepening American involvement in Vietnam? One can only speculate.

But because the thousand days of the Kennedy administration represented such a relatively brief span of time, new attention focused on the late president's style of leadership. Two comments by the late Arthur Krock indicate the tone of some of the things said about JFK immediately after his death. Krock, veteran correspondent of the *New York Times,* recalled:

For more than a decade in the prewar, wartime, and postwar period my wife and I had a farm, Limestone, on the west bank of the Shenandoah River, four miles west of Berryville, Virginia. I recall in particular a visit from John F. Kennedy before he departed for the service with the Navy in the Pacific from which he emerged a hero—and with the spinal injury that plagued him for the rest of his life. . . .

When the young ensign drove out of the gate . . . to report to Washington for sea duty, I could conceive of the sequel of war hero, United States Representative, and Senator from Massachusetts. But not that we had drunk a stirrup cup with a future President— only with one of the most shining youths I had ever encountered.

Krock also commented: "The death of John F. Kennedy, after less than three years in office, deprived his contemporaries as well as history of the full record required for a balanced judgment of Presidential capabilities."[39]

The emergence of the Camelot theme relative to the Kennedy administration originated with a widely read essay by Theodore H. White in *Life* magazine shortly after the assassination. In the first volume of his memoirs, White relates the story of how he concluded the interview with the president's widow and concludes:

So the epitaph on the Kennedy Administration became Camelot—a magic moment in American history, when gallant men danced with beautiful women, when great deeds were done, when artists, writers and poets met at the White House, and the barbarians beyond the walls held back.

Which is, of course, a misreading of history. The magic Camelot of John F. Kennedy never existed. Instead, there began in Kennedy's time an effort of government to bring reason to bear on facts which were becoming almost too complicated for human minds to grasp. No Merlins advised John F. Kennedy, no Galahads won high place in his service. The knights of his round table were able, tough, ambitious men, capable of kindness, also capable of error, but as a group more often right than wrong and astonishingly incorruptible. What made them a group and established their companionship was their leader. Of them all Kennedy was the toughest, the most intelligent, the most attractive—and inside, the least romantic. He was a realistic dealer in men, a master of games who understood the importance of ideas. He assumed his responsibilities fully. He advanced the cause of America at home and abroad. But he posed for the first time the great question of the sixties and seventies: What kind of people are we Americans? What do we want to become?[40]

Three members of the Kennedy White House staff wrote about his administration within a brief time after it ended. Theodore C. Sorensen, who had been the president's chief counsel and principal adviser and speechwriter, wrote in *Kennedy:*

In my view, the man was greater than the legend. His life, not his death, created his greatness. In November, 1963, some saw it for the first time. Others recalled that they had too casually accepted it. But the greatness was there, and it may well loom even larger as the passage of years lends perspective.[41]

Similar tributes were written by Arthur Schlesinger, Jr., and Pierre Salinger. Schlesinger, who told of Kennedy's leadership skills in *A Thousand Days,* his account of the Kennedy administration, also told this author that President Kennedy had a personal magnetism and an ability to get people to work together that marked him as an outstanding leader.[42] Salinger wrote in his memoirs of the Kennedy era:

Since leaving Washington, I have given as much of my time as I can speaking to student audiences. The question I receive most often is whether I believe John F. Kennedy will go down in history as a great President. The question is difficult to answer. He, certainly, was not at all satisfied with the record of his administration. He regarded the nuclear test ban treaty as his most important achievement, and Vietnam as the most frustrating of his foreign policy endeavors. In the domestic field, he was disappointed that he had not been able to push either Medicare or a comprehensive civil rights bill through the Congress. Yet there can be no question that the groundwork he laid for both was a factor in their eventual enactment under President Johnson.

I am, of course, a prejudiced witness. But I believe that future generations of Americans will rank him as one of our greatest Presidents—not because of his specific accomplishments, and there were many, but because he brought to a world, cynical after almost two decades of cold war, the hope that a better life was possible.[43]

Controversy arose over a volume by journalist William Manchester entitled *The Death of a President*. This book detailed some accounts of friction between the Kennedy and Johnson staffs after the assassination and brought denials from some of those who were the object of various statements. Some felt that Manchester had sensationalized frictions that were inevitable at a time of rapid transition of administrations.[44]

KENNEDY FROM THE 1970S

Inevitably, changing political climates and changing expectations of the public tend to dim legendary perceptions, and a period of debunking and deprecation follows adulation.

Because the Vietnam experience engendered a great deal of disillusionment and critical writing about executive actions during the 1960s, a good deal of critical scholarship focused on President Kennedy during the 1970s. One of the critics, Bruce Miroff, author of *Pragmatic Illusions,* suggested that there was a note of insincerity in Kennedy's advocacy of civil rights reforms and charged also that in his treatment of the Berlin Crisis and the Bay of Pigs in 1961 and the Cuban missile crisis in 1962, Kennedy had needlessly fostered a crisis mentality. Miroff wrote:

Socialized well before they reach the White House, Presidents confront an array of pressures which effectively reinforce their orthodoxy. We have witnessed, in the career of John Kennedy, the continuous interplay between political demands and personal desires that typifies the modern Presidency. Thus, proponents of economic, political, and military expansionism find willing agents in Presidents fascinated by their own opportunities for global action. Sophisticated leaders of industry and finance deal with self-proclaimed partners anxious to make the corporate economy thrive on its own terms. Entrenched power-holders bargain with cautious White House politicians concerned, even when responding to the grievances of the powerless, to maintain the dominance of the existing power elite.

The record of the Kennedy Presidency should serve as a warning to those who still believe that major changes in American society can be instituted if only the right liberal makes it to the White House. Liberals will no doubt regain the Presidency in the future. But they will hardly refashion it into an instrument for the progressive transformation of American politics. That transformation can be accomplished only by those who have a stake in change. It is likely to be impeded by Presidents—who are, after all, the most successful products of the existing order.[45]

Richard Walton, a foreign policy critic, spoke of Kennedy as a bold warrior and counterrevolutionary. He felt that JFK's foreign policy positions did not materially differ from those of Eisenhower. Walton tended to play down the settlement of the Cuban missile crisis and the test ban treaty as matters of much less historical importance than they appeared to be during the Kennedy years. Walton wrote:

What a tragedy that the anti-communist impulse in Kennedy prevailed over his idealism, his genuine sympathy for the poor peoples of the world. One final irony: although neither could say so, both Robert and Edward Kennedy have campaigned against the foreign policies of their brother John.

. . . Kennedy was not one to attempt to change America's sentiment; rather he was one to respond to its mood and exploit it. He moved back, not ahead as he had promised. A few years later, when the mood of the nation was changing, he might have successfully guided us through the difficult transition period, for his political gifts were unequaled. But that possibility, like what he might have done given another five years in office, is speculation.

There is tragedy enough in the Kennedy story, but if his admirers are correct, if he would have learned from the first years of Vietnam and changed the nation's course away from escalation, then the greatest tragedy of all is that Lyndon Johnson, with Kennedy's advisers at his side, carried on, at increasing and terrible cost, a policy that Kennedy himself would have abandoned as indefensible. But that, too, is speculation. All we are left with are those three short years. The record seems clear. Whatever his achievements in less significant areas, whatever he might have done later, John F. Kennedy as President

was Cold Warrior and counterrevolutionary. Cuba, Berlin, Vietnam—those are his monuments.[46]

Still another critic of the entire approach taken during the Kennedy and Johnson
years is David Halberstam, author of *The Best and the Brightest:*

John Kennedy was dead. His legacy was a mixed one. He had come at the latter part of
the Cold War: at the beginning, he had not challenged it, though he had, in the last part
of his Administration, begun to temper it. On Vietnam his record was more than cloudy.
More than any other member of his Administration, he knew the dangers of a deep U.S.
involvement, the limits of what Caucasian troops could achieve on Vietnamese soil, and
yet he had significantly deepened the involvement. He had escalated the number of
Americans there to 16,900 at the time of his death, with more than 70 dead (each dead
American became one more rationale for more dead Americans): more important, he had
markedly escalated the rhetoric and the rationale for being there. Although he seriously
questioned the wisdom of a combat commitment, and at the end had grave doubts about
the viability of the counterinsurgency program, whether we should be there at all, he had
never shown these doubts in public, from the rostrum of the bully pulpit. The only thing
he expressed doubts about was the Diem regime, that and little more. His successor had
to deal not so much with Kennedy's inner doubts, so carefully and cautiously expressed,
but with his public statements, all supportive of the importance and significance of
Vietnam. In addition, his speeches and programs had raised the importance of Vietnam
in American minds; his commitment had, by the publicity his Administration gave it,
become that much more vital, and had led to that many more speeches, that many more
newspaper stories, that many more television stories on the Huntley-Brinkley show.[47]

Lewis J. Paper, in seeking to make "an objective assessment" of Kennedy's
presidency, concluded:

It is, of course, impossible to determine whether Kennedy would have succeeded in
fulfilling the promise he offered in 1961 if he had survived two terms in the White House.
It is not entirely clear how he would have responded to evolving problems and changing
circumstances. But it is clear the additional five years would have allowed Kennedy to
clarify and perhaps change the decisions of those first three years and pose different
choices for his successors.
    Kennedy's response to the hostilities in Vietnam is illustrative. His growth in the White
House may have enabled him to draw upon his lessons with the Laotian settlement and
the detente with the Soviet Union to realize the dangers of the growing American involvement in that conflict. As noted earlier, there is much evidence to suggest that Kennedy
was in fact becoming more sensitive to these dangers. In short, in judging the soundness
and foresight of Kennedy's actual decisions in exercising leadership, one should also
consider the possible direction of those decisions, the degree to which they would mesh
with the trends of history, and the extent to which he would grow with his experiences.
For Kennedy's politics, like a nation's politics, did not know the absolute demarcations
which define the end of one policy and the inception of another—demarcations which
could guide analyses and facilitate indisputable conclusions. American politics is a continuum, and each president is part of that continuum.

For three years, the promises of Kennedy's performance were considerably compromised by the limitations of the presidential office and by his own attitudes. Yet after the funeral procession faded from memory, his ideals lingered on, with millions of people in this country and around the world grasping for the promise that remained unfulfilled. The finality of any judgment would, in some ways, be as tenuous as a similar analysis of Abraham Lincoln if he had died after delivering the Gettysburg Address. And as with Lincoln, the tragedy of Kennedy's untimely death was that his effect on the continuum of American politics was suspended. "He was a man who could have become great or who could have failed," Norman Mailer said shortly after Kennedy's death, "and now we'll never know. That's what's so awful. . . . Tragedy is amputation: the nerves of one's memory run back to the limb which is no longer there."[48]

One comment on the Kennedy myth, made in a study of JFK's precongressional years by Joan and Clay Blair, Jr., should be added to the comments of his more recent critics:

As we have reported, it was wartime censorship and Joe Kennedy's contacts at *Reader's Digest* that were primarily responsible for Jack receiving so much credit during this episode (the *PT-109* incident). He was, in effect, a "manufactured" war hero. Here, we believe, the Washington Press Corps deserves a failing grade. It blindly accepted Jack's version of his combat record, or the incomplete, censored wartime accounts, with no independent investigation. It was not until Jack was already President that Robert Donovan told the full story, and even then he distorted certain portions of it to put Jack in a more favorable light.[49]

Commenting on the Kennedy record on the important domestic issue of civil rights in a 1970s study, Carl M. Brauer says:

Certain ideas guided Kennedy. As an American nationalist, he was troubled by the damage racial intolerance was inflicting upon his country's image abroad, particularly in the Third World where he hoped to expand American influence. . . . Racial discrimination offended him intellectually. Hence, he shared with the civil rights movement a fundamental belief.

Personal factors also shaped Kennedy's handling of civil rights. His grace and style charmed Black delegates in personal meetings. Sensitivity and empathy contributed to his making symbolic gestures, such as calling Coretta King, and permitted him to comprehend, on more than [an] intellectual level, the struggle for equal rights. Finally, Kennedy needed to feel that he was leading rather than being swept along by events. As President, he was uncomfortable playing a passive role. Therefore, when in the spring of 1963 he perceived that he was losing the reins of leadership, he boldly reached out to grasp them once again.

Kennedy's exercise of leadership probably helped instill in many potential civil rights activists a confidence and daring that they would not otherwise have had. . . .

One could well draw up a balance sheet of Kennedy's civil rights record. On the minus side, one might list the appointment of segregationist judges in the South, the delay in the housing order followed by the promulgation of the narrowest possible one, as well as numerous instances of executive cautiousness. . . .

The plus side of the ledger would be considerably longer. It would include a large number of executive actions, such as the appointment of Blacks to high offices and the gains in federal employment generally. . . . High on the list would be the many accomplishments relating to law enforcement, including the use of marshals to prevent mob rule in Montgomery, the application of legal pressure to bring about desegregation in transportation terminals, and the persistent implementation of court orders to effect desegregation at the universities of Mississippi and Alabama. . . . Because the administration played a role in the creation of the Voter Education Project, it might be afforded partial credit for its accomplishments. By April, 1964, the VEP had registered nearly 580,000 new voters in the South. President Kennedy's proposal of a broad civil rights bill in 1963 and his preliminary successes in getting that bill through Congress would also deserve places on the plus side of the ledger. Finally, Kennedy's exercise of moral leadership, through rhetorical advocacy and through personal example, would certainly merit inclusion in the positive column.

A balance sheet does not convey Kennedy's full importance, however. Kennedy was significant not only for what he did, but for what he started. His Presidency marked a profound change from the inertia that had generally characterized the past. In a tragically foreshortened term of less than three years, he instituted a vigorous and far-reaching effort to eliminate racial discrimination in American life. Operating within the bounds of a democratic political system, Kennedy both encouraged and responded to Black aspirations and led the nation into its Second Reconstruction.[50]

Finally, recent criticism of JFK's foreign policy and its impact on his image includes these comments by David Detzer in *The Brink,* an account of the 1962 Cuban missile crisis:

John Kennedy himself and his brother Robert received most of the praise that followed the crisis, perhaps rightly so. Yet what made them succeed—in addition to Russia's own rationality—was America's governmental machinery which in general ran smoothly. The military, particularly the Navy, performed well. The CIA seems to have done a fine job. But the part of the government which worked best during this period was that much-maligned department which John Kennedy had once compared to Jell-O: the Department of State. Here was Dean Rusk supervising a remarkably complex series of diplomatic maneuvers. Here were Chip Bohlen and Llewellyn Thompson, perceptive and prudent analyzers of the Soviet Union. Here was Ed Martin's Latin American desk; and the USIA which delivered a torrent of information to the world; and Roger Hilsman, the brainy and literate intelligence man; and George Ball, the organizer of peace; and Adlai Stevenson at the UN. They were a terribly impressive lot.[51]

Defenders of the Kennedy record have suggested, as the late Kenneth O'Donnell did in a press interview, that there was never any intent on the part of JFK to broaden the commitment to Vietnam. Former Senate Majority Leader Mike Mansfield, later ambassador to Japan, said that Kennedy told him it was his (JFK's) intention to withdraw American troops from South Vietnam in 1965.

KENNEDY FROM THE 1980S

Reference should be made to two brief efforts at a more balanced appraisal of the Kennedy record. Garry Wills says in *The Kennedy Imprisonment:*

The love of risk, the taste for compromising intrigues and hair-breadth escapes, may lead to an "interesting" life; but it can lead, as well, to international trouble if indulged in the White House. Kennedy admired risk-takers, not only on the football field or the field of battle, but in everyday life. People around him were constantly challenged to display their macho. . . .

Admiration for the courage that takes risks can have odd policy consequences. . . . But this very love of dash and freedom had conspicuous exceptions on the "new frontier." The Kennedy Administration, brashly taking on bureaucrats, was timorous if not obsequious with the oldest bureaucrat in town, J. Edgar Hoover.[52]

In Herbert S. Parmet's recent JFK biography covering the presidential years principal concerns of reviewers of the volume have dealt with deceit alleged to have been used in relation to Kennedy's health (the alleged presence of Addison's disease) and allegations of liaisons with women. Of this Carroll Kilpatrick wrote:

It is clear that the public was deceived about the extent of the President's back problems and about the need for steady cortisone dosages to control Addison's disease. . . . Also at the time there were hints about the President's pursuit of women. But only J. Edgar Hoover's network had the evidence. . . . Finally, there is the unanswered question of what Kennedy would have done in Vietnam beyond what he did in his lifetime . . . "Still, for him to have withdrawn [from Vietnam] at any point short of a clear-cut settlement would have been most unlikely," Parmet concludes from the available evidence.[53]

Much of the image that comes through in this body of criticism of JFK depicts him as the "heavy"—the cold warrior looking for a crisis to exploit, the male chauvinist who had to prove his macho image (views particularly expressed by Miroff, but also by Wills), the leader in search of a crisis so that he could show his leadership skills.

A 1983 Louis Harris survey showed that of the modern presidents Kennedy remained the most popular with the general public despite doubts expressed by historians and political scientists.[54]

All this controversy about the effectiveness of JFK's programs and the changing image of his White House service should be viewed in context. The distortions of time seem to get in the way of our view of an earlier era. It seems possible in this interpretation that perfectly natural actions of any president in one era may lead to vehement criticism in a different period. Each generation views these historical figures through the prism of its own experiences. To gain a better understanding of the Kennedy era, one must remember that the nation had not yet gone through the traumas of Vietnam and Watergate. There was a stronger rapport between the nation's leadership and the public. That kind of relationship may now be difficult if not impossible to restore.

During the 1980s it appears that a more balanced view of JFK and his strengths and weaknesses is beginning to emerge. Joan and Clay Blair's *The Search for JFK,* previously quoted, and Herbert Parmet's two-volume biography, *Jack: The Struggles of John F. Kennedy* (prepresidential) and *JFK: The Presidency of John F. Kennedy,* are examples of an effort to move beyond both adulation and debunking to attempt a realistic appraisal of JFK's historical image.

CONCLUSIONS ABOUT JFK'S POPULAR IMAGES

It is inevitable that after more than twenty years certain reassessments will occur. The aura created by the assassination and its controversies over whether or not Lee Harvey Oswald was part of a conspiracy is beginning to wear off. The foreign and domestic policy controversies of the Kennedy era can now be viewed in the light of newer problems and controversies—the undoing of some of the New Deal, New Frontier, and Great Society domestic programs which many thought were firmly rooted, the international controversies dealing with Afghanistan, Iran, Poland, Lebanon, El Salvador, and Nicaragua. Viewed from the vantage point of these problems as opposed to the immediate post-Vietnam period, does Kennedy appear in a different light? Inevitably he does, but it remains for more definitive analysts to make the contrasts and conclusions. Viewed from the Reagan era, what can we say about JFK's leadership style? Was it similar to that of Ronald Reagan, only used toward a different end?

Two decades after his death, controversy remains around the figure of President John F. Kennedy. While the Camelot legends and myths have perhaps left only a residue, there are both strongly positive and strongly negative feelings toward Kennedy's record and about his image.

The image of President Kennedy can be contrasted with those of his brothers. The image of young Joe Kennedy, the war hero, never developed in mature adulthood because he died as a young man. JFK's image seems to be one of coolness and dispassionate calmness toward events, while many saw Robert Kennedy as a more involved, more combative, activist political leader. JFK also dealt with different problems than those dealt with by Ted Kennedy, who has spent most of his political career in the U.S. Senate, although he was defeated in the 1980 presidential primaries and announced that he would not campaign in 1984.

One might conclude, then, in view of all that has been written and said about him, and despite the difficulties arising from the legends growing out of the assassination, that John F. Kennedy was an authentic American hero, flaws and all. He did use the impact and force of his personality to "get American moving" and to make his contribution toward the quest for peace. It is clear after two decades that his accomplishments, marred as they may have been by some of his failures, cannot be ignored.

NOTES

1. Andrew Turnbull, ed., *The Letters of F. Scott Fitzgerald* (New York: Dell Publishing Co., Laurel edition, 1966), p. 43.

2. Interestingly enough, Kennedy has been compared with another president of Irish background, Ronald Reagan, in this regard.

3. Democratic National Committee (DNC) files, March 25, 1960, Memorandum, John F. Kennedy Presidential Library, Boston.

4. DNC files, March 14, 1960, Memorandum, John F. Kennedy Presidential Library.

5. The Goldwater campaign of 1964 also used Simulmatics technology. In *The Ticket-Splitters,* Walter DeVries and Lance Tarrance argue that the main shortcoming of Simulmatics is that it tends to be bound by historical artifacts, i.e., it is predicated on the expectation that voters will continue to respond to issues, personalities, and party symbols as they have in the past.

6. The study of right-wing political activities, prepared by Myer Feldman of the White House staff during Kennedy's presidency, contains fascinating data. It was commented on independently by Fred W. Friendly in *The Good Guys, the Bad Guys and the First Amendment: Free Speech vs. Fairness in Broadcasting* (New York: Vintage Books, 1977), especially Chapter 9, "The Paid-Time Case: The President's Use of Television," pp. 121–141. Friendly questions whether the White House was unfairly taking advantage of the existing Federal Communications Commission (FCC) "fairness doctrine" in opposing the right-wing movement's attacks on the Kennedy administration. It is possible to suggest that the administration's response was perfectly natural.

7. Paul C. Light, *The President's Agenda: Domestic Policy Choice from Kennedy to Carter* (Baltimore: Johns Hopkins University Press, 1982). Note that discussion of approval ratings for Kennedy are based on published public opinion data found in the *Gallup Political Almanac,* Report No. 182, October-November 1980.

8. *Time,* November 16, 1960, "Men of the New Frontier," pp. 5–7.

9. "T.R.B. from Washington," *New Republic,* 142, no. 22 (November 21, 1960): 2.

10. "Who Lost the Election?" *National Review,* 9, no. 20 (November 19, 1960): 298, 299.

11. "The First Days: Opening the Door," *Newsweek,* Special Inauguration Section, 57, no. 5 (January 30, 1961): 16–18.

12. "On with the New," *National Review,* 10, no. 3 (January 28, 1961): 38, 39.

13. "Grand Illusion," *Time,* 37, no. 18, (April 28, 1961).

14. "Action Stations?" *National Review,* 13, no. 18 (November 6, 1962): 340, 341.

15. "T.R.B. from Washington," *New Republic,* 147, no. 18 (November 3, 1962): 2.

16. "JFK in the 'Bully Pulpit,' " *Newsweek,* 61, no. 25 (June 24, 1963): 27, 28.

17. Ibid., pp. 29, 30.

18. "R.I.P." *National Review,* 15, no. 24 (December 17, 1963): 511.

19. "Another Beginning," *New Republic,* 149, no. 23 (December 7, 1963):3.

20. For an excellent recent account of the fiasco at the Bay of Pigs, see Peter Wyden, *Bay of Pigs: The Untold Story* (New York: Simon and Schuster, 1979).

21. See Carl M. Brauer, *John F. Kennedy and the Second Reconstruction* (New York: Columbia University Press, 1977), especially "Conclusion: John F. Kennedy and the Second Reconstruction," pp. 311–320.

22. Schlesinger said in a personal interview with the author (previously published) that there was much esprit de corps among all Kennedy's staff members. He attributed this to Kennedy's personal magnetism and charm. Interview with Schlesinger, July 12, 1978, at his office, Graduate Center, City University of New York, quoted in William C. Spragens et al., *From Spokesman to Press Secretary* (Lanham, Md.: University Press of America, 1980), p. 149. Schlesinger also praised JFK's ability to recruit staff members who worked well together.

23. In a paper titled "John F. Kennedy and His Advisory Staff," presented in Chicago at the 1979 annual meeting of the Midwest Political Science Association, the author quoted several Kennedy staff aides to this effect. For example, Schlesinger: "In recruitment of talent, President Kennedy picked people who were mature people; they . . . worked relatively well together. Kennedy himself facilitated this good working relationship." Myer Feldman, a special assistant to the president:

It was a very informal and close relationship. . . . It was easy for the staff to obtain access to President Kennedy and to work directly with him. . . . JFK discussed matters while they were with him. One got used to taking up his list of items. JFK had a small staff, not much larger than FDR's. . . . There was never a more dedicated staff than the one that served President Kennedy.

In the author's book, *From Spokesman to Press Secretary* (p. 35), Salinger commented about working for JFK:

I was very comfortable working with him. He had a way of putting people who worked with him at ease; when I would have my first meeting with him, there wasn't just serious talk. At the beginning we would joke and gossip about things that were happening and you felt totally comfortable about President Kennedy. You weren't in awe of him, and you didn't feel restrained.

Quotation from interview with Salinger at ABC Paris Bureau, 22 Avenue d'Eylau, Paris, September 18, 1979.

24. For one example, see "Action Stations?" (editorial), *National Review,* 12, no. 18 (November 6, 1962): 340, 341. For a different view, see "Cuba and Berlin" (editorial), *New Republic,* 147, no. 18 (November 3, 1962): 1, 3. While *National Review* expressed dismay that Kennedy had delayed action so long, *The New Republic* was concerned lest Kennedy should overreact.

25. Memorandum, "The Simulmatics Corporation," from Democratic National Committee files for 1960 Presidential Campaign, John F. Kennedy Presidential Library. The memo is undated but was obviously prepared at the beginning of the 1960 campaign.

26. Simulmatics Report No. 1, May 15, 1960, "Negro Voters in Northern Cities" (Preliminary Edition), in DNC files, 1960 Presidential Campaign, John F. Kennedy Presidential Library.

27. Simulmatics Report No. 2, August 25, 1960, Copy No. 15, "Kennedy Before Labor Day," in DNC files, 1960 Presidential Campaign, John F. Kennedy Presidential Library.

28. Theodore C. Sorensen, *Kennedy* (New York: Bantam, 1966), pp. 270–272.

29. James MacGregor Burns, *Leadership* (New York: Harper and Row, 1978), p. 19. For Burns' comments about Kennedy as a presidential candidate in 1960, see James MacGregor Burns, *John Kennedy: A Political Profile* (New York: Harcourt, Brace, 1960). Burns says in a concluding comment: "To [the battle for survival], Kennedy could bring bravery and wisdom; whether he wold bring passion and power would depend on his making a commitment not only of mind, but of heart, that until now he has never been required to make" (p. 281).

30. See Salinger interview in Spragens et al., *Spokesman,* pp. 28–36.

31. From Oral History Interview, Peter Lisagor, John F. Kennedy Presidential Library, Boston, quoted in William C. Spragens, *The Presidency and the Mass Media in the Age of Television* (Washington, D.C.: University Press of America, 1978), p. 306.

32. Joe McCarthy, *The Remarkable Kennedys* (New York: Dial Press, 1960), p. 127.

33. Ibid., pp. 30, 31.

34. Roy Hoopes, *The Steel Crisis: 72 Hours That Shook the Nation* (New York: John Day Co., 1963), pp. 288, 289.

35. Grant McConnell, *Steel and the Presidency—1962* (New York: W. W. Norton and Co., 1963), pp. 114, 115.

36. Nelson W. Polsby, ed., *The Modern Presidency* (New York: Random House, 1973); Joseph Kraft, "Kennedy's Working Staff," pp. 146–157, especially p. 155.

37. Grant McConnell, *The Modern Presidency* (New York: St. Martin's Press, 1967), "Myth and Symbol," pp. 1–15.

38. M. Wolfenstein and G. Kliman, eds., *Children and the Death of a President* (Stanford: Stanford University Press, 1963).

39. Arthur Krock, *Memoirs: Sixty Years on the Firing Line* (New York: Funk and Wagnalls, 1968), p. 355.

40. Theodore H. White, *In Search of History: A Personal Adventure* (New York: Harper and Row, 1978), pp. 524, 525.

41. Theodore C. Sorensen, *Kennedy* (New York: Harper and Row, 1965), p. 758.

42. Spragens et al., *Spokesman,* pp. 149–151.

43. Pierre Salinger, *With Kennedy* (Garden City, N.Y.: Doubleday and Co., 1966), p. 758.

44. William Manchester, *The Death of a President* (New York: Harper and Row, 1965).

45. Bruce Miroff, *Pragmatic Illusions: The Presidential Politics of John F. Kennedy* (New York: David McKay Co., 1976), pp. 294, 295.

46. Richard J. Walton, *Cold War and Counter-revolution: The Foreign Policy of John F. Kennedy* (New York: Viking Press, 1972), pp. 233, 234.

47. David Halberstam, *The Best and the Brightest* (New York: Random House, 1972), pp. 233, 234.

48. Lewis J. Paper, *The Promise and the Performance: Leadership of John F. Kennedy, an Objective Assessment* (New York: Crown Publishers, 1975), pp. 379, 380.

49. Joan Blair and Clay Blair, Jr., *The Search for J.F.K.* (New York: Berkley Publishing Corp.; G. P. Putnam's Sons, 1976), p. 587.

50. Carl M. Brauer, *John F. Kennedy and the Second Reconstruction* (New York: Columbia University Press, 1977), pp. 317–320.

51. David Detzer, *The Brink: Cuban Missile Crisis, 1962* (New York: Thomas Y. Crowell, 1979), p. 260. Also on the Cuban missile crisis, see Elie Abel, *The Missile Crisis* (Philadelphia: Lippincott, 1966); Robert F. Kennedy, *Thirteen Days* (New York: Norton, 1969); and Henry M. Pachter, *Collision Course* (New York: Praeger, 1967).

52. Garry Wills, *The Kennedy Imprisonment: A Meditation on Power* (Boston: Atlantic Monthly Press/Little, Brown, 1982), p. 35.

53. Herbert S. Parmet, *JFK: The Presidency of John F. Kennedy* (New York: Doubleday/Dial, 1983), quoted in review by Carroll Kilpatrick, retired *Washington Post* White House correspondent, Book World of the *Washington Post,* March 29, 1983, pp. 6, 11.

54. Poll cited in Hedley Donovan, *Roosevelt to Reagan: A Reporter's Encounter with*

Nine Presidents (New York: Harper and Row, 1985), p. 85. The Harris poll showed JFK with a higher approval rating in its sample than even Ronald Reagan. Kennedy's numbers were in the 30 percent range, but none of the others were above the 20 percent range. Finally, for a typical retrospective survey, see "Kennedy Remembered: After 20 Years, a Man Lost in His Legend," *Newsweek,* November 28, 1983, pp. 60–91.

ANNOTATED BIBLIOGRAPHY

Books

Barber, James David. *The Presidential Character: Predicting Performance in the White House.* Englewood Cliffs, N.J.: Prentice-Hall, 1972.
  Chapter 9 contains a discussion of "John F. Kennedy and Active-Positive Commitment."
Boller, Paul F., Jr. *Presidential Anecdotes.* New York: Penguin Books, 1982.
  Contains some insightful stories about JFK in Chapter 34, "John F. Kennedy, 1961–63."
Bradlee, Benjamin C. *Conversations with Kennedy.* New York: Norton, 1975.
  The *Washington Post* executive editor's description of private talks he had with President Kennedy when Kennedy was off duty, relaxing with friends.
Burns, James MacGregor. *John Kennedy: A Political Profile.* New York: Avon, 1960.
  A political campaign biography, Burns' work is more sophisticated and more analytical than others of this genre; it is a useful source for information about JFK's prepresidential career. Burns is essentially friendly to JFK.
Detzer, David. *The Brink: Cuban Missile Crisis, 1962.* New York: Thomas Y. Crowell, 1979.
  The most recent and quite detailed case study of the Cuban missile crisis. Well written and quite readable.
Epstein, Edward Jay. *Inquest.* New York: Viking Press, 1966.
  One of the better written accounts of the Kennedy assassination and the post-assassination inquiries.
Gadney, Reg. *Kennedy.* New York: Holt, Rinehart and Winston, 1983.
  A British author's popular biography on which the 1983 television miniseries on NBC was based.
Hilsman, Roger. *To Move a Nation.* New York: Delta Books, Dell Publishing Co., 1967.
  An account of the Kennedy foreign policy by an important diplomatic figure in the Kennedy State Department.
Kennedy, Robert F. *Thirteen Days.* New York: Norton, 1969.
  Published posthumously, this account by the president's brother about the Cuban missile crisis is a valuable first-hand account by a key participant.
Lane, Mark. *Rush to Judgment.* New York: Viking Press, 1966.
  A bitter attack on the Warren Commission's conclusions by the Oswald family's attorney.
McCarthy, Joe. *The Remarkable Kennedys.* New York: Dial Press, 1960.
  This campaign biography places much emphasis on JFK's family. See also Richard J. Whalen, *The Founding Father* (New York: New American Library, 1964); Hank Searls, *The Lost Prince* (New York: World Publishing Co., 1969), a bi-

ography of Joseph P. Kennedy, Jr.; Joseph Dinneen, *The Kennedy Family* (Boston: Little, Brown, 1960); Jack Newfield, *Robert Kennedy: A Memoir* (New York: Dutton, 1969); Edwin Guthman, *We Band of Brothers* (New York: Harper and Row, 1971); David Halberstam, *The Unfinished Odyssey of Robert Kennedy* (New York: Random House, 1969); Gail Cameron, *Rose* (New York: Putnam, 1971); David E. Koskoff, *Joseph P. Kennedy* (Englewood Cliffs, N.J.: Prentice-Hall, 1974); Rose F. Kennedy with Robert Coughlan, *Times to Remember* (Garden City, N.Y.: Doubleday, 1974); James MacGregor Burns, *Edward Kennedy and the Camelot Legacy* (New York: Norton, 1976); Arthur Schlesinger, Jr., *The Life and Times of Robert F. Kennedy* (Boston: Houghton Mifflin, 1978); Arthur Beschloss, *Kennedy and Roosevelt* (New York: Harper and Row, 1980); James H. Davis, *The Kennedys: Dynasty and Disaster* (New York: McGraw-Hill, 1984); Doris Kearns Goodwin, *The Fitzgeralds and the Kennedys: An American Saga* (New York: Simon and Schuster, 1987); Peter Collier and David Horowitz, *The Kennedys* (New York: Summit Books, 1984).

Manchester, William. *The Death of a President*. New York: Harper and Row, 1967.
The controversial account of the Dallas assassination and its aftermath which resulted in a legal dispute between the author on the one hand and Jacqueline and Robert Kennedy on the other.

———. *Remembering Kennedy: One Brief Shining Moment*. Boston: Little, Brown, 1983.
A pictorial review of the early career and presidency of John F. Kennedy.

Martin, Ralph H. *JFK: A Hero for Our Time*. New York: Harper and Row, 1983.
Similar in content to the Parmet book; detailed discussion of JFK's health problems.

Miroff, Bruce. *Pragmatic Illusions: The Presidential Politics of John F. Kennedy*. New York: McKay, 1976.
An effort to make a revisionist approach to the Kennedy administration, this analysis criticizes JFK's Cold War foreign policy and his civil rights policy as being too conservative, but it recognizes his public opinion skills and other positive leadership qualities.

O'Donnell, Kenneth P. and David Powers. *"Johnny, We Hardly Knew Ye!"* Boston: Little, Brown, 1972.
An account by Kenneth O'Donnell, now deceased, and David Powers of their longtime staff relationship with John F. Kennedy.

Paper, Lewis J. *The Promise and the Performance: The Leadership of John F. Kennedy*. New York: Crown Publishers, 1975.
One of the first revisionist views of the Kennedy administration to strike a fairly good balance between JFK's strengths and weaknesses.

Parmet, Herbert S. *JFK: The Presidency of John F. Kennedy*. New York: Doubleday/Dial, 1983.
Another attempt at a balanced appraisal of the JFK presidency; it succeeds fairly well if perhaps a bit on the harsh side. It is a companion volume to *Jack: The Struggles of John F. Kennedy* (New York: Doubleday/Dial, 1977), in which the prepresidential career of JFK is analyzed.

Schlesinger, Arthur M., Jr. *A Thousand Days: John F. Kennedy in the White House*. Boston: Houghton Mifflin, 1965.
This account of the Kennedy administration was written in lively style by the

Pulitzer Prize-winning historian who served on JFK's senior staff. Discussion of the Bay of Pigs and the Cuban missile crisis is particularly good.

Sidey, Hugh. *John F. Kennedy, President*. New York: Atheneum, 1963.
A contemporary journalist's account of the JFK administration.

Sorensen, Theodore C. *Kennedy*. New York: Harper and Row, 1965.
Written by Kennedy's chief counsel and chief speechwriter, generally considered JFK's closest adviser with the possible exception of Robert Kennedy.

Thompson, Josiah. *Six Seconds in Dallas*. New York: Random House, 1968.
One of the better written accounts among the many discussions of the assassination.

United Press International and American Heritage. *Four Days: The Historical Record of the Death of President Kennedy, Nov. 22–25, 1963*. Rev. ed. New York: Simon and Schuster, 1983.
An updated version, with an introduction by Theodore H. White, of a popular account of the assassination published in 1963. (A similar illustrated book written by Saul Pett and published by the Associated Press, *The Torch Is Passed,* is also available.)

Warren Commission. *The Official Warren Commission Report on the Assassination of President John F. Kennedy*. Garden City, N.Y.: Doubleday, 1964.
This is the official publication which stirred great controversy with its denial that a conspiracy had occurred when Lee Harvey Oswald murdered JFK.

Wills, Garry. *The Kennedy Imprisonment: A Meditation on Power*. Boston: Atlantic Monthly Press/Little, Brown, 1982.
An essay about the effect of the JFK legend on Robert and Edward Kennedy's political careers.

Wyden, Peter. *Bay of Pigs*. New York: Morrow, 1979.
A detailed case study of the abortive Bay of Pigs invasion of April 1961.

Television Documentaries

The twentieth anniversary of the Kennedy assassination in November 1983 brought a spate of television documentaries about President Kennedy. The best of these probably included:

Dickerson, Nancy. "Being with John F. Kennedy." Syndicated and viewed on Channel 50, Detroit, November 18, 1983, 2 hours.
"Insider" movies from the archives.

Jennings, Peter. "JFK: A Realistic Appraisal." ABC News, November 15, 1983, 90 minutes.
An effort to balance JFK's role in history; e.g., Jennings points out that the Cuban missile crisis, a "victory" at the time in 1962, may have intensified the U.S.-Soviet arms race.

"Kennedy: A Three-Part Miniseries." Based on Reg Gadney's BBC Production. Aired for three nights on NBC, November 20, 21 and 22, 1983.
This "docudrama" (in itself the object of controversy) depicted Kennedy as seen from a British author's viewpoint. It focused on both policy and JFK's private life and painted a scathing portrait of the late J. Edgar Hoover, director of the FBI, played by Vincent Gardenia. (This production was preceded by an ABC production in 1978 called "The Missiles of October" starring William DeVane.)

Videotape Production

"JFK: A Videotape Portrait." Produced in 1981 by the CBS News Division. Walter
   Cronkite, narrator.
   Includes well-edited coverage of the Kennedy administration and the assassination.

18 LYNDON B. JOHNSON

William C. Spragens with Melinda Swan

THE BACKGROUND OF LYNDON BAINES JOHNSON

One of the most intriguing and controversial presidents of the twentieth century was Lyndon Baines Johnson. The controversy swirling around him grows out of at least two factors—the seemingly endless war in Vietnam, and also Johnson's off-and-on relationships with principal staff aides. He possessed tremendous drive, managing to cram two work days into each of the days he worked as president. He was very emphatic about his policy positions; he also mastered the art of persuasion, which (especially in his legislative days) he refined into something known in Washington as "the treatment."

Lyndon Johnson was a political figure who was larger than life in the sense that he literally dominated Washington while he was president. He also possessed a master's knowledge of the intricacies of the Capitol Hill process—both the public perception of the legislative process, and the backroom maneuvering necessary to achieve success. Such recent biographers as Robert Caro have tried to sort myth from fact regarding LBJ; their efforts have stirred much controversy.

Two themes are particularly important in examining the myth and legend of Lyndon Johnson, his background as a product of the Texas Hill Country and a family involved in politics in his father's generation, and the manner in which his presidency fell between the deaths of the Kennedy brothers. From JFK's assassination in November 1963 until Robert Kennedy's assassination in June 1968, after Johnson already had withdrawn as a candidate for reelection, LBJ seemed to be obsessed with the need to reestablish his own political identity beyond the shadows of the Kennedys.

In relationships with presidential staff aides and other subordinates, he had a paradoxical unpredictability—one day caustically critical, the next day making amends in an unexpected way, such as a symbolic apology.

Part of Johnson's character can be understood by understanding the character of his native Texas Hill Country. In the early twentieth century the Hill Country still had a strong flavor of the frontier. Both his parents reflected the Texas culture, though in different ways, and each imparted to him either hereditary or environmental characteristics that influenced his basic political makeup.

Alfred Steinberg, Doris Kearns Goodwin, Ronnie Dugger, and Robert Caro all suggest that there was a tension in the shaping of Johnson's image during his formative years. Sam Johnson stimulated his eldest son's interest in politics and perhaps some of the political genius LBJ exhibited in his career. Friends described Sam Johnson as a plunger—as much of a failure as a success at farming, but one with a loyal political following even though in Johnson City, Texas, his faltering finances provoked controversy. Caro and Kearns also refer to the high expectations held for LBJ by Rebekah Baines Johnson, his mother, because her own father, Joseph Wilson Baines, of Blanco, Texas, had been an attorney, an educator, and a Baptist lay preacher, as well as a member of the Texas legislature and secretary of state. Sam Ealy Johnson, his father, a member of the Texas legislature (1904–1908, 1918–1924) had, according to Doris Kearns, been a strong opponent of the Ku Klux Klan and a strong civil libertarian. Caro argues that Sam was more willing to take unpopular positions than Lyndon, and he argues that Lyndon "went whichever way the wind blows," that Lyndon was more than a pragmatist—that he simply lacked political principles. There has been plenty of dispute about this assessment of the LBJ image in the early reviews of the first volume of Caro's projected trilogy.

Johnson's first experience in exhibiting political skills came as an undergraduate at San Marcos State Teachers College in the late 1920s; there he parlayed a position as student receptionist in the college president's office into an influential campus role; he also founded a secret society known as the White Stars, which competed with the previously dominant Black Stars. Because of divided opinion, there remains heated dispute about this more than a half century later. After a brief stint as a debate coach in Houston, Johnson went to Washington as secretary to U.S. Representative Richard Kleberg of the King Ranch family. As a Kleberg aide he quickly won the speakership of an aides' organization known as the "Little Congress" and quite early sought to become a political protégé of President Franklin D. Roosevelt. He was appointed Texas administrator of the National Youth Administration during the New Deal, then was elected to Congress in 1937. As a congressman, he became an ally of Speaker Sam Rayburn. LBJ unsuccessfully sought election to the Senate against Governor Wilbert Lee (Pappy) O'Daniel in 1941 in a contest in which it is widely believed he was "counted out" in a ballot fraud. He volunteered for service with the Army Air Corps in the Pacific (where he won a Silver Star) until called back to Congress at President Roosevelt's request in 1942. He remained in the House until he won a U.S. Senate seat in 1948, defeating Governor Coke Stevenson by 87 votes out of 900,000 in a contested election. In 1951 he became Democratic whip in the Senate and in 1953 became minority leader. Two years later he became majority leader, a post he held until after his election as vice president in 1960. From January 20, 1961, to November 22, 1963, he served as vice president and was given several significant assignments by President John F. Kennedy, including a mission to West Berlin during the 1961 Berlin crisis and the chief role in the development of the space program.

After becoming president in 1963, Johnson won election in his own right by defeating Senator Barry Goldwater in a landslide in November 1964. His administration was marked by the Great Society cluster of programs—civil rights advances for minorities and women, an omnibus federal aid to education bill, the federal War on Poverty, and other measures considered in retrospect to have just about completed the New Deal agenda begun by FDR in 1933. However, the greatest controversy of the Johnson years proved to be the war in Vietnam, which split his party down the middle. In January 1968 he announced that he would not seek reelection so that he could devote the rest of his term to seeking an honorable end to the war.

Johnson had a quiet retirement on his Texas ranch, turning his organizational and other talents to management of his agricultural interests. On his way to the top politically, he and Lady Bird Johnson had developed a successful broadcasting business, which began with Radio Station KTBC in Austin and expanded into television at the time of that industry's early growth. Just prior to his death in January 1973, LBJ had received a telephone message from President Nixon about the Vietnam truce.

Against this background, what can be said of LBJ's image?

SOME KEYS TO UNDERSTANDING THE LBJ IMAGE

The background and youth of Lyndon Johnson had a lasting impact on his efforts for progressive political causes. His dogged espousal of the war in Vietnam and his dealings with friends in the oil industry caused some to consider him as having become more liberal as president than he had been as a congressman and senator. However, since he was a pragmatic politician, his ideological view must be considered to have been influenced by his constituencies. It is not surprising, then, that he moved toward a more liberal position after he was elected by a national constituency as opposed to a Texas constituency. Furthermore, one must recognize that the picture of LBJ as a conservative congressman friendly with the oil interests is simplistic. From the very beginning of his years in Washington, LBJ was strongly influenced by the ideas and programs of Franklin Delano Roosevelt and perhaps even more by the progressivism of Speaker Sam Rayburn, also a Texan.

One story is related by Caro amid accounts of the intrigues of Texas politics. When Johnson was teaching Hispanic children in the rural school at Cotulla, he agreed to teach English to the Hispanic janitor. This he did, according to Caro, despite the taunts and jeers of the town bullies. According to this story, it was during this time that LBJ developed an empathy with the underclass that marked the true origins of his War on Poverty and the beginning of an attitude that would come to fruition with the adoption of the Voting Rights Act of 1965.[1]

As senate majority leader, Johnson became identified with the passage of the civil rights bills of 1957 and 1960. He also played a large role in the development of the interstate highway program. He and Speaker Rayburn developed a system of bipartisan cooperation with President Eisenhower. During this time, Johnson's image seemed more that of a centrist Democrat than a vanguard progressive.

By 1956 it was generally believed in Washington that Senator Johnson had presidential aspirations. But in that era, it was believed that there was little chance that a southerner could be elected. While Johnson liked to hone his image as a westerner, it was true that he had been close to several southern legislators, including Senator Richard Russell of Georgia, considered a member of what William S. White called the Senate's "Inner Club." After Johnson became president, the public began to adjust its image of him as the Texas cowboy, the legislative magician, to fit its notions of the presidency.

In the later years of his presidency, the public's attention became divided between the events in Vietnam and the U.S. reaction to the war. The draft had proved unpopular, partly because there never had been a formal declaration of war and partly because opinion about Vietnam was badly divided. Demonstrations against the draft and teach-ins about the war had occurred on college and university campuses as early as 1965.

An example of the divisiveness of the war occurred during the Democratic National Convention in Chicago in August 1968, when demonstrations took place both outside the convention arena and in downtown Chicago. Police attacked demonstrators with billy clubs, and the scene was televised to a much-concerned national audience. The melee distracted attention from the convention, where an anti-Vietnam amendment to a platform resolution was debated, then defeated in a close vote.

The Johnson administration reflected the end of an era in the development of the Democratic party as the cluster of constituencies comprising the different factions within the party seemed to undergo a transformation and rearrangement because of the Vietnam War.

The Great Society could be considered in many ways as the peak of trends toward extensive government social programs. Medicare, aid to education, civil rights enforcement, consumer protection regulations, and the like seemed to have reached the height of popularity under Johnson, whose image was that of a Democratic president who had inherited the New Deal and the New Frontier and had moved forward in developing programs to deal with social concerns.

As issues changed, it became more apparent that the elements of the old Democratic coalition, including minorities, labor, intellectuals, and other reform-oriented groups, tended to be centrifugal, that is, always in danger of flying apart. To the extent that it held together, it was cemented by opposition to the common political foe, the conservative status quo interests which in recent times had looked largely to the Republican party for the articulation of their interests. The development of Vietnam as a divisive issue split this old coalition in such a way that it would never again consist of quite the same clustering of groups.

Johnson's effectiveness and lack of effectiveness as president were closely related to the public's perception of him. It was suggested that he was not as articulate a communicator as some of his predecessors. This problem doubtless arose out of Johnson's press relations; he did not view the media as an enemy to the extent that Nixon did, and, in fact, in his early days in the White House courted the media. But he seemed to feel a need to persuade the working press to become his supporters and even partisans. Certainly, friendly columnists such as William S. White and often Drew Pearson wrote favorably about him, but most Washington correspondents wrote both pro and con, as is the norm for any president. No president has ever liked criticism, but Johnson sometimes seemed to take it personally. Thus, he lacked some of the rapport that President Kennedy usually was able to maintain with the media.

Yet, ironically, it was through the media, especially television, that the public gained some positive impressions of Johnson. This can be explained by the coverage he had in the prepresidential years, when legends developed about his feats as Senate majority leader.

Lady Bird Johnson had a largely positive impact on the public's perception of her husband as president. She was widely known for her interest in beautification projects and in humanitarian causes, but she did not have quite the activist public image that Eleanor Roosevelt or more recently Rosalynn Carter seemed to have.

Partisan images of LBJ may differ somewhat from personal images. He had a somewhat different image in his role as a campaigner than in his role as president, but the personal images were those he had long before becoming an incumbent, and some of them remained throughout his presidency.

LYNDON JOHNSON'S SELF-IMAGE

Johnson's own apparent view of himself—at least in an official sense—can be found in various places in *The Vantage Point,* his autobiographical account of his presidency. Reflecting in retirement at his ranch in Texas, he wrote of his final moments in office:

Now, as I rode in my final presidential procession through Washington, I knew that although I was leaving, this city would be part of me forever. The Marine band saluted me for the last time with "Hail to the Chief" as I took my place in the inaugural stands in front of the Capitol. . . .

As I watched the ceremony, I reflected . . . on how inadequate any man is for the office of the American Presidency. The magnitude of the job dwarfs every man who aspires to it. Every man who occupies the position has to strain to the utmost of his ability to fill it. I believe that every man who ever occupied it, within his inner self, was humble enough to realize that no living mortal has ever possessed all the required qualifications.[2]

PUBLIC OPINION POLLS ABOUT JOHNSON

As had been true of any president since the advent of modern public opinion polling and survey techniques, President Johnson was highly concerned with his approval ratings. In LBJ's era, the surveys included both public and privately commissioned surveys analyzed by strategists for candidates and examined carefully by officeholders for clues about how their issue positions and stands were viewed by the public.

As illustrated in Figure 18.1, Johnson's approval rating fluctuated considerably during his presidency. It hit a high point at the height of activity by the eighty-ninth Congress in the adoption of his Great Society legislation, and it hit its low during the final year of his presidency after his policies in Vietnam had become highly unpopular.

Two factors may have contributed to an artificially high approval rating for Johnson during his first eighteen months in office: sympathy toward him after he had to take over the White House responsibilities very quickly after the assassination of President Kennedy, and the fact that his Republican opponent for the presidency in 1964 was Senator Barry Goldwater, who was viewed as an extremist right-wing candidate by much of the American public.

The Louis Harris Survey released by the *Los Angeles Times* Syndicate on August 10, 1964, indicated that 84 percent of those polled backed President Johnson's position on the Gulf of Tonkin incident, a key factor in American escalation of the war in Vietnam.[3]

On April 8, 1965, in a memorandum to LBJ, Jack Valenti of the White House staff gave these figures on LBJ's approval rating, as reported by John Brice's Philadelphia poll:[4]

Number of Respondents = 600

January 1964	April 1964
66%—good	57%—good
6%—all right	6%—all right
17%—fair	20%—fair
3%—could be better	3%—could be better
3%—bad, poor	9%—bad, poor
4%—don't know	4%—don't know

Raw figures from public opinion surveys do not adequately portray the public's perception of LBJ without analytical comments. First, for even the most popular presidents there is a dropping off in popularity from the beginning or honeymoon period of their terms to the end. Another long-term trend has been that each successive president since Kennedy has started out with a slightly lower popularity rating, though Nixon hit 23 percent at the nadir of the Watergate crisis, and there are individual exceptions.

Allowing for this, one must consider how the public viewed Johnson. As surveys became more sophisticated they began to go beyond simple questions about whether the voter thinks the president is doing a good job to asking voters how they view the traits of the president at issue. Voters were inclined to view Johnson as professional and able, but they came to doubt his credibility as the

Figure 18.1
Approval Ratings for Lyndon B. Johnson

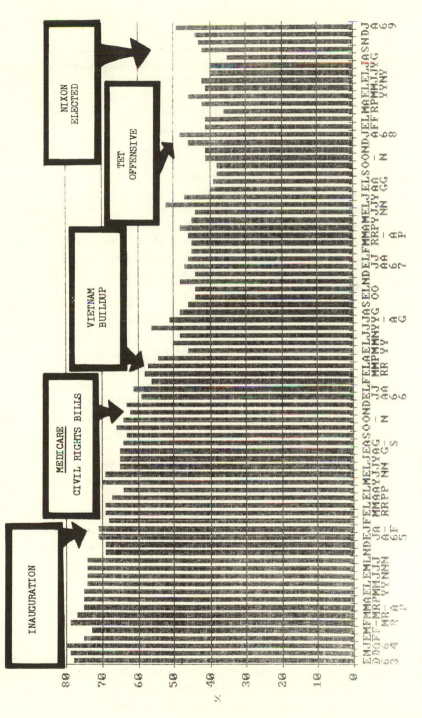

Source: Gallup Opinion Index, September–October 1980.

Vietnam issue moved to the forefront of public awareness. His scores were generally higher on domestic than on foreign policy issues.

The Johnson White House kept voluminous files on public opinion surveys about the president. Material available to scholars at the Lyndon Baines Johnson Library indicates that published polls were filed in the form of the news releases mailed out by the syndicates that distributed the polls (an indication that the White House usually saw these polling results before they were published); in the form of clippings sent to the White House by Johnson supporters around the country; commissioned reports (about both the presidential campaign and the off-year campaign of 1966); and special reports made when specific geographical areas were polled for particular political reasons.

Johnson's following had certain regional aspects. The core of his support came from Texas and the Southwest, but he also had a loyal following of traditional Democrats and New Dealers with a considerable degree of long-run party loyalty. Johnson had supporters in labor and in the business community, and he drew on some of the same sources of support given to Kennedy (as a Democrat), but he also relied on different occupational and demographic sources of support than those relied on by President Kennedy.

Material from the Johnson Library, based on Gallup data, shows somewhat higher approval in mid-1966 for President Johnson by men than women, and higher approval among those with grade-school education. He was most popular among manual workers in the occupational categories and those in the most youthful age cohorts, Democrats in partisan terms, Catholics by religious preference, the East in regional terms, the $3,000 to $4,999 annual income bracket, and in urban-rural terms residents of cities of 500,000 and over.

The Gallup polling data on Johnson from 1963 to 1969 indicate that his overall average popularity was 55 percent, meaning that more than half the population approved of his presidential policies and judgments.

The peak period in Johnson's popularity seems to have come in the immediate post-Camelot time segment from December 1963 to December 1965, with the highest in January 1964, at 80 percent. Johnson's subsequent election victory nearly a year after taking office gave him an additional honeymoon period which ended in 1966 (something comparable to the post–shooting incident period of good will toward Ronald Reagan in 1981). Besides the honeymoon factor, Johnson achieved an outstanding performance during 1965 because of his ability to push through Congress the Great Society programs.

The decline in Johnson's popularity during 1966 and 1967 coincided with several events, including the civil rights backlash and urban rioting, major Republican gains in the off-year election coupled with the administration's difficulty in achieving fair housing legislation, and, perhaps most tellingly, the increasing escalation in Vietnam. In the latter part of 1967, LBJ enjoyed a temporary recovery similar to that of Jimmy Carter during the few months after Camp David. By January 1968 Johnson's ratings had edged back up to 48 percent.

However, he soon sank to his lowest acceptance level ever. Four major events occurred within the first eight months of 1968 which aroused the public's consternation, and as usual the president became a scapegoat. The *Pueblo* crisis, the Tet offensive, the president's announcement that he would not run for re-election, and the assassination of Martin Luther King (as well, perhaps, as that of Senator Robert F. Kennedy) all contributed to LBJ's lowest approval rating during his presidential years—35 percent in August 1968.

Johnson finished his presidential career with a 49 percent rating. Once again, nearly half the population approved of his political stance, perhaps because the public by this time knew that no matter what Johnson had done, he was no longer to be president. Therefore, they were better able to empathize and give him a higher rating. (By this time, the Paris truce negotiations were in session.)

JOHNSON AS SEEN BY HISTORIANS, POLITICAL SCIENTISTS, AND JOURNALISTS

Rexford G. Tugwell, the political scientist who had served as a principal aide to Franklin D. Roosevelt, wrote of Johnson:

[Eric] Goldman . . . saw, as he watched, that Johnson was offending some extremely vocal people with access to the media—they were academicians, literati, and artists, mostly—and he himself was there to transmit their ideas and make them helpful in the country's governance. His obvious failure resulted in faint praise for Johnson's achievements and thunderous denunciations for the policies disapproved of by Goldman's constituency. [Goldman was a Princeton historian on leave in the White House.]

Johnson's tragedy was only partly that he adopted policies inimical to the national interest; his predecessors had done that too. It was said also that he did it in arbitrary ways, seeing himself as the embodiment of final power and then refusing to acknowledge the causes of the turn against him.[5]

Arthur M. Schlesinger, Jr., the historian who served President Kennedy, published a collection of essays that included comments by Ambassador John Bartlow Martin, who wrote of Johnson:

Aware that his every move was compared with "what Kennedy would have done," President Johnson at times seemed uncertain. It seemed that he felt he was, somehow, a usurper in his own White House. Comparisons of his "style" with Kennedy's hurt him. People talked about his vulgar idiom, his habit of swimming nude, his dislike of the intellectuals and of long position papers and analyses. And the more President Johnson attempted to hold the grip on the American imagination that John F. Kennedy had held, the more he repelled those whose imaginations Kennedy had held most firmly.[6]

Doris Kearns, the political scientist and onetime staffer for Johnson, wrote a political psychology analysis after indepth interviews with the retired Johnson at the LBJ Ranch in Texas. Unlike Caro, who interviewed Lady Bird Johnson but mostly wrote from documentary sources and interviews with numerous persons who knew Johnson, Kearns is more charitable. She states:

Lyndon Johnson found (in "continual motion and limitless ambitions") the source of his achievement in power and control. Yet control is not the only road to success, even in public life. For Johnson, however, control fulfilled another need as well: mastery of the outer world was necessary to mastery of the self. . . . control of the external world was . . . the only way of containing the powerful mixture of hate, rage, and love he experienced at various times toward his mother, his father, and himself. Mastery of the outer world was necessary to mastery of the self. And the drive for control was a surrogate for his urgent childhood desires to control the earliest of his environments and change his position within his parental family, thus enabling him to compel love and prevent conditions that prevented inner conflicts, dangers, and fears.

This understanding of the inward forces that contributed to Johnson's pursuit of power should not diminish respect for his extraordinary achievements; on the contrary, it should increase our regard for the masterful way in which—most of the time—he was able to harness and direct his personal needs toward constructive, social ends. . . .

It is also important to recognize that, while the demands of psychic structure led Johnson to pursue power, they did not determine that politics would be the avenue of that pursuit. The larger social setting provided content for Johnson's ambitions. Had his father and his father's friends been engaged in business or finance, one can imagine Johnson pursuing a very different career. But the options for a poor boy from a poor place in central Texas were limited. . . . Politics was the one profession that seemed to offer both a reasonable chance of entry and a limitless future. In short, the same drives set in a different society or another age might have led to very different pursuits.

And one thing is certain: his childhood relationships . . . may have shaped and energized his ambitions, but they did not, and could not ensure their realization.

Johnson's success and achievements—his performance—were made possible, to a very large extent, by his unusual capacities, his intellect, energy, talent, and insight into men and the nature of institutions, through which he developed techniques of incredible and intricate subtlety. To his knowledge and skill he applied an innovative genius to construct a large variety of instruments which increased the coercive powers that enabled him to impose his will. And that very success only strengthened and increased his ambition.[7]

While Kearns finds LBJ to have the image of neither a hero nor a villain, Caro, author of *The Years of Lyndon Johnson,* seems to project the image of at least the young LBJ as a kind of real-life J. R. Ewing in politics. While granting Johnson great ability and ambitions, Caro basically paints him as an egotistical, selfish manipulator of other men and ideas who was ruthless enough to hand out cash to Hispanic voters during a Texas election and thought nothing of exploiting the friendship and guidance of Sam Rayburn; Charles Marsh, publisher of the *Austin American-Statesman,* and even of FDR—using Rayburn to gain status in the eyes of FDR and the White House staff, using Marsh to conduct an alleged liaison with Marsh's purported mistress, and using FDR's friendship to climb the ladder of national politics. Such an image of unrelieved villainy is in contrast to Kearns' image of a mixture of greatness and pettiness and to the image painted by journalist George Reedy of a great man who was very difficult to work for and petty at times.

Caro suggests that he began with this view but that he found more and more about Johnson that was detestable. Caro maintains that Johnson, through the imposition of secrecy and through intimidation, sought to impose his own image on the history of his times. Regarding this, Caro writes:

Essential though it may be to understand Lyndon Johnson—his character and his career—this understanding is hard to acquire. He made it hard. Enlisting all his energy and all his cunning in a lifelong attempt to obscure not only the true facts of his rise to power but even of his youth, he succeeded well. He told stories readily and repeatedly (filling them with vivid, convincing detail) about the year he spent in California as a teenager, about his college girlfriend and the denouement of their relationship, about his father, whom he sought to portray as a drunken ne'er-do-well—about, in fact, a hundred aspects of his youth. And not merely many but most of these stories were false. Aiding in his success, moreover, was an aspect of his temperament with which, during his Presidency, Washington was to become familiar; an extraordinary preoccupation with, and talent for, secrecy[8]

Reedy, Johnson's first press secretary in the White House after Pierre Salinger's departure, knew Johnson longer and no doubt better than Doris Kearns, and he knew more of Johnson's character and image, apparently, than Caro (who does, however, provide useful insights). Of Johnson, Reedy has written recently in a remarkable essay:

The unhappy ending of the Johnson political story . . . cannot detract from the man's fascination. He was a tremendous figure—a combination of complexities and simplicities that bewildered all observers. He could be extremely shrewd in dealing with political contemporaries and astoundingly gullible in the selection of his personal advisers. He was capable of taking tremendous risks in some directions and exhibiting extraordinary timidity in others. He had a deep and compassionate understanding of the economic underdog but no comprehension of the feelings of those who felt they had been displaced by the machinations of mass society. The fact that a generation of Americans could be alienated from the values of their forefathers was something beyond his ken . . .

Regardless of how things have changed, however, Lyndon Baines Johnson was *the* consummate political leader of his era. Despite his weaknesses, he had a profound understanding of the workings of America's governmental system. For this alone, he is worth careful scrutiny. The present can be understood only in terms of the past, and there is an important slice of our past in which he was the principal moving force. He acted and the nation reacted. How future history will treat his Presidency is anyone's guess. . . . Of one thing, however, I am confident. No one will ever be able to look at him without concluding that he was either the most, or one of the most, fascinating of the presidential personalities of the Twentieth Century. . . .

The problem of finding the real Lyndon B. Johnson was further complicated by the advent of television film and tape. This gave him an opportunity to study his public appearances and, Pygmalion-like, seek to change his image. This meant a series of hair stylings; continual changes in the cut of his clothes; and interminable arguments over the merits of horned rim versus rimless glasses. For a while he tried contact lenses but the shape of his eyeballs was wrong. He could not stand the agony—particularly under the glare of television and newsreel lights.

Nevertheless, a real Lyndon B. Johnson could be found not by listening to his words but by watching what he did. There were political issues upon which he never deviated and in these are the clues to what was genuine about his personality. At bottom it was a burning desire to make life easier for those who had to struggle up from the bottom. . . .

The point emerges with sharp clarity in an examination of his views on education. Nothing was in his thoughts more often. He sought guarantees that every boy or girl in the United States "could have all the education he or she can take." He was actually superstitious about the subject. . . .

He did not wear the mantle of age with any grace because he never learned to enjoy anything but sensual activity. He could think, but not reflect; devise ingenious schemes for achieving goals but not ponder the validity of the goals; outguess his fellow human beings in playing the great game of one-upmanship without realizing that the game might not be worth playing. In short, he had none of the contemplative qualities which in old age, can compensate for the loss of youthful vigor. A few weeks after his heart attack in 1955, he summed up the whole problem when he told a conference of doctors, gathered to evaluate his condition, that he enjoyed nothing but whiskey, sunshine, and sex. Without realizing what he was doing, he had outlined the tragedy of his life. . . .

Were there nothing to look at save LBJ's personal relationships with other people, it would be merciful to forget him altogether. But there is much more to look at. He may have been a son of a bitch, but he was a colossal son of a bitch. By sheer size he could dominate any landscape. And no one could avoid the feeling of elemental force at work when in his presence. One did not know whether he was an earthquake, a volcano, or a hurricane but one knew that he possessed the force of all three combined and that whatever it was, it might go off at any moment. . . .

At his best, he also possessed the finest quality of a politician. It was a sense of the direction of political power—the forces that were sweeping the masses. He did not merely content himself by getting ahead of these forces. He mastered the art of directing them. . . .

Of all his qualities, however, the most important was that he knew how to make our form of government work. That is an art that has been lost since his passing and we are suffering heavily as a result.[9]

THEMES IN THE JOHNSON IMAGE

Although Robert Caro tends to describe Lyndon Johnson's skills in a critical vein, it is important to observe LBJ in the context of his own times, as well as in the context of the political arena in which he moved. Whatever his faults, Johnson possessed tremendous capabilities, as evidenced by his performance in securing passage of the Omnibus Civil Rights Act of 1964 and the Voting Rights Act of 1965, in the Senate censure of Joseph McCarthy, and in the cluster of Great Society programs.

Reedy's *Lyndon Johnson: A Memoir* explains in detail LBJ's prowess in political maneuvering. As contemporaries, Rowland Evans and Robert Novak commented on Johnson's skills in *LBJ: The Exercise of Power:*

Throughout his long climb upward, Johnson's posture had always been deliberately and necessarily flexible. There was, first, his shifting constituency in Texas. Representing the barren hill country of poor farmers and small town merchants still impoverished by the Depression, Johnson was Franklin Roosevelt's young protege, a New Deal stalwart. Then, seeking the larger constituency of all of Texas—including the new Texas of oil and big money—Johnson became a labor-baiting, Southern-style freshman senator. And in the Senate, Johnson survived in two worlds: that of Senate Majority Leader, a national party spokesman, and that of a Texan who was never quite sure of survival in his home base. And finally, the emancipation from that Texas constituency to become Vice-President, free now at last to be as liberal as necessary for his national constituency. Up that long and tortuous path, his flexibility of ideology was necessary to maximize his power.

He had magnified those pitifully small prerogatives of the Majority Leader's office and made that office, while he held it, one of the mightiest in the land. Once in the White House, he had further stretched and refined to new dimensions the powers of an office inherently more powerful than any in the world.[10]

Thus, we see Johnson as, not a man with no beliefs, but rather as a cautious politician who sought to serve his constituency. He was a man of high ideals; yet, he was not so inflexible that he couldn't realize that his own ideals must be superseded by those of the public he was elected to serve. It seems that Johnson believed that if he wished to gain power, he must not alienate those to whom he was responsible on his way. This strategy is not so different from that of any other professional politician, especially of the period. Johnson is worthy of some admiration at least for his understanding of the political process. It also is important to remember that when Johnson reached the pinnacle of power and felt free to exercise his own conscience, he did so in ways he believed would be best for society.

Lyndon Johnson was a man of complex character. One of the more intricate facets of his character was his intense interest in the media. His behavior toward the news media was quixotic at best, negative at worst. Although Johnson became the owner of a television station in Texas, it did not seem to make him any more tolerant of the media. He often expressed the feeling that the media seemed bent on defaming him, especially during the worst of the so-called credibility gap that resulted from his Vietnam policies.

Sarah McClendon wrote in *My Eight Presidents:*

I was not the only newspaper reporter to find out that Johnson could love you one day and hate you the next. I even saw Lyndon Johnson get angry at Tex Easley, the original mild-mannered reporter, who covered Washington for eighty-five Texas newspapers—a man who went out of his way not to print anything derogatory about anyone. In contrast, I felt it was my patriotic duty to expose everything I saw and heard. . . .

Johnson's attempts to manipulate the media did not stop with newspapers. His power over the television and radio stations was absolute. His influence with the national networks was formidable. Although Johnson's station in Austin was a CBS affiliate, all three networks did many favors for Johnson and gave him plenty of coverage. They also sought out his advice when they created new network affiliates in his home state.[11]

For a man who was described by one of his closest friends as a "huge, unique, personal force,"[12] a man who attempted to dominate every aspect of life, it must have been frustrating not to control the media. Information suggests that Johnson indeed had strong media control levers. For example, in a twenty-five-year longitudinal study of White House press coverage, Doris Graber found that "one is struck by how favorable they [the media] are. Each organization (CBS, New York *Times* and *Time)* presented two favorable stories about the White House for each that was unfavorable."[13] Johnson himself never seemed to perceive the media as favorable to him. He believed that the media represented an unbreakable foe despite the fair coverage they gave him, especially during his first year and a half in office.

Perhaps Johnson's failure to view the press objectively stemmed from his own feelings that the press itself lacked objectivity. He was a man of power, and perhaps the press to him was a usurper of power. Doris Kearns wrote:

Johnson's expansion of the President's power over the Cabinet and the party was accompanied by an energetic campaign to build his influence with the press to consolidate his claims. For he believed that no President could lead for very long if the media did not support him; unfriendly media would make him vulnerable to assaults on the power he was building. Johnson regarded members of the press as similar to the membership of any other interest group. And he acted on the assumption—congenial to his natural traits and conduct—that he could find a way to bargain with them for good coverage and favorable stories. "Reporters are puppets," Johnson said. "They simply respond to the pull of the most powerful strings. Every reporter has a constituency in mind when he writes his stories. Sometimes it is simply his editor or his publisher, but often it is some political group he wants to please, or some intellectual society he wants to court. The point is, there is always someone. Every story is slanted to win the favor of someone who sits somewhere higher up. There is no such thing as an objective news story. And if you don't control the strings to that private story, you'll never get good coverage no matter how many great things you do for the masses of the people. There's only one sure way of getting favorable stories from reporters and that is to keep their daily bread— the information, the stories, the plans and the details they need for their work—in your own hands, so that you can give it out when and to whom you want. Even then nothing's guaranteed, but at least you've got the chance to bargain."[14]

Much of Johnson's frustration with the media may have stemmed from the fact that JFK managed to do so well. George Christian, the third and last Johnson White House press secretary, said:

Ever since Johnson, there's been a lot of experimentation. Manufacturing of events in order to satisfy a public need for a President they feel they can trust. . . . President Kennedy didn't have to create this. He had a natural ability to deal with his constituency. He had a keener political sense than most presidents and knew how to sell himself. Everybody since then has tended to compare himself to the Kennedy style and fret about not being as adept at capturing the public's imagination. This has afflicted every President since Kennedy. . . . All worry about it too much and create an artificial atmosphere that's not really reflective of their own character or ability or way of running the Presidency; when a President has to "ham it up" for public consumption, this has always failed.[15]

Johnson reflected on his problems with the Kennedy image during a CBS News special broadcast:

I had many problems in my conduct of the office being contrasted with President Kennedy's conduct of the office, with my manner of dealing with things and his manner, with my accent and his accent, with my background and his background. He was a great public hero and anything that I did that someone didn't approve of, they would always feel that President Kennedy wouldn't have done that—that he would have done it in a different way, that he wouldn't have made that mistake. And when I had some minor Bay of Pigs, or missile crisis, or difficulties as he had with Khrushchev in Vienna and came back and added many billions to the defense budget and recommended to us and the Congress that we call up the Reserves—which we did to get ready for a crisis that didn't really develop—but when I had those things happen to me there was a group in the country, and very important, and influential molders of opinion, who I think genuinely felt that if President Kennedy had been there those things wouldn't have happened to him.[16]

Doris Graber quotes a media analyst: "Said one, 'Johnson was a less-than-ideal television candidate. According to Edward Chester, Johnson on television projected an unappealing physical appearance along with a "slow drawl." ' Joe McGinniss saw him as 'heavy and gross' and 'syrupy' as he 'stuck to the lens.' "[17]

So heavy was Johnson's reliance on polls that he even used them to sway important personages. Dom Bonafede wrote:

During the 1964 presidential campaign . . . Johnson invited industrialist Henry Ford II to the White House. . . . Ford had made up his mind not to endorse the Republican nominee, Senator Barry Goldwater of Arizona, but was undecided whether to support Johnson or remain neutral.

As Bill Moyers, Johnson's press secretary, recalls the incident: "LBJ pulled out one poll after another, one from New York, one from California, one from Ford's home state of Michigan, and said, 'You don't want to be left out in the cold, do you? Everybody will be driving the highways in your cars and you'll be hitching a ride. You better get aboard.' It was an unassailable, unrelenting barrage of statistical evidence."

Shortly afterward, Ford publicly came out in support of Johnson.[18]

The Austin files also contain extensive impressions and letters from helpful friends who sought to build and improve LBJ's public persona. One of these letters, from James Nicholson, a strong LBJ and Democratic party supporter, discussed his luncheon with five attorneys:

Naturally, the discussion got around to my candidacy, our party, and its future. Each of these gentlemen felt the same as I did—that one of the tragedies of this campaign of

1966 was the abuse which was given to the President; and their sympathy and support of him as a person was clear. We all concluded, however, that one of the tragedies was the inability of the President, whether due to people, speech writers or what, to communicate his sincerity and dedication to each of us. I say to you in honesty and with affection for the President that the impression that people have of him is one who pushes to achieve results but one who does not lead.

Something must be done to enable the force of his personality to come across to the ordinary person. He has traditionally been most effective in the small group at the conversational level, and I wonder if something ought not to be done to enable him to make the same kind of projection to each of us.[19]

Vietnam was the issue that clouded all of Johnson's presidency and most of the writings about him since. It is difficult, even now, to be objective regarding Vietnam and its effects on Johnson's image as more damning material emerges. The worst part of Vietnam for Johnson, in image terms, was the credibility gap that surfaced when reporters noted a vast difference between Johnson's campaign speeches on Vietnam and his actions in office. Regarding this, George Edwards III wrote:

The number of prevarications expanded considerably in the Johnson Presidency. Thus, shortly after taking office, Johnson let his secretary of defense mislead the American people about the situation in South Vietnam as he [McNamara] later told the press that the South Vietnamese could cope (on the same day he told the President that South Vietnam might fall to the Communists even with U.S. aid).

Nineteen-sixty-five found several lies emanating from the Johnson Administration. First, the day before he appointed Abe Fortas to the Supreme Court, Johnson told reporters he had not even considered whom to appoint. Second, the U.S. claimed a CIA agent never offered a $5 million bribe to the prime minister of Singapore. Unfortunately for the U.S., the prime minister produced a letter of apology from Secretary of State Dean Rusk—predating the disavowal. Finally, the President justified our invasion of the Dominican Republic as necessary to save American lives (because "some fifteen hundred innocent people were murdered and shot, and their heads cut off. . . . ") and the U.S. ambassador there had phoned the President while sitting under his desk as bullets were whizzing overhead. None of this was true, nor was the claim that we were neutral. We really invaded the island to prevent the possible Communist takeover.[20]

Prevarications were not unknown to LBJ. In fact, Caro argues that LBJ was known for them. While in college his propensity for exaggeration was widely recognized, according to the biographer of Robert Moses, in this account: "He was given the public nickname 'Bull.' 'That was what we called him to his face,' said Edward Peils, a classmate. 'Because of his constant braggadocio. Because he was so full of bullshit, manure that people didn't believe him. Because he was a man who could just not tell the truth.' "[21]

According to many reports, Johnson's ability at least to embroider the truth or engage in deceptions continued throughout his life. Yet, he was a man deeply concerned about those he was elected to serve. Why lie to them about Vietnam?

Johnson himself later admitted that perhaps he had not handled the Vietnam War correctly. Of course, his reasoning differs from that of his critics:

I don't think the American people—I think I did a poor job of pointing up to the American people that one time, two times, a dozen times, we made substantial overtones to Ho Chi Minh—willing to go anywhere, anytime, talk about anything; just please let's talk instead of fight. And in not one single instance, not one, did we get anything but an arrogant, tough, unyielding rebuff. And yet the next day, I would be attacked that I hadn't handled it the right way—and not one word about Ho Chi Minh.[22]

The result? In Johnson's own words:

The reaction in South Vietnam was quite different from what it was in this country. The people there rose up in arms and I think for the first time brought about a degree of unity that never existed before. So the people of South Vietnam pulled up their socks, enlistments increased, and the folks started coming in and saying, "Come on, let's stop the kinds of things that have happened to us during Tet and let's all rally behind the leadership." In this country our folks did somewhat the opposite. Because immediately the voices just came out of the holes in the wall and said, "Let's get out." And that's what Ho Chi Minh had meant to do all the time—to win in Washington, what he had not won in Paris. To win in this country, in the homes of this country, what he could not win from the men out there that represented us.[23]

Johnson's image will remain tarnished for many years to come by Vietnam. The quick, lithe, strategic brain that was once so admired quickly fell from grace to become seen as that of a scheming liar. The votes are still not all in as to what Lyndon Johnson will eventually mean to history, but perhaps David Halberstam's comments sum up the current view as well as any:

There were many Lyndon Johnsons, this complicated, difficult, sensitive man, and among them were a Johnson when things were going well and a Johnson when things were going poorly. Most of the Kennedy men, new to him, working with him since Dallas, had only seen Johnson at his best. Moving into the post-assassination vacuum with a certain majesty, he had behaved with sensitivity and subtlety, and that challenge had evoked from him the best of his qualities. Similarly, during the planning on Vietnam, during the time he had been, as a new President, faced with his most terrible dilemma, he had been cautious and reflective. If there was a bluster it was largely a bluster on the inside; on the outside he was careful, thoughtful, did his homework, and under certain conditions could be reasoned with.

But when things went badly, he did not respond that well, and he did not, to the men around him, seem reasonable. There was a steady exodus from the White House during 1966 and 1967 of many of the men, both hawks and doves, who had tried to reason with him and tried to affect him on Vietnam. . . . In the late fall of 1965, Johnson learned the hard way that the slide rules and computers did not work, that the projections were all wrong, that Vietnam was in fact a tar baby, and that he was in for a long difficult haul. . . . At that time Lyndon Johnson began to change. He began to sulk, he was not so open, not so accessible, and it was not easy to talk with him about the problems and difficulties in Vietnam. McNamara's access was in direct proportion to his optimism; as he became more pessimistic, the President became reluctant to see him alone. Johnson did not need other people's problems and their murky forecasts; he had enough of those himself. He was, sadly, open-minded when things went well, and increasingly closed-minded when things went poorly.[24]

Perhaps, in the final analysis, the public's image of Johnson is similar to that of Johnson's attitude. When things were going well, the nation felt very open-minded and generous in its respect and praise; when things were going poorly, the country was closed-minded and negative toward all he stood for. Because of Vietnam, it is still easy to forget the other image of Johnson—the great political skillsman who sought to make America a "Great Society."

CONCLUSIONS ABOUT THE LBJ IMAGE

Six conclusions may be drawn about Lyndon Johnson's image. First, two conflicting images of LBJ's political stance emerge from the analysis. One of these images, which we do not accept, but which some observers do, is that of the totally pragmatic—some might even say Machiavellian—political operative who lacked any lasting beliefs of his own. The other, described in William S. White's book, *The Professional,* is the description of LBJ as the consummate professional politician, a political leader with tremendous abilities, who, in terms of domestic politics at least, correctly gauged the sentiment of the Congress and the public in achieving great strides for the downtrodden.

Second, Johnson can be viewed as a product of his own time, the mid-twentieth century. This is why some of Caro's criticisms appear unfair. The ethics and standards of politics in Johnson's period were different from those we hold today, and it is not reasonable to measure Johnson's career between his election to Congress in 1937 and the end of his presidency in 1969 by those benchmarks.

Third, we find Johnson's great concern with his public image reflected in his preoccupation with his treatment by the media and his uncommonly intense interest in the media, which could be described as almost a morbid fascination. He kept three television sets in the Oval Office so that he could see simultaneously what all three networks were reporting about his administration; for a time he also kept a live camera in the White House so that he could appear live on the evening news.

Fourth, Johnson kept struggling for a more effective public image. In a sense, perhaps without realizing it, he was striving to be another JFK. Instead of emphasizing his own best qualities, he made the mistake of trying to emulate his predecessor, a very different president with very different leadership qualities. For a man who was able to control many of the events of his own life, it must have been incredibly frustrating not to be able to control his own image. Johnson tended to look on press secretaries as cheerleaders, perhaps one reason why as president he was served by three after Salinger, a JFK holdover. He also tended to expect Washington correspondents to be cheerleaders, which by the nature of their occupation they of course could not be. A misperception of the role of the national press was a serious flaw in LBJ's approach to the building of his image.

Fifth, Johnson's image winds up as a dichotomy between the "Legislative Wizard" and the "Great Manipulator" of his congressional career and "The Man Who Botched Up Vietnam." His foreign policy successes in other areas— and eventually his domestic policy successes—were overshadowed by the public perception of his "failure" in Vietnam.

Finally, a sixth point is that LBJ's image today seems to be ambivalent. It is that of a gifted, talented leader who accomplished much in domestic policy only to have his historical reputation blemished in a dirty war. Perhaps future generations will be kinder to Lyndon Johnson than his contemporaries were.

NOTES

1. Robert Caro, *The Years of Lyndon Johnson: The Path to Power* (vol. 1) (New York: Alfred A. Knopf, 1982), pp. 166–173. See especially the anecdote about Thomas Coronado on p. 169.

2. Lyndon Baines Johnson, *The Vantage Point: Perspectives on the Presidency 1963– 1969* (New York: Holt, Rinehart and Winston, 1971), pp. 564–567.

3. Release from *Los Angeles Times* Syndicate, Louis Harris Survey, August 10, 1964, White House Central Files, EX PR 15 Public Opinion Polls, Lyndon Baines Johnson Library, Austin, Texas.

4. John Brice's Philadelphia poll, cited in memorandum from Jack Valenti to President Johnson, April 8, 1965, White House Central Files, EX PR 17 Public Opinion Polls.

5. Rexford G. Tugwell, "The Historians and the Presidency," *Political Science Quarterly,* 86, no. 2 (June 1971): 183–204.

6. John Bartlow Martin, "Election of 1964," in Arthur M. Schlesinger, Jr., *The Coming to Power: Critical Presidential Elections in American History* (New York: Chelsea House, 1977), pp. 458–487, especially p. 479. Also see p. 400.

7. Doris Kearns, *Lyndon Johnson and the American Dream* (New York: Harper and Row, 1976), Author's Postscript, pp. 369–371.

8. Caro, *Path to Power,* pp. xviii, xix. David Herbert Donald of Harvard in a review in the *New York Times* Book Review, November 21, 1982, pp. 1, 35–38, concluded:

Johnson's achievements are slighted, and the book becomes a dark chronicle of consuming personal ambition. For readers who want to believe that the President Johnson of the Vietnam war years not merely was, but always had been an unprincipled monster, *The Path to Power* will be rewarding reading. For those who seek to understand this remarkably complex, singularly gifted and tragically limited man, Mr. Caro's book will see more like a caricature than a portrait.

Robert Sherrill of the *Texas Observer* said in a review in the *Washington Post* Book World, November 21, 1982, pp. 1, 2, 10, 11:

One gets an overwhelming sense of *deja vu.* We are hearing exactly the same accusations that were made a generation ago by left-wing Democrats in Texas, bitter from being crushed throughout the 1950's and 1960's by Johnson's forces, the same accusations made by right-wing Texans such as

J. Evetts Haly in 1964 *(A Texan Looks at Lyndon)*, infuriated by Johnson's pious destruction of Barry Goldwater.

Of Caro's style, Sherrill writes: "This isn't simply a biography. It's a production." Bruce Morton of CBS News interviewed Robert Caro, Emmette Redford, and Willard Deason on the Caro book controversy and stated, "The real argument between Caro and his critics is over motive" (segment of CBS Sunday Morning News with Charles Kurault, 9:00–10:30 A.M. EST, Sunday, March 27, 1983).

9. George E. Reedy, *Lyndon Johnson: A Memoir* (New York: Andrews and McMeel, 1982), pp. 9, 10, 22, 52, 158, 159.

10. Rowland Evans and Robert Novak, *LBJ: The Exercise of Power* (New York: New American Library, 1966), pp. 599, 600.

11. Sarah McClendon, *My Eight Presidents* (New York: Wyden Books, 1978), pp. 136, 137.

12. Caro, *Path to Power,* p. 164.

13. Doris A. Graber, ed., *The President and the Public* (Philadelphia: Institute for the Study of Human Issues, 1982), p. 89.

14. Kearns, *LBJ and American Dream,* pp. 258, 259.

15. William C. Spragens with Carole Ann Terwoord, *From Spokesman to Press Secretary: White House Media Operations* (Lanham, Md.: University Press of America, 1980), p. 51.

16. Lyndon B. Johnson, CBS News Special, "LBJ: Tragedy and Transition," broadcast on Saturday, May 2, 1970, 7:30–8:30 P.M. EDT. Produced by CBS News and narrated by Walter Cronkite.

17. Graber, *President and Public,* p. 123.

18. Dom Bonafede, "Carter and the Polls—If You Live by Them, You May Die by Them," *National Journal,* August 9, 1978, p. 1312.

19. Letter to W. Marvin Watson from James Nicholson of Indianapolis, November 18, 1966 (dictated November 16, 1966), exchange of correspondence between Watson and Nicholson, Aides' Files, Office Files of James R. Jones, Box 1, Lyndon Baines Johnson Library, Austin, Texas.

20. George Edwards III, "Presidential Manipulation of Public Opinion," in Thomas E. Cronin, ed., *Rethinking the Presidency* (Boston: Little, Brown, 1982), pp. 207, 208. See also John M. Orman, *Presidential Secrecy and Deception: Beyond the Power to Persuade* (Westport, Conn.: Greenwood Press, 1980), covering the period from the Kennedy administration through the Ford administration. See particularly Chapter 4, "Bureaucratic Secrecy: Lyndon B. Johnson," pp. 97–122.

21. Caro, *Path to Power,* p. 160.

22. CBS News Special, "LBJ: The Decision to Halt the Bombing," broadcast February 6, 1970, 10:00–11:00 P.M. EST. Produced by CBS News and narrated by Walter Cronkite.

23. CBS News Special, February 6, 1970.

24. David Halberstam, *The Best and the Brightest* (New York: Random House, 1972), pp. 622, 623.

ANNOTATED BIBLIOGRAPHY

Books

Caro, Robert. *The Years of Lyndon Johnson: The Path to Power.* Vol. 1. New York: Alfred A. Knopf, 1982.

This first volume of a projected trilogy has ignited great controversy. It contains documentation of LBJ's fund-raising as a congressman in the precomputer era.

Dugger, Ronnie. *The Politician: The Life and Times of Lyndon Johnson: The Drive for Power—from the Frontier to Master of the Senate*. New York: W. W. Norton, 1982.

This book is valuable for two things—its insight into the Texas culture from which LBJ derives his political essence, and the author's willingness to examine Johnson as a flesh-and-blood politician engaging in all the nitty-gritty activities (e.g., fund-raising) that political practitioners must engage in.

Evans, Rowland, and Robert Novak. *Lyndon B. Johnson: The Exercise of Power*. New York: New American Library, 1966.

A journalistic account by two columnists who were contemporaries of Johnson, this book gives a good idea of the image projected by LBJ at the midpoint of his term.

Halberstam, David. *The Best and the Brightest*. New York: Random House, 1972.

This critique covers Vietnam decision-making during the distressing war period.

Johnson, Lyndon Baines. *The Vantage Point: Perspectives of the Presidency (1963–1969)*. New York: Holt, Rinehart and Winston, 1971.

In Lyndon Johnson's own words, he leaves his impressions of his presidency. The book reads somewhat like an official document and does have a self-justifying tone, but it is a valuable reference for determining Johnson's basic issue positions on both domestic and foreign policy.

Kearns, Doris. *Lyndon Johnson and the American Dream*. New York: Harper and Row, 1976.

This insightful volume is part biography, part political psychology. Kearns worked for LBJ near the end of his administration, but during his retirement she conducted a series of interviews with him at the LBJ Ranch in Texas. Kearns provides useful insights into the formative years of LBJ, the influence of his parents on his development (particularly his mother), and the impact of the Texas culture on his political career.

Redford, Emmette S. *An Administrative History of the Lyndon B. Johnson Administration*. Austin: University of Texas Press, 1982.

This is the first book of its kind. The treatment of departmental matters is good and well documented; there is some lack of integration of material, but this may be inevitable in such a study.

White, Theodore H. *The Making of the President 1964*. New York: Atheneum, 1965.

One in a series of narrative accounts of presidential elections, this book by the noted journalist relates details of the Johnson-Goldwater election campaign of 1964. Useful in placing the campaign in context.

———. *America in Search of Itself: The Making of the President 1956–1980*. New York: Harper and Row, 1982.

A kind of summary of the *Making of the President* series, this book gives a good synthesis from White's perspective of the political significance of the Great Society and the impact of television in the 1964 election.

Recordings and Tapes

Cronkite, Walter. narrator. "I Can Hear It Now/The Sixties." Written and edited by Fred Friendly and Walter Cronkite (associated in production: J. G. Gude and John

M. Patterson). Columbia Masterworks MSX 30353.

Three-record set. Includes LBJ taking presidential oath in Dallas, first address to Congress, November 27, 1963, acceptance at Atlantic City, August 27, 1964, announcement that LBJ will not seek another term, March 31, 1968.

————. "Vietnam: Chronicle of a War." CV500049/CB500049.

A videotape history of the war in Vietnam, narrated by the anchorperson of whom LBJ is reported to have said, "If Cronkite says we've lost the war, we're in trouble."

Huntley Chet, and David Brinkley, narrators. "A Time to Keep: 1964." RCA Victor, LOC-1096.

Includes events of 1964 campaign against Goldwater.

————. "A Time to Keep: 1965." RCA Victor, LOC-1097.

Includes Johnson's 1965 inaugural address, Selma appeal at night session of Congress in 1965.

19 RICHARD M. NIXON

Frank Kessler

In a January 1973 interview with *Time* magazine, President Richard M. Nixon, embarking on his second term, commented, "I have probably the most unusual opportunity, the greatest opportunity of any President in history." Even accounting for Nixon's tendencies to exaggerate the significance of many of the events of his life in his early memoirs with the appropriately overstated title, *Six Crises,* Nixon was convinced of his place in the folklore of American politics. He saw in the next four years a chance to take advantage of a fortuitous set of circumstances in the sweep of world history to put into place a new structure of world peace. Comments such as these were hauntingly reminiscent of Woodrow Wilson's dream of decades past that envisioned the League of Nations as the insurance that World War I would, in fact, be "the war to end all wars."

Ironically, Nixon's niche in history was assured not through his profound international initiatives or breakthroughs on the domestic or economic policy fronts. Unfortunately for Nixon, his legacy seems destined to be Watergate and its myriad examples of betrayal of the public trust.

This chapter will examine how Nixon's image as an overwhelmingly victorious candidate in 1972 deteriorated within months into that of a broken man, limping, albeit with theatrical gallantry, from the nation's constitutional pinnacle to the virtual oblivion of his San Clemente estate in the short space of two years. It pursues the factors that contributed to the fall from public grace of a president and how images affect careers, especially when the image of the person is contrived and does not fit his character. As we examine the ways in which Nixon damaged his own image as he administered the office, we shall show how his administration encouraged an assertive Congress and in the process weakened both public perceptions of the presidency and the potential freedom of action of his successors.

NIXON'S CHILDHOOD INSECURITIES

As one of the sons of Frank and Hannah Nixon, Richard Nixon spent his childhood in Southern California. According to James David Barber, Nixon's

mother Hannah had a strong Quaker influence on his life. His father Frank was
a trolley operator who had moved from Columbus, Ohio, to Southern California.
He was as stern with the boys as the mother was loving and understanding.
Nixon also faced tragedy as a child with the death of two young brothers, Harold
and Arthur. This disrupted the home life of the rest of the family, as Hannah
was away at a tuberculosis sanatorium caring for the sick brothers.

Nixon's other brothers were Edward and Donald. Of Richard, Donald said:

Dick always planned things out. He didn't do things accidentally. . . . He wouldn't argue
much with me, for instance, but once, when he had had just about as much of me as he
could take, he cut loose and kept at it for half to three quarters of an hour. He went back
a year or two listing things I had done. He didn't leave out a thing. I was only eight,
and he was ten, but I've had a lot of respect ever since for the way he can keep things
in his mind.

Richard Nixon also had to deal with a father who was a curmudgeon who suffered
from bleeding ulcers and deafness.

There is little doubt that Richard went through traumatic experiences when
each of his brothers died. This perhaps gave him the melancholy countenance
which stayed that way much of the time. At the time of the Teapot Dome scandals
of the 1920s, Richard read much about these in the newspapers and told his
mother, "Mother, I would like to become a lawyer—an honest lawyer, who
can't be bought by crooks."

As a student at Whittier College he took to the stage. He played an innkeeper
in *Bird in Hand*. An audience turned him on, as William Rogers and Rose Mary
Woods both noticed later, since Richard was usually shy in crowds.

Barber warns that too much should not be made of Richard's successes at
Whittier College and states:

Overall, Richard won respect in his college years, but little affection, no close friends.
In a college yearbook cartoon other students are shown talking and laughing around the
central figure—Richard Nixon—neat, solemn, and alone. As a senior he ran for student
body president and won. Part way into the campaign, he visited a professor's mother and
told her he was withdrawing from the race. His duties at the store [his father's store] had
not given him enough time to get known, so he thought he stood no chance of winning.
She persuaded him to continue; the "about to quit" pattern had its beginnings there.

After graduation from Whittier, Nixon attended Duke University Law School
and graduated with honors. A story is told about how he later confessed that he
was so concerned to learn what his grades were that he and a classmate broke
into a professor's office to examine the gradebook. Apparently the break-in was
not discovered at the time and was not disclosed until much later.

After Duke, Nixon worked for the Office of Price Administration (OPA) in
wartime Washington. Perhaps because of his shyness, he had been rejected on
applying for a job within the Federal Bureau of Investigation; nor had he had

any better luck when applying to the John Foster Dulles law firm in New York City, Sullivan and Cromwell.

CONGRESS AND THE ALGER HISS CASE

After returning home to Whittier to practice law, and meeting and marrying Patricia (Thelma) Ryan, Nixon answered a newspaper ad and was chosen as the Republican nominee for Congress from the Whittier district in 1946. He was elected in a controversial campaign against the popular Representative Jerry Voorhis. At the age of thirty-two he defeated the New Deal–oriented Voorhis with a hard campaign and with the aid of a political climate in which even a New Dealer like Voorhis could be made to look something like a communist. Earl Mazo and Stephen Hess, Nixon's biographers, have described how Nixon "won" a debate with Voorhis by waving papers in Voorhis' face after a Nixon advertisement had declared: "A vote for Nixon is a vote against the Communist-dominated PAC [Political Action Committee of the CIO] with its gigantic slush fund."[1]

As a congressman from California, Nixon won fame and notoriety through his membership on the House Un-American Activities Committee (HUAC), which investigated communists and fellow-travelers (communist sympathizers). The HUAC investigation ultimately led to the conviction of Alger Hiss, who had served FDR at Yalta and was a secretary at the United Nations founding conference in San Francisco.

Questioning of Alger Hiss by the committee established that Whittaker Chambers, a *Time* editor, had testified that he and Hiss were members of a communist group in Washington in the 1930s, and Chambers later produced the controversial "pumpkin papers"—actually microfilms of State Department documents of the 1930s he said Hiss had copied and turned over to him as a Soviet agent. Hiss denied knowing Chambers, at least under that name, and later charged that the "pumpkin papers" (hidden on microfilm in a pumpkin on Chambers' Maryland farm) were forged by typewriter—a claim the courts never accepted. In the late 1970s, Hiss was still making an unsuccessful effort in the courts to clear his name through documents released to him under the Freedom of Information Act of 1967, but he had been readmitted to the bar. For Richard Nixon the principal importance of the Hiss case was that it made him nationally known.

Nixon asserted in his memoirs that "people were now alerted to a serious threat to our liberties" because of the Hiss case. Nixon also observed: "I think that Foster Dulles expressed the real lesson of the Hiss case when he said, 'The conviction of Alger Hiss is human tragedy. It is tragic that so great promise should have come to so inglorious an end.'"

Having first vanquished Jerry Voorhis and then Alger Hiss, Richard Nixon took on and defeated Helen Gahagan Douglas, a popular liberal congresswoman, in the 1950 California Senate race. This was the widely noted "pink lady" campaign in which Nixon tagged Congresswoman Douglas with having voted many times with Vito Marcantonio, the American Labor Party congressman from New York City, who was considered a fellow-traveler of the communists of that day. Murray Chotiner, the political "fixer," was a principal campaign aide to the Nixon organization, which distributed a pink sheet carrying a comparison of Helen Douglas' votes in the House with those of Marcantonio. Nixon won in a landslide.

NIXON AS VICE PRESIDENT

Richard Nixon only served about two years as senator because in 1952 he was tapped by the Republican hierarchy to be the running mate for General Dwight D. Eisenhower. As a vice presidential candidate, he was the object of a controversy about a secret campaign fund he had operated to which oil men and others contributed. The campaign fund was similar to those used by many senators to supplement travel funds and to avoid spending tax dollars for what were more purely political purposes than their normal activities. But it was attacked immediately by the Democrats. There was some talk of Nixon resigning from the GOP ticket after the fund was made known in a nationally syndicated column by Peter Edson of the Newspaper Enterprise Association. Nixon was reported to have been perturbed by the insistence of General Eisenhower that he would have to be "clean as a hound's tooth" to remain on the ticket. But Nixon went on nationwide television with talk of the fund, of his loyal wife Pat who wore "a good Republican cloth coat" (President Truman's aides had been the object of scandals involving mink coats), and also about Nixon's family dog Checkers, a gift from Texas admirers. "No matter what they say, we're gonna keep him," Nixon said of his children's dog. The public reaction was overwhelmingly positive; Nixon stayed on the ticket, and he was welcomed in Wheeling, West Virginia, by Eisenhower, who now said of him, "He's my boy."

The Eisenhower-Nixon ticket swept to an unprecedented landslide victory in 1952 on the K1C2 slogan—Korea, Communism, and Corruption. Nixon was the "point man" for the Republicans, traveling about the country to speak for the party faithful. On the road in campaigns in 1954, 1956, and 1958, Nixon sometimes got carried away with partisan rhetoric and at one time accused former President Truman of being "a traitor to the high principles of the Democratic party." This made Speaker Sam Rayburn furious. Although Rayburn spoke frequently with President Eisenhower, he would hardly speak to Nixon at all.

In 1956 there was controversy over whether Nixon would remain on the ticket with Eisenhower, who had offered him a chance to become a cabinet officer instead. Nixon nearly quit in disgust but decided to attempt to remain on the ticket, and his grateful friends in the party easily derailed an attempt by Eisenhower aide and former presidential candidate Harold Stassen to replace Nixon with someone else. In 1958 Nixon was the target of a communist-led mob of rock-throwers and spitters in Caracas, Venezuela, which made him a hero to many conservative Americans. In 1959 he went to the American exhibition at a Moscow fair and engaged in the famous "kitchen debate" with Nikita Khrushchev in which they discussed such matters as American technological superiority and the availability of color television sets. Again this aided Nixon's popularity with many of the more conservative American voters.

LOSING RACES FOR PRESIDENT AND GOVERNOR

In 1960 Richard Nixon was nominated by the Republican party to run for president as Eisenhower's successor. He was engaged in four television debates with John F. Kennedy, and while there was some controversy about the last three debates, the consensus of observers was that Kennedy "won" the first debate. Nixon looked ashen and tired, and his stubbly beard showed because the compound used for makeup had not been applied heavily enough, according to most accounts. He also was somewhat obsequious toward Kennedy in trying to erase the image of the "old Nixon"—the unpresidential partisan campaigner for the Republican party.

After being defeated by Senator Kennedy in one of the closest presidential elections in American history, Richard Nixon attempted a comeback by running for California governor in 1962. He was defeated by Edmund G. (Pat) Brown, father of "Jerry" Brown and predecessor of Ronald Reagan at Sacramento in the governor's chair. Then Nixon moved to New York to practice law and waited for another chance to run for president. This came in 1968.

THE VICTORIOUS 1968 CAMPAIGN

Richard Nixon was nothing if not tenacious, so in 1968, after Senator Barry Goldwater had been soundly defeated in 1964, Nixon ran for and received the Republican nomination at Miami Beach, defeating Governor Nelson A. Rockefeller of New York and Governor Ronald Reagan of California for the nomination. He had learned a good deal of humility in the preceding eight years, and while never a favorite of American reporters, probably had the nearest to a good press in this campaign that he ever had.

Nixon's 1968 opponents were Vice President Hubert H. Humphrey, the Democrat who waited too long to declare his independence from Lyndon B. Johnson's policy of pressing the war in Vietnam, and Governor George C. Wallace of Alabama, who was known for his anti–civil rights positions. Wallace at one time had a level of support approaching 20 percent in the polls, but his following faded as the election neared. Nixon ran a conservative campaign, seeking to cling to his slim lead, and Humphrey made a headlong rush at the end of the campaign. But Nixon won in a close contest. It was later charged that Nixon's friends sought to influence President Nguyen Van Thieu of South Vietnam not to participate in the Paris peace conference; the Republicans rejoined that Thieu was intelligent enough to realize that his country would get a better deal from Nixon and the Republicans.

NIXON: THE FIRST ADMINISTRATION

During his first administration, President Nixon dealt with two chief problems: domestic economic policy and the "winding down" (a popular term) of the war in Vietnam. According to some sources, chiefly Seymour Hersh, Nixon, through his national security adviser, Henry A. Kissinger, reached a truce in Vietnam in 1973 that could have been had in 1968 or 1969. Republican defenders of Nixon have maintained that he had to achieve "peace with honor" by allowing an "honorable" American withdrawal from South Vietnam. At any rate, American participation in the war ended effectively in January 1973, and Saigon (and the rest of the country) fell to the communists in 1975. Nixon tenaciously held throughout his tenure to the "domino theory"—that a communist victory in one country would eventually lead to communist victories elsewhere.

In domestic policy, Nixon in 1971, after saying that he would never take such a step, introduced temporary wage and price controls to get the economy under control and to stabilize what threatened to be serious inflation. He was also known for paring down domestic programs and for what seemed an endless series of vetoes of education bills. The liberal establishment opposed him vigorously, but he had in the first term the support of most of the business community.

However, it was the controversy between Nixon and the peace movement that led to some of what John Mitchell, Nixon's first attorney general, came to call the "White House horrors." This also led to the cluster of scandals known collectively as Watergate.

EXPLAINING WATERGATE IN IMAGE TERMS

Richard Nixon reached the peak of his popularity at 67 percent shortly after the signing of the Vietnam truce in January 1973. The Gallup "approval ratings" also show that the low point of his popularity came in July and August 1974, when it reached 24 percent. (The lowest rating for anyone was President Carter's 23 percent in 1979.) This unpopularity came to Nixon largely because of public revulsion at the reelection tactics of his 1972 campaign and even more because of what came to be known as the "smoking gun" evidence (on an audio tape) that he conspired—if unwittingly, as he maintained—in the obstruction of justice in the Watergate case.

One of the best studies of President Nixon and Watergate is the recently published *The Battle for Public Opinion* by two political sociologists, Gladys Engel Lang and Kurt Lang. It suggests that there was a bitter battle between the Nixon administration and the news media over the agenda-setting process. Agenda-setting is defined as the placing of priorities on issues for public discussion. Normally both the White House and the news media have a great deal of influence on this process.

The Langs suggest that it was Nixon's defeat in the battle for public opinion that forced him to retreat at crucial points when political survival depended on agenda-setting. The Langs note:

In February 1973 Nixon was enjoying peak ratings. It was the beginning of his second term and just after the peace agreement was signed with North Vietnam on January 25, resulting in the return of the American prisoners of war after years in North Vietnam. He was bound to slip from the pinnacle of popularity even with the cease fire.

They also observe that "Watergate was not a significant factor in the outcome of the 1972 election."

The Langs note that some five months after the presidential election fewer people than before thought that Watergate was only a political squabble. There had been some erosion in the president's credibility, but even at this stage people, unable to understand what was going on, still wanted to believe in Nixon as their elected president. It was when the media and the opposition began to get at the truth of Watergate that Watergate at last became an issue.

There were soon others who believed that there was a scandal. Nixon's actions, however, were motivated by his overriding concern for national security, in the opinion of many voters even at this time.

The Langs observe:

The news should be treated as if it were a map of the political landscape. Such a map is, to be sure, a complex map with contours of political figures, public failures, expanding problems, and threats. Inevitably it depicts the world from a partisan perspective regarding what is selected and highlighted. The labels it gives to events locate obtuse unknown events and tend to make the world appear more familiar. . . .

These media maps have to be a focus of investigation. They make up the symbolic environment that creates interest not only from the mass public but also reflects the views of the circle of insiders who also depend on the media in charting their political courses. Although the image has become more vivid and more personal, the image still is refracted. Some elements are blown up; others appear distorted or are diminished in their size by their proximity to the vanishing point. The same applies to the images of public perception. The indirect role of public opinion has changed over the years and the image of the public depicted through the media has become a most important reference group not only for political actors (elected officials, etc.) but also for the public itself and even for the media.[2]

EXPLAINING THE DEFLATION OF NIXON'S IMAGE

To fully understand the deflation of Nixon's somewhat contrived political image, one must examine it in the context of factors that tend to weaken any president's status in the American public's eyes. Public perceptions of an incumbent president may differ markedly from the more aloof and, it is hoped, objective, scholarly perspectives seen from ten or more years later. An examination of the Nixon years should serve as a poignant case study to buttress

Richard Neustadt's contention that "a particular President's influence on government hinges to a great extent upon what the public thinks of him."

On the eve of Nixon's unprecedented decision to resign, a disconsolate president called in Secretary of State Henry A. Kissinger to the Oval Office, ostensibly to discuss "relations with the Soviet Union and China." Kissinger, unlike the president, recalled that August 7 more as a period of reminiscing which found the president seeking assurance that he had made major foreign policy contributions during his administration. (The moves toward recognition of China may look more significant in the 1980s than the conclusion of the SALT treaty with the Soviet Union, but few would doubt that Nixon left a lasting mark on American foreign policy.)

Secretary Kissinger's words of consolation could ultimately apply to most presidents. Dwight Eisenhower, for example, would find his record, considered mediocre in his lifetime, recently assessed more favorably by scholars as disparate as Fred I. Greenstein, Stephen Ambrose, and Cornelius Cotter.

In the Preface to this volume the editor notes Thomas Cronin's view that mass media and our educational system have contributed substantially to the exaggerated image of the chief executive, which has been variously labeled the "imagined," "the mythical," or the "textbook" presidency.[3]The same people who helped fashion giant perceptions of occupants of the White House during the FDR, Truman, Kennedy and early Johnson years began castigating the abuses of the "imperial" presidency which peaked during Nixon's tenure. Ultimately, Nixon's drive for success in reaching his foreign policy and domestic political goals, no matter what the cost, led to his resignation. It also awakened a sleeping congressional giant.

Both Richard Nixon and Lyndon Johnson left the White House under pressure of increasingly unfavorable public opinion. What is it about a particular president that might encourage him to leave office before his time? Some evidence points to the erosion of Nixon's self-image as a reason for early departure (aside from the obvious legal and constitutional reasons).

In his influential *War, Presidents and Public Opinion* (1973), John Mueller found that public perceptions of the state of the economy, war-peace international issues, and the personality of the president (as the public perceived it) were the key factors in shaping opinion about any particular president. The *Gallup Opinion Index* in its September-October 1980 study, "Presidential Popularity: A Forty-three-Year Review," reached similar conclusions. (See Figure 19.1.)

Examining Nixon's unceremonious exit, his own personality, character, and image increasingly played a major part in his woes as they had throughout his political career. Henry Kissinger affirmed this view in his memoirs:

At the moment of his fall, I felt for Nixon a great tenderness ... for the tremendous struggle he had fought with his own complex personality, for his anguish, great aspirations defeated in the end by weaknesses of character that became destructive because he had never come to grips with them.

Figure 19.1
Approval Ratings for Richard M. Nixon

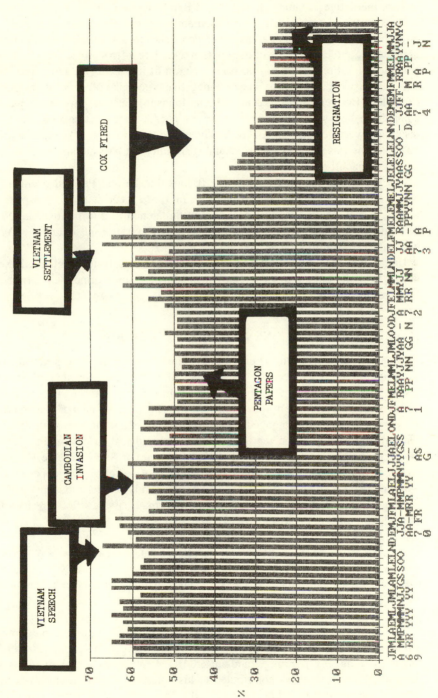

Source: Gallup Opinion Index, September–October 1980.

With predictive accuracy, James David Barber wrote in 1971 that "one need only read over his speech on the Cambodian invasion (1970) with its themes of power and control, its declaration of independence, its self-concern, its damning of doubters, and its coupling of humiliation with defeat [to see] . . . this character could lead the President on to disaster." Nixon fit into Barber's active-passive, positive-negative typology as an active-negative type. Like other active-negative examples (Hoover, Wilson, and Lyndon Johnson), Nixon gave evidence of compulsive behavior, expending enormous energy in everything he did as a result of low self-esteem and out of fear he would not succeed. Like other active-negatives, he was prone to a siege mentality, rigidity, and pessimism. In addition, he was frequently maudlin.

In 1954 Nixon reportedly told close friends that he and Pat had decided he would retire after his term ended in 1957. In 1956, faced with the prospect of being "demoted" to a cabinet post, Nixon threatened to quit politics. In 1962 he held his famous "last press conference" in which he told reporters, "You won't have Nixon to kick around anymore."

Unlike Hoover, Wilson, or Lyndon Johnson (all rigidly ideological), Nixon had an "investment not in values, not in standing for some principle . . . [rather] his investment was in himself."

IMAGES: CREATING ONE AND HIDING OTHERS

Though Nixon invested his energies in himself, the product was not always a saleable commodity because the wrapper often failed to disguise what was inside. Biographers have described his days from childhood through his political career as a never ending effort to compensate for his own feelings of inadequacy. His low self-esteem encouraged him to project an image of strength; his aunt remembered him lying on the lawn gazing skyward lost in daydreaming. (As president, he also secluded himself at Key Biscayne or San Clemente.)[4]

Barber found that Nixon's world view was that of a skeptic who expected the worst of people. In Nixon's own writings, he rarely appears disappointed in those grim expectations. He wrote of the aftermath of the 1960 presidential campaign:

I have seen many men become bitter after an election defeat when they saw friendships melt away. . . . And what really hurt worst was that those for whom they had done the most were often the first to desert. I was not unprepared for this reaction because I had already gained that experience during my mercurial career.

To Nixon, most people were lazy and lacking in drive, daring, and courage. Unlike his self-image, others lacked will power, personal mobilization capacities, and the willingness to struggle and suffer. His skeptical view of human nature and emphasis on its flaws contributed to his tendency to play no-holds-barred politics. He seemed to believe that he had to *do unto others* before they had a chance to *do unto him*. This seemed exemplified in his campaigns against Jerry Voorhis (for Congress) and Helen Gahagan Douglas (for the Senate). Adlai Stevenson viewed this philosophy of politics as giving Nixon an image of ''smash and grab and anything to win.''

In later years criticism was leveled at the 1972 Committee to Re-elect the President (CRP) for a sign that hung over the door of its Washington office declaring, ''Winning in politics isn't everything, it's the only thing.'' Combativeness was his very way of life. He once commented: ''I believe in the battle, whether it's the battle of the campaign or the battle of this office. . . . It's always there wherever you go. I perhaps carry it more than others because that's my way.''

Though shy and introverted as a youth, at Whittier College he participated in debate, drama, student government, and football as outlets for his drive to succeed. He terms sports ''the most exciting kind of combat imaginable.''

Nixon was a gambler, and his combativeness led him to do things others considered foolhardy. His wife Pat remembered that he wanted badly to ice skate despite lack of agility. Dick ''almost broke his head two or three times but he just kept on going.'' His stubbornness was illustrated by his decision to debate Jerry Voorhis in the congressional campaign of 1946 when all his advisers had opposed this move.

Nixon appeared to have a poor sense of self because of abuse heaped on him by his temper-prone father, Frank Nixon. He learned a masculine role model of bantam rooster.[5] In *Six Crises* Nixon says that he tried to please his father with good performance in school. But it was to his mother, Hannah, that he turned for affection. She provided him with a model of cool, controlled, capable personality. Because of her example, Nixon concluded that ''the ability to be cool, confident, and decisive in crisis is not an inherited characteristic; but is the direct result of how well an individual has prepared himself for battle.''

The New York physician Arnold Hutschnecker responded to questions about Nixon's character by suggesting that Nixon, whom he saw as vice president, had a controlled-adjusted personality. Henry Kissinger remembered a call he received from Nixon on August 8, 1974, on the eve of the president's resignation, in which Nixon said, ''Please, Henry, don't ever tell anyone that I cried, that I was not strong.'' About human frailties, Nixon himself observed in *Six Crises:* ''I have found leaders are subject to all human frailties: they lose their tempers, become depressed. . . . Even strong men will cry.'' At school Nixon learned to overcome tendencies toward introversion when they got in the way of translating daydreams into success. In debating, he learned to mask true feelings and to act in a cool and calculated way.

THE CONTRIVING OF AN IMAGE

Before his 1968 race for the White House, Nixon had great difficulty leaving the type of impression he wanted to leave with the American electorate. Joe

McGinniss, who served on the Nixon public relations team in 1968 for a time, became known as author of *The Selling of the President 1968*. In this volume McGinniss seeks to explain the image problem the former vice president experienced in his effort to defeat Vice President Hubert Humphrey. McGinniss and his cohorts felt that the public viewed Nixon as a loser either because there was something about him that they did not like, or they felt that he spelled loser, or because so many other people they knew felt he was a loser. Their solution to the image problem was to show his best side (without 5 o'clock shadow or running mascara as in the 1960 presidential debates) and a human side the public might not have recognized before. The "new" Nixon should project spontaneity, kindness, and a low-key, less tense image. Even the previously critical Theodore H. White could write of 1968: "As I approached the campaign of 1968, I tried to tuck away records, files, and utterances of the Richard Nixon of the 1950's. The Nixon of 1968 was so different than the Nixon of 1960 that his whole personality required re-exploration." Later, in his *Breach of Faith*, White seemed to be writing a post-Watergate mea culpa to atone for such effusive comments about the Nixon of the 1968 and 1972 campaigns.

The public relations practitioners "created" the public "personality" of the "new" Nixon by restructuring his encounters with the public. They used staged "spontaneous" happenings with the belief that gut voter reaction toward the candidate could be made more favorable. "It's not the man we have to change; but rather the *received impression* and that impression often depends more on the medium . . . than it does on the candidate himself." A Nixon producer said:

Let's face it, a lot of people think Nixon is dull. . . . He's a bore, a pain in the ass. . . . They figure other kids got footballs for Christmas, Nixon got a briefcase and loved it. . . . He looks like someone hung him up in a closet overnight and he jumps out in the morning with his suit all bunched up and starts running around saying "I want to be President."

As he had used anticommunism, the popularity of Eisenhower, and the truce in Korea as issues in earlier campaigns, Nixon sought to persuade the public that just as Eisenhower had achieved a truce in Korea so he could attain a truce in Vietnam. A centerpiece of his campaign was to avoid totally debates with Humphrey and George Wallace; this was to maintain total control of his image. He deviated from this strategy only once—to make a previously planned appearance on "Meet the Press" on NBC shortly before the election.[6]

WINNING REELECTION IN 1972

True to form in 1972, the winning Nixon Rose Garden strategy—relatively new at that time—was little more than a minor variation on the format that had worked so well in 1968. (The format became a little ragged and did not work so well later for Gerald Ford or Jimmy Carter.) The major difference was that he was president this time so that he did not have to rely on the Eisenhower mantle. He also had a $60 million war chest for the campaign. He had little real opposition in the primaries, and he could focus all the attention of the public on Senators Edmund Muskie and George McGovern—his likely opponents in November. Instead of town meetings and question and answer sessions in New Hampshire, he was now able to campaign by being filmed at work in the White House. In addition, he had all the political levers available to the incumbent president. Despite this advantage, temptations were great—given the fact that he was running behind in some polls in 1971—to return to techniques used in opposing Voorhis, Helen Douglas, and Alger Hiss for probing for weaknesses in the opponent's armor. In 1960, for example, the Nixon campaign had carefully researched all John Kennedy's campaign statements looking for inconsistencies. Once again, Nixon sought to compensate for feelings of inadequacy.

If the break-in at the Watergate complex did nothing else to the Nixon administration's image, it dispelled the notion that Nixon was in charge of his own destiny. As Nixon put it to his chief aide, H. R. Haldeman: "I hate things like this. We're not in control." Espionage had been part of all Nixon campaigns, according to John Ehrlichman. In 1968 Murray Chotiner sought to place a "mole" in the Humphrey campaign. Ehrlichman wrote: "Almost every day Chotiner's mole on the Humphrey press plane would send us lengthy reports describing the morale, internal operating problems, and off-the-record or unreported comments of the opposition campaign staff and candidate and . . . the candidate's wife." It was ironic that these efforts backfired to further besmirch the image and reputation of Richard Nixon himself.

In *The Palace Guard,* Dan Rather and Gary Paul Gates stated that they sought to show H. R. Haldeman as a principal agent in the Watergate disasters. But in doing so, they had no intention of taking Richard Nixon off the hook. Nixon later admitted to the American public that he chose his own staff and thus had to take responsibility for their actions.

The "us versus them" mentality led to the "Enemies List." Charles Colson made up the original list of those who would not be invited to White House gatherings and galas. Later John Dean, the president's nemesis, told of an August 1971 memo:

This memorandum addresses the matter of how we can maximize the fact of our incumbency in dealing with persons known to be active in opposition to our Administration. Stated a bit more bluntly . . . how can we use the available federal machinery to screw our political enemies?

As names were added to the list, it swelled to over 300. But a mere 20 were on the prime list.

According to a taped conversation of September 15, 1972, with John Dean (as given in edited transcripts) President Nixon said:

I want the most comprehensive notes on all those who tried to do us in. They didn't have to do it. If we had a very close election and they were playing the other side, I would understand this. No—they were doing this quite deliberately and they were asking for it, and they are going to get it. We have not used the power in this first four years as you know. We have never used it. We have not used the Bureau [FBI] and we have not used the Justice Department, but things are going to change now.[7]

It was clear that those not loyal to or cooperative with the president could find themselves the subject of IRS audits, FBI security checks, or, in Daniel Ellsberg's case, the target of attempted character assassination.

USING THE WHITE HOUSE TO LOOK PRESIDENTIAL

Historians might find that the image of Richard Nixon and his administration, and even the luster of the presidency itself, began to fade after June 17, 1972, the date of the Watergate break-in by E. Howard Hunt, Frank Sturgis, Eugenio Martinez, and others at the Democratic National Committee headquarters. The burglars had used CIA equipment for the illegal breaking and entering, according to later reports, and this had been with the blessing of high-ranking Nixon aides.

As the cocoon so neatly spun around the operation began to unravel, key personnel left themselves liable to charges of perjury and obstruction of justice. During an attempt to cover up White House ties to the operation, John Dean testified later that he spoke on March 21, 1973, to the president and Haldeman about the "cancer on the Presidency." Dean referred to problems in getting "hush money" for Hunt and others and the accompanying perjury; but it was much more involved than that. The cancer had been festering since the first days of the administration; a number of factors had contributed to the impact of Watergate on public perceptions and to poor judgment which would bring down the administration. First, one must examine the nature of the presidency as Nixon saw it. Next, one should consider the "old buddies" staffing system with its excessive emphasis on loyalty, team players, and isolation at the top created by hierarchical staffing patterns. Third, one should examine White House attempts to politicize the bureaucracies, abusing their investigative arms, and finally keeping White House control over supposedly nonpolitical bureaucracies (as Richard Nathan put it, "The Plot That Failed").

The president's obsession with control was reflected in this testimony before the Senate Watergate Committee:

He was very interested in meals and how they were served, and the timing of serving by the waiters. . . . He was interested in who introduced him to guests and he wanted it done properly. . . . [He was] interested in the details of the drive up the walkway, whether the military should be on the right or the left . . . whether or not the Secret Service would salute during "The Star Spangled Banner."

Early in 1970, after a trip to Europe, Nixon ordered the White House police garbed in military-style uniforms including tunics, patent leather holsters, formal shoes, and pointed Prussian helmets. Peals of press laughter forced the outfits into mothballs. In retrospect the incident seems anything but laughable since it showed the president's insensitivity to democracy and his lack of good judgment.

In choosing his staff, Richard Nixon used the old buddies network (sometimes called the BUGAT or BOSGAT system) to hire top aides like Haldeman. This produced team players who knew that their loyalties belonged to the president. The emperor does not want to be told that he has no clothes. White House aide Jeb Stuart Magruder recalled:

I had bounded around for several years, not having a job I really liked. . . . and now I had a job I loved. "Jeb," I told myself, "you're not going to screw this one up. You like this job and you're going to do what they tell you." Although I was aware that they were illegal, and I am sure others knew . . . we had become somewhat inured to using some activities that would help us in accomplishing what we thought was a legitimate cause.

Getting along meant doing what Haldeman wanted done. He was in many respects an alter ego to the president. The president let Haldeman handle details of administration including work as the president's resident hatchet man. Haldeman said of his role, "Every President has his SOB and I guess I'm Nixon's."[8]

Haldeman was nicknamed "the Berlin Wall." According to Magruder and others, he controlled the flow of both information and people into the Oval Office. Even though the real danger to the presidency is isolation from reality, Nixon feared the opposite. Haldeman served as a final filter for memoranda, deciding whether they should reach the president's desk.

Henry Kissinger suggested that the needs of Nixon's personality called for a Haldeman-type operation:

The vaunted Haldeman procedures were an effort to compensate for . . . weaknesses. Access to the President was restricted because even a tightly limited schedule of appointments brought forth constant Presidential complaints. A White House staffer sat in on every meeting with an outsider so as to assure some follow-up on Presidential promises (and to be aware on occasion of the need to disavow them). As much staff business as possible was conducted by memoranda because Nixon was much more likely to express his real views in writing rather than face to face.

The staffing system which handled the "tough issues" like the decisions to break in at the Watergate kept the president from getting his hands soiled, though it may have damaged his public image later; but it permitted less image-conscious aides to make decisions which demonstrated that the presidency might not be such a heroic seat of governance as mythology suggested.

THE BUREAUCRACIES AND NIXON'S IMAGE

Nowhere was Richard Nixon's need to be in control of things more apparent than in the image he projected to the federal bureaucracy. When he entered the

White House in 1969, Kennedy-Johnson appointees had been added to the bureaucracy over the past eight years. These appointees held key positions up and down the employee lists of federal agencies. When one proposes, as Nixon did, to cut budgets, career civil servants do not stand in line to offer suggestions. They do not lack the ability to act as budget bloodhounds and sniff out savings, but they surely have little incentive to cut off their own noses. To make the bureaucracies more responsive, Nixon tried to put his own appointees into key positions in agencies and departments to the point of almost politicizing the civil service ranks in certain domestic departments like Health, Education and Welfare, which had grown greatly under Kennedy and Johnson. Nixon realized that he could not depend on cabinet secretaries he had appointed to ride herd over careerists in their departments because their bureaucrats showed great alacrity in co-opting their bosses. The plot to seize control of the bureaucracies from within might have had some success as it had for JFK in the early 1960s had not Watergate intervened.

In another attempt to gain control over the government, Nixon decided to use the Budget Bureau (renamed the Office of Management and Budget [OMB]) as a club over the head of the departments and agencies. The new OMB had a more activist role in this area. He also created a Domestic Council to act as a co-ordinating instrument.

Though the administration did not succeed in creating controls over all departments and agencies, it did successfully use some of them to political advantage. The administration sought to call off the FBI from Watergate through the efforts of Attorney General John Mitchell. Political opponents and investigative journalists often felt the hot breath of an IRS audit encouraged by the Nixon White House. Daniel Schorr of CBS News was even told that an FBI security check was made of him "because the Administration was considering him for an appointment." As his reporting had been frequently critical, no one seriously believed this story.

When an agency or its chief got in the way of the Nixon administration's "game plan," White House aides played "political hardball." When Federal Reserve Board Chairman Arthur Burns refused to lower interest rates at the Fed unless the administration balanced the federal budget, a White House staffer said in a press "leak" that the White House was considering an expansion in the size of the Fed. This ploy was reminiscent of FDR's court-packing plan. The administration also leaked the impression that Nixon planned to reject Burns' request for a $20,000 salary increase during a time of recession and economic distress. Nixon later exonerated Burns by apologizing for the unfair shot taken at him, since Burns had not only not asked for a raise for himself, but had suggested that no government official get a raise. This episode further tarnished the president's image.

Nixon and his aides not only sought to control nominally independent agencies; they shifted spending patterns in such agencies as the Office of Economic Opportunity, a Johnson-created agency, and the Job Corps, another Johnson-holdover agency. The president, instead of vetoing appropriations legislation, circumvented apparent legislative intent by making massive impoundments of funds, seeking to override nearly two centuries of fiscal traditions.

In the foreign policy area, Nixon authorized the invasion of or "incursion" into Cambodia and the secret bombing of Cambodia, and expanded the emergency powers of the president in prosecuting the war in Vietnam, as in the "carpet bombing" of North Vietnam at Christmas 1972.

On one of the Watergate tapes we learn of another way that the administration tried to circumvent Congress in foreign affairs, by using documents classification to withhold information. The president did the following thinking aloud in a meeting with Haldeman, Ehrlichman, and aide Egil (Bud) Krogh:

Maybe another approach to it would be to set up . . . a new classification system. . . . Don't use *Top Secret* for me ever again. I never want to see *Top Secret* in the God damn office. . . . shall we call it uh, John, what would be a good name? *President's secure?* . . . *Eyes Only* is a silly thing too. It doesn't mean anything anymore.[9]

SUMMARY

In the light of the security maze erected around President Nixon, and hierarchical patterns designed to free him from endless meetings, a daydreamer like he was might find it hard to believe that his own political capital had sunk so low that he should consider resigning.

Since so much critical material has been written on Watergate and the abuses surrounding the White House staff and the Committee to Re-elect the President, it is tempting to overlook Nixon's foreign policy successes, such as negotiating arms control with the Soviets and opening trade relations and initiating dialogues with the Chinese Communists. Somehow, it seems, the White House hoped that its successes on the international scene might blunt criticism of Watergate and other failings. Until almost the very end, Nixon and his chief of staff Haldeman expected good public relations to work to cover a multitude of transgressions, including some as monumental in scope as the Watergate scandal. Still, beneath the packaging of the "new" Nixon, near the surface remained the character of a man with an insatiable appetite for success, desire for control, and a latent, though real, need to be approved of and loved.

For a man burdened with such a need to achieve and such a sense of history, how unfortunate it is that the abuses of presidential power and the tarnishing of the public perceptions of the presidency stand to be the principal legacy he leaves the nation. All the foreign policy achievements could not change the fact that he resigned in the face of impeachment. Thus Nixon's image is a complex one— a striver, but one who deceived himself as well as the public in his leadership role.

NOTES

1. *Time,* January 3, 1973, p. 15, as cited in James David Barber, *The Presidential Character: Predicting Performance in the White House,* 1st ed. (Englewood Cliffs, N.J.: Prentice-Hall, 1972), p. 441. On Nixon's theatrical capacities, see Bruce Mazlish, *In Search of Nixon* (New York: Basic Books, 1972), p. 70. For a more favorable view, see Bela Kornitzer, *The Real Nixon* (Chicago: Rand McNally, 1960), p. 107. Also see Earl Mazo and Stephen Hess, *Nixon: A Political Portrait* (New York: Popular Library, 1968), p. 19, and David Abrahamsen, *Nixon v. Nixon: An Emotional Tragedy* (New York: New American Library, 1978). On Hannah Milhous Nixon, see Barber, *The Presidential Character,* p. 400. On scolding by RN, see ibid., p. 398. On Frank Nixon, see ibid., p. 399. On Nixon as loner, see ibid., p. 402. On Teapot Dome comment, see ibid., pp. 405, 406. On reaction to audiences, see ibid., p. 411. On student body president race, see ibid., p. 411. Campaign ad quoted in ibid., p. 415.

2. A full account of the Hiss case may be found in Alistair Cooke, *A Generation on Trial: U.S.A. v. Alger Hiss* (Baltimore: Penguin Books, 1952); Whittaker Chambers, *Witness* (New York: Random House, 1952); Alger Hiss, *In the Court of Public Opinion* (New York: Alfred A. Knopf, 1957); and Richard Nixon, *Six Crises* (New York: Pyramid Books, 1968). On "threat to our liberties," see Richard Nixon, *RN: Memoirs of Richard Nixon,* 2 vols. (New York: Grosset and Dunlap, 1978), 1:57. On Hiss case, see ibid. 1:86. Nixon's own account of the 1950 Senate campaign is carried in ibid., 1:87–95. Nixon is critical of Helen Gahagan Douglas' "stridency." An account of the same campaign from her viewpoint is given in an interview in *Ms.* magazine, Lee Israel, "Helen Gahagan Douglas," *Ms.,* October 1973, pp. 55–59, 112, 115–119. This article is highly critical of Nixon and his "pink lady" campaign techniques. Accounts of the Kennedy-Nixon debates of 1960 can be found in many places including Nixon, *Six Crises;* Barber, *The Presidential Character,* p. 384; Theodore H. White, *The Making of the President 1960* (New York: Atheneum Publishers, 1961); Sidney Kraus, ed., *The Great Debates* (Bloomington: Indiana University Press, 1961); Theodore C. Sorensen, *Kennedy* (New York: Harper and Row, 1965), pp. 195–206; Arthur M. Schlesinger, Jr., *A Thousand Days* (Boston: Houghton Mifflin, 1965); and Herbert Parmet, *JFK: The Presidency of John F. Kennedy* (New York: Dial Press, 1983). Principal sources for what happened in the 1968 campaign are Nixon, *RN,* vols. 1 and 2; Hubert H. Humphrey, *The Education of a Public Man: My Life and Politics* (Garden City, N.Y.: Doubleday and Co., 1976); Theodore H. White, *The Making of the President 1968* (New York: Atheneum Publishers, 1969); Henry A. Kissinger, *The White House Years* (Boston: Houghton Mifflin, 1979); Seymour Hersh, *The Price of Power: Kissinger in the Nixon White House* (New York: Summit Books, 1983). For polling data on approval ratings see *Gallup Opinion Index,* September-October 1980. Also see Gladys Engel Lang and Kurt Lang, *The Battle for Public Opinion: The President, the Press and the Polls During Watergate* (New York: Columbia University Press, 1983), especially Chapter 6, "The Battle of the Polls: October 1973–May 1974," pp. 94–136. On peak of RN popularity, see ibid., p. 6. On media map, see ibid., pp. 6, 41, 24, 25.

3. Richard Neustadt, *Presidential Power* (New York: John Wiley, 1976), pp. 160, 161, as cited in Stephen J. Wayne, "Great Expectations: What People Expect from Their Presidents," in Thomas E. Cronin, ed., *Rethinking the Presidency* (Boston: Little, Brown, 1982), p. 186. On Kissinger visit see Nixon, *RN,* 2:1066. On Nixon international moves,

see Henry A. Kissinger, *Years of Upheaval* (Boston: Little, Brown, 1982), pp. 1206, 1207. On reevaluation of Eisenhower, see Fred I. Greenstein, "Eisenhower as an Activist President: A New Look at the Evidence," *Political Science Quarterly*, 94 (Winter 1979–1980): 575–596. Also see Stephen Ambrose, "The Eisenhower Revival," in Cronin, *Rethinking the Presidency*, pp. 103–114; and Cornelius Cotter, "Eisenhower as Party Leader," *Political Science Quarterly*, 98 (Summer 1983): 255–284. On "imagined" presidency, see Louis Koenig, *The Chief Executive*, 3rd ed. (New York: Harcourt, Brace, 1975), p. 11. On "mythical" presidency, see Frank Kessler, *Dilemmas of Presidential Leadership: Of Caretakers and Kings* (Englewood Cliffs, N.J.: Prentice-Hall, 1982), p. 5. On "textbook" presidency, see Thomas Cronin, "The Textbook Presidency," in Charles Peters and John Rothschild, *Inside the System* (New York: Praeger, 1973), pp. 6–19.

4. Arthur Schlesinger, Jr., *The Imperial Presidency* (Boston: Houghton Mifflin, 1973). Regarding the "sleeping congressional giant," for a discussion of the limits of the budgetary process see Lance T. LeLoup, "Fiscal Chief: Presidents and the Budget," in Stephen A. Shull and Lance T. LeLoup, eds., *The Presidency: Studies in Policy Making* (Brunswick, Ohio: Kings Court, 1979), p. 211. The aroused Congress placed restrictions on budgeting and impoundment of federal funds and the president's authority as com-mander-in-chief, and helped produce a spate of legislative vetoes, wait and report pro-visions, and similar legislative roadblocks for the White House. Some of these were impacted by a 1983 Supreme Court ruling in *Chadha* v. *INS*, but the situation has not been fully clarified. Thomas E. Cronin even suggests that Nixon left in his wake an "imperilled Presidency." For a further discussion of this concept, see Koenig, *Chief Executive*, pp. 10–12. On public perceptions, see John Mueller, *War, Presidents and Public Opinion* (New York: John Wiley, 1973). On shifting approval ratings of Nixon, see American Institute of Public Opinion, *Gallup Opinion Index*, Report #182, September-October 1980, entire issue. On "tenderness" toward Nixon, see Kissinger, *Years of Upheaval*, pp. 1206, 1207. For prediction of "disaster," see Barber, *The Presidential Character*, p. 441. On "last press conference," see Mazlish, *In Search of Nixon*, p. 70. On "investment in himself," see Barber, *The Presidential Character*, p. 349. On feelings of inadequacy, see ibid., p. 441. A good discussion of Nixon's self-image is found in Mazlish, *In Search of Nixon*, pp. 109–126.

5. On Nixon worldview, see Barber, *The Presidential Character*, pp. 416, 417. On "mercurial career," see Nixon, *Six Crises*, p. 425. On Voorhis campaign, note Jerry Voorhis, *The Strange Case of Richard Milhous Nixon* (New York: Paul Erikkson, 1972). On campaign against Helen Gahagan Douglas, see Theodore H. White, *Breach of Faith* (New York: Atheneum Publishers, 1975), p. 64. On "anything to win," see ibid., p. 64. On "it's the only thing," see Theodore H. White, *The Making of the President 1972* (New York: Bantam Books, 1973), p. 442. "I believe in the battle" quoted in Erwin C. Hargrove, *The Power of the Modern Presidency* (New York: Alfred A. Knopf, 1974), p. 177. On excitement of sports, see Nixon, *RN*, 1:119. "Almost broke his head" in Mazo and Hess, *Political Portrait*, pp. 18, 19; also see Mazlish, *In Search of Nixon*, p. 49. On poor sense of self, see Barber, *The Presidential Character*, pp. 396, 397.

6. On pleasing Frank Nixon, see Mazlish, *In Search of Nixon*, p. 27. "Ability to be cool" in Nixon, *Six Crises*, p. 318. Dr. Hutschnecker's view in Mazlish, *In Search of Nixon*, p. 9. "Please, Henry" quotation in Carl Bernstein and Bob Woodward, *All the President's Men* (New York: Simon and Schuster, 1975), p. 424. "I have found leaders" in Nixon, *Six Crises*, p. xiv. On masking feelings in debate, see Barber, *The Presidential Character*, p. 419. On loser image see Joe McGinniss, *The Selling of the President 1968*

(New York: Pocket Books, 1969), pp. 203–205. On "new Nixon" of 1968, see White, *Making of the President 1968,* see p. 179. On importance of evening television news, see McGinniss, *Selling of the President*, p. 167. On "received impression" see White, *Breach of Faith,* pp. 323–343. "Someone hung him up" in McGinniss, *Selling of the President,* p. 202.

7. On search for JFK inconsistencies, see White, *Making of the President 1968,* pp. 164, 165. "We're not in control" quoted in ibid., p. 167. Report on Chotiner's role in John Ehrlichman, *Witness to Power: The Nixon Years* (New York: Pocket Books, 1982), p. 32. For Haldeman's role, see Dan Rather and Gary Paul Gates, *The Palace Guard* (New York: Warner Books, 1975), p. 368. Nixon's view of responsibility in *New York Times,* May 1, 1973, p. 32. For more details on Colson and the "Enemies List," see Kessler, *Dilemmas of Presidential Leadership,* p. 4. "Screw our political enemies" quoted in White, *Breach of Faith,* p. 152. For pictures and listings of occupations of those on the enemies list, see Marvin Miller, *The Breaking of the President* (Covina, Calif.: Classic Productions, 1975), pp. 79–99. "Things are going to change now" quoted in Washington Post Staff, *The Presidential Transcripts* (with commentary by Bob Woodward, Carl Bernstein, Haynes Johnson, and Lawrence Meyer) (New York: Dell, 1974).

8. On the Pentagon papers, see Neil Sheehan et al., *The Pentagon Papers: New York Times Edition* (New York: Bantam Books, 1971). Also see Daniel Ellsberg, *Papers on the War* (New York: Simon and Schuster, 1972). On "cancer on the Presidency," see Washington Post Staff, *Presidential Transcripts,* March 21, 1973, p. 141. Nixon view of bureaucracy in Richard Nathan, *The Plot That Failed: Nixon and the Administrative Presidency* (New York: John Wiley, 1975). On Nixon's attention to minor details, see Fred Greenstein, "A President Is Forced to Resign: White House Organization and Nixon's Personality," in Allan Sindler, ed., *America in the Seventies* (Boston: Little, Brown, 1977), pp. 89, 90. On Prussian helmets, see *New York Times,* January 19, 1970. "Old buddies network" described in Frederick Malek, *Washington's Hidden Tragedy* (New York: Free Press, 1978), p. 64. Also see Stephen Hess, *Organizing the Presidency* (Washington, D.C.: Brookings Institution, 1976), p. 9. On results of willingness to go along, see David Broder, *The Changing of the Guard* (New York: Penguin, 1981), p. 84. Also see John Dean, *Blind Ambition* (New York: Simon and Schuster, 1976). Haldeman's "alter ego" role described in Jeb Stuart Magruder, *An American Life: One Man's Road to Watergate* (New York: Atheneum Publishers, 1974), p. 56. Haldeman's work on administrative detail noted in Richard Pious, *The American Presidency* (New York: Basic Books, 1979), p. 245. "Every President needs his SOB" quoted in Ehrlichman, *Witness to Power,* p. 59.

9. Haldeman as "Berlin Wall" noted in Rowland Evans, Jr., and Robert D. Novak, *Nixon in the White House: The Frustration of Power* (New York: Vintage, 1972), p. 47. For comments on president's isolation, see Joseph Califano, *The Presidential Nation* (New York: Norton, 1975), p. 192. On Haldeman as final filter, see Magruder, *An American Life,* p. 59. On Nixon memo-writing, see Evans and Novak, *Nixon in the White House,* p. 48. On civil servants' attitude toward Nixon, see ibid., p. 48. On IRS audits, see Kissinger, *The White House Years,* pp. 95, 96. For Arthur Burns episode, see Hugh Heclo, *A Government of Strangers* (Washington, D.C.: Brookings Institution, 1977), p. 260. On the Daniel Schorr case involving retaliation against a CBS News correspondent, see White, *Breach of Faith,* p. 167. For Nixon "thinking aloud" on classification system, see William Safire, *Before the Fall* (Garden City, N.Y.: Doubleday, 1975),

pp. 492–495. Also see Morton Halperin and Daniel N. Hoffman, *Top Secret* (Washington, D.C.: New Republic Books, 1977), p. 28.

BIBLIOGRAPHIC ESSAY

Alistair Cooke, *A Generation on Trial: U.S.A. v. Alger Hiss* (Baltimore: Penguin Books, 1952), is one of the more thorough accounts of Nixon's role in the House Un-American Activities Committee investigation of Alger Hiss and the two Hiss trials (the investigation first put Nixon into the national headlines).

Bela Kornitzer, *The Real Nixon* (Chicago: Rand McNally, 1960), is an admiring campaign biography by a naturalized citizen.

Richard M. Nixon, *Six Crises* (Garden City, N.Y.: Doubleday, 1962), is Nixon's first autobiographical volume. It contains much material about the 1960 election and the "kitchen debate" with Khrushchev as well as the Caracas attack of 1958 during Nixon's Latin tour.

Earl Mazo and Stephen Hess, *Nixon: A Political Portrait* (New York: Popular Library, 1968), is a basically friendly but somewhat analytical campaign biography from the second, victorious presidential campaign.

Lewis Chester, Godfrey Hodgson, and Bruce Page, *An American Melodrama: The Presidential Campaign of 1968* (New York: Viking Books, 1969), is a London *Sunday Times* team's view of the 1968 campaign; it is critical of Robert Kennedy and explains Nixon from their own conservative viewpoint.

Theodore H. White, *The Making of the President 1968* (New York: Pocket Books, 1970), was the first account of the 1968 presidential campaign to mention the contacts made by Anna Chenault with President Thieu of South Vietnam during the early Paris negotiations.

Neil Sheehan et al., in *The Pentagon Papers: The New York Times Edition* (New York: Bantam Books, 1971), provide one version of the published and edited report made for Secretary of Defense Robert McNamara on why the United States got involved in Vietnam and how it happened.

Jerry Voorhis, *The Strange Case of Richard Milhous Nixon* (New York: Paul Erikkson, 1972), depicts Nixon's political career through the eyes of the man he defeated for Congress in 1946; at writing, the author was still bewildered by the experience.

Daniel Ellsberg, *Papers on the War* (New York: Simon and Schuster, 1972), consists of polemics written by the former marine turned peace activist who turned over the Pentagon Papers to the *New York Times* and whose psychiatrist's office was rifled by the "plumbers."

Rowland Evans, Jr., and Robert D. Novak, *Nixon in the White House: The Frustration of Power* (New York: Vintage, 1972), provides a mildly friendly view of Nixon from two syndicated columnists.

Richard Whalen, *Catch the Falling Flag* (Boston: Houghton Mifflin, 1972), is a conservative Republican activist's critique of Nixon's opportunism.

John Mueller, *War, Presidents and Public Opinion* (New York: John Wiley, 1973), places Nixon's Vietnam leadership in the context of case studies of previous presidents and the relationship between presidential foreign policy decision-making and public opinion.

Theodore White, *The Making of the President 1972* (New York: Bantam Books, 1973), provides a narrative of Nixon's landslide victory over McGovern in 1972.

In Theodore H. White, *Breach of Faith* (New York: Atheneum Publishers, 1975), the author apologized for his praise of Nixon in the 1973 volume.

John Newhouse, *Cold Dawn* (New York: Holt, Rinehart and Winston, 1973), carries a detailed account of the SALT I negotiations, some of it reportedly from Kissinger "leaks."

Henry Brandon, *The Retreat of American Power* (Garden City, N.Y.: Doubleday, 1973), provides a conservative British columnist's view of Nixon-Kissinger diplomacy.

Erwin C. Hargrove, *The Power of the Modern Presidency* (New York: Alfred A. Knopf, 1974), explains the cultural matrix of the Nixon era and its diplomacy and domestic policy.

Washington Post Staff, *The Presidential Transcripts* (with commentary by Bob Woodward, Carl Bernstein, Haynes Johnson, and Lawrence Meyer) (New York: Dell, 1974), summarizes the officially released portions of the infamous Nixon Watergate tapes.

Jeb Stuart Magruder, *An American Life: One Man's Road to Watergate* (New York: Atheneum Publishers, 1974), gives an account of a White House aide's involvement in Watergate and his appearance before the Ervin select committee.

Marvin Kalb and Bernard Kalb, *Kissinger* (Boston: Little, Brown, 1974), provides an admiring but well-written biography of Nixon's national security adviser and (from 1973 to August 1974) secretary of state. (Bernard Kalb served in 1985 and 1986 as spokesman for the Reagan State Department.

Thomas Eagleton, *War and Presidential Powers* (New York: Liveright, 1975), presents a critical view of Watergate by the senator who withdrew from George McGovern's 1972 presidential ticket.

Carl Bernstein and Bob Woodward are the authors of *All the President's Men* (New York: Simon and Schuster, 1975) and *The Final Days* (New York: Simon and Schuster, 1976). The first volume by the *Washington Post* investigative team details the unraveling of the mystery (it was made into a movie starring Jason Robards, Dustin Hoffman, and Robert Redford). The second volume presents the pathetic but controversial account of Nixon's forced resignation and events leading up to it.

Marvin Miller, *The Breaking of the President* (Covina, Calif.: Classic Productions, 1975), makes a case for underworld connections with figures in the Nixon administration.

Dan Rather and Gary Paul Gates in *The Palace Guard* (New York: Warner Books, 1975) provide a description of the Nixon staff's involvement in Watergate from the vantage point of CBS News' White House beat.

Richard Nathan, *The Plot That Failed: Nixon and the Administrative Presidency* (New York: John Wiley, 1975), gives a Nixon administration economist's view of Nixon's failed experiment with the super-cabinet which fell victim to the Watergate crisis.

William Safire in *Before the Fall: Inside the Pre-Watergate White House* (Garden City, N.Y.: Doubleday, 1976) provides a Nixon's speechwriter's account, perhaps the best, of policies and personalities in the Nixon White House prior to the scandal.

Richard Neustadt, *Presidential Power: The Politics of Leadership with Reflections on Johnson and Nixon* (New York: John Wiley, 1976), is the first of two revisions of a "classic" study of reputation and its influence on power in Washington; it is useful for its insights into Nixon's modus operandi.

Jonathan Schell, *The Time of Illusion* (New York: Alfred A. Knopf, 1976), a book-length essay which first appeared in *The New Yorker,* depicts the mood of Washington in the Nixon years.

J. Anthony Lukas, *Nightmare: The Underside of the Nixon Years* (New York: Viking Press, 1976), depicts a chilling disregard of the Constitution in the Nixon era.

John Dean, *Blind Ambition* (New York: Simon and Schuster, 1976), gives the view of a pivotal figure in the "uncovering" of Watergate who served as the president's counsel; Dean tells how he decided to "blow the whistle" rather than become merely a scapegoat. In 1982 Dean wrote a follow-up memoir, published about the time of Charles Colson's *Born Again*.

Elmo Zumwalt, *On Watch* (New York: Quadrangle Books, 1976), deals with military policy-making and politics; the author, an admiral, did not concur in all the Nixon policies.

Morton Halperin and Daniel N. Hoffman, *Top Secret* (Washington, D.C.: New Republic Books, 1977), is by the authors of a legal study, *Freedom vs. National Security: Secrecy and Surveillance* (New York: Chelsea House, 1977). They give an account of wiretaps as experienced by a former National Security Council aide and his collaborator.

Roger Morris, *Uncertain Greatness* (New York: Harper and Row, 1977), is a critical, though not savage, biography of Nixon's second secretary of state, Henry Kissinger.

Paul E. Sigmund, *The Overthrow of Allende and the Politics of Chile, 1964–76* (Pittsburgh: University of Pittsburgh Press, 1977), provides a scholarly analysis of Kissinger's diplomacy in Chile.

David Abrahamsen, *Nixon v. Nixon: An Emotional Tragedy* (New York: New American Library, 1978), is a psychoanalyst's effort at writing psychobiography.

Richard M. Nixon, *RN: Memoirs of Richard Nixon* 2 vols. (New York: Grosset and Dunlap, 1978), is the postpresidential autobiography which preceded *The Real War*. (Robert Sam Anson has also written *Exile,* an account of Nixon in retirement.)

Bruce Buchanan, *The Presidential Experience* (Englewood Cliffs, N.J.: Prentice-Hall, 1978), instead of looking at the impact presidents have had on the presidency, examines what impact a president's environment has on the incumbent; especially useful in explaining Nixon's arrogant behavior.

Nicholas von Hoffman, *Make-Believe Presidents: Illusions of Power from McKinley to Carter* (New York: Pantheon Books, 1978), takes a satirical look at modern presidents, including Nixon.

Sarah McClendon, *My Eight Presidents* (New York: Wyden Books, 1978), gives a veteran Washington syndicated correspondent's view of Nixon as one of her eight subjects, in a typically critical fashion.

Louis Fisher, *The Constitution Between Friends* (New York: St. Martin's Press, 1978), provides one of the best available accounts of the Nixon battle with Congress over impoundment.

Frederick Malek, *Washington's Hidden Tragedy* (New York: Free Press, 1978), provides a Nixon aide's view of Watergate.

Tad Szulc, *The Illusion of Peace* (New York: Viking Books, 1978), probes beneath the truce in Vietnam signed in 1973.

Jacob Beam, *Multiple Exposure* (New York: W. W. Norton, 1978), presents a diplomat's view of arms control talks and other issues of the Nixon era.

David Wise, *The American Police State* (New York: Random House, 1978), is a journalist's view of abuses by the CIA and FBI during the Nixon era as covered by the Church Committee investigation and his own reporting.

Arturo Valenzuela, *The Breakdown of Democratic Regimes: Chile* (Baltimore: Johns Hopkins University Press, 1978), analyzes the fall of Salvador Allende and the American influence on the outcome.

Henry A. Kissinger, in *The White House Years* (Boston: Little, Brown, 1979) and *Years of Upheaval* (Boston: Little, Brown, 1982), provide his view of the National Security Council and State Department through 1974; Kissinger provides the rationale for his various policy actions and details the Paris truce negotiations.

William Shawcross, *Sideshow* (New York: Simon and Schuster, 1979), explains the author's view that American involvement in Cambodia prolonged the war in Vietnam.

James David Barber, *The Pulse of Politics: Electing Presidents in the Media Age* (New York: W. W. Norton, 1980), analyzes cycles in presidential election imagery and is especially valuable for Chapter 14, "Richard Nixon 1968," pp. 287–308.

William Gulley, *Breaking Cover* (New York: Simon and Schuster, 1980), gives a view of Nixon from the former head of the White House military office.

Gerard C. Smith, *Doubletalk: The Story of SALT I* (Garden City, N.Y.: Doubleday, 1980), gives the diplomat's version of the arms control negotiations which led to the Moscow treaty in 1972.

Harrison Salisbury, *Without Fear or Favor* (New York: Times Books, 1980), a history of the recent operations of the *New York Times,* includes a detailed account of the Pentagon Papers controversy.

G. Gordon Liddy, *Will* (New York: St. Martin's Press, 1980), contains the Watergate burglar's view of the episode after he ended his oath of secrecy.

Frank Kessler, *Dilemmas of Presidential Leadership: Of Caretakers and Kings* (Englewood Cliffs, N.J.: Prentice-Hall, 1982), a presidency text written by the author of this chapter, contains much material on the Nixon years.

John Ehrlichman, *Witness to Power: The Nixon Years* (New York: Pocket Books, 1982), is a review of the 1969–1974 period by Nixon's principal domestic aide.

Roger Morris, *Haig: The General's Progress* (Chicago: Playboy Books, 1982), contains an account of General Haig's service as chief of staff to Nixon in 1973 and 1974 and as a Kissinger aide.

Seymour Hersh, *The Price of Power: Kissinger in the Nixon White House* (New York: Summit Books, 1983), is a highly critical view of Kissinger's stewardship under Nixon by a prize-winning journalist.

20 GERALD R. FORD

William C. Spragens

Gerald Ford holds a unique position in the history of the American presidency. He is the only "unelected president" in the nation's history: unlike other vice presidents who succeeded to the office on its being vacated by his predecessor, he was appointed rather than elected.[1]

Gerald Ford also is distinguished by his role as a "healer" in the beginning of the post-Watergate presidency.[2] This did not exempt him from controversy because his pardon of former President Richard M. Nixon was highly controversial.[3] To get a better understanding of how Gerald R. Ford acted as president, it is necessary to sketch a bit of his prepolitical background as well as to note his career in Congress. Later in the chapter, his media relations and his approval as well as the issues he dealt with and his activities as an elder statesman will be discussed.

FORD'S PREPOLITICAL BACKGROUND

Gerald R. Ford was born as Leslie Lynch King in Omaha, Nebraska, on July 14, 1913. His parents were Dorothy Gardner King and Leslie King, who was a wool dealer. It was a failed marriage, and in 1915 his natural parents were divorced. His mother returned to her parents' Grand Rapids home when Ford was a small child. She remarried, and the stepfather's name was Gerald R. Ford. He adopted young Leslie, and on adoption his name was changed to Gerald Rudolph Ford.[4] After he became president, the story was widely told of Ford's first encounter with his real father at the age of seventeen. He previously had not known of his adoption.

Young Gerald attended South High School in Grand Rapids, a community with a strong flavor of the Dutch Reformed Church, to which many of its earlier settlers belonged. Because his family attended Grace Episcopal Church, he was not exposed to quite such a rigorous background. Gerald, Sr., was active in community affairs, as was Ford's mother, Dorothy Gardner King Ford. After the 1929 stock market crash, the elder Ford lost his home when his savings were wiped out.[5]

An early interest of Gerald Ford was athletics; he developed football skills under coach Clifford Gettings at South High, where Jerry played the position of center. He had a respectable academic record and in 1930 made his first trip to Washington by train for five days of sightseeing.[6]

Following graduation from South High in 1931, Gerald Ford was successfully recruited for college football by Harry Kipke, noted football coach at the University of Michigan in Ann Arbor. Jerry found a job waiting tables in the interns' dining room at University Hospital in Ann Arbor.

Early in his football career, Ford was distressed by the banning of a black teammate, Willis F. Ward, from the Georgia Tech game at a time when total segregation was enforced in southern athletics. Another highlight of his gridiron days was an appearance in the San Francisco East-West Shrine Game on January 1, 1935. He also played against the Chicago Bears as a College All-Star.

After graduation from Michigan in 1935, Ford rejected pro football offers. Instead he enrolled at Yale Law School and became assistant to the Yale football coach, Ducky Pond. Ford completed law school in the upper third of his class; he then worked briefly for the Harry Conover Model Agency in New York.[7]

In partnership with Philip Buchen, a friend from his Michigan days, he opened a law office in Grand Rapids late in 1941. But by April 1942 he had enlisted in the navy and received an ensign's commission. He participated in the navy's V-12 program at Chapel Hill, North Carolina, and eventually was assigned to the Third Fleet in the Pacific. There, in December 1944, he narrowly escaped death when a typhoon hit his ship, the U.S.S. *Monterey*. After forty-seven months on active duty with the navy, Ford returned to Grand Rapids in 1945.

In 1948 Ford ran as an upstart candidate against the Michigan Fifth District congressman, Bartel J. Jonkman. He defeated Jonkman in the September 14 Republican primary, then went on to win a congressional seat in the November 2 general election. In between the two votes, on October 15, he married Elizabeth Bloomer Warren, who became widely known as Betty when she became First Lady.[8]

FORD AS FRESHMAN CONGRESSMAN

Early in 1949 Ford began work in his office in what is now the Cannon Office Building across from the Capitol. He chose as his administrative assistant John P. Milanowske, originally from Grand Rapids and a recent graduate of Catholic University Law School in Washington. Senator Arthur Vandenberg, the Republican legislator from Grand Rapids, was then at the peak of his career and became something of a mentor and source of advice for Ford. The senator stressed to Ford the importance of doing good committee work and paying careful attention to constituents' needs.[9]

In his memoirs, Gerald Ford explains how his war experience had changed his outlook on legislation:

I had changed. Before the war, I'd been an isolationist. Indeed, while at Yale, I had expressed the view that the U.S. ought to avoid "entangling alliances" abroad. But now I had become an ardent internationalist. My wartime experiences had given me an entirely new perspective.[10]

While his views were internationalist on foreign policy, Ford was a conservative Republican on domestic policy issues. He soon won assignment to the House Appropriations Committee, where his Republican views about small government and low taxes reflected the sentiments of his district as well as his own convictions. Ford worked closely at times with his subcommittee chairman, Congressman George Mahon of Texas, who headed the Defense Appropriations Subcommittee. The young congressman once said, "We are not military strategists, but we can render considered judgments" about defense spending.

In his first two terms, Ford's record was essentially moderate. He favored enlarging the Rules Committee, a move opposed by staunch conservatives, but he did vote against repeal of the Taft-Hartley Act, in opposition to public housing, and against the minimum wage legislation of the Truman administration. He also voted to kill the poll tax.[11]

CONGRESSIONAL SERVICE UNDER EISENHOWER

After Republican gains were made in the 1950 election, prospects brightened for a Republican administration, and in 1952 Dwight D. Eisenhower's election meant that Ford would be able to work with a president of his own party in power. Ford was one of eighteen Republican congressmen who in February 1952 urged Eisenhower to return to the United States to run for president.

In the Eisenhower election of 1952 Ford won his third term in the House. He was also pleased about the election of Richard Nixon as vice president, as Nixon, a former colleague of Ford's in the House, was handling most party affairs for Eisenhower. Ford rejected various overtures to run for the U.S. Senate and instead in 1954 won election to his fourth term in the House. By 1956 he had declined an opportunity to run for governor of Michigan, again in order to stay in the House. During 1956 he worked for other Republican candidates, since his seat was in a district considered "safe" for his party.

Ford won his fifth term in 1958 in a year of Democratic gains. He supported Richard Nixon for the 1960 presidential nomination and was the object of a boomlet by his friends for the vice presidential nomination at the Chicago convention at which Nixon was nominated.[12]

FORD AS OPPOSITION LEADER

After the election of John F. Kennedy, who took office in January 1961, Ford assumed a growing role in the opposition party in the House. He was in his sixth term and seventeenth in seniority among House Republicans; he was also second-ranking minority member on the Foreign Operations Subcommittee.

Ford took a bipartisan stance in support of President Kennedy after the abortive Bay of Pigs operation in April 1961. In 1961 Ford also won a Distinguished Service Award from the American Political Science Association. An event of 1962 was the Cuban missile crisis of that fall after which Republicans failed to do well in congressional elections.

This factor prompted a revolt by some Republicans at the beginning of the Eighty-eighth Congress in January 1963. They sought to show their displeasure with Minority Leader Charles Halleck of Indiana. As a result they selected Ford to displace Representative Charles Hoeven of Iowa as chair of the House Republican Conference. In the 1964 presidential election year, Ford threw his support to Governor George Romney of Michigan until Romney withdrew from the race after telling a television interviewer he had been "brainwashed" during a visit to South Vietnam. Ford loyally supported the party's nominee, Senator Barry Goldwater, who lost in a landslide to President Johnson.[13]

From a starting point as GOP House Conference chairman, Ford decided to contest the leadership with Halleck in January 1965 and was the winner in a ballot that gave him the narrow edge of seventy-three to sixty-seven caucus votes. Thus began his term as House minority leader, which continued until he left the House near the end of President Richard Nixon's presidency.[14]

During this period the war in Vietnam became more and more unpopular, and as opposition leader Ford viewed the LBJ record on Vietnam as one of "shocking mismanagement." Ford's party did well in the 1966 off-year elections, and after the withdrawal of President Johnson in February 1968, followed by the assassination of Robert Kennedy and the Chicago Democratic debacle at the convention, Ford saw the GOP nominee, Richard M. Nixon, capture the White House in 1968.[15]

One controversy in which Ford was involved in 1968 was that over the open housing legislation, which was passed with a bipartisan coalition after some defections from the Republican opposition. Ford's opposition, he said, was based on procedures rather than on the principle of open housing, which he said he favored.

During the 1968 Miami Beach Republican National Convention at which Nixon and Spiro T. Agnew were nominated as the GOP slate, Ford was permanent chairman. He attacked the Johnson administration for "having blundered into a war in Vietnam." He campaigned for numerous other Republican candidates and was once again returned to the House from his "safe" district.

FORD IN THE LEADERSHIP UNDER NIXON

Ford was reelected in 1969 as minority floor leader in the House, but was now joined by John Anderson, the Republican congressman from Illinois, who replaced Melvin Laird of Wisconsin, Nixon's secretary of defense. Anderson was chairman of the Republican House Conference.

Occasions on which Ford was obliged to defend the Nixon administration included a controversy over the selection by Health, Education and Welfare Secretary Robert Finch of Dr. John H. Knowles, director of Massachusetts General Hospital, as assistant secretary for health and scientific affairs. A major fight arose over this choice, and Ford helped to convince President Nixon that he should withdraw the nomination. Knowles was unacceptable to the conservative leadership of the American Medical Association.

Another controversy in which Ford was involved was the unsuccessful effort to impeach the liberal Supreme Court justice, William O. Douglas. Still another Republican controversy in this period was about the dismissal of Interior Secretary Walter J. Hickel. Ford again loyally supported the administration.[16]

Ford continued his record of party loyalty in backing Nixon and Agnew for reelection in 1972. Then came the Watergate scandal, and in another scandal in 1973 Agnew was forced to resign in the face of an impending federal prosecution on charges of bribery.

The resulting vacancy in the vice presidency prompted Richard Nixon to follow the procedures established by the Twenty-fifth Amendment to fill vacancies in the vice presidency. Although it was reported that Nixon would like to have chosen his treasury secretary, John B. Connally of Texas, after canvassing Republicans in Congress and the nation, Nixon announced his selection of Ford as vice president–designate on October 12, 1973. Thus was to begin a trying time for Ford as the Nixon administration approached its last days.

FORD'S BALANCING ACT AS VICE PRESIDENT

During Ford's tenure as vice president, Nixon's popularity and approval ratings declined as disclosure after disclosure was made about the Watergate scandal. Ford loyally defended Nixon in his role as vice president, but it seems apparent now that he had not been told the extent of the president's involvement in the cover-up efforts following the Watergate break-in.

Before Ford had been confirmed as vice president, he was grilled in a Senate confirmation inquiry and required to explain an allegation made by lobbyist Robert N. Winter-Burger, but Ford was exonerated by the committee. Winter-Burger had accused Ford of exchanging favors in return for campaign contributions. Ford's finances were also carefully examined. To cap this controversy, Ford won bipartisan approval in the Senate by a 92–3 roll call vote on November 27, 1973, after a favorable vote by the committee.

On the House side, the full Judiciary Committee recommended him on November 29 by a vote of 29–8. The full House approved his appointment on December 6 by a vote of 387–35, which was put on record. Even one black congressman, Representative Andrew Young, Democrat of Georgia (later ambassador to the United Nations), supported Ford, despite attacks made on Ford's civil rights record by other black legislators. Young voiced "faith and hope" that his vote would be vindicated by Ford.[17]

The replacement of Agnew by Ford brought increased demands from many quarters for Nixon's resignation, because the inquiry into Nixon's affairs had by this time become more incriminating. The Watergate scandals had placed Ford in a difficult position. He was expected to be loyal to President Nixon, who appointed him, but he was also expected to uphold his own record for integrity. This prompted him to involve himself in a balancing act which was indeed difficult.

It was believed that Ford had behind-the-scenes differences with White House aides about the release of evidence about Nixon's behavior, and this prompted him to toughen his stance in his dealings with the Nixon staff. Jerald ter Horst, later Ford's press secretary for a brief period, states that Ford felt he might have been "used" by the White House staff during this period.[18]

FORD SUCCEEDS TO THE PRESIDENCY

On Monday, August 5, under pressure from the United States Supreme Court, Nixon released transcripts which provided the so-called smoking gun evidence of his early implication in the Watergate cover-up. The previous day in New Orleans Ford had made a statement of loyalty to Nixon but had been notified by Nixon chief of staff Alexander Haig that matters at the White House were "unraveling" rapidly and that Ford might expect a major event within the next three days or so.

At this point, with the likelihood growing of a Nixon resignation, the so-called Ford transition group went into action to prepare for such an eventuality. Finally the resignation was announced. Thursday, August 8, 1974, was to be Nixon's last full day in the White House. On Friday, August 9, Ford would take the oath of office as Nixon was flying back to California.[19]

In a brief inaugural statement in the East Room that Friday, Ford voiced the view that "truth is the glue that holds government together" and expressed relief that "our long national nightmare is over." Then he expressed another hope, that "our former President, who brought peace to millions, find it for himself."[20]

By August 20, Ford had announced his designation of former Governor Nelson A. Rockefeller of New York to serve as his vice president. Rockefeller would of course have to go through the confirmation process in Congress as Ford had done. Asked in his first televised news conference about what code of ethics he would adopt for the new administration, Ford replied, "The code of ethics that will be followed will be the example that I set."

FOREIGN POLICY EVENTS OF FORD'S TERM

The image of Gerald Ford can be measured to some degree by his various approval ratings (dealing with public perceptions of his effectiveness as president) as they coincide in time with some of the major events of his term. Each of these events will be discussed briefly along with a reference to Ford's approval rating at the time, with some interpretive information. Foreign policy events will be discussed first.

The beginning point and high mark of Ford's approval rating was approximately 70 percent, where it stood in August 1974. After Ford's January 1975 State of the Union address, in which he discussed his foreign policy, his approval rating stood at 39 percent.

A major event in April 1975 was the fall of Cambodia; at this point, Ford's popularity curve, which had been 43 percent, slipped back to the 39 percent mark. Then there occurred the incident of the U.S.S. *Mayaguez* off the coast of Cambodia. The American ship was seized by pirates and recaptured by U.S. Marines; Ford's approval rating rose to 51 percent by the end of May 1975, the month of the *Mayaguez* incident.

After Egypt and Israel signed a disengagement agreement, a positive foreign policy development, Ford's approval rating stood at 47 percent as August 1975 ended. Another major foreign policy development was Ford's trip to the Far East. He met at Vladivostok with Premier Leonid Brezhnev of the Soviet Union and traveled to China. Ford also received favorable coverage of the China trip, and at that time (early December 1975) his approval rating moved up from a low point of 42 percent to 46 percent.[21] (See Figure 20.1 for approval ratings).

Foreign economic policy and the balance of trade were major foreign policy concerns during Ford's tenure. He also participated in the Helsinki Conference at which an agreement was signed by the Western powers with the Soviet Union in which the West agreed to accept the World War II boundaries in Eastern Europe in exchange for a Soviet pledge regarding human rights. Much controversy followed this agreement, and on repeated occasions after Helsinki the Republican party's right wing was critical of Ford for signing the agreement.

President Ford's basic approach was to follow a policy of detente similar to that of Richard Nixon. While more hard-line than the policy desired by some of the opposition Democrats, it was not quite so strident a policy as that followed by the Reagan administration since 1981. In some ways this policy was more moderate than that followed in the latter part of the Carter era, especially after the 1979 invasion of Afghanistan.

DOMESTIC POLICY EVENTS OF FORD'S TERM

Despite the importance of foreign issues, many analysts feel that, absent a major foreign policy crisis, a president's approval rating is more quickly affected

Figure 20.1
Approval Ratings for Gerald R. Ford

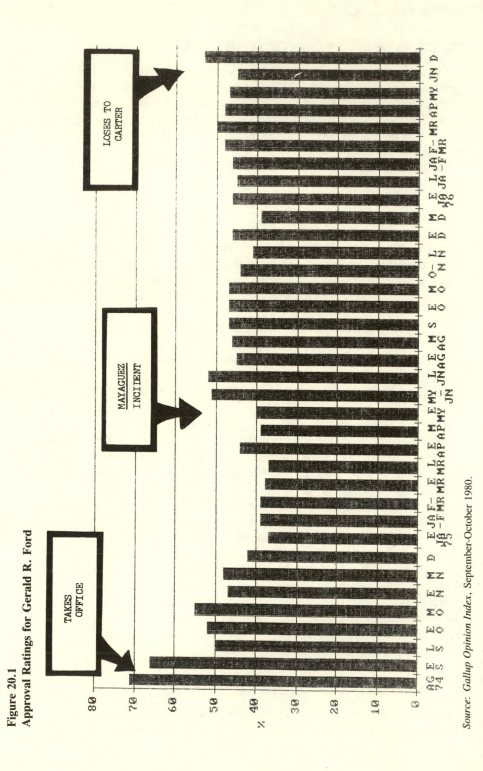

Source: Gallup Opinion Index, September–October 1980.

by reaction to his domestic policy decisions, always a bellwether of presidents' popularity with the general public.

In the Ford term, a landmark event occurred in early September 1974, not long after the former Michigan congressman and vice president had taken office. This was Ford's decision to pardon Richard Nixon, who had resigned from office but had not yet been the object of a grand jury investigation focused on him rather than his subordinates. Nor had Nixon been charged with any crimes at this point.

At any rate, the pardon was quite controversial, particularly the timing of it. Ford argued that nothing else of importance on the national agenda could be properly dealt with until the pardon issue was disposed of. His critics argued that by acting prematurely, Ford allowed the concealment of information the public should have had about the misdeeds of the Nixon administration.

Following a media outcry about the pardon, Ford's approval rating dropped from its peak of 71 percent in August 1974 to 50 percent in September after the pardon. When Ford went before a congressional committee to testify on his decision to grant the pardon, his approval rating rose slightly, back up to 54 percent.

But other factors were affecting Ford's approval ratings. Announcement of a 6 percent unemployment rate, a politically sensitive barometer, brought another downward slide in Ford's approval rating. This coincided with his effort to fight inflation, which was much publicized. After the 6 percent unemployment announcement, and prior to the January 1975 State of the Union Address, Ford's approval rating hit a low point of 37 percent, a level to be reached at only one other moment in his term.

FORD'S PUBLIC RELATIONS: PROBLEM OF "KLUTZ" IMAGE

On Ford's accession to the presidency, he received sympathetic coverage from much of the news media. During the brief period before he moved into the White House, reporters depicted him coming to the door of his suburban Virginia home in robe and pajamas to pick up his own morning paper, and preparing his own English muffins for breakfast. Since there had been much talk prior to Ford's tenure about the "imperial presidency," Ford was seeking to project a somewhat more populistic image. This can be seen in his reference to "a little plain talk among friends" in his inaugural remarks in August 1974.

As president, however, Ford faced a quite different problem in his "image" relationship to the American public than did Richard Nixon. Ford was bland where Nixon was controversial; when Ford did take controversial positions, he seemed to have greater ability at defusing them than did his immediate predecessor.

Ron Nessen, Gerald Ford's press secretary, had this to say about Ford's image problems:

Gerald Ford's biggest continuing problem in the White House—and mine, as the overseer
of his press relations—was the portrayal of him in the media as a bumbler. This false
image was perpetuated by news reports, photographs and TV film clips that magnified
every presidential stumble. Alleged physical clumsiness was subtly translated into suggestions of mental ineptitude. Such ridicule in the press and on television undermined
public respect for Ford as a leader and damaged his chances in the 1976 election. After
all, no one wants a clown for president.

Ford was depicted, literally, as Bozo the Clown in a retouched photo on the cover of
New York magazine. Chevy Chase, an unknown television comedian, became a household
word by doing pratfalls in supposed imitation of Ford. . . .

It was a sorry and mindless performance by the press. The idea that Ford was a not-
very-bright klutz was just plain wrong, a false image spread [by] journalism at its worst.

In his sixties, Ford was a youthful, graceful, athletic man, skiing, golfing, swimming
and playing tennis. He had finished in the top third of a brilliant Yale Law School class.[22]

President Ford was depicted as falling down in the snow while skiing; another
unfortunate episode occurred when he was arriving in Vienna on a state visit—
an old football knee injury gave way and Ford tumbled down the ramp stairway
of Air Force One. This episode was shown and reshown on evening television
news programs.

Still another example of this kind of image projection occurred when Ford
was on a state visit to the Far East; his itinerary included a visit with Emperor
Hirohito of Japan. Since Ford was obliged to wear morning clothes for this call
on the Emperor, he was photographed along with Hirohito in this garb. The only
problem was that the trousers that Ford wore appeared too short, and there was
comment on this fact.

Ford was embarrassed in image terms by at least two other episodes that
occurred during his administration. One was the investigation of the Central
Intelligence Agency and the Federal Bureau of Investigation by a Senate investigating committee headed by Senator Frank Church of Idaho. Disclosures were
made about CIA schemes with the underworld—developed under earlier presidents—for the "elimination" of such foreign leaders as Premier Fidel Castro of
Cuba. The FBI was disclosed to have sent threatening letters to the late Dr.
Martin Luther King. All this activity prompted Ford to designate a commission
headed by Vice President Nelson A. Rockefeller to investigate the domestic and
foreign intelligence agencies. William Scranton was replaced by George Bush
(former United Nations ambassador) as director of the CIA. William Ruckle-
shaus, a hero of the "Saturday Night Massacre," briefly headed the previously
discredited FBI.

TWO ATTEMPTS ON FORD'S LIFE

Two attempts, both unsuccessful, were made to assassinate President Ford.
Both of these incidents occurred in California:

On September 5, 1975, President Ford was on the Capitol grounds in Sacramento en route to an appearance before the California General Assembly when Lynette (Squeaky) Fromme emerged from a crowd of handshakers with a pistol in hand. The weapon was deflected before a shot could be fired, according to witnesses. . . .

On September 22, 1975, Sara Jane Moore shot at and missed the President as he was emerging from the St. Francis Hotel on Post Street in San Francisco, near Union Square. Ms. Moore, 47, was reported to have used a five-shot revolver.

After the close brush with death or injury, President Ford said at a news conference on his return to Washington:

" . . . We have talked to our four children, and I guess they are kind of happy that we are back here all right.

"But let me say most emphatically, I thank the Secret Service for doing a super job again. . . .

" . . . The most important thing is that I don't think any person as President or any person in any other major political office ought to cower in the face of a limited number of people, out of 214 million Americans, who want to take the law into their own hands. The American people expect . . . [and] want a dialog between them and their other public officials. And if we can't have that opportunity of talking with one another, seeing one another, shaking hands with one another, something has gone wrong in our society."[23]

Both "Squeaky" Fromme and Sara Jane Moore were arrested, incarcerated, and tried, and both have been serving time in federal prisons. Both seemed identified with the radical left and apparently accepted a caricature of Ford as an uncaring beneficiary of the wealthy.

THE 1976 ELECTION: PRIMARY CONTEST WITH REAGAN

President Ford had not gone through a national election before his accession to the White House; he was unique in this, since all previous vice presidents succeeding to the office had been participants in a national campaign.

Ford, unlike the others, had only participated in contests in the Fifth Congressional District in Michigan, which he represented. This meant that he had to build a national constituency for the election, a special and unprecedented problem.

Furthermore, the president faced a strong challenge within his own party from the candidacy of former Governor Ronald W. Reagan of California. This contest went right down to the wire. Ford won a close victory in the New Hampshire primary, but Reagan ran well in Florida and other southern states. Ford seemed to be gaining the edge until Reagan went on national television with a fund-raising appeal, then ran strongly in the North Carolina and Indiana primaries. All of a sudden Ford was engaged in a neck-and-neck contest with Reagan. The California primary, in which Reagan was all but certain to be the victor, came near the end of the primary season.

The nomination outcome narrowed down to uncommitted delegates, and it was not certain until a test vote had been taken on Reagan-supported rules changes at the national convention in Kansas City that Ford would be the nominee. Reagan, however, had damaged his credibility with lifelong Republicans and hard-liners serving as delegates when he proposed Senator Richard Schweiker of Pennsylvania as a running mate. Schweiker was then viewed as a moderate or progressive Republican, not to the taste of some of Reagan's ultraconservative backers. Ford then triumphed at the convention, and Reagan pledged to campaign for his fellow conservatives running for the Senate and the House.

During the convention itself, one effort was made to have Ford look truly presidential. A very aggressive-looking presidential portrait was placed on Ford billboard displays outside the Kemper Arena, the Kansas City convention site. Delegates, alternates, and the press saw this each time they entered the arena.

Another effort was made by the administration to placate foreign policy conservatives concerned about the Ford/Kissinger so-called detente policy toward the Soviet bloc. Secretary of State Henry Kissinger was brought to the convention to glad-hand delegates, and it was also announced late in 1975 by Vice President Rockefeller that he would not seek Ford's blessing. Rockefeller was regarded by some delegates as too progressive for another term. In the end Ford's choice for vice presidential running mate in 1976 was the reliable conservative Senator Robert Dole of Kansas (later to serve as Senate majority and minority leader and a 1988 presidential candidate).

FORD AND THE CARTER DEBATES

The Ford image as perceived by the voters was developed in part in his debates with Governor Jimmy Carter in the fall 1976 campaign, particularly the second debate. In discussing foreign policy in the second debate, Ford made the figurative statement that the people of Poland and Eastern Europe could never be dominated by the Soviet Union. This obviously flew in the face of the existing satellite status of these nations, and when asked about his statement, Ford repeated it in the debate. It was several days before a clarification was issued by the White House.

The controversy over the Eastern Europe statement was ill-timed from President Ford's viewpoint, as he was rapidly gaining on Carter (who had a twenty-point lead in the polls after the conventions). Ford's gains resulted from published remarks made by Carter to a *Playboy* interviewer after Carter ostensibly thought the tape recorder was turned off at the end of an interview.

Ford was also a participant, along with his opponent, in another awkward moment during the first debate, which was held in Philadelphia. During this debate, as Ford's opponent was making his closing statement, the microphones failed. Both men stood stiffly at their lecterns for nearly half an hour while the technical problem was resolved by engineers. The problem resulted from the American Broadcasting Company lack of foresight in not bringing backup equipment to the debate, held at the Walnut Street Theater, but the net effect was to make both candidates look a bit stiff.

THE 1976 ELECTION: GENERAL CONTEST WITH CARTER

The debates have just been described. But apart from these Ford made an all-out effort, described by campaign communication aide Malcolm MacDougall in his work *We Almost Made It,* to improve his image; negative advertising seeking to denigrate the Carter record as governor of Georgia was used as well as positive advertising showing Ford at the Vladivostok summit, speaking at the Kansas City convention, visiting Emperor Hirohito, and making his appearances at the Helsinki Conference of 1975.

Some students of campaigning processes have compared Ford's campaign effort of 1976 with that of Hubert Humphrey in 1968. Ford was nearly 20 percentage points behind Carter in the national polls at the time of the Kansas City convention; this prompted Ford to challenge Carter to a series of debates when Ford gave his acceptance speech in Kansas City. The president knew that he had nothing to lose at that point.

Certainly partisan dissension within Republican ranks had something to do with Ford's defeat. But Ford's image as the Washington "insider" also helped to cause his loss to an obvious "outsider." In this election, as in the 1980 one, it was an asset to be an outsider, and Ford's Washington experience, which would previously have been an asset, worked against him.[24]

FORD AS FORMER PRESIDENT: FORD LIBRARY ACTIVITIES

After his defeat President Ford established his headquarters in Palm Desert, California, where he lived in a resort home called Rancho Mirage. However, Ford maintained his Michigan activities through the operation of the Ford Library in Ann Arbor and the Ford Museum in Grand Rapids. At the library, for example, he and former President Carter appeared at a joint dinner in 1983, and on another occasion the former president was host to a conference on foreign policy attended by former secretaries of state William Rogers, Dean Rusk, and Alexander Haig and former National Security Adviser Zbigniew Brzezinski.

Ford Museum activities included the appearances of several former first ladies and members of presidential families in a program at the museum in Grand Rapids. In 1985 President Ford himself was host and delivered the keynote address at an academic conference of the Center for the Study of the Presidency.

The former president also maintained some of his political activities. Unlike his immediate predecessor, he appeared at the Republican convention in Dallas in 1984 and presented a speech that was a predictable attack on Democratic policies and praise for the Reagan record.

Comfortable with his golfing and skiing activities and participation in these conferences, Ford seemed to be settling easily into the role of elder statesman. He also sat on several corporate boards of directors.

His postpresidential period also saw the publication of his memoirs, entitled

A Time to Heal, in 1979. This detailed his account of his presidency and his view of the pardon controversy of 1974, as well as his assessment of the major events of the Ford years.

CONCLUSIONS ABOUT THE FORD PRESIDENCY— TRANSITIONAL MIDDLE AMERICAN—LAST OF LESS IDEOLOGICAL REPUBLICANS?

What, then, can be concluded about Gerald R. Ford's brief tenure in the White House and the image he left with the American public?

Ford left office with some admiration and respect but may have left only a slight impact on the office, partly because of his relatively brief tenure. The Ford presidency was clearly a transitional one in which the nation was adjusting downward its expectations of what its presidents could achieve for the public. Congress was reasserting its power perhaps more than at any time since the 1920s or in the latter part of the New Deal era; Ford was a transitional president in that he and his successor were moving away from the "imperial presidency" image that had been prevalent from FDR through Nixon.

Ford was also transitional in that the balance of forces within his own party seemed to be shifting from dominance by internationalist Republicans with an eastern base to more hard-line Republicans with a Sun Belt base. Ford was a traditional conservative in the pattern developed after the end of the FDR era; but in the decade of the 1980s ideological conservatives were to have a greater impact on the party. Thus members of the opposition who saw Ford as quite conservative within a decade could look back with nostalgia at his relatively moderate positions, particularly in the realm of foreign policy.

Ford did indeed carry a "Middle America" image as the spokesman for the interests of the average middle-class American. His nonpartisan hero in terms of image was Harry Truman, who, along with Senator Arthur Vandenberg of Michigan and some of the other leaders of Ford's early congressional years, left an impact on his views, particularly in foreign policy. Ford was a fiscal conservative and, like other Republican presidents, was noted for vetoing spending bills that he thought were too extravagant. He was, however, somewhat more likely than the others to bargain with the Democratic Congress. Indeed, he was obliged to do so perhaps more than Presidents Nixon and Reagan if he wanted his legislation passed.

An intriguing question about Gerald Ford as he is compared with the other Republican presidents who have served since 1953—four up to 1985, compared with three Democrats—is whether he might be the last of the less ideological Republicans elected to the office for some time. Ford was a pragmatist and was not as inclined as his more recent successor of his own party to aim his remarks at the far right of the Republican party.

In sum, then, he was a transitional figure who, having begun his legislative career in 1948, was one of the few remaining links to the Truman period. Those in public life who recall the events of that era are rapidly dwindling in numbers; there may indeed be a nostalgia for Ford and the 1970s as the world's and the nation's problems grow more complex.

His image, then, was that of a quite typical American with emphasis on American values; he was also a creature of the Congress in which he spent so many years, as well as a representative of America's heartland.

NOTES

1. Gerald R. Ford, *A Time to Heal* (New York: Harper and Row, 1979), pp. 27, 28, 33–35. Here can be found Ford's personal reflections on the succession and his sentiments on the Nixon resignation speech. See also J. F. ter Horst, *Gerald Ford and the Future of the Presidency* (New York: Third Press, 1974), pp. 183–185, for an account of pre-transition discussions and Ford and Nixon's pretransition briefing.

2. Marc Landy, ed., *Modern Presidents and the Presidency* (Lexington, Mass.: Lexington Books, D. C. Heath and Co., 1985), p. 202; comment by John J. Rhodes, former GOP House leader. This is fairly typical of reaction at the time. Ford's successor, Jimmy Carter, thanked the retiring president at the 1977 inauguration for "all he has done to heal our land."

3. On the Ford pardon of Nixon, see Ron Nessen, *It Sure Looks Different from the Inside* (New York: Playboy Press/Simon and Schuster, 1978), pp. 9, 10, 30, 33, 34, 198, 356; Ford, *Time to Heal*, pp. 168, 171, 172, 175; ter Horst, *Ford and Future*, p. 236 (letter of resignation); John Osborne, *White House Watch: The Ford Years* (Washington, D.C.: New Republic Books, 1977), p. 7; William C. Spragens et al., *From Spokesman to Press Secretary: White House Media Operations* (Lanham, Md.: University Press of America, 1980), pp. 67, 68; Sarah McClendon, *My Eight Presidents* (New York: Wyden Books/Simon and Schuster, 1978), p. 190. McClendon says that the only two major decisions Ford made were those related to the *Mayaguez* and the Nixon pardon.

4. For an account of Ford's first meeting with his real father, see Ford, *Time to Heal*, p. 46. For a more detailed account of Ford's childhood see ter Horst, *Ford and Future*, pp. 27–35.

5. Ter Horst, *Ford and Future*, p. 35.

6. Ibid., pp. 35–37.

7. Ibid., pp. 38–46.

8. Ibid., pp. 46–51.

9. Ibid., pp. 53–55.

10. Ford, *Time to Heal*, p. 59.

11. Ter Horst, *Ford and Future*, pp. 57–62.

12. Ibid., pp. 63–73.

13. Ibid., pp. 81–86.

14. Ibid., pp. 81, 82.

15. Ibid., pp. 101–113.

16. Ibid., pp. 101–127.

17. Ibid., pp. 131–169; Ford, *Time to Heal*, pp. 102–104.

18. Ter Horst, *Ford and Future*, pp. 171–180; Ford, *Time to Heal*, pp. 104–117.

19. Ter Horst, *Ford and Future*, pp. 183–187; Ford, *Time to Heal*, pp. 113–120, 1–6.

20. Ford, *Time to Heal,* pp. 38–40.

21. Ford's approval ratings are taken from Gallup Poll data.

22. Nessen, *It Sure Looks Different,* p. 163.

23. William C. Spragens, ''Political Impact of Presidential Assassinations and Attempted Assassinations,'' *Presidential Studies Quarterly,* 10, no. 3 (Summer 1980): 336–347.

24. Probably the best account of the 1976 campaign can be found in Jules Witcover and Jack Germond, *Marathon: The Pursuit of the Presidency 1972–1976* (New York: Viking Press, 1977). Other accounts can be found in the Ford and Carter memoirs and in Theodore H. White, *America in Search of Itself* (New York: Harper and Row, 1982).

21   JIMMY CARTER

Dennis M. Anderson

CARTER: PREPRESIDENTIAL IMAGES

In December 1973, when Jimmy Carter was completing the third full year of his single four-year term as governor of Georgia, he was so unknown to the public outside his native state that when he appeared as a guest on the popular "What's My Line?" television show, four unblindfolded celebrities on the panel were unable to guess his identity.

However unknown he was to the American public, Governor Carter had ambitions and a plan. The plan for capturing the Democratic presidential nomination, devised by his political aide Hamilton Jordan, called for Carter to start early and to devote his campaign effort to states whose primaries and caucuses would receive disproportionate media attention early in the campaign—Iowa, New Hampshire, Florida, and Illinois. Accordingly, in December 1974, the self-styled "peanut farmer" and "nuclear engineer," former naval officer, state legislator, and little-known one-term governor of a state from a region which had not produced a president in over a hundred years announced his candidacy for president of the United States.

Carter traveled extensively, cultivating local press, attending even minor party functions, establishing contacts, and building the rudiments of an organization. Although a lead in a "straw poll" of attendees at an October 1975 Jefferson-Jackson Day dinner in Ames, Iowa, gave him national coverage which had eluded him in his first several months of campaigning, Carter was still barely surfacing in national opinion polls by the end of 1975.

Jimmy Carter moved into large-scale national notice when 27.6 percent of the Iowa Democratic activists who turned out for neighborhood caucuses in January 1976 designated him as their choice. While Carter's 27 percent was twice that of the second place candidate, Senator Birch Bayh of Indiana, it was considerably less than the 37 percent who voted "uncommitted." On the strength of this ambiguous showing, Carter was hailed by influential organs of the national press as a "major contender" or even "the Man to Beat."

Two weeks later Carter edged out his principal rivals for first place in the New Hampshire primary by a few thousand votes. With no conservative candidates in the race, Carter's plurality victory (30 percent) over four liberals came from conservative Democrats.

In the next set of primaries, damaging defeats in Massachusetts and New York were offset by victories in Florida and North Carolina over former Alabama governor George Wallace; a plurality victory in Illinois, where his principal opposition was not entered; and a narrow victory over Congressman Morris Udall in Wisconsin. Betty Glad notes that the press failed to call into question the electoral viability of a Democratic candidate who could not come out ahead of major competition in two large northeastern industrial states.

With momentum from these victories, Carter's "Peanut Brigade" of volunteers, backed with adequate money for a media blitz, moved into Pennsylvania, which was to be the crucial "shoot-out" with Senator Henry Jackson of Washington, who had been the winner in New York and Massachusetts. While Jackson had half-hearted support from labor leaders whose first love was Hubert Humphrey, much of the state's political establishment remained neutral, not wanting to burn bridges to a candidate who might turn out to be their nominee. Of the one-third of the registered voters who went to the polls, 37 percent voted for Carter and 25 percent for Jackson, with Udall and Wallace trailing.

Still not believing in the inevitability of Carter's nomination, Idaho's Senator Frank Church, shortly followed by California's Governor Edmund G. (Jerry) Brown, Jr., entered the race. Between early May and June 1 Carter was beaten by Governor Brown or Senator Church in half a dozen late primaries. Even a victory by 1 percent over Udall in Michigan, where Carter had momentum and support from much of the state's establishment, was so close as to be an embarrassment. However, because he had chosen to run in every primary, the impact of each of his defeats was minimized by victories elsewhere. In spite of the adverse turn in Carter's fortunes during the late spring primary contests he had amassed a commanding lead in delegates.

Carter secured the Democratic party nomination by winning only one of three big contests in the final set of primaries. Abandoning California and New Jersey to the opposition, the Carter campaign managed to get the press to treat Ohio—where Carter had organization, endorsements, and a divided opposition—as the crucial test. Mayor Richard Daley of Chicago said that Carter would have the nomination in his grasp if he won Ohio. With that and a 52 percent victory in Ohio the media hailed Carter as the inevitable nominee. In the next few days and weeks the other candidates released their delegates.

The grass-roots support that brought Carter his nomination was less impressive than his delegate lead. Carter's image as a winner in most of his primaries was based on plurality, not majority, victories, and his following multiplied as he received votes of people for whom he had been second or third choice but whose first choices had dropped out or were perceived as unable to win. Carter actually won "a relatively small plurality of the 15.6 million votes cast in Democratic primaries." Moreover, Carter's electoral strength depended on whom he faced. Against opponents on his right (primarily Wallace) he was strong, and against opponents on his left (primarily Udall, Brown, and Church) he was weak. The media concentration on individual wins and losses tended to overlook this weakness. His only consistent group support came from blacks and southerners. During the primaries Carter had been first choice of between 30 and 40 percent of Democrats, and only in mid-June, when his nomination was assured, did he become first choice of over 50 percent. Carter's appeal thus rested on a softer base than was apparent to most observers of his triumphal nomination at the Democratic Convention in New York. Jimmy Carter became the 1976 Democratic standard-bearer through a nominating process that did not require strong support from party elites or core constituencies of the Democratic party.

Several bits of luck help to account for Carter's victory: Humphrey's non-candidacy; the lack of great popular enthusiasm for any of the 1976 primary candidates; the fortuitous division of the vote among his opponents; the failure of the opposition to get behind Senator Jackson in Pennsylvania in the mistaken belief that there would be sufficient time later; and the nature of media coverage of the primaries.[1]

The Carter campaign's appeal stressed qualities of character far more than issues: trust, love, compassion, a government "as good as its people" which would be restored by an "outsider" uncorrupted by the old crowd of Washington insiders. It would take someone who had not been part of the evils of the "bloated" and "confused" Washington bureaucracy to clean it up. Yet, while Carter's campaign theme emphasized trust, polls showed that "there was no more trust placed in him by voters than in any of the other candidates."

At the time of his nomination, remarks of friends and supporters stressed Carter's administrative abilities, intelligence, morality, curiosity, personal discipline, persistence, and loyalty. His enemies suggested that Carter was stubborn, tactless, ruthless, a poor administrator, lacked a sense of humor, and possessed a self-righteous streak. *Newsweek* suggested that Carter had "skillfully applied ... the South's traditional sense of place, family and community to national politics." David Halberstam attributed Carter's success to his ability to reassure those "deeply threatened" by rapid change.[2]

Carter's nomination in Madison Square Garden was a media triumph, and he entered the general election campaign with a united party behind him and a substantial lead over Gerald Ford in the polls. But by election day President Ford had narrowed the Carter lead to about 2 percent with an effective media campaign stressing his known qualities against Carter's unknown qualities, alleged "fuzziness," and lack of experience. Carter's rapid emergence on the national scene had left many people with the feeling that they knew too little about him as a person, and many had misgivings about his fundamentalist religious orientations. Betty Glad cites the "softness" of Carter's 1976 electoral support as evidence of "widespread uncertainty in the electorate about what Jimmy Carter stood for and about what he would do as President."

Probably because of each side's emphasis on the personal qualities of its candidate and because issue differences between Carter and Ford mirrored traditional party positions on economic management, party identification counted for more in explaining the division of the vote than it had in 1972. Carter won support from many traditional Democratic voting groups (such as blacks and union households), which was comparable to that won by Democratic candidates in the previous twenty-five years.[3] "Small pluralities" of the electorate gave Carter the edge over Ford in reducing unemployment, and in reducing the size and improving the efficiency of the federal government. Neither candidate was thought to be more likely to reduce inflation. Notwithstanding Carter's emphasis on trust, Ford enjoyed public perceptions of greater trustworthiness.

Carter's 51 percent was less than the "normal" or expected vote for a Democratic candidate based on the fact that there were far more people in 1976 who identified with the Democratic party than the Republican party. Jimmy Carter received the smallest percentage from independent voters (38 percent) of any winning candidate in twenty-four years. It is fair to conclude that his victory in November 1976 had less to do with his personal appeal and was based instead on the fact that he was the nominee of the Democratic party.

CARTER'S PRESIDENTIAL IMAGE

Sometimes satire captures an overall image with more richness (and certainly more wit) than public opinion polls. One of Russell Baker's columns written well over a year after Carter had taken office perhaps best captures his initial image on the eve of his inauguration.

There was a mean street, Pennsylvania Avenue. At one end stood, not a saloon, but a Capitol, filled with gun-toting poker players who could skin the innocent slicker than a hickory elm. At the other, not a general store run by Mister Big who was behind all the cattle rustling, but the White House, where the things that had been going on for years were a scandal to God-fearing folks.

Here . . . was a town ripe for the arrival of a stranger, a lone rider pure of heart, galloping in from the purifying grandeur of the great open countryside. In a room full of bourbon guzzlers, he would order sarsparilla, and afterward clean up the town.[4]

Baker credits his metaphor of the lonely and virtuous outsider coming in to clean up a mean town to Henry Kissinger, who had observed that American attitudes toward government had been shaped by cowboy movies in which the lone hero, against all odds, makes everything right in the end.

Populistic symbols were prominent at Jimmy Carter's inaugural. Three hundred thousand invitations to attend the free events of the inaugural celebration were sent to Carter supporters. Carter wore an "ordinary three piece business suit" for the swearing-in ceremony, took his oath of office on his family's Bible and, in a pedestrian inaugural address, called for "fresh faith in the old dream."

And, as Russell Baker put it, "He didn't ride a white horse but he walked down Pennsylvania Avenue as bravely as Gary Cooper at high noon."

In his early actions and pronouncements as President, Carter continued his "populist" emphasis on being an open president close to his public. His daughter Amy was enrolled at a predominantly black public school near the White House; "Ruffles and Flourishes" and "Hail to the Chief" were deleted from ceremonies; chauffeur service for White House aides was eliminated; government regulations would be written in "plain English"; and visiting foreign leaders would be greeted with less pomp and ceremony. And to symbolize his concern for energy conservation, Carter wore a cardigan sweater during his first "fireside chat." The new president was quoted through a press aide as "determined to stay in touch with the people."

He stayed in touch by graciously answering questions from ordinary citizens on a call-in show, by including "average Americans" as 5 or 10 percent of the guests invited to state dinners, and by subjecting himself to question and answer sessions at town meetings around the country. In these trips Carter would demonstrate his closeness to the people by staying overnight at the homes of typical Americans, calling an individual in the area who had written the White House about some problem, or visiting an elementary school class. In February 1977, 20 percent more of the public chose a description of Carter saying he "sides with the average citizen" than in preelection polls.

Figure 21.1 shows levels of approval or positive job ratings throughout President Carter's term by the Gallup Organization, Louis Harris and Associates, and the Eagleton Institute at Rutgers (a poll of New Jersey residents). Among these three polls, Carter's generally higher ratings from Gallup are the result of differences in question wording. The Gallup poll asks, "Do you approve or disapprove of the way Jimmy Carter is handling his job as President? Harris asks, "Would you say he is doing an excellent, pretty good, only fair, or a poor job?" Harris then counts only the respondents who chose "excellent" or "pretty good" as positive and "only fair" and "poor" as negative.

The Eagleton poll's wording is essentially the same as Harris' except that its second is "good" instead of Harris' "pretty good"—a slightly more demanding judgement. Another reason to expect somewhat lower ratings from the Eagleton poll is because its sample is drawn only from residents of New Jersey, and Carter's greater popularity in the South than elsewhere increased his popularity in national polls.

In order to avoid clutter, "disapproval" or negative ratings ("only fair" or "poor") are not plotted in Figure 21.1. Since 10 to 15 percent of Gallup's respondents have "no opinion," President Carter's Gallup disapproval mentions tend to exceed his Gallup approval mentions when his approval ratings sink to about the middle-to-lower 40 percent range. In contrast to Gallup, the Harris poll tends to have no more than 1 or 2 percent "no opinion."

After reaching his peak ratings of 70–75 percent in March, Carter's approval levels edged downward to a 60–67 percent range, where they remained from

Figure 21.1
Approval Ratings for Jimmy Carter

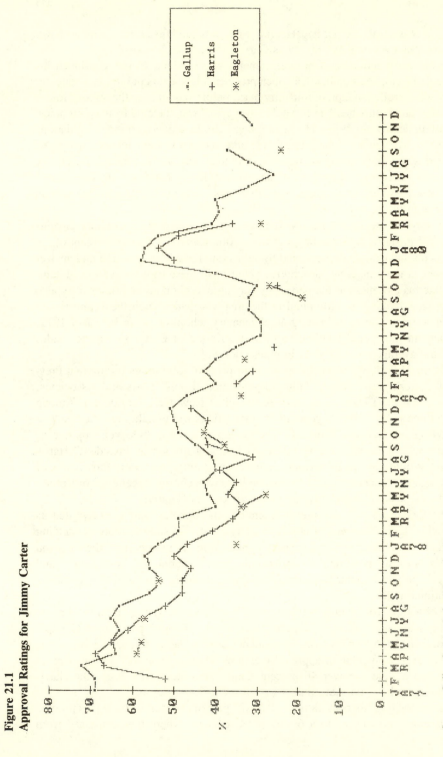

Source: Gallup Opinion Index, November-December 1980; Louis Harris Associates; Eagleton Public Affairs Center.

April until late summer of 1977. In its summary of the Carter presidency, Gallup suggests that there were three reasons for the early popularity of the Carter administration: 1) a positive rating of Carter's handling of the economy and energy situation (his first principal policy initiative was his "moral equivalent of war" energy speech), 2) "his image as a leader," and 3) a perception of his political position as moving closer to the public's own moderate "political philosophy."

Table 21.1 allows us to examine the changes in the different components of President Carter's image in order to see what lies beneath the overall "on balance" job approval ratings in Figure 21.1. In Table 21.1 respondents were asked to select the term which best describes Jimmy Carter on a series of pairs of opposite traits described in "phrase portraits." Percentages of respondents who selected the more favorable (positive) of each of the pairs of opposites are shown for the last three of Gallup's samplings in 1980. A Percentage Difference Index (PDI) is used for the first six samplings (from right to left). The PDI is calculated by subtracting the percentage of people endorsing the negative phrases from the percentage of positive respondents. For example, under "Positive Phrases," "Decisive, sure of himself" is matched with "Negative Phrases," "Uncertain, indecisive, unsure." In January 1980 Carter received a 39 percent positive rating in this category, as may be seen in Table 21.1; 48 percent (not shown) chose the negative term. Subtracting the negative from the positive percent gives us −9 for our percentage difference index score on this item. PDIs were not calculated for the last two of Gallup's samples because the negative percentages were not available. Because of this, both PDIs and positive percentages are shown for purposes of comparability for the January 1980 sampling.

At the bottom of Table 21.1 are listed the average percentages of "no opinion" respondents. In sharp contrast to all the later samplings, nearly three-fifths of the sample in February 1977 declined to select either the positive or negative description of President Carter. This is probably a reflection of the new president's poorly crystallized image at the time of his inauguration and an indication of his "fuzziness" problem. Although fewer in number, the February 1977 respondents who gave an opinion were overwhelmingly favorable ("Bright, intelligent," 43 percent; "not too bright," 2 percent), presumably reflecting Carter's high early job approval ratings.

Favorable press coverage during his "honeymoon" period reinforced these positive feelings and presumably began to lead to the development of a more fully crystallized image as President Carter settled into the job during the spring and summer of 1977. Martha Joynt Kumar and Michael B. Grossman report that tributes to Carter's "skill as a leader of public opinion were widespread in the media."[5] In comments drawn from five leading magazines and newspapers, Bruce Miroff reports stories citing humility, "down home" modesty, openness, candor, and lack of pretension in the Carter White House. These "soft" images provided the necessary balancing of "hard" characteristics. Among these were

Table 21.1
Components of Carter's Image: A "Phrase Portrait"

Positive Phrases	Positive Percentages			Percentage Difference Index (PDI)					
	Sept. 1980	June 1980	Jan. 1980	Jan. 1980	July 1979	Jan. 1979	July 1978	Sept. Oct. 1977	Feb. 1977
Decisive, sure of himself	35%	28%	39%	−9	−28	−7	−17	+33	+32
Has strong leadership qualities	29%	26%	34%	−20	−40	−17	−22	+35	+27
Displays good judgment in a crisis	51%	62%	74%	+63	+46	+40	+38	+57	+30
Well-defined program for moving the country ahead	25%	21%	31%	−25	−54	−35	−35	−1	+13
Offers imaginative, innovative solutions to national problems	34%	30%	41%	−2	−21	−12	−6	+21	+21
Bright, intelligent	70%	62%	71%	+53	+43	+52	+52	+68	+41
A person of exceptional abilities	n.a.	24%	29%	−30	−42	−25	−40	−8	+4
Says what he believes even if unpopular	54%	53%	57%	+26	+24	+21	+30	+35	+19

Table 21.1 (continued)

	Sept. 1980	June 1980	Jan. 1980	Jan. 1980	July 1979	Jan. 1979	July 1978	Oct. 1977	Sept. Feb. 1977
Positive Phrases									
Puts country's interests ahead of politics	n.a.	46%	58%	+30	−2	+7	+7	+27	+27
You know where he stands on issues	31%	23%	33%	−22	−47	−36	−38	−5	+6
Takes moderate, middle-of-the-road positions	76%	70%	77%	+68	+52	+55	+54	+48	+22
A likeable person	n.a.	68%	71%	+54	+44	+52	+57	+66	+33
Sides with the average citizen	52%	41%	49%	+13	−4	−5	+11	+25	+25
Sympathetic to concerns of poor	64%	55%	58%	+30	+16	+14	+33	+36	+32
A man you can believe in	n.a.	34%	50%	+13	−21	−9	−6	+15	+19
A man of high moral principles	79%	75%	78%	+68	+60	+67	+67	+70	+38
A religious person	82%	78%	78%	+67	+65	+70	+69	+71	+40
Average percent No Opinion	−	−	−	13%	7%	7%	7%	12%	58%

Source: Gallup Opinion Reports: no. 163, p. 51; no. 174, p. 12; no. 181, p. 31.

praise for his intelligence, self-confidence, determination, toughness, effectiveness, and skill as a manager and "problem-solver."

These hard and soft features represented what was, from the administration's point of view, a helpful balancing of several contradictory desires Americans have toward their president: he should be fair but tough, kindly but forceful. As Miroff concludes, "Jimmy Carter was presented by the press largely in the symbolic terms that he and his aides were working diligently to establish." Increases in Carter's favorable percentage differences (PDIs) in September-October 1977 in all but four of the phrase portrait categories presumably reflect this favorable coverage as well as the development of a more fully crystallized image as people moved away from the "no opinion" position.

Bruce Miroff argues that the beginning of the end of President Carter's predominantly favorable coverage in the national press and the destruction of his favorable image with the public should be traced to the president's mishandling of the Lance affair. Bert Lance, Carter's budget director and a longtime Georgia associate, had come under scrutiny from the Senate Governmental Affairs Committee and then the press over his banking practices. There were questions about the propriety of overdrafts and proper collateral for large loans. Lance's troubles dominated press coverage of the Carter administration from midsummer 1977 until late September, when he resigned.

President Carter's "dogged defense" and premature exoneration of Lance led many influential journalists to begin to call into question Carter's political judgment and managerial ability. Miroff quotes James Reston as saying that "some of the early magic had been lost" and Hedrick Smith as contending that the Lance case "robbed the President of . . . moral authority with the public."[6] What had been Carter's special claim to symbolic novelty and power was now in doubt.

By October Carter's Gallup approval ratings showed a 10 percentage point shift toward disapproval compared to his pre–Lance affair ratings of late spring and early summer. A new set of images had begun to appear in the press. Toughness had been supplanted by vacillation; the politically savvy manager now lacked both a sense of direction and priorities; the president who had appeared as master of the Capitol was now too weak to conquer the Washington establishment and appeared to be carried along by events rather than being their shaper. The press also reported stories of administrative confusion among the White House staff, public relations ineptitude by President Carter, and waning public enthusiasm for the president.

In Figure 21.1 the Eagleton poll shows a precipitous drop in Carter's positive job ratings between late fall 1977 and January 1978, while Gallup's and Harris' ratings suggest that Carter's decline came in two stages separated by a temporary plateau during the early winter of 1977/78.[7] The specific character of the damage to Carter's image is evident in Table 21.1's July 1978 sampling, where we see sharp declines in the choice of positive phrases which describe hard components of his image. While the positive PDIs—for the most purely hard traits such as strong/weak leadership and "sure (unsure) of himself"—shift sharply in a negative direction, the most pure soft traits ("high moral principles," "religious person," "likeable person") show very little or no erosion.

According to Miroff, the Lance affair, unlike other political embarrassments, had the capacity to set in motion such catastrophic changes in Carter's image because Carter's handling of it was so contrary to the reigning imagery that it possessed shock value, and one such instance can lead to a devastating alteration. Another example of such an alteration is Ford's pardon of Nixon.

As the disastrous effects of the Lance affair sank in, a new "prevailing image" began to govern Carter's overall popularity which, as we see in Figure 21.1, declined more or less steadily from late 1977 to April 1978, when he landed at a low of 40 percent approval. But while these job approval ratings were destined to rise and fall again, the deterioration in the hard components of Carter's image in Table 21.1 were to prove permanent. By mid-1978 this "prevailing image" of weakness in hard traits and strength in soft traits is established; it persists essentially unchanged throughout his presidency.

The weakness in the hard components of Carter's image manifested itself in lower expectations. In a CBS News/*New York Times* poll more people felt that "anybody—some other president or another branch of government"—would be more likely than Carter to "balance the federal budget within the next few years," make the government "more efficient," reduce unemployment, and handle "energy problems effectively." The gap between "possible for anybody" and Carter widened throughout 1977 as optimistic expectations about Carter declined.[8]

Godfrey Sperling described a popular feeling very consonant with the weak-hard, strong-soft pattern in the July 1978 phrase portraits in Table 21.1. While people were "rooting for [Carter] to succeed" it was difficult to find "anyone who wasn't less than satisfied with the President's performance." Carter was no longer seen as "the Carter of old" who would bring fresh, new approaches to problems in Washington. Other polls confirmed these feelings of ambivalence and disappointment. An Associated Press-NBC News poll found that while 80 percent agreed that Carter was "an honest man" and "a hard working President," 63 percent rejected the assertion that "Carter has shown that he can get things done."

Mixed public feelings toward Carter may also be seen in Figure 21.1, where Carter's ratings from Gallup are better than those from Harris or Eagleton. Gallup's respondents were more willing to "approve" Carter's job handling than Harris' respondents were to give him at least an evaluation of "pretty good." As we noted when we introduced Figure 21.1, "only fair" ratings do not get counted as "positive" by Harris or Eagleton. When asked the Gallup questions, many of Harris' "only fair" respondents said that they "approved." Popular ambivalence was also reflected in the fact that a majority of Harris poll respondents who gave Carter an "only fair" rating gave him a "C" when asked to grade him on a scale of "A" through "F".

The announcement of peace agreements between Egypt and Israel at Camp

David was followed immediately by a rapid rise in Carter's popularity which broke his ratings out of the trough they had been in since the spring. After his "weeks of perseverance and eventual triumph" in negotiating a Middle East peace agreement President Carter's Camp David based popular resurgence— which Cliff Zukin and J. Robert Carter, Jr., characterize as a "modest 'thank you' "—lasted only through January 1979, after which his ratings began another long slide.[9]

One reason improvements in Carter's job approval ratings were short-lived was because there was no fundamental change in the weakness of his underlying image. Just as presidential images are, as Miroff points out, sufficiently stable that "single policy failures or political setbacks" are unlikely to radically alter a president's image in a negative way, successes in foreign policy which do not touch people directly cannot strengthen a presidential image whose underlying contours are inherently weak.

In a similar vein, Zukin and Carter argue that it is the "prevailing image rather than close assessment of a president's particular actions, to which elites, and especially 'ordinary' citizens, usually refer when they discuss and evaluate an incumbent president." Consequently, it is probably fair to say that discrete events of the early Carter presidency such as his embarrassing abandonment of his $50 tax rebate plan, the rebuff of an unrealistically constructed arms control proposal in the spring of 1977, and later the ratification of the Panama Canal Treaties as well as his decision to defer production of the neutron bomb did not, by themselves, have any appreciable adverse effect on the long-term trend of Carter's popularity. In a similar way, when the news was good the public gave Carter a brief "thank you" in the form of improved job approval ratings (Figure 21.1) for Camp David but did not change its basic feelings about him, as evidenced by the small and temporary character of the improvements in the post–Camp David phrase portraits (Table 21.1).

The Eagleton poll findings suggested that Carter had not been exempted from the adverse effects of the vicissitudes of domestic politics even during the short-lived resurgence of good feelings over Camp David. Zukin and Carter indicate that during this period from October 1978 to January 1979, Democratic support of President Carter dropped by 12 percentage points while Republican support was essentially "stable," actually "rising a mere two points." The result of this was an overall decline in the Eagleton poll. (See Figure 21.1.) They suggest that the only event which "might account for this movement" was a "blistering attack" on the Carter domestic policies by Senator Edward Kennedy at the Democratic Midterm Conference. Consistent with this argument also is the fact that the only parts of Carter's phrase portrait where there are noticeable declines between July 1978 and January 1979 are in two items that many of the core constituencies of the Democratic party might be especially sensitive to: "sides with the average citizen" and "sympathetic to problems of the poor."

Factors with more salience and broader public impact than his lift from Camp David or Senator Kennedy's criticism were at work during the second major decline in Carter's standing with the public, which began in early 1979 and extended throughout most of the year. Zukin and Carter's New Jersey poll data contained seven components of President Carter's performance ("overall performance, handling the economy, foreign affairs, energy, honesty and general competence," among others). Of these, "competence" had the strongest negative impact on the president's approval rating even during the time of his Camp David resurgence in late 1978. Polls throughout this period suggested Carter's ongoing image problem. In February 1979 an ABC News-Harris survey found that only 28 percent had "a great deal of confidence" in Carter, and in the fall 64 percent of a Gallup survey said that they had "no confidence" in President Carter's "ability to handle . . . the nation's most critical problem."

Next to his "competence," the best predictor of Carter's job rating was the poor evaluation of his handling of the economy which, in the New Jersey poll, was never positive at any time during his presidency. Inflation is one of the most potent factors pulling down presidential approval ratings. Throughout the Carter years the public mentioned the "cost of living" as its most important concern.[10] The unprecedented double-digit inflation of Carter's last two years helped to lock in concrete the public's negative judgements about his competence and his problem-solving ability. Zukin and Carter also found that President Carter's ratings on his handling of energy problems tended to parallel his ratings on the economy, which also could have contributed to his "steady decline."

Very low in their ability to predict presidential job approval were popular evaluations of foreign policy, an area whose headline impact is not matched by any direct impact on people's daily lives and whose weakness is attested to by the temporary character of President Carter's Camp David resurgence.

Carter's post–Camp David decline reached bottom in the summer of 1979. The average Gallup approval rating for this second low plateau of Carter's (June through October 1979) was 30.2 percent approval and 56 percent disapproval, with about 13.5 percent expressing "no opinion." In mid-July Carter gave his "crisis of the American spirit" speech, in which he argued that there was a "malaise" gripping the country. Temporary up-ticks in favorable judgements of the president quickly faded away. While the public did not appear to place primary blame on Carter for the gasoline crisis, the frustrations associated with the long gas lines of the summer of 1979 may have added to the public's disposition to give the president low marks.[11]

In the Eagleton poll Carter's popularity hit its low point of 19 percent in September. His September Gallup ratings did not seem to be further adversely affected by the resignation of Andrew Young as U.N. ambassador or the removal of three cabinet members. In early October Gallup reported that the public was closely divided on Carter's response to the discovery of a Russian combat brigade in Cuba.

By the fall of 1979 Carter's ratings in Figure 21.1 show a pattern of rather steady decline throughout his time in office, with only one noticeable upswing of four to five months duration at the time of the Camp David peace agreement.

While presidents typically lose support over time, President Carter's decline by 1979 was more extreme than for most of his predecessors. Humphrey Taylor of the Louis Harris organization has suggested regular phases which define the public's progressive disenchantment with its presidents. According to Taylor, three trends or phases in public opinion are typical for recent presidents:

First, people start to criticize the President's inability to make things better, and his ratings on specific domestic and economic policies fall.

Second, the President's overall job rating falls as people increasingly doubt the performance will live up to the promise. . . . The faith lingers on that his objectives and policies are praiseworthy, but that he sadly lacks what it takes to implement them.

Only at the very end, and with great reluctance do the American people stop thinking well of the President himself as a person.[12]

Figure 21.2 may be interpreted as a kind of time-lapse photograph of the changing relationships among the dimensions of President Carter's image at different phases of his presidency. Carter's initial low rating for problem-solving in December 1977 suggests that Phase 1 was well underway before his first year in the White House was completed. In Table 21.1, Carter's ratings on the two most problem-solving oriented phrase portraits (having "a well-defined program" and "imaginative . . . solutions to national problems") had already begun to decline in the fall of 1977 and summer of 1978. In Figure 21.2 the widening gap between the ratings for trust and confidence in the man and the problem-solving rating suggests increasing doubt about the president's ability to perform or "implement" solutions to the nation's problems or to achieve his praiseworthy "aims and objectives." Carter's perceived inability to deal effectively with problems becomes increasingly important as the apparent regulator of the level of his overall (Gallup) job approval rating, while trust and confidence in Carter as a person become increasingly irrelevant to his approval rating. Finally, the greater buoyancy of the "trust and confidence . . . in the man" measure in Figure 21.2 (compared to the two job-related measures)—and the continuing high ratings on the soft phrase portrait traits in Table 21.1—suggest that Carter never did fully reach Phase 3 even when his overall job approval ratings were at their lowest levels.

On the eve of the hostage crisis, President Carter, presumably late in Phase 2, enjoyed "high confidence" in his ability "to lead the country" from 23 percent of Democrats, 11 percent of independents, and 9 percent of Republicans. Thus, before the Iranian hostage seizure, Carter's standing with the public and with Democrats did not augur well for his chances for reelection or even renomination.

When the American Embassy in Teheran was seized in early November Carter's approval rating had remained "remarkably stable" for the preceding six months but mired in its second major trough around 30 percent. However, the imprisonment of the American personnel by the Iranian militants led to a "rally-

Figure 21.2
Changing Dimensions of Carter's Image

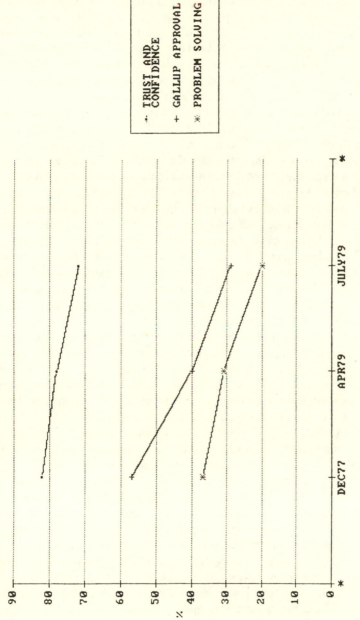

Trust and Confidence: "How much trust and confidence do you have in President Carter, the man—a great deal, some, hardly any, or none?" Percentages include "a great deal" and "some."

Problem Solving: "How would you rate President Carter's record to date—do you think he's done an excellent job in dealing with the problems facing the nation, a good job, a fair job, or a poor job?" Percentages include "excellent" and "good."

Source: Gallup Organization; Louis Harris Associates; Eagleton Foundation.

round-the-flag'' effect that increased President Carter's overall positive job ratings more rapidly than had ever occurred in four decades of the Gallup poll.

By early December Carter's Gallup approval rating reached 61 percent, and he led Senator Kennedy (who had announced his candidacy for the Democratic presidential nomination in early November) among Democratic voters by approximately 2 to 1, reversing the ratio, which had been in the senator's favor in October. Seventy-seven percent of Gallup's respondents said that they approved of Carter's handling of the Iranian crisis in December, with 19 percent disapproving. By New Year's, approval of the president's handling of the crisis had begun to decline, but was still favorable by a 2 to 1 ratio.

The hostage crisis gave President Carter "diffuse support," which the public had not rewarded him with after the Camp David accords. For the first time, according to Zukin and Carter, foreign affairs had more influence on President Carter's overall approval ratings than did the economy. However, while the hostage crisis temporarily altered the alignment of forces that governed the levels of the president's ratings, Zukin and Carter's data suggested to them that the public's rally-round-the-flag-induced high ratings for Carter did not mean that the public thought he had become more competent. The public merely felt that in time of crisis it should support the president. Corroborating Zukin and Carter's conclusions is evidence that popular perceptions of Carter had not been fundamentally altered. No permanent strengthening of hard traits occurred (Table 21.1), and, although Carter led Kennedy two to one, he lost to the senator in comparative assessments of the hard traits and trailed Kennedy as a "strong leader" even among his own supporters.

Lacking the staying power that might have been provided by a stronger underlying image, Carter's approval ratings began their inevitable decline before the new year was well under way, slipping to 55 percent approval (with 36 percent disapproval) by early February. Majorities approved of Carter's handling of foreign policy but disapproved of his handling of domestic problems. Those who disapproved of Carter's handling of foreign policy were more likely to say that he was "not tough enough" with the Soviet Union rather than "too tough"—a traditional sentiment among Americans, probably made more salient by the Soviet Union's invasion of Afghanistan in late December.

In the subsequent months, President Carter was to undergo a "severe decline in popularity as he rolled to the nomination." According to the Eagleton poll, favorable impressions declined sharply after the Massachusetts and Vermont primaries in early March. Scott Keeter and Cliff Zukin report that Carter's popularity stabilized in April but then declined further in May and June, with larger declines among Democrats than Republicans. The aborted hostage rescue mission in April appeared to have little immediate adverse effect on the president's standing. However, still lower approval ratings in late May suggested a delayed reaction from the failed rescue mission; as Keeter and Zukin suggest, "The finality of its failure and the apparent lack of options ultimately undermined confidence in the President."[13]

Although the president by late spring had obtained a commanding lead in convention delegates, Senator Kennedy continued his campaign for the nomination, and this probably slowed down the process of reconciliation of Democrats to their probable nominee. Carter's popularity hit the all-time low of 21 percent approval for any Gallup poll in mid-July. Carter then enjoyed a modest recovery to 32 percent approval in August and 37 percent in September as the fall election campaign against Ronald Reagan began in earnest.

Polls during the campaign measuring the strengths and weaknesses of the two candidates (see Table 22.1 in the next chapter on Ronald Reagan) confirmed the familiar pattern of Carter's weakness in leadership and problem-solving, particularly in comparison with Reagan. Probably because of desperation born of his low standing in the polls and inability to make visible progress on the problems of the economy and toward the release of the hostages held by Iran, Carter campaigned aggressively, attacking Reagan in a more negative way than would normally be advisable for an incumbent president running for reelection.[14]

Carter culminated a series of strident attacks on Reagan with a statement in Chicago on October 6 that Reagan's election might disunify the country's "blacks from whites, Jews from Christians, North from South, rural from urban." Reagan reacted mildly, and Carter suffered from much negative press comment. Reagan's strategists felt that "the President's overblown attack rhetoric stuck him with the tag of 'dirty campaigner' for the remainder of the election."[15] In an ABC interview with Barbara Walters, Carter promised to stop being nasty. Carter probably also lost ground when he refused to participate in a debate on September 21 arranged by the League of Women Voters on the grounds that John Anderson, an independent candidate who had begun the fall campaign with about 15 percent support, had been included.

Given the voters' desire for "strong leadership" and Reagan's advantage over Carter on this dimension, Carter's defeat in November by nearly 10 percentage points, while not predicted by most preelection polls, should not have been surprising. Apparently many voters waited until after the Carter-Reagan debate in Cleveland in the last week of the campaign before coming down solidly in Reagan's favor. Given Carter's strategy of painting Ronald Reagan as a mean, racist, war-mongering ogre, the debate confrontation between the two candidates, where Reagan appeared credible, could only help Reagan and seal Carter's fate.

CARTER'S POSTPRESIDENTIAL IMAGE

Carter's loss by 8.5 million votes to a candidate with many negatives of his own while running as an incumbent president and candidate of the majority Democratic party must be counted as the most negative possible judgment on his presidency.

In postelection opinion polls pluralities placed Carter in the middle categories on any question rating "the job [he has] done" or how he "will go down in history." However, the remaining respondents were more than twice as likely to place him below rather than above the average categories. The public assessment of Carter was somewhat weaker than the ratings given President Ford when he left office four years earlier. In summary, the public's initial "historic" judgment tended to be moderately negative.

However, the specific negatives of the Carter presidency were still present. In a Harris poll listing of eight recent presidents, more than three times as many respondents rated Carter as "least able to get things done" (44 percent) than gave this dubious appellation to any of the other presidents. Only negligible percentages rated Carter as "best on domestic" or "foreign affairs."[16]

Journalistic opinion was less severe. The MacNeil/Lehrer Report, a Public Broadcasting Service program, interviewed four prominent journalists on a "Carter Retrospective" a few days before he left office. They tended to believe that Carter on balance had been judged a bit too severely and agreed that there "were more pluses than minuses" in foreign policy: the Israeli-Egyptian peace treaty, the Panama Canal settlement, normalization of relations with China, an effective policy toward black Africa, and improvement of relations with many Third World countries. In domestic policy his inability to translate good instincts into effective policy leadership was made worse by the lack of relevant national experience of his "trusted Georgia allies" in the "immediate White House circle." Several times these journalists noted Carter's central problem: he did not inspire and could not articulate "a vision with respect to domestic affairs." In economic management there was less agreement but a more critical judgment; in particular, Carter's failure to stay with a consistent economic policy.

They finally agreed that excessive image consciousness in the Carter White House had brought trouble upon him, leading him to role play at the job of being president and to telegraph to the public "that there was no substance to some of what he did."[17]

In one survey conducted by the *Chicago Tribune* in the spring of 1982, presidential scholars ranked Carter "tenth worst" among presidents. This low rating prompted a close Carter friend, Atlanta mayor Andrew Young, to blast the scholars for "insensitive elitism." Another survey of historians in late 1982 placed Carter in the average category along with John F. Kennedy and Gerald Ford.[18]

Public speculation as to whether former President Carter's endorsement of Walter Mondale's candidacy for the 1984 Democratic presidential nomination would hurt or help Mondale, even in Georgia, and the initial reluctance of many Democrats to accord Carter a speaking time at the 1984 Democratic Convention during prime TV time are indications that, for his first four years out of office, Jimmy Carter was a political pariah, particularly among his former supporters. The strong support for President Reagan in 1984 among younger voters whose historic memories do not extend beyond the Carter years may also turn out to be Jimmy Carter's unappreciated but lasting legacy to his party.

The first indications that Jimmy Carter's public image might be undergoing the expected postpresidential rehabilitation did not appear until mid-summer of

1985. A *Washington Post*/ABC News poll found a 55 to 39 percent "favorable" over "unfavorable impression" of Carter, "almost the reverse" of his ratings in December 1980.[19] Carter's ratings compared favorably with several other Democratic political leaders and showed special strength among some groups that had been especially disillusioned with him as president: Democrats and liberals.

During the MacNeil/Lehrer Report in January 1981, one of the journalists (Eugene Patterson) commented that Carter's problem was that he "bored us." In early 1983 the International Dull Men's Club announced that Jimmy Carter had "almost made" their annual 1983 list of the Ten Dullest Americans.[20]

NOTES

1. This discussion of the Carter prenomination campaign draws heavily from Betty Glad's biography, *Jimmy Carter: In Search of the Great White House* (New York: W. W. Norton, 1980), pp. 231, 233, 238–239, 247, 248–249, 254–256; F. Christopher Arterton, "The Media Politics of Presidential Campaigns: A Study of the Carter Nomination Drive," in James David Barber, ed., *Race for the Presidency: The Media and the Nominating Process* (Englewood Cliffs, NJ: Prentice-Hall, 1978), pp. 36–45; William E. Bicker, "Network TV News and the 1976 Presidential Primaries," ibid., pp.106, 108; Donald R. Matthews, "Winnowing: The News and the 1976 Presidential Nomination," ibid., pp. 63, 78.

2. *Newsweek,* July 19, 1976, pp. 18–30; David Halberstam, "The Coming of Carter," *Newsweek,* July 19, 1976, p. 11.

3. The discussion of the nature of Carter's support draws from Warren E. Miller and Theresa Levitan, *Leadership and Change: Presidential Elections from 1952 to 1976* (Cambridge, Mass.: Winthrop Publishers, 1976), pp. 196–205, 220–225. See also Glad, *Jimmy Carter,* pp. 254–256.

4. Russell Baker, "Washington Is a Tough Town," *Toledo Blade,* May 22, 1978.

5. The description of the symbolism of the Carter inauguration and of the first months of the Carter presidency comes from Glad, *Jimmy Carter*. The discussion of Carter's image and the content of his press coverage during his first year is greatly indebted to a 1981 American Political Science Association convention paper by Bruce Miroff, "The Media and Presidential Symbolism: The Woes of Jimmy Carter," a content analysis of the elite press. Martha Joynt Kumar, Michael B. Grossman, and Leslie Lichter-Mason, "Images of the White House in the Media," in Doris Graber, ed., *The President and the Public* (Philadelphia: Institute for the Study of Human Issues, 1982), also discusses the early image and press coverage of President Carter.

6. Many contradictory desires of Americans toward their president may be found in Thomas Cronin's discussion of twelve "paradoxes" in Chapter 1 of *The State of the Presidency,* 2nd ed. (Boston: Little, Brown, 1980), pp. 3–22. In addition to Miroff, the discussion of public opinion about Carter in this chapter rests upon polls from the *Gallup Political Index,* Nos. 163, 167, 169, 170, 171, 174, 175, and 182. The Gallup poll typically conducts two or three samplings in a month, occasionally one. The percentages shown in Figure 21.1 are averages of each month's polls.

7. The Eagleton poll is the data base for a perceptive article by Cliff Zukin and J.

Robert Carter, Jr., "The Measurement of Political Popularity: Old Wisdoms and New Concerns," in Graber, *The President and the Public,* pp. 207–241.

8. Stephen J. Wayne, "Expectations of the President," in Graber, *The President and the Public,* p. 22. See also "Opinion Roundup—Solving the Problems: Can Carter Do It? Can Anyone Else?" *Public Opinion,* (May/June 1978): 34.

9. Sperling's observations came after traveling through the South and Midwest that spring and are from his column, "President's Image Still Confusing," *Toledo Blade,* June 17, 1978, p. 5. See Barry Sussman, "Distortion in Popularity Polls," *Washington Post,* February 12, 1978, pp. A1, A10; Gary R. Orren, "Opinion Roundup," *Public Opinion,* (May/June 1978): 35. Much of the remaining discussion of the effect of Camp David on the Carter popularity levels relies on Zukin and Carter's analysis of the Eagleton poll data.

10. "Opinion Roundup—Inflation: A Wipe-out Issue," *Public Opinion,* January/February 1979, p. 27; Miroff "The Media" p. 156; Zukin and Carter, "Measurement of Political Popularity," pp. 220, 221.

11. Only 11 percent blamed Carter, while 42 percent blamed the oil companies. Gallup, No. 167, June 1979, p. 23.

12. Morton Kondracke, "White House Watch—History Resumes," *New Republic,* January 20, 1982, pp. 10, 12–13, quoting Humphrey Taylor at a conference sponsored by *Opinion Outlook* magazine.

13. The dynamics of President Carter's popularity during the 1980 prenomination struggle are ably discussed by Scott Keeter and Cliff Zukin, "New Romances and Old Horses: The Public's Images of Presidential Candidates," in Graber, *The President and the Public,* pp. 39–82. Keeter and Zukin's analysis rests on Eagleton poll data. Data from Gallup polls are also relied upon in the discussion of the prenomination phase.

14. Much of the discussion of the 1980 campaign draws from Paul R. Abramson, John H. Aldrich, and David W. Rohde, *Change and Continuity in the 1980 Elections* (Washington, D.C.: Congressional Quarterly Press, 1982).

15. Richard Wirthlin, Vincent Breglio, and Richard Seal, "Campaign Chronicle," *Public Opinion,* 4 (February/March 1981): 43–49. On the "meanness" issue, see also Hamilton Jordan, *Crisis! The Last Year of the Carter Presidency* (New York: Putnam, 1982).

16. "Opinion Roundup," *Public Opinion,* 4 (February/March 1981): 35; *Gallup Opinion Index,* Nos. 182 and 186.

17. The four journalists interviewed on the MacNeil/Lehrer Report's "Carter Retrospective," aired on January 15, 1981, were Brian Dickenson of the *Providence* (Rhode Island) *Journal-Bulletin,* Robert Maynard of the *Oakland* (California) *Tribune,* Eugene Patterson of the *St. Petersburg* (Florida) *Times,* and Lois Wille of the *Chicago Sun-Times.* Library No. 1384, Show No. 6144.

18. The *Tribune* survey is summarized by *U.S. News & World Report,* June 15, 1982. A UPI story carried the second survey of historians: "Historians Rate Lincoln as the No. 1 President," *Daily Sentinel-Tribune* (Bowling Green, Ohio), December 14, 1982, p. 15.

19. Barry Sussman, "Kennedy, Hart Top Poll on Democrats Likeliest to Run in 1988," *Washington Post,* Sunday, August 11, 1985, p. A4. Two other efforts to rehabilitate Carter's record are Reo M. Christenson, "Carter and Truman: A Reappraisal of Both," *Presidential Studies Quarterly,* 13, no. 2 (Spring 1983): 313–323, and Hodding Carter III, "Jimmy Carter Recalled: Good President, Bad Communicator," *Wall Street Journal,* September 5, 1985, p. 23.

20. "Gerald Ford, Lawrence Welk Top Dull List," *Toledo Blade,* January 9, 1983, p. 3. Instances of continuing hostility to Carter are cited by Meg Greenfield in "Shunned," *Washington Post National Weekly Edition,* April 2, 1984, p. 29.

BIBLIOGRAPHIC ESSAY

The first biographies of Jimmy Carter grew out of his need to publicize himself during the 1976 campaign, and any value they possess rests on Carter's importance, not their own merit. Carter's autobiography, *Why Not the Best* (Nashville: Broadman, 1976), demonstrates (in his "own words") his fatuous technocratic approach to political problem-solving. His policy discussions in a *A Government as Good as Its People* (New York: Simon and Schuster, 1977), while rooted in naivete, are demogogic in character. Two other early campaign biographies are Tom Collins, *The Search for Jimmy Carter* (Waco, Tex.: Word Books, 1976), and Leslie Wheeler, *Jimmy Who? An Examination of Presidential Candidate Jimmy Carter: The Man, His Career, His Stands on the Issues* (Woodbury, N.Y.: Barron's Educational Series, 1976). Collins gives some sense of the meaning of Carter's southern origins and has lots of interesting pictures, many of them courtesy of the Gerald Rafshoon Agency. Wheeler's book is a generally uncritical account of Carter's life, with transcripts of some of his major pronouncements, issue positions, and testimonials.

The first of the more serious biographies of Carter published early in his presidency was Kandy Stroud's *How Jimmy Won: The Victory Campaign from Plains to the White House* (New York: Morrow, 1977). This is an anecdotal treatment of Carter, his family, close friends, early career, and the 1976 campaign. A forgettable examination of Carter's early life in rural Georgia is cousin Hugh Carter's gossipy treatment of Carter family relationships in *Cousin Beedie and Cousin Hot: My Life with the Carter Family of Plains* (Englewood Cliffs, N.J.: Prentice-Hall, 1978). James Wooten's biography (which took Carter's first secret service code name as its title), *Dasher: The Roots and the Rising of Jimmy Carter* (New York: Summit Books, 1978), covers his early life and family plus the first eight months in office in a sympathetic but balanced fashion. Another informative work which is unfortunately limited to the early days is Robert Shogun, *Promises to Keep: Carter's First 100 Days* (New York: Crowell, 1977). Another favorable treatment is William Lee Miller's *Yankee from Georgia: The Emergence of Jimmy Carter* (New York: Times Books, 1978), which examines the influence of Reinhold Niebuhr on Carter and sees him more as a puritan than a stereotypical southerner.

Two biographies with the same subtitle *(The Man and the Myth),* Peter Meyer's *James Earl Carter* (Kansas City: Sheed, Andrews and McMeel, 1978) and Victor Lasky's *Jimmy Carter* (New York: Marel, 1979), are both undiscriminatingly critical. Meyer's book contrasts campaign promises with behavior in office, and Lasky's is a boring polemic that recounts every accusation ever made. Clark R. Mollenhoff rehashes minor scandals in *The President Who Failed: Carter Out of Control* (New York: Macmillan, 1980), and argues that Carter turned out to be the same kind of expedient politician he promised he would replace. None of these three works provides any insight into public policy problems, Carter, or his people. A different kind of criticism comes from Lawrence H. Shoup, *The Carter Presidency and Beyond: Power and Politics in the 1980s* (Palo Alto, Calif.: Ramparts Press, 1980), which argues that Jimmy Carter was essentially a tool of the eastern corporate establishment. Like most such exposés this thesis of elite corporate domination of policy-making is not subjected to rigorous enough analysis to be convincing.

Among the best books on Carter is Haynes B. Johnson's *In the Absence of Power: Governing America* (New York: Viking Press, 1980). Johnson provides much detail about the troubled relations between Carter and the Washington community (Congress, the bureaucracy, and the press) during the years prior to the hostage crisis, but his book is less adequate in explaining the "whys" of Carter's failure. A general biography that falls into the psychological genre is Betty Glad's *Jimmy Carter: In Search of the Great White House* (New York: W. W. Norton, 1980). This is the most complete and thorough biography of Carter, rich in critical insights into his self-image and his stylistic populism. It is suitable for the general reader who does not want to read more than one book on Jimmy Carter.

Two books in the psychological genre that do not add much to our understanding of Carter are Bruce Mazlish and Edwin Diamond's *Jimmy Carter: A Character Portrait* (New York: Simon and Schuster, 1980), and Lloyd deMause and Henry Ebel's edited volume, *Carter and American Fantasy: Psychohistorical Explorations* (New York: Two Continents, 1977).

Among more specialized works are two that focus on Carter's religious beliefs and upbringing: David Kucharsky, *The Man from Plains: The Mind and Spirit of Jimmy Carter* (New York: Harper and Row, 1976), and James T. Baker, *A Southern Baptist in the White House* (Philadelphia: Westminster Press, 1977). Gary M. Fink's *Prelude to the Presidency: The Political Character and Legislative Leadership Style of Governor Jimmy Carter* (Westport, Conn.: Greenwood Press, 1980) sympathetically examines Carter's years as governor with heavy emphasis on governmental reorganization. The initial staffing of the Carter administration is examined in detail in *Promise and Performance: Carter Builds a New Administration* (Lexington, Mass.: Lexington Books, 1979) by Bruce Adams and Kathryn Kavanaugh. Lawrence E. Lynn and David de F. Whitman's *The President as Policymaker: Jimmy Carter and Welfare Reform* (Philadelphia: Temple University Press, 1981) tells much about Carter's problems as political leader and administrator by examining why his welfare reform plan failed.

Among more general works on the Carter administration, the Congressional Quarterly's yearly volumes, *President Carter* (Washington, D.C.: Congressional Quarterly), contain many handy reference materials including summaries of major events by subject, messages, statements, and news conferences. Two books of scholarly essays provide a good review of events and policies of the Carter years for those whose memories of the time have faded. *The Carter Years: The President and Policy Making* (New York: St. Martin's Press, 1984), edited by M. Glenn Abernathy et al. covers various policies as well as Carter's relations with different Washington political institutions. *Eagle Entangled: U.S. Foreign Policy in a Complex World* (New York: Longman's, 1979), edited by Kenneth A. Oye et al., examines different aspects of Carter administration foreign policy in the context of international politics. For the serious student of public opinion and the Carter presidency, Doris Graber, ed., *The President and the Public* (Philadelphia: Institute for the Study of Human Issues, 1982), is a source of many insights.

Supplementing the foregoing scholarly analyses are the memoirs of the participants. Carter's own memoirs, *Keeping Faith: Memoirs of a President* (New York: Bantam Books, 1982), give much detail but little sense of his larger purposes; there is much discussion of foreign policy, less of domestic. Carter's petty denigration of trusted and, one would have thought, respected associates gives us a disappointing measure of the man. Zbigniew Brzezinski, *Power and Principle: Memoirs of the National Security Advisor 1977–1981* (New York: Farrar, Straus and Giroux, 1983), provides informative coverage of the major foreign policy events of the Carter years. Carter's Chief of Staff Hamilton Jordan candidly recounts his role in *Crisis: The Last Year of the Carter Presidency* (New York: Putnam, 1982). Press secretary Jody Powell's *The Other Side of the Story* (New York: Morrow, 1984), while containing some truth, is a one-sided excoriation of the press coverage of the Carter administration which leaves the suggestion that the media and not Carter's own ineptitude did him in. Rosalynn Carter's memoirs, *First Lady from Plains* (Boston: Houghton Mifflin, 1984), cover her life but focus on her activities as First Lady. Mrs. Carter cannot acknowledge that anything that went wrong might have been Jimmy's fault.

While most of the Carter biographies deal with the 1976 campaign, readers principally interested in the minutiae of Carter's campaign may want to read Martin Schram's anaecdotal *Running for President* (New York: Stein and Day, 1977). Two works focus on the 1976 Carter-Ford debates in the context of the campaign: Sidney Kraus, ed., *The Great Debates: Carter vs. Ford 1976* (Bloomington: Indiana University Press, 1979), and Lloyd Bitzer and Theodore Rueter, *Carter vs. Ford: The Counterfeit Debates of 1976* (Madison: University of Wisconsin Press, 1980). Interesting anecdotal coverage of the 1980 campaign may be found in Jack W. Germond and Jules Witcover, *Blue Smoke and Mirrors: How Reagan Won and Why Carter Lost the Election of 1980* (New York: Viking Press, 1981). For a more broadly focused scholarly analysis of the 1980 election, see the essays in *The American Elections of 1980* (Washington, D.C.: American Enterprise Institute for Public Policy Research, 1981), edited by Austin Ranney. Jimmy Carter, his colorful family and southern origins have stimulated attempts at satire—peanut jokes, puns on southern pronunciation, outhouse humor, and iconoclastic comments on Carter and southern life and customs: Roy Blunt, *Crackers: This Whole Many-Angled Thing of Jimmy, More Carters, Ominous Little Animals, Sad-Singing Little Women, My Daddy and Me* (New York: Knopf, 1980); John H. Corcoran, *True Grits* (New York: Dell, 1977); Alan Coren, *The Peanut Papers in Which Miz Lillian Writes* (New York: Dell, 1977); and William Edward Maloney, *The Jimmy Carter Dictionary* (Chicago: Playboy Press, 1977). Considering what they had to work with, the surprise is that these books are, on the whole, not particularly funny.

22 RONALD REAGAN

Dennis M. Anderson

RONALD REAGAN: PREPRESIDENTIAL IMAGE

Ronald Wilson Reagan grew up with the values of small-town America: good fellowship, flag-waving patriotism, religion, a Horatio Alger-like faith in the future, hard work, plain and simple tastes, and a suspicion of the America that was developing in its distant growing cities. His older brother "Moon" recalls that the Reagans' world "couldn't have been more all-American." While the reality for the Reagan family was the "pinched near side of poverty," the times are remembered by Ronald Reagan in a rosy, nostalgic glow. The Reagan parents, Jack and Nelle, managed to avoid making their boys feel poor. As Ronald Reagan was to recount it, "The government didn't keep coming around telling you you were poor." His biographies recount the usual boyish hi-jinks, a passion for sports, particularly football, and school plays. At Eureka College, a small, impecunious Christian Church institution, young "Dutch" Reagan was more all-round man on campus than scholar.

By the time the Republicans were gathering in Detroit in 1980 to give him their nomination, which had twice before eluded him, Reagan brought a record and an image shaped by his Midwest small-town values, and experiences as sportscaster, motion picture star, union leader, TV personality, corporate pitch man, and banquet speaker as well as eight years as governor of California. Despite having been a political presence on the national scene for sixteen years and a celluloid presence in movie houses for nearly thirty years before that, there was some suggestion among journalists that he remained something of an enigmatic figure to the mass public. As *Newsweek* put it, "at the very hour of his coronation . . . as the Republican nominee, he remains only hazily known to millions of his countrymen."[1]

Ronald Reagan came to his active involvement in electoral politics fairly late in life, moving to it through his presidency of the Screen Actors Guild and the encouragement of his and his second wife Nancy's well-connected and well-heeled friends. He had been a liberal New Deal Democrat, like his father Jack, until the early 1950s, but after he gave his nationwide televised appeal on behalf of Barry Goldwater's doomed presidential candidacy in 1964, he had become the leading spokesman for what was to become an increasingly dominant conservative point of view in the Republican party.

As governor, Reagan did not achieve his goal of reducing the size of the California bureaucracy but did halt its growth and made marginal savings in the cost of state government. By the time he was well into his second term he had also learned to apply skills he had first used as president of the Screen Actors Guild, bargaining hard but compromising when he finally had to. While he learned to govern in the real world, "his record," as *Newsweek* put it, "bore little resemblance to the rhetoric he wrapped it in. . . . he was more interested [in] and more successful at painting his word pictures of the world than at making the world conform to his pictures."

After having been barely edged out for the Republican presidential nomination by an incumbent president in 1976, Reagan entered the 1980 Republican nomination battle with a solid plurality of support in polls of Republican party supporters. After being unexpectedly upset by his principal challenger, George Bush, in the Iowa precinct caucuses, Reagan turned the first primary into a crucial turning point by doing two things he had not done in Iowa: campaigning hard and meeting his opponents in debate. Reagan, with TV cameras rolling, championed the right of four other candidates to join a debate scheduled between him and Bush, while the latter sat mute. The result was to make Bush look like a spoilsport and to reestablish Reagan as front runner. He defeated Bush two to one in New Hampshire.

Reagan victories in subsequent primaries removed all of his other rivals for the nomination except Bush. While Bush ran strongly in several large, industrial states, Reagan's solid base among conservative Republicans, nurtured over the years on the party fundraising banquet circuit, could not be overcome.

At the convention in Detroit, Reagan-type conservative sentiment predominated, and the Republican delegates endorsed supply-side economic policies, a much harder line against the Soviet Union, and uncompromising positions on several social issues even though the policies in all three areas represented significant departures from the more traditional conservatism of the Nixon and Ford administrations.[2]

The Reagan campaign strategists were confident of a substantial victory in spite of the public polls calling the race close. In a confidential memorandum they set their focus on Reagan's "image strengths that enbody the presidential values a majority of Americans think are important: Leadership, Competence, Strength and Decisiveness. At the same time we must minimize the perception that he is dangerous and uncaring."[3] Coupled with this emphasis on Reagan's strengths and minimization of his weakness was an attack "through our media and spokespersons" on Jimmy Carter's major weakness as an "ineffective and error-prone leader." Their memo outlined a "can do" scenario based on findings that voters were optimistic that the "nation could be put back on the right track through the selection of good leaders.'' Reagan surrogates attacked Carter in September and through the first week of October along these lines.

Both candidates, however, faced difficulties during the campaign. Reagan's problems arose from increasingly critical press scrutiny of some of his earlier policy proposals and from becoming caught in contradictory and/or factually erroneous statements (on such matters as the amount and source of air pollution). His propensity for making embarrassing impromptu statements created trouble at the beginning of the campaign. After a politically costly remark denouncing Carter for opening his campaign in Tuscumbia, Alabama, which Reagan erroneously said was the birthplace of the Ku Klux Klan, Reagan's handlers kept him away from the press. This exclusion from the press became a talking point for the Democratic campaign.

A Carter attack on Reagan in Chicago that Reagan would divide the country along racial, religious, and sectional lines backfired on the embattled president, undermining some of his positive personal image. Carter probably also lost ground when he refused to participate in a debate on September 21 on the grounds that John Anderson had been included. Both Anderson and Reagan projected competence during this debate.

Table 22.1 shows that Reagan's greatest advantages over Carter were in public perceptions of leadership, competence, and problem-solving ability, particularly reducing inflation. These were the very traits that had become the most pronounced, permanent weaknesses in Carter's public image and that had become the criteria on which the public judgement in November would rest most heavily. The two candidates were basically even on personal attributes (understanding, judgment, intelligence), and Reagan trailed Carter only on policy moderation and the more sympathetic traits at the bottom of Table 22.1.

Given the levels of public dissatisfaction with Carter as president, all that was necessary to give Reagan victory was to assuage public misgivings about him, something accomplished by his credible performance in the only debate between the two major party candidates, which was held one week before the election. Students of voting behavior agreed that Reagan's victory was more of a negative repudiation of Jimmy Carter than a positive endorsement of Reagan or his policies.

RONALD REAGAN: PRESIDENTIAL IMAGE

President-elect Reagan did not enjoy the usual pre-inaugural elevation of his popularity typically enjoyed by most of his predecessors. His failure to expand his support beyond those who had voted for him was all the more noteworthy considering the fact that in Jimmy Carter, Ronald Reagan ''had an easy act to follow.''[4]

President Reagan began his administration with a more modest approval rating than any of his predecessors in the previous forty-five years. Immediate post-inaugural approval ratings by Gallup in the low 50 percent range were followed

Table 22.1
Contrasting Images of Reagan and Carter, Fall 1980

	Reagan	Carter	Net Advantage
*The best hope to reduce inflation	71%	14%	57R
*Has strong leadership qualities country needs	61	18	43R
Has strong leadership qualities	65	31	34R
Decisive, sure of himself	69	37	32R
*He is competent	48	25	23R
You know where he stands on issues	54	33	21R
A colorful, interesting personality	70	50	20R
*He would provide honest and moral leadership for the country	45	27	18R
The kind of person who can get the job done	56	39	17R
Offers imaginative solutions to national problems	52	37	15R
Has modern, up-to-date solutions to national problems	45	36	9R
Has clear understanding of the issues facing the country	55	50	5R
*He is trustworthy	33	32	1R
Would display good judgment in a crisis	55	55	0
Bright, intelligent	73	73	0
Says what he believes even if unpopular	54%	57%	3C
Sides with the average citizen	43	56	13C
Sympathetic to problems of the poor	41	68	27C
Takes moderate, middle-of-the-road positions	48	82	34C

*From Decision/Management/Information telephone survey, November 5–8, 1980. See Richard Wirthlin et al., *Public Opinion*, February/March 1981, pp. 45, 46. The other questions are from Gallup, September 12–15, 1980, sampling.

by 60 percent approval after two months in office. (See Figure 22.1.) At the same time, Reagan's disapproval percentages were rising more rapidly than his approval ratings during his first two months, probably because of the announcement of his administration's economic plan near the end of his first month in office.

Insofar as a significant minority of the public saw the Reagan administration's economic policies as threatening the social "safety net" for lower-income families, it had the effect of polarizing public opinion early in his term, thus reducing the customary highs of approval most of his predecessors enjoyed during their "honeymoon" periods. Reagan's disapproval ratings were considerably higher than the early ratings of Carter, Nixon, Kennedy, or Eisenhower. In addition, larger proportions of the public approved or disapproved of Reagan's performance "strongly" than "not so strongly"—a pattern also strikingly at variance with that of his predecessors, who received fewer ratings at the extremes. Moreover, in strong contrast to Carter, Reagan's early support was also sharply polarized along partisan lines. This partisanship gap was larger for Reagan than for his fellow Republicans, Nixon and Ford. In summary, President Reagan's appeal, at least in comparison to his recent predecessors, was more divisive than consensual.[5]

After surviving his wounding by John Hinckley at the end of March, President Reagan's favorable standing in the polls rose to a point where two of three Americans gave him favorable ratings for his handling of his job. These ratings leveled off with roughly six in ten Americans approving through the spring and summer of 1981. While the effect of the assassination attempt was to prolong the president's honeymoon period, its end was signalled by some new falling off in favorable ratings at the end of the summer of 1981.

The president's positive job approval ratings moved downward rather rapidly during the fall and winter of 1981/82, presumably reflecting the disintegration of the early sanguine hopes that the Reagan administration's economic plans would lead quickly to growth and prosperity. The declines in job approval were paralleled by very sharp declines in the public's confidence in the president's handling of the economy.

In March 1982, for the first time, President Reagan's Gallup disapproval rating virtually matched his approval rating at 46 to 45 percent. Because its test of positive feelings is more rigorous and is more immediately sensitive to changes in the environment, the Harris Poll had turned negative four months earlier.[6] Declines from the previous fall in the public's already low ratings of his handling of specific problem areas such as the economy, inflation, and unemployment continued.

President Reagan's Gallup approval rating remained in the mid-40 range through early summer, then slipped down into the low 40s by midsummer, where it was to remain until the Israeli invasion of Lebanon and the president's opposition to a trans-Siberian gas pipeline desired by America's Western European allies. These events might have contributed to the decline in Reagan's ratings for

Figure 22.1
Approval Ratings for Ronald Reagan

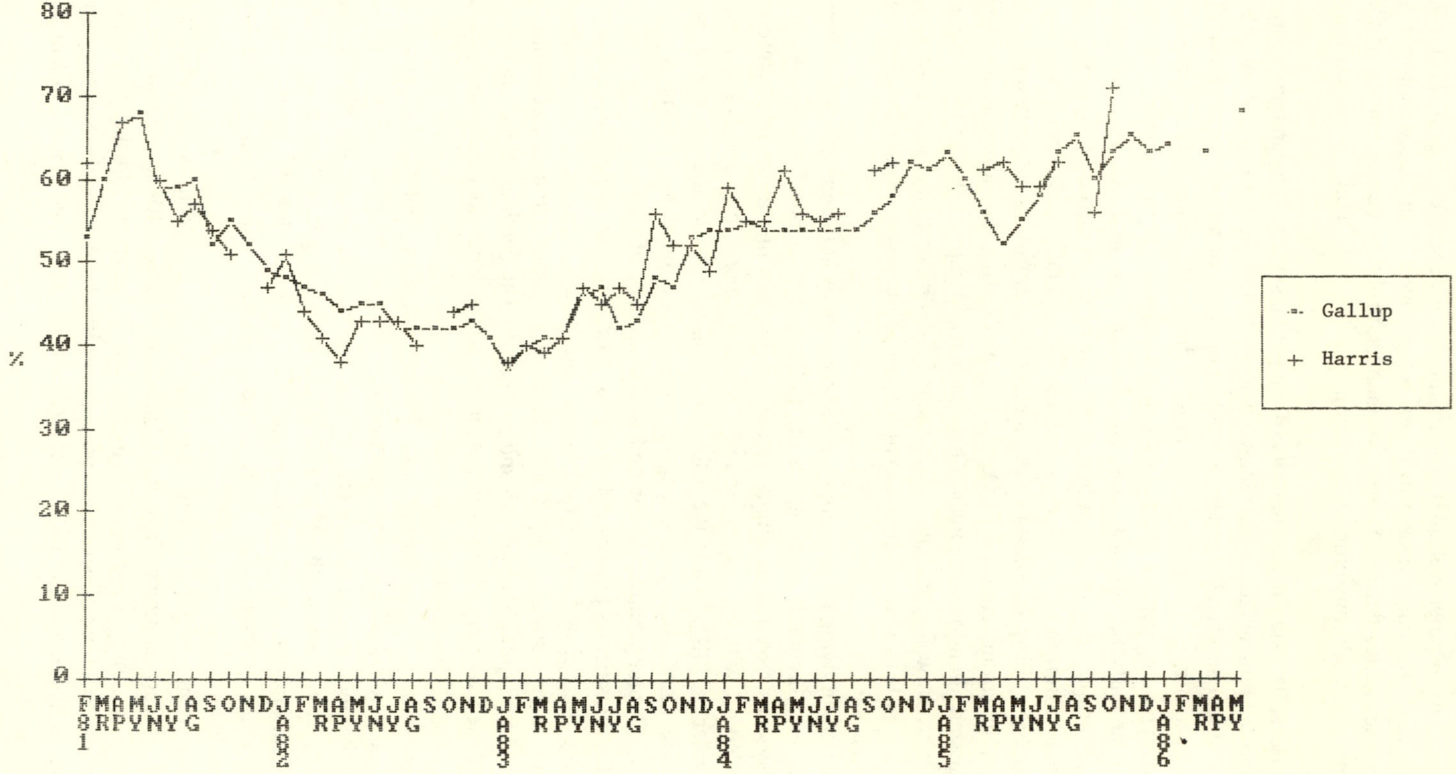

Source: Gallup Organization; Louis Harris Associates.

handling of foreign affairs, but feelings about his handling of the problems of the economy were governing the level of his overall job approval. In summary, from March 1982 until late winter/early spring 1983, the president's standing declined very gradually as the ravages of the recession became more widely felt.

The recession was at its worst at the time of the November midterm congressional elections of 1982. In the face of polls showing two-thirds majorities opposing decreases in "government spending for social programs" and over three-fifths citing unemployment as "the most important problem" facing the country, the Republicans lost twenty-six seats in the House of Representatives in the 1982 elections while maintaining their existing margin of control in the U.S. Senate (fifty-four seats to forty-six) by winning several close races. The twenty-six seat loss for the president's party was higher than the average midterm loss for the party of a president in his first term but lower than the predicted loss based on the condition of the economy. Public attitudes at the time of this midterm election setback for the president were pessimistic about the current economic situation, skeptical about the benefits of Reaganomics, but somewhat less negative about the long-term efficacy of the Reagan economic program. By a 10 percent margin the Democratic party was seen as the party which "will do the better job of keeping the country prosperous."

The nadir of Reagan's job approval ratings came in January 1983 after unemployment had been over 10 percent for four months. William C. Adams shows that Reagan's Gallup poll approval ratings moved downward and later upward in tandem with the employment rate, with "every one point increase in unemployment" being associated with a 6 percent decrease in Reagan's popularity.[7]

By the spring of 1983 there was a noticeable improvement in his approval ratings. While skeptics still outnumbered believers by a 4 to 3 ratio, there were noticeable increases since January in economic optimism.

In the late winter of 1983 the *Washington Post*/ABC News poll asked thirty-two questions about Ronald Reagan, all of which were based on comments volunteered about him by respondents in earlier polls.[8] In Table 22.2 an index of advantage has been calculated by subtracting the less favorable from the more favorable response for each agree-disagree question. The extent of the positive or negative percentage differences (PDIs) are indicated at the extreme left, where the index of advantage ranks the items from most to least favorable. A plus (+) immediately before each statement indicates that agreement constitutes the favorable response; a minus (−) indicates that disagreements constitute the favorable response. General categories in which each response falls have also been indicated in parenthesis.

Six of President Reagan's eight most positive PDI scores express feelings of trust or competence in him as a person. Sixty percent, for example, agreed (as opposed to 37 percent disagreeing) that he was a "strong leader." Only on some highly specific, and possibly idiosyncratic, personal items pertaining to campaign promises, personal rigidity, and vacations were the president's positive and negative ratings more evenly divided.

Table 22.2
Reagan's Image, February-March 1983

Index of

Advantage

+50	+He is an honest person	(personal-trust)
+37	+He's making a real effort to repair the economy	(economic management)
+36	+He sticks to his principles	(personal-trust)
+34	-He's not sincere, he is a faker	(personal-trust)
+30	-He will cause a war	(war-peace)
+27	-He doesn't know what he is doing	(personal-competence)
+23	+He is a strong leader	(personal-competence)
+23	-I just don't trust him	(personal-trust)
+19	-He is far behind the times	(policy views)
+18	+He is cutting waste in government	
+15	-He is bringing the country into a depression	(economic management)
+13	-He is not trying to reduce unemployment	(economic management)
+12	+He is doing better than Carter	(general)
+11	+He is starting to change the country in a good way	(general)
+ 8	+His long term plan will surely work out	(general)

Table 22.2 (continued)

Index of

Advantage

+8	-He has a negative view on	
	women's rights	(policy views-fairness)
+6	-He takes too much vacation	(personal-effort)
+5	-He is unfair to old people	(fairness)
+1	+He is cleaning up the mess	
	that was left behind	
+3	+"He has controlled inflation well"	(economic management)
-4	-He is too rigid to accept advice	(personal-competence)
-11	-He is creating an arms race	(war-peace)
-11	+He is keeping his campaign	(personal-trust)
	promises	
-13	+He will keep us out of war	(war-peace)
-15	-He is unfair to the middle class	(fairness)
-21	-He has created big budget	(economic management)
	deficits	
-24	-He has no idea what people who	(fairness-compassion)
	aren't wealthy are going through	
-25	-He is unfair to blacks	(fairness)
-26	-President Reagan is unfair to	(fairness)
	the poor	
-34	-He is a rich man's President	(fairness)
-37	+He has good ideas for changing the	
	Social Security system	(fairness-policy)
-41	+He is cutting back only those programs	
	that should be cut back	(fairness)

Source: Barry Sussman, "A Report Card for Ronnie," *Washington Post*, March 13, 1983, p. B5.

Reagan's largest negative as manager of the economy was for "big budget deficits," followed secondarily by his failure to receive majority endorsement for having "controlled inflation well." However, on the positive side, the public stopped short of endorsing the more extreme negatively worded suggestions that "he is not trying to reduce unemployment" or that he is "bringing the country into a depression." Finally, perhaps reflecting the same optimism found in earlier polls, respondents tended to be most positive when asked the most general questions about "making a real effort to repair the economy." In addition, some of the respondents may have been thinking of the economy when they gave moderately positive answers to the questions which had no explicit economic referent: "starting to change the country in a good way" and "his long term plan surely will work out."

Two of the three war and peace questions were moderately unfavorable to Reagan, suggesting a worried ambivalence. A third question is highly positive but only because its wording is extreme: "He will cause a war."

Finally, Reagan's most negative assessments have primarily to do with what has been characterized as the "fairness issue." The perception that the Reagan administration lacks compassion, represents special privilege, or that its policies call for disproportionate sacrifices to be borne by average or less fortunate Americans is suggested by the answers to several of the questions toward the bottom of the list in Table 22.2. The judgments are negative about program cutbacks and Reagan's "ideas for . . . Social Security" and agree with expressed beliefs that he is a "rich man's President," "is unfair to the poor," "to blacks," "to the middle class," and has no empathy for those who "aren't wealthy." On only two negatively worded fairness questions pertaining to old people and women's rights did President Reagan elicit marginally positive PDI scores.

A few weeks after the *Washington Post/* ABC poll, Gallup found majorities or large pluralities saying that the Reagan administration was treating the following groups "unfairly": "People like you," "The Average Citizen," "Poor people," "Small business people," "Elderly people," "Farmers," and "Middle-income people." However, only 31 and 36 percent, respectively, felt that women and blacks were being treated unfairly (55 and 50 percent "fairly"). There was a consensus on the fair treatment only of "Wealthy people" (90 percent "fairly") and "Business executives" (78 percent "fairly").

Even before the publication of these polls the fairness issue had become a subject of press comment and a serious concern of the White House staff. While the fairness issue was a weak spot in Ronald Reagan's image before he became president (see Table 22.1), it gained salience in 1981. In February, when asked whether Reagan cared more about serving upper-income, middle-income, or poor people as opposed to "serving all people," two-thirds said that he "cares equally about serving all people," with less than a fourth saying upper-income, 6 percent middle-income, and 3 percent the poor. But by the end of 1981 majorities were saying that Reagan "cares more about serving . . . upper income people'' rather than ''all people.'' And by August 1982, 59 percent felt that he ''cares about . . . upper income people'' and 31 percent ''all people.''[9] These responses suggest, as did the two earlier polls, that the categories the public uses to think about fairness tend to be defined not in racial or sexual terms but in socioeconomic class terms.

While the mass public did not appear to define Reagan's ''unfairness'' as applying to women in particular, women themselves tended to react to President Reagan in a noticeably less favorable way than men. Although Reagan carried the vote among women in both 1980 and 1984, they were less likely than men to have voted for him in both elections and were less positive toward him than men in approval ratings and trial heats throughout his first term. The size of this difference, which was labeled the ''gender gap'' by the press, typically tended to run around 8 or 9 percent. Among the possible explanations offered have been women's traditionally greater distrust of aggressiveness and the use of force, the economic impact of Reaganomics on poor families headed by women, and the personal witnessing of the impact of Reaganomics on the less fortunate by middle-class women, who tend to dominate the helping professions such as nursing and social work.

If one assumes that the cause of the gender gap is not that women dislike Reagan, but that men like him more, then the explanation may simply be a macho image more appealing to men. As a physically fit, wood-chopping, wise-cracking septuagenarian with a ''tell-it-to-the-marines'' rhetoric and a full head of hair who once played tough cowboys in the movies, Ronald Reagan would appear to possess several elements of a macho image. He played many of the scenes of his presidency the way a tough macho cowboy would: 1) making a joke to his wife about failing to duck after having been shot by an assassin; 2) as a commander-in-chief taking tough stands against the Soviets, Congress (on the AWACS sale to Saudi Arabia), unions (breaking the air controllers union by firing all striking air traffic controllers); 3) ordering an ''invasion'' to ''save'' frightened medical students in Grenada; and 4) showing a controlled, sensitive, emotional masculinity in decorating others for heroism, which, had it been done by Jimmy Carter, would have simply been weepy.[10] Support for the macho interpretation of the gender gap is suggested by evidence that some groups traditionally highly responsive to macho appeals, such as Latinos, voted for Reagan in 1984 in greater proportions than one would otherwise expect.[11]

Reagan's job approval ratings in late winter 1983, however negative, were an improvement over his beginning of the year lows (see Figure 22.1) and were to prove to be the first step in an impressive resurgence in his approval ratings during his third year in office as the economy rebounded and public optimism grew. While Reagan's ratings for specific aspects of his presidency (economy, Social Security, social program cuts, foreign affairs, military spending) were all still negative, his enhanced job handling rating was matched by improvements in trial heats, pulling nearly even with Walter Mondale and John Glenn. The president's two top aides (James A. Baker III and Edwin Meese III) strongly suggested that Reagan would seek a second term and would announce his intentions in the autumn.[12]

By late summer Reagan was running virtual dead heats in "trial runs" against Mondale and Glenn. In a Gallup "personality profile" of Reagan, Mondale, and Glenn, the president received more positive evaluations stressing leadership and sense of purpose: "says what he believes," "knows where he stands," and "has a well-defined program." But he trailed his potential Democratic rivals under the more empathetic categories: "being sympathetic to the poor," "siding with the average citizen," and "takes moderate positions." A comparison of President Reagan with Senator Glenn and former Vice President Mondale on a "Stapel Scalometer" (a ten-point scale used by the Gallup Organization with ratings from +5 to −5) showed mild but approximately equal net enthusiasm for all three men. But consistent with earlier polls indicating Reagan's polarized image, the president received three to six times as many "highly unfavorable" (−4 and −5) ratings as his rivals.

In the fall, President Reagan's approval percentages were, by modest margins, running ahead of his disapproval percentages in most polls. Then three attention demanding events occurred: the shooting down of a Korean passenger airliner (KAL Flight 007) by the Soviets in early September, and in late October the car bombing of a marine barracks at the Beirut, Lebanon, airport with the killing of 236 American servicemen and wounding of others, closely followed by the invasion of Grenada, a small Caribbean island with a Marxist government.

There was the predictable rallying around the flag after the KAL 007 incident. The Harris Survey attributed an eleven-point rise (from 45 to 56 percent positive) to Reagan's "moderate but firm" response.

The bombing of the marine barracks with its traumatic loss of American lives was followed two days later (on Tuesday, October 25) by the surprise invasion of Grenada by American armed forces under cover of an unprecedented news blackout. On the Thursday evening after the Grenada invasion, Reagan delivered a televised address that apparently went a long way toward reassuring the misgivings of a nervous and, given the character of the rapid sequence of events, understandably confused public. Public opinion polls before and after the speech showed significant shifts toward the president's position on both Grenada and Lebanon. The president's October 27 speech elicited larger gains among groups that already tended to be more supportive: the affluent, the college-educated, and men (thus widening the gender gap).[13]

Despite these favorable shifts in public opinion, a familiar soft spot in the public perception of Reagan in foreign policy matters was also visible: he was still perceived as being too readily disposed to the use of force. While his October speech caused dramatic declines in the percentages of Americans who expressed disapproval of his handling of foreign policy, the percentages still worried that his policies were increasing the chances of war declined only slightly, and, as the next month's surveys were to show, only temporarily.

The Harris Survey observed that the president's positive ratings had twice risen from the mid-40 range to over 50 percent during the fall in response to international events: from positive ratings in the mid-40s in August to 56 percent positive after the KAL 007 incident in early September; back to 47 percent positive in early October, only to rebound to 56 percent in the aftermath of the Beirut marine barracks tragedy, invasion of Grenada, and TV address, all of which took place in one week. After the events of late October, Harris found the president's positive marks settling to 52 percent in November and 49 percent in December. His approval ratings in the Gallup poll (which is a less sensitive barometer of opinion change) showed a more consistent gain as the year ended. The sources of what Harris described as "volatile and quite unstable" public opinion about the president probably are in public ambivalence: rallying around the flag for quick, conclusive, and relatively cost-free military actions such as the Grenada invasion, yet worried about the president's perceived "trigger happy" propensities.[14]

The large loss of American lives in the marine barracks tragedy would probably have led to a significant negative impact on the president's popularity had it not been for the fortuitous (from the administration's viewpoint) timing of the highly popular Grenada invasion, coming as it did only two days later, thus diverting attention from the heavy American losses in Beirut.

President Reagan ended his third year in office with his highest Gallup approval rating in two years. These third-year gains compare very favorably to the records of his predecessors. Carter, Nixon, and Kennedy all underwent significant erosion in their approval ratings during much of their third year in office.

In January 1984 President Reagan made the expected announcement that he would seek reelection in November. The successful mission by the Reverend Jesse Jackson to free an American pilot, Lieutenant Robert Goodman, Jr., held prisoner in Syria, and positive commentary on the White House welcoming home ceremony for them, brought President Reagan's ratings a beginning of the year boost.

In early 1984 Gallup reported that "satisfaction" with the "way things are going" in the country had reached a five-year high. Although falling a little below his overall job handling rating, late winter opinion polls gave the president positive marks of 52 and 53 percent for "handling the economy," with weaker ratings for handling unemployment and the budget deficit. In March the sharpest negative public judgments were on Reagan policy in Lebanon and Central America. Judgments about the handling of relations with the Soviet Union and "foreign policy" were closely divided.[15] The president's overall job handling rating was in the low-to-middle 50 percent range during this time, a level he had reached in late 1983 and which continued until the late summer of 1984, at which point it began a further rise.

During the spring of 1984 the news media were filled with reports of internecine warfare among the Democratic presidential hopefuls contesting for their party's White House nomination. In order to avoid distracting public attention from the

Democratic fratricide, the White House staff decided to pursue a low-visibility "situation room campaign" with no partisan campaign travel and minimal public appearances in Washington by the president.[16] Instead of campaign travel, therefore, President Reagan's spring itinerary stressed foreign travel: a trip to China in late April with stops in Hawaii and Guam on the way over and a meeting with Pope John Paul II in Alaska on the way home; a European trip in early summer that included stops in Ireland (his ancestral homeland), at a memorial ceremony on the fortieth anniversary of the D-Day landings in Normandy, and at an economic summit in London. Thus, in contrast to the rancor of the Democrats, the media coverage of the president featured noncontentious ceremonial events at which he was shown to best advantage.

While his visit to China was viewed positively, Reagan's overall foreign policy and the fairness issue were his greatest vulnerabilities. The ceremonial role, however, was the president's strongest suit. In April the Republicans took an unaccustomed lead over the Democrats as the party best for prosperity. In June Gallup reported that the public was bullish on the economic recovery, and by September the economic optimists predominated over the pessimists.

The improved economic conditions made it possible for the Reagan reelection strategists to run a "Feel good about America" campaign. The common theme of his commercials was "It's morning in America." While close association with self-serving special interest groups could have been a problem for candidate Reagan under less rosy economic conditions, it was his opponent, Walter Mondale, who emerged from the bruising Democratic nomination contest with the image of being the candidate of special interests and the "old politics." The generally positive feeling about Reagan and the country meant that the events of Campaign '84, like the specific events of most campaigns, counted for little. A midcampaign Mondale surge based on a victory on points over the president in the first of two October debates quickly faded away. Most polls indicate that the race was stable throughout the campaign, and the final 59–41 percent victory of the president was the predictable outcome which had not been materially altered or reshaped by the events of the campaign.

While Reagan's 1980 victory had been based heavily on anti-Carter sentiment, the 1984 victory was based primarily on positive feelings about Reagan and his record, primarily economic. "His economic policies" were the most frequently cited reasons people gave for casting their votes for Reagan. The septuagenarian president received strong support from young voters, an abrupt reversal of the pattern of the several preceding elections. Sixty percent of the new voters voted Republican, while Mondale's best showing was among voters sixty-five and over. While the vote among blacks was as monolithically Democratic as ever, the president demonstrated again his ability to cut into other elements of the old Democratic coalition, running more strongly in the South than in any other section of the country and carrying a majority of white trade union voters. The gender gap remained at 9 percent, however, with an even wider gap occurring among young men and women.

"FEELING GOOD ABOUT AMERICA" CAMPAIGN

President Reagan's "feeling good about America" campaign gave little hint about his second-term agenda. Consequently, his reelection did not create any fresh mandate for his policies. The Reagan administration was forced to take defensive postures on many of the issues of 1985, fending off challenges to his MX missile program and his aid to the contras in Nicaragua. On other issues the administration had to improvise catch-up solutions in response to new political forces: trade relief, continuing bad times in the farm belt, sanctions against the white racist government of South Africa, audible congressional complaints about waste in defense procurement.[17]

After initial postelection highs in the 60 percent range, the president's Gallup poll standings began to decline in March, the month when he vetoed a popular farm bill. His Gallup approval ratings then remained in the 50 percent range until midsummer. In early May ceremonies commemorating the end of World War II were held. A decision to pay his respects to German war dead at a cemetery at Bitburg, West Germany, where it was discovered that soldiers from Nazi SS units were buried, produced widespread criticism that President Reagan was morally insensitive. This imbroglio probably did his ratings no permanent harm.

The incarceration in Beirut of thirty-nine Americans whose TWA jetliner had been hijacked provided the occasion for crowd-pleasing macho rhetoric as the nation rallied around the president in the crisis. Probably also enhancing his standing and counterbalancing his macho rhetoric was the administration's circumspect behavior, which helped lead to the release of the hostages after seventeen days.

In July doctors removed a cancerous tumor from Reagan's colon. After his successful surgery his Gallup job approval ratings rose above 60 percent, where they were to remain until midway (1986) in the second term.

The end of 1985 brought with it the temporary derailing of tax reform by the president's fellow Republicans in the House of Representatives and the passage of the Gramm-Rudman automatic budget-balancing bill.

By late winter 1985–86 Reagan's political position contrasted with that of early 1985 in that he was now characterized as being "in command." While he had suffered some reversals, he had, through tenacious stubbornness, prevailed in changing policy and the terms of political debate on a range of issues from aid to the Nicaraguan contras to lowering maximum tax rates to 35 percent.

In late March 1986 American air and naval forces attacked Libyan gunboats, missile installations, and Libyan leader Moammar Khadafy's headquarters as a reprisal for earlier acts of terrorism sponsored by Libya. While the public rallied to support the president's action, large majorities opposed further military strikes and preferred restricting additional moves against Khadafy to the economic and diplomatic spheres.

After the first year and a half of his second term President Reagan received favorable job handling ratings from roughly two-thirds of the public, rivaling his honeymoon period highs. Most other two-term presidents have suffered declines in their popularity in their fifth year, and no president since the advent of modern opinion polling has shown fifth-year job approval ratings as high as Reagan's. Two explanations for the unprecedented buoyancy of his popularity over time are the strong economy and his alleged Teflon qualities.

THIRD YEAR OF ECONOMIC GROWTH

By the winter of 1985/86 the country was enjoying the third year of economic growth, which had begun at the end of the 1981–82 recession. As president, Reagan received credit for the decline in inflation rates (engineered by Federal Reserve chairman Paul M. Volcker) from double digits in 1979 and 1980 to 4 percent and less in the mid-1980s. The 1981 tax cut was also popular, eventually adding to personal disposable income which is second only to controlling inflation as the economic variable most strongly related to presidential popularity.

Since he was first dubbed the "Teflon president" by Representative Patricia Schroeder (D-Col.), many observers believed Reagan's popular standing was virtually immune to any kind of policy disaster. Steven Weisman suggested that "by concentrating on general themes and by projecting an upbeat spirit" the president was able to separate himself from vexatious national problems and unpopular policies and could act as a mediator between government and people just as he had once, as the genial host for GE Theater, acted as "a kind of mediator between the company and the audience." Certainly every effort was made to present the president positively and to distance him from negative imagery. When unemployment was high in 1981–1982 the president never appeared in black tie but was photographed signing bills in denims, visiting job training centers, or loading sandbags with flood control workers. Any bad news from the White House was announced by a written statement.[18]

Many writers have called into question the Teflon hypothesis, and Michael Robinson and Maura Clancey put it to the test by asking respondents in a national survey how often Reagan "attends church service" after the press had carried a story in which the White House had admitted that the president had not formally visited a church in nine months.[19] Robinson and Clancey reported that his church-goer image with the public was far superior to the reality. Some respondents told them that "Reagan must go to church every week, given the way he talks about prayer." Robinson and Clancey also discovered that 40 percent of the public gave marginally or wholly negative responses when asked if Reagan adhered to "strict ethical principles," but the public was, however, more likely to attribute "strict ethical principles" to Reagan than to his staff. They concluded that "Ronald Reagan is only stick-resistant, not stick-proof."

Calling President Reagan Teflon may simply be an acknowledgement that his image is strong or that he has a hold on American consciousness that is not fully captured in public opinion polls. Lou Cannon thought his "resonant performance'' in the wake of the assassination attempt "endowed him with a mythic quality that became an underestimated ingredient of his political success." Gary Wills once suggested that Reagan's strength grew out of the fact that he had been part of the American scene as a politician or an actor for so long that people who had grown up with him felt comfortable with him; that his age reassured people that the "past perdures." And after five years of the Reagan presidency Kevin Phillips argued that President Reagan's "job approval had really lost its job quotient" and it had "become a 'father-figure' rating, and that's not going to go down."[20] One source of such strength may be in the emotional catharsis provided by the graceful way in which Reagan presides in his role as chief of state over ceremonies of remembrance for fallen heroes, whether they are the seven crew members of the ill-fated space shuttle *Challenger* or the dead at the Normandy beachhead on the occasion of the fortieth anniversary of D-Day. In addition, Reagan's consistency and tenacity in pursuing his purposes, combined with his upbeat temperament, probably contributed to the strength of the "strong leader" component of his image. This "hard" image, as was noted in the chapter on Jimmy Carter, is inherently better fitted to weathering political adversity than an image composed of "soft" elements.

One of the reasons Reagan is called the "Teflon president" is because high job approval ratings persist even in the face of popular majorities disapproving many of his policies. While President Reagan's Gallup job approval ratings have been above 50 percent since late 1983, his ratings for some specific policy areas have been negative. For the last half of 1985 and the first half of 1986, his overall Gallup approval rating exceeded his disapproval ratings by more than thirty points. At the same time the balance of opinion on his "handling of the federal deficit," "nuclear arms reduction negotiations with the Russians," and "the situation in Central America" was negative, sometimes strongly so. Barry Sussman offered an explanation of "How Reagan Stays Popular Even When His Policies Aren't," which he called the "porcupine theory." The porcupine is not aggressive and extends its quills only when attacked and prefers to let the world go by. Similarly, the public will give good marks even to leaders about whom they may have misgivings as long as the economy is healthy and the nation is not at war. While the public sees injustice, worries about military adventurism, and disapproves of the deficit, such issues have not been salient enough to cause it to extend its prickly quills. The public has "distinguished Reagan and his economic success from the rest of his programs."[21] The positive ratings for his handling of the economy during this period suggest the limits of both the Teflon and porcupine theories.

SUMMARY AND CONCLUSIONS

It is dangerous to attempt any final summation for a president more than two years before his scheduled departure from office. Dom Bonafede, however, did make such an estimate of what future scholars might say of Ronald Reagan's presidency when he surveyed presidential scholars in 1985. The better than half of Bonafede's respondents who rated Reagan "good, near great or great" cited his leadership qualities and success in building trust and confidence. Many scholars made contingent judgments, and the substantial minority who were more critical worried about Reagan's postponing of problems. This latter view was advanced by Bert Rockman, who argued that much of Reagan's popularity was because, directly opposite from Carter, Reagan generated "tangible benefits in the present with vague . . . costs" postponed to the future.[22]

Certain characteristics of Reagan's image persist: on the negative but less salient side are his tendency to polarize people, worry about his propensity to military adventurism, and a persistent feeling that he is unfair to average and less privileged Americans; on the positive but currently more salient side are his strength in hard leadership ("macho"?) traits very probably deriving in significant part from his boldness, optimism, tenacity, and clear purpose, augmented by his untempered, "go for it" rhetoric. But for all his image strength, his public approval, like that of other presidents, has waxed and waned with the condition of the economy.

AFTERWORD

The above assessment of the Reagan administration was completed in the spring of 1986. Since then the accomplishments of President Reagan have been placed in jeopardy by two major developments: first, the Iran-*contra* scandal involving arms sales to Iran in exchange for hostages, who were taken in Lebanon at the probable instigation of Iran, and the diversion of some of the proceeds of these sales to the Nicaraguan *contras;* and second, the stock market crash of October 1987.

Somewhat counterbalancing these negative developments were the Reagan administration's three summit conferences, held in Geneva with Soviet President Mikhail Gorbachev in 1985, in Reykjavik, Iceland, with Gorbachev in 1986, and in Washington with Gorbachev in December 1987. The latter was the occasion for the completion and signing of the INF (intermediate nuclear force) arms control treaty.

During the final period of the Reagan administration the president's approval ratings hovered around the 50 percent range, dipping most noticeably during December 1986 and January 1987 when the impact of the hostage scandal was at its most damaging.

Despite second-term difficulties, Ronald Reagan proved an effective president in achieving many of his goals.

NOTES

1. Reagan's early life and career and the country's perception of him at the time of his 1980 nomination in Detroit are summarized in *Newsweek,* July 21, 1980, pp. 3, 29, 30. See also Lou Cannon, *Reagan.* (New York: Putnam, 1982).

2. Much of the discussion of the 1980 campaign draws from Paul R. Abramson, John H. Aldrich, and David W. Rohde, *Change and Continuity in the 1980 Elections* (Washington, D.C.: Congressional Quarterly Press, 1982).

3. The confidential memo, "Seven Conditions of Victory," dated October 9, 1980, is in Richard Wirthlin, Vincent Breglio, and Richard Seal, "Campaign Chronicle," *Public Opinion*, 4 (February/March 1981): 43–49.

4. William A. Sabo, "Establishing Expectations: Public Response to Reagan's Early Term," *Politics and Policy*, 5 (1985): 37–57; Jack Germond and Jules Witcover, "Reagan's Popularity Stands Unchanged," *Cincinnati Enquirer*, January 12, 1981.

5. In the discussion of the Reagan presidency the following issues of *The Gallup Report* have been used: Nos. 186, 188, 195, 199, 203, 206, 211, 212, 213, 217, 219, 223, 225, 227, 228, 232, 233, and 234.

6. Of Harris' four ratings, "excellent," "pretty good," "only fair," and "poor," the latter two ratings are both counted as negative. See the discussion of the effects of question wording differences in the "Prepresidential Image" section of Chapter 21.

7. William C. Adams, "Recent Fables About Ronald Reagan," *Public Opinion* 7 (October/November 1984): 6–9.

8. Half the sample of 1,504 Americans was asked sixteen of the questions and half was asked the other sixteen questions. The average "No Opinion" percentage was nearly 6 percent, with a range of 2 to 13 percent. "The poll was conducted from February 25 to March 2." Barry Sussman, "A Report Card for Ronnie," *Washington Post*, March 13, 1983, p. B5. See also "Opinion Roundup—Reagan's Ratings," *Public Opinion*, 5 (April/May 1983): 42, 43.

9. "Opinion Roundup—The Fairness Factor," *Public Opinion*, 5 (April/May 1983): 37.

10. Danny M. Adkison, "Reagan and the Gender Gap: Macho To Do About Nothing," paper delivered at the Popular Culture Association/American Culture Association meeting, Louisville, Kentucky, April 3–6, 1985, pp. 10, 11.

11. Representative Robert Garcia (D-N.Y.) suggested that in view of the fact Reagan had not "done anything substantive for the Hispanic community," his surprisingly high vote among Hispanics (44 percent) was a response to "the macho image" he portrayed. "Victors and Vanquished Give Their Reasons Why," *U. S. News & World Report*, November 19, 1984, pp. 88–93.

12. David Hoffman, "Aides Suggest President Is Likely to Announce He'll Seek a 2nd Term," *Washington Post*, April 15, 1983, pp. A1, A9.

13. Barry Sussman, "Polling: Why the GOP Pays Richard Wirthlin One Million a Year," *Washington Post National Weekly Edition*, December 26, 1983, p. 35; "Opinion Outlook—Trends Affecting Government Policy," *National Journal*, December 3, 1983, p. 3548.

14. The "volatile" public opinion is noted in the Harris Survey, "Reagan Ratings on Roller Coaster," *Cleveland Plain Dealer*, March 21, 1984, and the ambivalence on foreign policy by William Schneider, "Despite Foreign Policy Popularity Boost, Doubts About Reagan Persist," *National Journal*, November 9, 1983, p. 2448.

15. "Opinion Outlook," *National Journal*, April 4, 1985, p. 991.

16. Lou Cannon, "Reagan's 'Situation Room Campaign,' " *Washington Post National Weekly Edition*, April 1, 1984, p. 23.

17. David Broder, "Reagan's '84 Smart Tactic Proven Wrong," *Toledo Blade*, No-

vember 7, 1985, p. 20; David Broder, "After Year Five Reagan Still Looms Large," *Toledo Blade,* December 22, 1985, p. D4.

18. Steven R. Weisman, "Can the Magic Prevail?" *New York Times Magazine,* April 29, 1984, pp. 39–42.

19. Michael Jay Robinson and Maura Clancey, "Teflon Politics," *Public Opinion,* 7 (April/May 1984): 17, 18.

20. Lou Cannon, "The Best Advice: Rest a While," *Washington Post National Weekly Edition,* August 5, 1985, p. 35; Gary Wills, "Ron and Destiny: Scene 2; Where Will He Lead Us, This Embodiment of Our Everyday Experience?" *Esquire,* August 1980, pp. 37, 38. The Kevin Phillips statement is quoted by Rich Jaroslovsky, "Reagan Gets High Ratings as 'Father Figure,' but Polls Don't Translate into Support on Issues," *Wall Street Journal,* February 26, 1986, p. 50.

21. David Gergen, "Following the Leaders: How Ronald Reagan and Margaret Thatcher Have Changed Public Opinion," *Public Opinion* 8 (June/July 1985): 16, 55–57; Barry Sussman, "The 'Porcupine Theory': Explaining Contradictory Opinions," *Washington Post National Weekly Edition,* August 5, 1985, p. 37. See also William C. Adams, "Recent Fables About Ronald Reagan," *Public Opinion,* 7 (October/November 1984): 7–9.

22. Dom Bonafede, "Presidential Scholars Expect History to Treat the Reagan Presidency Kindly," *National Journal,* April 6, 1985, pp. 743–747; Bert A. Rockman, "A Tale of Two Presidents: Carter, Reagan, and Lessons for Public Morality," *Presidency Research,* 8, no. 1 (Fall 1985): 8.

BIBLIOGRAPHIC ESSAY

Because he is our contemporary, many of the books on Ronald Reagan are either incomplete, highly specialized, unbalanced, and/or superficial. Scholars of the future seeking historical perspective will need to look skeptically at today's bibliographic offerings on Reagan. Particularly deserving of skepticism are five early works with the apparent purpose of applying goose grease generously to their subject. They include Lee Edwards, *Reagan: A Political Biography,* rev. ed. (Houston: Nordland, 1980); Frank Van der Linden, *The Real Reagan: What He Believes; What He Has Accomplished; What We Can Expect from Him* (New York: W. W. Morrow, 1981); and the particularly sticky *Star to Guide Us* by Don C. McGlothin (Wheeling, Ill.: Presidential Publications, 1982). All these are long on trivial Reagan anecdotes, but very short on critical analysis. The prize for idolatrous treatment of Ronald Reagan goes to his wife for her autobiography (with Bill Libby), *Nancy* (New York: W. W. Morrow, 1980), a compendium of simplistic comments on family life. Also uncritical is Rowland Evans and Robert Novak, *The Reagan Revolution* (New York: Dutton, 1981), on his early career, the 1976 and 1980 presidential campaigns, and the new administration's proposed policy changes.

Critical reviews of the Reagan gubernatorial record by his predecessor in Sacramento are Edmund G. Brown, Sr., *Reagan and Reality: The Two Californias* (New York: Praeger, 1970), and Edmund G. Brown, Sr. (with Bill Brown), *Reagan: The Political Chameleon* (New York: Praeger, 1976). Lou Cannon, *Ronnie and Jesse: A Political Odyssey* (New York: Doubleday, 1970), describes Reagan's early political career and that of his 1970 gubernatorial opponent, Speaker Jesse Unruh.

Reagan's own autobiography, *Where's the Rest of Me?* (New York: Duell, Sloan and Pearce, 1965), written with Richard C. Hubler before he entered politics, has new information only occasionally, mostly in portions dealing with motion picture strikes and communists in Hollywood. Its title comes from his most famous line in what is generally believed to be his best movie, *King's Row*. Photographs and summaries of all fifty-three of his films are carried in Tony Thomas, *The Films of Ronald Reagan* (Secaucus, N.J.: Citadel Press, 1980).

The first serious postelection biography with any detachment is Bill Boyarsky, *Ronald Reagan: His Life and Rise to the Presidency* (New York: Random House, 1981), a readable and moderately unfriendly account of his early life and political career, concluding with a brief chapter on the early Reagan presidency. A much fuller account of the Reagan administration's first two years (dealing with policies and staff relationships) is Laurence I. Barrett, *Gambling with History: Reagan in the White House* (Garden City, N.Y.: Doubleday, 1983), written by a *Time* correspondent. The best overall biography is Lou Cannon, *Reagan* (New York: Putnam, 1982), a thorough and fair-minded account of Reagan's life and political career by the *Washington Post* White House correspondent, which also includes vignettes of Reagan's close aides. Cannon's conclusions are positive, although he does not neglect Reagan's shortcomings.

Unlike these three biographies, two others, which also cover the First Lady, fail to qualify as serious works. The theme of Laurence Leamer's gossipy and occasionally catty *Make-Believe: The Story of Nancy and Ronald Reagan* (New York: Harper and Row, 1983) is that the Reagans see the world as a sound stage. Bill Adler, *Ronnie and Nancy: A Very Special Love Story* (New York: Crown Publishers, 1985), lives up to the promise of schmaltz in its title.

Two "psychological" biographies of Ronald Reagan are Lloyd de Mause, *Reagan's America* (New York: Creative Roots, 1984), which uses a heavy-handed Freudianism to attack the Reagan administration and to speculate about hidden fantasies in America; and Robert Dallek, *Ronald Reagan: The Politics of Symbolism* (Cambridge, Mass.: Harvard University Press, 1984), a readable psychobiography which argues that Reagan's conservative purposes as president have been motivated by the desire to re-create the idealized world of his youth.

Ronnie Dugger describes his *On Reagan: The Man and His Presidency* (New York: McGraw-Hill, 1983) as a policy biography. His book is a perhaps overlong but well-documented critique of Reagan from a liberal viewpoint. Its most valuable new contribution is the inclusion of transcripts of five-minute radio broadcasts Reagan made between 1975 and 1979, which contain an unvarnished right-wing candor and which presumably are expressions of the real, "vintage" right-wing ideologue in Reagan before he fell into the hands of politically calculating aides and protective White House assistants.

Congressional Quarterly's yearly volumes on *President Reagan* and its *Reagan's First Year* (Washington, D.C.: Congressional Quarterly, 1982) are very handy sources of basic information: presidential messages, news conferences, issue positions, policies, personal profiles, election summaries, relations with Congress and the courts, and chronologies of events.

Several books focus chiefly on Reagan administration policies. Two early such works which analyze foreign/defense and domestic/economic policy are Fred I. Greenstein, ed., *The Reagan Presidency: An Early Assessment* (Baltimore: Johns Hopkins Press, 1983), and Hedrick Smith et al., *Reagan, the Man, the President* (New York, Macmillan, 1980). Of the two volumes, Greenstein's contains the more sophisticated analysis. An objective and thorough analysis of the first four years of Reagan administration's domestic policies and their effect on American society may be found in John L. Palmer and Isabel V.

Sawhill, eds., *The Reagan Record: An Assessment of America's Changing Domestic Priorities* (Cambridge, Mass.: Ballinger, 1984). Several cuts below the Palmer and Sawhill book is Wayne Valid, ed., *The Future Under President Reagan* (New York: Arlington House, 1981), an undistinguished and blatantly partisan collection of essays by administration loyalists. Among more specialized policy studies are two books on Reaganomics. Bruce R. Bartlett, *Reaganomics: Supply-Side Economics in Action* (New York: Arlington House, 1981), is a readable but shallow treatment by a committed supporter. William Craig Stubblebine and Thomas D. Willett, eds., *Reaganomics: A Mid-term Report* (San Francisco: ICS Press, 1982), is a collection of economists' papers on Reaganomics. Ably done criticisms of administration health and arms control policies are found, respectively, in Joan Claybrook, *Retreat from Safety: Reagan's Attack on America's Health* (New York: Pantheon, 1984), and Strobe Talbott, *Deadly Gambits: The Reagan Administration and the Stalemate in Nuclear Arms Control* (New York: Knopf, 1984). A different kind of book on issues and events of the Reagan years is Herbert Block, *Herblock Through the Looking Glass* (New York: W. W. Norton, 1984), which contains a narrative of events and 490 cartoons whose sarcasm is largely directed at the Reagan administration. Another critical work using (sometimes unintended) humor—Mark Green and Gail MacColl, *There He Goes Again: Ronald Reagan's Reign of Error* (New York: Pantheon Books, 1983)—takes Reagan's own words to demonstrate that there are large gaps in his knowledge.

The only high-ranking Reagan administration officials to have written memoirs by early 1986 were its first secretary of state, Alexander M. Haig, *Caveat: Realism, Reagan and Foreign Policy* (New York: Macmillan, 1984), and David Stockman, *The Triumph of Politics: The Failure of the Reagan Revolution* (New York: Harper and Row, 1986). Haig exposes to our view the bureaucratic politicking behind the formulation of foreign policy during his year and a half in office. Stockman takes the reader behind the scenes of the formulation of budget and tax policy in describing the ''supply-side revolution'' of the first Reagan term and giving his explanation of why it failed to prevent a $200 billion a year deficit.

Many volumes deal with the 1980 and 1984 campaigns. F. Clifton White and William J. Gillis, *Why Reagan Won: A Narrative History of the Conservative Movement* (Lake Bluff, Ill.: Regnery/Gateway, 1982), is the first of two strongly pro-Reagan books on the 1980 election. They place the story of Reagan's road to the 1980 nomination in a context of what they describe as a growing conservative movement. Peter Hanneford, *The Reagans: A Political Portrait* (New York: Coward-McCann, 1983), is a pollyannaish account of Reagan presidential campaigns by a former speechwriter who moves cardboard characters before the reader. Two recountings of the 1984 campaign of interest to politics buffs are Peter Goldman et al., *The Quest for the Presidency 1984* (New York: Bantam Books, 1985), and Jack W. Germond and Jules Witcover, *Wake Us When It's Over* (New York: Macmillan, 1985). These are in the who-said-what-to-whom genre of political reporting. Two other chronicles of the 1984 election argue that political outcomes are manipulated by elite actors. Roland Perry, *Hidden Power: The Programming of the President* (New York: Beaufort Books, 1984), argues that pollsters manipulate the politicians, and William A. Henry III, *Visions of America: How We Saw the 1984 Election* (Boston: Atlantic Monthly Books, 1984), emphasizes ways press reporting (especially on television) affected popular perceptions. A noteworthy exception to this tendency to ignore the well-crystallized substantive concerns of the public and to overemphasize elite actions during the campaign is Jeff Greenfield, *The Real Campaign: How the Media*

Missed the Story of the 1980 Campaign (New York: Summit Books, 1982). He persuasively argues that no amount of image manipulation through the media could overcome the fact that the American public in 1980 wanted Jimmy Carter to go away. Richard Reeves, *The Reagan Detour: Conservative Revolutionary* (New York: Simon and Schuster, 1985), is a succinct explanation of Ronald Reagan's overwhelming victory in 1984. It concludes with a stimulating discussion of directions for the future.

23 CYCLES IN THE PUBLIC PERCEPTION OF PRESIDENTS

Kim Ezra Shienbaum
and William C. Spragens

How does one make sense of the fluctuating tide of public opinion with respect to presidential performance?

Ever since the institution of the presidency was established, historians and political scientists have been developing theories to explain these patterns of cyclical behavior in the public's perception of presidents.

Michael Grossman and Martha Kumar have suggested a repetition of a short-term cycle in each administration. In this view, most presidents go through a build-up phase in which a less well known figure or an unknown principal becomes a celebrity; a phase in which disillusionment sets in and muckraking occurs; and a phase which amounts to a stand-off.[1]

In a similar vein, a three-stage cycle of "consensus," "conflict," and "conciliation" has been posited by James David Barber in *The Pulse of Politics*. Some critics have suggested that Barber has strained to fit some administrations into this construct, but it remains a useful heuristic device.

James Davis in *The American Presidency* cites a summary of public support for modern presidents that originally appeared in John H. Aldrich, Gary J. Miller, Charles W. Ostrom, Jr., and David Rohde, *American Government: People, Institutions, and Policies,* and which appears here in Table 23.1. Davis suggests that all modern presidents were most popular during their first year in office. Their support tended to decline during years two and three and increased during the final year of each term.

All this is but background for the analysis of public opinion polls, which indicate that distinct sets of cycles occur with respect to public opinion of presidential performance at a given time. Gallup polls suggest that whereas public opinion assessments of presidential candidates prior to an election are about evenly divided (the closeness of post–World War II vote patterns bears this out in such years as 1960, 1968, and 1976), public estimation of the winning candidate dramatically increases after the election. This is the case even when the approval ratings of the incumbent president running for reelection are at a low ebb. He too, upon gaining reelection, is accorded a boost in his public opinion

Table 23.1
Public Support for Modern Presidents: A Summary

	Average Approval Rating			
Administration	Year 1	Year 2	Year 3	Year 4
Truman (1949–1952)	58.5	41.0	28.3	29.6
Eisenhower (1953–1956)	69.3	65.4	71.3	73.3
Eisenhower (1957–1960)	65.0	54.6	63.3	61.1
Kennedy (1961–1963)	76.0	71.6	63.5	____
Johnson (1964–1968)	66.4	41.2	44.0	41.5
Nixon (1969–1972)	61.4	56.9	49.9	56.4
Nixon (1973–1974)	41.8	25.9	____	____
Ford (1974–1976)	____	53.9	43.1	48.1
Carter (1977–1980)	62.4	45.5	38.1	39.5
Reagan (1981–1984)	57.0	43.7	44.6	54.3

Source: Gallup Opinion Report, no. 182, October-November 1980; Gallup Opinion Report, no. 225, June 1984. Reprinted, with permission, from John H. Aldrich et al., *American Government: People, Institutions, and Policies* (Boston: Houghton Mifflin, 1986), p. 490.

ratings (although there was a long gap between 1964 and 1984 when political turbulence either ruled out second terms or aborted them). In part, this phenomenon affects all winners and has been termed the fait accompli effect, whereby winners tend to experience a marked rise in public estimation and losers a concomitant decline. However, in the case of the president, this upward surge in public opinion ratings has been attributed to the "honeymoon period," which may last for up to a year after the inauguration, but which usually disappears fairly rapidly.

Evidence on honeymoon periods indicates that these are of differing durations. Also, the level of intensity of the opposition's feelings continues even when approval ratings are high. The Skaggs analysis of George Washington in Chapter 1 indicates that this pattern occurred in the Washington administration. The president came to New York with plaudits and by the end of his second term had witnessed the division of opinion into the rudiments of the party system. Scurrilous attacks were made on the retiring president, who left office in 1797. The Hatzenbuehler analysis of Jefferson is focused on Jefferson's application of Lockean ideology to practical politics, but nothing in it seems to refute the suggestion that, like Dwight Eisenhower, the author of the Declaration of Independence had an anticlimactic White House tenure.

The Reed analysis of Andrew Jackson stresses his strength and his contro-versiality. The Bursey analysis of Lincoln suggests that there are exceptions to the "honeymoon rule" as reflected in the minority election of Lincoln, the criticism of Lincoln by Seward and others who wanted a more radical policy and, of course, by his Confederate enemies. The icon of Lincoln has only emerged with the passage of time, Bursey suggests, with the greater detachment of modern times making possible a stronger appreciation of both Lincoln's political shrewdness and his saintly qualities.

In the Fishel analysis of Hayes, the aftermath of the Reconstruction is reflected. The detachment of Hayes and his aloof stance on racial divisions reflected his political realism and what the author appears to view as cognizance of the need for a period of consolidation and healing. The fraudulent contest of 1876–1877 was not conducive to a normal honeymoon, but the deviation from the theoretical pattern was apparently less than in 1861 because of conflict weariness similar to that which makes 1980s politicians chary of Nicaraguan involvements.

The superb analysis of Cleveland's terms, during a time of close party division and alliances between conservative Democrats and Republicans across sectional lines, indicates that integrity and negative qualities perceived to be used in the public interest can contribute to a president's popularity, even if he comes from a minority party. There was a conservative consensus in Cleveland's time even as in modern times, but it was also a time of caretaker government, which even the conservatively activist "Reagan revolution" has not been able to reproduce.

The modern pattern seems more clearly to emerge with William McKinley, who, in John Latcham's view, was a transitional figure to the more modern institutional form of the presidency. McKinley clearly had a honeymoon which in the Latcham analysis required his deft manipulation of war-producing currents and the handling of the Spanish-Cuban crisis in such a way as to ward off hostilities until opinion had consolidated behind the administration—a pattern similar to that of Franklin Roosevelt in the isolationist era of the 1930s.

Theodore Roosevelt followed a pattern more modern in nature as the recipient of public sympathy following the McKinley assassination. This reflected more the experiences that Calvin Coolidge, Harry Truman, and Lyndon Johnson had after sudden transitions (as well as that following the first prepardon month of the Gerald Ford term) than the turbulent succession of Chester Arthur, troubled as it was by his spoilsman reputation and by Republican factionalism. Roller and Latcham give insights into the evolution of image-building which contributes to the "honeymoon" aura.

The Natoli analysis of the Wilson presidency suggests that the Wilson New Freedom legislative program found Woodrow Wilson going into the White House on what was perhaps the crest of the Progressive movement. The author's view is that Wilson fits this pattern, and she points to the Walworth and other bio-graphies suggesting that as president of Princeton University and as governor of New Jersey Wilson went through similar cycles, partly because of his rigid leadership style, partly because of the fickleness of public opinion. This view is corroborated in the work of Alexander and Juliet George, who pioneered in the writing of psychobiography.[2]

Jennings' view of "normalcy politics" in the Harding era and the disillusionment that followed the Teapot Dome investigation seems to fit the model suggested above. So does the good will given to Calvin Coolidge despite the disillusionment that set in at the turn of the decade, which Franklin Roosevelt termed "nine long years at the ticker, three long years in the breadlines."

Herbert Hoover, in the analysis of Spragens and Lear, appears more as a precursor of modern trends locked into his "rugged individualism" ideology than as the cardboard creation of Democratic publicist Charles Michelson. But it is true that he entered office hailed as a hero and was booed at a baseball game in 1932.

The Gilbert analysis gives examples of masterful media manipulation and image-building in the Franklin Roosevelt era in describing the staging of Rooseveltian appearances. The tactics of Roosevelt's media managers might have been impossible in the age of the satellite but were successful in the era of more genteel politics, Gilbert notes. Again, the evolution through up and down cycles is evident in the "forgotten man" speech, the "Hundred Days," the Supreme Court battle, and later the Yalta recriminations, which doubtless contributed to the Twenty-second Amendment.

More sophisticated interpretation of polls became possible in the Truman era. One of the most thoroughgoing sudies in this volume, that of Sternsher, seems to suggest that Truman's term fits the pattern of the aborted honeymoon partly because of the stature of his immediate predecessor.

President Eisenhower had the benefit of the beginning of television technology and the pattern-molding skills of James C. Hagerty, which to a considerable extent set the basic pattern of efforts to influence public perceptions that have continued up to the era of David Gergen, Larry Speakes, and Patrick Buchanan. Both Eisenhower and John F. Kennedy had to deal with the civil rights conflict, and both men dealt with it in gingerly fashion, much as Hayes dealt with racial issues in the 1870s.

President Kennedy, according to various views, was swept along with the tide of the civil rights revolution or waited until there was a consensus he could exploit (much in the pattern of Franklin Roosevelt's pre–Pearl Harbor leadership on foreign policy). Whatever interpretation one chooses, it is clear that JFK's rhetoric brought about a temporary euphoria. Republican critics later charged that he raised unrealistic expectations, while Kennedy's defenders suggested that he had redefined idealism in American life. But he did enjoy a brief honeymoon despite his narrow victory margin. Lyndon Johnson's period of good will lasted briefly, also, and was marred by his concept of the media as cheerleader, a view he shared with Richard Nixon. The feats of Lyndon Johnson in congressional cloakroom manipulation were not matched in the area of public relations, where Kennedy was clearly his superior. Neither fit the model of the ideal president who can handle both superbly, but then none of the thirty-nine incumbents through Ronald Reagan has.

Richard Nixon experienced a brief "Bring Us Together" period after the 1968 election, but the turbulence of Vietnam and the vocal minority who opposed imperialism in Vietnam, along with the news media (much of which he alienated by his penchant for secrecy), helped to bring about his downfall at the time of Watergate.

The Gerald Ford who toasted his own English muffins and picked up his newspaper at his door in his pajamas quickly gave way to the postpardon Ford who was castigated by members of his own party who were bitterly opposed to detente with the Soviet Union.

It would be oversimplifying things to describe Jimmy Carter, the first Deep South president since Zachary Taylor (1848–1850), as a "Democratic Hoover," but the oil shock of 1979, the Iranian crisis, the Ted Kennedy factionalism, and Carter's "good old boy" cultural roots combined to make things difficult for him. To his opponents, he was a weak and indecisive leader; to his supporters, he was too "good" to be an effective political practitioner. But the Carter honeymoon was ended by the Bert Lance affair in 1977. It appears, too, that Carter lacked the political skills that enabled Ronald Reagan to survive turmoil at the Environmental Protection Agency, the Hinckley attack (which of course prolonged his own honeymoon), the economic distress of 1982, the resignation of Labor Secretary Raymond Donovan under a cloud, turmoil over Nicaragua, El Salvador, and Lebanon, and the like.

It may be said in later eras that, like Eisenhower, Reagan shoved some troublesome problems under the carpet, but Ronald Reagan was more likely the beneficiary of the traditional desire to see a president succeed after nearly two decades of turbulent times.

HONEYMOON AND DECLINE: SOME EXPLANATIONS

From the high point of the honeymoon period, several studies have shown that the approval ratings of each incumbent president have deteriorated significantly. Several observers have attempted to explain each of these cycles. The honeymoon period, for example, has been attributed by James Stimson to the "restraint of political critics and the enthusiasm of presidential friends which combine to produce a public portrait of the new president on a super-human scale." To be sure, the media, early in any presidential term, work to popularize, even glamourize, the new incumbent, reporting in great detail his preferences, habits, and the like—for example, Ronald Reagan's penchant for jelly beans, Jimmy Carter's preference for cardigan sweaters, or Gerald Ford's fondness for English muffins. The public, too, is given to a burst of initial optimism based on a groundswell of respect for the office and public hopes for the future.

If the honeymoon is understandable, how do we account for the often rapid deterioration in presidential popularity that both historical data and public opinion polls reveal? To be sure, the generosity of the press evaporates all too soon, after which presidents generally become the butt of media carping and criticism, if not caricature. Recent presidents subjected to such press treatment include Gerald Ford, who rapidly became the "bumbling buffoon," and Jimmy Carter, who was tagged as "wishy washy"—appellations both found hard to escape.

The most persuasive explanation of this phenomenon has been provided by John Mueller, who has attributed these recurrent declines to a "coalition of minorities" which builds up over time. Each decision a president makes, he argues, tends to alienate certain groups and, as time goes on, more and more groups are alienated, accounting for a president's low popularity at the end of his term.[3] (On average, declines of 29 percent have been experienced by recent incumbents, regardless of performance.)

Mueller's explanation, plausible though it is, does not address, nor does it explain, a second peculiarity in the presidential-public opinion cycle—the fact that polls have recorded a secular downtrend in which each successive president starts out with lower ratings than his predecessor and ends with even lower ratings. (See Figure 23.1). While it cannot be determined for certain whether the complexity of modern problems or the relatively increased sophistication of voters has brought this about, this secular downtrend is evident in the poll data over the past forty years.

Samuel Kernell, Peter Sperlich, and Aaron Wildavsky, for instance, provide a systemic answer by surveying the impact of demographic trends.[4] They begin by identifying those population groups that might be expected to provide a priori support for the institution. They speculate that such groups would be among the least connected to the political system and thus need to rely on an easily recognizable symbol.

They identify such groups as the elderly, the less well educated, and the religious fundamentalists. The elderly, they hypothesize, have been socialized into a more deferential political culture, which stressed patriotism, while religious fundamentalists, they speculate, are more likely to have stronger needs for guidance and order than others. The less well educated, on the other hand, tend to have little political information and to be weakly motivated to participate in the political process. They are thus more likely to rely on a single cognitive link to the political system—and the president fills this role.

The core of support that these groups provided waned during the 1960s, when the population was younger, more educated, and more likely to be psychologically flexible. More recent demographic trends, however, suggest an aging of the U.S. population and a revival of religiosity. Should these trends continue, support for the presidency can be expected to become resurgent, with the Reagan presidency considered a watershed.

Other observers seek to account for the downtrend in popular support for the presidency by focusing exclusively on educational trends. They point out that scholarly presentations of the presidency (which had been laudatory in the past)

Figure 23.1
Ratings of Presidents on "Keeping the Economy Healthy"

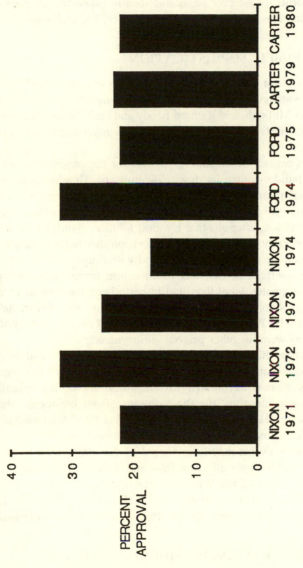

Source: Harris Report, 1973–1975; Public Opinion, April-May 1980.

have been counterbalanced by the revisionist perspective in the wake of Watergate. Such "popular" works as Garry Wills' *Nixon Agonistes* and *The Kennedy Imprisonment* have served to demystify both a popular as well as an unpopular president. Moreover, few of the more recent academic interpretations of the presidential office could ever be as uncritically supportive as earlier observers such as Clinton Rossiter and Arthur Schlesinger, Jr., had been.

GREATER PUBLIC SOPHISTICATION

In any case, there is increasing evidence of greater public sophistication, even cynicism, toward government in general, documented in studies by Edward Muller, Lester Milbrath, and Richard Brody and Paul Sniderman, among others.[5] All have reported steep declines in the "trust in government" indicator in recent years.

Still others explain the declining support for the presidency in terms of the tendency to build up, then let down, incumbents. This has been compounded by the greater intimacy between the president and the media, as well as the greater potential for such intimacy provided by a visual medium like television. It was on television, after all, that Lyndon Johnson displayed the scar from his gall bladder operation, and it was on television that Betty Ford spoke publicly about her problems with breast cancer and with drugs and alcohol.

Newspaper journalism, too, has taken a turn toward revealing presidential weaknesses in greater detail than had hitherto been the case as recently as the Kennedy era. Nixon's alleged drunkenness during the Watergate crisis was starkly reported by Woodward and Bernstein in *All the President's Men* and *The Final Days,* as were his other personal idiosyncracies.

What effect has this greater public intimacy had on the office of the presidency? Michael Robinson argues that television has rendered it both less legitimate and, paradoxically, more powerful. Why? Robinson argues that it is because television allows us to see, close up, the shortcomings of our presidents, thereby deromanticizing them. He concludes with the paradox that "television has helped to make [presidents] more important but less popular."

Finally, recent events may have served to demythify presidents—at least to reveal them as less than all-powerful—and thus to undermine their popular support. The impact of the Watergate episode should not be underestimated. The tapes, in particular, revealed, for the first time, the inner, and brutally cynical, workings of the presidential office and did so in embarrassing detail.

IMPACT OF EVENTS ON PRESIDENTIAL IMAGES

In addition, beginning perhaps with Vietnam, recent international events have shown the president to be a weak figure in dealings, not only with major allies such as Great Britain and France, but also with minor but recalcitrant (and domestically popular) foreign heads of state such as Ho Chi Minh, the Ayatollah

Khomeini, Daniel Ortega of Nicaragua and, of course, Colonel Moammar Khadafy of Libya. Terrorism, in particular, highlights the fact that certain acts are beyond the control of the president and reveals, only too clearly, his impotence.

For all these reasons, it is difficult to envision a rapid upturn of the secular downtrend in public assessments of presidential performance in office. Nevertheless, it is possible to speculate that a "bottoming out" or stabilization of the secular downtrend occurred during the Reagan years, now coming to a conclusion.

CATEGORIES OF MYTHS (SCHOLARLY AND POPULAR) AND COMPARISONS BETWEEN ADMINISTRATIONS

General themes about the presidency can be summarized in terms of both scholarly and popular myths, as well as through comparisons between administrations. In the literature on the presidency as a central institution of American life, scholarly opinion (as opposed to the kinds of popular attitudes reflected in the Louis Harris /Newsweek polls taken on the twentieth anniversary of the Kennedy assassination) has made an impact on the lasting images of American presidents. So have literary and artistic contributions such as the St. Gaudens Lincoln statues and the 1984 Gore Vidal novel, Lincoln, part of a broader series of political novels.

In the remainder of this chapter we explore categories of myths—both popular and scholarly—about past presidents. Some of these mythic images include the "military hero" versus the civilian; the "log cabin to White House" myth discussed by Donald Pessen and others versus the "patrician presidents"; and the "outsider" versus the "insider."

Interestingly, although contexts change, there have been recurring patterns of these images. One of the most enduring mythologies has been the "log cabin to White House" president, much more common than the "patrician president," scion of the upper classes.[6] Frankly "patrician presidents" were the rule only in the early years of the Republic. Thus David Skaggs, author of the chapter on George Washington, writes that Washington was born into a Virginia gentry family and that "by the age of forty he was one of the most substantial and influential citizens of the Northern Neck of Virginia." Even so, Thomas Jefferson, Robert Hatzenbuehler notes, was much more self-effacing, describing himself as "coming from a *natural* aristocracy . . . the grounds of which are virtue and talent" rather than "inherited wealth, birth or religious succession."

Subsequent "patricians," relatively few in number, have all sought to identify strongly with the common man. These include Theodore Roosevelt, his cousin Franklin D. Roosevelt, and John F. Kennedy. David Roller found that although Theodore Roosevelt belonged to America's squirearchy, TR grew up with a distinct vision of what was unjust about society and had a sense of duty to correct these injustices. As state assemblyman, the young Theodore Roosevelt shocked his peers by introducing a bill of impeachment against Judge Theodore Westbrook for corrupt dealings with Jay Gould, a wealthy New York financier, "in opposition to some of the Roosevelt family's more distinguished friends and the leadership of the state's Republican party."

In a similar vein, Robert Gilbert, writing about FDR, stresses Franklin Roosevelt's life of personal wealth and affluence and his cloistered and privileged youth on his Hyde Park estate. John F. Kennedy, though his father was a self-made millionaire, also had a privileged, even pampered, upbringing. Yet all three men espoused the cause of the common man and embraced policies many of their social class deemed detrimental to their own interests.

The first president to break the patrician mold was Andrew Jackson, his candidacy coinciding with the first national convention of a major party to choose a presidential nominee. Jackson had a "frontier image." Albert Gallatin, a contemporary, described him unflatteringly as "having the manners and deportment of a backwoodsman." Jackson, however, proved to be a trendsetter, and subsequent presidents have emphasized the plebeian, rather than the patrician, in their backgrounds.

The supreme symbol of the common man remains Abraham Lincoln. In his first major political speech he frankly stated, "I was born and have ever remained in the most humble walks of life." Unlike William Henry Harrison, who was the first president to use the "log cabin" metaphor, Lincoln had actually been born in one. Bursey writes that his "humble origins, ungainly appearance and lack of formal education fitted the image of a common man."

The log cabin imagery did not end in the nineteenth century. With modifications it has continued into the twentieth century. Herbert Hoover, a Stanford graduate and self-made millionaire, was the son of a blacksmith, while Harry S Truman emphasized his common beginnings as the haberdasher from Kansas City who had been a farm boy. More recently, Lyndon Johnson, the scion of a prominent political family in Texas, assiduously cultivated his image as a poor boy from a poor place, while Jimmy Carter's campaign biography described him as a "simple barefoot boy grown up to be a peanut farmer."

POPULARITY OF "OUTSIDER" IMAGE

A second image in which presidential candidates frequently cast themselves is that of the "outsider" new to Washington. Early presidents were not, of course, outsiders. Both Washington and Jefferson had served in the Virginia House of Burgesses. Washington had served as president of the Constitutional Convention in 1787 and Jefferson as secretary of state in Washington's first cabinet. In fact, prior to Andrew Jackson, all presidents had moved up the political ladder by way of the office of secretary of state (except for Washington himself and John Adams, his immediate successor).

Andrew Jackson was the first rank outsider and the first to be elected from the West. It should be noted, however, that Jackson, while an outsider to Washington politics, was not a political neophyte. Reed states that he had entered state politics in Tennessee in 1790, some thirty years before becoming president, serving both as state senator and state representative before resigning to become state superior judge. Yet despite Jackson's political experience, some 60 percent of his key men were outsiders, not only to Washington, but also to the societies from which they initially came. It is interesting that although a lack of national experience would be considered a political liability in other countries, in America it has been considered a political "plus." Of Jackson, Woodrow Wilson commented that "it was unprecedented that one so conspicuously outside the ranks of administrative and legislative service should seek the highest civil office."

However, by the time Lincoln took office, the outsider image had been fully legitimized. Lincoln, says Bursey, had never held top national office, despite one congressional term, and had been defeated in three attempts to win more prominent posts. Lincoln further legitimized the political unknown. Unlike any president before him (including Jackson, also an outsider, but one known nationally for his military exploits) Lincoln had no real claim to public greatness before he became President, as Bursey notes. He was chosen, as others after him would be chosen (for example, Harry Truman over Henry Wallace as candidate for vice president in 1944), because he was the *least objectionable* among his rivals.

IKE BEST KNOWN MODERN OUTSIDER

Of modern presidents, Dwight D. Eisenhower is the best known outsider, a man so apolitical that he was courted by both Republicans and Democrats in 1948. He reluctantly accepted the Republican nomination in 1952 only after he became convinced that the Republican party was about to be captured by its isolationist wing—a trend he considered dangerous in the postwar world.

The postwar rise of entrepreneurial politics, encouraged by changes in party rules, first by the Democrats and then by the Republicans in the early 1970s, particularly the increasing importance of presidential primaries in the nominating process, opened up the presidency to real outsiders. The most prominent of these was Jimmy Carter, virtually unknown in national polls in 1975, yet Democratic presidential nominee and then president hardly more than a year later. Carter deliberately stressed an anti-Washington campaign theme. Dennis Anderson sums up: "It would take someone who had not been part of the evils of the 'bloated' and 'confused' Washington bureaucracy to clean it up." He was the "lone stranger" from out of town. Carter's theme was usurped by Ronald Reagan in 1980, not so much as a personal description of candidate Reagan, but as the rallying cry for a Republican ideology that had wanted for some time to stop the growth of federal bureaucracy and government spending. (Ironically, the southern wing of the Democratic party had always espoused local autonomy and states' rights, paving the way for a potential future electoral alliance). Thus Reagan, although in politics since 1964 and governor of California between 1966 and 1974, campaigned as an outsider, promising to get "government off the backs of the American people."

HAYES, WILSON CULTIVATED OUTSIDER IMAGE

So persuasive is this outsider theme that some presidents have cultivated, somewhat disingenuously, the outsider image. Rutherford B. Hayes, for example, stayed aloof from the Republican party hierarchy and made little sustained effort to create a party coalition around himself. Nevertheless, the Republican party chose him, nominating him for Congress in Ohio's Second District while he was in the army. Indeed, Leslie Fishel, in Chapter 5 suggests that Hayes was not a partisan Republican. Nevertheless, Hayes accepted their help. Woodrow Wilson, too, cultivated the image of being a loner, although he owed his first start in politics to the political bosses of New Jersey, through the good offices of his mentor, George Harvey, editor of *Harper's Weekly* and a man with ties to the bosses and industrialists. The bosses supported Wilson's nomination as governor of New Jersey after he assured them that "the last thing I would think of would be building up a machine of my own." Then, after being attacked by reformers in the Democratic party, and feeling pressure from the electorate at large, Wilson "astounded both boss and critic alike by clearly proclaiming his independence the night of the nomination." He subsequently campaigned on a reformist platform, favoring primaries—a reform that had the effect of reducing the power of the bosses who had earlier endorsed him.

Then there was Warren Harding, who began as an outsider demanding a youth movement in the Republican party, but was co-opted into the Republican fold as a faithful party worker in return for the political support of the bosses he had earlier opposed. Indeed, the "Ohio Gang," as they came to be called, worked hard to promote Harding's political aspirations. It is important to note, however, that prior to the recent changes democratizing party rules, outsiders had to have some other claim to fame—some other status that gave them public recognition. Thus most, if not all, outsider presidents have been war heroes. Andrew Jackson, for example, served in the War of 1812, where he earned the widely recognized nickname "Old Hickory." After winning the "Battle of Horseshoe Bend" in 1804 over the Indians, Jackson gained instant national fame. His defeat of the British at New Orleans created a heroic national image that was an important factor in propelling him toward the presidency. From William Henry Harrison (who immortalized the election slogan "Tippecanoe and Tyler Too") to Eisenhower, military hero status has been an important component of name recognition for outsiders.

INSIDERS AS PRESIDENTS AND THEIR EXPERIENCE

More typically, however, until the recent disenchantment with big government and the moves to democratize the nominating methods of both parties since 1972, presidents have often been "insiders" with some national experience and strong party ties.

William McKinley, for example, was elected seven times to Congress, played a major role in three party conventions (1884, 1888, and 1892), and allied himself with two major power brokers in Ohio politics, John Sherman and Mark Hanna (the latter called the first national political boss in the United States).

Several twentieth century presidents were insiders. They include Herbert Hoover, who served as director of food relief, then as secretary of commerce in the Harding and Coolidge administrations, before winning the Republican presidential nomination in 1928. His successor, Franklin D. Roosevelt, though never a member of the Democratic "inner club," allied himself with reform Democrats and served in state politics before Woodrow Wilson appointed him assistant secretary of the navy under Navy Secretary Josephus Daniels. Only after serving as governor of New York State between 1928 and 1932 did he become the Democratic nominee for president in 1932.

Roosevelt's third vice president, Harry S Truman, got his start in politics in 1922 under "Boss Tom" Pendergast, an association which would later haunt him when he became president. Indeed, a Roper poll in 1948 enumerated the following reasons, given by respondents, for disliking Truman:

He is tied up with the Pendergast machine.

He is just a politician and not a statesman.

Lyndon B. Johnson was, without question, an insider. According to Spragens, Johnson's family had been involved in Texas politics, and Johnson himself went to Washington early in his political career as secretary to U.S. Representative Richard Kleberg of Texas. LBJ quickly became a political protégé of FDR, was elected to Congress in his own right in 1937, and then came under the influence of a fellow Texan, Speaker Sam Rayburn. After his slim election to the Senate in 1948, LBJ served in several important party posts: as Democratic whip in 1951, minority leader in 1953, majority leader in 1955, and then as vice president from 1961 to 1963. (His chief opponent for the Democratic nomination in 1960, John Kennedy, had also been on the national scene for more than a decade but must be classified as an outsider because party leaders had to be persuaded to support him. It was the emerging party primaries which Kennedy entered, and won, which helped considerably to enhance his candidacy at the Democratic Convention in Los Angeles.)

CONTEMPORARY VERSUS HISTORICAL IMAGES OF PRESIDENTS

We turn now to a discussion of contemporary (popular) versus historical images of presidents. We have already noted that popular images are subject to cycles as well as changing biases. For example, scholars like Fred I. Greenstein have

noted that the public is prone to evaluate presidents in terms of their image—
that is, in purely personal terms—rather than in terms of their accomplishments.
Scholars, too, display bias in their assessments of presidents, though it is bias
of a different sort. They have tended to equate presidential greatness with presidential "activism." The Robert Murray poll of historians, for example, places
Lincoln, FDR, George Washington, and Thomas Jefferson on top of the list of
great presidents; each served during a period of national crisis. The Schlesinger
polls reveal similar biases. Moreover, scholarly perceptions have, over time,
been subject to periods of revisionism during which bad presidents have been
rehabilitated and good presidents have their warts revealed. Over time, the cycle
repeats itself.

As we indicated above, most presidents have been less popular at the end of
their presidential terms than at the beginning. David Skaggs states that George
Washington was at the peak of his popularity at the time of his inaugural, but
inevitably a clash of personalities and political interests, especially over foreign
policy, led to a decline in his popularity, even though Washington himself tried
to stay aloof from the political fray. Contemporary observers were critical of
his "concerned remoteness," aloofness, and cautiousness. Despite this popular
assessment, after he had left office, Washington's mythic image grew into that
of the "Father of His Country." He was immortalized by Mason Locke Weems,
who created a folk hero. After Washington's death, public perceptions became
preoccupied with his prepresidential image as a war hero. Nineteenth-century
scholarship tended to support the mythic image, and it was not until early in the
twentieth century that a few historians painted a dissenting portrait. In the muckraking tradition, Skaggs describes W. E. Woodward's *George Washington: The
Image and the Man* as having a "derisive antihero bias," as did Rupert Hughes'
uncompleted *George Washington*.

Thomas Jefferson has had an ambiguous image for scholars. At first Jefferson
was ranked low as president, but a rehabilitation of his image reached a climax
in the 1940s, and Jefferson was ranked as a "great president" in both the
Schlesinger and Murray polls. Jefferson now came to be characterized as the
first effective party leader—and one who inaugurated some fundamental changes
in the management of government.

Andrew Jackson has also had an ambiguous contemporary—and scholarly—
image. During his tenure, the opposition called him ignorant, weak, and a despot
who was unqualified for public office. Yet Reed notes that Jackson, overall, had
a positive contemporary image—"magnetic, romantic, and colorful." Historians
who have been critical pointed to the "spoils system" associated with the Jackson
presidency. Then, under the influence of Frederick Jackson Turner at the close
of the nineteenth century, there was a massive shift among historians to a pro-
democratic orientation, and Jackson became a beneficiary of this historical twist.
In more recent times, Arthur Schlesinger, Jr.'s, book, *The Age of Jackson*,
sparked another pro-Jackson mood, so much so that Jackson was ranked as a
"near-great" president in the Murray poll. The Jackson era has not, however,

been without its critics. Richard Hofstadter has viewed it as a phase of exploding laissez-faire capitalism.

Abraham Lincoln remains a favorite of historians. He was ranked first in the Murray poll, in both Schlesinger polls (1948 and 1962), and in the *Chicago Tribune* poll of 1982. In the public mind, Lincoln achieved a saint-like status after his assassination. The only negative scholarly commentary comes indirectly in Arthur Schlesinger, Jr.'s, work, *The Imperial Presidency,* in which it is argued that the president operates like a dictator in times of war. Since Lincoln played a significant role in the definition and use of these war powers, it is hard to see how the Schlesinger interpretation can avoid implying that Lincoln's presidency gave the first major impetus to the "imperial presidency" Schlesinger decried. Schlesinger, however, softens his criticism by noting that Lincoln, though a despot, did not become one lightly.

Rutherford B. Hayes has been regarded among scholars as a forgotten president, in part because he had neither war nor depression to fight. In addition he had no charismatic personality and was generally viewed as a weak leader.

In the view of Vincent De Santis, Grover Cleveland's strength of character made him heroic, but in a negative sense. This was due to his resistance to an aggrandizing and overbearing Congress.

Contemporary and historical perceptions of the McKinley presidency diverge. A popular president in his own day, McKinley was elected twice and presided over a booming economy and the spoils of the Spanish-American War. Historians, however, have chosen to view McKinley as a tool of business and a puppet of Boss Hanna. McKinley's image suffered a long decline. In the Murray poll he was ranked "below average," and in the Schlesinger poll of 1948 he was ranked tenth out of twenty-nine presidents. By 1982 McKinley's image had risen sufficiently that in the *Chicago Tribune* poll of historians and political scholars he was ranked tenth, but this time out of a total of thirty-nine. Although this was an improvement in McKinley's standing, it is still in the "mediocre" category.

McKinley's partial rehabilitation with scholars can be attributed, in part, to Margaret Leech's *In the Days of McKinley* (1959), Wayne Morgan's *William McKinley and His America* (1963), and Lewis Gould's *The Presidency of William McKinley* (1980). The latter argued that McKinley was the first modern occupant of the office and that he presided over a prosperous age and had good relations with Congress.

Woodrow Wilson fared fairly well in the Murray poll, being ranked as a "near great" president. Natoli, however, views Wilson as an elitist who gave lip service to the notion of following public opinion. It was his character flaws, particularly his obstinacy, that she feels contributed to his defeat over the League of Nations issue.

Warren Harding was ranked "below average" in the Murray poll. His presidency was, of course, mired in scandal, and the debunking views of historians are still the most common. Nevertheless, even the Harding image is subject to historical revisionism, the rehabilitation process having begun with the release of the Harding Papers by the Ohio Historical Society, as described by Jennings in his assessment.

Herbert Hoover's contemporary popularity was high when he first took office, but sank as he did not realize the gravity of the impending disaster and then blamed international events for causing the economic ills that marred his administration. He was overwhelmingly defeated by Franklin Roosevelt and left office with his reputation badly tarnished. His public image remains, even today, that of the man who misguidedly clung to his principles of rugged individualism even as the nation sank into a morass of despair. Schlesinger views him as inflexible and self-righteous, and this view is echoed by the majority of historians.

The consensus of historical opinion surrounding Franklin Roosevelt is as laudatory as Hoover's has been negative. FDR has been ranked as a "great president" in all three polls of historians. During his presidency, however, there was not nearly as much unanimity with respect to his performance. His fellow Democrats attacked him for acting against the party platform, while the upper classes reviled him as a tool of the "Negroes and Jews." To others, FDR was a "savior and miracle worker." FDR was certainly a pragmatic politician, and the course he charted was at times erratic. Yet his image, one of "dynamic determination," has been one that historians have been willing to endorse.

Although the Murray poll ranks Harry Truman as a "near great," Truman's contemporary popular image was very negative. That this image lingers in the public mind is reflected in a Louis Harris poll in 1972 in which Truman was ranked last among postwar presidents. Bernard Sternsher notes that, during his term of more than seven years in office, Truman enjoyed two minor honeymoons with the public, one when he assumed office after FDR died and one after his own election in 1948. However, he also managed to end his first year in office with one of the lowest public opinion ratings of any president. He seemed, to his contemporaries, to lack stature and aptitude and was viewed as a bad manager and a tool of the Pendergast machine. Among historians, however, Truman is enjoying a minor reassessment.

The Eisenhower presidency marks the beginning of an important contemporary trend affecting the public images of presidents. Eisenhower was the first president to make use of television in his campaign and later during his presidency. Because of television and the strong personalization of the office that has occurred, we now see the advent of presidents who have better (and in some cases worse) contemporary images than their respective policies would warrant, and from which they seem almost disassociated. It is through the prism of television images that we can best view the popular presidencies of Kennedy, Reagan, and, of course, Eisenhower himself, as well as the personally unpopular presidencies of Nixon, LBJ, Carter, and Ford, who presented far less visually appealing images of themselves to the public. Historians who denigrate public relations skills as opposed to achievement in office (which is of course a valid position) appear to overlook the centrality of image in a television/cable/satellite era, although, as we have noted earlier, this heavy exposure of presidents is a two-edged sword because along with greater power and importance it enhances the vulnerability of presidents and demystifies them, presenting some legitimacy problems.

In Kennedy's case, the dramatic use of television to project a favorable image of himself and his family and their private and personal times together served to increase his personal popularity and to divert public attention from his policies, many of which were bogged down in Congress. Because of television, Kennedy became a glamorous and telegenic media celebrity or star. Television magnified his youthfulness, vigor, and poise. The televising of his assassination and funeral served to convert Kennedy from a popular president into an enduring national myth, sparking a sort of national love affair which has still not ended.

But Kennedy did not beguile only the public. His personal relationship with historians, aides, and scholars such as Arthur Schlesinger, Jr., Theodore Sorensen, and Theodore White resulted in a wealth of favorable commentaries about his presidency. Victor Lasky's unfavorable *J.F.K.—The Man and the Myth*, written while the president was alive, remains a minority view among academics. Only the changing political climate of the 1970s, which brought with it disillusionment over executive actions, particularly with respect to Vietnam, produced a critical revisionist perspective on Kennedy.

In 1976 Bruce Miroff, in *Pragmatic Illusions*, accused Kennedy of fostering a crisis mentality over the Bay of Pigs, the Cuban missile crisis, and Berlin. Richard K. Walton, in *Cold War and Counter-revolution*, characterizes Kennedy as a "Cold Warrior" and counterrevolutionary, while David Halberstam's *The Best and the Brightest* accuses Kennedy of deepening American involvement in Vietnam. Most recently, Garry Wills has even attacked the Kennedy persona, painting him as a philanderer and dilettante.

During the 1980s, it appears that historians are moving toward a more balanced view of Kennedy, particularly with respect to his prepresidential years—witness Joan and Clay Blair's *The Search for JFK* and Herbert Parmet's *Jack: The Struggles of John F. Kennedy*.

For subsequent presidents television has worked to their detriment—with the notable exception of Ronald Reagan (an ex-actor). In LBJ's case, the public forgot the achievements of the Great Society once the visual horrors of the Vietnam War began entering the living rooms of the shocked American television viewers through the nightly news broadcasts. This, plus LBJ's unphotogenic image, "his unappealing physical appearance and slow drawl," soon congealed his initial public support into implacable public hostility. He now seemed cynical and deceptive, lacking in credibility. Doris Kearns, a sympathetic observer, blames LBJ's decline in public sympathy on his inability to project himself on television—and LBJ himself blamed the media for creating the "credibility gap."

Kearns apart, other professional observers—historians, political scientists, and journalists—have not been kind to LBJ, viewing him as "abrasive," "abusive," and "evasive." To intellectuals who had been personal friends of John F. Kennedy, LBJ by contrast seemed vulgar, vain, and insecure. John Bartlow Martin theorized that LBJ had "only the loosest grasp on national politics, especially of the national mood, purpose and will. In the end this defeated him." Doris Kearns concludes, more charitably, that LBJ was neither a hero nor a villain, but simply the captive of frustrating historical circumstances that turned against him.

LBJ's image among other scholars continues to be ambivalent. He is seen as either a Machiavellian pragmatist or a consummate politician. Robert Caro views him as a "scheming liar" and an "egotistical, selfish manipulator of other men and ideas." George Reedy, LBJ's first press secretary, on the other hand, describes him as a fascinating blend of complexities and simplicities, while Rowland Evans and Robert Novak see him as a skilled politician, pure and simple.

LBJ's successor, Richard Nixon, had problems with the media that went back a long way. He is said to have lost the election of 1960 due to his unflattering image on television during the debate with Kennedy. Nixon's inability to project a credible image instead earned him the nickname "Tricky Dick." His administration finally came unstuck during the long and unfavorable Watergate Senate hearings, which were televised. The public subsequently ignored his international initiatives and domestic and economic breakthroughs.

Professional Nixon watchers focus on the repercussions of his presidency on the presidential office and its powers. It was because of Nixon that Congress placed restrictions on the president's ability to wage war and impound congressionally appropriated funds. His image as unscrupulous, ruthless, and combative still remains among scholars and, as yet, no revisionist view of Nixon has emerged. It may well be that, as Henry Kissinger consoled Nixon, "history will treat you more kindly than your contemporaries have," but it is still too soon to tell.

Gerald Ford's negative image was reinforced, if not created, by television, which presented him as a bumbling caricature of himself, tripping down the stairs and sometimes even over his own words. For instance, in a televised campaign debate with Jimmy Carter in 1976, he claimed that Poland was not under Soviet domination—and never would be so long as he was president.

Jimmy Carter sought to use television to demythify what he regarded as a bloated and self-important presidency. His populist view was broacast by the media. Carter was seen in jeans and sweaters, visual symbols of his folksiness and frugality. In the end, however, the diminutive presidency Carter created diminished his own public image, swallowed his own achievements, and undercut his authority and legitimacy. Television reinforced his image as a vacillating, weak, and confused leader. After the disastrous Bert Lance affair, the media began reporting a pattern of embarrassing incidents that rapidly transformed his presidential image which, in any case, was vulnerable since it was "thin and ungrounded" in any public past. A Harris poll in 1980 listed the names of presidents since Roosevelt with the question: "Which President was least able to get things done?" Carter, then Ford, were ranked as the least able. A year earlier, polls revealed that what the public wanted was "strong leadership" and not what they saw as Carter's strengths—honesty, caring and compassion.

Elite opinion was only marginally more favorable than Carter's public image. A survey of historians, journalists, and political scientists conducted in the *Chicago Tribune* in 1982 (after Carter had left office) ranked Carter as the tenth worst president. William Safire, a former Nixon speechwriting aide, characterized Carter as having a "weathervane philosophy of government," and Carter's lack of any overall vision or philosophy, combined with his deliberate efforts to demythify the presidential office, ensured that even professional opinions are not very likely to improve with time.

Of all postwar presidents (with the possible exception of Kennedy and Eisenhower), Reagan is the most personally popular, aided as he has been by a television image of strength and toughness combined with affability. His popularity seems immune to misstatements of fact and even to unfavorable events which would have destroyed Carter—for instance, the massive killings of American troops in a car bombing in Beirut in 1983. As to the "Teflon-coated" president, a *Newsweek* poll taken during the 1984 campaign indicated that people liked Reagan even though they disagreed with his stand on issues and, in some cases, even attributed positions to him that had, in fact, been taken by his Democratic opponent Walter Mondale.

Reagan also used television, both during and after his campaigns, to project themes of optimism and hope about the future, combined with a consistent sense of direction—in sharp contrast to his predecessor, Carter. Informed observers like Garry Wills say that Reagan, as a celebrity, has brought authority to an institution which, like other institutions in American society, had lost legitimacy and authority. Wills, however, also sees Reagan as preferring the symbolic over the substantive, in some cases using symbols to mislead. Other critics have also pointed to his adroit use of empty gestures combined with artful theatrical posturing. Dennis Anderson concludes, however, that as far as the public is concerned, "hard" images are more appealing to the public than "soft" images. In other words, Carter's honesty and compassion are less appealing, to the public and even to some professional observers, than Reagan's toughness and sense of direction. Reagan could also be the beneficiary of a more conservative trend in the writing of history, as libertarian and conservative historians become more prominent in historiography using newer approaches.

In conclusion, it should be noted that although many presidential reputations have undergone historical revisionism, not all have. A minority—Lincoln, for example—have been immune thus far. Scholarly assessments differ with respect to the emphasis they place on character and events and in assessing presidential performances. Some presidents have been subject to criticism because of failures of character—for example, Woodrow Wilson and Rutherford B. Hayes. Others, like Nixon and Lyndon Johnson, have been indicted due to a combination of character and circumstances. All presidents whose reputations bear the marks of scholarly tarnish can wait and hope for the cycles of historical revisionism to rescue them.

NOTES

1. Michael B. Grossman and Martha J. Kumar, *Portraying the President* (Baltimore: Johns Hopkins University Press, 1981).

2. Abner Falk suggests in "Aspects of Political Psychobiography," *Political Psychology*, 6, no. 4 (December 1985): 605–619:

Some politicians are also artists or writers, like Disraeli; and, as the Georges' study of Wilson (George and George, 1966) and subsequent psychobiographies culminating in Volkan and Itzkowitz's (1984) monumental study of Kemal Ataturk have shown, political action can be deeply influenced and determined by unconscious conflict or fantasy as can a literary creation. Political actions, however, must in some way accord with reality. If they cease to do so, the political leader no longer functions in his role.

Falk cites Hitler's aberrations as the products of a diseased mind. Although the univariate analysis of Lloyd de Mause in *Reagan's America* (New York: Creative Roots Publishers, 1984) seeks to show the impact of fantasy on the Reagan presidency, the impact of Senate Republican leaders on economic policy, as in 1982 and 1987, and the advice that led to the recognition of the Corazon Aquino regime in the Philippines indicate that there are limits to this view.

3. James Stimson, *To Be a Politician* (New York: Pocket Books, 1959); John Mueller, *War, Presidents and Public Opinion* (New York: John Wiley and Sons, 1973), and "Presidential Popularity from Truman to Johnson," in *American Political Science Review*, 64 (1970): 21, 22.

4. Samuel Kernell, Peter W. Sperlich, and Aaron Wildavsky, "Public Support for Presidents," in Aaron Wildavsky, ed., *Perspectives on the Presidency* (Boston: Little, Brown, 1975), pp. 148–164.

5. See Lester Milbrath et al., *Political Participation* (Chicago: Rand McNally, 1977); Edward Muller and Thomas Jackson, "On the Meaning of Political Support," *American Political Science Review*, 71, no. 4 (December 1977): 1561–1595; and Richard Brody and Paul Sniderman, "From Life Space to Polling Place," *British Journal of Political Science*, 7 (1977): 337–360.

6. Michael J. Robinson, *Over the Wire and on TV CBS and UPI in Campaign '80* (New York: Russell Sage, 1983). The dichotomy between "plebeian" and "patrician" presidents is not, of course, a complete accounting. Some presidents fit neither category, but must be classified as "Middle Americans," the most recent of which was Gerald R. Ford. The state of Ohio has produced more than its share of "Middle American" presidents, e.g., Rutherford B. Hayes, William McKinley, Warren G. Harding, and William Howard Taft, all of whom were comfortably middle class.

SELECTED BIBLIOGRAPHY

Barber, James David. *The Presidential Character*. 2nd ed. Englewood Cliffs, N.J.: Prentice-Hall, 1977.

Draws on biographical sources to produce psychological interpretations of political behavior from the early twentieth century to the Carter era.

Benedict, Michael Les. *The Impeachment and Trial of Andrew Johnson*. New York: Norton, 1973.

Discusses the trial of the chief executive, prefaced by analysis of Reconstruction and including discussion of the politics of impeachment, the Senate trial, and verdict.

Berger, Raoul. *Impeachment: The Constitutional Problems*. Cambridge, Mass.: Harvard University Press, 1973.

Discusses how impeachments were brought about and their effect on government officials. Specifically discusses the impeachment of Justice Samuel Chase and President Andrew Johnson.

Burns, James MaGregor. *Leadership*. New York: Harper and Row, 1977.

Develops theory on the power of leadership and the crucibles of political leadership, in a broader context. He also uses a psychological matrix and social sources in discussing the origins of leadership.

Cronin, Thomas E. *The State of the Presidency*. 2nd ed. Boston: Little, Brown, 1980.

Analyzes political values and political pressures that shape presidential performance; also analyzes and interprets the promise of the presidency and constraints on presidential leadership.

Edwards, George C.,III. *The Public Presidency: The Pursuit of Popular Support*. New York: St. Martin's, 1983.

Public opinion and media relations aspects of the presidency.

Goldsmith, William M. *The Growth of Presidential Power: A Documented History*. 3 vols. New York: Chelsea House, 1974.

A three-volume set beginning with origins of the presidency and concluding with Nixon's resignation.

Greenstein, Fred I. *Evolution of the Modern Presidency: A Bibliographical Survey*. Washington, D.C.: American Enterprise Institute, 1977.

This volume of 2,500 bibliographic entries identifies and classifies significant works on the evolution of the American presidency since 1932.

Hardin, Charles M. *Presidential Power and Accountability: Toward a New Constitution*. Chicago: University of Chicago Press, 1974.

Deals with party government's constitutional potential, the problem of bureaucracy, the nature and influence of military bureaucracy, the feasibility of party government, and reform.

Hargrove, Erwin C. *The Power of the Modern Presidency*. Philadelphia: Temple University Press, 1974.

Written during the Watergate crisis, this study of the presidency combines the approaches of earlier analyses dealing with issues of leadership and authority in the presidency.

Heclo, Hugh, and Lester A. Solomon, eds. *The Illusion of Presidential Government*. Boulder, Colo.: Westview Press, 1981.

Analyzes the president's managerial role; includes final report of the National Academy of Public Administration's Panel on Presidential Management.

Hodgson, Godfrey. *All Things to All Men: The False Promise of the Modern American Presidency*. New York: Simon and Schuster, 1980.

Discusses the paradox of presidential and congressional power and politics without strong parties. Analyzes the Carter period and the president's relationship with the public.

Hoxie, R. Gordon. *Command Decision and the Presidency: A Study in National Security Policy and Organization*. New York: Reader's Digest Press, 1977.

Military policies from FDR through the Truman era, the Cold War, and the Korean War as well as policy decision-making until Eisenhower's final year, detente, command decisions, crisis management, and related topics through the early Carter era.

Hughes, Emmet John. *The Living Presidency*. New York: Coward, McCann, and Geoghegan, 1973.

The resources and paradoxes of the ideas and mysteries of the presidency, the restraint and range of presidential power.

James, Dorothy. *The Contemporary Presidency*. New York: Pegasus, 1974.

Deals with the president's use of media to influence the public; increasing economic, foreign, and military responsibilities; also foreign policy and presidential prospects for the future.

Meltsner, Arnold, ed. *Politics and the Oval Office*. San Francisco: Institute of Contemporary Studies, 1981.

Analyzes recent trends in the presidency—institutional and attitudinal trends of the public, the parties, the media, Congress, the bureaucracy, and the courts. Also deals with the key issue areas of defense, energy, and the economy.

Nash, Bradley D., ed. *Organizing and Staffing the White House*. New York: Center for the Study of the Presidency, 1980.

A former subcabinet official under Eisenhower edited these essays dealing with administrative history, the contemporary presidency, and prescriptions for administrative reform. Includes some incisive comments by Milton Eisenhower.

Neustadt, Richard. *Presidential Power: The Politics of Leadership from FDR to Carter*. New York: Wiley, 1980.

A second revision of a classic work first published in 1960, appraising the president and his powers with emphasis on reputational analysis and transition problems.

Page, Benjamin I., and Mark P. Petracca. *The American Presidency*. New York: McGraw-Hill, 1983.
> A good recent general text which deals with the White House up through the early Reagan era.

Pious, Richard. *The American Presidency*. New York: Basic Books, 1979.
> Discusses creation of the presidency, presidential powers, prerogative powers, and administrative powers. Also deals with economic and foreign policy and the war-making power.

Reedy, George E. *The Presidency in Flux*. New York: Columbia, 1973.
> A lecture on mass society with the basic theme that there has been a decline in the classic democratic dialogue in our society, with an unhealthy effect on our national life. It also deals with how political techniques used in mass communication have tended to make the presidency more separated from the people.

Relyea, Harold C. ed. *The Presidency and Information Policy*. New York: Center for the Study of the Presidency, 1981.
> An analysis of executive branch information policy Freedom of Information Act and its amendments.

Schlesinger, Arthur M., Jr. *The Imperial Presidency*. Boston: Houghton Mifflin, 1973.
> Deals with a shift in the constitutional balances, with the contemporary presidency appropriating powers reserved by the Constitution to the Congress for the presidential war-making power.

Sorensen, Theodore C. *Watchmen in the Night*. Cambridge, Mass.: MIT Press, 1975.
> Discusses the Nixon presidency, the facade of unlimited presidential power, and how to make the president more accountable to the Congress, the courts, and the people.

Strum, Phillipa. *Presidential Power and American Democracy*. Pacific Palisades, Calif.: Goodyear, 1979.
> Examines the relationship between the president and the Congress, analyzing different types of power and differing approaches to the governing process, as well as problems of presidential isolation and the chief executive's conception of his role.

INDEX

CONTRIBUTORS

DENNIS M. ANDERSON (Ph.D., Northwestern, 1970) has taught in the Political Science Department at Bowling Green State University since 1968. He received his B.A. (1957) and M.A. (1964) from Oberlin College. His research interests are primarily in public opinion and electoral politics.

L. GERALD BURSEY is associate professor of political science at Northeastern University, Boston, and is a doctoral graduate of Harvard University.

MALCOLM LEE CROSS (Ph.D., University of Missouri–Columbia, 1980) is assistant professor of social science at Tarleton State University, Stephenville, Texas. He earned a B.A. in government and international relations from Carleton College, Northfield, Minnesota (1972), and an M.S. in public administration from the University of Missouri–Columbia (1975). He has served on the staffs of the city managers of Berkeley, Missouri, and Portage, Michigan. His areas of interest include organization theory and design, political and administrative history, and leadership.

EMIL DANSKER, director of communication programs and professor of journalism at Central State University (Ohio), was formerly at Bowling Green State University, where he received a doctorate in communications. He has been a reporter and editor for thirty years on various newspapers, including the *Toledo Blade,* and has done freelance writing. He has made numerous scholarly presentations. His publications include "How Reporters Evaluate the Credibility of Their Sources" in the *Newspaper Research Journal,* and two videotape studies: "Kent 1970: Covering the Confrontation," which examines print and broadcast coverage of the killing of four students at Kent State University by Ohio National Guardsmen, and "Expelled from Iran," a similar examination of coverage of the 1979–1981 hostage crisis in Iran. He was among reporters for the *Dayton Daily News* whose work on housing concerns was submitted for a Pulitzer Prize in 1970. With Dr. Spragens, he was codirector of the National Conventions

Project, an apparently unique program under which students have worked for the media at the Democratic and Republican national nominating conventions since 1976.

VINCENT P. DE SANTIS has taught American history at the University of Notre Dame since 1949. He is a former Guggenheim Fellow and Fulbright Professor, and he has written a number of books and articles on United States history since 1865. His recent publications include a full-length study of American foreign policy from the American Revolution to the present and essays on Presidents Hayes, Truman, Eisenhower, Kennedy, and Carter.

LESLIE H. FISHEL, JR., received an undergraduate degree from Oberlin College and graduate degrees from Harvard University. Mr. Fishel has specialized in black history in the late nineteenth century. He has taught at the Massachusetts Institute of Technology, Oberlin College, Heidelberg College, and Bowling Green State University, and has served as director of the State Historical Society of Wisconsin, president of Heidelberg College and, currently, director of the Rutherford B. Hayes Presidential Center in Fremont, Ohio.

ROBERT E. GILBERT (Ph.D., University of Massachusetts) is professor of political science and chairperson, Department of Political Science, at Northeastern University. A specialist on the American presidency and on the political effects of the mass media, he is the author of *Television and Presidential Politics* (1972) and has published articles in such journals as *Presidential Studies Quarterly, Journal of Social, Political and Economic Studies, Mass Communication Review, Il Politico,* and the *UMKC Law Review.*

RONALD L. HATZENBUEHLER is a professor of history, Idaho State University. He has written extensively on the early national history of the United States and is coauthor of *Congress Declares War: Rhetoric, Leadership, and Partisanship in Early America.*

R. GORDON HOXIE (Ph.D., Columbia University, 1950) is a founder and chief executive officer of the Center for the Study of the Presidency. He is also editor of *Presidential Studies Quarterly.* Earlier Dr. Hoxie served as president of C.W. Post College and chancellor of Long Island University. He is the author, contributor, or editor of more than a dozen volumes on the American presidency.

DAVID H. JENNINGS (Ph.D., Ohio State University, 1958) received his B.A. in 1941 from Bates College and his M.A. in history from Syracuse University in 1946. He taught and coached in New England prep schools from 1941 to 1946. From 1946 to 1981, he taught history at Ohio Wesleyan University, concentrating on recent American history and foreign policy.

FRANK KESSLER is professor of political science at Missouri Western State College and the author of a textbook, *Dilemmas of Presidential Leadership: Of Caretakers and Kings*. He was recipient of the Distinguished Professor Award in 1983–1984 and has also been a Danforth Foundation Associate. He has lectured extensively on the American presidency in both the United States and Canada. He has published articles in *Presidential Studies Quarterly, Current History, Mid-West Quarterly,* and *Universitas*. He is currently president of the Missouri Political Science Association and was a member of the National Endowment for the Humanities Seminar for College Teachers on the Presidency at New York University in 1976.

JOHN S. LATCHAM is associate professor of political science at Kent State University, Trumbull Campus, Warren, Ohio. He is the author of a forthcoming book on Mark Hanna and has published extensively in *Presidential Studies Quarterly, Political Psychology,* and other journals. He has done extensive research in leadership psychology and has presented papers on political psychology for the American Political Science Association, Midwest Political Science Association, and the International Society for Political Psychology.

LINDA J. LEAR is adjunct associate professor in the Department of History of the George Washington University. She is the author of *Harold L. Ickes: The Aggressive Progressive 1874–1933* (1981) and is at work on a full-scale biography of Interior Secretary Harold L. Ickes. Additionally, she has written on natural resource and environmental history topics, most recently "Boulder Dam: A Crossroads in Natural Resource Policy," *Journal of the West* (forthcoming).

MARIE D. NATOLI, associate professor of political science at Emmanuel College in Boston, was awarded a doctorate at Tufts University in 1975. Her primary research area is the American presidency and vice presidency, on which she has lectured, written, and published extensively. Her book, *American Prince, American Pauper: The Contemporary Vice Presidency in Perspective,* was published by Greenwood Press. In faculty development, she has hosted a weekly television course, "Simulation Games for the Classroom Teacher," and has been selected by the American Political Science Association as a participant in the APSA Faculty Development Program. Dr. Natoli is the recipient of grants from the National Science Foundation (NSF), the Lilly Endowment, the Fund for the Improvement of Post Secondary Education (FIPSE), and the Ford Foundation, as well as two Emmanuel College faculty development grants. She is cited in the *Directory of American Scholars, Who's Who Among American Women,* the *World's Who's Who of Women,* and the *International Who's Who in Education*. She is a member of the John F. Kennedy Library Academic Advisory Committee and the editorial board of the *Presidential Studies Quarterly*.

JOHN J. REED, professor emeritus of history, formerly was chairman of the Department of History and director of American Studies at Muhlenberg College, after teaching at Lehigh and Temple universities and Moravian College. He is currently lecturer in history at Allentown College (Center Valley, Pa.) where, among other things, he gives a course in the history of the presidency. He has recently done reviews for the *Pennsylvania Magazine of History and Biography* and the *Journal of the Early Republic,* and selections of Theodore Dwight Weld, the Grimké sisters, and Walt Whitman for a projected encyclopedia of American reformers. He is currently preparing a study of the first national nominating convention of the Whig party and is revising a manuscript on the emergence of the Northern Whigs. His final draft of the antebellum chapter on the history of Allentown, Pennsylvania (to be published by the Lehigh County Historical Society), has been accepted.

DAVID C. ROLLER is associate professor of history at Bowling Green State University. He is coeditor of an encyclopedia on American history, an active member of the BGSU faculty senate and a popular classroom professor.

KIM EZRA SHIENBAUM is an associate professor of political science at Rutgers University–Camden. She is author of *Beyond the Electoral Connection: A Reassessment of the Role of Voting in Contemporary American Politics,* published in 1984. She is editor of a book entitled *Legislative Morality: Private Choices on the Public Agenda,* published in 1985, and is recipient of a grant from the state of New Jersey for a public affairs radio interview program.

DAVID CURTIS SKAGGS is a professor of history at Bowling Green State University, where he has taught since 1965. During 1985–1986 he served as a William C. Foster fellow of the U.S. Arms Control and Disarmament Agency in Washington, on assignment to the Bureau of Multilateral Affairs. He is the author of *Roots of Maryland Democracy* (1973) and the editor of *The Old Northwest in the American Revolution* (1977) and *The Poetic Writings of Thomas Cradock, 1718–1770* (1983). He is the author of more than two dozen scholarly articles dealing with colonial and revolutionary America in such periodicals as the *Journal of American History, William and Mary Quarterly, Maryland Historical Magazine, Virginia Magazine of History and Biography, Military Affairs,* and *Military Review.* He currently edits the *Northwest Ohio Quarterly.*

WILLIAM C. SPRAGENS (Ph.D., Michigan State University, 1966) is coauthor and editor (with Robert W. Russell) of *Conflict and Crisis in American Politics* (1970), as well as the author of *The Presidency and the Mass Media in the Age of Television* (1978) and (with Carole Ann Terwoord) *From Spokesman to Press Secretary: White House Media Operations* (1980). A professor emeritus of political science at Bowling Green State University in Ohio, where he taught full-time from 1969 to 1986, he is also political science book review editor for

Presidential Studies Quarterly and has contributed to such journals as *The Western Political Quarterly, Midwest Journal of Political Science, Political Science Quarterly,* and *Journal of Negro History.* He held a Falk Fellowship in 1960–1961, was a Ford legislative intern in the Michigan General Assembly, 1961 Session, and in 1978 was a Summer Seminar Fellow at a National Endowment for the Humanities seminar at the City University of New York. He has also received two Moody grants from the Lyndon Baines Johnson Foundation. He was a visiting professor at the American University in Washington in 1980–1981 and has done research at several presidential libraries.

BERNARD STERNSHER, University Professor of History at Bowling Green State University, is the author of *Rexford Tugwell and the New Deal* (1964) and *Consensus, Conflict and American Historians* (1975). Recent publications reflecting his interest in politics and voter behavior are "Reflections on Politics, Policy, and Ideology," in Robert H. Bremner and Gary W. Reichard, editors, *Reshaping America: Society and Institutions 1945–1960* (1982), and "The New Deal Party System: A Reappraisal," *Journal of Interdisciplinary History* (Summer 1984).

MELINDA SWAN, a graduate of Bowling Green State University, is press secretary to Ohio attorney general Frank Glebezze and has worked with public relations firms in Florida.